SCOTS LAW

A STUDENT GUIDE

SCOTS LAW

A STUDENT GUIDE

Nicole Busby   Bryan Clark
Richard Mays   Roderick Paisley   Paul Spink

Edited by Richard Mays

Members of the LexisNexis Group Worldwide

United Kingdom	Butterworths, a Division of Reed Elsevier (UK) Ltd, 4 Hill Street, EDINBURGH EH2 3JZ and Halsbury House, 35 Chancery Lane, LONDON WC2A 1EL
Argentina	Abeledo Perrot, Jurisprudencia Argentina and Depalma, BUENOS AIRES
Australia	Butterworths, a Division of Reed International Books Australia Pty Ltd, CHATSWOOD, New South Wales
Austria	ARD Betriebsdienst and Verlag Orac, VIENNA
Canada	Butterworths Canada Ltd, MARKHAM, Ontario
Chile	Publitecsa and Conosur Ltda, SANTIAGO DE CHILE
Czech Republic	Orac sro, PRAGUE
France	Editions du Juris-Classeur SA, PARIS
Hong Kong	Butterworths Asia (Hong Kong), HONG KONG
Hungary	Hvg Orac, BUDAPEST
India	Butterworths India, NEW DELHI
Ireland	Butterworths (Ireland) Ltd, DUBLIN
Italy	Giuffré, MILAN
Malaysia	Malayan Law Journal Sdn Bhd, KUALA LUMPUR
New Zealand	Butterworths of New Zealand, WELLINGTON
Poland	Wydawnictwa Prawnicze PWN, WARSAW
Singapore	Butterworths Asia, SINGAPORE
South Africa	Butterworths Publishers (Pty) Ltd, DURBAN
Switzerland	Stämpfli Verlag AG, BERNE
USA	LexisNexis, DAYTON, Ohio

© Reed Elsevier (UK) Ltd 2001

A CIP Catalogue record for this book is available from the British Library.

First published by T & T Clark Ltd 2000
Reprinted 2001

ISBN 0 567 00561 5

Typeset by Fakenham Photosetting Limited, Fakenham, Norfolk
Printed and bound in Great Britain by Unwin Brothers Ltd, Woking

Visit Butterworths LexisNexis *direct* at : www.butterworthsscotland.com

FOREWORD

It is said that in the rarefied atmosphere of RAE assessments, student books do not rate very highly. If that is so, it is unfortunate, as it can be more difficult to write a good student text than something designed for other readerships.

Equally, it is often assumed that a "student" text is written only for, and will be used only by, those at college or university; the fact that laymen will often consult such a text to "get a flavour" of an issue is frequently overlooked.

Whether or not this book is intended only for college or university students, it is to be commended. The authors have succeeded in setting out the law in clear terms, and while the necessary condensation involved in such an exercise can make for obfuscation, that is not so here.

I have no hesitation in commending this book to the "student", in whatever guise he or she is to be found.

D.J. Cusine
Peterhead

June 2000

PREFACE

This book attempts to summarise in clear and concise terms key areas of law in Scotland. It is written principally with our own students (current and future) in mind, although we hope that other students throughout Scotland will use it as well. We are not the first authors to attempt to cover multiple areas of law in a single volume. In preparing our text, we have come to appreciate the task that others have undertaken, and their achievements, all the more. Law does not lend itself to neat compartmentalism: principles just will not be principles. The law is replete with exceptions to rules and caveats to general positions. Extracting the basics is often more difficult than giving in-depth coverage to a topic.

All of the authors are experienced teachers of law. We have sought to bring our individual knowledge, and our collective experience of teaching students (particularly non-LLB students), to bear in producing the text. It is not an attempt to cover all the laws of Scotland, but rather the core subjects taught in universities and colleges throughout Scotland.

The book was written during the months of November 1999 to March 2000. We have attempted to state the law at 1st March 2000. Law is dynamic: it changes and grows rapidly. However, by adhering to a strict timetable and with a publisher committed to speedy publication we have tried to ensure that not too much has changed during the period that the book was in production.

There are, as always, many people to thank. Chapters were read by Colin Campbell, David Christie, James Connelly, Sam Middlemiss, Veronica Strachan, Iain Taylor, Linda Tyler (all of the Robert Gordon University), Michael Christie and Professor Michael Meston (both formerly of the University of Aberdeen), Donna McKenzie Skene (senior lecturer in law at the University of Aberdeen), Professor Joe Thomson (currently a Scottish Law Commissioner), and Philip Morris, senior lecturer in law at the University of Stirling. Each made helpful suggestions which have improved the end product, but, of course, responsibility for any errors or omissions remains with the authors.

We would also like to thank Euan Roberts (research), and Audrey Howie and Eileen Ord (Secretarial) (all of the Robert Gordon University) for their assistance. We are also indebted to Christine Gane for preparing the index, Heather Palomino for copyediting and proofreading, and Mhairi Paterson for preparing the tables.

In addition, the support and enthusiasm for the project that we received from law publisher, Dr Carole Dalgleish, were tremendous. She really was the sixth member of the team, making helpful suggestions on format, presentation and content. She commissioned the idea, supported it throughout, and drove us on. The publishers, T & T Clark Ltd, are to be congratulated too, for ensuring that the book has been produced at a price affordable to most students.

Working together as a team, we have tried to present the law in an accessible way, which we hope will facilitate the learning and understanding of law. We, ourselves, are enthusiasts and hope that this book may encourage those who read it to explore the law beyond the basics. It is our sincere hope that this book will find a place in student affections as their first law book (if there can be such a thing as affection for a law book!).

Nicole Busby
Bryan Clark
Richard Mays
Roderick Paisley
Paul Spink

March 2000

THE AUTHORS

Nicole Busby is a lecturer in law at the Robert Gordon University and has held the post since 1997. She previously worked at the University of Glasgow. She has taught company law and employment law across a wide range of courses. She has worked as a consultant on the implementation of both of these areas of law, particularly in the context of SMEs. Her main research interests are in the fields of European and employment law and she has published widely in both reference works and academic journals. Recent publications include: "Division of Labour: Maternity Rights in Europe" (2000) *Journal of Social Welfare and Family Law* 3; and "Arbitration: A Suitable Mechanism for Adjudication of Unfair Dismissal Claims?" (1999) 18 *Civil Justice Quarterly* 149.

Bryan Clark is currently a lecturer in business law at Heriot Watt University. He holds a B.A. (Hons.) from the Robert Gordon University and an LL.M. in Petroleum Law and Policy from the University of Dundee. His main teaching and research interests are company law and civil justice. He has published widely in these and other areas in a number of academic and professional journals. Recent publications include: "The Director's Duty of Care: Subjective, Objective or Both?" (1999) 27 SLT (News) 239; "Unfairly Prejudicial Conduct" (1999) 38 SLT (News) 321; and "Fiduciary Duties under the Joint Operating Agreement" (1999) 20 *Business Law Review* 150.

Richard Mays is a senior lecturer in law at the Robert Gordon University and has held that post since 1994. He is a qualified solicitor and holds a Ph.D. from the University of Edinburgh. He is author of *Summary Cause Procedure in the Sheriff Court* (1995); *Social Work Law in Scotland* (with Veronica Strachan and Vikki Smith) (1999); and the General Editor of *Scottish Social Work Legislation* (looseleaf). In addition, he has published numerous peer-reviewed journal articles. His latest article is "The Criminal Liability of Corporations and Scots Law—The Lessons of Anglo-American Jurisprudence" (2000) 4 *Edinburgh Law Review* 46.

Roderick Paisley is Professor of Commercial Property Law at the University of Aberdeen. He is also a qualified solicitor and previously worked in private practice in Glasgow and Aberdeen, mainly in the field of commercial conveyancing. His areas of research and teaching include land law, conveyancing, succession and trusts. He is also co-author (with Sheriff Douglas Cusine) of *Servitudes and Rights of Way* (SULI, 1998), and contributes regularly to *Scottish Law & Practice Quarterly*. Current research activities include a book on unreported Sheriff Court cases on property law with commentaries and a book on property law in Scotland.

Paul Spink is a lecturer in law at the University of Stirling. His main research interests are in the fields of competition law, EU law and the law of the single market. Recent publications include: "Comparative Advertising in the European Union" (1998) 47 *International Comparative Quarterly* 855 (with R. Petty); "Enforcing EC Competition Law: Fixing the Quantum Fines" (1999) *Journal of Business Law* 219; and "Challenging Environmental Tobacco Smoke in the Workplace" (2000) 1 (4) *Environmental Law Review* 243.

CONTENTS

      An Emerging Nation
      The Eleventh, Twelfth and Thirteenth Centuries
      The Fourteenth, Fifteenth and Sixteenth Centuries
      The Seventeenth Century
      The Eighteenth Century
      The Nineteenth Century
      The Twentieth and Twenty-First Centuries

      Historical and Philosophical Sources
      Formal Sources

      Overview
      The Civil Courts
      The Criminal Courts
      The European Court of Justice
      Courts of Special Jurisdiction
      Alternatives to the Court
      Legal Personnel

      Overview
      The Essential Elements of a Contract
      Gratuitous Undertaking
      Formation of Contract
      Formalities of Contract
      Defective Contracts

TABLE OF CASES

TABLE OF STATUTES

TABLE OF STATUTORY INSTRUMENTS

1 THE HISTORY OF SCOTS LAW

Few legal systems can boast of a heritage quite as rich or diverse as the Scottish. Built **1–01** on foundations one thousand years old, it has drawn selectively from a wide variety of sources, including foreign schools of legal policy typically characterised as mutually exclusive. An immutable symbol of nationhood, the independence of Scots law has been assiduously guarded since the time of David I. Even after Union with England in 1707, the Scottish legal system retained its own distinctive character. As a consequence, Scots law today combines a unique blend of doctrine and principle.

AN EMERGING NATION

During the Iron Age, Celtic tribes migrated north from mainland Europe and settled **1–02** in the territory that would eventually become Scotland. They brought with them a well-established legal system predicated on the observance of consuetudinary, or customary, practice. Although this largely unwritten law exercised influence that can be traced in the Highland and Island communities of the Middle Ages, it has left no enduring mark on modern Scots law.

The Romans came to Britain in 43 AD, but Scotland was never conquered despite the empire's sporadic attempts at subjugation. Almost four hundred years of skirmishing followed but, perhaps ironically, given their subsequent susceptibility, large parts of the native population emphatically rejected the influence of Roman culture and law.

In the "dark ages" that followed the end of the Roman occupation of southern Britain, four distinct peoples fought over the territory of the north. The Picts, whose arrival may have preceded even the earliest Celtic immigrants, arguably qualify as Scotland's indigenous tribe. They occupied the land north of the Forth-Clyde line, excluding Argyll. From Irish Dalriada came an ambitious and aggressive people known as the Scots. After establishing a base in Argyll they expanded into Galloway and the Western Isles before meeting fierce resistance. The Angles, a Germanic tribe imported into Britain by the Romans in an attempt to stabilise the border provinces, had established themselves in the Northumbrian Lothians. The Britons formed a kingdom at Strathclyde, extending from its capital at Dun Breatann (modern Dumbarton) to the shires of Ayr and Stirling.

In 843 Kenneth MacAlpin was crowned king of the Scots. He also had a contested claim to kingship of the Picts and, according to legend, he eliminated rival claimants to that throne with brutality. By 847 he had united the two tribes and forged the new kingdom of Alba (or Scotia), which encompassed all the territory of Scotland north of the river Forth.

With more powerful kingdoms to the north and south, the Angles of Northumbria and the Britons of Strathclyde fell into gradual decline. However, in time, the language of the Scottish Angles became entrenched in the south and east of Scotland. That language was English. The primacy of "Scots" English over the Celtic dialects was to prove a crucial factor in the future development of the emerging nation's legal system.

MacAlpin and his successors were soon confronted by a new threat. By the middle of the ninth century, Scotland, like the rest of Britain, was subject to attack by raiders from Scandinavia. The young kingdom survived this onslaught, but in the years that followed Vikings established extensive settlements in Orkney, Shetland and the Western Isles, and on the coastal fringes of the northern mainland. Accordingly, it was Norse law and custom that governed these territories. This well-developed legal system exercised great influence over Orkney and Shetland long after Scotland eventually acquired the islands in 1468–69. Indeed, traces of udal law (on land rights and ownership) from the thirteenth-century Gulathing Code of the Norwegian king, Magnus IV ("the Law-Mender"), have survived to see occasional application in modern times.

By 1016, England was in a state of turmoil, under the weak and ineffectual leadership of Ethelred ("the Unready") and beset by Danish invaders (led by King Canute). The Scottish king, Malcolm II, capitalised on this situation by allying with Owen, the titular king of Strathclyde, and striking against the Northumbrian army. The Battle of Carham, fought in either 1016 or 1018, saw Malcolm capture the Lothians. At the battle, or soon after, Owen of Strathclyde died. His kingdom was thereafter subsumed within the kingdom of Alba, and the new Scottish nation (excepting those areas still under Viking control) achieved its modern territorial boundaries.

THE ELEVENTH, TWELFTH AND THIRTEENTH CENTURIES

EARLY INFLUENCES

1–03   On the death of Malcolm II a bitter and bloody struggle for power ensued between his descendants and Macbeth, the earl of Moray. Malcolm Canmore ("Big Head" or "Great Chief"), an heir of the original royal line, finally prevailed. He was crowned king, Malcolm III, in 1058. His reign has been portrayed as the era in which English influence first took hold in Scotland, but this paints a rather crude picture of history. Fundamentally, and certainly in terms of the development of law, there was no significant "English" factor, even in England, for several generations after this period. Malcolm married the Saxon princess, Margaret, in 1070, and as a consequence many Anglo-Saxon, and some Norman, practices were adopted in Scotland, in particular via the Church. This alliance also marked the beginning of an era in which the political heart of the Scottish monarchy became detached from the Celtic, Gaelic-speaking North and drew closer to the Teutonic, English-speaking South. However, the Scottish king harboured dreams of conquest and his reign is best characterised by conflict, rather than co-operation, with England's new Norman masters. On at least five occasions Malcolm invaded the north of England. Each time he was driven back, and on his final campaign in Northumberland in 1093 he met his end.

FEUDALISM

The Norman conquest of England in 1066 had no immediate impact in Scotland. **1-04**
However, while several kings, including Duncan III (1093–94 and 1094–97) and Alexander
I (1107–1124), attempted to stem the tide, Norman influence and institutions began to
permeate Scottish society. This process, which has been referred to as Anglicisation, but
is more accurately rendered Anglo-Normanisation,[1] accelerated under David I, who was
king from 1124 to 1153. David had spent his youth in England and trained as a knight
under the English king, Henry I. He was much impressed by the Anglo-Norman system
of government that had so quickly and effectively pacified his host country.

David's own royal court, the Church and, in particular, the nascent Scottish legal
system came to be styled on the Norman model. That said, David's reign should not
be depicted as one of bland mimicry of his larger, more powerful neighbour.
Although much was borrowed, the manner of its adoption was by no means slavish.
Although substantive variation was rare, David took steps to ensure that Norman
principle and policy were tailored to suit Scotland.

It was at this time that the feudal system of land tenure, by which vassals held lands
from lords-superior on condition of certain (usually military) services, was implemented in Scotland. By the process of subinfeudation, land was in turn passed on
in smaller parcels to sub-vassals in return for the performance of feudal duties (in
England, this was prohibited by Edward I in 1290; in Scotland subinfeudation remains
competent—but, by the abolition of Feudal Tenure etc (Scotland) Act 2000 it will shortly
become incompetent). Above all, stood the king, from whom the whole, intricate web of
obligation and fealty emanated. Through this structure, he disseminated his law.

BARON, SHERIFF AND JUSTICIAR

Usually the tenant-in-chief (the first recipient of land—often styled as baron) enjoyed **1-05**
the right to a seat at the king's council (*Curia Regis*) and to hold court, in both civil and
criminal matters, over his own feudal tenants. Procedure in the Scottish feudal courts
is described in the *Quoniam Attachiamenta*, which was written in the latter part of the
fourteenth century. It was this system of justice that governed the everyday life of
the common Scot. Over time, certain barons were entrusted with considerably more
expansive powers of public justice, including the Crown Pleas of murder, rape, incest
and arson. Other royal privileges were also bestowed and these most favoured barons
became holders *in regalitatem*. A "regality" was therefore a barony with extended
jurisdictional and administrative powers—in a sense, a kingdom within a kingdom.

The office of sheriff was also introduced during David's reign. Loosely based on the
Anglo-Saxon *shire-reeve*, this post was transformed under the early Norman kings.
Appointed from the lower tiers of the royal council, the sheriffs administered civil and
criminal justice, in a manner complementary but technically superior to the jurisdiction of the tenant-in-chief, in the king's name. They also exercised important tax
collection powers. It was some considerable time before these officers penetrated the
far reaches of the country, but by the end of the thirteenth century the whole of
Scotland had been divided into sheriffdoms.

---

[1]   Some commentators prefer the term Scotto-Normanisation.

Above the sheriff, and second only to the king's court in the new judicial hierarchy, stood the justiciar (or justice-ayre). These high officers, again of Norman origin, oversaw the work of the sheriffs. They had extensive judicial powers, dealing in particular with the four pleas of the Crown. They dispensed justice in matters of civil and criminal law that fell between the jurisdiction of the sheriff and the attention of the king's court. The justiciars, who were appointed from the ranks of the nobility, eventually came to neglect their judicial role. Records indicate a lack of enthusiasm for travel in the regions on circuit or ayre, and by the fifteenth century the justiciars' courts were sporadic in operation. The civil jurisdiction of the justiciar was thereafter swallowed up by other courts, but after the intervention of James VI in 1587 they continued to play an important part in the administration of criminal justice until the foundation of the High Court of Justiciary in 1672.

In short, by about 1150 the superstructure of Scotland's legal system was in place. The feudal or baronial courts had an extensive jurisdiction over the day to day affairs of the community. These courts were supervised by the sheriffs, who themselves enjoyed wide jurisdiction, and were in turn watched over by the justiciars. The king's council sat as the final appellate court from the justiciar. It also dealt with matters concerning the magnates at first instance. An early form of trial by jury was introduced during this period. Although differing in emphasis and in the minutiae of law, the emerging Scottish and English legal systems shared a similar, Norman-engineered, feudal beginning.

A PEACEFUL INVASION

1–06 At the time of David I, and for sometime thereafter, broad allusion to the concept of "Scottishness" is as unhelpful as any contemporary reference to "Englishness", in the context of the evolution of the respective states' legal systems. Each country played host to a cosmopolitan population, and, on both sides of the border, most of those with the power to influence the development of the law were Norman. An often over-looked but important feature of this period was the royal policy of importing Norman nobility. With the promise of land and power, David, himself an Anglo-Norman nobleman, enticed into Scotland those French families that would come to form its ruling class. It was by this means that the families of Balliol, Brus (or Bruce) and Stewart, among many others, came to establish themselves in Scotland. This migration of minor French nobility underpinned what became a strong and durable alliance between the two countries. While native chieftains were tolerated, they were unques-tionably sidelined. David lavished favours on these Norman incomers, intent on exploiting their expertise in military and political affairs to consolidate his own position.

THE BURGHS

1–07 Another feature of David's reign was the emergence of the Scottish burghs. Burghal courts, with jurisdiction over land and merchant disputes, delivered local justice under the authority of the guilds and the protection of the king. The Chamberlain went on ayre to supervise these courts (there were 20 burghs by 1153) and a final appeal lay to the "Parliament" of the burghs, which ultimately declared the law to be applied. The "Four Burghs" of Edinburgh, Roxburgh, Stirling and Berwick implemented the *Leges Quatuor Burgorum*, a body of law of Anglo-Saxon origin, overlaid with the pick of local custom and incorporating some Norman doctrine and terminology. The *Leges*, perhaps the earliest surviving collected body of law in Scotland, contain regulations of an economic and administrative nature for the control of burghal life.

CANON LAW

From the middle of the twelfth century onwards, Church courts, which administered the Canon law of Rome, began to establish themselves. Operating alongside the royal and burghal justice systems, clerical judges-delegate came to enjoy wide civil and criminal jurisdiction, and dominated the broad field of family law. Decisions were frequently reviewed on appeal to Rome. As a consequence, there is no evidence that distinctively Scottish rules evolved prior to the Reformation in the sixteenth century. **1–08**

It was by reason of pressure from the Fourth Lateran Council[2] that certain ancient practices, including trial by ordeal, fell into desuetude. The fundamental Scots law precept of the binding gratuitous promise also owes its existence to the influence of the Canonists. Thus, the modern Scots law of contract, unlike its English counterpart, incorporates no doctrine of consideration. Clerical lawyers schooled in the Canon law participated in the administration of lay, as well as ecclesiastical, courts (including royal councils) until the Reformation. During this period they provided formative contributions in almost all spheres of law. The procedure of the Court of Session, established in 1532, was based on the highly developed Romano-Canonical model, and these new rules gradually filtered down into the sheriff courts. It is through the reception of Canon law that Roman law first influenced the development of the Scottish legal system. As is shown below, its impact was both profound and long-lived.

FROM ANGLO-NORMAN TO SCOTO-ROMAN LAW

The period leading up to the Wars of Independence, in particular the reign of Alexander III (1249–86), saw strong and stable government under which the feudal, burghal and church courts flourished. Relations with England, which had deteriorated after the death of Henry I, were repaired. As the contemporary text *Regiam Majestatem* testifies, Scotland remained content to adopt the best of the Anglo-Norman legal system. Gradually, however, the two systems of law began to diverge. Several factors contributed to this process. **1–09**

From the early part of the thirteenth century, English justices, having at their disposal burgeoning volumes of juristic material, set about the task of refining and elaborating the law. The relative simplicity of Norman law rapidly became overlaid with innumerable technicalities. Precedent piled on precedent to create, within a remarkably short period, an intricate labyrinth of case law.

Even if Scottish lawyers had wished to stay abreast, the logistics of the situation, including the probable absence of any comprehensive system of law reporting in Scotland and difficulties of communication with Westminster, now mitigated against close co-ordination. In any event, by the middle of the thirteenth century, the growth of the church courts and the activism of clerical lawyers had ensured that Canon and

---

[2] A general council of the Western Church held in the Lateran Basilica, Rome in 1215, regarded by Roman Catholics as ecumenical.

Roman law had gained a strong foothold in Scotland. The emerging legal profession became indoctrinated with the civilian idiom of legal thought, which demands deductive reasoning from general principle to specific application. This systematic process is the antithesis of the precedent-driven common law system that was developing south of the border. The empirical English system requires not a deductive approach, but inductive logic enabling the lawyer to extrapolate from specific instances to derive a general principle capable of application in future cases.

The English common law courts created specific forms of action for each individual type of claim. Procedural intricacy, and thus rigidity, quickly built itself into the system. This route was not followed in Scotland, where early forms of action, known as brieves (based on the English writ), gave way to a more flexible procedural form (the summons) which could be adapted to fit numerous different types of claim.

As these fundamental methodological and procedural differences entrenched themselves, divorce of the two legal systems became a political objective for a Scottish monarchy eager to assert its independence against an increasingly hostile and expansionist England. With the accidental death of Alexander III in 1286, so ended the amiable, if tentative, relationship between the two countries. Alexander had taken steps to ensure that his granddaughter Margaret ("Maid of Norway") would be recognised as his heir, but she was only three years old at the time of his death. In 1290, as she made her way to her new realm, she died in Orkney.

THE STRUGGLE FOR INDEPENDENCE

1–10   The Scottish nobility again turned in on itself to compete for the throne. No fewer than 13 candidates presented themselves for consideration. In a bid to minimise the threat of invasion from the south, Edward I, the hawkish king of England, was invited to sit in judgment on the claimants. Edward narrowed the field to the two best claims, those of John Balliol and Robert Bruce, and then, with a vested interest, chose the lesser man in Balliol. The new king was enthroned at Scone on St Andrew's Day, 1292.

THE FOURTEENTH, FIFTEENTH AND SIXTEENTH CENTURIES

ROBERT BRUCE

1–11   Edward immediately launched a campaign to undermine John. Within days of the coronation, contrary to an earlier undertaking to respect the independence of Scots law, the English king began overruling judgments delivered in Scottish courts. John had no response. The new king proved himself both weak and malleable, and Edward proceeded to heap humiliation upon him. Eventually, in 1295, as Edward prepared for war with France, the Scottish magnates rose up and allied themselves with the French king, Philip IV. John played a passive role in this endeavour. Edward, on the other hand, was a formidable soldier and widely recognised as the foremost king of the Christian world. His reputation as the "Hammer of the Scots" is well deserved. Marching north in 1296, he quickly suppressed the rebellion, before ceremonially stripping John of the throne. In the summer of 1298 he dealt a similarly decisive blow to the guerrilla forces of William Wallace at the Battle of

Falkirk. This left a power vacuum in Scotland and the country fell under English administration.

After years of political strife, Robert Bruce, grandson of the earlier claimant, took the throne in 1306. However, with a view to clearing the path to his succession, Robert had conspired in the murder of John Comyn, who arguably had a stronger claim to kingship. The new king was defeated at Methven by the English, and then again by Comyn's supporters at Dalrigh, near Tyndrum. As Scotland teetered on the brink of civil war, Robert was forced into hiding. Edward again journeyed north to reassert his authority, but the aging English king died before he could crush the new uprising. Robert Bruce survived to consolidate his position.

The new king of England, Edward II, lacked the tenacity of his father and allowed Robert the freedom to prosecute a long war of attrition in Scotland. The Scots won a decisive victory at Bannockburn in 1314, but it was not until 1328, after Edward had been deposed, that the war ended. The Treaty of Edinburgh, which guaranteed Scotland's independence, was signed on 17th March 1328.

AFTER BRUCE

Predictably, the Wars of Independence accelerated the divergence of the Scottish and **1–12** English legal systems. There was no abrupt termination of Anglo-Norman influence, but increasingly Canonical-Roman law became the model from which Scotland borrowed. The optimism engendered by the signing of the Treaty of Edinburgh was short-lived. After King Robert's death in 1329, Scotland, which had benefited from a period of reconstruction and consolidation in the latter part of his reign, descended into another dark and turbulent age. Political infighting and a series of ineffectual kings diminished the authority of the crown and destabilised the country to a degree that was not conducive to the healthy development of its legal system.

The Treaty of Edinburgh was soon forgotten. Edward III renewed England's campaign against Scotland and relations between the two countries deteriorated once again. Over the following centuries both countries had a hand in perpetuating what became an almost constant state of hostility. Scotland's alliance with France, itself in conflict with England, was rejuvenated. However, although French influence was strong, and in many respects positive, it was small compensation for Scotland's troubled relationship with its southern neighbour. Conflict with England had a debilitating effect on all aspects of Scottish life. Internecine clan warfare and widespread poverty further served to hamper the administration and refinement of Scots law. Although the term has now fallen into disrepute, this is a period that has been referred to by many commentators as the "Dark Age" of Scottish legal history.

The feudal structure that underpinned Scotland's government and legal system deteriorated as the power of the monarchy dwindled. Socio-economic malaise and political decay provoked the implementation of regressive legal policies. Numerous attempts were made to recapture what was perceived to be the thirteenth-century "golden age" of Scots law, but these were frustrated because the necessary legal infrastructure did not exist. Those primitive practices that were resurrected actually had the effect of stultifying modernisation. The administration of justice was organised on an ad hoc basis, at a local level. Unqualified judges drawn from the minor nobility followed their own fluctuating interpretation of the law, often delivering judgments in their own interest, and public confidence was undermined. The absence of a supreme court ensured a lack of supervision, uniformity and central co-ordination. This in turn allowed further inefficiencies and corruption to infect the system. It became common to oversimplify great tracts of substantive law. While some patchy social reform was undertaken during the period, this was undeniably an era in which many aspects of Scottish society, in particular the legal system, suffered considerable stagnation.

THE EARLY PARLIAMENT

1–13 All that said, the picture was perhaps not quite as dark as some have painted. A Parliament, comprised of the "Three Estates" of the clergy, burgesses and tenants-in-chief, came into being. This assembly established itself in the fourteenth and fifteenth centuries. From an early stage in its development it exercised some broad judicial functions, hearing appeals from a variety of courts. The practice of holding regular judicial sittings, or "Sessions", was formalised in 1426 as part of a package of measures adopted by Parliament to improve the machinery of government and the administration of justice. Many of these refinements had an English pedigree. By the end of the fifteenth century, Scotland's legislative base had expanded considerably, although it was still far from complete.

THE COURT OF SESSION

1–14 Scotland continued to suffer extended periods of war, religious upheaval and civil unrest (including Cromwellian occupation from 1651–1660) until the end of the seventeenth century, but the promise of a new dawn in the development of its legal system was signalled by the foundation of the College of Justice in 1532. The College, which grew out of the judicial committees of Parliament, was funded by the Church (another sign of the impotence of the Crown), and, in recognition of this, seven of the 14 appointed Senators and the President of the College were prelates (this practice was abrogated by 1579). These 15 judges constituted the Court of Session, which came to exercise supervisory control over all subordinate courts and remains the supreme civil court of Scotland today. Based on a Roman model, the Court of Session provided Scotland with a permanent, professional judiciary trained in Canon and Civil law. (It is important to note that the word "civil" has two different meanings. It may describe that branch of law that is not criminal law; alternatively, it may describe a body of legal doctrine founded on Roman law.) These "Session" judges modelled the developing law of Scotland in the image of their own education and experience. Accordingly, at this important formative stage, it was canonical procedure and the civilian doctrines of continental Europe that predominated in the new court.

PRACTICKS

1–15 While the court was still in its infancy, judge-made and practitioner-made case notes began to emerge. At the behest of James V, these notes, which became known as *Practicks*, were compiled in volumes and circulated among members of the profession. Later they provided a model for the earliest published law reports. Other *Practicks*, including those of Balfour and Hope, attempted a complete digest of the law, incorporating statutory, foreign and historical materials alongside case notes and a practical commentary. Courtroom reference to previous decisions became commonplace and a growing tendency to respect earlier judgments manifested itself. These practices did not, however, come to crystallise in the form of a perfected doctrine of *stare decisis*—which requires a judge to abide by a decided case on the same point of law. It was probably the influence of Roman law, with its emphasis on principle over precedent, that resulted in Scottish courts not going the same way as the English in this regard.

LEGAL EDUCATION

The growing legal profession established both the Faculty of Advocates and the Society of Writers to the Signet in this period. The third branch of the profession, which comprised of the Notaries Public, also developed during the sixteenth century. However, those that aspired to practice found a lack of adequate instruction in the Scottish universities. As a consequence, from the middle of the sixteenth century, Scots students flocked in great numbers to the universities of France, and later the Netherlands, to receive schooling in Roman law, where the discipline had flourished since the early days of the Renaissance. When these budding lawyers returned home, it was largely to civilian principle and authority that they turned when confronted with an issue on which Scots law was silent. In this fashion, Roman law both inspired and underpinned innovative legal argument in proceedings before Scottish courts.

1–16

THE REFORMATION

The Reformation of 1559–60 brought an end to the church courts and to the study of Canon law in Scotland. Commissary courts were set up to take over the family law jurisdiction of their ecclesiastical predecessors, and from 1609 appeal lay to the Court of Session. All law that conflicted with the Protestant religion was annulled by Parliament in 1567 and, *inter alia*, judicial divorce was introduced. Only Canon law that had hitherto been assimilated into the Common law of Scotland, including certain aspects of the law of marriage, survived this act of expurgation.

1–17

On the other hand, the Scottish Protestants, led by John Knox, held Roman law in high esteem. Calvin had much admired it, and its influence is readily discernible in his work. The "Auld Alliance", which had come into existence in 1295 when Scotland and France shared a common enemy in England, now faltered. Indeed, putting mutual hostility temporarily aside, for a time the Scots and the English collaborated to mitigate the threat that Catholic France posed to their new religion.

THE SEVENTEENTH CENTURY

UNION OF THE CROWNS

On the death of Queen Elizabeth in 1603 the crowns of Scotland and England were united under James VI of Scotland and I of England. James immediately left Edinburgh for London, and thereafter governed Scotland through close control of the Privy Council.

1–18

In March 1604, James enthusiastically addressed the Westminster Parliament with plans for complete union between Scotland and England. His proposal received a cool reception on both sides of the border. In deference to the wishes of the king, commissioners were appointed to investigate the project, but it was clear from the outset that the weight of political and public opinion in both countries was opposed to unification. The commissioners, including the eminent lawyer Sir Thomas Craig (author of *Jus Feudale*, 1655), returned a favourable report. However, the project was shelved in the face of continued public apathy, if not outright animosity.

James did at least achieve the repeal of English Acts treating Scotland as a hostile state. In *Calvin's Case*,[3] he secured the principle of dual nationality for those born after his accession. Furthermore, in a successful attempt to tighten his control of the region, James abrogated the *Leges Marchiarum*, or laws of the Borders. By this unique legal system the oft-disputed lands between the two countries had been governed since the twelfth century.

Inspired by the "laudable custom of England", the office of Justice of the Peace was expanded to include the functions of a local magistracy in 1609. For many years this post was unpopular. An insufficient number of justices were appointed to meet the workload, and the powers accorded to them were inadequate to fulfil their extensive judicial and administrative duties. Justices suffered intimidation, to the extent of armed bands invading sittings, and they were often undermined by local barons, who saw them as "rivals for the profits of justice". It was not until the system was reorganised after the Act of Union that justices began to play the role originally envisaged for them.

Another important development during the reign of James VI was the establishment in 1617 of the General Register of Sasines. The Sasine Register maintained a public record of all transactions relating to land in Scotland until 1979 when land registration became competent in some areas.

SCOTLAND UNDER CROMWELL

1–19 Scottish forces fought on both sides of the English Civil War, but the country was ultimately outraged by Cromwell's execution of Charles I in 1649. Thereafter, the Scots rallied to support the cause of Charles II, who was proclaimed king in Edinburgh. This brought Cromwell north with his well-trained and experienced army. Led by David Leslie, the Scottish royalists were routed at Dunbar in September 1650. Cromwell proceeded to subjugate the country, a task he carried out with brutal efficiency. Scotland offered little resistance to the occupation he instituted. Commissioners were appointed to undertake the work of the Privy Council and the Court of Session. Ironically, these functions were performed in a highly competent and diligent manner, and Scotland benefited from a period of stable government and effective justice. However, Scottish representation in the Commonwealth and Protectorate Parliaments was limited to a derisory 30 members and an inveterate attitude of mutual distrust did nothing to further Cromwell's plan for full union between the two countries. After Cromwell's death in 1658, the political environment and administration he had so carefully engineered rapidly deteriorated. English rule in Scotland came to an end, and the restoration of the Stuarts quashed all hopes of early union.

THE RESTORATION

1–20 Charles II ruled Scotland from London by decree in similar fashion to his grandfather, James VI. Not once during his 25-year reign did he visit Scotland. A hand-picked

---

[3]　1608 7 Co Rep 1a.

Scottish Parliament reconvened in 1661 to restore by legislation the authority of the Crown. An Act Recissory annulled all Acts passed since 1633. The Court of Session was also reinstated. Charles' instrument of control was the Privy Council, which came to enjoy extensive legislative and judicial powers under the royal prerogative. As a result, Parliament and the Court of Session were sidelined, to some extent, during this period.

HIGH COURT OF JUSTICIARY

1–21 The High Court of Justiciary was established by statute in 1672. Descended from the Court of the Justiciar, the High Court remains the supreme criminal court of Scotland today. Based in Edinburgh, the Court is presided over by the Lord Justice-General. This office was, until 1830, an honorary position conferred by the Crown on a succession of noblemen who were not legally trained. Now, the position is held by the Lord President of the Court of Session, Scotland's most senior judge. The day to day work of the court was undertaken by the Lord Justice-Clerk and five Senators of the College of Justice (Court of Session judges), who, in this capacity, took the title Commissioners of Justiciary. Unlike the Court of Session, which is permanently established in Edinburgh, it was provided that the High Court would travel on circuit to the major towns of Scotland to try the more serious crimes (although this practice was not fully implemented until the middle of the eighteenth century). The High Court is endowed with privative or exclusive jurisdiction over the Crown pleas, and exercises appellate jurisdiction over all subordinate courts in the criminal justice system. No appeal lies from the High Court to the House of Lords at Westminster.[4]

The development of criminal justice did not proceed apace with that of the civil law. Although the same respected judges of the civil courts also dispensed criminal justice, the quality of the latter seldom matched that of the jurisprudence formulated in the Session. By way of example, "witches" were still being burned in the 1720s in Scotland.

THE INSTITUTIONAL WRITERS

1–22 The latter half of the seventeenth century saw legal writing assume an increasingly important function. Over the next 150 years a series of monumental works set about the organisation and consolidation of Scots law. Unless contradicted by modern case law or legislation these are still reliable sources of law. The first to come to print was Sir Thomas Craig's *Jus Feudale* in 1655. This text expounds the feudal land law of Scotland and draws close comparison to English law. In 1681 Viscount Stair published *The Institutions of the Law of Scotland*. Foremost among the so-called "institutional writers" Stair, a former Lord President of the Court of Session, is celebrated as the architect of modern Scots law. In his work, Stair presented an original amalgamation of the ostensibly disparate laws of Scotland. He consolidated strands of Roman, Canon, feudal and customary law with the primary sources of statute and case law, deducing a comprehensive set of rules to underpin the civil system of justice. Adopting a style inspired by the sixth-century *Institutes* of the Roman Emperor Justinian, Stair advanced in his jurisprudence an emphasis on the ordered and harmonious development of first principle. Although Stair's work is now of diminishing

---

4 *Mackintosh v Lord Advocate* (1876) 3 R (HL) 34.

significance in the day to day business of the law, it was of fundamental importance in establishing the shape, identity and philosophical base of modern Scots law.

Among the other writers recognised as authoritative, Erskine stands second only to Stair. His *magnum opus, An Institute of the Laws of Scotland* (1773), offers an elegant analysis of classical Scots law, again deduced from first principles. His work is more accessible than that of Stair and has been cited more frequently in modern times.

George Bell must also be considered a jurist of the first rank. His *Commentaries on the Law of Scotland and on the Principles of Mercantile Jurisprudence* (1804) provides a systematic and insightful exposition of the law merchant and, again, is regularly cited.

In the field of criminal law David Hume is pre-eminent. His work, *Commentaries on the Law of Scotland Respecting Crimes* (1797) is of the highest authority on the subject, and is redolent of Stair's own endeavour in civil law. George Mackenzie, a contemporary of Stair, made an early contribution to the literature with *The Laws and Customs of Scotland in Matters Criminal* (1678), but his work is largely overshadowed by that of Hume.

THE EIGHTEENTH CENTURY

THE ACT OF UNION

1–23 The eighteenth century ushered in new crises for Scotland. Queen Anne, the last of the Stuart monarchs, was, incredibly, predeceased by all of her 17 children. Prevarication over the question of the succession provoked another serious deterioration in relations between England and Scotland. However, it was clear that neither country could countenance war. Scotland was poor and its population afflicted by famine. After the catastrophic collapse of the Darien colonial trading venture, trade with England offered the only realistic lifeline. England, on the other hand, was already at war with France and needed to keep its northern boundary secure.

Despite public opposition in Scotland, a joint commission met in London in April 1706 to discuss the terms for union. The English conceded unfettered freedom of trade and the Scots agreed to recognise Sophia, Electress of Hanover, and her Protestant heirs as successors to Anne as Queen of Scotland. When the terms for union were presented to the Scottish Parliament on 12th October there were riots in the streets of Edinburgh, Glasgow and Dumfries. Many members spoke passionately against what they perceived to be "the murder of Scotland", but economic pragmatism ultimately prevailed over nationalist sentiment. In the words of William Seton of Pitmedden, "this nation, being poor, and without force to protect its commerce, cannot reap great advantage by it, till it partake of the trade and protection of some powerful neighbour nation".

On 25th March 1707, James Douglas, the "Union Duke", adjourned the Scottish Parliament. The first Parliament of Great Britain met at Westminster in October of the year, with Scotland represented by 45 members of the House of Commons and 16 peers in the House of Lords. The Scottish Privy Council was abolished in 1708.

As a postscript on the original Scottish Parliament, it is pertinent to note that, unlike its English counterpart, it never even purported to represent popular opinion. By the middle of the fifteenth century a small committee known as the Lords of the Articles had been appointed. This body came to enjoy virtually unchecked legislative power and its existence denied Parliament the opportunity to attain a state of functional maturity. Once the Crown had assumed the power to appoint to this committee in 1612, Parliament became "a mere registry for the royal will".

Under the Act of Union Scotland retained its own system of law with two provisos. First, the revenue laws of England in regard to trade, customs and excise were to apply in Scotland. Second, and perhaps more importantly, it was declared that Scots law could be altered by the new Great Britain Parliament—absolutely in the case of public rights of policy and civil government, but only for the "evident utility of the subjects of Scotland" in the case of private rights.

The 1707 Act also guaranteed the maintenance and jurisdiction of Scotland's courts. The question of the judicial role of the House of Lords was avoided in the Treaty, but the House quickly assumed jurisdiction to hear appeals from the Court of Session.[5] This decision was disputed in Scotland, but many appeals followed. The House of Lords is now recognised as the final court of appeal for Scotland in civil cases.

ENGLISH INFLUENCE RESTORED

Aimed at a restoration of the Stuart dynasty, the two Jacobite rebellions of 1715 and **1–24** 1745 were quickly suppressed. In the aftermath of the "Forty-Five", the heritable jurisdictions (of barony and regality) vested in the feudal lords, now so clearly at odds with the exercise of the central authority of the State, were abolished by Parliament. The hereditary office of sheriff was also replaced by Crown appointed, legally qualified, sheriffs-depute (a close equivalent of the modern sheriff principal).

Scotland settled into a more peaceful, and more prosperous, age. Domestic stability enabled the steady development of Scots law, a process fortified by the endeavour of the institutional writers. Much legislation was enacted and the courts dynamically interpreted and amplified the law in their decisions. As the Scottish legal system matured in partnership with the English, the need for constant reference to Roman law diminished. Erskine habitually draws on Roman law in his work, published in 1773, but as time passed Roman law came to be "more frequently cited from the Bar than applied by the Bench". Until the middle of the eighteenth century the traditional mode of entrance to the Scottish Bar was by examination in civil law. In 1750, however, an examination in Scots law was made compulsory for all entrants.

Trading activity increased sharply during the latter half of the eighteenth century. England, which was overwhelmingly Scotland's most important market, had already developed a comprehensive and sophisticated body of commercial law and, in the absence of native authority, it was to this system that the Scottish judiciary turned. Bell's *Commentaries* (1804) is peppered with references to English authority and, while some fundamental differences remained, the jurisprudence of the Roman school was to a great extent marginalised in this important sphere.

Having established this broad avenue of influence, English law began to flow, first into the tributaries of mercantile law, and later into unconnected areas of civil law. English authority was commonly introduced into Scottish courts as a by-product of the process of litigation, often by lawyers seeking to develop fertile lines of counter-

---

[5]   *Greenshields* v *Magistrates of Edinburgh* (1710–11 Rob 12).

argument. Bell urged caution in this respect, stressing that any law so adopted should be consistent with natural justice and in conformity with existing principles of Scots law. In the main, the Scottish courts were vigilant in their rebuttal of attempts to duplicate the technicalities of English law.

THE NINETEENTH CENTURY

1–25 During the nineteenth century, English common law traditions gradually eroded the pre-eminence of Roman law in several branches of the Scottish legal system. This process was expedited by the legislative activity of the Westminster Parliament and by the appellate function of the House of Lords in Scotland's civil system of justice. The onset of the Napoleonic wars curtailed foreign study and accelerated this trend.

Writing at the beginning of the nineteenth century, Bell's analytical style bears comparison with that of contemporary English commentators. Perhaps this is to be expected, given that his early work addresses the English-engineered sphere of mercantile law. Founded on a deconstruction of decisions and the often fine points they establish, Bell's endeavour was clearly instrumental in Scotland's subsequent adoption of the English doctrine of *stare decisis*. This is one of the characteristics of modern Scots law that prevents its classification as a traditional, Roman-based system.

The administration of civil and criminal justice underwent extensive reform in this period. In particular, in 1808, the Court of Session was restructured, broadly to achieve its modern shape. The "Outer House" of the Court came to deal with cases at first instance; while the "Inner House", itself organised into two divisions of four judges each, was made an appellate court. From 1821, Inner House judgments were compiled and published in annual volumes known today as Session Cases. Procedural reform implemented in the Court of Session Act 1850 reduced the role of written pleadings, and the Court of Session Act 1868 facilitated the use of shorthand notes, which further expedited the work of the court. The Criminal Procedure (Scotland) Act 1887 and the Summary Jurisdiction Act 1907 respectively streamlined and simplified procedures in the solemn and summary criminal courts. A measure of administrative devolution took place in the latter half of the nineteenth century. In 1885 the Scottish Office was formed to assume the tasks previously undertaken by the Lord Advocate and the Home Secretary at Westminster. The following year saw the establishment of the post of Secretary of State for Scotland.

THE TWENTIETH AND TWENTY-FIRST CENTURIES

1–26 The modern period of Scots law is characterised by the increasing importance of precedent and by the expansion of statute into fields hitherto governed by the common law. Over the course of the twentieth century the Scottish legal system drifted further away from the continental school of policy and the influence of English law became ever more profound. Legislation from the Westminster Parliament extended into almost every area of traditional public and private law, and previously unregulated aspects of society fell subject to close statutory control. Most of this new legislation was designed for UK-wide applicability and English doctrine predominated. As a consequence, the mass of twentieth-century legislation bore little affiliation to established principles of Scots law and the latter underwent extensive modification over the period.

The legislative programme of court reform and consolidation embarked on during the nineteenth century continued throughout the modern period. The District Court was established in 1975.[6] The new court replaced the Justice of the Peace Courts and the Burgh Police Courts. Generally speaking, twentieth-century reforms kept faith with the original goals of simplification and rationalisation of procedure.[7] Cautious refinement, rather than innovation, became the standard. That said, this period saw rapid growth in the use of specialised tribunals, such as the Lands Tribunal for Scotland and Employment Tribunals,[8] and these ultimately made substantial inroads in the jurisdiction of the courts.

EUROPEAN INTEGRATION

In 1973 the UK joined the European Economic Community. Formed in the long shadow of   **1–27** the Second World War (1939–45) this supranational organisation was established by the Treaty of Rome 1957. The architects of the Community were driven by a desire to safeguard the fragile peace in Western Europe by integrating the economies of, and promoting co-operation between, the great continental powers. Over the years following the accession of the UK the Community grew to encompass 15 Member States and a still wider European Economic Area, and transformed itself from an economic entity founded on a single market into a political union with an expansive jurisdiction and overtly federalist ambitions.

It was the Treaty of Maastricht,[9] which entered into force on 1st November 1993, that established the European Union. As a consequence, the European Community was integrated into a broader political and institutional framework. After some initial resistance among the national courts of the Member States it is now almost universally acknowledged that EU law, in all its forms, prevails over national law, and that EU remedies must be given full effect in national legal systems.[10] Previously in the shade of the European Council and the European Commission, the democratically elected European Parliament gradually assumed greater legislative power in the latter part of the twentieth century and now has a central role in the law-making processes of the Union. The development of the European Union is likely to prove a crucial factor, perhaps the single most important factor, in the further evolution of the Scottish legal system.

THE NEW SCOTTISH PARLIAMENT

Despite the formation of Scottish Standing and Grand Committees (in 1894 and 1948   **1–28** respectively) the Westminster Parliament was long criticised for failing to accord due consideration to the Scottish perspective in the performance of its legislative function. Concerns centred on two main issues. First, it was argued that insufficient parliamentary time was dedicated to the consideration of Scottish affairs: for example,

---

[6] District Courts (Scotland) Act 1975.
[7] See, eg Sheriff Courts (Scotland) Act 1971 and Court of Session Act 1988.
[8] Formerly Industrial Tribunals—renamed by the Employment Rights (Dispute Resolution) Act 1998.
[9] The Treaty on European Union, Maastricht, 7th February 1992.
[10] C-213/89 R v Secretary of State for Transport, ex parte Factortame Ltd [1991] 1 AC 603.

throughout the whole of the 1990s the House of Commons debated the Scottish Health Service for a total of only three hours. Second, Scottish MPs, even if unanimous, require the acquiescence of the majority of the House to legislate for Scotland. Too often, the time-starved Parliament extended legislation modelled on the English legal system and tradition to Scotland without due concern for the inherent differences that still distinguish the two jurisdictions.[11]

In September 1997, a referendum on devolution produced a large majority in favour of the establishment of a Scottish Parliament with a wide range of legislative competencies, including the power to vary tax rates. A much smaller majority supported the establishment of an Assembly, with more modest powers, in Wales. On 6th May 1999 the people of Scotland voted in their first national parliamentary elections. Under a voting system that combined the traditional first-past-the-post system with proportional representation, the Labour Party won the largest number of seats, albeit an insufficient number to command an overall majority. Accordingly, Labour negotiated a coalition with the Liberal Democrats to achieve a working majority. The new Parliament, which remains ultimately subordinate to Westminster, assumed its full legislative powers on 1st July 1999.[12] After a slightly unsteady start, the new Parliament is now settling into its legislative function. Bills in progress at the time of writing include: Abolition of Feudal Tenure, etc (Scotland) Bill; Abolition of Poindings and Warrant Sales Bill; Adults with Incapacity (Scotland) Bill; and, Standards in Scotland's Schools, etc Bill.

Future developments can be monitored at the following internet sites:

Scottish Parliament: http://www.scottish.parliament.uk/
Scottish Courts: http://www.scotcourts.gov.uk/index1.htm

---

[11] One notorious example being the Truck Act (1831), which was designed to replace earlier English legislation but proved largely unintelligible to Scottish lawyers.
[12] See Chapter 2.

SUMMARY

AN EMERGING NATION

- The Battle of Carham (1016 or 1018) settled the territorial boundaries of the Scottish nation.

THE ELEVENTH, TWELFTH AND THIRTEENTH CENTURIES

- The period 1058–1250 saw strong Anglo-Norman influence. In particular, the Scottish legal system came to be styled on the Norman model. Early Scottish kings took steps to ensure that Norman principle and policy were tailored to suit Scotland.
- During the reign of David I (1124–1153) the feudal system of land tenure, by which vassals held lands from lords-superior on condition of certain (usually military) services, was implemented in Scotland. The offices of sheriff and justiciar were introduced.
- Burghal law and Canon law were well established by the end of the twelfth century.
- From 1250 the Scottish and English legal systems began to diverge.

THE FOURTEENTH, FIFTEENTH AND SIXTEENTH CENTURIES

- The Wars of Independence drove Scotland towards their enemy's enemy, France. Although French influence was positive it did not compensate for Scotland's troubled relationship with England. Conflict with England, clan warfare, primitive practices and widespread poverty served to stultify the further modernisation of the Scottish legal system.
- The Scottish Parliament established itself in the fourteenth and fifteenth centuries. Comprised of the "Three Estates" of the clergy, burgesses and tenants-in-chief, this assembly loosely exercised some broad judicial functions, hearing appeals from a variety of courts.
- The College of Justice grew out of the judicial committees of Parliament and the Court of Session was established in 1532.
- The Reformation of 1559–60 brought an end to the church courts and to the study of Canon law in Scotland.

THE SEVENTEENTH CENTURY

- James VI's plans for union between England and Scotland was shelved in 1604–5.
- The office of Justice of the Peace was expanded to include the functions of a local magistracy in 1609.
- The General Register of Sasines was established in 1617.
- The supreme criminal court of Scotland, the High Court of Justiciary, was established in 1672.

- From the latter half of the seventeenth century legal writing became increasingly prolific and influential. Viscount Stair published *The Institutions of the Law of Scotland* in 1681.

THE EIGHTEENTH CENTURY

- Erskine produced *An Institute of the Laws of Scotland* in 1773.
- The Act of Union of 1707 merged the English and Scottish Parliaments at Westminster. The Act guaranteed the maintenance and jurisdiction of Scotland's courts. The question of the judicial role of the House of Lords was avoided in the Treaty, but the House quickly assumed jurisdiction to hear appeals from the Court of Session: *Greenshields* v *Magistrates of Edinburgh* (1710–11 Rob 12).
- As the Scottish legal system matured in partnership with the English in the eighteenth century, the need for constant reference to Roman law diminished. English law began to flow, first into the tributaries of mercantile law, and later into unconnected areas of Scots civil law.

THE NINETEENTH CENTURY

- During the nineteenth century, English common law traditions gradually eroded the pre-eminence of Roman law in several branches of the Scottish legal system. This process was expedited by the legislative activity of the Westminster Parliament and by the appellate function of the House of Lords in Scotland's civil system of justice. The onset of the Napoleonic wars curtailed foreign study and accelerated this trend.

THE TWENTIETH AND TWENTY-FIRST CENTURIES

- In the twentieth century, legislation emanating from the Westminster Parliament predominated in almost every field. Existing common law was modified and previously unregulated activities and aspects of society fell subject to close statutory control.
- The UK joined the European Economic Community in 1973.
- The new Scottish Parliament, which exercises legislative power devolved from the Westminster Parliament, was established on 1st July 1999.

FURTHER READING

Lord Cooper, *The Scottish Legal Tradition* (The Saltire Society and the Stair Society, 1991) (edition by Meston and Sellar)

Gordon (ed) *Legal History in the Making* (Hambledon Press, 1991)

The Laws of Scotland: Stair Memorial Encyclopaedia (Law Society of Scotland/ Butterworths), Vol 22, "Sources of Law (General and Historical)"

Sellar, *Scottish Legal History* (Butterworths, 2000)

Walker, *A Legal History of Scotland*, Vols I–V (T&T Clark, 1988–1998)
Walker, *The Scottish Legal System* (7th edn, W Green, 1997)
White and Willock, *The Scottish Legal System* (Butterworths, 1993)

2 SOURCES OF SCOTS LAW

HISTORICAL AND PHILOSOPHICAL SOURCES

A fundamental issue in any legal system concerns the origin and validity of legal **2–01** principles. Historically, the development of Scots law has been shaped through the centuries by a wide variety of sources, including Canon (or church) law, English law and, perhaps most notably, Roman law. Philosophically, social mores, politics and economics are influential factors in the formation of legal principles. Although these historical and philosophical influences account for the origins of Scots law, they do not explain where the current binding rules of law derive their authority from. Any specific binding rule of law must be derived from one or more sources of law, known as "formal sources".

FORMAL SOURCES

Formal sources of law arise in a number of different forms including: **2–02**

- Legislation
- Common law
- Institutional writings
- Custom
- Equity.

LEGISLATION

Legislation is the primary source of law and is the result of the expression of will of a **2–03** parliamentary or rule-making body. The amount of legislation affecting Scotland has increased dramatically over the last 50 years or so. Modern life is a complex affair, requiring legislation to regulate and facilitate activities in society. In the aftermath of the Industrial Revolution of the 1850s, successive governments found it necessary to enact laws in areas such as employment, housing, health and social services, education and the environment. Recent times have also seen an increase in the number of bodies empowered to legislate for the people of Scotland. As will be noted below, this power to legislate arises either constitutionally or by legislation itself. Those bodies empowered to enact laws applicable to Scotland include the UK Parliament, the Scottish Parliament, the European Union and various individuals and bodies delegated the right to enact legislation.

UK legislation

2–04   Legislation enacted by the UK parliament is known as a statute. This represents the will of the highest law-making power in the UK—the Queen in Parliament. The UK has what is known as a parliamentary democracy. In constitutional terms this means that, except in prescribed areas where it has conceded power (for example, those issues governed by European Union legislation and those devolved to the new Scottish Parliament), the UK Parliament is the supreme legislative body in the UK and in theoretical terms is legally empowered to pass any legislation it sees fit. Unlike legislative bodies in other countries (such as the USA), the UK Parliament is not bound to bow to any higher authority such as a written constitution.[1]

Statutes applicable to Scotland

2–05   After the Act of Union of 1707 that brought about the union of the old Scottish and English Parliaments, Scotland was entitled to retain its own separate laws and legal system. Acts of the old Scottish Parliament may still apply in Scotland today (for example, the Articles of Regulation remains of relevance to the practice of arbitration in Scotland). Many Acts of the old Scottish Parliament have, however, been repealed by subsequent legislation or have fallen into desuetude (disuse). Desuetude occurs when an Act has fallen out of use or has become totally inappropriate given changing social standards and ways of life in modern society.

Not all UK Parliamentary legislation is automatically applicable to Scotland. Since the Union of the Parliaments in 1707, however, all legislation of the UK Parliament has applied to Scotland as well as England unless it has been expressly stated that it does not apply to Scotland. Given a lack of parliamentary time, it has been common for UK-wide Acts of Parliament to include additional Scottish sections designed to take account of different legal rules and concepts that exist north of the Border.[2]

Some Acts of the UK Parliament apply *only* to Scotland. This is denoted by the word 'Scotland' appearing in brackets towards the end of the title of the Act—for example, the Land Registration (Scotland) Act 1979.[3] The scope for Scotland-only Acts of the UK Parliament has been greatly reduced by the advent of the new devolved Scottish Parliament which has the exclusive right to legislate for Scotland in a number of areas.[4]

---

[1]   Although the UK Parliament is under an obligation to consider the terms of the Human Rights Act 1998—discussed below at para 2–27.
[2]   Much criticism, however, has been aimed at this practice (colloquially known as "putting a kilt" on the Act) in that it has served to erode the uniqueness of Scots law by largely disregarding the nuances of Scots law by the wholesale importing of English legal principles.
[3]   See Chapter 7.
[4]   Discussed below at para 2–10.

Types of statutes

Broadly speaking, statutes can be divided into general Acts, local Acts and personal   **2–06**
Acts. By far the most common and the most important is the general Act which applies
to the whole community. Local Acts, by contrast, are restricted to a particular locality
and personal Acts are relevant only to a particular person or group of persons.

All general Acts begin life as Public Bills. Public Bills are generally introduced to
Parliament by a Government minister responsible for the relevant area of law. Some
Public Bills, however, are brought forward by individual Members of Parliament
(MPs). These are known as Private Members' Bills. Given the lack of parliamentary
time, very few of these Bills become Acts unless they receive support from the
Government.

Local and personal Acts begin life as Private Bills. It is important that Private Bills
are not confused with Private Members' Bills. Private Bills are promoted by
individuals or groups that are seeking some sort of benefit for themselves. Such Bills
are brought by petitioning parliament—a process which is akin to a court hearing. The
Bills are normally referred to a Private Bill committee where the promoters of the Bill
seek to establish a case to obtain the necessary parliamentary powers.

Purpose of Acts

In a sense it is true to say that the purpose of all Acts of Parliament is to enact new law.   **2–07**
Some Acts, however, do have specific technical and legal purposes. Codifying Acts are
designed to assimilate all existing law in a given area and bring it within the aegis of
one piece of legislation. An example is the Partnership Act 1890 which brought
together the Scots common law (judge-made law) and set it out in statute. Similarly,
Consolidating Acts serve to bring various strands of previous legislation together in
one Act. An example is the Health and Safety at Work etc Act 1974 which brought
together provisions set out in a spate of old Acts (including the Factories Act 1961 and
the Offices, Shops and Railway Premises Acts 1963), making the law clearer and more
accessible.[5] A declaratory Act is a government tool to restate the law, particularly in
the aftermath of a controversial, unpopular or inconvenient court decision. The War
Damage Act 1965 is a pertinent example. This piece of legislation was designed to
nullify the effects of a House of Lords' decision which compelled the government of
the day to pay compensation for their destruction of British-owned oil fields in the
Korean War.[6]

Amendment Acts are those with the specific purpose of amending a previous piece
of legislation. For instance, the Companies Act 1989 amended the Companies Act 1985.
If any ambiguity exists between the provisions of the original Act and the amending
legislation, the provisions of the latter will be enforced as they represent the latest
expression of the will of Parliament.

Statute Law Revision Acts are designed to repeal previous legislation which has
become obsolete or fallen into disuse. By contrast, a Law Reform (Miscellaneous
Provisions) Act is a common method by which minor amendments can be made to
various areas of law at the same time.

---

[5] See Chapter 12.
[6] *Burmah Oil Co (Burma Trading) Ltd v Lord Advocate* 1964 SC (HL) 117.

The legislative process for Public Bills

Pre-parliamentary procedure

2–08 Public Bills begin their life outside Parliament. Pre-parliamentary aspects are a very significant stage in any fledgling Bill's life. The law-making process begins by the Government considering what legislative measures it wishes to put to Parliament. At this stage, advice may be obtained and consultation sought from a number of internal and external bodies. Government departmental and inter-departmental committees are a common method by which such advice and representations can be obtained. Law reform bodies such as the Law Commissions of England and Wales and the Scottish Law Commission also have an important role to play in a number of areas.[7] Independent pressure and interest groups representing certain occupational, demographic or cultural groups in society may also seek to influence the policy-making process. The more powerful groups are able to make representations at an early stage to policy-makers before any legislative intentions are made public. Such interest groups can be said to hold insider status.

Consultation is also carried out openly in public. Governments often issue Green Papers which set out broad policy themes and invite representations from the public. In a similar fashion White Papers may also be issued. These set out more defined expressions of legislative intent. Generally speaking, consultation does not extend to allowing the public to vote on any proposed piece of legislation. A rare example of such consultation, however, was the recent referendum to approve the introduction of the Scotland Act 1998 and the setting up of the new Scottish Parliament.

After consultation, a Bill representing the Government's legislative intentions must be drafted prior to presentation to Parliament. The drafting is carried out by specialised legal personnel employed by the Government known as Parliamentary Counsel in co-operation with the Government department concerned. This can amount to a long and arduous process spanning many months until the Bill is drafted in such a fashion as meets the legislative requirements of the Government.

Parliamentary stages

2–09 A Bill may be introduced in either of the two houses within Parliament: the House of Commons which is the elected chamber housing Members of Parliament (MPs); or the unelected House of Lords. Given that the bulk of legislation stems from the Government, the vast majority of Acts begin life in the House of Commons. Indeed, Bills relating to certain areas of the law, including taxation and finance, must be introduced in the Commons. It should also be noted that, at the time of writing, the House of Lords is undergoing a process of reform and its future legislative powers are unknown.[8]

The Bill is presented to either house for its first reading. This is merely a formal

---

[7] See, for example, the recent Law Commissions' report into Directors' Duties: *Company Directors: Regulating Conflicts of Interests and Formulating Statement of Duties* (1999) Report no 261 (Scottish Report no 173).

[8] The House of Lords is presently in a phase of transition. All hereditary Peers, except 92 retained by way of a ballot of members, have been abolished (House of Lords Act 1999). At the time of writing the current Labour Administration has still to make its intentions for the future of the House of Lords known in any great detail. A recent report by a Royal Commission set up to make proposals for reform of the Lords has suggested that in future the House should be made up of 450 appointed and 100 elected members (*A House for the Future: Royal Commission on the Reform of the House of Lords*, Cm 4535 (2000).

exercise which allows the Bill to be published for the first time. The first real parliamentary debate on the Bill takes place in the subsequent second reading where a detailed discussion of the Bill's main policy themes takes place. Perhaps the two most important stages of a Bill's life in Parliament, however, are the Committee stage and the Report stage. After the second reading the Bill is considered by a special committee made up of MPs reflecting the balance of power in the House concerned. The Committee, in a long, drawn-out process, analyses the detail of the bill. When this has been completed, the Committee reports back to the House with a number of proposed amendments which are debated and voted on in the House. At the ensuing Third Reading, the Bill is read a third time, which in practice amounts to a motion that it be passed.

If the Bill survives this journey (and because of the government majority in the House of Commons, most government Bills do) then it passes to the other House for a similar process.[9] After this has occurred, the Bill must be forwarded to the Monarch for Royal Assent before it can become law.

Normally the Act will come into effect (or commence) on the date of Royal Assent. It is common, however, for provision to be made for the Act to come into force at a later time—either at a date set in the Act itself or where the Act empowers a Minister or some other person to fix a date for the commencement of the Act.

Legislation under the new Scottish Parliament

It is an interesting time for law and law-making in Scotland. At the time of writing, the **2–10** Scottish Parliament set up under the aegis of the Scotland Act 1998, is making its first tentative steps in legislating for the people of Scotland.[10]

Unlike its UK counterpart, the law-making powers of the Scottish Parliament do not arise constitutionally. The Scottish Parliament's legislative power is, by contrast, a devolved one facilitated by UK legislation (ie the Scotland Act 1998). The Scottish Parliament's powers are therefore subordinate to the authority of the UK Parliament.

The Scotland Act empowers the new Parliament (under the guiding hand of the governing Scottish Executive[11]) to enact law in all Scottish matters except certain reserved areas which remain the exclusive preserve of the UK Parliament. These reserved areas include UK constitutional issues, foreign affairs, defence, fiscal and economic policy (although after much debate the Scottish Parliament was granted limited tax-raising powers), social security and employment. Any proposed Scottish legislation which encroaches upon any reserved matter is deemed to be "not law".[12] The areas that remain do, however, represent great scope for legislating by the new Scottish body.

Legislative procedure

The legislative procedures used in the Scottish Parliament differ somewhat from those **2–11** of its UK counterpart. The Scotland Act itself provids rather little detail about the

---

[9] The House of Lords can merely delay a government bill for up to one year. The Lords is, however, undergoing a period of reform and its future powers to veto Commons' Bills are not yet known.
[10] At the time of writing only four Acts have been passed by the Scottish Parliament—the Mental Health (Public Safety and Appeals) (Scotland) Act 1999; Public Finance and Accountability (Scotland) Act 2000; the Budget (Scotland) Act 2000; and the Census (Amendment) (Scotland) Act 2000. Another 10 Bills are currently being considered by Parliament.
[11] Currently a Labour/Liberal Democrat coalition.
[12] Scotland Act 1998, s 29(1).

legislative process, except that the Parliament adopt Standing Orders to ensure that a Bill is subject to three readings prior to adoption.[13]

When a Bill is presented to the Scottish Parliament it must be accompanied by a written statement from the Presiding Officer outlining his* view on whether the proposed legislation falls within the remit of the Parliament's powers. The Presiding Officer's role is, generally, to ensure that the legislative process runs in an orderly and effective fashion. If the Bill is introduced by the Scottish Executive (an Executive Bill), it must also be accompanied by a written statement from the Minister promoting the Bill that, in his view, the proposed legislation falls within the ambit of Parliament's legislative powers. In addition, the Bill should be accompanied by a memorandum outlining, amongst other things, the policy objectives of the proposed legislation and any consultation which has preceded it.

The three designated Parliamentary stages for Bills are outlined below:

Stage 1: After the Bill is presented to Parliament, it is forwarded to a committee (known as "the lead committee") whose remit is to consider the general principles of the Bill and report back to Parliament. The Parliament then considers the general principles of the Bill in light of the committee's report.

Stage 2: Once Parliament has agreed upon the general principles of the Bill, it is then sent back to the lead committee or alternatively to a committee of the whole Parliament, where the Bill's provisions are examined in detail and amendments to the Bill can be made.

Stage 3: The Parliament will then decide whether the Bill will be passed or not.

Once a Bill is passed by the Parliament, the Presiding Officer will forward it to the Monarch for Royal Assent. Prior to this, however, and within four weeks of the passing of the Bill, the Advocate General, the Attorney General or the Lord Advocate can refer the Bill to the Judicial Committee of the Privy Council to examine whether the Bill falls within the legislative scope of the Parliament.[14] Also, the Secretary of State for Scotland (of the UK Parliament) may issue an order forbidding the Presiding Officer from forwarding the Bill for Royal Assent.[15]

Delegated legislation of the UK Parliament

2–12   With the need for legislation growing significantly in recent years, it has been impossible for successive governments to find the time and resources required to enact all necessary laws and regulations through the complex and time-consuming Parliamentary law-making process.

For this reason, many statutory provisions do not arise directly from Parliament but come into being by way of what is termed "delegated legislation". Basically speaking, the term delegated legislation means that the right to legislate has been delegated by

---

* 'he' implies 'she' throughout unless the contrary is apparent.
[13] Standing Orders of the Scottish Parliament, Edition 2 (20/01/00). Available at http://www.scottish. parliament.uk/parl_bus/sto1.htm.
[14] Scotland Act 1998, s 33. The Advocate General is the Scottish Law Officer of the UK Parliament; the Attorney General is the chief law officer of the UK and the Lord Advocate is both a member of the Scottish Executive and the head of the legal system in Scotland. The Privy Council is in many ways a Constitutional anomaly. Although it began life as an advisory body to the Monarch and is nominally a part of the UK Executive it is a court consisting of the Lord Chancellor (head of the English legal system) and House of Lords' judges (Lords of Appeal in Ordinary). See Chapter 3.
[15] Scotland Act 1998, s 35.

Parliament and exercised by some other body or person. There are two main types of delegated legislation: Statutory Instruments and Byelaws.

Delegated legislation is fundamentally controlled by Parliament in the sense that all such legislative measures must fall within the parameters of a guiding or enabling Act of Parliament (ie the delegated legislation must be within the powers bestowed by the enabling Act (or *intra vires*)).

Statutory Instruments

Under the aegis of an enabling Act of Parliament, Government ministers are **2–13** empowered to formulate their own regulations within their area of responsibility.[16] The Act of Parliament may set out a general policy framework which is in many senses "brought to life" and implemented in specific situations by the Minister concerned by making delegated legislation. Since 1948 these Ministerial legislative measures have been termed Statutory Instruments.[17]

In addition to these statutory powers, Ministers of the Crown may also make Orders in Council. Some of these orders are made in pursuance of what is termed the "Royal Prerogative"—residual powers of the Monarch which the government can lay claim to given its constitutional status as "the Queen in Parliament". In other cases, the right to make Orders in specified situations is delegated to "Her Majesty in Council" in Acts of Parliament. For example, the Emergency Powers (Defence) Act 1939 empowered the Monarch (and, in practice, therefore the government) to make Orders in Council to ensure public safety after an outbreak of war.

Byelaws

Local authorities are delegated powers by Parliament to pass local byelaws which **2–14** apply to their geographical area of governance.[18] These powers are necessary to enable the local authority to carry out its governing functions and tackle nuisances and disorder within its local government area. This may include laws to govern such activities as restricted areas for drinking alcohol, public house licensing hours, the licensing of saunas, and the prohibition of ball games in public parks.

Generally speaking, byelaws do not come into being until they are confirmed by some governmental authority (usually a government Minister).

Similarly, the right to make byelaws is also granted to certain public corporations such as British Gas, Railtrack and British Telecom, allowing them to carry out their functions and regulate their interaction with members of the public.

Acts of Sederunt and Acts of Adjournal

Power is conferred by certain Acts of Parliament on the Scottish Courts to enact rules **2–15** for court procedure. The Court of Session can exercise this power (relating to procedure in both the Court of Session and the sheriff courts) by the passing of an Act of Sederunt. The power to pass an Act of Sederunt stems from the Administration of Scotland Act 1933, s 16. In addition, the Court of Session derives similar powers from other statutes pertinent to particular situations.[19]

---

[16] For example Health and Safety at Work etc Act 1974. See Chapter 12.
[17] Statutory Instruments Act 1946.
[18] Primarily under the Local Government (Scotland) Act 1973 (as amended).
[19] Including the Sheriff Courts (Scotland) Act 1971.

The High Court of Justiciary can also exercise similar powers relating to the administration of the criminal courts in the form of Acts of Adjournal made under authority set out in the Criminal Procedure (Scotland) Act 1975.[20]

Sub-delegated legislation

2–16   Generally speaking, an enabling Act only allows one level of delegation. Indeed, there is a presumption that Parliament intended that the person or corporation authorised to craft delegated legislation is not authorised to sub-delegate that power to a third party. This presumption stems from the common law rule of agency that a delegate cannot delegate.[21] In some cases, however, where the enabling Act is set out in very general terms this gives rise to rather general delegated legislation which in turn requires more specific sub-delegation. The most striking example of this sub-delegation arises from the Emergency Powers (Defence) Act 1939. This piece of legislation was enacted at the outbreak of the Second World War and empowered Ministers to make orders, which provided authority for certain directions which, in turn, allowed the issuing of licences in particular cases.

Controlling delegated legislation

2–17   There are a number of checks and balances that exist in relation to delegated legislation. Apart from ensuring that suitable guidelines are set down in the enabling Act, there are other additional parliamentary checks.[22] Statutory instruments must be laid before either House of Parliament which makes them available to MPs for a three-week period prior to coming into effect. In addition to this, the instrument may be subject to one of two procedures—negative or affirmative resolution procedure. More commonly, the negative procedure will apply which means that a parliamentary vote can nullify the instrument. Rarely, the affirmative procedure will apply which will mean that the instrument cannot come into being unless it is approved by Parliament.

In addition to these checks, instruments may also be examined by a Joint Committee on Statutory Instrument made up of members from both the House of Commons and the Lords. The Committee can refer the instrument back to either House on any of nine specified grounds.

The Courts can also play a monitoring role in respect of delegated legislation. If it appears that a particular statutory instrument is beyond the powers of its enabling Act (*ultra vires*), then a court can undertake what is known as the judicial review of the provision and may strike the instrument down.

Delegated legislation of the Scottish Parliament

2–18   In strict terms, all Acts of the Scottish Parliament are delegated legislation in the sense that the Scottish Parliament's powers to pass laws are devolved from an Act of the UK Parliament (Scotland Act 1998). As was noted above,[23] when a Bill is passed it may be subject to the review of the Judicial Committee of the Privy Council to ensure that it falls within the Parliament's legislative powers prior to the Bill receiving Royal Assent.

---

[20] ss 282 and 457.
[21] See Chapter 6.
[22] Primarily under ss 4–7 of the Statutory Instruments Act 1946.
[23] See para 2–11.

Even after the legislative measure receives Royal Assent and becomes law it can be challenged in the courts on the grounds that it is beyond the powers bestowed by the UK Parliament.[24]

The Scottish Parliament can also delegate legislative powers to its Ministers by the granting of such powers in an enabling Act. Any instrument made by a Minister must be laid before Parliament. The instrument will then be referred to either the lead committee—that is, a committee of the House within whose remit the instrument falls—or a special Subordinate Legislation Committee. The committee then examines the instrument to ensure, amongst other things, that it is *intra vires* or within the powers set out in the enabling Act, properly drafted, and does not encroach upon an issue reserved for the UK Parliament. The committee then reports back to Parliament.

In addition to committee reviews, in common with the UK Parliament, instruments are subject to one of two Parliamentary procedural checks. Some instruments will become law after the lapsing of a 40-day period unless a motion is passed that the instrument not be made. In other cases, instruments will not receive the force of law unless they are expressly approved by Parliament.

Delegated legislation: pros and cons

Delegated legislation has been described as a "necessary evil". Its principal advantage **2–19** is that it solves the problem of the lack of parliamentary time and resources necessary to legislate in all necessary circumstances. Delegated legislation has the merits of speed and flexibility and legislation can be crafted quickly to meet the needs of new, novel situations and to take into account new technologies and social circumstances. It can also be used in emergency situations where swift action is required, for example in war-time. In addition, in especially technical matters delegating the right to legislate to those with specialised knowledge can save a great deal of Parliamentary time debating such matters.

Despite these positive attributes, delegated legislation has been the subject of a great deal of criticism. The main concerns have centred on the lack of control over delegated legislation—in particular, legislative powers wielded by Government Ministers. As outlined above, UK Parliament has some means of control over instruments passed by Government Ministers but given the lack of parliamentary time and resources devoted to the monitoring committees it has been seriously doubted whether in practice they are of much effect. It is too early to comment on the effectiveness of the Scottish Parliament's monitoring of statutory instruments.

In addition, the Court of Session can only exercise its power of judicial review when a case is specifically referred to it and even then the power to grant a remedy arises only after the damage has been done which is not entirely satisfactory. In many cases, the Court of Session may find itself "straight-jacketed" in reviewing the ministerial power. This is because courts can never challenge the merits of any given ministerial action; in general terms, delegated legislation can only be challenged on the basis that it is *ultra vires* of the rights bestowed by the enabling Act. Given the tendency in enabling Acts to grant wide discretionary legislative powers to ministers, there may be little scope for challenging a ministerial action.

---

[24] Or indeed, contrary to EC law or Convention rights set out in the Human Rights Act 1998: see paras 2-20–2-27.

EC legislation

2-20 The European Economic Community (EEC) was formed by the Treaty of Rome in 1957. This built upon the previous European Coal and Steel Community (ECSC) of 1951 and sought to facilitate common economic policies and remove all trade barriers between the subscribers to the Treaty ("Member States").

The UK joined the EEC in 1973 and as a consequence of creating a single European market and promoting increased economic and social cohesion (the EEC was later renamed the European Community (or EC)), UK citizens have since found themselves increasingly subject to EC legislative measures which have sought to unify many different areas of the law across the Member States.[25]

The Treaty of Rome was followed by two subsequent treaties—the Single European Act (SEA) of 1986 with the purpose of establishing a single European internal market and the Treaty on European Union (TEU) of 1992 (the Maastricht Treaty) which brought about the notion of the European Union (EU) to umbrella all existing Community powers and activities and bring about increased political co-operation.

The treaties represent the primary legislation of the EU and, importantly, have paved the way for a spate of secondary legislation. Notwithstanding the creation of the EU, the secondary legislation still tends to be referred to as European Community or EC legislation and arises in various different forms including regulations, directives and decisions.

As a general point it must be noted that the secondary legislation must not be inconsistent with the Treaties themselves. By contrast, all EC law takes precedence over Member States' domestic legal provisions. Therefore, where a conflict arises between an aspect of EC law and Scots law, the EC provision will prevail.[26]

Regulations

2-21 Regulations are binding rules which are directly applicable to Member States. This means that unless specified otherwise, States do not require to enact any domestic legislation to bring the provision into force. Indeed, States are prohibited from enacting any domestic provisions which are inconsistent with the regulation. Regulations also have what is known as "direct effect". This means, for example, that Scottish citizens can enforce such regulations directly through the Scottish domestic courts.

Directives

2-22 Directives, by contrast, are far more flexible provisions. Directives do not automatically become part of the domestic law of Member States. Rather, States are required to craft domestic legislation to bring a particular area of law into line with the directive. This bestows upon States a measure of discretion as to how the provisions are to be brought into domestic law. A directive may be brought into force by the passing of an Act of Parliament or by some form of delegated legislation.[27] Generally speaking, directives do not have direct effect. Thus, Scottish citizens cannot enforce

---

[25] About a third of UK domestic legislation is now based on Community law.
[26] *R v Secretary of State for Transport, ex parte Factortame* [1990] 2 AC 85.
[27] For example, the 1989 European Directive on Insider Dealing (89/592/EEC) was implemented by Part V of the Criminal Justice Act 1993—See Chapter 11.

the provisions of a directive through the Scottish courts until the directive has been incorporated into domestic law.

There have been instances, however, where the European Court of Justice (ECJ) has held that a citizen of a Member State could enforce a directive against a public body which is an organ of the State. This will occur in circumstances where the time limit for implementation of the directive has passed but it has not yet been incorporated into the Member State's domestic law. In addition, the directive must be sufficiently definite and precise, so the Member State has little discretion as to how the directive should be implemented.

The ECJ has also allowed directives to be directly enforced against private individuals of Member States in very limited circumstances although the case law to date is far is from uniform.[28] In addition, the ECJ has held that a citizen may bring an action for damages for the failure of his or her Member State to bring its domestic law into line with a directive.[29]

Decisions

In this sense we mean administrative decisions of the Commission or Council of Ministers, rather than decisions of the European Court of Justice.[30] Many hundreds of these are passed each year. These are addressed either to Member States or specified corporations or individuals. They become automatically binding on the addressee alone.   **2-23**

How EC law is made

The way in which EC law is enacted is somewhat complex and very different to the UK's domestic legislative process. EC legislation is made by way of an interactive process between the EU's three main political organisations (known as Institutions).   **2-24**

The Institutions

The European Commission is composed of 20 Commissioners each responsible for a particular area of EU activity. Commissioners must be EU nationals acting in an independent capacity from their Member States. This makes the Commission an overtly European body. The Commission has a number of functions, the chief of which is that it is responsible for bringing forth proposals for legislation. It also acts as protector of the Treaties and can bring any Member State to the European Court of Justice for failure to comply with the provisions set out in the Treaties.   **2-25**

The Council of Ministers is made up of Ministerial representatives drawn from each of the 15 Member States, and is therefore much more concerned with protecting Member States' own interests. The Council is very much at the heart of the legislative process and generally acts upon proposals tendered by the Commission.

The European Parliament is not a parliament in the traditional sense; it is not the main legislative body of the EU. It is a democratic body made up of some 626 members elected by the 15 Member States in national elections. The Parliament is primarily an

---

[28] See *Colson v Land Nordrhein-Westfalen* [1986] 2 CMLR 430 and compare with *Marleasing SA v La Comercial Internacional de Alimentacion SA (Case No 106/89—Decision 13 November 1990)*.
[29] *Francovich v Italian Republic* [1992] IRLR 84; *Porter v Attorney General for Northern Ireland* (settled out of court on 26th June 1995).
[30] See Chapter 3.

advisory body but, as explained below, this body does have a co-operative and consultative role to play in the law-making process.

General legislative procedure

2–26   Generally speaking, the Commission is responsible for suggesting new legislative measures. Once a proposal is drafted, a copy is sent to the Council of Ministers, which in turn is forwarded to the European Parliament. The Parliament may then review the proposals and take further representations from the Commission prior to passing on its own views to the Council of Ministers. The proposal is then reviewed by one of a number of Council working groups manned by civil servants drawn from all Member States. After further review, the final form of the provision can be given binding force by the Council.

In other cases, the European Parliament can flex legislative muscles more in keeping with its name. The Single European Act 1986 introduced a new co-operation procedure which allows the Parliament to either accept, reject or amend the position (known as a common position) taken by the Council. If the Parliament rejects the common position, this can only be ignored by the Council by an unanimous vote. In the case of a Parliament amendment to the common position, a qualified majority of the Council may override the amendment.

The Treaty on European Union of 1992 further increased the Parliament's legislative power. The co-decision procedure vests in the Parliament greater powers of consultation and, in effect, allows it to veto the Council's decision and thereby block legislation.

The European Convention on Human Rights (ECHR) and the Human Rights Act 1998

2–27   Special mention must be made of the effect of the Human Rights Act 1998. This piece of UK legislation incorporated the European Convention on Human Rights (ECHR) into domestic law. The ECHR sets out a number of fundamental freedoms and basic human rights. The Human Rights Act absorbs the articles of the Convention, termed Convention rights.[31] The Convention Rights are far-reaching and include: general legal protection of life; protection against slavery, torture or inhumane treatment; the right to liberty and protection against unlawful arrest; the right to a free trial; and the right to freedom of thought and expression.

The UK became a signatory to the ECHR in 1950 and ratified it in 1951. Being an international treaty, ratification of the ECHR did not mean that its terms would automatically become incorporated within UK domestic law. In this sense, the Convention itself could not strictly speaking be viewed as a formal source of law.[32] In practical terms this meant that individuals seeking to enforce any of the provisions (articles) of the ECHR could not pursue a claim through the UK courts. Aggrieved individuals had to take their case to the Court of Human Rights in Strasbourg.

As the Human Rights Act 1998 served to incorporate the provisions of the ECHR into domestic law, the result is that those seeking to rely on Convention rights are now able to pursue actions through the domestic courts.

---

[31]   And the first and sixth protocols to the Convention (except certain derogations and reservations).
[32]   See *Kaur v Lord Advocate* 1980 SC 319, 1981 SLT 322; *Moore v Secretary of State for Scotland* 1985 SLT 38. Although where there appears to be any ambiguity in UK legislation, the principles of the Convention could be referred to as an aid to statutory interpretation—*R v Secretary of State for the Home Department, ex parte Brind* [1991] 1 AC 696; *Anderson v HM Advocate* 1996 JC 29.

It is also noteworthy that the new Act has a special status in that it is designed to take precedence over all other sources of law. Indeed, in accordance with section 19 of the Act, prior to the second reading of any UK Parliamentary Bill, the government Minister responsible for the legislative proposals must state that in his opinion the provisions of the Bill are not incompatible with the Convention Rights. UK legislation incompatible with Convention rights is not disbarred, however, and a Minister may state that the government is nonetheless prepared to proceed with a Bill even though its provisions are not wholly consistent with Convention rights.

Under section 31(1) of the Scotland Act, the member of the Scottish Executive responsible for the promoting of the bill must state that its terms are not incompatible with the Convention. Unlike its UK counterpart, however, the Scottish Parliament is forbidden to enact legislation which is contrary to Convention rights.[33]

COMMON LAW

In plain terms, the common law was originally law that was common to the land. Such **2–28** laws arose from old customary practices, and were often influenced by, and at times imported from, external sources, such as Canon law, English law and Roman law and were accepted and upheld by the courts in particular cases. Indeed, many areas of Scots law (for example, contract law[34]) are not based primarily upon legislation but are largely derived from common law principles.

Judicial precedent

The second major source of Scots law after legislation is the common law derived from **2–29** the decisions of courts or judicial precedent. This represents rules produced by the courts without reference to legislation. At the heart of the notion of judicial precedent is the idea of standing by court decisions (or *stare decisis*). In general terms what this concept means is that a court is bound to follow the previous decision of a superior court. Any previous decision which must be followed is known as binding. A decision which the present court can choose to follow or not is known as persuasive.

Historically, Scotland did not operate a strict system of judicial precedent akin to that south of the border. Largely caused by a growth of case-reporting, and arguably the influence of the House of Lords, in the eighteenth century Scotland gradually adopted a more rigid system of precedent.[35]

When is a case binding?

If a decision of a previous court is to be binding on the present court then, broadly **2–30** speaking, it must be a decision from a court of higher authority.

The civil court hierarchy[36]

The European Court of Justice sits at the top of the civil court hierarchy and its **2–31** decisions bind all courts in the UK although it does not bind itself.

---

[33] Scotland Act 1998, s 57(2).
[34] See Chapter 4.
[35] Although some of the Institutional Writers (see below at para 2–37) rejected a strict system of judicial precedent, in 1828 the Court of Session accepted that a prior decision of the Court was binding; see Smith, *The Doctrines of Judicial Precedent in Scots Law* (W. Green, 1952).
[36] See Chapter 3 for a detailed examination of the court structure in Scotland.

The House of Lords will only hand down precedents for Scotland in relation to Scottish appeals or those that relate to the interpretation of UK-wide statutes. Again, the House of Lords reserves the right to depart from its own decisions.

The Court of Session is divided into the Outer House (a court of the first instance) and the Inner House (primarily an appeal court). The decisions of the Inner House bind both itself and the Outer House and the inferior Sheriff Court. Where a decision has been reached by one division of the Inner House, however, it can be reversed by a bench of seven Inner House judges. Outer House and Sheriff Court judgments are never binding; they may, however, be persuasive.

The criminal court hierarchy

2–32 Judicial precedent has never been applied as strictly in the Scottish criminal courts. The High Court of Justiciary, when sitting as an appeal court, does not regard itself as being bound by its own decisions. Furthermore, while sheriff courts are likely to view decisions of single High Court judges with respect, and, in practice, will generally follow their rulings, they are not formally bound to adhere.

Cases to be in-point

2–33 In addition to the decision being heard in a superior court, before a subsequent case is bound by the former decision, it must be in-point. For a case to be in-point, it is not necessary to be similar factually, rather it must be concerned with the same point of law which the decision in the previous case turned upon. This is known as the *ratio decidendi* or simply the *ratio*. It is only the *ratio* of a case that is binding.

The *ratio* must be distinguished from all aspects of the court judgment. In any judgment the court may embark on a lengthy and complex discussion of the various legal issues relevant to the case. Many hypothetical questions and historical legal points may be raised, discussed and examined in detail. All such remarks and opinions made in the court's judgment are known as *obiter dicta* or *obiter*. While in no way binding, these additional *obiter dicta* statements may nonetheless be viewed in a persuasive light, particularly if they are made by a senior court.

Case reports

2–34 In order for any system of precedent to function, it is necessary that previous decisions and judgments are recorded and capable of being cited by the parties and scrutinised by courts in subsequent cases. To facilitate this, most modern legal regimes have developed a system of case-reporting which records the decisions of courts and the opinions of judges in court cases. In Scotland, the most authoritative series of case reports is *Session Cases* which reports decisions (and judgments) of the Court of Session and Scottish appeals to the House of Lords. Other reports include *Scots Law Times* which include case reports from all the Scottish Courts including the Court of Session, High Court of Justiciary and the sheriff courts.

Decisions of foreign courts

2–35 It may be that a particular case throws up a novel situation of which no useful guidance can be gleaned from sources of Scots law. In such cases it is permissible to look to the decisions of courts of other legal systems. In particular, the decisions of English courts are often examined, particularly in areas where Scots law is largely similar to its southern counterpart, such as commercial and industrial law. English law has provided the foundations for many other legal systems, including the USA and Commonwealth nations, and decisions of the courts and statutory rules in these jurisdictions may also be of use in certain cases.[37]

Precedent: pros and cons

The first advantage of judicial precedent is that it provides consistency and fairness in **2–36** the law. Without a system of precedent, the law would be more uncertain and it is likely that more court actions would be brought in the face of conflicting views on the state of the law. Judicial precedent is also intrinsically concerned with the idea of natural justice—in particular, the idea that all should be treated in the same fashion by the courts of the land. Related to this is the idea that inferior courts are less likely to make errors in their interpretation of the law if they are handed down precedents from the superior courts.

Another important feature of judicial precedent is that it allows the law to develop in a uniform and logical fashion where courts can apply recognised legal principles to meet new situations without the need for Parliamentary intervention.

Despite these positive attributes, there are drawbacks to judicial precedent. First, the legal system may become too rigid and inflexible if courts are restrained by previous decisions, some of which may not be considered to have been properly decided and hence represent "bad" law.

It is also contended that the system of precedent is not, in practice, always followed; in a bid to evade a previous decision, the court may strive to find artificial distinctions with a previous case which would otherwise be binding. Moreover, it may not necessarily be easy to isolate the *ratio* of any case. In reaching a decision, a judge may follow two or more legal principles in determining his decision. Where a case is heard by more than one judge on appeal the different judges may prefer to take different lines of argument with the result that the case may produce more than one *ratio*.

Another problem is that there is no comprehensive system of reporting and many cases remain unreported. Thus, many precedents go unnoticed and this leads to a haphazard system of law development and, in practice, makes searching for a precedent that supports your own case a difficult, and at times random, process.

It is worth noting that the reporting situation has been improved in recent years. There has been a spate of new case reporting series in various areas of the law (for example, *Butterworths Company Cases*) and with technological advancements more and more cases are reported on the internet, thus increasing the accessibility of many precedents.

INSTITUTIONAL WRITINGS

Institutional writings are bodies of work written by eminent jurists of their day **2–37** providing comprehensive discussions of various areas of Scots law as it was developing at that time. These works drew upon the early decisions of the courts, Scottish customary practices and the laws of other jurisdictions including Roman law, Canon

---

[37] In a similar fashion, the courts may examine other sources of the rules and principles of foreign legal systems (for example, legislation or legal writings) when Scots law does not provide a solution. In particular, reference to legal writings on Roman law, which has influenced Scots law in a number of areas, may be of use.

law and English law. In times before any standardised system of case reporting was in place, such writings came to be relied upon as definitive sources of Scots law.

Even today, in the absence of any conflicting rule set out in either legislation or case law, institutional writings remain a valid source of Scots law and can be cited in court. With the vast increase in legislation from various sources and adoption of a doctrine of judicial precedent backed up by a comprehensive system of case reporting, the importance of institutional works as a formal source of law has diminished greatly. Nonetheless, these works remain of great historical importance, particularly in establishing the origins of many areas of Scots law and in determining how the Scots legal system has been influenced by other schools of legal thinking.

While the first institutional writing was Sir Thomas Craig's discussion of property law in *Jus Feudale* in 1655, the most influential of the early legal jurists was the first Viscount Stair (James Dalrymple). His *Institutions of Scots Law*, first published in 1681, provided the cornerstone upon which much of Scots law was built. This work focused on a whole range of areas of Scots law including the law of obligations, property and succession and drew upon many sources including Scots customary rules, early decisions of the Scottish courts, legislation of the old Scottish Parliament, Roman law, the Bible and general principles of equity and reason.

Other important institutional writings include:

> Sir George Mackenzie, *The Laws and Customs of Scotland in Matters Criminal* (1678)
> Lord Bankton, *An Institute of the Laws of Scotland* (1751–53)
> Professor John Erskine, *An Institute of the Laws of Scotland* (1773)
> Baron David Hume, *Commentaries on the Law of Scotland respecting Crimes* (1797)
> Professor George Bell, *Commentaries on the law of Scotland and on the Principles of Mercantile Jurisprudence* (1810); *Principles of the Law of Scotland* (1829)

Non-institutional works

2–38 Law writing today is rife and countless books, articles and commentaries on various areas of Scots law are produced every year. Strictly speaking, legal writings of a non-institutional nature cannot be regarded as a source of law. Historically, such writings could only be mentioned in legal argument in court to support the speaker's view of the law. In modern times, however, many of the more scholarly works are cited in both legal argument and in judgment, although the opinions of writers in non-institutional literature are never binding sources of law. Such writings are merely persuasive and the more established and revered the work is, the more persuasive it is.[38] A work can gain authority as a source of law only in the sense that it has been approved by the court—ie, it is the court's view that is the authority, not the writer's opinion itself.

CUSTOM

2–39 The old customary law of Scotland had a major historical influence on our present legal system. Many of the old Scottish customary practices, embraced by institutional writers and accepted and developed by the courts of the land, became established principles of law.

---

[38] Some of the most influential works include, Gloag on *Contract* and Gordon's *Criminal Law*.

Custom as a source of new law

Aside from this historical influence, a custom can still act as a formal, binding source **2–40** of new law. This occurs very rarely today given that many customary practices have been blended into the law by means of adoption by the courts or being set out in statute. Nonetheless, a court will be bound to give legal effect to a particular practice if it can be shown to be well-established; recognised and practised; well-defined and certain; fair and reasonable; and not inconsistent with recognised principles of law.[39]

Although not strictly speaking giving rise to an authoritative source of law, particular customs can bestow legal rights in individual cases. A particular business practice or custom, for example, can be held by the courts to become an implied term of a business contract. Again, before the business practice can be imported into the contract, it must be widely accepted within the trade, definite and certain, reasonable and not inconsistent with the terms of the contract.[40]

A custom may also bestow certain legal rights in the context of land law. For example, what is termed a public right of way[41] may be established when the public has customarily crossed a piece of ground to arrive at a destination. After a prescribed period of use which has not been objected to by the landowner, the public may gain a legal right to pass through the land.

EQUITY

The term "equity" conjures up notions of fairness or justice. While any civilised legal **2–41** system would hope that this principle would run to the heart of its laws, equity has a precise meaning within the context of sources of law. Here, the Scottish legal system differs from the English. Whereas, historically, England developed separate systems of law and equity (including the separate Chancery Court of equity), this has never been the case in Scotland. Generally speaking, it is probably better in Scotland to think upon equity not so much as a source of law itself, but more a mechanism by which the more stringent aspects of the law can be softened in practice. In this way, the Scottish courts developed equitable remedies to be granted to parties in deserving cases including those of specific implement[42] and interdict.[43]

In addition to this, vested in the Scottish superior courts (the Court of Session and the High Court of Justiciary) is the power of *nobile officium* (literally, equitable power). The *nobile officium* allows the court (albeit in very limited circumstances) to grant a remedy where it deems it equitable to do so even where, strictly speaking, the law does not provide one.

---

[39] See *Bruce* v *Smith* (1890) 17 R 1000 where the test of reasonableness failed.
[40] A recent case where a custom was held to be incorporated into a contract was *Stirling Park & Co* v *Digby Brown & Co* 1995 SCLR 375, 1996 SLT (Sh Ct) 17. See Chapter 4.
[41] See Chapter 7.
[42] To compel a specified act by a party.
[43] To prohibit certain acts by parties.

SUMMARY

FORMAL SOURCES

- The term "sources of law" can hold different meanings. The term "formal source" refers to the source which confers binding force on any given legal rule.
- The formal sources are: Legislation; Common law (Case law); Institutional writings; Custom; and Equity.

LEGISLATION

- Legislation is the primary source of law. It has increased dramatically in recent times and arises in a number of different forms including: Acts of the UK Parliament; Acts of the Scottish Parliament; European Community legislation; and Delegated legislation.

ACTS OF THE UK PARLIAMENT

- The UK Parliament is, in constitutional terms, the supreme law-making body in the UK, although it has given away rights in certain areas (for example to the EU). Legislation passed by the UK Parliament is known as "statute".
- UK Parliamentary Bills must be scrutinised by way of a lengthy parliamentary process in both the House of Commons and the House of Lords before they can be passed to the Monarch for Royal Assent.

ACTS OF THE SCOTTISH PARLIAMENT

- Under the Scotland Act 1998, the Scottish Parliament is empowered to enact laws for the people of Scotland. Certain areas have been "reserved", however, and remain in the hands of UK Parliament.

DELEGATED LEGISLATION

- Delegated legislation arises when the right to make laws has been delegated by Parliament to some other person or body.
- Delegated legislation is subject to the control of both the UK and Scottish Parliaments and the 'judicial review' of the civil courts.

EC LEGISLATION

- Since the UK joined the EEC in 1973, it has been subject to an increasing amount of EC legislation.
- EC legislation is formulated by way of a complex process of interaction between the European Commission, Council of Ministers and European Parliament. EC law generally takes precedence over domestic legislation.

THE EUROPEAN CONVENTION ON HUMAN RIGHTS

- The ECHR, setting out a number of fundamental rights and freedoms, has been incorporated into Scottish domestic law by the Human Rights Act 1998. Scottish citizens can now seek to enforce "Convention Rights" through the Scottish courts.

COMMON LAW

- Common law is the next important source of law after legislation. Court decisions operate as a source of law by way of the doctrine of judicial precedent or "standing by decisions" where the decisions of superior courts become binding on inferior courts. A past decision will only be binding if the *ratio decidendi*, *ie* the legal principle upon which that case was decided, is the same as the *ratio* in the present case. Other hypothetical or "by the way" remarks made in a judgment are known as *obiter dicta* and are merely persuasive.

INSTITUTIONAL WRITINGS

- Institutional writings are the works of eminent legal jurists who wrote about Scots law predominantly in the sixteenth, seventeenth and eighteenth centuries. The scope of these works as valid formal sources of law has been eroded in recent times by increased legislation and the adoption of judicial precedent.

CUSTOM

- There is very little scope now for custom to operate as a source of new law. For this to occur the custom should be well-established; recognised and practised; well-defined and certain; fair and reasonable; and not inconsistent with recognised principles of law.

EQUITY

- Equity denotes fairness or justice. Equity is more a method by which the law can be softened, than a source itself. Courts have developed the equitable remedies of "specific implement" and "interdict" and the superior Scottish courts have a limited power of *nobile officium* which allows them to grant a remedy even if the law does not provide one.

FURTHER READING

Burrows (ed) *Greens Guide to European Law in Scotland* (W Green, 1995)
Deans, *Scots Public Law* (T&T Clark, 1995)
Gloag and Henderson, *The Law of Scotland* (10th edition, W Green, 1995)
The Laws of Scotland: Stair Memorial Encyclopaedia (Law Society of Scotland Butterworths), Vol 22, "Sources of Law (Formal)"

McFadden and Lazarowicz, *The Scottish Parliament: An Introduction* (T&T Clark, 1999)

Paterson, Bates and Poustie, *The Legal System of Scotland: Cases and Materials* (4th edn, W Green, 1999)

Walker, *The Scottish Legal System* (7th edn, W Green, 1997).

White and Willock, *The Scottish Legal System* (2nd edn, Butterworths, 1999)

3 THE JUDICIAL SYSTEM

OVERVIEW

Under the Act of Settlement of 1707, which brought about the union of the Scottish **3–01** Parliament with its English counterpart, Scotland was granted the right to retain an independent and distinct judicial system.[1] This chapter provides an overview of the Scottish judicial system and its legal personnel. It also discusses some of the alternative mechanisms for the resolution of disputes, such as tribunals, arbitration and mediation.

In most legal systems there are, fundamentally, two types of court—the civil court and the criminal court. The civil courts are provided by the state as a forum in which citizens can resolve their disputes without recourse to violence or disorder. When parties are unable to resolve their differences by amicable means then one party (the "pursuer") may raise an action in the appropriate civil court against the other (the "defender"). In very simple terms, after hearing arguments from both parties, the court then rules in favour of one or other of the parties and grants a remedy accordingly. This process is known as litigation.

In contrast to the civil courts, the function of the criminal courts is to act as a forum in which the state can punish those who have acted contrary to the criminal law. In plain terms, the criminal law lays down a minimum prescribed standard of behaviour required by the state.[2] The state prosecutes those (known as "accused" persons) who allegedly have acted in a manner which falls below the minimum acceptable standards and such persons are "tried" in the criminal courts. If found guilty of a crime by the court the accused may be punished (or "sentenced") accordingly.

In both civil and criminal courts, the parties must bring forth arguments of both fact and law. That is to say that each side presents evidence of its view of the facts of the case and also sets forth legal arguments based on its interpretation of particular rules of law which are central to the case (for example, a piece of legislation or a principle of common law).[3]

Generally speaking, the legal arguments are decided on by the presiding judge who

---

[1] Although civil appeals are heard in the House of Lords – see para 3–20.
[2] See Chapter 14.
[3] See Chapter 2.

may also decide on factual issues. In some courts, however, the facts of the case are determined by a jury drawn from members of the general public. In criminal cases, the sentence (a fine or a period of imprisonment) is decided upon by the judge. Similarly, in civil cases, the remedy (the extent of damages that one party must pay to another) is determined by the judge.

THE CIVIL COURTS

CIVIL JURISDICTION

3–02   A court has no right to hear a case if the action does not fall within its jurisdiction. The jurisdiction must be held by the court in two ways: first, the court must have jurisdiction to hear the type of case which is referred to it; and second, the court must have jurisdiction over the parties to the action. In Scotland, the court must exercise jurisdiction over the defender: the doctrine *actor sequitur forum rei* (the pursuer is bound to "follow the court of the defender") applies.

There are three UK civil courts which have jurisdiction in Scotland:

The Sheriff Court

The Court of Session

The House of Lords.

THE SHERIFF COURT

3–03   In terms of structure, sheriff courts are organised into six geographical areas known as "sheriffdoms". Based upon the old regional local government areas these are Grampian, Highlands and Islands; Tayside, Central and Fife; Lothian and Borders; Glasgow and Strathkelvin; North Strathclyde; and South Strathclyde, Dumfries and Galloway.

The sheriffdoms are broken up into 49 sheriff court districts. Each sheriff court district has a sheriff court and a number of sheriffs who man the courts. Each sheriffdom is headed by a sheriff principal who is responsible for the overall administration and organisation of the sheriff courts therein. In addition to this, the sheriff principal hears appeals from the decisions of sheriffs in civil matters and may also sit as a sheriff.

Sheriffs are appointed by the crown under the Sheriff Courts (Scotland) Act 1877 and are either advocates or solicitors of at least 10 years' standing.[4] The sheriff principal is also empowered to appoint honorary sheriffs who need not hold legal qualifications.[5] Until recently, the Lord Advocate[6] was empowered to appoint temporary sheriffs as and when required to ease the workload of the sheriff courts. In

---

[4] See paras 3–48 to 3–51.
[5] Sheriff Courts (Scotland) Act 1907. Honorary sheriffs who are not legally qualified in practice seldom sit in court.
[6] See para 3–53.

the aftermath of a recent ruling of the High Court of Justiciary,[7] however, all temporary sheriffs were dismissed.[8] The reason for this was that the control over the appointments of temporary sheriffs by the head of the prosecution service, the Lord Advocate, was deemed contrary to the right to a fair trial enshrined in the Human Rights Act 1998.[9] An additional 12 full-time sheriffs have since been appointed to alleviate the shortage in judicial manpower which resulted from the demise of temporary sheriffs.

Jurisdiction of the sheriff court

Jurisdiction over the defender

The sheriff court can exercise jurisdiction over the defender in a number of different ways. **3–04**

Under the Sheriff Courts (Scotland) Act 1907, the court holds jurisdiction over the defender if he is resident within the sheriffdom in which the sheriff court is situated or, having resided there for at least 40 days, the defender has ceased to reside there for less than 40 days and has no known address within Scotland. Additionally, where a defender is of no fixed abode, the Civil Jurisdiction and Judgments Act 1982 provides that he can be personally cited to appear in the court.[10]

Alternatively, where the defender carries on business within a sheriffdom, the 1907 Act provides that he be cited personally by the court or cited at his place of business. Similarly, the 1907 Act provides that the court can claim jurisdiction if the defender is the owner of heritable property[11] and the action relates to that property.

Finally, in matters relating to breach of contract or commission of a delict (legal wrong[12]) then the 1982 Act empowers the court to exercise jurisdiction over a defender if either the contract is performed or the delict is committed within that court's sheriffdom.

Jurisdiction over subject-matter

The sheriff court enjoys a wide jurisdiction in respect of the types of cases that it can **3–05** hear.[13] The sheriff court holds exclusive (or "privative") jurisdiction over certain types of cases: this means that such cases cannot be brought in any other court. By contrast, a small category of cases must be brought in the superior Court of Session.[14]

Sheriff court procedures

Depending on the type of case being brought, the pursuer must bring one of three **3–06** different forms of court action—the "small claim", the "summary cause" or the "ordinary cause".

---

[7] See para 3–24.
[8] *Starrs* v *Ruxton* 2000 SLT 42.
[9] See Chapter 2 for a brief discussion of the Human Rights Act 1998.
[10] *ie*, personally summoned to appear at court.
[11] See Chapter 7.
[12] See Chapter 5.
[13] See Beaumont, *Anton and Beaumont's Civil Jurisdiction in Scotland* (2nd edn, 1996).
[14] These are discussed below at para 3–13.

Small claims

3–07 The small claims procedure (which is technically a species of the summary cause) was introduced by way of the Law Reform (Miscellaneous Provisions) (Scotland) Act 1985. A small claim is the appropriate action when the monetary value of the claim is below £750. This type of court procedure is the most truncated and informal—for example, some of the strict rules regarding the admissibility of evidence are relaxed. The premise behind the small claim is that the informality of the proceedings will mean that the process will be both speedy and cost-effective and that parties will not require legal representation.[15] Reflecting the cheap and informal nature of the proceedings, no legal aid (state-provided financial assistance[16]) is available in respect of a small claim. As a final point, given that Scottish courts generally stipulate that the loser pays the winner's costs, it is important to note that such costs are generally limited to £75 in defended cases.[17]

The sheriff may treat a small claim as a summary cause or an ordinary cause if he is of the opinion that there are complex questions of law involved or on the joint motion of the parties.[18]

Summary cause

3–08 The summary cause procedure is regulated by the Sheriff Court (Scotland) Act 1971. This procedure is applicable to actions where the monetary value sought is between £750 and £1500 and also actions relating to eviction from heritable property. Again reflecting the limited importance of the types of actions brought thereunder, the summary cause is a truncated form of court process. The action begins by the pursuer filling out a pre-printed claim form. If the defender does not return his portion of the form by a specified day (known as the "return day") decree will be granted by the court automatically.[19] Otherwise, a date for proof (a trial) is set for a later date.[20]

A summary cause must be treated as an ordinary cause where the parties issue a joint motion to this effect. If one party motions to this effect, the sheriff may make such an order and, in relation to actions regarding the recovery of possession of moveable or heritable property, the sheriff may, of his own accord, give such a direction.

Ordinary cause

3–09 All other actions must be brought as an ordinary cause action. This is the most legalistic, time-consuming and hence expensive court procedure in the sheriff court.[21] This type of action is commenced by the way of an "initial writ"—a document which sets out the pursuer's grounds of claim. This will, in turn, be met by corresponding "defences" from the defender. After a period of adjustments between the parties (which may take the form of admissions by either party and agreements as to the

---

[15] There is evidence that small claims are often run by sheriffs like any other court and hence, in practice, solicitors are invariably hired by parties to represent them in court proceedings—see Mays and Clark, "ADR and the Courts" (1997) 2 SLPQ 57.
[16] Regulated by the Legal Aid (Scotland) Act 1986.
[17] See, generally, Kelbie, *Small Claims Procedure in the Sheriff Court* (1994).
[18] Law Reform (Miscellaneous Provisions) (Scotland) Act 1990.
[19] Although actions relating to eviction from heritable property do not have return days.
[20] See, generally, Mays, *Summary Cause Procedure in the Sheriff Court* (1995).
[21] The procedure must conform to the Sheriff Courts (Scotland) Act 1907.

issues relative to the case between the parties) any remaining grounds of dispute will be determined at a subsequent court hearing.

Appeals in the sheriff court

The right to an appeal will depend on the type of procedure under which the case has **3–10** been heard. In a small claim, the only right of appeal is to the sheriff principal on a point of law by "stated case". This procedure is so termed as the sheriff is bound to state the reasons for his determination of the case. Similarly, in a summary cause, an appeal may be made to the sheriff principal by stated case on a point of law. There may, however, be a further right of appeal from the sheriff principal to the Inner House of the Court of Session. This is only available if the sheriff principal grants leave for the appeal. In the ordinary cause there is a right to appeal to the sheriff principal with a further subsequent appeal available to the Inner House of the Court of Session. Alternatively, however, an initial appeal from the decision of the sheriff in an ordinary cause may be made directly to the Court of Session thus leap-frogging the sheriff principal phase.

THE COURT OF SESSION

The Court of Session sits in Edinburgh and is split into two sections or "houses"—the **3–11** Outer House which is a court of the first instance (that is, where cases are brought for the first time); and the Inner House which primarily acts as an Appeal Court. The Court of Session was established in 1532 and has been radically reformed over the years. The Court of Session's present constitution was largely established in the early nineteenth century and is now regulated in the main by the Court of Session Act 1988.

Jurisdiction of the Court of Session

Jurisdiction over the defender

Akin to the position as regards the sheriff court, the pursuer is bound to follow the **3–12** court of the defender and, as such, the Court of Session must hold jurisdiction over the defender in some way. Unlike the sheriff court, the Court of Session enjoys jurisdiction over cases spanning the whole of Scotland. The main way in which jurisdiction is founded is on the basis that the defender is permanently or habitually resident in Scotland.[22] Alternatively, jurisdiction may be claimed on the basis that the defender is the tenant or owner of heritable property in Scotland (the action need not relate to that property).

There are special rules regarding jurisdiction in relation to consistorial matters (for example, matrimonial actions including divorce, separation and nullity of marriage). In such cases, the Court of Session can claim jurisdiction when either party to the marriage is "domiciled" (has a permanent home) in Scotland on the date the action commenced, or was habitually resident in Scotland throughout one year immediately prior to the commencement date.

---

[22] Civil Jurisdiction and Judgments Act 1982.

Jurisdiction over subject-matter

3–13 A small category of cases must be brought to the Court of Session. This category has diminished in recent years but includes actions relating to personal status, actions of reduction, actions relating to the tenor of lost documents and petitions to wind up a registered company where the share capital is more than £120,000. In addition, actions reviewing the decisions of government ministers, local authorities and public bodies must be brought in the Court of Session. Finally, any appeal to the *nobile officium* ("equitable power") is available only in the Court of Session.[23]

By contrast, some actions are privative to the sheriff court—*ie* those where the monetary value of the claim does not exceed £1,500 and actions relating to eviction from heritable property—and thus recourse to the Outer House of the Court of Session will be unavailable. In most civil cases, however, the pursuer will be free to make a choice between the Court of Session and the sheriff court. In cases which are of more importance in legal or financial terms, the Court of Session is more likely to be chosen as its decisions have a higher legal status. There are, however, a number of concerns that must be taken into account before raising an action in the Court of Session. Given the protracted nature of the court process, litigation is likely to incur more time and greater costs than an equivalent action in the sheriff court. In addition, in the Court of Session, parties must engage advocates in addition to solicitors to represent them in the courts which adds considerably to the expense of the action.[24]

The Outer House

3–14 In the Outer House, a case is heard by a judge sitting alone, known as a "Lord Ordinary". In a very limited range of cases (primarily those involving claims for damages in respect of industrial accidents), a jury of 12 may also sit to determine the facts of the case. Those eligible for appointment as a Lord Ordinary include suitably experienced Queen's Council (QCs), former sheriffs of five years standing or solicitor-advocates of five years' standing. Legislation framed under the Maximum Number of Judges (Scotland) Order 1999 has recently increased the number of Court of Session judges to 32.[25]

Outer House procedure

3–15 Proceedings in the Outer House are normally commenced by a written summons which, if defended, is done so by a corresponding set of defences. The parties then enter into a period within which pleadings are adjusted between them in a similar fashion to ordinary cause procedure in the sheriff court—known as the "open record" ("record" is pronounced with the emphasis on the first syllable). Once the adjustments are completed, the record is said to be "closed". The case may then proceed to a proof (to determine the facts of the case) or it may be necessary for the court to convene a hearing to determine certain legal issues prior to proceeding to proof.[26]

---

[23] See Chapter 2.

[24] Although parties may alternatively engage a solicitor-advocate who has the right of audience in the Court of Session—see para 3–48.

[25] There were previously 27. The increase has been at least partly due to the loss of judicial time caused by the current trial of the Lockerbie bombing suspects taking place in a special court of Scottish jurisdiction in the Netherlands.

[26] There may be times where the court requires to ascertain certain facts of the case before it can determine a legal argument. Such a hearing is known as a "proof before answer".

In addition, certain actions are brought on petition. In basic terms, such actions (for example, for the court to appoint new trustees or wind up a company or partnership) are brought by one party petitioning the court for a remedy. The court may remit the petition to a suitably qualified third party to determine the merits of the petition and report back to the court.

Appeals from the Outer House

Appeals from the verdicts of the Outer House are generally brought to the Inner House by what is known as a "reclaiming motion". The appeal may, rarely, be on the facts of the case. It is more usual for appeals to be heard on a point of law. **3–16**

The Inner House

The Inner House is primarily an appeal court hearing appeals from the Outer House, sheriff courts and other tribunals. The Inner House sits as a court of the first instance on rare occasions where parties require interpretation of a point of law only—for example, taxation cases and certain petitions by limited companies. The Inner House consists of two divisions: the First Division which comprises the Lord President[27] and three other "Lords of Session"; and the Second Division comprising the Lord Justice-Clerk[28] and three Lords of Session. Each division is of equal status and the *quorum* (*ie* the minimum number of judges who sit at any one time) is three. It should be noted that in matters of particular importance the court may sit as a full bench of seven judges or may even augment this number by bringing in further judges from the Outer House. **3–17**

Inner House procedure

Generally speaking, evidence as to the facts of cases is rarely heard in the Inner House, although a transcript of the evidence led at the initial court hearing may be examined. The Court is generally confined to hearing argument as to a point of law which is central to the decision of the previous court. Depending on the difficulty of the legal issues being determined, the judges may deliver an instant decision orally or, alternatively, may adjourn proceedings (known as "making *avizandum*") and deliver a written opinion at a later date. It is common for one judge to issue a comprehensive opinion with the other judges issuing supplementary "concurring" opinions—which often simply state that the judge concurs with the leading opinion. Judges are not always in agreement, however, and a judge who does not agree with the decision of the majority may issue a dissenting opinion. **3–18**

Appeals from the Inner House

Appeals can be brought from the decisions (known as "interlocutors") of the Inner House by raising a petition "praying" that the House of Lords reverse the previous ruling. Appeals are generally only available on points of law. Additionally, the right of appeal will only normally arise when the Court of Session grants leave to this effect or where the judgment of the Inner House is not unanimous. **3–19**

---

[27] Scotland's senior judge.
[28] Depute to the Lord President.

THE HOUSE OF LORDS

3–20 The House of Lords in its judicial capacity should not be confused with the second legislative chamber of Parliament.[29] Although the two bodies have the same origin, the House of Lords sitting as a court comprises only the "judicial committee" of the House—the Lord Chancellor and a number of law lords known as "Lords of Appeal in Ordinary".[30] The Lords of Appeal must either have held high judicial office or be barristers or advocates of at least 15 years' standing.

In terms of its jurisdiction over Scottish matters, the House of Lords may hear appeals only from the Scottish civil courts.[31] It has no jurisdiction in criminal matters. Although the *quorum* of judges is three, in practice it is usual for a panel of five judges to hear any appeal. By convention, two of the Lords in the judicial committee must be of Scottish origin and experience. It does not necessarily follow, however, that a Scottish law lord will sit on any given appeal from the Scottish courts. Over the years, concerns have been voiced that the lack of Scottish legal input in appeals from courts north of the border has led to the erroneous imposition of English legal principles and the erosion of Scots law.[32]

As a final point it should be noted that, in technical terms, any decision by the House of Lords is only given legal force when the judgment is applied in the Inner House of the Court of Session.

THE CRIMINAL COURTS

3–21 There are three courts which enjoy jurisdiction over criminal matters in Scotland:

> The District Court
>
> The Sheriff Court
>
> The High Court of Justiciary.

THE DISTRICT COURT

3–22 The district court is the lowest in the hierarchy in terms of the importance of cases which are brought before it. Set up under the aegis of the District Courts (Scotland) Act 1975 which served to merge the previous minor criminal courts in Scotland—the Justice of the Peace courts and the Police Burgh courts—district courts deal with the least serious crimes in society, including such misdemeanours as drunk and disorderly, breach of the peace and road traffic offences.[33] In jurisdictional terms, the district court hears cases where the alleged crime was committed within its district.

---

[29] Discussed briefly in Chapter 2.
[30] By virtue of the Appellate Jurisdiction Act 1876.
[31] This was first established in *Greenshields* v *Magistrates of Edinburgh* (1710–1711) Rob 12.
[32] Although for a more luminous discussion on this issue, see Paterson, Bates and Poustie, *The Legal System of Scotland* (4th edn, 1999), pp 91–94.
[33] See Chapter 14.

In the main, district courts are not manned by legally qualified judges. Rather, a lay-judge known as a Justice of the Peace (or "JP") presides over the court. A JP is generally an upstanding member of the community who, after relevant training, is bestowed with the role of judging his fellow citizens in relation to minor offences. Given his lack of any legal expertise, the JP is assisted on points of law by a legally qualified clerk of court. The penalties that a JP can impose—60 days' imprisonment or a fine of £2,500—are somewhat limited and reflect the gravity of the offences heard in the court.

It is worth noting that in Glasgow a slightly different system which predated the advent of the district courts has been allowed to continue to operate. Unlike their counterparts elsewhere in Scotland, Glasgow's district courts are manned by legally qualified personnel appointed by the local authority known as "stipendiary magistrates". These magistrates enjoy greater sentencing power akin to a sheriff in summary proceedings[34]—a maximum fine of £5,000 and six months' imprisonment (12 months in a case of a second or subsequent offence of violence or dishonesty).

THE SHERIFF COURT

The sheriff court is the next step up in the criminal court hierarchy. Depending on the gravity of the offence that the accused is charged with, one of two court procedures will be adopted. In less serious crimes, the summary procedure will be adopted.[35] In summary procedure, the sheriff sits alone and determines both questions of fact and law. The penalties that a sheriff sitting in summary proceedings may impose are identical to the sentencing power of a stipendiary magistrate.[36] **3–23**

For more serious offences, solemn procedure will be adopted. In solemn procedure, cases are heard by a sheriff along with a jury of 15 members of the public. The sheriff determines legal issues while the facts of the case are determined by the jury. In solemn cases, the sheriff may impose an unlimited fine and a term of imprisonment up to a maximum of three years. If he is of the opinion that the crime warrants a harsher sentence than he is empowered to hand out, the sheriff may remit the case to the High Court of Justiciary for sentencing.

THE HIGH COURT OF JUSTICIARY

Established in 1672, the High Court of Justiciary is the supreme criminal court in Scotland. Unlike its civil counterpart, the Court of Session, there is no right of appeal therefrom to the House of Lords.[37] The High Court is a "circuit court" which means that it has no permanent base: rather it travels "on circuit" to cities throughout Scotland as required. **3–24**

The High Court consists of the Lord President of the Court of Session (called "Lord Justice-General" when acting in his High Court capacity), the Lord Justice-Clerk, and all the other Court of Session judges (called "Lords Commissioners of Justiciary").

The High Court deals with the most heinous crimes, including murder, rape and

---

[34] See para 3–23.
[35] This should not be confused with summary cause procedure in civil matters.
[36] See para 3–22.
[37] Established in *Mackintosh* v *Lord Advocate* (1876) 3 R (HL) 34.

treason. While sitting as a trial court, a solitary judge generally sits with a jury of 15 (who determine the facts of the case). In particularly complex or important cases, however, a bench of three judges may sit. There is no limitation on the sentencing power of judges in the High Court, although some sentences are imposed by statute— for example, if an accused person is found guilty of murder, the sentence that must be imposed is life imprisonment.

It should be noted that an Order in Council, the High Court of Justiciary (Proceedings in the Netherlands) Order 1998 has recently been made under the authority of the United Nations Act 1946. This has paved the way for the two Libyan "Lockerbie bombing" suspects to be prosecuted in a Scottish court in the Netherlands.

The High Court as an appeal court

3–25   The High Court also sits as an appeal court, hearing cases from its own trials and also from the sheriff court and district courts. All appeals are now heard in Edinburgh by a panel of three judges, although in particularly important cases a panel of five or more judges may sit.

Appeals are divided into two categories: summary appeals and solemn appeals. Summary appeals (on what is termed the "justiciary roll") are generally made by way of stated case.[38] The appeal may be against conviction, sentence or both. Similarly, the prosecutor may appeal but only on a point of law which has led to an acquittal. The appellant (but not the prosecutor) may bring forth fresh evidence but, generally, appeals are made on a point of law. Additionally, if some form of irregularity in the court procedure is being claimed, the parties may bring a special truncated form of appeal either by way of bill of suspension (by the accused) or bill of advocation (by the prosecutor).

The Court has a number of options: it may order a retrial or an acquittal; it may confirm the original verdict; or, it may reduce or increase the sentence (if the appeal was with regard to sentence).

In solemn appeals (on the "criminal appeal role") the accused may appeal against sentence and conviction (although he cannot appeal against a sentence which is fixed by law). Again, in cases where procedural irregularity is claimed, appeal may be made by bill of suspension and the prosecutor may raise such an appeal by a bill of advocation. The accused has no right of appeal against the verdict of the jury except that he may bring forth fresh evidence which may result in a retrial. If the prosecutor is of the view that the punishment handed down by the trial court is too lenient, he may appeal against the sentence. In addition, the Lord Advocate may appeal on a point of law if the accused has been acquitted.[39] Whatever the outcome of this appeal, however, it has no effect on the acquittal of the accused.

Previously, the Secretary of State for Scotland had the right to refer a case to the High Court for review if he felt it was in the interests of justice regardless of whether an appeal had already been held. This power may usefully be exercised where fresh evidence in a case has come to light. Under section 25 of the Crime and Punishment (Scotland) Act 1997, this power has been transferred to the Scottish Criminal Cases Review Commission—an independent body made up of members of the legal

---

[38] See para 3–10.
[39] Known as the "Lord Advocate's Reference" under the Criminal Procedure (Scotland) Act 1995, s 123.

profession, persons with experience of the criminal justice system and other appropriately qualified individuals.

THE EUROPEAN COURT OF JUSTICE (ECJ)

The domestic Scottish courts can, at any point, refer a point of law governed by EU rules to the European Court of Justice.[40] The ECJ sits in Luxembourg and consists of 15 judges and nine judicial advisers known as Advocates General. The Advocates General, which have no counterpart in the domestic courts of Scotland, are court officials whose remit is to provide advice to the judges in the form of a detailed opinion on the legal issues at hand. **3–26**

In addition to dealing with referrals from the domestic courts of Member States, the ECJ has jurisdiction in a number of other EC matters including taking action against Member States who are in violation of EC law and the judicial review of the acts of the institutions of the EU.[41]

The court generally sits "in plenary" which means that all the judges of the court hear the case. Less difficult cases, however, may be decided in chambers in front of three, five or seven judges. Any judgments of the ECJ become legally enforceable by their implementation in the domestic courts.

A Court of the First Instance was also set up under the aegis of the Single European Act 1988 (a piece of EC legislation) to help ease the workload of the ECJ. This court deals with a number of cases including those relating to competition law and judicial review.

COURTS OF SPECIAL JURISDICTION

There are a number of other courts which also claim jurisdiction in Scotland in certain specified situations. **3–27**

COURT OF THE LORD LYON

Although of little relevance to the general population, this ancient court which is presided over by the Lord Lyon King of Arms continues to exercise jurisdiction over matters such as heraldry, the right to bear arms and the use of clan badges. It enjoys both criminal and civil jurisdiction and is empowered to both fine and imprison offenders and seize any items of which use or possession is unauthorised. Decisions of this court may be appealed to the Inner House of the Court of Session and thereafter to the House of Lords. **3–28**

---

[40] If the House of Lords is faced with a question governed by a point of EC law it must seek the opinion of the ECJ.
[41] See Chapter 2 for a brief overview of the EC legislation and the institutions.

SCOTTISH LAND COURT

3–29   This court was originally set up to hear cases relating to small landholdings.[42] The court's jurisdiction has since been expanded and it now encompasses a wide range of cases relating to agricultural landholdings. The court consists of a legally qualified chairperson and a number of other members (up to a maximum of seven—one of whom must speak Gaelic). Either party to a case may appeal the court's decision by stated case on a point of law to the Inner House of the Court of Session.

LAND EVALUATION APPEAL COURT

3–30   As its name would suggest, this is an appeal court. This court hears appeals from decisions of local valuation appeal committees and the Scottish Lands Tribunal. The appeal is heard by one Court of Session judge or, in the case of an appeal from the Lands Tribunal, three Court of Session judges. The case is appealed to the court by way of a stated case on a point of law. There is no further right of appeal.

RESTRICTIVE PRACTICES COURT

3–31   This UK-wide court set up by virtue of the Restrictive Practices Act 1956 hears cases relating to monopolies, unfair pricing practices and price maintenance agreements.[43] The court comprises five judges, one of whom must be derived from the Court of Session and a number of lay members. When the court sits in Scotland, cases are heard by the Court of Session judge and two lay members.

CHURCH COURTS

3–32   Church courts deal exclusively with issues relating to church membership. The Church of Scotland has a number of legally established courts including the Kirk Session, Presbytery, Synod and General Assembly which exist independently from the Scottish courts. There is, accordingly, no right of appeal from the decisions of these courts to the Court of Session.[44] The courts of all other church denominations in Scotland do not enjoy this independent status.

COURTS MARTIAL

3–33   These are UK-wide courts which have been established within the armed forces to deal with disciplinary military matters. A Courts Martial Appeal Court consisting generally of three or five Lord Commissioners of Justiciary can hear cases referred from the courts martial in certain circumstances. A further appeal may be made in matters of public interest to the House of Lords.

---

[42]   See Chapter 7.
[43]   The Court's jurisdiction has been extended over the years, principally by the Resales Prices Act 1964 and the Fair Trading Act 1973.
[44]   *Logan* v *Presbytery of Dumbarton* 1995 SLT 1228.

CHILDREN'S HEARINGS

Established by the Social Work (Scotland) Act 1968, the children's hearing panel has long been admired as a method of dealing with children under the age of 16 who may be in need of compulsory measures of care. Every local authority in Scotland has a children's hearing panel consisting of a number of lay members. In any case, a chairman and two other members sit. To ensure a gender balance, both male and female members must be present at any panel. **3–34**

Cases are referred to the panel by the Principal Reporter, an official who is answerable to a public body known as the Scottish Children's Reporter Administration.[45] Previously, cases were referred to the panel by a local government official termed merely "the reporter" but the current scheme of arrangement came into being by way of the Local Government etc. (Scotland) Act 1994.[46]

The hearing is empowered merely to dispose of the case—that is, to decide what measures should be taken in respect of the child. Accordingly, the panel has no remit to decide on questions of law or fact. Any such matters must be referred to a sheriff to determine prior to the case being disposed of by the panel.

By way of the Children (Scotland) Act 1995, there is a right of appeal to the sheriff against the decision of the panel. Additionally, there is a right of appeal to the sheriff principal on a point of law or procedural irregularity. In either case, there is a further right of appeal to the Inner House of the Court of Session.

Not all cases relating to children under the age of 16 are dealt with by the panel. When a serious offence is alleged, a child may be charged in the usual way in either the sheriff court or the High Court of Justiciary. The court, however, may decide (and in some instances is compelled) to refer the matter back to the panel either for advice or for disposal.[47]

ALTERNATIVES TO THE COURT

The current judicial system in Scotland has been subject to a number of criticisms, not least in the sense that pursuing or defending an action through the civil courts is often too expensive, time-consuming, legalistic, adversarial and uncertain. It has been argued that there may be better ways of resolving many civil disputes and both the state and private bodies offer (and at times compel the use of) a range of alternatives to the court process. While some alternative mechanisms, such as tribunals and arbitration, are well established, others such as mediation are relatively new and untested.[48] **3–35**

---

[45] Under the guiding control of the Secretary of State.

[46] The children's hearing panel system has since been updated by way of the Children (Scotland) Act 1995.

[47] It has been suggested that the Children's Hearing Panel may be contrary to the right to a fair trial set out in the Human Rights Act 1998, in that the Principal Reporter both institutes proceedings against the child and acts as an adviser to the panel who decide on how the case is to be disposed of. Norrie "Human rights challenges to the children's hearing system" (2000) 4 JLSS 8.

[48] The court process in Scotland has been the subject of a number of recent reforms and other proposals for future reform have been suggested. In January 1994, the rules for the conduct of civil litigation in the sheriff courts were streamlined. See also Lord Cullen, *Review of the Business of the Outer House of the Court of Session* (1995); Sheriff Court Rules Council, *A Consultation Paper on the Proposed New Rules for Summary Cause and Small Claims in the Sheriff Court* (1998); Mays, *The Changing Landscape of Dispute Resolution in Scotland* (1997) Hume Papers on Public Policy, Vol 4, No 5.

TRIBUNALS

3–36 Given the undoubted increased state intervention in the lives of the public over recent years, scope for conflict between the state and its subjects over matters of public administration has increased dramatically. It would be impractical to attempt to resolve this huge range of disputes through the time-consuming and expensive court process, and, consequently, this has given rise to a host of tribunals designed to ensure the speedy and cost-effective resolution of disputes relating to administrative matters. Examples include Social Security Appeals Tribunals, National Health Service Tribunals, Education Appeal Committees and Immigration Appeals Tribunals. The perceived success of these tribunals in administrative issues has seen their form replicated in a number of other dispute areas including employment and agriculture.

Tribunal procedure

3–37 While the composition of the various tribunals differs they generally share a number of common characteristics. Generally, tribunals are chaired by a legally qualified chairperson who is assisted in hearing cases by a number of relevantly trained lay members. Most tribunals sit in local centres and are heard in public.

Although the procedures across the different tribunals vary considerably, they are generally designed to be more informal, flexible and less time-consuming than the formal court process. Despite the relative informality, it is common, however, for legal representation to be sought by parties appearing in tribunals.

By virtue of the Tribunals and Inquiries Act 1958[49] the guiding philosophy of administrative tribunals is that they should be underpinned by the virtues of openness, fairness and impartiality.[50] To ensure that tribunals are run in such a fashion, control over their functions is exercised by the Council of Tribunals (and, in particular, its Scottish committee), a public advisory body which reviews the conduct of tribunals and makes annual reports thereon to Parliament.[51]

In addition, the courts can exercise control over the decisions of tribunals in two ways—judicial review or appeals of decisions. These two types of judicial control are quite distinct. In basic terms, judicial review relates solely to situations where it is alleged that the tribunal has acted *ultra vires* (outwith its powers) or contrary to the principles of natural justice. Judicial review can only be exercised by the Court of Session and in general it will only do so if all other possible remedies have been exhausted by the applicant. The grounds for an appeal are far more wide-ranging and cases can be appealed on their merits—that is, on the basis that the case has been wrongly decided either in relation to a point of law or on the facts. Appeals may be made to a higher tribunal, a government Minister or a court.

Employment Tribunals

3–38 A special mention should be made of Employment Tribunals which, as currently provided by the Industrial Tribunals (Constitution and Rules of Procedure)

---

[49] Based on recommendations set out in the *Franks Report* of 1957 (Cmnd 218).
[50] In addition, the procedures must always follow the constitutional principles of natural justice—that is that no man be a judge in his own case and that both sides must be given reasonable opportunity to put forward representations.
[51] Set up under the aegis of the Tribunals and Inquiries Act 1958.

Regulations 1996, are empowered to hear an array of employment disputes including sexual and racial discrimination, equal pay and unfair dismissal.[52] The tribunal consists of a legally qualified chairperson assisted by two lay members, one of whom is a representative of an employers' association and the other a trade union representative.[53]

The 1996 Regulations also lay down the procedure for the raising and conduct of tribunal actions. Proceedings tend to be quite informal as panels are empowered to conduct them in any manner they deem most suitable.

Appeals against decisions ("awards") of the tribunal can be made on a point of law to the Employment Appeal Tribunal (EAT). The EAT consists of the Lord President of the Court of Session plus other members appointed on the basis of their skill and experience in employment matters. Further appeals may be made to the Inner House of the Court of Session and subsequently to the House of Lords.

ARBITRATION

Arbitration has long been a popular method of dispute resolution in business circles and has in fact existed in one form or another in Scotland since the thirteenth century.[54] **3–39**

Arbitration is essentially an adjudicative process whereby the parties appoint or agree upon the appointment of a private judge (or "arbiter") and accept his decision (known as "award") instead of resorting to litigation. Given that a primary purpose of arbitration is to avoid litigation, arbitration is a binding and legally enforceable process and the arbiter's award carries the full force of law with appeals to the courts available in only limited circumstance.[55]

Although arbitration is at times compelled by legislation (known as statutory arbitration),[56] in the main it is a voluntary process. Voluntary recourse to arbitration may come into being either by parties agreeing to submit to arbitration when a dispute arises or (commonly in the commercial context) by the inclusion of an arbitration clause in a contract stipulating that if a dispute arises relating to that contract, the matter will be settled by reference to arbitration.[57]

Conduct of arbitration

Although, there are a number of Acts of Parliament relevant to the practice of arbitration in Scotland,[58] arbitration is largely regulated by common law rules which, to a great extent, leaves the conduct of proceedings in the hands of the parties. **3–40**

---

[52] See Chapter 12.
[53] Although, by virtue of the Trade Union Reform and Employment Rights Act 1993, a chairperson may, on rare occasions, sit alone.
[54] See Hunter *The Law of Arbitration in Scotland* (1987). Indeed, as old a statutory provision as the 15th Article of Regulation, an Act of the Old Scottish Parliament, remains of relevance to the practice of arbitration in Scotland today.
[55] Explained below at para 3–41.
[56] *eg* the Agricultural Holdings (Scotland) Act 1991 provides that disputes between landlord and tenant will be settled by an arbitration procedure set out in the Act.
[57] Under the Employment Rights (Dispute Resolution) Act 1998, the Advisory and Conciliation and Arbitration Service (ACAS) is empowered to offer an arbitration programme in respect of unfair dismissal cases. At the time of writing, the arbitration scheme was not yet up and running.
[58] Including the Articles of Regulation 1695; the Arbitration (Scotland) Act 1894; the Administration of Justice (Scotland) Act 1972, s 3; and the Law Reform (Miscellaneous Provisions) (Scotland) Act 1990.

In theory, parties are free to appoint any person they wish to act as an arbiter. In practice, they will appoint a suitably qualified person such as a lawyer of some standing or someone with relevant expertise in the area of dispute such as an experienced accountant, architect, surveyor or chartered engineer. It is often thought that disputes can be resolved more effectively by arbiters who have experience and expertise in the particular area of dispute as time does not require to be expended explaining technical matters to them.

Choosing an arbiter is made easier by the fact that most of those who practise as such are members of a relevant professional body such as the Chartered Institute of Arbiters (Scotland) or the British Academy of Experts who maintain lists of accredited arbiters. Occasionally, parties may agree to appoint a particular office-bearer in the event of a dispute. In some cases it may be difficult for the opposing parties to agree upon the appointment of the arbiter. In such a case, it may be that both parties appoint their own arbiter. If this occurs and the two arbiters cannot come to an agreement it may be necessary to appoint a further individual—known as an "oversman"—to determine the final decision.

Appeals

3–41 An arbiter's award cannot be appealed on its merits.[59] Appeals of awards to the Court of Session are available only in very limited circumstances. The main grounds of appeal are as follows:

(a) "Corruption, bribery or falsehood": these grounds were first set out in the 25th Article of Regulation 1695 and allow the award to be set aside if it is tainted in this way. It has been held that this ground does not extend to the innocent mistakes of the arbiter in reaching his decision.[60]

(b) The arbiter must not have an undisclosed interest in the outcome of the proceedings.[61] The parties may, however, waive the right to object to the interest the arbiter holds.[62]

(c) The award has gone beyond its term of reference—("*ultra fines compromissi*"). The award must relate only to the questions put to the arbiter by the parties. Any other issues which the arbiter determines in his award are outwith his powers of reference and are not, therefore, binding on the parties.

(d) The award is defective. If the award is either unintelligible or in an improper form then the court may set it aside. If the award is merely ambiguous, then the court may place its own interpretation on it. The form that the award should take will be dictated by the terms of the arbitration proceedings the parties entered into.

(e) Defective procedure. The court may intervene if the arbitration procedure is defective in some way. This may mean that the process has not conformed

---

[59] First established by the 25th Article of Regulation 1695.
[60] *Adams* v *Great North of Scotland Railway* (1890) 18 R (HL) 1.
[61] See *Sellar* v *Highland Railway* 1919 SC (HL) 19.
[62] *Tancred, Arrol & Co* v *The Steel Co of Scotland Ltd* (1890) 17 R (HL) 31.

with that agreed upon by the parties or that it falls short of what is considered to be in the interests of natural justice.

Arbitration: pros and cons

While the procedures in an arbitration do vary somewhat, in the main, arbitration   **3–42** is touted as a speedy, cheap, more informal and private alternative to the court process.

Despite these positive attributes, arbitration has been subject to growing criticism over the fact it has in many senses become a mirror image of litigation. It is undeniable that commercial arbitration has become more legalistic, complex, and hence more time-consuming and expensive in recent years. The increased participation of lawyers in the process has been identified as one of the main contributing factors to this general malaise. As far as costs are concerned, in addition the arbiter, his legal clerk (if required) and the venue must be paid for by the parties to the arbitration, whereas in the courts, the costs of the court buildings and judges' salaries are borne by the taxpayer.

In order to alleviate some of these difficulties, it has been suggested that domestic arbitration in Scotland be underpinned by legislative measures.[63] A draft arbitration bill, setting out a range of terms which will complement parties' arbitration agreements has also been formulated.[64]

OTHER FORMS OF DISPUTE RESOLUTION: ADR

In recent times there have been moves to embrace new, alternative forms of dispute   **3–43** resolution ("ADR"). In the main, these processes seek to provide a more harmonious method of dispute resolution than the adversarial processes of litigation and arbitration. The main ADR process is known as mediation (also known in some contexts as "conciliation"). In plain terms, mediation is a process whereby the disputing parties are encouraged to reach their own resolution to their dispute assisted by a third party neutral (or mediator) who acts as a catalyst. Unlike litigation and arbitration the mediator does not impose his own solution or decision on the parties.[65]

Taking a lead from the employment sphere where such consensual methods of dispute resolution have been adopted by ACAS since 1974[66] a number of recent developments in ADR have occurred over different dispute areas including family, commercial and community disputes.

At the time of writing, at least outwith family and employment matters, there has been only a very limited take up of ADR services. A number of important issues relating to such matters as ensuring adequate regulation and standards of training will require to be resolved before ADR mounts a serious challenge to the courtroom in the arena of dispute resolution.[67] In addition, in the main, ADR is a voluntary process and, unlike litigation and arbitration, cannot guarantee settlement.

---

[63] Davidson, *The Practice of Arbitration in Scotland 1986–1990* (1993) Scottish Office Central Research Unit Report; Davidson, *The Future of the Scots Law of Arbitration* 1989 SLT (News) 213.
[64] Scottish Courts Administration, *Consultation Paper on Legislation for Domestic Arbitration in Scotland* (1997).
[65] On ADR generally, see Clark and Mays, *The Development of ADR in Scotland* (1996) 16 CJQ 26; Moody and Mackay, *Greens Guide to Alternative Dispute Resolution in Scotland* (1995).
[66] See Chapter 12.
[67] See Clark and Mays, *Regulating ADR—The Scottish Experience* [1996] 5 *Web Journal of Current Legal Issues*.

Mediation in family disputes

3–44 Mediation first took a hold in Scotland in the late 1980s when a mediation scheme in matrimonial matters (dealing with custody of, and access to, children arising on separation and divorce) was set up in the Lothian region. This initiative was swiftly replicated in a number of other areas in Scotland under an umbrella organisation, Family Mediation Scotland ("FMS"). A group of family lawyers offering mediation services, known collectively as "CALM" (Comprehensive Accredited Family Mediators), was subsequently set up in 1994. CALM mediators offer a mediation service on "all issues" arising from separation and divorce including custody of, and access to, children, and financial and property issues.

In matrimonial matters, both the sheriff courts and the Court of Session can refer parties to mediation if it is deemed suitable.[68]

Mediation in commercial disputes

3–45 In 1994, the Faculty of Advocates set up a service offering mediation to parties embroiled in commercial disputes. This was quickly followed in the same year by a mediation service (known as "ACCORD") set up by a group of solicitors trained in mediation techniques. Other professional groupings were quick to become involved and a self-regulating Mediators' Association was established in 1996. This body represents a number of trained mediators drawn from a diverse range of professional backgrounds including, architects, surveyors, accountants, lawyers and academics who are seeking to offer mediation services. Probably the flagship ADR organisation in the UK, the Centre for Dispute Resolution (or "CEDR"), launched "CEDR Scotland" in 1997, a body that retains lists of accredited mediators to which parties may have recourse in commercial disputes.

Mediation in community disputes

3–46 A number of neighbourhood and community programmes have been set up in Scotland (including pilot schemes in Edinburgh, Dundee, Kirkcaldy, Livingstone and Glenrothes) since 1995 under the auspices of such charitable concerns as Mediation UK and SACRO. These programmes, which are in the main manned by voluntary mediators, aim to help parties resolve an array of neighbourhood disputes which range from noise pollution, problems with the behaviour of children and pets, harassment and boundary issues.

Mediation as a diversion from prosecution

3–47 A number of pilot programmes have been developed throughout Scotland by SACRO which refer accused persons to mediation programmes where they attend face-to-face sessions with the victims of their crimes and provide some form of compensation to their victims instead of being prosecuted through the criminal courts.

---

[68] Under Ordinary Cause Rule 33.22 and Court of Session Rule 49.23.

LEGAL PERSONNEL

SOLICITORS

The term "lawyer" is a generic term and the Scottish legal profession is split into two **3–48** distinct streams of practitioner—solicitors and advocates. Solicitors have been described as "general practitioners" of the law. Most solicitors work in private practice either solely or, more commonly, in partnership with other solicitors. Some, however, work "in-house" for large commercial concerns, or for public and local authorities. Solicitors tend to deal with a wide range of legal issues such as tendering legal advice to the public, drawing up legal documents, handle the estates of deceased persons and facilitating the buying and selling of heritable property ("conveyancing").

In addition, many solicitors represent clients in both the civil and criminal courts. Traditionally, solicitors had rights of audience (the right to represent clients) only in the inferior Scottish courts—that is, the sheriff and district courts. Certain suitably qualified and experienced solicitors have, however, been granted extended rights of audience to appear in the superior courts—that is, the Court of Session, the High Court of Justiciary and the House of Lords—under the provisions of the Admission as a Solicitor with Extended Rights (Scotland) Rules 1992. Such individuals are known as "solicitor-advocates".

All solicitors are governed by the Law Society of Scotland (LSS) set up in 1949 and now regulated by the Solicitors (Scotland) Act 1980. Every practising solicitor is bound to be a member of the LSS and can only practise law when in possession of a current practising certificate issued by the ruling body. The LSS has a number of functions including responsibility for admission, education and training issues, regulating standards of practice and disciplining misconduct. The LSS is also responsible for the maintenance of a Guarantee Fund, to which all solicitors must contribute. The fund is used as a last resort to pay out compensation to those who have suffered financial losses at the hands of negligent solicitors. In addition to its regularity functions, the LSS also serves to promote the interests of solicitors in the wider political arena.

Training

Most solicitors have gained a law degree (LLB) from a Scottish University, prior to under- **3–49** taking a one-year Diploma in Legal Practice (Dip LP). The next step in the process is for the "trainee solicitor" to undertake a two-year "traineeship" with a private practice or public authority with a view to qualifying as a solicitor at the end of the training period. Solicitors are also bound to augment their professional skills by attending a certain number of hours of Common Professional Development (CPD) seminars per year.

ADVOCATES

Advocates arguably represent the elite of the legal profession in Scotland. As such, **3–50** they have traditionally enjoyed exclusive rights of audience in the superior Scottish courts. This has, however, been eroded somewhat of late by the advent of the solicitor-advocate. Advocates have become collectively known as "the Bar".[69] All advocates

---

[69] This term stems from the fact that in the Court of Session advocates stand behind a bar which runs along the length of the courtroom.

must be members of their ruling body, the Faculty of Advocates. There are two types of advocate—"junior counsel" and "senior counsel" also known as Queen's Counsel (or QCs).

All advocates practice alone. Unlike solicitors, advocates are not entitled to set up partnerships (although they may work together on a particular case). A particular peculiarity of the legal system is that a client is not able to contract or make any contact with an advocate directly. He may instruct an advocate only through the offices of a solicitor. Furthermore, at any meeting between the advocate and the client, the solicitor must be present.

In addition to representing clients in the superior courts, advocates are often consulted by clients through their solicitors to investigate a particular area of law or analyse a particular clause in a contract where a measure of doubt exists. The advocate then issues an opinion on the issue known as an "opinion of counsel". Such an opinion is likely to present parties contemplating a court action with a greater appreciation of their legal position and chances of success.

Training

3–51   The route to entry to the Bar is similar to that for solicitors. Most advocates hold a university law degree and diploma in legal practice which is followed by a year's traineeship in a legal office followed by a nine-month period "deviling" for an established advocate.[70]

CONVEYANCING AND EXECUTRY PRACTITIONERS

3–52   The Law Reform (Miscellaneous Provisions) (Scotland) Act 1990 paved the way for two new kinds of legal personnel—licensed conveyancers and executry practitioners. A Scottish Conveyancing and Executry Board was set up to provide a regulatory role. The provisions of the Act were shrouded in controversy amidst fears from solicitors that the conveyancing market would become saturated and fees would drop to unsustainable levels. Since the provisions have come into force, these new vocational opportunities have not, however, proved popular and at the time of writing only a handful of practitioners have been registered with the board.

LAW OFFICERS OF THE CROWN

3–53   The advent of the new Scottish Parliament has brought with it changes in the make-up of the law officers of the crown—the Crown's official legal advisers. Two of Scotland's crown law officers are now members of the Scottish Executive. Under the Scotland Act 1998, the Lord Advocate and the Solicitor General for Scotland are appointed by the Queen under the advice of the First Minister[71] and with the approval of the Scottish Parliament. Prior to the new Scottish Parliament, appointment was made by the Prime Minister. The Lord Advocate and the Solicitor General represent the Crown (now the Scottish Executive) in both criminal and civil matters. In addition, the Lord Advocate is the head of the Crown Office and thus has the ultimate responsibility for the

---

[70] For which the "devil" is generally not paid.
[71] The leader of the Scottish Executive.

prosecution of crimes in Scotland. He also appoints a number of "advocates depute" who, in practice, appear in all but the most important of High Court cases in which the Lord Advocate or the Solicitor General will themselves appear. Procurators fiscal (or more commonly their deputes) represent the Crown in cases in the inferior sheriff and district courts.

The Lord Advocate also has an active role in the appointment of judges and sheriffs.[72] The Scotland Act also made provision for a third Crown Law Officer—the Advocate General for Scotland. The Advocate General is a member of the UK Government and serves to advise the government on legal issues which affect Scotland.

THE JUDICIARY

There is no separate occupational group which constitutes the judiciary. The judiciary   **3–54** is merely drawn from suitably experienced and esteemed members of both branches of the legal profession. The relevant qualifications are outlined in the discussion on the courts above.

Scotland's most senior judges, the Lord President and the Lord Justice-Clerk are appointed by the Crown on the advice of the Prime Minister. Other Court of Session and High Court judges are appointed by the Crown on the recommendation of the Secretary of State for Scotland. Sheriffs are also appointed by the Crown on the advice of the Secretary of State. The Lord Advocate also has an active role in judicial appointments.[73]

JPs are also appointed by the Crown on the advice of the Secretary of State although some are appointed in an *ex officio* capacity by local authorities. Stipendiary magistrates are appointed by the local authority within which the relevant district court is situated.

---

[72] It seems likely that the Lord Advocate may lose all his powers of patronage as there are concerns that these powers run contrary to the right to a fair trial enshrined in the Human Rights Act 1998. An independent judicial appointments board is currently being mooted.
[73] But see note 72 above.

SUMMARY

- There are two main types of court in Scotland—the civil courts and the criminal courts.

THE CIVIL COURTS

- The courts that have jurisdiction in Scottish civil matters are the sheriff court, the Court of Session and the House of Lords.
- Sheriff courts are organised into six sheriffdoms and 49 sheriff court districts.
- The sheriff court enjoys a wide jurisdiction. Cases are presided over by sheriffs and are heard under one of three different procedures—the small claim, the summary cause and the ordinary cause.
- The Court of Session sits in Edinburgh and is split into two houses: the Outer House and the Inner House.
- The Outer House is a court of the first instance and has a wide jurisdiction to hear a range of civil cases throughout Scotland. Cases are heard by a judge (known as a "Lord Ordinary") who sits alone.
- The Inner House is primarily an appeal court and a panel of at least three judges hears appeals from the Outer House and the sheriff courts.
- The House of Lords consists of the "judicial committee" of the House comprising the Lord Chancellor and a number of law lords. This is the highest court in the UK and has jurisdiction to hear Scottish appeals in civil matters only.

THE CRIMINAL COURTS

- The Scottish criminal courts are the district courts, the sheriff courts and the High Court of Justiciary.
- The district courts, generally presided over by lay-judges known as Justices of the Peace, are the lowest in the criminal court hierarchy and deal with the most minor offences in society. The Justice is advised on legal issues by a legally qualified clerk of court.
- The sheriff courts deal with more serious crimes, and depending on the gravity of the offence, one of two procedures will be employed: summary procedure or solemn procedure. In summary cases the sheriff sits alone in hearing the case; in solemn proceedings, the sheriff determines issues of law and a jury of 15 members of the public determines the facts.
- The High Court of Justiciary is a circuit court which deals with the most serious offences such as rape, murder and treason. Cases are presided over by a single judge known as a "Lord Commissioner of Justice" and a jury of 15.
- The High Court also sits as an appeal court where a panel of three judges hears appeals of cases from the High Court itself, the sheriff courts and the district courts.

THE EUROPEAN COURT OF JUSTICE (ECJ)

- The Scottish courts may refer any issue governed by European Community law to the European Court of Justice (ECJ) to issue a ruling.

ALTERNATIVES TO THE COURT

- Tribunals are state-provided mechanisms where administrative and industrial disputes can be resolved in a flexible, speedy and informal manner.
- Arbitration is a method of dispute resolution by which disputes are resolved by a private judge known as an arbiter. Arbitration is a binding, legally enforceable process with appeals of decisions (known as "awards") available only in limited circumstances.

OTHER FORMS OF DISPUTE RESOLUTION: ADR

- A number of new, alternative means of resolving disputes (ADR) have been introduced in recent years. The main ADR process is mediation where parties are assisted to resolve their disputes by a neutral third party known as a mediator. A number of mediation services have been set up in different areas of dispute including, commercial, matrimonial and neighbourhood matters.

LEGAL PERSONNEL

- There are various types of legal professionals in Scotland including solicitors and advocates, solicitor-advocates and licensed conveyancing and executry practitioners.
- Solicitors have been termed "general practitioners" of the law and generally represent clients in the lower courts.
- Advocates have rights of audience in the superior Scottish courts and issue opinions (known as "counsel's opinion") on particular points of law.

FURTHER READING

Books

Beaumont, *Anton and Beaumont's Civil Jurisdiction in Scotland* (2nd edn, W Green, 1995)

Gloag and Henderson, *The Law of Scotland* (10th edn, W Green, 1995)

Hunter, *The Law of Arbitration in Scotland* (T&T Clark, 1987)

Kearney, *Children's Hearings and the Sheriff Court* (2nd edn, Butterworths, 2000)

Kelbie, *Small Claims Procedure in the Sheriff Court* (Butterworths, 1994)

The Laws of Scotland: Stair Memorial Encyclopaedia (Law Society of Scotland/ Butterworths), Vol 2 "Arbitration"; Vol 6 "Courts and Competency", "The House of Lords", "The High Court of Justiciary", "The Court of Session", "The Sheriff Court" and "The District Court"; Vol 13 "Legal Profession, Solicitors" and "The Modern Faculty of Advocates"

Mays, *Summary Cause Procedure in the Sheriff Court* (Butterworths, 1995).

Moody and Mackay (eds), *Greens Guide to Alternative Dispute Resolution in Scotland* (W Green, 1995)

Paterson, Bates and Poustie, *The Legal System of Scotland: Cases and Materials* (4th edn, W Green, 1999)

Stewart, *The Scottish Criminal Courts in Action* (2nd edn, Butterworths, 1997)

Walker *The Scottish Legal System* (7th edn, W Green, 1997)

White and Willock, *The Scottish Legal System* (2nd edn, Butterworths, 1999)

Reports

Mays and Clark, *Alternative Dispute Resolution in Scotland* (Scottish Office Central Research Unit Report, 1999)

4 CONTRACT

OVERVIEW

A contract is a legally enforceable agreement between two or more persons. Contracts **4–01** of one kind or another both govern and expedite our daily lives. Your home, your job, the food you eat, the clothes you wear and the services from which you benefit—all these things are underpinned, one way or another, by the law of contract. Life in a modern industrial society is typically sustained by the coexistence of dozens of separate contracts. Indeed, it is difficult to get through a day without making at least one new one. Banish from your mind the notion that a binding contract requires special formality or even to be made in writing. Most do not. Every time you buy a tin of baked beans or a newspaper from a shop, every time you order a pizza over the telephone, put a coin into a vending machine or pump fuel into your car on a garage forecourt you enter into a contract. The vast majority of the contracts you make are either verbal, or made solely by the implication of your actions and devoid of any particular formality. Go to a supermarket checkout and watch what people do. It is easy to make a contract.

THE ESSENTIAL ELEMENTS OF A CONTRACT

Be it for the purchase of a chocolate bar, a bus ticket or an ocean liner, every valid and **4–02** enforceable contract exhibits certain fundamental characteristics. In the absence of any one or more of the following essentials a contract may be void, voidable, or merely unenforceable:

MULTIPLE PARTIES

It takes two or more parties to make a contract; one cannot contract with oneself.[1] **4–03**

---

[1] *Church of Scotland Endowment Committee v Provident Association of London Ltd* 1914 SC 165.

Generally speaking there is no upper limit on the number of contracting parties, although in certain circumstances statute imposes a limit.[2]

OFFER AND ACCEPTANCE

4–04 An offer is a specific proposal to give or do something. The person making the offer is known as the "offeror"; the person to whom it is made is known as the "offeree". If an offer is met by the unconditional acceptance of the offeree, and all other requisite conditions are in place, a contract results.[3]

CAPACITY

4–05 Each party to the contract must have legal capacity to make the agreement. Generally speaking, an individual will have full contractual capacity. However, there are restrictions on the capacity to contract of the following categories of person.

Minors

4–06 Section 1(a) of the Age of Legal Capacity (Scotland) Act 1991 establishes the general rule that persons under the age of 16 do not have the capacity to enter into any transaction having legal effect. A contract so made will be void unless it falls within one of the exceptions provided by section 2 of the Act.[4] In particular, a person under 16 may be deemed to have legal capacity to enter into a transaction:

(a) of a kind commonly entered into by persons of his age and circumstances, and

(b) on terms which are not unreasonable.

This provision is constructed so as to expand in permissive scope as a child grows older and begins to enter into higher value and more sophisticated contracts. Whether a particular transaction is of a kind that might be entered into by a minor is a question that can be reduced to the simple application of commonsense. For example, whereas the purchase of computer game software (priced at £39.99) by a 15-year-old boy might be sanctioned, the purchase of a personal computer (priced at £999) on which to play the game probably would not. The same child's 10-year-old brother, however, might only be deemed competent to transact to buy the bus tickets to take them into town and the crisps and sweets they ate while shopping. The subject-matter and value of the putative contract, the age, maturity and social profile of the minor, and the wider context of the transaction are all relevant factors. As to the question of *reasonableness*, the court will err on the side of caution with a view to safeguarding the interests of the minor.

The 1991 Act provides that a person achieves full contractual capacity at the age of 16. However, in deference to the fact that young people mature at a different rate, section 3 of the Act permits a person under 21 to apply to the court to set aside a

---

[2] For example, s 716 of the Companies Act 1985 provides that no more than 20 people may enter into a partnership agreement.
[3] See paras 4–18 *et seq.*
[4] These include the power to make a will; consent to an adoption order; consent to medical treatment; or instruct a solicitor.

transaction entered into before he attained the age of 18. In so doing, the applicant must establish that it was a "prejudicial transaction", which is defined as a transaction that:

(a) an adult, exercising reasonable prudence, would not have entered into in the circumstances of the applicant at the time of entering the transaction; and

(b) has caused or is likely to cause substantial prejudice to the applicant.

Certain transactions cannot be set aside. In particular, these include transactions in the course of the applicant's own trade, business or profession.[5] If a party dealing with a person aged 16 or 17 is concerned that a transaction may later be challenged, a joint summary application may be made to the sheriff court to have it ratified under section 4 of the Act. All parties to the contract must concur in the application. Transactions so ratified cannot subsequently be called into question.

The insane

Generally speaking, a person of unsound mind has no contractual capacity. Most "contracts" made by an insane person are void, although if necessaries[6] are sold and delivered a reasonable price (not necessarily the contract price) must be paid for them.[7] If a *curator bonis* has been appointed to manage the insane person's affairs, the latter has no contractual capacity at all. If a *curator* has not been appointed and the person's mental state is fluctuating then his contracts will only be valid if made during a lucid interval. An ongoing contract does not necessarily lapse in the event of the supervening insanity of one party.[8] For example, a partnership contract is not automatically dissolved if a partner becomes insane. That said, however, mental incapacity is a ground on which the court may decree the dissolution of a partnership.[9] **4–07**

The intoxicated

Whether a person's capacity is affected by drugs, alcohol or other such means, in order to set aside a contract on grounds of intoxication it is necessary to establish that the intoxicated person has completely lost the capacity to consent to an obligation.[10] A condition that amounts to no more than "high spirits" or, say, a temporarily more relaxed approach to life, will not suffice to justify the avoidance of an obligation entered into. **4–08**

If a person's intoxication does reach a level that prevents him from forming the requisite intent, any contract he makes while his condition persists will be voidable. However, a contract can only be avoided if the intoxicated party takes steps to repudiate it as soon as he recovers his senses and realises what he has done.

---

[5] Other transactions that cannot be set aside include: any action in civil proceedings; consent to medical treatment; transactions into which the other party was induced by virtue of any fraudulent misrepresentation by the applicant as to his age or other material fact; transactions ratified by the applicant after achieving the age of 18; transactions ratified by the court.

[6] The term "necessaries" includes goods necessary to support life, such as articles of food and clothing, and *may* extend to articles necessary to maintain a person in his particular state and station of life at the time of delivery.

[7] Sale of Goods Act 1979, s 3(2).

[8] *Wink* v *Mortimer* (1849) 11 D 995.

[9] Partnership Act 1890, s 35.

[10] *Taylor* v *Provan* (1864) 2 M 1226.

Enemy aliens

4–09 This curious phrase refers to persons of any nationality (including home nationals), who in time of war reside or do business in an enemy country. Enemy aliens have no contractual capacity; indeed it is a crime to attempt to contract with such a party. Contracts in existence on the outbreak of war become void. On the restoration of peace it is possible to recover monies paid under a contract,[11] but the contract itself will not revive.

Corporate bodies

4–10 Generally speaking, the contractual capacity of a corporate body is determined by the terms of its constitution. The *ultra vires* doctrine[12] dictates that a corporate body may not contract on a matter that lies outwith the range of powers that have been conferred on it.

A corporate body established by royal charter may enter into any bona fide contract except those expressly excluded by the charter itself. The boundaries of the contractual competence of statutory corporations, including public corporations and local authorities, are typically marked out in the founding statute. Any attempt to contract outwith these parameters will be *ultra vires* and void *ab initio*. The most commonly occurring form of corporate body is the registered company which includes, in particular, the typical commercial trading company. The objects clause of a company's memorandum of association sets out its contractual capacity. The Companies Act 1989 abolished the *ultra vires* rule as previously applied to contracts entered into by registered companies to the detriment of innocent third parties, although the internal effects of the rule may still operate to impose personal liability on the party that entered into the transaction on behalf of the company.[13]

Unincorporated bodies

4–11 Associations, clubs, societies, most trusts and other such incorporated bodies do not have a distinct legal personality of their own. As a consequence, unincorporated bodies have no contractual capacity. Office bearers must carry out the business of the body in their own name.

Partnerships

4–12 In Scots law a partnership has a legal personality distinct from that of its partners,[14] but it is not a fully competent persona and has no contractual capacity. A partnership must therefore contract through its agents, or partners.[15] Generally speaking, the acts of partners in carrying out the ordinary business of the firm will bind the firm.

INTENTION TO CREATE LEGAL RELATIONS

4–13 It is necessary to establish that both parties entered into an agreement with the intention of creating legal relations. Entailed in every legal offer is an expression of

---

[11] See *Cantiere San Rocco* v *Clyde Shipbuilding Co* 1923 SC (HL) 105.
[12] Literally, "beyond the powers".
[13] s 35. See Chapter 11.
[14] Partnership Act 1890, s 4(2). In English law a partnership has no separate legal personality.
[15] The scope of a partner's authority to act is discussed in Chapter 10.

willingness to be bound on specific terms should those terms be accepted without qualification by the offeree. If the issue of intention is disputed the court will apply an objective test. In these circumstances it matters not what the parties had in their minds, but what inference a reasonable man would draw from their words and conduct. In deciding whether the parties had the intention to enter into a legal relationship, the court will consider, *inter alia*, the nature and context of the founding negotiations. In the case of casual social intercourse, domestic promises and most undertakings proffered in other non-commercial situations there will usually be a presumption that the parties lacked the requisite intent.[16] This presumption can of course be rebutted, in particular where a significant financial interest is involved.[17] On the other hand, where negotiations take place in a commercial context there will usually be a strong presumption in favour of an intention to establish a binding contract.[18] If the parties do not wish to bind themselves to an agreement made in a business setting they must clearly express their contrary intention. In *Rose and Frank Co v Crompton Ltd*[19] it was held that an "Honourable Pledge Clause" expressly denying legal jurisdiction fulfilled this purpose.

CERTAINTY OF TERMS

Unless an agreement is constituted in reasonably specific and definite terms no court will be able to entertain its enforcement. Where an obligation is not adequately defined or specified in a purported bargain there can be no agreement on that particular point (and thus no consensus—see below) between the parties. Consequently, the agreement, or that part of it affected by ambiguity if excision is possible, will be treated as void. It is for the court to satisfy itself as to the certainty of terms and again an objective test is applied. In *McArthur v Lawson*[20] Lord President Inglis stated that the terms of an agreement must be at least precise enough to allow a decree of specific implement to be framed. **4–14**

In *Gunthing v Lynn*[21] the offeror undertook to pay an additional sum for a horse at a later date if it proved "lucky" in the meantime. When the other party sought to enforce this promise he was unsuccessful. The term "lucky" is far too vague to be susceptible to judicial enforcement. Did it mean the horse had to win a race, or two races, or all its races, or just to place well?

That said, in general terms and in the context of a commercial agreement in particular,[22] a court will be reluctant to conclude that a purported agreement is void from uncertainty. If satisfied that the parties intended to create a binding agreement, the court will do its best to give precise meaning to looseness of expression. It may be possible to persuade the court to enforce a contract where an apparently ambiguous term can be made certain by obvious implication, by reference to a previous course of

---

16 *Balfour v Balfour* [1919] 2 KB 571.
17 *Campbell v Campbell* 1923 SLT 670.
18 *Wick Harbour Trs v The Admiralty* 1921 2 SLT 109. There are exceptions. In *Kleinwort Benson Ltd v Malaysian Mining Corporation* [1989] 1 All ER 785 it was held on appeal that a comfort letter (encouraging an offer of credit) created a moral rather than legal obligation.
19 [1925] AC 445.
20 (1887)4 R 1134.
21 (1831) 109 ER 1130.
22 See *Hillas & Co Ltd v Arcos Ltd* 147 LT 503; *Scammell and Nephew Ltd v Ouston* [1941] AC 251.

dealings between the parties, or by virtue of common usage within the relevant trade. If the plaintiff in *Gunthing* had been able to show that the term "lucky" was a recognised term of the horse-dealing trade with a specific and widely acknowledged connotation, he may well have recovered damages—assuming of course that the performance of the horse actually satisfied this particular criterion.

In *TWL Inc Ltd* v *Technology Leasing Ltd*[23] a contract for the provision of consultancy services was specific as to the fee payable but unclear as to the nature and extent of the service to be performed. The purported contract stated that services would be provided as "required by the client at such times and at such locations as the client and the consultant shall agree from time to time". Although the court was quite prepared to accept that the parties had intended themselves to be bound, it was impossible to determine exactly what the consultants were bound to do. It was held that an "agreement to agree" on the essential terms of a contract could not derive an enforceable bargain. This finding is consonant with Lord Jauncey's observation in *Neilson* v *Stewart*[24]: "It is trite law that an agreement which leaves a part, essential to its implementation, to be determined by later negotiation does not constitute a concluded and enforceable contract".

CONSENSUS

4–15 An effective acceptance must precisely match the offer made. The parties must reach *consensus in idem*—that is to say, there must be a meeting of minds, or agreement on the same essential terms. Consider the following example:

FOR SALE
Ferrari Testarossa, limited edition model,
one previous owner, mint condition,
£1750 ono.

This advert sounds tempting. If placed in a motor magazine it would doubtless solicit countless "sight unseen" offers. However, there is a good chance that many offerors would be disappointed to discover that the car in question comes in a presentation box 6 inches long and 4 inches wide.

In *Mathieson Gee (Ayrshire) Ltd* v *Quigley*[25] M offered to *supply* the equipment necessary for the removal of silt from a pond, but Q purported to accept an offer to *remove* the silt from the pond. It is frankly surprising that the case got as far as the House of Lords, but when it did it was held that no contract existed between the parties. M had offered one sort of contract, and Q had "accepted" a different kind of contract altogether. Therefore there was no consensus, no agreement to underpin a contractual relationship.

On occasion, a party (typically a company) will seek to deal on the basis of standard terms and conditions, and these are often voluminous. Where such a set of terms

---

[23] Glasgow Sheriff Court, 8th December 1999, unreported.
[24] 1991 SC (HL) 22.
[25] 1952 SC (HL) 38.

contains a clause of an unusual nature, the presence of which might not be anticipated by the other party, it is not sufficient that the offeror draws attention generally to the conditions. In *Montgomery Litho Ltd v Maxwell*,[26] although the defender had signed an application form, on behalf of a company, which contained the statement "I have read and accepted the company's standard terms and conditions", he was deemed not to have accepted the imposition of a personal obligation of guarantee. The existence of this term, which in the context was atypical and thus unforeseeable, had not been drawn specifically to his attention. This is consonant with *Interfoto Picture Library Ltd v Stiletto Programmes Ltd*,[27] which concerned a penalty clause that was so severe the court held it could not fairly be brought to the notice of the other party by indirect reference. The existence of such a term demanded explicit notification.

In *Beta Computers (Europe) Ltd v Adobe Systems (Europe) Ltd*[28] A ordered a computer software package from B. The software was delivered in a package which showed that the software was subject to strict end-user licence conditions. The conditions could be read through the wrapping. On the package it stated: "Opening the ... package indicates your acceptance of these terms and conditions". Consequently A attempted to return the package unopened, but B refused to accept its return and sued for payment of the price. It was held that there could be no *consensus in idem* until the conditions of use stipulated by the author were produced and accepted by the parties, and this could not come earlier than the stage at which B tendered to A an expression of those conditions. Accordingly, there was no concluded contract and A was entitled to reject the software.

A LEGAL OBLIGATION

The law does not recognise all obligations as enforceable. It should be obvious that **4–16** casual domestic arrangements and other personal and social agreements (for example, a promise to attend a coffee morning or a dinner date) will seldom generate a binding legal obligation.[29] The courts will also refuse to enforce agreements of an immoral, illegal or criminal nature. In *Pearce v Brooks*[30] a firm of coachbuilders agreed to hire a brougham carriage of "intriguing design" to a prostitute in the knowledge that she intended to use the carriage to ply her trade. She failed to pay the hire and the firm sued. It was held that the contract was ancillary to the promotion of sexual immorality and unenforceable as a consequence. A promise of payment to induce a woman to become a mistress was treated in similar fashion in *Benyon v Nettlefold*.[31] In *Barr v Crawford*[32] a woman paid in excess of £10,000 in bribes in an attempt to obtain the licence of a public house. When she later sued to recover the bribe money the action was dismissed.

Sponsiones ludicrae ("sportive promises"—betting or gaming agreements) are also unenforceable at law. It may come as a surprise to learn that your local bookmaker is

---

[26] 2000 SC 56.
[27] [1988] QB 433.
[28] 1996 SLT 604.
[29] See also para 4–13.
[30] (1866) LR 1 Ex 213.
[31] (1850) 3 Mac & G 94.
[32] 1983 SLT 481.

under no contractual obligation to honour your next big win.[33] As Lord Kames put it in his *Principles of Equity*[34]:

> "Many engagements of various sorts, the fruits of idleness, are too trifling, or too ludicrous to merit the countenance of law; a court whether of common law or equity, cannot preserve its dignity if it descends to such matters. Wagers of all sorts, whether upon horses, cocks or accidental events, are of this sort."

In *Kelly* v *Murphy*[35] K sued M, the promoter of a football pool, for monies to which he was entitled as winner of the pool. It was held that an action for recovery of a gambling debt could not be entertained by a Scottish court. The case of *Ferguson* v *Littlewoods Pools Ltd*[36] provides a graphic illustration of the rule. Here, a pools syndicate completed a coupon that would have won them a dividend of £2.5 million, but their celebrations were short-lived. It transpired that the pools agent with whom they dealt had failed to submit the winning coupon and pocketed the stake money. The syndicate sued Littlewoods but there was more disappointment ahead: Lord Coulsfield dismissed the action as founded on a *sponsio ludicra*.

GRATUITOUS UNDERTAKING

4–17   This is an issue on which there is divergence between the Scottish and English laws of contract. In Scotland a gratuitous contract, or promise, is binding, whereas in England it will fail to prove enforceable[37] for lack of consideration (that is, some element of valuable reciprocity). Indeed, it may be more accurate to refer to an undertaking of this kind as a *promise*, since it entails a unilateral obligation, rather than as a contract, which denotes a reciprocal obligation. In Scots law, with its origins in Roman law, consideration is not essential and an obligation to give or do something gratuitously is as enforceable as any mutual contract. The classic case is *Petrie* v *Earl of Airlie*,[38] where the Earl was offended by a placard and issued a proclamation offering a reward of 100 guineas to any person who could identify its author and printer. The proclamation stated that the reward would be paid on conviction. Petrie gave information that implicated his brother and claimed the reward. However, the Earl was advised that no indictable offence had been committed and no prosecution resulted. It was held that a unilateral voluntary obligation, such as a promise to pay a reward, is enforceable. Petrie was therefore entitled to the reward. Lord Corehouse stated: "The respondent having obtained from the advocator all that he stipulated for, he is not entitled to evade payment of the price which he offered for it, because it does not answer the purpose which he had in view." In *Morton's Trustees* v *Aged Christian Friend Society of Scotland*,[39] another case often cited

---

[33]   *Robertson* v *Balfour* 1938 SC 207.
[34]   p 22.
[35]   1940 SC 96.
[36]   1997 SLT 309.
[37]   Unless made by deed.
[38]   (1834) 13 S 68.
[39]   (1899) 2 F 82.

to illustrate this principle, M offered a subscription of £1,000, payable in 10 annual instalments, to a charitable society. M's offer was accepted by the society and he duly paid the first eight instalments, but he died before the next instalment became payable. When a dispute arose over the outstanding payments it was held that the obligation to meet them constituted a binding contract.

FORMATION OF CONTRACT

OFFER

An offer must by word or action carry with it an objectively verifiable intention to form **4–18** a binding contract, it must be communicated to another party and it must be in specific terms. An offer may be made to a specific person, a specific group of people, or it may be communicated to the world at large. In the renowned *Carlill v Carbolic Smoke Ball Co*[40] the defendants advertised in various newspapers that they offered to pay £100 to any person who contracted influenza after using a medical preparation known as "the Carbolic Smoke Ball" three times a day for two weeks. They also claimed they had deposited £1,000 at a specified bank "to show our sincerity in the matter". Mrs Carlill contracted influenza after using the ball as stipulated and sued for £100. The court dealt with three points of particular significance. First, the defendants argued that the advert was no more than "puffery" and that there was no intention to create legal relations. On this matter the court took the view that the deposit of £1,000 at a bank was clear evidence of an intention to pay claims. Second, the court confirmed that it is possible to make a legally effective offer to the public at large. Whether such a public statement will constitute a general offer is a question of construction. Essentially, the offer and entailed undertaking must be definite and set out in perfectly distinct and specified conditions. Finally, it was held that it was not necessary for Mrs Carlill to have communicated her acceptance to the company. Mrs Carlill's acceptance was, in the circumstances, to be inferred from her conduct in compliance with the terms of the advert.

The classic Scottish authority in point is *Hunter v General Accident, Fire and Life Assurance Corporation*.[41] Here an insurance company advertised in a diary that the sum of £1,000 would be paid to the owner of a diary who was killed in a railway accident within 12 months of registering himself with the company. The executor of a man who had been registered and had been killed in a train crash claimed the money. It was held that the advert constituted an offer and that a contract had been concluded on compliance with the conditions stated therein. Lord Kinnear stated[42]:

> "... when a general offer addressed to the public is appropriated to himself by a distinct acceptance by one person, then it is to be read in exactly the same way as if it had been addressed to the individual originally."

---

[40] [1893] 1 QB 256.
[41] 1909 SC (HL) 30.
[42] At 353.

INVITATION TO TREAT

4-19 It is important to distinguish between an offer and other representations or statements that may at first sight resemble offers, but which are not susceptible to acceptance so as to derive a binding contract. Foremost among these contractual "blind alleys" is the invitation to treat. An invitation to treat is an indication of a willingness to negotiate: in simple terms it is a signal that the party is "open to offers". Accordingly, whereas an offer can be accepted to create a contract, an invitation to treat cannot be accepted, although it may solicit an offer which might subsequently prove the basis of a contract. Examples of invitations to treat include goods displayed in a shop window, on a shop shelf or in a catalogue, good exposed for sale at an auction viewing or otherwise advertised for sale. When a well-known electrical goods retailer mistakenly advertised colour televisions for sale on its website at the very attractive price of £3.99 several hundred orders were received before the error was corrected. The retailer refused to meet a single order (the intended price was £399.99) and, in terms of the law of contract at least, it was on very safe ground. The advert constituted no more than an invitation to treat and the "orders" received were in fact offers to buy, which the retailer was fully entitled to refuse.

Fisher v *Bell*[43] provides a more traditional illustration of this concept. In the case a shopkeeper displayed a price-tagged flick knife in his window. He was charged with offering the knife for sale contrary to section 1(1) of the Restriction of Offensive Weapons Act 1959. However, it was held that the shopkeeper had not offered to sell the weapon, but merely indicated a willingness to negotiate. Accordingly, no offence had been committed. This straightforward principle of contract law was similarly overlooked in *Pharmaceutical Society of Great Britain* v *Boots Cash Chemists (Southern) Ltd.*[44] Here, Boots were charged with an offence under the Pharmacy and Poisons Act 1933, which stipulated that sales of poisons must take place under the supervision of a registered pharmacist. The problem, in the eyes of the prosecuting authority, was that Boots operated a self-service system with a pharmacist present only at the cash desk. If the act of selection of goods by the customer had been deemed acceptance of an offer to sell Boots may have been liable to conviction, but again it was held that no offence had been committed. The display of goods on the shelf was merely an invitation to treat to customers to make an offer to buy at the cash desk, at which point the pharmacist would accept the offer, derive a contract and hence supervise the sale.

OFFER OR PRICE QUOTATION?

4-20 Generally speaking an advance indication of the price of goods or services will be deemed to be a non-binding estimate, quotation or simply an expression of willingness to negotiate. In *Harvey* v *Facey*[45] H sent a telegram asking "Will you sell us Bumper Hall Pen? Telegraph lowest cash price". In response F telegraphed, "Lowest price for Bumper Hall Pen £900". H then telegraphed to F, "We agree to buy Bumper Hall Pen for £900 asked by you". H received no reply. The court held that no valid contract had been created. F's telegram constituted no more than the answer to a question. It was

---

[43] [1960] 3 All ER 731.
[44] [1953] 1 QB 401.
[45] [1893] AC 552.

merely a statement of the lowest price at which he was prepared to sell. It did not amount to an offer and therefore there was nothing for H to "accept". H's purported acceptance was in fact an offer to buy susceptible to acceptance by F.

Philip & Co v *Knoblauch*[46] provides a useful contrast. Here, K wrote to P: "I am offering today plate linseed for January/February and have pleasure in quoting you 100 tons at 41s. 3d. usual plate terms. I shall be glad to hear if you are buyers and await your esteemed reply". The following day P telegraphed: "Accept hundred January/February plate 41s. 3d". K responded with a further telegram rejecting P's attempt to contract. It was held that K's first telegram *was* an offer and that a contract had been formed by P's acceptance. Moreover, the fact that the acceptance tendered included no reference to the condition "usual plate terms" mentioned in the offer did not impair its effect. An acceptance need not expressly reiterate all the terms of an offer.[47]

REVOCATION OF OFFER

Generally speaking, an offeror may revoke an offer at any time prior to its acceptance **4–21** by the offeree. During this period the offeror is deemed to enjoy *locus poenitentiae* ("room for repentance"). This rule will apply unless the offeror has promised to hold the offer open for a specified period of time. In Scotland such an undertaking is binding.[48]

LAPSE OF OFFER

An offer lapses if: **4–22**

    (a) it is rejected;

    (b) a counter-offer is made[49];

    (c) a time limit fixed by the offeror for acceptance expires;

    (d) the subject-matter of the contract is destroyed or materially altered;

    (e) the proposed contract is made illegal or otherwise becomes impossible to perform;

    (f) either party dies or the offeror[50] becomes insane;

    (g) it is not accepted within a reasonable time.

To expand on the last criterion, what is a reasonable time will vary depending on the circumstances of the case, the nature of the proposed transaction and, if applicable, the practice or custom of the relevant trade. Offers concerning perishable goods or commodities that command a fluctuating market price will clearly have a much

---

[46] 1907 SC 994.
[47] See also *Erskine* v *Glendinning* (1871) 9 M 656.
[48] *Littlejohn* v *Hadwen* (1882) 20 SLR 5.
[49] See "Acceptance", below.
[50] There is *obiter dicta* to suggest that the intervening insanity of the offeree will cause an offer to lapse: *Reynolds* v *Atherton* (1922) 127 LT 189 (HL).

shorter shelf-life than those relating to a less volatile subject-matter or service. In *Glasgow Steam Shipping* v *Watson*[51] it was deemed that an offer made on 5th August to supply coal at 7s per ton was no longer open to acceptance on 13th October, by which time the price of coal had risen to 9s per ton. Similarly, in *Wylie and Lochhead* v *McElroy and Sons*[52] there was a delay of five weeks before an attempt was made to accept an offer to undertake ironwork. Over the intervening period the price of iron had risen sharply. It was held that the offer had not been timeously accepted.

ACCEPTANCE

4–23   The offeror is fully entitled to state the method by which acceptance should be communicated. In the absence of any such stipulation, the mode of acceptance will generally be dictated by the nature and context of the offer. Acceptance may be made in writing or it may be oral, and more often than might be imagined acceptance may be inferred merely from the conduct of the offeree. Taking money in response to an offer to buy, dispatching goods, issuing a ticket or putting a coin into a slot machine are all examples of acceptance by performance.[53] As stated above, an acceptance will only derive a binding contract if it corresponds precisely to the essential terms of the offer: there must be *consensus in idem*. In other words, acceptance must be absolute and unconditional. A "qualified acceptance" is no acceptance. Any response to an offer, whether couched in terms of an "acceptance" or not, which seeks in any way to alter or add to the terms of the original offer, is no more than a counter-offer. A counter-offer cancels the original offer and no subsequent acceptance of the original terms is valid. In *Wolf & Wolf* v *Forfar Potato Co Ltd*[54] the status of the following exchange was at issue:

29/11/77	F sends telex to W—"I can offer 1,000 tonnes 'Desiree' … for late January. This offer is valid until 17.00hrs 30/11/77".
30/11/77	W sends telex to F—"We accept the offer *but* shipment should be in the week of 9 January 1978" (plus additional conditions).
30/11/77	W sends second telex to F—"We confirm that we have accepted your offer. We would also highly appreciate if you could take into consideration the points we have raised".

The key word in this scenario is *but*. W's first telex, although described as an acceptance, was in fact merely a counter-offer because it sought to vary the terms of the original offer. W's second telex suffers less equivocation, but it came too late. Given that the first "acceptance" was a counter-offer, its effect was to cancel the original offer. Accordingly, the second attempt at acceptance failed because there was nothing left to accept. At the end of the featured exchange the ball was firmly back in F's court. It fell to F either to accept W's counter-offer, or to vary its terms with a new offer. However, F refrained from so doing and the court held that no contract had been formed.

---

[51] (1873) 1 R 189.
[52] (1873) 1 R 41.
[53] See para 4–29.
[54] 1984 SLT 100.

COMMUNICATION OF ACCEPTANCE

The general rule is that acceptance is not effective until it is communicated to the **4-24** offeror. As a consequence, silence will not usually amount to acceptance. There may be an express or implied (by strong course of dealings etc) agreement between the parties that an offer is to be regarded as accepted unless it is expressly rejected within a specified time. Failure to refuse an offer may then constitute acceptance. However, this is highly unusual.[55] It would be necessary to adduce cogent evidence to convince the court that it is appropriate to sanction a transaction carried out on this basis.

In *Felthouse* v *Bindley*[56] the plaintiff offered to buy a horse and stated: "if I hear no more about it I consider the horse mine." The horse was later sold to another but it was held that the plaintiff had no valid claim. Acceptance could not be imposed on the offeree on the basis of his silence. As is so often the case, the exceptions to the rule that acceptance must be communicated generate the bulk of the law relative to the issue. In the following situations express, communicated acceptance is not necessary for completion of the contract.

Postal rule

Where the parties negotiate by post the general rule is that a letter of acceptance **4-25** becomes effective, completing the contract, as soon as it is dispatched. In *Dunlop* v *Higgins*[57] a letter of acceptance was delayed in the post and failed to reach the offeror by the appointed time, but because it had been posted on the day stipulated for acceptance it was held that a contract had been concluded. There is English authority to suggest that unless a letter is properly stamped and addressed the postal rule will not apply and there is no effective communication of acceptance until the letter arrives.[58] However, when the issue was addressed in Scotland the court was less pedantic. In *Jacobsen, Sons & Co* v *Underwood & Son Ltd*[59] a letter of acceptance in reply to an offer expiring on 6th March and posted on that day was insufficiently addressed[60] and delayed in the post until 7th March as a consequence. It was held that the postal rule applied and that the offer had been accepted on time.

Conversely, a letter of revocation is not effective until it reaches the offeree. If a letter of acceptance and a letter of revocation cross in the post, the contract will be deemed completed at the point of posting of the acceptance. In England, the position is that, even if a letter never arrives, the contract is deemed concluded on posting.[61] For obvious reasons this rule is susceptible to abuse and its application may foster consequent ambiguity. It has not found favour in Scotland.[62]

The postal rule is somewhat arbitrary and clearly has the potential to disadvantage the offeror. However, it is easy enough to exclude its operation. The rule can be avoided if the offeror stipulates that notice of acceptance must actually reach him by a certain date.[63]

---

[55] See *Barry, Ostlere & Shepherd* v *Edinburgh Cork Importing Co* 1909 SC 1113.
[56] (1872) 11 CB (NS) 869, 142 ER 1037.
[57] (1848) 6 Bell's App 195.
[58] *Re London and Northern Bank* [1900] 1 Ch 220.
[59] (1894) 21 R 654.
[60] The street name and number being omitted.
[61] *Household Fire Insurance* v *Grant* (1879) 4 Ex D 216.
[62] *Mason* v *Benhar Coal* (1882) 9 R 883.
[63] *Holwell Securities Ltd* v *Hughes* [1974] 1 All ER 161.

Table 4.1   The postal rule: a summary

	Proper and timeous posting	Letter delayed	Letter lost
Scotland	Acceptance on posting: *Dunlop v Higgins*	Acceptance on posting: *Jacobsen & Sons* v *Underwood*	Position uncertain but probably no valid acceptance: *Mason* v *Benhar Coal*
England	Acceptance on posting:*Adams v Lindsell*[64]	Acceptance on posting: *Adams v Lindsell*	Acceptance on posting: *Household Fire Insurance* v *Grant*

Internet contracts and the postal rule

4–26   Electronic bargains, negotiated and concluded over the Internet, have now become commonplace. There is nothing inherently special or unique about such contracts. All the essential rules of contract formation, validity and enforceability are applicable.[65] The Internet supports two primary forms of communication: electronic mail (e-mail), and web page interaction (click-wrap). Both of these are capable of sustaining contractual negotiations, and both must be considered in the context of the postal rule. At the time of writing, these matters have yet to be fully considered by the courts and the following commentary is largely speculative. Given the exponential growth in e-commerce it is unlikely these *lacunae* will survive for long.

E-mail acceptance

4–27   It can be argued that e-mail acceptances should benefit from the postal rule for two reasons. First, unlike the telephone, telex or fax, which are excluded from the ambit of the postal rule on the grounds that they are instantaneous methods of communication,[66] some margin of delay occurs in the transmission of an e-mail. This means that, like the traditional postal service, it is difficult to verify immediately that delivery has been successful. Second, due to the way in which e-mail is transmitted (which often involves the deconstruction and reconstruction of the message), the sender has no guarantee that it will reach its destination intact. If the transmission fails there may be a significant delay before notification of "undeliverable mail" is received.[67]

Click-wrap (website) acceptances

4–28   The technicalities are beyond the scope of this book but, in simple terms, it can at least be noted that, unlike e-mail, click-wrap communication is virtually instantaneous. In this regard, interaction on a website is more like a telephone conversation than an exchange of e-mails. The sender of an acceptance is capable of determining whether

---

[64] (1818) B & Ald 681.
[65] For a thoughtful and erudite analysis of the emerging law in this field see Murray, "Entering Into Contracts Electronically: The Real W.W.W." in *Law and the Internet: A Framework for E-Commerce* (2000).
[66] See, *eg*, *Entores v Miles Far East Corporation* [1955] 2 QB 327; *Brinkibon Ltd v Stahag Stahl GmbH* [1983] 2 AC 34; *Merrick Homes v Duff* 1996 GWD 9–508.
[67] Murray, n 65, refers to this as an "electronic return to sender".

his message has been received almost immediately. Accordingly it is submitted that there is no role for the postal rule in this context: click wrap acceptances require to be received to be effective.

Acceptance by performance

Sometimes the performance of an act may amount to effective acceptance without   **4–29** communication to the offeror. Consider a typical supermarket: a carton of orange juice displayed on a shelf in the shop constitutes an invitation to treat. When the carton is selected, taken to the checkout desk and put on the conveyor, an offer to purchase is made. Indeed the customer makes individual offers to purchase each of the goods selected. When the assistant, in one motion, scans the carton and slides it to the far end of the checkout for bagging, the offer to purchase is accepted. We have all witnessed this kind of transaction. How many times have you heard the assistant say, "I hereby accept your offer to purchase this carton of orange juice (details) at a price of £1.99 on behalf of Y Supermarket Ltd ..."? The chances are you have not. Imagine how long it would take to deal with an average trolley full of shopping. Acceptance is inferred by conduct.

The same analysis applies to many ordinary transactions—a pint of beer purchased in a pub, a ticket for the cinema, swimming pool or museum, an ice-cream from a van, a newspaper from a shop—the list is a long one and acceptance is almost always by performance, inferred by the act of processing the transaction.

An order for the supply of goods (for example, from a catalogue) does not require express communication of acceptance. Typically the offeror sends an order to the catalogue company and a few days later the goods arrive at the offeror's door. There is no automatic confirmation of acceptance in the intervening period. In this context, the act of processing the order and supplying the goods is acceptance by conduct.[68]

Goods sent "on approval" can be accepted by any act that is inconsistent with the ownership of the offeror: for example, using the goods, reselling the goods or doing any other act which infers acceptance. If a party is sent an expensive designer dress on approval from a fashion house it is anticipated that the recipient will try the dress on in order to decide whether to purchase it; that is what "on approval" means. However, if the recipient wears the dress out to a ball she will be deemed to have accepted it without the need for communication to the offeror.[69]

At auction the auctioneer signals acceptance of the highest offer by banging his gavel.[70] No verbal communication is necessary; in fact such would be unusual. Furthermore, it is not necessary that the bidder either sees or hears the gavel brought down.

Acceptance by performance also takes place when a party operates a vending or ticket machine. In this case the offer is typically borne on the machine or by it. The offeree can shout at the machine all he likes, but acceptance is by conduct, by the act of putting money into the slot.[71]

Lastly, it is may not be necessary to communicate acceptance of a general offer or advertisement. For example, in the context of a lost property reward poster the finding

---

[68] Bell, *Commentaries*, I, 344.
[69] See also the Sale of Goods Act 1979, s 35.
[70] See also *ibid* s 57(2).
[71] See *Thornton* v *Shoe Lane Parking* [1971] 2 QB 163.

and returning of the property is sufficient. It is not necessary to advise the offeror that you have decided to look for the property. *Petrie* v *Earl of Airlie*,[72] as discussed above, is good authority on this point. Likewise, as seen in *Carlill* v *Carbolic Smoke Ball Co*,[73] an offer to the world at large drawn in definite terms can be accepted by the performance of its conditions by any member of the public inclined to do so. Again, communication of acceptance is not required in order to derive a contract.

THE CREATION OF THE CONTRACT

4–30   At the moment of valid acceptance the contract comes into being. Once acceptance is given it cannot be withdrawn. One case that appears to suggest otherwise, *Countess of Dunmore* v *Alexander*,[74] where a letter of revocation was posted *after* a letter of acceptance but was still deemed effective, stands as dubious authority and is not deemed worthy of further comment here. It is not necessary that an acceptance expressly repeats all the terms of the offer. General acceptance of an offer that incorporates certain conditions will be treated as an acceptance of the offer *in extenso* in most circumstances, and in particular where the conditions are considered to be "standard" or foreseeable in the context of the offer in question.[75]

FORMALITIES OF CONTRACT

4–31   We have already established that most contracts require little or no formality. Most contracts may be made verbally or implied by virtue of the actions of the parties. If a contract comprises of the essential elements set out above it will generally be enforceable in the absence of any special formality. Moreover, there are no special requirements relating to the proof of most types of contract. Generally speaking any form of evidence, including the testimony of the parties or other witnesses to the transaction (which is known as "parole") may be adduced to establish the existence of a contract and the extent of its terms.[76]

However, the Requirements of Writing (Scotland) Act 1995 provides that certain contracts do require to be made in writing in order to be valid and enforceable. This Act abolished the old common law regime on formality of contract and has greatly simplified the law in this area. By section 1(2) of the 1995 Act a written document is required for:

> "(a)   the constitution of:
>
> > (i)   a contract or unilateral obligation for the creation, transfer, variation or extinction of an interest in land[77];

---

[72]   (1834) 13 S 68.

[73]   [1893] 1QB 256.

[74]   (1830) 9 S 190. This decision is flawed. The curious should exercise caution.

[75]   There are exceptions to this rule, in particular under the Unfair Contract Terms Act 1977 (see below): see also *Montgomery Litho Ltd* v *Maxwell* 2000 SC 56.

[76]   See the Contract (Scotland) Act 1997, s 1(2).

[77]   Note that writing is not required for the constitution of a lease granted for not more than one year.

(ii) a gratuitous unilateral obligation (but not a gratuitous contract) except an obligation undertaken in the course of business; and

(iii) a trust by which a person declares himself to be sole trustee of his own property or any property which he may acquire;

(b) the creation, transfer, variation or extinction of an interest in land otherwise than by the operation of a court decree, statute or rule of law; and

(c) the making of a will, testamentary trust disposition and settlement or codicil."

Section 2 of the 1995 Act provides that the only formality required for the constitution of these contracts is subscription by the granter (or by the signature of each granter if there is more than one). If a document is to be considered *probative* (that is "self-proving"—regarded as authentic without the need for the presentation of additional evidence), one of two conditions set down in the Act must be satisfied. The document must either be:

(a) *attested* (witnessed) (s 3)—the contract must be signed, or the signature acknowledged, by the granter before one mentally capable witness aged over 16 who knows the granter (a "testing clause" which states the name and address of the witness is included); or

(b) *endorsed with a court certificate* (s 4)—obtained by application to the sheriff court supported by an affidavit stating that the document was subscribed by the granter.

NOTARIAL EXECUTION

Where a granter is blind or otherwise unable to write, a procedure known as notarial **4–32** execution is available. By this procedure, unless the granter stipulates otherwise, the document is read out in the presence of the granter by a solicitor, advocate, justice of the peace or court clerk. The document is then signed by the latter party in the presence of the granter. If the document consists of more than one sheet it must be signed on each sheet. The document will be deemed invalid to the extent that it confers any benefit on the subscriber or the subscriber's family. In order to qualify as probative one of the conditions set out in section 3 or section 4 of the Act (as above), must be satisfied.

ELECTRONIC CONTRACTS

There is no difficulty in concluding everyday contracts and indeed the bulk of trans- **4–33** actions over the Internet. As stated, no special formality is required. Under the provisions of the Electronic Communication Act 2000, contracts required to be made in writing can now be accommodated in electronic form. Section 7 of the Act provides that electronic signatures incorporated into electronic communication and the certification by any person of such a signature shall be admissible in evidence in relation to any question as to the authenticity or integrity of the communication or data. Section 8 empowers Ministers to authorise and facilitate the use of electronic communications or electronic storage by order made by statutory instrument. By this means, legal efficacy and functional equivalence with more traditional forms of contract and endorsement may be accorded to electronic contracts and digital signatures. The 2000 Act established the foundations for full electronic freedom of contract.

DEFECTIVE CONTRACTS

4–34   An *ex facie*[78] valid contract may nonetheless harbour some defect that impairs its enforceability at law. Many factors may conspire to produce this result, including lack of capacity, illegality, error and misrepresentation. Depending on the nature of the defect, the contract may be rendered either void, voidable or merely unenforceable.

VOID "CONTRACTS"

4–35   In simple terms, if a putative "contract" is void there is no contract and never was one. Indeed, the phrase "a void contract" is a contradiction in terms because no contract ever existed. A contract deemed to be void is a nullity and can exercise no legal effect whatsoever. Such a "contract" cannot be enforced by the courts and no party can acquire rights or obligations through it. This means, for example, that the ownership of goods or property cannot pass under a void contract.

Common among transactions that are treated as null and void are: those defective on grounds of capacity, whether by reason of the age, insanity or intoxication of one of the parties; illegal contracts; contracts contrary to public policy; certain contracts entered into in error or induced by misrepresentation.

VOIDABLE CONTRACTS

4–36   In this context the term "voidable" means that at least one party can either "take the contract or leave it". A voidable contract is an agreement that creates an *ex facie* valid and enforceable contract, but which also contains some inherent flaw that is not immediately fatal but nonetheless renders the contract vulnerable to challenge by one of the parties to it. Such a contract generally remains valid unless and until the party entitled to avoid it takes steps to annul it or set it aside.

The right to challenge a voidable contract must be exercised timeously. If the party entitled to repudiate the contract acquiesces in the face of knowledge of its voidable status he may be taken to have affirmed the contract and accepted the obligations arising therefrom. Furthermore, it is a condition of reduction that *restitutio in integrum* (entire restoration) is both possible and carried out. If the parties are unable, for some reason, to restore each other to their original, pre-contractual positions then the right to cancel the contract may be lost.

Transactions that may be deemed voidable include: contracts concluded by undue

---

[78] "On the face of it".

influence; contracts by a person acting in breach of a fiduciary duty (for example, a contract entered into on behalf of a company by a director with a conflict of interests); some contracts by insolvents; some contracts by intoxicated persons where the level of intoxication suffered does not fully remove the power of rational consent; certain contracts entered into by error or misrepresentation.

UNENFORCEABLE CONTRACTS

These contracts may be valid in all respects—neither technically void nor voidable— **4–37** but by reason of their nature they prove unenforceable by legal process in the courts. Unenforceable contracts include agreements not intended to confer legal rights and obligations such as the typical "gentleman's agreement" and many social and domestic agreements. Another good example is the *sponsio ludicra*, or gaming contract.[79] Those contracts which required to be constituted in a form prescribed by statute must be so constituted or they will be unenforceable. Other contracts will be unenforceable due to a simple lack of evidence.

ERROR

If either or both parties enter into a contract in error the validity of the contract may be **4–38** affected. This is a complex area of law. As a first step it is important to distinguish between the two fundamental types of error: errors of law and errors of fact.

ERROR IN LAW

Errors as to law occur where a party misunderstands the legal effect of the contract or **4–39** his legal rights pertaining thereto. In accord with the familiar principle of law *ignorantia juris neminem excusat* (ignorance of the law excuses no one), the general rule is that error as to law will not impair the validity of the contract. That said, in *Morgan Guaranty Trust of New York* v *Lothian Regional Council*[80] it was held that a payment made under error of law is recoverable. However, it should be noted that a claim for repetition (or repayment) derives from the law of equity under the *condictio indebiti* (which supports an action for the repayment of money paid in the mistaken belief that it was owed) and not from the law of contract.

ERROR IN FACT

Errors as to fact arise where one or both parties are mistaken about some material **4–40** characteristic of the contract. In his *Principles of the Law of Scotland*,[81] Bell identifies the five major heads of error in fact, namely error as to: (1) the subject-matter of the contract; (2) the identity of the other party (where this is essential); (3) the price; (4)

---

[79] Discussed at para 4–16. See, *eg*, *Robertson* v *Balfour* 1938 SC 207.
[80] 1995 SC 151.
[81] s 11.

the quantity, quality or extent of the subject; (5) the nature of the contract itself. Errors in fact may affect the validity of a contract in a variety of ways depending on the circumstances of the error in question. Different forms of error and the legal consequences thereof are discussed below.

UNINDUCED ERROR

ERROR OF EXPRESSION

4–41 An error of expression may occur where the parties have reached a clear oral agreement but the contract so concluded is not accurately transferred into writing. In *Krupp v John Menzies Ltd*[82] there was a verbal agreement to pay an employee one-twentieth of net annual profits. However, when the written contract was subsequently drawn up this provision was represented as an agreement to pay one-fifth of net profits due to the simple arithmetical mistake of a clerk. The employee sued for payment of her share of the profits as provided by the written contract, but the court upheld the original agreement on evidence from the employer.[83]

At common law the courts are confronted with a stark choice between reducing or upholding the written contract; strictly speaking no amendment is permitted. However, the Law Reform (Miscellaneous Provisions) (Scotland) Act 1985 provides a straightforward procedure for the rectification of documents that misrepresent the intention of the parties.[84] Adjustments so made by the court will have retrospective effect. This power is subject to section 9 of the Act, which provides that the court must be satisfied that the interests of innocent third parties are not adversely affected by any proposed rectification.

An error of expression may also occur where the offeror unintentionally misstates the terms of his offer and the offer is accepted before correction can be made. If the offeree realises a mistake has been made—for instance, where the offeror quotes an unrealistically low price for goods—the "contract" is likely to be deemed void. However, where the offeree accepts in good faith, unaware of the misstatement, the legal position is ambiguous. In general terms, contracts made in such circumstances may be voidable, in particular where the offeree might reasonably have been expected to notice the mistake. In *Seaton Brick and Tile Co v Mitchell*[85] a contractor offered to do work for a lump sum, which, due to his own miscalculation, was smaller than it should have been. The offer was accepted but when he discovered his mistake the contractor refused to do the work. It was held that the contract was valid and binding. In the circumstances there was nothing to signal the existence of the error to the acceptor and he had justifiably acted on the offer. This case can be usefully contrasted with *Wilkie v Hamilton Lodging House Co*,[86] where a tradesman undercharged on his bill as a consequence of a miscalculation that was obvious on the face of the document. Given that

---

[82] 1907 SC 903.
[83] See also *Aberdeen Rubber Ltd v Knowles & Sons (Fruiterers) Ltd* 1995 SLT 870.
[84] s 8.
[85] (1900) 2 F 550.
[86] (1902) 4 F 951.

the other party should have noticed this mistake, it was held that the tradesman was entitled to charge the amount previously agreed. In *Steel's Trustees* v *Bradley Homes (Scotland) Ltd*[87] the offeree mistakenly accepted in writing an offer for the payment of a sum with interest accumulating from the wrong date. The court rejected his attempt to reduce the contract on this ground. The offeree's true intentions were unknown to the offeror, and it was not reasonable to infer this knowledge in the circumstances.

ERROR OF INTENTION

An error of intention occurs where one or both of the parties are mistaken as to the nature of the contract. Accordingly the error may be either unilateral or bilateral. **4–42**

Unilateral error

Generally speaking, if the error is of one party only the validity of the contract will not be impaired. A contract will not usually be reduced on the ground that one party is unaware of a material fact unless that party has been induced to enter the contract by misrepresentation or fraud, even if the other party is aware of the error. In *Spook Erection (Northern) Ltd* v *Kaye*[88] there was a mistaken belief on the part of one party that property was being sold subject to a 990-year lease when in fact it was subject only to a 90-year lease. It was held that this error would only be a ground for reducing the contract if it could be shown it had been induced. However, no misrepresentation was found and the contract was deemed to be valid. **4–43**

Nevertheless, a unilateral, uninduced error may well invalidate a gratuitous contract. As Lord Reid stated in *Hunter* v *Bradford Property Trust*[89] "a person should not be allowed to retain a gratuitous benefit given under essential error on the part of the person conferring the benefit". In addition, the general rule will not apply if the unilateral error is so fundamental as to have denied the parties achieving *consensus in idem*. In these circumstances the contract will not have come into existence: the transaction will be deemed void. Finally, it can be argued that unilateral error may provoke the reduction of a contract where the other party is aware that a mistake has been made and seeks to take unfair advantage of it. In *Steuart's Trustees* v *Hart*[90] the seller of land believed that it was burdened with an annual feuduty of £9.15s when in fact it was subject only to a feuduty of 3s. The buyer knew of the seller's error, which had depressed the price of the land, and sought to take advantage of it. The court reduced the contract. This authority is not uncontroversial and is not in harmony with the body of jurisprudence on unilateral uninduced error. It seems the court was attempting to do justice between the parties on the facts and *Steuart's Trustees* has been distinguished and doubted in later cases.[91] However, in *Angus* v *Bryden*[92] the court attempted to justify *Steuart's Trustees* as a case based on error of expression rather than error of intention.

---

[87] 1972 SC 48.
[88] 1990 SLT 676.
[89] 1970 SLT 173.
[90] (1875) 3 R 192.
[91] See, *inter alios*, *Brooker-Simpson* v *Duncan Logan Ltd* 1969 SLT 304; *Spook Erection (Northern) Ltd* v *Kaye* 1990 SLT 676.
[92] 1992 SLT 884.

Bilateral error

4–44   This class of error broadly subdivides into common error and mutual error.

Common error

4–45   Common error occurs where both parties make the same mistake about a fact connected to the contract. If the misconstrued fact is material, or fundamental, to the transaction the "contract" will be deemed void. For example, section 6 of the Sale of Goods Act 1979 provides that where there is a contract for the sale of specific goods and the goods without the knowledge of the seller have perished at the time the contract is made, the contract is void. *Couturier v Hastie*[93] is a case in point: here, a cargo of grain on board a ship was sold under a contract, but prior to the point of contract and unbeknown to the parties the grain had begun to rot. Some of the grain had been dumped overboard and the rest had been sold while still in a marketable state. The contract was void.

   Common error as to opinion, rather than fact, will not invalidate the contract. In *McGuire* v *Paterson*[94] the parties settled a claim for compensation, both having formed the opinion that the pursuer's injuries were relatively minor. In fact, the injuries were later found to be serious, but the original settlement was upheld. Similarly, in *Leaf* v *International Galleries*[95] both parties contracted over a painting in the mistaken belief that it was the work of a celebrated artist. The contract was held to stand. *Dawson* v *Muir*[96] concerned the sale of vats for their "scrap value" of £2. Later they were found to contain white lead valued at £300. The court refused to reduce the contract at the behest of the seller merely because it had transpired the goods were more valuable than the parties had previously anticipated. By the same token, common error in the context of a contract where it is apparent the parties consented to take a risk on some fact or state of affairs will not vitiate the contract; indeed the existence of error itself may be denied.[97]

Mutual error

4–46   Mutual error occurs where the parties misunderstand one another and each has formed a different impression of what has been agreed. Where the error goes to the heart of the transaction and is sufficiently serious to be counted as *essential* error, *consensus in idem* will be lacking and the "contract" will be treated as void. Where the misunderstanding is merely *incidental* the court may examine the bargain to determine which, if either, of the party's perceptions was informed by the most reasonable construction of the transaction. The contract may then be upheld on the basis of the favoured interpretation. The distinction between essential error, which is otherwise referred to as *error in substantialibus* ("error in the substantials"), and incidental error, which is otherwise known as *error concomitans* (or "collateral error"), is further discussed below.

---

[93]   (1856) 5 HL Cas 673.
[94]   1913 SC 400.
[95]   [1950] 2 KB 86.
[96]   (1851) 13 D 843.
[97]   *Pender-Small* v *Kinloch Trustees* 1917 SC 307.

Incidental error—error concomitans

Minor or peripheral errors do not prevent the formation of a consensus and a contract **4–47** will usually be upheld even if so affected. However, a contract may still be voidable if an incidental error is induced by misrepresentation. In *Cloup v Alexander*[98] a company of French comedians contracted for the hire of a theatre "for their performances". Later it was discovered that it was illegal for them to present their particular style of performance at that particular venue. The court enforced the contract because in its essentials it was sound. The contract had been solely for the hire of the theatre; there was no misrepresentation. No specific reference was made to the nature of the contemplated performances and this was therefore considered to be an incidental matter.

Essential error—error in substantialibus

As discussed above, this is error that goes to the essence of the contract. Such an error **4–48** denies the possibility of valid consent, or consensus, and typically renders the "contract" void. Bell's *Principles* identifies five types of essential error.[99]

(i) Error as to the subject-matter of the contract   This occurs where the parties do not **4–49** have the same item, goods or service in mind at the point of contract. In *Scriven v Hindley*[100] bales containing tow were sold at auction. The successful bidder was under the impression the barrel contained hemp, which is considerably more valuable, and as a consequence he was not held bound by the contract. *Raffles v Wichelhaus*[101] offers a famous illustration of the rule. In this case two ships were due to set sail with a cargo of cotton from the port of Bombay to England. One ship was to sail in October, the other in December. Both ships were named *Peerless*. A contract was formed for the purchase of cotton "to arrive ex *Peerless*", but while one party anticipated delivery on the October ship, the other party had the December ship in mind. It was held that there was no consensus and that no contract had been formed.[102]

(ii) Error as to the identity of the parties   Usually the identity of the parties is irrelevant **4–50** to the contract. However, on occasion it will constitute a material factor. This may be the case where the contract is for a personal service, or where one party has reason to fix his mind on a contract with another specific individual. The leading Scottish authority is *Morrisson v Robertson*.[103] M had a history of dealings with W. T, a confidence trickster, approached M and falsely represented that he was W's son. M was deceived into giving cattle to T on credit on the strength of this misrepresentation. T then sold them to another party and disappeared. It was held that the original "contract" was void and that M was entitled to recover the cattle. Identity had been of the essence of the contract. M would not have extended credit to T had he known of T's true status.

Morrisson remains good law, but it does not describe the general policy of the court on this issue. Identity is seldom fundamental to a contract, even where blatant deception is involved. *MacLeod v Kerr*[104] provides a useful contrast and perhaps a

---

[98] (1831) 9 S 448.
[99] s 11.
[100] [1913] 3 KB 564.
[101] (1864) 2 H & C 906.
[102] See also *Mathieson Gee (Ayrshire) Ltd v Quigley* 1952 SC (HL)38.
[103] 1908 SC 332.
[104] 1965 SC 253.

better guide to general judicial policy. In this case G, misrepresenting himself as C, purchased a car from K with a stolen cheque. G later sold the car to the proprietor of a garage, who bought it in good faith. The court held that the car now belonged to the garage proprietor. The first contract, under which G had obtained the car, had been voidable, not void. K was not in error as to the identity of the person in front of him at the point of contract: whether he called himself C or G or even X was irrelevant. The original contract had been rendered voidable through induced incidental error, but the power to reduce the contract was lost when ownership passed to the bona fide third party.

4–51 *(iii) Error as to price*   This occurs where the parties are at odds either as to the price fixed in the agreement, or as to the means of determining the price to be paid. Where the contract is silent as to price and obligations under it are performed, section 8(1) of the Sale of Goods Act 1979 provides that the price may be determined by examining any relevant course of dealings between the parties. Failing that a court has the power to fix a "reasonable price".

In *Wilson* v *Marquis of Breadalbane*[105] there was confusion about the price of cattle. The seller thought that the price was to depend on the quality of the cattle (which would have produced a price of £15 per head), whereas the buyer believed that the price had been settled at £13 per head. When the matter was disputed the court held the contract void. However, the cattle had already been slaughtered and eaten, which meant that *restitutio in integrum* (restoration of the pre-contractual position) was impossible. The buyer was consequently required to pay the market price of £15 per head. *Stuart* v *Kennedy*[106] concerned a contract for a quantity of coping stone, the price being agreed on a "per foot" basis. One of the parties had formed the impression that this was a reference to *lineal* feet, but the other party had *square* feet in mind. As a consequence there was a large discrepancy in the price. The court determined that no consensus had been achieved and the contract was thus void; because the coping stone had already been laid, the buyer was again required to pay the market price for it.

4–52 *(iv) Error as to the quantity, quality or extent of the subject*   An error of this kind, which may be regarded as a sub-species of error as to subject-matter (as discussed above), will only render a contract void if it is fundamental to the agreement. Peripheral or trivial mistakes will not suffice to reduce a contract. In addition, it is usually necessary to show that the error was induced by the misrepresentation of the other party to the contract.[107] In *Royal Bank* v *Greenshields*[108] G undertook to act as a cautioner for the debt of H. G later sought to defend an action for the payment of the debt on the ground that he had consented to act while in error as to the full extent of H's indebtedness. The court held that the contract stood. The bank owed no duty of disclosure and no inducement had taken place.

Occasionally the circumstances of a case may infer misrepresentation. In *Patterson* v *Landsberg & Son*[109] P purchased certain items of jewellery which purported to be antique. In fact the articles were merely reproductions. The contract was set aside on the basis of P's mistake as to the quality of the goods.

---

[105] (1859) 21 D 957.
[106] (1885) 13 R 221.
[107] *Menzies* v *Menzies* (1893) 20 R (HL) 108.
[108] 1914 SC 259.
[109] (1905) 7 F 675.

(v) Error as to the nature of the contract   This most commonly arises where a party is   **4–53** mistaken as to the nature of a document that he signs. For example, in *McLaurin* v *Stafford*[110] a man mistakenly thought he was signing a will, whereas in fact the document was a disposition, which had the effect of giving his property away immediately. The disposition was set aside. However, the law does not typically view with a benevolent eye those who sign documents and subsequently claim not to have understood them unless such parties have been induced so to act by misrepresentation. In *Stewart* v *Kennedy*[111] Lord Watson said: "... in the case of onerous contracts reduced to writing, the erroneous belief of one of the contracting parties in regard to the nature of the obligations which he has undertaken will not be sufficient to give him the right to rescind, unless such belief has been induced by the representations, fraudulent or not, of the other party to the contract".[112] In *Royal Bank of Scotland* v *Purvis*,[113] a wife signed a guarantee for money lent to her husband. When an action for payment was raised against the wife she sought to reduce the guarantee by claiming that she had signed the document in error as to its true nature. The court refused to set the guarantee aside: the wife knew she was signing a document that gave rise to obligations in favour of the other party, no inducement had occurred and no retrospective inquiry into her state of mind was possible.

INDUCED ERROR: MISREPRESENTATION

Error in the mind of one party may be induced by the misrepresentation of the other   **4–54** party. A misrepresentation is an untrue statement of *fact* made prior to, and usually designed to encourage, the formation of a contract. A statement of *opinion* ultimately found to misrepresent the subject-matter will not usually justify the reduction of the contract,[114] unless made in the course of business and reliance is reasonable in the circumstances. Depending on the circumstances a half-truth, or incomplete statement, may amount to fatal misrepresentation. In *Couston* v *Miller*,[115] C signed a deed that M had read over to him but it transpired that M had left out an essential part. This was found to be misrepresentation. In order to found a remedy the misrepresentation must ultimately lead to a contract and it must be material to the bargain struck. For example, in the context of negotiations over the sale of a car a false claim that the car has a new exhaust system would probably be material but a claim to the effect that the ashtrays have been emptied would not.

Where an error in the substantials is induced, the contract will be void; where an error *concomitans* is induced, the resulting contract is voidable. There are three classes of misrepresentation: innocent, negligent and fraudulent. It should be noted that fraudulent or negligent misrepresentation may found an action in damages, but innocent misrepresentation will not. No remedy will be available unless it can be

---

[110] (1875) 3 R 265.
[111] (1890) 17 R (HL) 25.
[112] *ibid* at 29.
[113] 1990 SLT 262.
[114] See, *inter alia, Flynn* v *Scott* 1949 SC 442.
[115] (1862) 24 D 607.

shown that the party receiving the misrepresentation was misled by it and has reasonably relied on it. A claim to the effect that a certain second-hand car "will take you to the moon and back" is merely a boast and would not be taken seriously as a misrepresentation at law. In other words, the misrepresentation must be a factor in leading the recipient into the contract.

INNOCENT MISREPRESENTATION

4-55   An innocent misrepresentation is a false statement made with an honest, although unfounded, belief in its truth. The party making the statement must have reasonable grounds for so doing if it is to be categorised as innocent. Unlike fraudulent and negligent misrepresentation, innocent misrepresentation is not a civil wrong and thus, as stated above, it does not found an action in damages. This means that a pursuer will be denied a remedy unless *restitutio in integrum* is possible and the contract can be set aside. Therefore, unless the parties can be restored to their original, pre-contractual position the court will not act against an innocent misrepresentation. *Boyd & Forrest* v *Glasgow and South-Western Railway Co*[116] offers a good illustration of this rule. Here, builders contracted to lay a stretch of railway track for a price of £243,000, which was determined after consideration of survey data provided by the railway company. The data was based on the work of independent surveyors, but the figures were altered by the railway company's engineer. In its altered state the data was inaccurate, in that it significantly underestimated the amount of rock to be removed; because of the additional rock the work actually cost £379,000 to complete. The House of Lords held that there was no fraud; the engineer had altered the notes because he genuinely believed them to be wrong. In the second action in this matter the House of Lords dismissed a claim for a remedy on the ground of innocent misrepresentation. The builders failed to prove that the statement had *induced* the contract. In addition, having discovered the falsity of the data they continued to work on the track, effectively barring themselves from reduction. Moreover, even if the contract had been deemed voidable, *restitutio in integrum* was impossible because the track had already been laid.

FRAUDULENT MISREPRESENTATION

4-56   Fraud, in this context as a civil wrong, was defined by Lord Herschell in *Derry* v *Peek*[117]: "... fraud is proved where it is shown that a false representation has been made (1) knowingly, or (2) without belief in its truth, or (3) recklessly, careless whether it be true or false ... To prevent a false statement being fraudulent there must ... always be an honest belief in its truth." This definition and the latter statement in particular was endorsed in *Boyd & Forrest* where, as stated above, accurate data was deliberately, but honestly, altered by an agent of the respondent.

As stated above, where the error induced by fraud is essential the contract is void; otherwise it is voidable. If reduction is not available due to the impossibility of *restitutio in integrum* the deceived party is entitled to sue for damages because fraud is a delict in itself. Indeed, *Smith* v *Sim*[118] suggests that damages may be claimed in

---

[116] 1912 SC (HL) 93, and for the second action in this matter see (*No 2*) 1915 SC (HL) 20.
[117] (1889) 14 App Cas 337.
[118] 1954 SC 357.

addition to reduction, and even in the alternative, where the option to reduce the contract is available as of right. In addition, the courts are generally less inclined to insist on perfect restitution in the context of fraudulent misrepresentation. In *Spence* v *Crawford*[119] there was an attempt to reduce a contract on the ground of fraudulent misrepresentation. In the circumstances it was difficult to afford precise *restitutio in integrum*, but the court permitted a cash readjustment to complete the process of restoration. Misrepresentation will not be deemed fraudulent unless it is possible to prove conscious *mala fides*. Mere carelessness or inadvertence will not suffice to justify an allegation of fraud, although such may amount to negligent misstatement.

NEGLIGENT MISREPRESENTATION

Negligent misstatement triggers delictual liability and is considered in more detail elsewhere in this text.[120] This form of misrepresentation occurs where one party makes a false statement honestly, but without reasonable grounds for so doing. Liability in negligence is defined by the parameters of the duty of care. In this context a duty of care is owed to those who may foreseeably and reasonably rely on a pre-contractual statement.[121] Usually it is necessary to show that the maker of the statement professes to have a special knowledge of the subject-matter and that he is aware that the recipient is both relying upon him and likely to suffer loss should the statement prove inaccurate. In *Esso Petroleum Co* v *Mardon*[122] E induced M to take the tenancy of a petrol station by representing to M that sales would be 200,000 gallons per year. In fact, in the first 15 months sales were only 78,000 gallons. As a consequence, M could not afford to pay the rent and he was sued by E. M counterclaimed against E, seeking damages, *inter alia*, in tort for negligent misstatement. It was held that E had special knowledge of the issue and that M's reliance on the erroneous statement had been reasonable in the circumstances. E therefore owed a duty of care to M and was found liable in damages for negligent misrepresentation. This ruling was endorsed as applicable in Scotland in *Kenway* v *Orcantic*,[123] which concerned false claims as to the capacity of a cargo ship.

4–57

Where error induced by negligent misrepresentation is essential the contract is void; otherwise it is voidable. If reduction is not available because *restitutio in integrum* cannot be achieved, the innocent party is entitled to sue for damages. Damages can be claimed in addition to, or as an alternative to, reduction.[124]

NON-DISCLOSURE AS MISREPRESENTATION

Although direct questions must be answered fairly and honestly,[125] there is, broadly speaking, no legal obligation on the parties to volunteer all the information relevant to a potential contract. As a general rule the parties are left to safeguard their own interests. The familiar principle *caveat emptor* ("let the buyer beware") is applicable.

4–58

---

[119] 1939 SC (HL) 52.
[120] See Chapter 5.
[121] See *Hedley Byrne & Co Ltd* v *Heller & Partners Ltd* [1964] AC 465.
[122] [1976] QB 801.
[123] 1979 SC 442.
[124] See Law Reform (Miscellaneous Provisions) (Scotland) Act 1985, s 10(1).
[125] *Aitken* v *Pyper* (1900) 8 SLT 258.

Indeed, the art of the bargain lies in knowing exactly what information to divulge, what information to withhold and what questions to ask. As a consequence, silence is not usually regarded as misrepresentation at law. Inevitably there are a number of exceptions to this general rule. A duty of voluntary disclosure may be found in the following situations.

Contracts *uberrimae fidei*

4–59   The parties are legally obliged to make full and frank disclosure in contracts *uberrimae fidei* ("of the utmost good faith"). Contracts of insurance (where the insurer must rely on full disclosure in order to evaluate risk) and partnership contracts (which are founded on mutual trust and confidence) fall into this category. The parties to such contracts owe a duty to disclose all material facts known. If a chain-smoker claims to have given up smoking when arranging life insurance, or a motorist neglects to mention his driving convictions when insuring his car, the respective contracts may be reduced when the true facts come to light.[126] In *The Spathari*,[127] Demetriades, a Greek ship broker, arranged for a ship to be transferred temporarily into the name of Borthwick, a Scotsman, so that the latter party could register and insure her. This scheme was employed because, at the time, Greek vessels were practically uninsurable due to a very poor safety record. Once insured the ship set sail for Greece to be resold. However, the ship sank on the voyage. It was held that the insurance company was entitled to refuse to pay out on the policy due to the non-disclosure of the Greek interest in the vessel.

Contracts involving a fiduciary relationship

4–60   A duty of voluntary disclosure is owed in contracts where the parties stand in a fiduciary relationship, namely a relationship founded on trust. These include contracts between parent and child, solicitor and client, principal and agent, director and company, trustee and beneficiary, and those between business partners. In *McPherson's Trustees* v *Watt*,[128] a solicitor named W arranged for a trust for which he acted to sell four houses to his brother. Unknown to the trustees, W had agreed to purchase two of the houses from his brother at a favourable price. When the trustees raised an action for reduction of the missives it was held that the contract should be set aside. W owed a fiduciary duty to the trust and the non-disclosure of his interest in the transaction rendered it void.

Material change of circumstances

4–61   Voluntary disclosure is expected where circumstances change or new facts come to light after initial representations have been made but before the contract is concluded. In *Blakiston* v *London and Scottish Banking and Discount Corporation Ltd*,[129] B took shares in a new company on the strength of a statement in the prospectus that S was to be a director. It later transpired that S had withdrawn from the post and B applied to have his name taken off the register on the ground that he was under error induced by the

---

[126] See, *eg*, *McCartney* v *Laverty* 1968 SC 207; *Standard Life Assurance Co* v *Weems* (1884) 11 R (HL) 48.
[127] 1925 SC (HL) 6.
[128] (1877) 5 R (HL) 9.
[129] (1894) 21 R 417.

neglect of the promoters to give him notice of the change in circumstances that occurred. Rectification of the register was granted.

Delusive subject

A duty of voluntary disclosure may also arise where the subject of the contract has by design taken on a misleading appearance. Contracts relating to modern reproductions of antiques[130] and reconditioned goods[131] fall into this category.   **4–62**

OTHER FACTORS IMPAIRING ENFORCEABILITY

FACILITY AND CIRCUMVENTION

Where one party is vulnerable due to old age, infirmity or some other impairment that   **4–63**
causes a weakness of mind which does not amount to insanity, and another party seeks to exploit that weakness by circumvention (which is misleading conduct falling short of fraud), the contract is voidable. In *Kerr Boyle* v *Wilson*,[132] K initially left her entire estate equally between her two sons. Over a period of years K executed various codicils, settling increasingly valuable bequests in favour of the defender. In 1994 a new will, drafted by the defender on his word processor and not in probative form, was signed by K. The new will nominated the defender as executor and directed that the defender should receive the whole estate, subject to some minor bequests to K's sons. It was held that the defender had acquired a position of considerable control and influence over K, both in relation to her financial affairs and in respect of her physical care. K's mental health was unquestionably impaired. She was physically dependent upon the defender. The defender was plainly possessive of K both emotionally and in terms of exercising control over her financial affairs. The court was satisfied that K's execution of the new will was procured by the defender's control and influence over her at a time when she was plainly in a state of facility (this rendered the will voidable). In any event, K was also found to be *incapax*, by reason of progressive senile dementia (this rendered the will void).

UNDUE INFLUENCE

Where a person exploits a position of trust or influence in order to induce a party to   **4–64**
enter into a contract that is contrary to their interests, the contract is voidable. *Kerr Boyle* v *Wilson*,[133] as discussed above, is as relevant to this issue as to the rules on facility. In *Ross* v *Gosslin's Executors*,[134] Lord President Clyde commented: "The essence of undue influence is that a person, who has assumed or undertaken a position of quasi-fiduciary responsibility in relation to the affairs of another, allows his own self-interest to deflect the advice or guidance he gives, in his own favour."[135] In *Forbes*

---

[130] *Edgar* v *Hector* 1912 SC 348.
[131] *Gibson* v *National Cash Register Co* 1925 SC 500.
[132] OH, 12th March 1999: http://www.scotcourts.gov.uk/index1.htm.
[133] OH, 12th March 1999 (see n 132).
[134] 1926 SC 325.
[135] At 334.

v *Forbes' Trustees*,[136] F entered into an ante-nuptial contract, contributing a total of £150,000 to a trust. This she did on the advice of her father, on whom she relied completely. Some years later F attempted to reduce the contract on the ground that her father had exercised undue influence over the matter. However, the court held that her father had been acting solely in her interests and that he had not abused her confidence in him. The contract stood. Lord Guthrie said: "It is essential to the conception of 'undue influence' in the law of Scotland that there has been a breach of fiduciary or quasi-fiduciary duty, confidence acquired and abused."[137]

FORCE AND FEAR

4-65   Where one party enters into a bargain under the influence of force or fear the purported contract is void for lack of true consent.[138] The essence of a case of force and fear as a ground of setting aside a transaction lies in one party bringing to bear threats or pressure which are either in themselves illegitimate or are deployed to achieve an illegitimate result, and in the other party agreeing to the transaction because of those threats or that pressure. The threat or force applied may be of any kind and may be directed at the party himself, to a close relation, or perhaps to any other person.[139] *Earl of Orkney* v *Vinfra*[140] provides a clear example: the Earl summoned Vinfra to his castle in Zetland and ordered him to sign a contract. Vinfra initially refused, at which point "The Earl was so offended that with terrible countenance and words, and laying his hand upon his whinger,[141] he threatened with excretable oaths to bereave Vinfra of his life, and stick him presently through the head with his whinger, if he subscribed not". Vinfra signed the contract, but not surprisingly it was later held to be null and void. If the threat is legitimate and justified then it does not count as force and fear, but there may be fine distinctions to draw on the nature and degree of such conduct and borderline cases may flirt with blackmail. In *Hislop* v *Dickson Motors (Forres) Ltd*,[142] H was accused of embezzlement by D, her employer. On admitting the allegation she agreed to repay the money. D obtained the key to her car and access to her savings account. Later, D discovered that H also had a current account. Other employees of D visited H at home and after a heated exchange H gave up a blank cheque to her current account. When the matter came to court, it was held that the transfer of the car and savings account withdrawals were voluntary acts and not reducible on the ground of force and fear. However, the signing of the blank cheque was set aside as an involuntary act induced by force.

In *Euan Wallace & Partners* v *Westscot Homes plc*,[143] the managing director of a company arranged for substantial consultancy fees to be paid to a firm in which he was principal partner. These payments were not authorised by the other directors of the company and the transaction was called into question. The company's solicitors advised that the payments might have been quasi-loans in breach of the Companies

---

[136] 1926 SC 325.
[137] At 331.
[138] *Priestnell* v *Hutcheson* (1857) 19 D 495.
[139] *Craig* v *Paton* (1865) 4 M 192.
[140] (1606) Mor 16481.
[141] A dagger!
[142] 1978 SLT (Notes) 73.
[143] 2000 SLT 327

Act 1985, s 330. The possibility of reporting the alleged breach to the procurator fiscal was mentioned by the other directors and the managing director agreed to reimburse the fees to the company. It was argued for the partnership that this agreement had been brought about through force and fear due to the threat to report the payments to the procurator fiscal being illegal and unwarranted. Although there had indeed been no breach of s 330 of the Companies Act, the court held that the legal advice was given in good faith and that it was neither illegal nor unwarrantable to report or threaten to report to the prosecution authorities actings which were genuinely believed to be criminal, even if the actings, viewed correctly, were not criminal. The circumstances did not support a claim of force and fear.

PACTA ILLICITA: ILLEGAL AGREEMENTS

The maxim *ex turpi causa non oritur actio* provides that no right of action arises from a disgraceful or immoral consideration. It is essential to the validity and enforceability of a contract that its object and performance are lawful. *Pacta illicita* are void and the court will not intervene to assist the parties in any way. As is expressed in the maxim *in turpi causa potior est conditio possidentis*, in a dispute involving an immoral purpose, the position of the possessor (or defender) is the better one. In other words, no recovery or remedy will be permitted: loss is left to lie where it falls.   **4–66**

However, where the parties are not *in pari delicto* (equally at fault) the court may be moved to assist the less culpable.[144] In *Cuthbertson* v *Lowes*,[145] C sold to L two fields of potatoes at a price of £24 per Scots acre. The potatoes were delivered but L refused to pay. The Weights and Measures Acts had declared any contract which used Scots measure instead of imperial measure void, therefore the present "contract", making reference to the Scots acre, was unenforceable. However, it was held that C was entitled to recover from L the market price of the potatoes at the time of their harvesting. To rule otherwise would have been to countenance the unjust enrichment of L.

STATUTORY ILLEGALITY

Statute can restrict the general freedom of contract and may declare certain types of agreement to be illegal and void, or merely unenforceable.[146] As illustrated in *Cuthbertson*,[147] the equitable doctrine of recompense may be invoked to do justice between the parties. The court may be moved to give effect to rights incidental to the "agreement" to prevent one side gaining an unfair advantage where the circumstances of a case are sympathetic to that end. If, however, there is *turpis causa* (immorality) in the agreement or its performance, the doctrine of recompense will not be applied.[148]   **4–67**

---

[144] *Macfarlane* v *Nicoll* (1864) 3 M 237.
[145] (1870) 8 M 1073.
[146] See, *eg*, Trade Union and Labour Relations (Consolidation) Act 1992.
[147] (1870) 8 M 1073.
[148] *Jamieson* v *Watt's Tr* 1950 SC 265.

ILLEGALITY AT COMMON LAW

4–68   A contract is *pactum illicitum* if its object is or entails the commission of a crime or a delict; if its purpose is in other respects immoral, for example aimed at the furtherance of sexual immorality[149]; or if it is detrimental to the national interest or contrary to public policy. It is the latter category in particular that deserves further elaboration.

Agreements contrary to public policy

4–69   Public policy, which in this context can be understood to mean the pursuit of the common good of the community, is a nebulous and fluctuating concept. In general terms, the following categories of agreement may be deemed contrary to public policy or the national interest and held to be void or otherwise unenforceable.[150]

Contracts with an enemy alien

4–70   This may include any kind of transaction with a person (even a home national) doing business in enemy territory.[151]

Contracts in conflict with national policy

4–71   These include "contracts" which would, if recognised, frustrate or stultify government policy.[152]

Contracts in conflict with the law or policy of a friendly state

4–72   Such contracts may be set aside even if unobjectionable in terms of *domestic* law and policy.[153]

Contracts inducing the corruption of a public office

4–73   This category includes any contract aimed at securing an improper advantage or benefit from the government, or fettering the exercise of the duties of a public official.[154]

Contracts interfering with or detrimental to the administration of justice[155]

4–74   This includes any contract aimed at perpetrating fraud against a court, and agreements excluding the jurisdiction of the court.

Contracts in restraint of individual liberty, in particular contracts in restraint of the freedom to work or trade

4–75   This important category is discussed in detail below.

Contracts in restraint of trade

4–76   The point of departure for the court is that contracts in restraint of trade and restrictive

---

[149] See, *eg*, *Pearce v Brooks* (1866) LR 1 Ex 213.
[150] This is not an exhaustive list.
[151] Bell, *Commentaries*, I, 323.
[152] *Trevalion v Blanche* 1919 SC 617.
[153] *Foster v Driscoll* [1929] 1 KB 470.
[154] *Stewart v Earl of Galloway* (1752) Mor 9465.
[155] *Walker v Walker* 1911 SC 163.

covenants are illegal and void as contrary to public policy. The court will only be moved to uphold a restraint if it can be established that:

(a) the party imposing the restriction has a legitimate interest to protect;

(b) the restrictions are reasonable as between the parties;

(c) the restrictions are in the public interest.

Restrictions in employment
In *Stewart* v *Stewart*,[156] R, the proprietor of a photographic business in Elgin employed **4–77** E as an assistant. E undertook not to carry on a photography business within 20 miles of Elgin. Later, E indicated that he intended to start his own photography business in the town. R sought to interdict him. The court held that the restraint was reasonably necessary for the protection of R's business interests and allowed its enforcement. The Lord Justice-Clerk stated:

> "The agreement imports no restriction on any business except that of photography, and that only in Elgin and the immediately neighbouring district. Such a restriction leaves it open to the defender to carry on any business he pleases, including photographic business, anywhere throughout the world except in a small town in the north of Scotland and a circle 20 miles round it. I cannot hold that either as regards the defender's own interests as a citizen or as regards the interests of the public in that district, there is anything that can be called unreasonable in restraint of trade, or more than a reasonable protection to the other contracting party … A photographer in a small town is desirous that [the defender] should not set up a rival business beside him and avail himself of the knowledge of the business and the customers of the existing establishment in which he has been an employee. That appears to me to be a most reasonable ground for such an agreement, not unduly restrictive of the liberty of the appellant to carry on business, and not detrimental to any interest in the community."[157]

So, a restrictive covenant may be enforced if the employer can show he is protecting a legitimate business interest. The question as to whether a restriction is reasonable between the parties depends on the nature of the restriction, particularly with reference to its geographic extent and temporal duration. In this regard, *proportionality* is key. The more extensive the exclusion and the longer its duration, the more likely it is that it will be struck down. A restriction must be no wider than is reasonably necessary to achieve the protection of the interests of the employer. In judging a restriction the court will weigh up a variety of other factors, including the following.

(i) The nature of the business Some businesses require more protection than others. It **4–78** is legitimate for an employer to seek to safeguard trade secrets or a vulnerable client/customer base. Consider, for example, a dental surgery in an ordinary provincial town. Typically, the individual dentists employed at the surgery will build a personal connection and relationship with attending patients. Each dentist is likely to cultivate their own group of "regular" personal patients, who in turn may be

---

[156] (1899) 1 F 1158.
[157] At 1163.

disposed to ascribe their goodwill and trust to the dentist instead of to the surgery itself. If one or two dentists were to leave the surgery to set up a practice in the next street it is more than likely that many of their regular patients would migrate with them, to the significant detriment of their ex-employer.

From another perspective it may be that the business in question is in the volatile high-tech or "ideas" industries, where research and development is the primary asset and commercial secrets determine success or failure. Compare a computer games development house with an arable farm. A farm worker is unlikely to be able to disclose much cutting-edge information on arable farming to a new employer. However, the development house may be entitled to restrict its ex-employees from working for a similar undertaking in light of the risk that their new ideas, gaming concepts and work-in-progress might be compromised. Of course, other factors must be considered before any restraint could be deemed reasonable. Although a wide geographical restriction might be tolerated, in light of the dispersed nature of the software development industry and the market it serves, it is unlikely that an excessive temporal restriction would be accepted. Commercial secrets, especially in software development, have a short shelf life: perhaps a six-month restriction would be reasonable, but three years, over which period the industry would more than likely have reinvented itself and its technology base two or three times, would almost certainly be considered draconian and unenforceable.

In *Prosoft Resources Ltd* v *Griffiths*,[158] a principal software engineer was subject to a restrictive covenant excluding him from working for a competitor within a certain area for a period of 12 months after termination of his employment. It was held that the pursuers had to aver and establish that the knowledge and information, which the defender retained when he left their employment, could properly be categorised as trade secrets deserving of protection. On the facts the pursuer failed to establish the unique nature of the defender's knowledge and the restraint was set aside.

4–79 *(ii) The seniority of the employee and in particular the sensitivity, importance or influence of his post* Generally speaking, an employer is entitled to take reasonable measures to protect his business connections and goodwill from abuse by an employee. It might be reasonable for a national fast food chain to impose a moderate restriction on the future employment activity of its marketing or finance director, who might be privy to sensitive commercial information. However, it is unlikely that the chain would be permitted to exercise the same control over an ex chip-fryer contemplating defection to a competitor. Likewise, the proprietor of a hairdressing salon may reasonably seek to put a restraint on her stylists because of the relationship they are able to cultivate with her clientele, but it would be entirely inappropriate to restrict the salon cleaner in similar fashion. In *PR Consultants Scotland Ltd* v *Mann*[159] a public relations company sought interdict against a former employee in terms of a restrictive covenant. The defender had given notice of resignation, during which period (throughout which the defender worked) a client of the pursuers transferred its account to a competitor. The defender was the person primarily responsible for that account. On termination of his employment with the pursuers, the defender accepted employment with the competitor as accounts executive responsible for said account. The covenant, which provided for a 12-month restriction on working for clients with whom the defender had dealings on behalf of the pursuers, was upheld by the court.

In *Bluebell Apparel Ltd* v *Dickinson*,[160] employee D had gained knowledge of trade secrets relating to the manufacture of "Wrangler" jeans. He was bound by a confidentiality clause and restricted from working for a competitor for a period of two years from the end of his employment. When D left his job to take up employment with Levi Strauss & Co, manufacturers of "Levi" jeans, it was held that the restraint was enforceable in light of the commercial value of the information to which he had become privy.[161]

(iii) The nature of the restricted area   A 20-mile exclusion zone might seem reasonable if **4–80** radiating from Crianlarich, which, although set amid beautiful mountain scenery, is frankly in the middle of nowhere so far as business is concerned. A small greengrocer business established in the village would be vulnerable to competition some distance away because of the isolation of the area and the lack of economic development. However, precisely the same restriction imposed by a similar employer based in Sauchiehall Street, Glasgow or in Princes Street, Edinburgh would almost certainly fail. In the latter cases a 20-mile exclusion zone would offer massively disproportionate protection to a greengrocer, encompassing millions of potential customers and ignoring the fact that possibly hundreds of similar businesses already flourish in the area.

In *Dallas McMillan & Sinclair* v *Simpson*,[162] a partnership contract prohibited partners in a Glasgow firm of solicitors from carrying on business as a solicitor within 20 miles of Glasgow Cross. The restraint was deemed unreasonable. Lord Mayfield held: "I find it difficult to conclude that it was necessary for the protection of the petitioner's interests that the respondents should not practice in any capacity, for example in East Kilbride, Hamilton, Motherwell or Airdrie to mention a few sizeable centres." Note in contrast that the 20-mile exclusion upheld in *Stewart* v *Stewart*,[163] applied to a sparsely populated region of northern Scotland.

(iv) The relative bargaining positions of the parties   The court will also be concerned to **4–81** verify that the parties are contracting on broadly equal terms by examining their negotiating power. It is difficult to justify a one-sided agreement, and the burden will be on the dominant party so to do. In *Schroeder Music Publishing* v *Macaulay*,[164] M, a young songwriter, entered into a contract with music publishers. The contract provided that the publishers held the exclusive rights to M's compositions for a period of five years, during which period the full, worldwide copyright would belong to the publishers. M's remuneration was to be by royalties alone and if his royalties exceeded £5,000 the agreement was to be automatically extended by a further period of five years. On the other hand, the publishers were under no obligation to publish any of M's songs and were entitled to terminate the agreement on a month's notice. M had no right to terminate the agreement. The House of Lords held that the agreement was

---

[160] 1978 SC 16.
[161] For further comment on the question of confidentiality clauses, see *TSB Bank plc* v *Connell* 1997 SLT 1254.
[162] 1989 SLT 454.
[163] (1899) 1 F 1158—see para 4–77.
[164] [1974] 1 WLR 1308.

grossly biased in favour of the publisher. As a consequence the restraint of trade imposed on M could not be justified.

Restrictions on the vendors of a business

4–82 When one party buys the business of another, in part he buys the *goodwill* and established customer base of the business. The value of these important assets would be diminished if the seller immediately found himself free to set up a new business in competition with his former undertaking. Accordingly, the common law concedes that it may be fair to allow the purchaser to impose reasonable restrictions on the future actions of the seller in this regard.

The court is usually more amenable to restrictions in this context than in the employment context, but the tests of *reasonableness* and *proportionality* are still applicable. The restraint must not cover a wider field of activity or extend for a longer duration than is absolutely necessary to safeguard the legitimate interests of the purchaser. In *Dumbarton Steamboat Co Ltd* v *MacFarlane*[165] a firm sold a carrier business to D. On taking up employment with D, partners of the vendor firm, including M, undertook not to solicit customers of the business or to carry on a similar business in the United Kingdom for a period of 10 years. About three years later, M was dismissed by D and M proceeded to set up a carrier business of his own in the Dumbarton area. It was held that M could be interdicted from canvassing former customers of the firm but that the restriction against carrying on business anywhere in the UK was unreasonable and therefore unenforceable. Furthermore, the court stated that it could not remodel the restriction so as to confine it to a more limited area. Lord Trayner said:

> "The business which the defender sold to the pursuers was the business of a carrier between Dumbarton and the Vale of Leven and Glasgow, and it was for the pursuers' protection in carrying on that business that the restriction or restraint now sought to be enforced was put on the defender. I think that restraint was unreasonable having regard to the subject-matter of the contract in which it is introduced. Its unreasonableness appears from this, that it would prevent the defender from carrying on business as a carrier, between say Liverpool and Manchester, or between Galashiels and Selkirk, both localities so distant from the place or places where the pursuers carry on the business bought by them that rivalry or competition between them and the defender is entirely out of the question. A restraint operating over so wide an area is greatly more than necessary for the pursuers' protection, and cannot therefore, in my opinion, be sustained."[166]

It is useful to contrast *Dumbarton Steamboat* with the often-cited English case of *Nordenfelt v Maxim Nordenfelt Guns and Ammunition Co Ltd*.[167] Here, the vendor of an armaments business undertook not to engage in the trade or business of an arms manufacturer anywhere in the world for a period of 25 years following the sale. This was clearly a far more onerous restriction than that set aside in *Dumbarton Steamboat*, but the agreement was upheld. The court reached this conclusion in light of the highly specialised nature of the business and the limited pool of customers for the product, which included national governments all over the world.

---

[165] (1899) 1 F 993.
[166] At 997.
[167] [1894] AC 535.

Tying-in: solus agreements

In some sectors it is common to come across agreements whereby a retailer or **4-83** distributor agrees to sell goods from only one manufacturer, usually in return for some special discount or advantage conferred by the latter. This practice is known as "tying-in" and the resulting contract is known as a *solus*[168] agreement. A good example is the tied public house, where a publican agrees to buy all or most of the beverages he sells from a single brewer. Typically the brewer will own the public house and lease it to the publican on favourable terms in return for this undertaking.

Whatever the context, *solus* agreements are prima facie void at common law as restraints of trade. If such an agreement is to be upheld before the court it must again satisfy criteria based on reasonableness and proportionality. In this context in particular, duration is a key factor. In *Petrofina (Great Britain) Ltd v Martin*,[169] M, the proprietor of a garage, entered into a *solus* agreement with the pursuer to the effect that M would purchase all his fuel from the pursuer in return for a discounted rate. The agreement was to run for 12 years, or until M had sold 600,000 gallons of petrol, whichever was the longer period. Later, on realising he was trading at a loss, M decided to incorporate his business and struck a new deal with an alternative fuel supplier. When the pursuer attempted to enforce the original contract by means of an injunction the agreement was set aside. The court held that the 12-year tie-in was unjustifiably long and that it was unreasonable to compel M to persist with a loss-making business merely to fulfill the contract.

It should be noted that European Community competition law intervenes to exempt and sanction some *solus* agreements, in particular beer supply and service station agreements, where it is perceived that the benefits entailed in the operation of the agreements outweigh their anti-competitive impact on the market and where certain specific criteria are fulfilled.[170]

The Competition Act 1998

Modelled on the competition rules of the Treaty of Rome, the Competition Act 1998 **4-84** has introduced a clearly defined anti-restrictive practices mechanism and brought UK domestic competition law into close alignment with the EC regime. The Act establishes effects-based prohibitions of anti-competitive agreements and may be invoked to regulate contracts in restraint of trade. Under section 2 of the 1998 Act (which echoes Art 81(1)[171] EC):

"(1) ... an agreement between undertakings, decisions by associations of undertakings or concerted practices which
(a) may affect trade within the United Kingdom, and
(b) have as their object or effect the prevention, restriction or distortion of competition within the United Kingdom,
are prohibited unless they are exempt in accordance with the provisions of this Part."

---

[168] Lit "alone".
[169] [1966] Ch 146.
[170] Formerly a block exemption was provided by Commission Regulation (EEC) 1984/83 on exclusive purchasing agreements: [1983] OJ L173/5. This regulation has now expired. Now see Commission Regulation (EC) 2790/99 of 22nd December 1999 on the application of Art 81(3) of the Treaty to categories of vertical agreements and concerted practices: [1999] OJ L336/21–25.
[171] Renumbered by the Treaty of Amsterdam: formerly Art 85 EC.

Section 4 of the Act provides that the Director General may grant an exemption from prohibition in domestic law[172] if a party to the relevant agreement makes a request for an exemption and the agreement meets the criteria laid out in section 9. Section 9 (which mirrors Art 81(3) EC) provides that an agreement must:

> "(a) contribute to
>   (i) improving production or distribution or,
>   (ii) promoting technical or economic progress,
>   while allowing consumers a fair share of the resulting benefit; but
> (b) does not
>   (i) impose on the undertakings concerned restrictions which are not indispensable to the attainment of those objectives; or
>   (ii) afford the undertakings concerned the possibility of eliminating competition in respect of a substantial part of the products in question."

Section 60 stipulates that matters arising under the Act are dealt with in a manner consistent with the treatment of corresponding provisions of Community competition law. In a field of policy that has occasionally suffered somewhat lacklustre implementation in the past, this mechanism should not only ensure UK conformity with the competition *acquis communautaire*, but also facilitate the maintenance of a dynamic harmony with European Court jurisprudence as it develops.

Contracts in restraint of trade: severability of terms

4–85 Where more than one restriction is imposed by an agreement the court may, if the structure of the contract permits, choose to sever the offending parts and allow the remainder to be enforced. In *Mulvein v Murray*[173] the pursuer engaged the defender under an agreement binding the defender "not to sell or to canvass any of [the pursuer's] customers, or to sell or travel in any of the towns or districts traded in by [the pursuer] for a period of twelve months from the date of the termination of this engagement." Later the defender terminated his employment and took up similar employment in Ayr. The pursuer brought an action for interdict. The court held that the restriction on selling to or canvassing the pursuer's customers was justified, but the other restrictions were found to be unreasonable and void.[174] Accordingly, the reasonable restriction was severed from the others and upheld.

In *Mulvein* it was possible to sever terms, but, generally speaking, if one unreasonable restraint is inextricably linked to other fundamental conditions of the contract, the whole agreement is open to challenge and likely to be rendered void. Most modern restrictive covenants anticipate and try to mitigate this risk by careful drafting and by incorporating a condition that purports to facilitate severability and establish the parties' provisional consent thereto. From the perspective of the party seeking to enforce a restraint it is better that an agreement survives in part than to see the entire contract set aside because of one unacceptable term.

---

[172] The European Commission has the exclusive power to grant exemption from the parallel Community regime under Art 81(3).
[173] 1908 SC 528.
[174] The exclusion was open-ended. The pursuer may have traded in every district of Scotland and England too. Moreover, it is difficult to define the word "district".

EXEMPTION CLAUSES

An exemption (or exclusion) clause is a contractual term that purports to exempt or **4–86** limit the liability (particularly for negligence) of a party in breach of the agreement. Exemption clauses may be incorporated on a notice or ticket and are often included in so-called "standard form" contracts. Either way, the party in the stronger bargaining position usually imposes them, and he does so for his own benefit. Whatever the origin or nature of the exemption clause, three questions must always be asked.

    (a) Is the exemption clause effectively incorporated into the contract?
    (b) Does the exemption clause cover the breach?
    (c) Does the Unfair Contract Terms Act 1977 permit the exclusion of liability?

IS THE EXEMPTION CLAUSE EFFECTIVELY INCORPORATED INTO THE CONTRACT?

As stated, the contract is made at the *moment* the offer is met by a valid acceptance. At **4–87** that point in time the terms, rights and obligations entailed in the agreement crystallise. Thereafter the contract cannot be unilaterally varied in any way. It is important, therefore, to verify that the party seeking to incorporate the exclusion clause has effectively brought the term to the attention of the other party *prior* to the point of contract formation. In *Thornton v Shoe Lane Parking Ltd*,[175] T was permitted to enter a car park after taking a ticket from a machine at the gate. The ticket issued by the machine referred to the applicability of certain conditions. These conditions, one of which purported to exclude liability for damage to cars and personal injury, were displayed on a notice inside the car park. T suffered injury while in the car park and sued for compensation. The operators of the car park sought to rely on the aforementioned exemption but the court ruled that it was ineffective. The contract was formed when T took a ticket from the machine at the gate,[176] before he gained access to the car park and before he took sight of the notice detailing the disclaimer.

    Olley v Marlborough Court Ltd[177] was resolved in similar fashion. Here, a couple arrived at a hotel and paid for a room in advance at the reception desk. On the wall of their room there was a notice purporting to exclude the hotel's liability for articles lost or stolen. A thief later gained entry to the room and stole valuables. It was held that the hotel could not avoid liability because the disclaimer had not been made until after the contract had been formed.

    Where an exemption clause is printed on a ticket its enforceability depends on whether the ticket is recognised as integral to the contract. Railway tickets, and other contracts of carriage, have been held to be contractual,[178] as have tickets for the deposit of property.[179] However, where a ticket is treated merely as a receipt or voucher, as

---

[175] [1971] 2 QB 163.
[176] See para 4–29.
[177] [1949] 1 All ER 127.
[178] *Thompson v London Midland and Scottish Railway Co* [1930] 1 KB 41. But note that exemption clauses in contracts of carriage are now subject to the Unfair Contract Terms Act 1977, as amended by the Law Reform (Miscellaneous Provisions) (Scotland) Act 1990.
[179] *Alexander v Railway Executive* [1951] 2 KB 882.

will often be the case, any disclaimer printed on it will be legally ineffective. In *Taylor v Glasgow Corporation*,[180] T received a ticket after paying for entry to public baths. The ticket was to be used as a voucher to hand over to an attendant inside. A disclaimer excluding the defender from liability for personal injury and damage to property was printed on the back of the ticket. Later, T injured herself and sued G for damages. The court held that G could not rely on the exclusion clause. The ticket was merely a voucher or receipt; it had been issued post-formation and could have no contractual effect.

Even where a ticket is found to be integral to the contract the conditions set out on it will not be enforceable unless they are drawn effectively to the attention of the recipient. In *Williamson v North of Scotland Navigation Co*[181] a condition was printed on the face of a steamer ticket, but in the smallest type known. Finding the condition unenforceable, Lord Justice-Clerk Scott Dickson said: "Nothing was done to direct attention to the condition printed on the face of the ticket in small type, which for any passenger must have been difficult to read, and for many passengers impossible to read without artificial assistance and very favourable surroundings."[182] An exemption clause printed, albeit legibly, on the back of the ticket was at issue in *Henderson v Stevenson*.[183] There was no reference to the additional clause on the face of the ticket and the court held that it had not been incorporated into the contract.

Hood v *Anchor Line Ltd*[184] provides a useful contrast. Here, the envelope containing a ticket bore a conspicuous notice on its front requesting the passenger to read the conditions of the enclosed contract. The ticket itself had on its face a notice in bold type making reference to further conditions and at the foot of the ticket a further notice, printed plainly in capital letters, directed passengers to read the conditions. It was held that the stated conditions had been incorporated into the contract.

Where a party actually signs a contractual document containing an exclusion clause he is usually bound by it, even if he did not read the contract.[185] This rule will apply unless that party's consent was induced by the misrepresentation of the other party,[186] or, possibly, where the exclusion is so unusual or extreme as to warrant specific and explicit notification.[187]

DOES THE EXEMPTION CLAUSE COVER THE BREACH?

4–88   At the outset it should be noted that the *contra proferentem*[188] rule applies to the interpretation of exclusion clauses. This requires that any ambiguities in a clause should be construed *against* the interests of the party seeking to enforce it. The courts typically take quite a strict line on the issue. For example, a mildly ambiguous

---

[180] 1952 SC 440.
[181] 1916 SC 554.
[182] At 561.
[183] (1875) 2 R (HL) 71.
[184] 1918 SC (HL) 143.
[185] *L'Estrange* v *Graucob* [1934] 2 KB 394.
[186] *Curtis* v *Chemical Cleaning & Dyeing Co* [1951] 1 KB 805.
[187] *Montgomery Litho* v *Maxwell* 2000 SC 56.
[188] Lit "against the person putting it forward".

exclusion clause relating to liability for property damage in an insurance contract was construed against the insurers in *Plews v Plaistead (No. 2)*.[189] The exclusion provided that the insurers would not be liable for damage to property which was "not stored at least 12 inches above floor level". The pursuer had decided to paint some shelves, on which videotapes were kept, and had removed the tapes to the floor near the shelves, intending to replace them the following day. In the meantime he dropped a large tin of paint over the tapes. The insurers were held liable because the word "stored" implied a degree of permanence and did not cover articles temporarily placed on the floor.

In *Bovis Construction (Scotland) Ltd v Whatlings Construction Ltd*,[190] W introduced a term into a construction contract with B that purported to limit W's liability in relation to "time-related costs" to £100,000. In the event, W failed to carry out the contracted work. When B terminated the contract and claimed compensation amounting to £2.7 million, W purported to rely on the limitation clause. The House of Lords held that it was appropriate to interpret the clause strictly, in light of the fact that it was W that had introduced it. The term "time-related costs" was held to apply to losses incurred as a consequence of a delay in performance, but not to those arising from non-performance. W was guilty of the latter and therefore the clause was not applicable. W was liable without limit for the breach.

There is a question as to whether it is possible to exclude liability for a fundamental breach, or a total failure to perform the contract. In *Photo Productions Ltd v Securicor Transport Ltd*,[191] P hired S to provide security for P's factory. The parties contracted on S's standard terms, which included an expansive exclusion clause to the effect that S was exempt from liability even in the event of damage caused by its employees. Later, one security guard deliberately started a fire at the premises. The fire got out of control and caused substantial damage to the factory. S disclaimed liability on the basis of the exclusion clause. Reversing the decision of the Court of Appeal, the House of Lords held that, even interpreted *contra proferentem*, the exclusion clause was wide enough to cover the incident that had occurred and P's case failed. In *Ailsa Craig Fishing Co Ltd v Malvern Fishing Co Ltd*,[192] which also involved Securicor Ltd and its standard form contract, negligent supervision led to the loss of two fishing vessels. The House of Lords held that the applicability of the exclusion clause after a fundamental breach was a matter of construction. Again, on the facts the limitation clause was deemed wide enough and clear enough to cover Securicor against liability for its own negligence.

It should be noted that the contracts entered into in *Photo Productions* and *Ailsa Craig* were made prior to the entry into force of the Unfair Contract Terms Act 1977. Under section 17 of the 1977 Act the issue of fundamental breach has been reduced to a question of whether the clause was fair and reasonable at the point of formation.

---

[189] 1997 SLT 1371.
[190] [1995] NPC 153.
[191] [1980] AC 827.
[192] 1982 SC (HL) 14.

DOES THE UNFAIR CONTRACT TERMS ACT 1977 PERMIT THE EXCLUSION OF LIABILITY?

4–89   Contrary to the impression conveyed by its title, the 1977 Act focuses specifically on the regulation of unfair exclusion clauses, both contractual and non-contractual. Part II of the Act[193] applies to Scotland. In general terms, the Act applies to:

> (a) *Consumer contracts*: where one party does not deal in the course of a business and the goods are of a type normally supplied for private use or consumption.[194]

> (b) *Standard form contracts*: where a contract is offered only on the basis of one party's standard terms. This may include contracts between businesses, although many will also be consumer contracts. It is for the court to identify this form of contract; no definition is provided in the Act.

Section 15 provides that the Act extends to contracts relating to goods or services of any kind, employment or apprenticeship, the use of land or the liability of the occupier of land. The Act does not apply to contracts of insurance or contracts relating to the formation, constitution or dissolution of any body corporate, unincorporated association or partnership.[195]

By section 16, where a contractual term purports to exclude or restrict liability for breach of duty arising in the course of any business or from the occupation of any premises used for business purposes of the occupier, that term:

> "(a) shall be void in any case where such exclusion or restriction is in respect of death or personal injury;

> (b) shall, in any other case, have no effect if it was not fair and reasonable to incorporate the term in the contract ..."

Section 17 stipulates that the incorporation of exclusion clauses and quasi-exclusion clauses (that is a condition permitting future variation of performance) in consumer contracts and standard form contracts will be void unless inclusion was *fair and reasonable* in the circumstances.

UNFAIR TERMS IN CONSUMER CONTRACTS REGULATIONS 1999

4–90   These Regulations[196] provide that a consumer[197] may set aside a contract for goods or services by showing that it is unfair. The Regulations apply to any term in a contract concluded between a seller or supplier[198] and a consumer where the term has not been

---

[193] ss 15–25.
[194] s 25(1).
[195] s 15(3).
[196] SI 1999/2083.
[197] Reg 3 defines "consumer" as any natural person acting for purposes which are outside his trade, business or profession.
[198] Reg 3 defines "seller or supplier" as "any natural or legal person who, in contracts covered by these Regulations, is acting for purposes relating to his trade, business or profession, whether publicly owned or privately owned."

individually negotiated. According to regulation 5(1) a contractual term is unfair if it is contrary to the requirement of good faith and causes imbalance in the parties' rights and obligations arising under the contract to the detriment of the consumer. Regulation 6 provides that the unfairness of a contractual term should be assessed, taking into account the nature of the goods or services for which the contract was concluded and by referring, at the time of conclusion of the contract, to all the circumstances attending the conclusion of the contract and to all the other terms of the contract or of another contract on which it is dependent. Schedule 2 to the Regulations contains an indicative list of terms that may be regarded as unfair.

Regulation 7 requires a seller or supplier should ensure that *all* written terms are set out in "plain, intelligible language". This provision operates in similar fashion to the common law *contra proferentem* rule: where there is doubt as to the meaning of any term, the term will be construed in favour of the consumer.[199] The "plain English" requirement has provoked companies in many sectors to reappraise their standard contracts and has had a major impact on the banking and insurance industries in particular.

A term found to be unfair will not bind the consumer, but the contract will continue to bind the parties if it is capable of continuing in existence without the unfair term.[200] Regulation 6(2) excludes the central provisions of subject-matter and price or remuneration from assessment in terms of fairness, although these provisions must still be set out in plain English.

The Regulations oblige the Director General of Fair Trading to consider any complaint made to him about the fairness of any contract term drawn up for general use. The Director General may, if he considers it appropriate to do so, seek an interdict to prevent the continued use of that term or of a term having like effect.[201] The Regulations provide that a "qualifying body" named in Schedule 1 (including statutory regulators, trading standards departments and the Consumers' Association) may also apply for an interdict to prevent the continued use of an unfair contract term provided it has notified the Director General of its intention at least 14 days before the application is made (unless the Director General consents to a shorter period).[202] Regulation 13 empowers the Director General and public "qualifying bodies" to require traders to produce copies of their standard contracts, and give information about their use, in order to facilitate investigation of complaints and ensure compliance with undertakings or court orders.[203]

BREACH OF CONTRACT

Where either party fails to fulfill his side of the bargain without justification a breach **4–91** of contract occurs. This entitles the innocent party to sue for damages or obtain some other remedy to compensate him for the loss he has suffered as a consequence of the breach.

---

[199] reg 7(2).
[200] reg 8.
[201] regs 10 and 12.
[202] reg 12.
[203] For comment, see Ervine, "The Unfair Contract Terms Regulations Mark II", 1999 SLT (News) 253.

REMEDIES FOR BREACH

Damages

4–92   Where a breach is established it is always open to the innocent party to seek monetary compensation by way of a claim for damages. Given that damages are intended to make restitution between the parties, to compensate for loss sustained as a consequence of breach of contract, it must be shown that some form of loss has actually been caused. However, if no direct loss is suffered the court may still be moved to award nominal damages in recognition of any consequent inconvenience or other disturbance.[204]

In general terms, no damages will be awarded unless there is a causal link between the breach and the loss suffered. In *Seton v Paterson*,[205] P hired a horse from S and, in breach of contract, rode it at a gallop. As a result the horse broke a bone and was confined to stables. The horse later died from inflammation of the bowels. In a controversial ruling, the court presumed that the death was attributable to a lack of exercise caused by the confinement of the horse and held that P was liable. *Seton* has been criticised on the grounds that no clear connection between the original injury and the death was proved. However, once the gateway criterion of causation has been established, recoverability of loss is governed by two principles, the application of which serves to restrict and quantify damages claims. First, it is necessary to show that the loss sustained was a reasonably foreseeable consequence of the breach (remoteness of damage). Second, there is a duty on the injured party to take all reasonable steps to mitigate their loss. These are discussed below.

Remoteness of damage

4–93   Generally speaking, the innocent party will only be permitted to recover damages for losses that should have been in the contemplation of both parties as a reasonably foreseeable consequence of breach at the time the contract was made. In *Hadley* v *Baxendale*,[206] a mill owner engaged the defendant carrier to take a broken crankshaft to be used as a pattern for a replacement. The defendant delayed in delivering the shaft and this caused the mill to be out of action for longer than anticipated. Hadley sued in respect of loss of profits during the period of additional delay. The court observed that it was common practice for millers to keep spare shafts. Typically, a spare would be utilised during the intervening period to enable the mill to continue operations. However, there was no spare and the carrier had not been advised of this fact. The court drew a distinction between *general* and *special* damages and ruled that damages could only be awarded in respect of:

(a) losses which arise naturally, in the ordinary course of things (general damages) or

(b) losses arising from special circumstances of which the defendant has been made aware at the point of contract (special damages).

---

[204] *Webster & Co v Crammond Iron Co* (1875) 2 R 752.
[205] (1880) 8 R 236.
[206] (1854) 9 Exch 341.

The above formulation is often referred to as "the rule in *Hadley* v *Baxendale*". On the facts no recovery could be permitted. No damages were awarded under the first head because in the normal course of things the mill owner would have fitted a spare shaft and therefore suffered no loss from the delay. The fact that the mill owner did not possess a spare shaft was a special circumstance of which the carrier had no knowledge at the point of contract; because the carrier was not aware of the abnormal situation he could not be made liable for the abnormal consequences and losses that followed.

In *Den of Ogil Co Ltd* v *Caledonian Railway Co*,[207] a 4,000-ton steamer was lying at Plymouth with a broken piston. A replacement was cast at Port Glasgow and dispatched by passenger train to Plymouth. The defender railway company had been advised that the carriage was urgent and that delay would prevent the ship from sailing. However, the defender was not informed of the size of the ship, which had a crew of 57 on board, or that the casting was a piston. In the event a delay was incurred and the ship owners sued for damages. It was held that the railway company was liable for general damages in respect of part of the outlays arising naturally from the delay but not for special damages in the form of additional losses connected to the exceptional and unanticipated size of the ship. Underlining the point that any relevant special circumstances must be fully disclosed, Lord President Kinross said:

> "If the defenders had been made aware of the size of the 'Den of Ogil' and the number of her crew I think that the pursuers would have had a strong claim for the whole of such outlays during the period of detention, as it has been said that in such cases the measure of the damages is the amount of the loss which might naturally be expected by the parties in the state of knowledge which they had when they entered into the contract to result from a breach of it."

In *Victoria Laundry (Windsor) Ltd* v *Newman Industries*[208] a boiler to be supplied by N to V was delivered late. As a consequence V lost (a) profits likely to have been made on the extra business the new boiler would have allowed them to take on, and (b) a valuable government contract which depended on the installation of the new boiler. It was held that N was liable in damages for the loss of general business described in (a), which was reasonably foreseeable in the circumstances, but not liable for the loss of the government contract, which was a special and unforeseeable factor that had not been disclosed at the point of contract.

In *Balfour Beatty Construction (Scotland) Ltd* v *Scottish Power plc*,[209] B were engaged in the construction of a concrete aqueduct and S had agreed to supply the necessary electricity. The building works required a long continuous pour of cement, but when the electricity supply failed this was interrupted. As a result the aqueduct had to be demolished and rebuilt at a cost of approximately a quarter of a million pounds. The House of Lords dismissed B's claim for special damages. In the ordinary course of events a power cut would not have had such costly consequences. The special circumstances had not been adequately communicated to S and it was not reasonable to attribute to S the requisite level of technical understanding of construction techniques

---

[207] (1902) 5 F 99.
[208] [1949] 2 KB 528.
[209] 1994 SLT 807.

that might have enabled them to have foreseen the likely result of a failure of the electricity supply.

The duty to mitigate loss

4–94   On discovering that the other party is in breach of contract, the innocent party is under a duty to take reasonable steps to minimise any resulting losses so as to mitigate his subsequent claim for damages. Damages will only be recoverable to an extent commensurate with the level of loss that reasonable preventive measures could not avert. A pursuer need not mitigate if to do so would be to damage his commercial credit or business reputation.[210] Moreover, it is not necessary for the pursuer to resort to extraordinary or exceptional measures or incur substantial expenditure in order to mitigate his loss. In *Gunter* v *Lauritzen*,[211] one party purchased goods having given notice that they were intended for resale. On delivery the goods were rejected on the ground that they were not in conformity with the contract. The intending purchaser sued for damages, claiming the loss of profit he would have made on resale. The goods in question were not obtainable on the open market in the form contracted for, but they were available in three separate lots from private sellers in different parts of the country. It was held that the pursuer was not obliged to take anything other than ordinary measures to replace the goods. He was entitled to recover from the seller the full loss of profit.

Rescission

4–95   Whereas the remedy of damages provides compensation within the framework of the contract, the remedy of rescission allows the party to withdraw, or resile, from the contract completely, without having to perform any obligations under it. Available where the other party has wrongly induced, repudiated, or committed a material breach of the contract, rescission terminates or cancels the contract. Note that this is merely an option at the disposal of the innocent party. It is always open to waive the breach, ask for performance and seek damages in the alternative.

Rescission is only justified where the breach is *material*—that is where it goes to the heart of the contract. The contract itself will often identify fundamental conditions, but in the absence of express guidance it is for the court to evaluate a particular term in all the circumstances of the case.[212] In *Wade* v *Waldon*,[213] the parties entered into an agreement by which, in March 1908, Wade was to perform at the Palace Theatre, Glasgow. One term of the agreement required artistes to give 14 days' notice prior to their performances and to supply "bill matter" (publicity material) at the same time. In the event, Wade neither gave the requisite notice nor supplied the bill matter and Waldon refused to allow him to perform, purporting to rescind the contract. The court held that Wade's breach of contract was not sufficiently material to entitle Waldon to rescind the contract, and Waldon was thus liable in damages for repudiating the contract. Lord President Dunedin said[214]:

---

[210] *Banco de Portugal* v *Waterlow & Sons Ltd* [1932] AC 452.
[211] (1894) 31 SLR 359.
[212] *Forslind* v *Bechley-Crundall* 1922 SC (HL) 173.
[213] 1909 SC 571.
[214] At 576.

"... in any contract which contains multifarious stipulations there are some which go so to the root of the contract that a breach of those stipulations entitles the party pleading the breach to declare that the contract is at an end. There are others which do not go to the root of the contract, but which are part of the contract, and which would give rise, if broken, to an action in damages."

The Lord President added[215]:

"It is quite in the power of the parties to stipulate that some particular matters, however trivial they may be, yet shall, as between them, form conditions precedent. If they have said so, then their agreement in the matter will be given effect to, but where they have not said so in terms ... then the Court must determine, looking to the nature of the stipulation, whether it goes to the essence of the contract or not."

Specific implement

The remedy of specific implement—the close equivalent of which is known as specific **4–96** performance in England—allows the innocent party to apply to court for an order directing the party in breach to carry out the contract. An order compelling the performance of an act is enforced by decree *ad factum praestandum*.[216] Where an order restricting the performance of an act is sought—for example, to enforce compliance with a restrictive covenant—an interdict is appropriate. Failure to comply with a court order renders the subject liable to a fine or imprisonment for contempt of court.

The court will always consider the alternative option of an award of damages where this constitutes a sufficient, appropriate and adequate remedy in the circumstances.[217] Moreover, there are a number of situations in which the remedy of specific implement is not available. In the following cases the court may refuse to grant a decree *ad factum praestandum*.

    (a) Where the obligation is to pay a sum of money the appropriate remedy is an action for payment and diligence. Generally speaking it is not competent in Scots law to grant an order that could lead to imprisonment for non-payment of a civil debt.[218]

    (b) Where the contract involves a personal or intimate relationship the court usually takes the view that forced compliance would be worse than non-compliance. For example, the fulfilment of an employment or partnership contract typically requires mutual trust and co-operation between the parties; where this has been lost the court will not act in vain. In *Skerret* v *Oliver*[219] a presbyterian minister sought a decree *ad factum praestandum* to compel the church to reinstate him, but the court refused the remedy. However, in *Peace* v *City of Edinburgh Council*[220] the court accepted that a remedy amounting to specific implement was appropriate in the context of an employment contract

---

[215] At 576
[216] Lit "for the performance of an act".
[217] *McArthur* v *Lawson* (1877) 4 R 1134.
[218] There is an exception where the contract is with a company to take up and pay for debentures of the company: Companies Act 1985, s 195.
[219] (1896) 23 R 268.
[220] 1999 SLT 712.

where the parties were in general agreement as to the subsistence of the contract and the provisions could be put into effect without requiring any greater degree of contact and mutual co-operation than the parties were prepared to accept. In addition, note that an Employment Tribunal may order the reinstatement of an employee unjustifiably dismissed.

(c) Where the subject of the contract lacks *pretium affectionis* (some special characteristic or quality), the court is likely to prefer to award the innocent party damages to enable the goods to be purchased from another source. While the court may order specific implement to enforce a contract concerning the sale of an antique oil painting, which is unique and irreplaceable, it is unlikely to do so where the contract involves generic goods easily obtainable elsewhere.

(d) Where compliance with the decree is impossible: *lex non cogit ad impossibilia*.[221] Specific implement will not be available where a party is bound to do something that he cannot do or something that amounts to an unlawful act.

(e) Where a decree would be unenforceable—for example, where the defender is outwith the jurisdiction of the Scottish courts.

(f) Where the court is of the view that grant of the decree would cause exceptional hardship, or where it would be unjust or inequitable to make such an order in all the circumstances.

(g) Where it is necessary to enforce the long-term performance of a general and possibly fluctuating duty as opposed to a specific act.

Retention

4–97   Retention is the withholding by the innocent party to a contract of performance of his obligations under the contract, usually the payment of a money debt, until the other party performs his reciprocal obligations. This defensive measure is only available in the following circumstances:

(a) where both obligations arise under the same contract[222]—for example, where defective goods are delivered the recipient may choose to withhold payment until the defect is remedied;

(b) where *compensation* can be pleaded. This involves the extinction of mutual similar claims by setting one off against the other, that is both debts must be liquid (*ie* of an ascertained amount and actually due) and there must be *concursus debiti et crediti* (*ie* the parties must be debtor and creditor in the same capacity at the same time).

(c) where the creditor in a money debt is bankrupt—it would be inequitable to oblige a debtor to pay the full amount of a debt in circumstances that dictate that he will only receive part payment of the debt owed to him by the other party.

---

[221] Lit "the law does not compel the performance of what is impossible".
[222] *Gibson and Stewart v Brown* (1876) 3 R 328.

Lien

Lien is the retention of moveable property until a debt due by its owner is paid. There **4–98** are two types of lien: special and general. The special lien is most common and is exercised against goods specific to the contract to be enforced. For example, a garage may seek to exercise a right of lien against a car on which it has done repair work until its bill has been paid. A general lien allows the person in possession of an article to retain it until an unconnected debt owed by the owner is paid. Certain trades and professions enjoy an acknowledged right to exercise a general lien. These include mercantile agents, solicitors, bankers and hoteliers.

Contractual remedies: liquidate damages

The parties to a contract may prefer to determine at the outset the damages payable in **4–99** the event of a breach. Such contractual provisions are known as "conventional" or "liquidate damages" clauses. If a breach subsequently occurs the innocent party has a claim for the specified sum, regardless of whether the actual loss suffered is greater or less than that amount. However, a clause of this nature will only be enforceable if the court is convinced that it represents a genuine pre-estimate of the loss likely to be suffered as a consequence of the breach in question.

If the court believes that a clause is designed *in terrorem*,[223] to intimidate or punish the party in breach by incorporating a draconian sanction, it will be treated as a penalty clause and set aside. In these circumstances the court will revert to ordinary practice and ascertain the amount of damages to be awarded on the basis of the standard rules of remoteness and mitigation discussed above. In deciding whether a clause should be treated as a genuine pre-estimate of loss or penalty, the court will adopt the perspective of the parties at the point of formation of the contract, not at the time of the breach.[224] The effect of the provision is of particular relevance. The label put on the clause by the parties is largely irrelevant. In *Lord Elphinstone* v *Monkland Iron and Coal Co*,[225] a lease contained an undertaking to soil-over deposits of slag by a certain date under a "penalty" of £100 per imperial acre for all ground not so restored. Despite the reference to a "penalty" it was held that this sum was a reasonable pre-estimate and enforceable as liquidate damages.[226]

In particular, where a clause stipulates that one fixed sum is payable in the event of a number of different breaches of varying seriousness, it is unlikely to be deemed a genuine pre-estimate and will probably be discounted as penal. In *Dingwall* v *Burnett*,[227] a lease contained several obligations, of varying importance, with a provision that £50 be paid in the event of a breach of any of them. The landlord claimed in excess of £300 in response to the tenant's breach, but the tenant argued his liability was restricted to the fixed sum. It was held that the £50 clause was an unenforceable penalty, because no effort had been made to link the sum to the

---

[223] Lit "as a threat".
[224] *Dunlop* v *Pneumatic Tyre Co* v *New Garage and Motor Co* [1915] AC 79.
[225] (1886) 13 R (HL) 98.
[226] See also *Cameron-Head* v *Cameron & Co* 1919 SC 627. Note that nowadays it is fairly unusual to encounter a contractual term of this nature described as a "penalty". For obvious reasons the court is typically confronted by an express claim that a clause provides solely for liquidate damages.
[227] 1912 SC 1097.

seriousness of the breach. Resorting to normal contractual principles, and perhaps somewhat ironically, the court awarded the landlord his full claim.

Occasionally, the court will acknowledge that it was impossible for the parties to make an accurate pre-estimate of loss. In these circumstances the court may uphold an apparently arbitrary sum if it appears it was fixed at a reasonable level. In *Clydebank Engineering and Shipbuilding v Castaneda*,[228] the Spanish Government ordered four torpedo boats (at the time of contract Spain was trying to suppress a rebellion in Cuba and anticipated hostile action from the United States of America) on the basis of a contract that contained a penalty for late delivery of £500 per week for each vessel. In the event, the boats were many months late and an action for £75,500 was brought against the shipbuilder. It was held that the clause was to be regarded as liquidate damages and not as a penalty given the difficulty in ascertaining the loss likely to be suffered as a consequence of delay. As Lord Moncrieff put it[229]: "The loss sustained by a belligerent, or an intending belligerent, owing to a contractor's failure to furnish timeously warships or munitions of war, does not admit of precise proof or calculation."

TERMINATION OF CONTRACT

4–100 Most contracts are quietly discharged by the performance of the reciprocal obligations they establish. However, there are a variety of other ways in which a contract may come to an end.

ACCEPTILATION

4–101 This occurs where one party voluntarily accepts the partial performance, defective performance or even non-performance of the other party as if it were full performance. Typically, this term is used where a creditor discharges a debtor without full payment being made. Acceptilation may also be mutual, in which case each of the parties agrees to waive performance by the other.

NOVATION

4–102 Novation takes place when a new obligation is expressly substituted for a prior obligation. The effect of this is to extinguish all liability flowing from the prior obligation.[230] Novation must be by mutual agreement; any unilateral attempt to substitute an obligation will be void as a matter of course. The parties must take care to set out the full consequences of the transaction and the discharge of the original obligation. There is a presumption at law that the new obligation will be additional to, and not in place of, the original obligation and this must be rebutted by clear evidence to the contrary.

---

[228] (1904) 7 F (HL) 77.
[229] At 84.
[230] See *De Montfort Insurance Co plc v Lafferty* 1998 SLT 535.

DELEGATION

This species of novation involves the substitution of a new debtor rather than the **4–103** substitution of a new obligation. Again, delegation is only valid if by mutual agreement. An intent to transfer the whole obligation and extinguish the liability of the original debtor must be clearly established or the court may presume that the latter party is still obliged to perform the obligation.

CONFUSION

Sometimes known as *combination*, confusion occurs where the same person becomes **4–104** both debtor and creditor, in the same capacity, under a contract. Since a person cannot be his own debtor, the obligation to make payment is extinguished *confusione* (by confusion). This situation rarely presents an issue for the courts. However, if, for example, a father loans money to his son and then dies leaving his entire estate to that son before the loan is repaid, the original debt would be extinguished by confusion.

PRESCRIPTION

Negative prescription provides for the expiry of rights which have not been exercised **4–105** after a certain period of time. Under the Prescription and Limitation (Scotland) Act 1973 most contractual obligations prescribe after five years (short negative prescription).[231] Long negative prescription of 20 years applies to certain other rights, including in particular rights of ownership in land.

The prescription clock is stopped and reset on the occurrence of either a "relevant claim" (where the creditor raises an action) or a "relevant acknowledgment" (where the debtor acknowledges his obligation in writing or takes steps towards performance). If either form of interruption takes place a new five-year prescription period commences. For the sake of completeness it should be noted that positive prescription allows for the creation of rights after the passage of a period of time, but this is not relevant here.

COMPENSATION

Where the parties to a contract owe each other money the respective debts may be set **4–106** off against each other so as to extinguish the obligation of one of the parties and reduce the obligation of the other.[232] For example, if Tom, a nightclub owner, owes "The Black Widows" £1,000 for a musical performance but the band ran up a bar bill of £250, Tom can plead compensation to the extent of the £250 the band owes him, with the result that Tom's liability is reduced to £750.

Compensation is only valid if the following conditions are fulfilled:

   (a) compensation must be pleaded in response to an action for recovery of a debt;

---

[231] The prescription period for obligations arising from defective products is 10 years from the date the product was first put into circulation.
[232] See the Compensation Act 1592.

(b) both debts must be liquid (*ie* of an ascertained amount and due for payment), unless both debts arise from the same contract or one party is bankrupt; and

(c) there must be *concursus debiti et crediti* (the parties must be debtor and creditor in the same capacity at the same time).

FRUSTRATION: IMPOSSIBILITY AND ILLEGALITY

4–107   A "contract" that is impossible to perform at the point of formation is no contract. A bargain of this kind is void *ab initio* (void from the beginning). Where a valid contract is formed but subsequent events beyond the control of the parties render performance impossible—and it must be *impossible*—additional inconvenience will not suffice[233]; the contract may be deemed frustrated. A similar fate may befall a contract that, post-formation, becomes illegal to perform. In addition, frustration may operate where a supervening change in circumstances so fundamentally alters the nature of performance that fulfilment of the original consensus is no longer possible. It is important to note that an event or incident will not serve to frustrate a contract if either party has a hand in its occurrence. If frustration is induced by one of the parties that party is likely to be liable for wrongful repudiation.[234] Where genuine frustration does occur the contract is reduced and no liability in damages will arise. That said, any monies paid over must be repaid, subject to deductions for part performance.[235]

Supervening impossibility

4–108   Clearly, where the subject-matter of the contract or something essential to performance of the contract is destroyed, the contract will be brought to an end by frustration. This is known as *rei interitus* ("the destruction of a thing"). In *Taylor* v *Caldwell*,[236] Caldwell agreed to let a music hall to the plaintiff for a series of concerts. Before the first concert was due to take place, and through no fault of the owner, the hall was destroyed by fire. Taylor sued for breach of contract. It was held that the destruction of the hall had made performance impossible and, therefore, the defendant was not liable under the contract.

Actual destruction of the subject is not a prerequisite for frustration. In *London and Edinburgh Shipping Company* v *The Admiralty*,[237] the fact that a ship had been very badly damaged, although it had not actually sunk, was sufficient to frustrate a contract for charter. A contract may also be terminated by frustration where the subject merely becomes unavailable to the parties. In *Mackeson* v *Boyd*,[238] B granted M a 19-year lease, commencing in 1926, of a mansion house. In 1940 military authorities requisitioned the property and M claimed the lease was frustrated. The court agreed. As the government's requisition had made it impossible for M to occupy the house there was *constructive* total destruction of the subjects let. Accordingly, M was permitted to

---

[233] See *Davis Contractors* v *Fareham Urban District Council* [1956] AC 696, where bad weather and inflation made the performance of a construction contract more difficult and expensive than had been anticipated, but by no means impossible.
[234] See *Maritime National Fish Ltd* v *Ocean Trawlers* [1935] AC 524.
[235] See *Cantiere San Rocco* v *Clyde Shipbuilding Co* 1923 SC (HL) 105.
[236] (1863) 122 ER 309.
[237] 1920 SC 309.
[238] 1942 SC 56.

abandon the lease. *Mackeson* was resolved, in particular, on the authority of the earlier *Tay Salmon Fisheries* v *Speedie*,[239] where a salmon fishing lease on a stretch of the River Tay was terminated when the Air Council declared that part of the river an aerial bombing zone.

Where a contract embodies an element of *delectus personae* (that is where the choice of a specific person is material to the contract), a change in the personal circumstances of the subject may constitute frustration. The obvious and most clear-cut example is intervening death, but insanity, illness, injury or bankruptcy may suffice. In *Condor* v *Barron Knights*,[240] C contracted to be the drummer in a pop group with a busy schedule of performances. After he became ill his doctor advised him that he should play only four nights a week, not every night as bound by his contract. It was held that the contract was frustrated due to the deterioration in C's health. Similarly, in *Robinson* v *Davison*,[241] a pianist's contract was terminated on the onset of illness.

Supervening illegality

If a valid contract is formed but a change in the law or the political situation— **4–109** including, as discussed above, the outbreak of war—renders performance illegal, the contract is terminated. It is not sufficient to show that a change (for example, the imposition of a new tax or regulation) makes performance more expensive or burdensome than had been anticipated: performance must be prohibited. In *Fraser & Co Ltd* v *Denny, Mott & Dickson Ltd*,[242] D contracted to supply pine wood to F. As a result of the outbreak of war restrictions were imposed on transactions of that type of timber, although the wood was available. It was held that performance was frustrated by supervening illegality.

Supervening change in circumstances

Sometimes events may occur or circumstances may change post-contract, rendering **4–110** performance impossible. The "Coronation cases", which involved litigation arising from the postponed coronation of Edward VII, offer famous examples of the application of this rule and may, in particular, be described as examples of frustration of purpose. In *Krell* v *Henry*,[243] H hired rooms in Pall Mall to view the King's coronation procession. Unfortunately, the King caught pneumonia and the ceremony was cancelled. When K sued for the hire charge, the court held the contract frustrated. Although the subject of the contract (*ie* the rooms) was intact, and no mention was made of the Coronation in the contract, the court agreed that the essence and object of the bargain, which was the observation of the procession, had been lost.

It is often necessary to draw a fine line in this context and *Krell* can be usefully contrasted with the contemporaneous *Herne Bay Shipping Co* v *Hutton*.[244] In this case a naval review was cancelled when the King fell ill. A pleasure boat had been hired "for the purpose of viewing the naval review and a day's cruise round the fleet". In this instance, the court held that the contract was *not* frustrated. The contract had two

---

[239] 1929 SC 593.
[240] [1966] 1 WLR 87.
[241] (1871) LR 6 Exch 269.
[242] 1944 SC (HL) 35.
[243] [1903] 2 KB 740.
[244] [1903] 2 KB 683.

purposes, one of which was still open to performance—namely the cruise around the fleet.

Unforeseen delay may frustrate a contract where so much time is lost that performance, typically in a business sense, is radically altered. In *Jackson* v *Union Marine Insurance Co Ltd*,[245] a ship was hired (by charterparty) to take a cargo of iron rails from Newport to San Francisco to be used in the construction of a railway. Long before it reached Newport, the ship ran aground and was damaged. Repairs took eight months to complete, by which time the charterers had hired another ship to carry the rails. Despite the fact that the contract had provided an indemnity in regard to "the perils of the sea", the court held that the contract had been frustrated. The delay dictated that the outcome of the eventual performance would have been very different from that originally contemplated by the parties.

---

[245] (1874) LR 10 CP 125.

SUMMARY

THE ESSENTIAL ELEMENTS OF A CONTRACT

- All valid and enforceable contracts incorporate certain essential characteristics.
- It takes at least two people to make a contract.
- A contract is formed when a legally effective offer is met by a valid acceptance.
- The parties must have the capacity to contract.
- Restrictions apply to the capacity of the following: minors; the insane; the intoxicated; enemy aliens; corporate bodies; unincorporated bodies; partnerships.
- It is necessary to establish that both parties entered into an agreement with the intention of creating legal relations.
- Unless an agreement is constituted in specific and definite terms no court will be able to entertain its enforcement.
- The parties must reach *consensus in idem*—that is to say, there must be a meeting of minds, or agreement on the same essential terms.
- The law does not recognise all obligations as enforceable. Among others, casual, domestic, social, criminal, immoral and betting agreements will not be enforced by the court.

GRATUITOUS UNDERTAKING

- In Scotland a gratuitous contract, or promise, is binding. In England a gratuitous contract is unenforceable due to a lack of consideration.

FORMATION OF CONTRACT

- An offer must by word or action carry with it an objectively verifiable intention to form a binding contract, it must be communicated to another party and it must be in specific terms. An offer may be made to a specific person, a specific group of people, or it may be communicated to the world at large.
- It is important to distinguish between an offer and an invitation to treat. Whereas an offer can be accepted to create a contract, an invitation to treat cannot be accepted, although it may solicit an offer which might subsequently prove the basis of a contract.
- Usually, an offer may be revoked at any time prior to acceptance and it may lapse automatically in a number of circumstances.
- Generally speaking, acceptance is not effective until it is communicated to the offeror.
- A "qualified acceptance" is no acceptance. Any response to an offer which seeks to alter or add to the terms of the original offer, is a counter-offer. A counter-offer cancels the original offer and no subsequent acceptance of the original terms is valid.
- Where the parties communicate by means of the postal service, the "postal rule" operates to determine that acceptance takes place at the moment the letter of acceptance is posted. The ordinary rules of contract formation apply to contracts concluded over the Internet.

- At the moment of valid acceptance the contract comes into being. Once acceptance is given it cannot be withdrawn.

FORMALITIES OF CONTRACT

- Under the Requirements of Writing (Scotland) Act 1995 certain contracts must be made in writing and signed by the parties. This is the exception to the general rule that no special formality is required.

DEFECTIVE CONTRACTS

- Defective contracts may be void (of no legal effect), voidable (valid but susceptible to cancellation) or simply unenforceable at law.

ERROR

- There are two fundamental types of error: errors of law and errors of fact. Generally speaking, error as to law will not impair the validity of the contract. Errors in fact may affect a contract in a variety of ways depending on the nature of the error in question.

UNINDUCED ERROR

- Where error of expression occurs the courts will typically seek to enforce the original intention of the parties. The Law Reform (Miscellaneous Provisions) (Scotland) Act 1985 permits the rectification of documents.
- Where an offeror unintentionally misstates the terms of his offer the "contract" is likely to be deemed void if the offeree seeks to exploit the mistake. However, where the offeree accepts in good faith, unaware of the misstatement, the contract will usually be deemed voidable.
- Error of intention occurs where one or both of the parties are mistaken as to the nature of the contract. A contract will not usually be reduced on the ground that one party is unaware of a material fact unless that party has been induced to enter the contract by misrepresentation or fraud.
- Common error occurs where both parties make the same mistake about a fact connected to the contract. If the misconstrued fact is material to the transaction the "contract" is void.
- Mutual error occurs where the parties misunderstand one another and each has formed a different impression of what has been agreed. Where the error is material the "contract" is void.
- Minor errors (error *concomitans*) do not prevent consensus and a contract will usually be upheld if so affected. However, a contract may still be voidable if incidental error is induced by misrepresentation.
- Essential error (*error in substantialibus*) typically renders the contract void. Five types of essential error are identified: error as to subject-matter; identity; price; quantity, quality or extent; nature of the the the contract.

INDUCED ERROR

- A misrepresentation is an untrue statement of *fact* made prior to, and usually designed to encourage, the formation of a contract.
- Where an error in the substantials is induced, the contract will be void; where an error *concomitans* is induced, the resulting contract is voidable.
- There are three classes of misrepresentation: innocent, negligent and fraudulent.
- Fraudulent and negligent misrepresentation may found an action in damages, but innocent misrepresentation will not.
- Silence is not usually regarded as misrepresentation at law, but full and frank disclosure is required, in particular, in contracts *uberrimae fidei* and fiduciary contracts.

OTHER FACTORS IMPAIRING ENFORCEABILITY

- A contract tainted by circumvention or undue influence is voidable.
- Where one party enters into a bargain under the influence of force or fear the purported contract is void for lack of true consent.

PACTA ILLICITA: ILLEGAL AGREEMENTS

- It is essential to the validity and enforceability of a contract that its object and performance are lawful. *Pacta illicita*, including agreements contrary to public policy, are void.
- Contracts in restraint of trade are void unless the restrictions are reasonable between the parties and not in conflict with the public interest.
- The question as to whether a restriction is reasonable between the parties depends on the nature of the restriction, particularly with reference to its geographic extent and temporal duration. In this regard, *proportionality* is key.
- The Competition Act 1998 may be invoked to regulate contracts in restraint of trade.
- Where more than one restriction is imposed by an agreement the court may choose to sever the offending parts and allow the remainder to be enforced.

EXEMPTION CLAUSES

- When assessing the applicability of an exemption clause it is necessary to ask whether the exemption is incorporated into the contract, whether it covers the breach, and whether the Unfair Contract Terms Act 1977 permits the exclusion.
- The Unfair Terms in Consumer Contracts Regulations 1999 provide that a consumer may set aside a contract for goods or services by showing that it is unfair. A contractual term will be deemed unfair if it is contrary to the requirement of good faith and causes imbalance in the parties' rights and obligations arising under the contract to the detriment of the consumer. *All* written terms in a consumer contract must be set out in "plain, intelligible language".

BREACH OF CONTRACT

- Where either party fails to fulfill his side of the bargain without justification a breach of contract occurs.
- Where a breach is established it is always open to the innocent party to seek monetary compensation by way of a claim for damages. It is necessary to prove: (a) causation; (b) that the loss sustained was a reasonably foreseeable consequence of the breach (remoteness of damage); and (c) that there is a duty on the injured party to take all reasonable steps to mitigate their loss.
- Rescission allows the party to withdraw, or resile, from the contract completely, without having to perform any obligations under it. Available where the other party has wrongly induced, repudiated, or committed a material breach of the contract, rescission terminates or cancels the contract.
- The remedy of specific implement allows the innocent party to apply to court for an order directing the party in breach to carry out the contract. An order compelling the performance of an act is enforced by decree *ad factum praestandum*.
- Retention is the withholding by the innocent party to a contract of performance of his obligations under the contract—usually the payment of a money debt—until the other party performs his reciprocal obligations.
- Lien is the retention of moveable property until a debt due by its owner is paid.
- The parties to a contract may determine at the outset the damages payable in the event of breach. Such contractual provisions are known as conventional or liquidate damages clauses. A clause of this nature will only be enforceable if the court is convinced that it represents a genuine pre-estimate of the loss likely to be suffered as a consequence of the breach in question.

TERMINATION OF CONTRACT

- Most contracts are discharged by performance. Other ways in which a contract may be terminated include: acceptilation, novation, delegation, compensation, confusion, prescription and frustration.
- Where a valid contract is formed but subsequent events beyond the control of the parties render performance impossible, the contract may be deemed frustrated. A similar fate may befall a contract that, post-formation, becomes illegal to perform. In addition, frustration may operate where a supervening change in circumstances so fundamentally alters the nature of performance that fulfilment of the original consensus is no longer possible.

CASE DIGEST

Gratuitous undertaking [see para 4–17]
  Morton's Trustees v *Aged Christian Friend Society of Scotland* (1899) 2 F 82
M offered a subscription of £1,000, payable in 10 annual instalments, to a charitable society. M's offer was accepted by the society and he duly paid the first eight

instalments, but he died before the next instalment became payable. When a dispute arose over the outstanding payments it was held that the obligation to meet them constituted a binding contract.

General offer [see para 4–18]

Hunter v *General Accident, Fire and Life Assurance Corporation* 1909 SC (HL) 30
An insurance company advertised in a diary that the sum of £1,000 would be paid to the owner of a diary who was killed in a railway accident within 12 months of registering himself with the company. The executor of a man who had been registered and had been killed in a train crash claimed the money. It was held that the advert constituted an offer and that a contract had been concluded on compliance with the conditions stated therein.

Invitation to treat [see para 4–19]

Pharmaceutical Society of Great Britain v *Boots Cash Chemists (Southern) Ltd* [1953] 1 QB 401
Boots were charged with an offence under the Pharmacy and Poisons Act 1933, which stipulated that sales of poisons must take place under the supervision of a registered pharmacist. The problem, in the eyes of the prosecuting authority, was that Boots operated a self-service system with a pharmacist present only at the cash desk. If the act of selection of goods by the customer had been deemed acceptance of an offer to sell Boots may have been liable to conviction, but it was held that no offence had been committed. The display of goods on the shelf was merely an invitation to treat to customers to make an offer to buy at the cash desk, at which point the pharmacist would accept the offer, derive a contract and hence supervise the sale.

Offer and acceptance [see para 4–20]

Philip & Co v *Knoblauch* 1907 SC 994
K wrote to P: "I am offering today plate linseed for January/February and have pleasure in quoting you 100 tons at 41s. 3d. usual plate terms. I shall be glad to hear if you are buyers and await your esteemed reply". The following day P telegraphed: "Accept hundred January/February plate 41s. 3d". K responded with a further telegram rejecting P's attempt to contract. It was held that K's first telegram *was* an offer and that a contract had been formed by P's acceptance. Moreover, the fact that the acceptance tendered included no reference to the condition "usual plate terms" mentioned in the offer did not impair its effect. An acceptance need not *expressly* reiterate all the terms of an offer.

Acceptance: the effect of a counter-offer [see para 4–23]

Wolf & Wolf v *Forfar Potato Co Ltd* 1984 SLT 100
This case involved a telexed offer and a telexed response couched in terms of an "acceptance" that varied the terms of the offer. A second unequivocal acceptance followed. Given that the first "acceptance" was a counter-offer, its effect was to cancel the original offer. The second attempt at acceptance failed because there was nothing left to accept.

Postal rule [see para 4–25]

Jacobsen, Sons & Co v Underwood & Son Ltd (1894) 21 R 654

A letter of acceptance in reply to an offer expiring on 6th March and posted on that day was insufficiently addressed and delayed in the post until 7th March as a consequence. It was held that the postal rule applied and that the offer had been accepted on time.

Error as to subject-matter [see para 4–49]

Raffles v Wichelhaus (1864) 2 H&C 906

Two ships were due to set sail with a cargo of cotton from the port of Bombay to England. One ship was to sail in October, the other in December. Both ships were named *Peerless*. A contract was formed for the purchase of cotton "to arrive ex *Peerless*", but while one party anticipated delivery on the October ship, the other party had the December ship in mind. It was held that there was no consensus and that no contract had been formed.

Misrepresentation [see para 4–55]

Boyd & Forrest v Glasgow & South-Western Railway Co 1912 SC (HL) 93; (*No 2*) 1915 SC (HL) 20.

Builders contracted to lay a stretch of railway track for a price of £243,000, which was determined after consideration of survey data provided by the railway company. The data was based on the work of independent surveyors, but the figures were altered by the railway company's engineer. In its altered state the data was inaccurate, in that it significantly underestimated the amount of rock to be removed; because of the additional rock the work actually cost £379,000 to complete. The House of Lords held that there was no fraud; the engineer had altered the notes because he genuinely believed them to be wrong. In the second action in this matter the House of Lords dismissed a claim for a remedy on the ground of innocent misrepresentation. The builders failed to prove that the statement had *induced* the contract. In addition, having discovered the falsity of the data they continued to work on the track, effectively barring themselves from reduction. Even if the contract had been deemed voidable, *restitutio in integrum* was impossible because the track had already been laid.

Restraint of trade: employment [see para 4–77]

Stewart v Stewart (1899) 1 F 1158

R, the proprietor of a photographic business in Elgin employed E as an assistant. E undertook not to carry on a photography business within 20 miles of Elgin. Later, E indicated that he intended to start his own photography business in the town. R sought to interdict him. The court held that the restraint was reasonably necessary for the protection of R's business interests and allowed its enforcement.

Restraint of trade: sale of business [see para 4–82]

Dumbarton Steamboat Co Ltd v MacFarlane (1899) 1 F 993

A firm sold a carrier business to D. On taking up employment with D, partners of the vendor firm, including M, undertook not to solicit customers of the business or to carry on a similar business in the UK for a period of 10 years. About three years later, M was dismissed by D and M proceeded to set up a carrier business of his own in the Dumbarton area. It was held that M could be interdicted from canvassing former customers of the firm but that the restriction against carrying on business anywhere in the UK was unreasonable and therefore unenforceable. Furthermore, the court stated that it could not remodel the restriction so as to confine it to a more limited area.

Remoteness of damage [see para 4–93]
   Hadley v Baxendale (1854) 9 Exch 341
In this case a distinction was drawn between general and special damages. It was held that damages could only be awarded in respect of:

(a) losses which arise naturally, in the ordinary course of things (general damages), or

(b) losses arising from special circumstances of which the defendant has been made aware at the point of contract (special damages).

FURTHER READING

Field and Gordon, *Elements of Scots Law* (2nd edn, W Green, 1997)

Gloag and Henderson, *The Law of Scotland* (10th edn, W Green, 1995), Chaps 4–15

Gordon, *Contract Law* (Law Basics) (W Green, 1998)

Huntley, *Contract: Cases and Materials* (W Green, 1995)

The Laws of Scotland: Stair Memorial Encyclopaedia (Law Society of Scotland Butterworths), Vol 15, Black *et al*, "Obligations"

McBryde, *The Law of Contract in Scotland* (W Green/SULI, 1987)

MacQueen and Thomson, *Contract Law in Scotland* (Butterworths, 2000)

Marshall, *Scottish Cases on Contract* (2nd edn, W Green, 1993)

Walker, *The Law of Contracts and Related Obligations in Scotland* (3rd edn, T&T Clark, 1995)

Willett and O'Donnell , *Scottish Business Law* (2nd edn, Blackstone Press, 1996)

Woolman, *Contract* (2nd edn, W Green, 1994)

5

DELICT

DEFINITION

A delict is a civil wrong committed by a person in deliberate or negligent breach of a **5–01** legal duty, from which liability to make reparation for any consequential loss or injury may arise.[1] So if, for example, someone eats something or uses something that does harm to him, or if someone does something or says something that causes someone else to suffer loss, the law of delict may provide a remedy. A delict should be distinguished from a breach of contract, where the obligation of which a breach is alleged originates in an agreement between the contracting parties. It is also important to draw a distinction between a delict (a civil wrong) and a crime (a criminal wrong). A crime is deemed to have a detrimental impact on the general community and, typically, the State will act to prosecute the accused in a criminal court. The prime objective of the criminal law is punishment of the offender. A delict, on the other hand, will give rise to a claim for damages against the wrongdoer in a civil court, and compensation of the injured party is the primary goal.

THE NATURE OF DELICTUAL LIABILITY

In order for delictual liability to arise, injury must be suffered as a consequence of a **5–02** legal wrong, which in turn must be caused by fault (*culpa*) on the part of the wrongdoer. This formula is expressed in the maxim *damnum injuria datum* ("loss caused by a legal wrong"), which can be broken down as follows:

- *damnum*—loss or injury suffered by the pursuer;
- *injuria*—conduct by the defender amounting to a legal wrong;
- *datum*—a causal link between *damnum* and *injuria*.

---

[1] The Scots law of delict broadly equates to the English law of tort.

DAMNUM

5–03 All claims in delict must be underpinned by proof that the pursuer has sustained some legally recognised form of loss (*damnum*). The *damnum* suffered may comprise, *inter alia*, physical injury, nervous shock, distress, damage to reputation, loss of earnings and other forms of economic loss. Where wrongful conduct fails to cause a relevant injury (*injuria sine damno*),[2] no case can be made out in delict. In *McFarlane v Tayside Health Board*,[3] a husband and wife sought damages from a health board alleging that after the husband's vasectomy they were given negligent advice that they could safely resume sexual intercourse without contraceptive precautions. The wife became pregnant and after a normal pregnancy gave birth to a healthy child. The question as to whether pregnancy, childbirth and the cost of bringing-up the child constituted recoverable loss was central to the case. The Lord Ordinary rejected this assertion, but on appeal the Second Division allowed recovery of the pursuers' whole claim. A compromise was struck by the House of Lords. It was held that the wife was entitled to *solatium* (compensation) for the pain and suffering associated with pregnancy and childbirth because they were physical consequences arising from negligence, and that the claim should extend to the costs of medical expenses, clothing and loss of earnings due to pregnancy and birth. However, the costs of the child's upbringing were not recoverable because the issue was one of pure economic loss[4] and it was not fair, just and reasonable to impose such liability on the defenders in the circumstances.[5] It was left to the dissenting Lord Millett to argue that the law should rightly take the birth of a normal, healthy baby as a blessing, not a detriment, and that while individuals might decide that their own interests lay otherwise, it would be repugnant to society's sense of values not to regard the balance as beneficial.

INJURIA

5–04 *Damnum* must be suffered as a result of an act by the defender in breach of a legal duty. The relevant wrongful act is known as the *injuria*. Of course, some acts that cause harm to a third party do not constitute breach of a legal duty and will not be treated as delicts. For example, an employer may dismiss an employee and the latter may suffer loss as a consequence but, in the ordinary course of things, such behaviour is not classed as wrongful and is not actionable in law. Legal duties giving rise to delictual liability may be derived from the common law[6] or imposed by statute.[7]

CAUSATION

5–05 The co-existence of *damnum* and *injuria* will not suffice unless a causal connection can be established. The range and scope of causation is a crucial issue and one that sustains a fertile field of litigation. In *Kay's Tutor v Ayrshire & Arran Health Board*[8] a child

---

[2] For example, where negligent advice is ignored.
[3] 2000 SLT 154.
[4] See below at para 5–33.
[5] See below at para 5–17.
[6] See, for example, *Donoghue v Stevenson* 1932 SC (HL) 31.
[7] See, for example, Occupiers' Liability (Scotland) Act 1960.
[8] 1987 SLT 577.

suffering from meningitis was negligently given an overdose of penicillin. On recovery, the child was found to be deaf. The assertion that the overdose had damaged the child's hearing was, however, rejected. Whereas meningitis itself is a recognised and common cause of deafness, the pursuer was unable to point to a single case in which penicillin in any dosage has been found to cause such an injury. Although *damnum* and *injuria* are conspicuous on the facts, the court was compelled to dismiss the action in the absence of any causal link between the two. In simple terms, the Health Board was exonerated because the negligent act for which it was responsible did not cause the injury suffered by the pursuer.

MODES OF DELICTUAL LIABILITY

PERSONAL LIABILITY

In delict, personal liability is the general rule. Delictual liability is usually imposed directly and exclusively on the wrongdoer, namely the individual responsible for the *injuria* which gives rise to the *damnum* incurred by the pursuer. It is a fundamental principle of law, and of delict in particular, that fault attaches to its author ('*culpa tenet suos auctores*'). Broadly speaking, it is not possible to attribute liability for the wrongs of one person to another. There are, however, important exceptions to this rule.[9] **5–06**

JOINT AND SEVERAL LIABILITY

The Law Reform (Miscellaneous Provisions) (Scotland) Act 1940 provides that where a court finds that two or more persons have contributed to the loss suffered by the pursuer they may be held jointly and severally liable.[10] This makes each wrongdoer individually liable to the pursuer to the full extent of the claim. Typically, the wrongdoer with the most money will thereafter become the focus of the pursuer's attention. The 1940 Act permits the chosen defender to bring an action against fellow wrongdoers to recover a contribution to the damages paid that reflects their share of responsibility for the pursuer's loss.[11] **5–07**

VICARIOUS LIABILITY

This form of liability is defined by the maxims *respondeat superior* ("let the superior answer") and *qui facit per alium facit per se* ("he who does something through another does it himself"). Vicarious liability may arise in a partnership or between a principal and agent, but litigation most commonly occurs in the context of an employment relationship.[12] In the latter case, vicarious liability operates to render an employer liable for the delicts of his employee. The employee remains personally liable for his **5–08**

---

[9] These are considered below.
[10] s 3(1).
[11] s 3(2). See *Drew v Weston SMT* 1947 SC 222, where two parties separately contributed to a fatal road traffic accident. See also *Stirling v Norwest Holst Ltd (No 2)* 1998 SLT 1359 at 1360.
[12] See Chapter 12.

actions and, accordingly, vicarious liability is also a good example of joint and several liability. As a consequence, a vicariously liable employer (who will usually be the target of any litigation by virtue of his insurance cover and greater ability to meet a claim) has a right of action against the wrongdoer for any damages paid.[13]

Employee/employer

5–09 In order to establish the vicarious liability of an employer it is necessary to satisfy the court that:

(a) a complete case in delict can be laid against the wrongdoer in person;

(b) the wrongdoer is an employee of the defender; and

(c) the delict was committed in the course of the wrongdoer's employment.

Given that the employer, for reasons stated above, will generally be the focus of any litigation, it is tempting to sacrifice due consideration of condition (1) in the rush to apply conditions (2) and (3), which certainly feature more prominently in most textbooks. The former issue is, however, fundamental to the success of a case. It is clearly necessary to establish an actionable claim in law against the wrongdoer himself before any question of vicarious liability can be raised.

Employee or self-employed?

5–10 In many cases, the second condition will prove a simple matter to resolve. It will often be easy to point to an established and well-defined employment relationship that is underpinned by a contract of service. The distinction between a contract *of service* and a contract *for services* is an important one. Where a wrongdoer is classed as self-employed, or as an independent contractor under a contract for services, the person who engages him in work is unlikely to be made liable for his delicts.[14] Notwithstanding this general rule, the latter party may be held personally (although not vicariously) liable where:

(a) he retained substantial direction and control over the way in which the work was done;

(b) he lacked the personal authority to delegate, or perhaps even to undertake, the task;

(c) work set was inherently risky, dangerous or unlawful;

(d) the contractor was selected negligently; or,

(e) personal liability is imposed by statute.

Where a wrongdoer's status is not immediately obvious, a number of factors may indicate whether a person is employed or self-employed. Where a person is paid a wage or salary and works fixed hours for a single "employer" he is likely to be deemed

---

[13] See n 11 above. See also *Lister Romford Ice & Cold Storage Ltd* [1957] AC 555.
[14] *McLean v Russel, Macnee & Co* (1850) 12 D 887.

an employee. On the other hand, where remuneration usually takes the form of commission or a lump sum and the worker is free to determine his own hours of work, possibly dividing his time between different "employers", he is more likely to be treated as an independent contractor. However, consideration of these factors does not prove conclusive in every case. The courts have developed a number of general tests to assist in the determination as to whether a wrongdoer qualifies as an employee or not.

The control test

This test measures the degree of control held by the putative employer over the work   **5–11**
of the wrongdoer. The greater the control actually exercised, the more likely it is that the wrongdoer will be deemed an employee. In particular, a wrongdoer may be treated as the employee of another where it can be shown that the latter has the right to dictate not only the terms of work done but also, to a significant extent, the manner of its performance.[15] In *Stephen v Thurso Police Commissioners*,[16] the pursuer was injured after stumbling over rubbish negligently left in a street. The commissioners argued that they had contracted with a carter for the removal by him of all rubbish from the street and that he should therefore be liable for the injury. However, the court found that, because the commissioners retained substantial control over the way in which the carter performed his work, he should properly be deemed an employee. As a result, the commissioners were held vicariously liable for the injury.

This test has its limitations. In some circumstances, an employer exercises very little control over the *modus operandi* of highly skilled or highly trained workers who are, none the less, manifestly employees. The issue arose in *Walker v Crystal Palace Football Club*,[17] where a professional footballer was ultimately held to be an employee. Although his club could not dictate specifically how he should play football he was bound to obey all general directions of the club and, on the pitch, obliged to follow the instructions of the team captain or other delegate of the club's authority. The exercise of control *per se* is clearly not a reliable guide in every case. Consider, for example, the status of an airline pilot, university lecturer, research scientist, head chef or surgeon, all of whom enjoy considerable autonomy at work. Other tests have been developed to address the weakness of the control-centred approach.

The integration test

This test measures the extent to which the work of the alleged employee is integrated   **5–12**
with the employer's business. A worker may qualify as an employee if he is deemed to perform an integral function for the organisation for which he works. Although work may be undertaken on behalf of a business, if that work is not fully integrated within the business but only accessory to it, then the worker in question may be treated as an independent contractor.[18] It should be noted, however, that not all persons closely integrated in the business of an organisation can be regarded as employees. Directors of a company and partners in a firm would fall into this category.

---

[15] *Yewens v Noakes* (1880) 6 QB 530.
[16] (1876) 3 R 535.
[17] [1910] 1 KB 87.
[18] *Stevenson, Jordan and Harrison Ltd v Macdonald and Evans* (1952) 1 TLR 101.

The multiple test

5–13 In recognition of the increasingly complex and diverse nature of modern employment relationships, this approach, which advocates consideration of *all* relevant factors rather than adherence to a single general rule, has gained currency in recent times. In *Ready Mixed Concrete (South East) Ltd v Minister of Pensions and National Insurance*,[19] the court rejected the notion that any test based on a single criterion deserved universal applicability. Mackenna J concluded that the issue of status could only be determined by looking at the working relationship as a whole. He set out three conditions necessary to support the existence of a contract of service:

(1) an agreement to provide work in consideration for a wage or other remuneration;

(2) an agreement that in performance of his work the worker will be subject to the employer's control; and

(3) all other provisions of the contract are consistent with its being a contract of service.

In *Lee v Chung*,[20] the status of a stonemason was at issue. He worked without supervision, was paid by the job, was free to work for others and did so. However, the respondent supplied his equipment and managed the work he undertook. When other jobs clashed with work for the respondent he gave priority to the latter, without making arrangements for assistant labour to fulfil his other commitments (as might be expected of an independent contractor). It was not his responsibility to price jobs (which, again, is normally a feature of the business approach of a sub-contractor); rather he was paid either a piece-work rate or a daily rate according to the nature of the work. Stressing the folly of reliance on a single test, the Privy Council concluded that the stonemason was an employee.

Numerous cases confirm that the labels put on a relationship by the parties will be treated with caution by the courts.[21] Self-description is influential only where other indicators are ambiguous[22] and never deemed conclusive *per se*.[23] In *Express & Echo Publications Ltd v Tanton*[24] it was held that where a person who works for another is not required to perform his services personally the relationship between the worker and the person for whom he works is not, as a matter of law, that of employee and employer. In the absence of such a conclusive factor, courts are increasingly choosing to focus on the nature and extent of the burdens, rights and expectations underpinned by the working relationship between the parties. In *Nethermere (St Neots) Ltd v Taverna*[25] the Court of Appeal stressed that the essence of an employment relationship is derived from a mutuality of obligations which may, *or may not be*, of a legal or formal

---

[19] [1968] 2 QB 497.
[20] [1990] ICR 409 (PC).
[21] See, *inter alia*, *Young and Woods v West* [1980] IRLR 201.
[22] See *Massey v Crown Life Insurance Co* [1978] 2 All ER 576.
[23] *Ferguson v John Dawson & Partners (Contractors) Ltd* [1976] 3 All ER 817; cf *Young and Woods v West* [1980] IRLR 201.
[24] [1999] ICR 693.
[25] [1984] IRLR 240.

nature—that is, the employer must be committed to offer work and the employee must be committed to provide his services. If mutuality is lacking, it is unlikely the court will find a contract of service. In *Carmichael v National Power plc*,[26] Lord Irvine concluded that a worker engaged as a casual tour guide could not be held to be an employee due to the absence of firm, reciprocal commitments between the respective parties.[27] The Court of Appeal had earlier ruled that terms giving rise to mutual obligations could be implied into the contract between the parties to give it "business efficacy", and that the casual workers thus qualified as employees, but the House of Lords dismissed this argument.

Acting in the course of employment?

In order to attribute vicarious liability to an employer it is also necessary to demon-   **5–14**
strate that the wrongdoer was acting in the course of his employment when he committed the delict. There is considerable case law on this question and the line between what is within and what is outwith the scope of employment can be a difficult one to draw. In *Century Insurance Co v N I Transport Board*[28] a tanker driver caused a fire after lighting a cigarette while in the act of pumping petrol into a tank in a garage. The employer denied liability for the subsequent damage, arguing, *inter alia*, that smoking in such circumstances was contrary to regulations and strictly prohibited by the employer's own instruction. However, although the court acknowledged that smoking was clearly an unauthorised act, because the act was committed while the employee was actually carrying out his duties, the employer was held vicariously liable. Contrast this case with *Kirby v NCB*[29] in which an explosion injured several miners when one of their number lit a cigarette, again contrary to regulation, during a break. This time, it was held that the wrongdoer was acting outwith the course of his employment and no vicarious liability was found. The fact that the wrongdoer was on a break probably influenced the court in its deliberations, but *Kirby* should not be taken as authority that a worker on a break will always be deemed outside the scope of his employment. In his judgment, Lord President Clyde offered the following guidance:

> "In the first place, if the master actually authorised the particular act, he is clearly liable for it. Secondly, where the workman does some work he is appointed to do, but does it in a way which his master has not authorised and would not have authorised had he known of it, the master is nevertheless still responsible, for the servant's act is still within the scope of his employment. On the other hand, in the third place, if the servant is employed only to do a particular work or a particular class of work, and he does something outside the scope of that work, the master is not responsible for any mischief the servant may do to a third party. Lastly, if the servant uses his master's time or his master's tools for his own purposes, the master is not responsible."[30]

Where an employee commits an act that is so far removed from the ordinary course of his employment as to be outwith its scope he may be deemed to be, in the language

---

[26] House of Lords, 18th November 1999. See also *O'Kelly v Trusthouse Forte plc* [1983] IRLR 369.
[27] See also *Express and Echo Publications v Tanton* [1999] IRLR 367.
[28] [1942] AC 509.
[29] 1958 SC 514.
[30] At 532.

of the court, "on a frolic of his own" and his employer will thus avoid vicarious liability. *Keppel Bus Co v Sa'ad Bin Ahmad*[31] provides a graphic example. In this case, a bus conductor employed by the appellants became embroiled in an altercation with a passenger. Eventually, the conductor lost his temper and hit the respondent with his ticket machine, breaking his glasses and blinding him in one eye. Such an act of personal malice could not be associated with the conductor's employment and it was held that the appellants were not vicariously liable.

However, actions reasonably incidental to an employee's job may be deemed within the course of his employment, in particular if intended to further or safeguard the employer's business. In *Neville v C & A Modes Ltd*[32] two sales assistants wrongly accused a shopper of shoplifting. The innocent shopper sued the store for defamation. It was held that, although the employees in question were not store detectives, their actions were incidental to their main duties and the store was therefore vicariously liable. In *Rose v Plenty*[33] milkmen had been warned that they must not in any circumstances use children to help them to deliver milk or give children lifts on milk floats. Plenty ignored this instruction and a boy was injured as a consequence of his negligent driving. Because the prohibited act was done for the purpose and benefit of the employer's business, it was held that the employer was liable. *Poland v John Parr & Sons*[34] contrasts neatly with *Keppel Bus*. In *Poland* a delivery man struck a boy he thought was stealing from the back of his employer's van. As in *Keppel Bus*, in isolation it is difficult to imagine an act further removed from the job of the employee, but in this case the employer was held liable, because the act was directed at protecting the employer's property. Of course, there are limits to this argument. In *Warren v Henlys Ltd*,[35] a similar act of employee violence was not attributed to the employer, because *personal* vengeance and malice, rather than protection of the employer's business, were found to be the key motivating factors.

Many accidents occur while employees are on the road; either commuting to and from their place of work, or otherwise in the ordinary course of their job. In *Smith v Stages*[36] the House of Lords held that an employee who was paid *wages* (not merely travelling expenses) by his employer to travel between his home and place of work was acting "in his employer's time" and thus in the course of his employment. Lord Lowry commented:

> "The paramount rule is that an employee travelling on the highway will be acting in the course of his employment if, and only if, he is at the material time going about his employer's business. One must not confuse the duty to turn up for one's work with the concept of already being 'on duty' while travelling to it."[37]

Consider, in this context, the case of *Compton v McClure*.[38] In this case, an employee was late for work. He drove at an excessive speed onto his employer's premises and

---

[31] [1974] 1 WLR 1082.
[32] 1945 SC 175.
[33] [1976] 1 WLR 141.
[34] [1927] 1 KB 236.
[35] [1948] 2 All ER 935.
[36] [1989] 1 All ER 833.
[37] At 840.
[38] [1975] ICR 378.

negligently injured the plaintiff. Although it could be argued the employee was still on his journey to work, his employer was found vicariously liable because the accident occurred onsite, inside factory gates manned by security guards where a 5 mph speed limit was in force. If the accident had happened just yards away on the street outside the premises it is likely the employer would have avoided liability.

Further guidance is provided by *Williams v A & W Hemphill Ltd.*[39] In this case a driver, who was under his employer's instructions to transport passengers from Benderloch in Argyll to Glasgow, was persuaded to deviate first to Stirling and then to Dollar by certain of those passengers.[40] The vehicle was involved in an accident on the road near Dollar and another passenger was injured. The court found that when the accident occurred the driver was in breach of an implied duty to make the journey by a direct route, but held that his overall duty to deliver his passengers safely to Glasgow still subsisted. Had the driver been driving an empty lorry, a substantial deviation might well have constituted a frolic of his own, but the presence of passengers, whom the driver was charged to deliver to an ultimate destination, served to refute the conclusion that the deviation for an ulterior purpose of the driver. The safe transport of the passengers was the dominant purpose of the authorised journey, and although a devious route was taken, that purpose continued to play an essential part. Consequently, the employer was held liable.

NEGLIGENCE

In the diverse realm of delict, which embraces, among other actions, assault, nuisance, defamation, and seduction, negligence is king. Negligence is the most commonly litigated delict, and its range and scope are immense. In the celebrated case *Grant v Australian Knitting Mills*[41] itchy underpants were at issue. Someone tried to inflate an apprentice motor mechanic in *Smith v Crossley Bros Ltd*[42] and *Cameron v Hamilton's Auction Marts Ltd*[43] concerned an adventurous cow. (Although it is arguable that many delictual actions deserve mention, a book of this nature affords insufficient scope to do them justice and, accordingly, negligence is the focus of this chapter.)   **5–15**

In a claim based on this delict, the pursuer will seek to prove that he has suffered loss or injury as a consequence of the defender's negligence. Negligence is conceptualised as behaviour falling below the standard to be expected of "the reasonable man". The notional reasonable man constitutes an objective measure of conduct, a societal yardstick against which the actions of the defender will be judged. Baron Anderson offered the following definition in *Blyth v Birmingham Waterworks Co Ltd*[44]: "Negligence is the omission to do something which a reasonable man, guided upon

---

[39] 1966 SC (HL) 31.
[40] The passengers were members of the Boy's Brigade, some of whom were intent on a liaison with members of a company of Girls' Guildry, who were bound for Dollar after a camping holiday in Benderloch.
[41] [1936] AC 85.
[42] (1951) 95 SJ 655.
[43] 1955 SLT (Sh Ct) 74.
[44] (1856) 11 Ex 781.

those considerations which ordinarily regulate the conduct of human affairs, would do, or doing something which a prudent and reasonable man would not do."[45]

In *Lochgelly Iron and Coal Co Ltd* v *McMullan*[46] Lord Wright elaborated on the legal framework in which the concept sits: "In strict legal analysis negligence means more than heedless or careless conduct, whether in omission or commission: it properly connotes the complex concept of duty, breach and damage thereby suffered by the person to whom the duty was owing."

In order to ground such an action the following points must be established by the pursuer:

(a) **duty of care**: the defender must owe the pursuer a legally recognised duty of care;

(b) **breach of duty**: the defender must breach that duty of care, *ie* commit a negligent act;

(c) **damage**: the pursuer must suffer some legally recognised form of damage;

(d) **causation**: the defender's breach of duty must be the cause of the damage suffered; and

(e) **remoteness**: the damage suffered must fall within the range of loss deemed recoverable in law.

An action in negligence is a house of cards. If you remove any one essential component it will collapse. It is necessary that all the above criteria are met. If the pursuer is unable to satisfy any one element of his claim then, no matter how compelling the case for the other four, the claim will fail.

DUTY OF CARE

Foundation authority

5–16   Although, as we will see, the law has now developed beyond this classic position, the range and scope of the duty of care in negligence was long defined by the "neighbour principle" as enunciated by Lord Atkin in the celebrated case *Donoghue* v *Stephenson*.[47] The facts of *Donoghue* belie its significance as the cornerstone of the modern law of negligence. It all happened at a café in Paisley. Donoghue was in the process of drinking the contents of a bottle of ginger beer, which had been purchased by her friend, when the said friend poured the remainder of the ginger beer into a glass. At this point a partially decomposed snail emerged from the bottle. As a consequence, Donoghue suffered injury and subsequently sought to recover compensation.

The law of contract provided the traditional means of redress, but this did not help Donoghue. She was not a party to the contract for the purchase of the ginger beer which subsisted between her friend and the keeper of the café and therefore she had no *locus* to sue under it. The House of Lords, however, held that Donoghue was

---

[45] At 784.
[46] [1934] AC 1 at 25.
[47] 1932 SC (HL) 31.

entitled to sue the manufacturer, Stevenson, in delict. Lord Atkin found that Stevenson owed Donoghue a duty of care, justifying his conclusion as follows:

"... a manufacturer of products, which he sells in such a form as to show that he intends them to reach the ultimate consumer in the form in which they left him, with no reasonable possibility of intermediate examination, [the ginger beer bottle was opaque] and with the knowledge that the absence of reasonable care in the preparation or putting up of the product will result in an injury to the consumer's life or property, owes a duty to the consumer to take that reasonable care."[48]

Lord Atkin set out the parameters of the duty of care owed by the manufacturer in terms that resonate through the law of negligence to this day:

"The liability for negligence, whether you style it such or treat it as in other systems as a species of 'culpa', is no doubt based upon a general public sentiment of moral wrong-doing for which the offender must pay. But acts or omissions which any moral code would censure cannot in a practical world be treated so as to give a right to every person injured by them to demand relief. In this way rules of law arise which limit the range of complainants and the extent of their remedy. *The rule that you are to love your neighbour becomes in law, you must not injure your neighbour; and the lawyer's question, Who is my neighbour? receives a restricted reply. You must take reasonable care to avoid acts or omissions which you can reasonably foresee would be likely to injure your neighbour. Who, then in law is my neighbour? The answer seems to be—persons who are so closely and directly affected by my act that I ought reasonably to have them in contemplation as being so affected when I am directing my mind to the acts or omissions which are called into question.*"[49] [emphasis added]

This is the neighbour principle. It both identifies and restricts that class of people to whom a duty of care is owed in any particular circumstances. This element of negligence is often employed as a so-called "threshold device" to filter claims. Under *Donoghue*, a duty of care arises if it is reasonably foreseeable that the acts or omissions of the defender may affect the pursuer. Consider, for example, the position of a motorist. It is obvious that he owes a duty of care to other road users, pedestrians and the owners of property abutting the road—but which ones? As he travels along the road that group of people to whom he owes a duty is constantly changing. Broadly speaking, everyone illuminated in the headlights of the motorist's car is owed a duty of care. They may foreseeably be affected by the motorist's actions, because the car is both proximate and travelling towards them. However, in this case the duty owed is fleeting. Once the car has passed a particular pedestrian it is unlikely (that is, not *reasonably foreseeable*) that the acts or omissions of the motorist will affect that pedestrian and therefore he is no longer owed a duty of care—unless of course the motorist turns the car around, in which case the pedestrian will once again be illuminated in its headlights.

The outcome of *Bourhill* v *Young*[50] was determined on these grounds. Bourhill, a pregnant woman, was alighting from a tram in Edinburgh when Young, a

---

[48] At 57.
[49] At 44.
[50] 1942 SC (HL) 78.

motorcyclist, negligently overtook the tram, travelled a short distance (15 metres) beyond and collided with a car. Young died in the accident. After his body was removed Bourhill saw blood on the road. She suffered nervous shock, which caused her to miscarry. The House of Lords held that her action against Young's executor must fail, because Young owed no duty of care to persons whom he could not reasonably anticipate would suffer injury as a result of his conduct on the highway. The occupants of the car were, but the pursuer was not, deemed to be within the range of the duty owed by Young. Lord Macmillan stated:

> "Young was clearly negligent in a question with the occupants of the motor car with which his cycle collided. He was driving at an excessive speed in a public thoroughfare and he ought to have foreseen that he might consequently collide with any vehicle which he might meet in his course, for such an occurrence may reasonably and probably be expected to ensue from driving at a high speed in a street. But can it be said that he ought further to have foreseen that his excessive speed, involving the possibility of collision with another vehicle, might cause injury by shock to the appellant? The appellant was not within his line of vision, for she was on the other side of a tramcar which was standing between him and her when he passed, and it was not until he had proceeded some distance beyond her that he collided with the motor car."[51]

So, it is pertinent that at the time of the accident Young had already passed Bourhill and, in any event, the latter was on the far side of the tramcar. She was not within the area of potential risk—in terms of the above analogy, she was not in his headlights. It was not foreseeable that she would be affected by Young's actions and therefore he did not owe her a duty of care.

The evolving law

5–17   In *Gibson* v *Orr*[52] floodwater in the River Kelvin caused the Gavell Bridge to collapse. Police officers were directed to the north side of the bridge, which they promptly coned off. The officers proceeded to position their Land Rover vehicle on the north side with its blue light flashing and its headlights illuminated so as to be visible and to give warning to any persons approaching the south side of the bridge. Some time later, and before they had received confirmation that any barrier or warning was in place on the south side of the bridge, the constables withdrew their vehicle. Within a few minutes of their departure, the car in which the pursuer was travelling made its approach from the still unmarked south side and fell into the river. The pursuer suffered injury and sued the police.

Lord Hamilton reflected on the appropriate test to be applied in determining whether a duty of care was owed to the pursuer by the defender. He considered *Caparo Industries plc* v *Dickman*,[53] where the House of Lords applied a test involving three elements. Lord Bridge said:

> "What emerges is that, in addition to the foreseeability of damage, necessary ingredients in any situation giving rise to a duty of care are that there should exist between

---

[51] At 88.
[52] 1999 SC 420.
[53] [1990] 1 All ER 568.

the party owing the duty and the party to whom it is owed a relationship characterised by the law as one of 'proximity' or 'neighbourhood' and that the situation should be one in which the court considers it fair, just and reasonable that the law should impose a duty of a given scope upon the one party for the benefit of the other."[54]

Rejecting the traditional approach laid down by Lord Atkin in *Donoghue*, Lord Hamilton ruled that this tripartite test fell to be applied in Scotland in personal injuries actions based on a duty of care as well as in other actions of damages so based.[55] The significance of *Donoghue* was acknowledged, but only as a milestone in the development in the law, not as a destination in itself. In the opinion of the court there was no logical justification for applying a different test for the existence of a duty of care in respect of personal injury from that applicable relative to physical damage, to property or to economic loss.

So, whatever the nature of the harm sustained by the pursuer, it is necessary to decide the matter not only by inquiring about foreseeability but also by considering the nature of the relationship between the parties, and to be satisfied that in all the circumstances it is fair, just and reasonable to impose a duty of care.[56] These are not to be treated as wholly separate and distinct requirements but rather collectively, as a guide to the pragmatic question whether a duty should be imposed in any particular case.

Negligent statements

Where a negligent statement causes physical injury the ordinary rules of liability are applicable.[57] However, an additional legal framework applies where a negligent statement results in purely financial loss. The criteria necessary to support the existence of such a duty were laid down in *Hedley Byrne & Co Ltd* v *Heller & Partners Ltd*.[58] Hedley Byrne wanted to ascertain the creditworthiness of a client called Easipower and approached Heller, Easipower's bankers, for a reference. In reply, Heller stated that Easipower was creditworthy, but added a disclaimer to the effect that this statement was made without responsibility on their part. Subsequently, Easipower went into liquidation and Hedley Byrne sued Heller. The action failed due to the disclaimer, but the House of Lords held that, in principle, liability in negligence may extend to negligent misstatement. Lord Reid stipulated that such liability would only arise where there was a "special relationship" between the parties. He explained that a special relationship would exist:

5–18

> "where it is plain that the party seeking the information or advice was trusting the other to exercise such a degree of care as the circumstances required, where it was reasonable for him to do that, and where the other gave the information or advice when he knew or ought to have known that the enquirer was relying on him."[59]

---

[54] At 573–574.
[55] See also *Coleridge* v *Miller Construction* 1997 SLT 485; *Forbes* v *City of Dundee District Council* 1997 SLT 1330; *British Telecommunications plc* v *James Thomson & Sons (Engineers) Limited* 1999 SLT 224.
[56] See *McFarlane* v *Tayside Health Board* 2000 SLT 154.
[57] See *Clay* v *AJ Crump & Sons Ltd* [1964] 1 QB 533.
[58] [1964] AC 465.
[59] At 486.

Subsequent case law has built extensively on the rule set out in *Hedley Byrne*. In *Caparo Industries plc v Dickman*[60] accounts were prepared that negligently overvalued the stock in a company. Shares were bought by a third party, in reliance on the accounts, to facilitate a takeover bid. The House of Lords concluded that *Caparo* could be distinguished from *Hedley Byrne* because the key feature of the latter case was that the defendant was fully aware of the nature of the transaction that the plaintiff was contemplating. This is at odds with the *Caparo* scenario, where accounts put into general circulation could be relied upon by strangers for any one of a variety of different purposes. In a ruling designed to restrict the scope of *Hedley Byrne*, it was held that auditors of a public company's accounts owed no general duty of care to existing shareholders or to members of the public at large (potential shareholders). In addition to the points raised by Lord Reid in *Hedley Byrne* it was deemed necessary to prove that the defendant knew his statement would be communicated to the plaintiff as an individual or as a member of a determinate class of people, and that the defendant knew the particular use to which it was intended his statement would be put.

Martin v Bell-Ingram[61] concerned a claim against a firm of surveyors after a house survey failed to identify serious faults with the roof. Although the surveyor had attached a disclaimer to the report, the pursuer successfully sued for negligent misstatement. The pursuer had acted on a verbal report before purchasing the house and did not get notice of the written report until after the transaction was complete, so the disclaimer was ineffective.

Public authority liability

5–19   The House of Lords conceded the principle that a public agency can be liable in negligence if it exercises its statutory powers without due care in *X and Others (Minors) v Bedfordshire County Council*.[62] However, this ruling indicates that broad policy decisions requiring the exercise of statutory discretion are unlikely to be justiciable and that even negligence at an operational level may not sustain liability unless the decision is wholly outside the ambit of the authority's discretion. In general terms, delictual liability cannot be superimposed on the exercise of a statutory duty if adherence to the common law duty is inconsistent with, or has a tendency to impede, the statutory function of the authority. This rule is commonly applied in practice: *Elguzouli-Daf v Commissioner of Police of the Metropolis*.[63]

Stovin v Wise[64] concerned a traffic accident at a dangerously obstructed road junction. Norfolk County Council, the local highway authority, had the power to order work to be carried out by the landowner to clear the junction of obstructions to sight. Despite a series of accidents and an internal decision to instruct remedial works, no action was taken and the accident on which this litigation founded occurred. While rejecting the concept of immunity from policy decisions, the House of Lords held that a failure to implement a decision did not suffice to establish liability in damages. Lord Hoffmann suggested that a duty of care may arise where a public agency fails to use a discretionary statutory power if: (1) inaction was irrational; and (2) it is the policy of

---

[60] [1990] 2 AC 605.
[61] 1986 SC 208.
[62] [1995] 3 All ER 353 (HL).
[63] [1995] 1 All ER 833.
[64] [1996] AC 923.

the legislation to afford the injured party a claim in damages if the power is not exercised.

In recent times, the courts have displayed a marked reluctance to hold that public authorities owe a duty of care in respect of the exercise or non-exercise of a statutory power.[65] That said, simple administrative failings which are pursuant to the lawful exercise of a discretion can be subject to a duty of care, even if some element of discretion is involved. In *Barrett v Enfield London Borough Council*[66] the House of Lords refused to dismiss a claim against a local authority brought by a man who had spent his childhood in care. The plaintiff alleged he had suffered psychiatric illness as a result of the authority's failure to provide appropriate care for him. It was held that a decision on whether to take a child into care was not reviewable by way of a claim in damages for negligence. However, once a child is taken into care the new element of proximity might sustain a common law duty of care and it is irrelevant that the local authority's decision involves the exercise of discretion on the part of social workers.

The conventional criteria for the establishment of a duty of care (as discussed above)[67] are broadly applicable in this context. Courts typically decline to impose a duty of care on public agencies because of the lack of proximity between the parties,[68] or on the broader grounds of the fair, just and reasonable criteria.[69] In practice, however, the attribution of liability will depend largely on an assessment of the policy arguments for and against the imposition of liability in all the circumstances of the case. In this regard, relevant factors will include the exact nature of the loss, the relationship between the parties and the practical consequences of the recognition, or denial, of a duty of care. Public policy considerations (in particular the concept of distributive justice) were certainly at issue in *McFarlane v Tayside Health Board*,[70] which concerned the attribution of liability to a health board after negligent advice that resulted in an unwanted pregnancy. In *Gibson v Orr*,[71] the police authority were found to owe a duty of care over the control of the hazard caused by the collapsed bridge. The police constables at the site were deemed proximate to road users likely to be affected by the hazard. Furthermore, there were no obvious policy reasons, such as might exist in the context of a criminal investigation or prosecution, to suggest it would not be fair, just and reasonable to impose the duty.

Osman v United Kingdom,[72] concerned a claim for damages arising from the alleged negligence of a police authority in crime prevention and detection. The Court of Appeal struck out the claim on the ground that it was not fair, just and reasonable to impose a duty of care in the circumstances of operational police work.[73] Consonant with the sentiment expressed in *Stovin*, the European Court of Human Rights held that "blanket" public policy immunity of this kind is a breach of the plaintiff's rights under

---

[65] See, *eg Kinsella v Chief Constable of Nottinghamshire*, [1999] TLR 624; *Hussain v Lancaster City Council* [1999] 2 WLR 1142 (CA); *Palmer v Tees Health Authority*, [1999] TLR 496.

[66] [1999] 3 WLR 79.

[67] See *Caparo Industries plc v Dickman* [1990] 2 AC 605.

[68] See *Capital and Counties plc v Hampshire County Council* [1997] 2 All ER 865.

[69] See *Hill v Chief Constable of West Yorkshire* [1989] AC 53.

[70] 2000 SLT 154.

[71] 1999 SC 420.

[72] (1998) 1 LGLR 431.

[73] See *Hill v Chief Constable of West Yorkshire* [1989] AC 53.

Article 6 of the European Convention on Human Rights.[74] *Osman* suggests that all relevant factors should be weighed in the balance and Scottish courts are, in future, likely to be less inclined to dismiss claims against public agencies as a consequence.

The standard of care

Generally

5–20 In order to discharge a duty of care the defender must measure up to the standard of care expected of the hypothetical "reasonable man" in all the circumstances of the case. The issue is not whether the defender did the best he could, but whether his actions meet this benchmark.[75]Although occasionally tempered by judicial interpretation, this is essentially an objective test. In *Nettleship* v *Weston*[76] a learner driver collided with a lamppost and injured the plaintiff (her driving instructor). At first instance the plaintiff's claim for compensation was dismissed. The defendant was deemed to have been doing all she could to control the car. However, the Court of Appeal held that the standard of care required of a learner driver is the same as that required of any other driver—that of a reasonably competent and experienced driver. A driver's incompetent best would not suffice. The court dismissed the notion that a variable (subjective) standard based on competence, experience and other personal factors would either be appropriate in the circumstances or workable in any wider context. If this seems a little harsh, it is as well to note that an objective standard may also be imposed on a defender whose conduct becomes impaired by the onset of illness (for example, after suffering a stroke); but only where the defender retains at least some degree of control over his actions.[77]

Compliance with approved practice

5–21 Sometimes, however, an objective standard is not applicable. If you were about to go under the knife for a heart bypass it is unlikely you would be reassured by the fact that the surgeon wielding the knife exercises all the skill and competence expected of an ordinary reasonable man. If you wanted to commission the building of a private jet, the chances are you would look for a company with a better grasp of aeronautical engineering than that traditionally accorded to the typical reasonable man.

Accordingly, where a person holds himself out as a professional or as having any special skill he will be judged not by the standard of the reasonable man but by the higher and more exacting standard of the reasonably competent professional in that field or exponent of that particular skill. This was confirmed in *Hunter* v *Hanley*,[78] where medical negligence was alleged: "The true test for establishing negligence in diagnosis or treatment on the part of the doctor is whether he has been proved to be guilty of such failure as no doctor of ordinary skill would be guilty of if acting with ordinary care."[79]

In *Bolam* v *Friern Hospital Management Committee*[80] a patient suffered injury during

---

[74] Article 6(1) provides that "In the determination of his civil rights and obligations ... everyone is entitled to a fair and public hearing."
[75] *Muir* v *Glasgow Corporation* 1943 SC (HL) 3.
[76] [1971] 3 All ER 581.
[77] *Roberts* v *Ramsbottom* [1980] 1 WLR 823.
[78] 1955 SLT 213.
[79] Per Lord President Clyde at 217.
[80] [1957] 2 All ER 118.

electro-convulsive therapy due to a failure to use muscle relaxants and restraints. There was a divergence of opinion within the medical profession as to whether such precautions were beneficial. It was held that a doctor is not negligent if he acts in accordance with a practice accepted as proper by a responsible body of medical men skilled in that particular art. In this regard it is not necessary that the practice in question is in conformity with the majority view within the profession.[81] This was confirmed in *Maynard* v *West Midlands Regional Health Authority*,[82] in which Lord Scarman added that "a doctor who professes to exercise a special skill must exercise the ordinary skill of his speciality".

Similarly, the operator of a trade or business is, generally speaking, expected to exercise care commensurate with the prevailing standards of the industry in question. However, the significance of this test should not be overstated. It should be thought of as establishing a rebuttable presumption. Evidence that a defender has acted in accord with common practice does not necessarily abrogate a finding of negligence[83] and by the same token the fact that a defender has departed from common practice is not conclusive of negligence *per se*.[84]

The standard of care expected of a reasonable person will vary widely, depending on the facts of the case in question. For example, a mountain guide would be expected to exercise greater diligence when leading a party of schoolchildren than when escorting a party of experienced, adult climbers.

BREACH OF DUTY

At the heart of the law of negligence lies the concept of breach of a legally recognised duty of care. Indeed, in one sense, breach of duty is the very essence of negligence itself. In turn, the question as to what is and what is not negligent generally falls to be determined by reference to the notional conduct of the "reasonable man". As discussed above, this objective yardstick was defined in *Blyth*.[85]

5–22

The pertinent question is: how do we ascertain what a reasonable man would have done in the circumstances of any particular case? Thankfully, this process is fairly straightforward. Certain key factors are weighed up against each other and balanced in the wider context of the case. The good news is that the decision generated by this process generally owes considerably more to plain common sense than pedantic legal principle. It is for the court "to weigh on the one hand the magnitude of the risk, the likelihood of an accident happening and the possible seriousness of the consequences if an accident does happen, and on the other hand the difficulty, expense and any other disadvantage of taking precautions.[86] The application of this formula is often rather grandly styled a "calculus of risk". In simple terms, this means the judge will typically ask the following questions, take account of all other relevant factors, and then make a decision.

---

[81] *De Freitas* v *O'Brien* [1995] TLR 86.
[82] [1984] 1 WLR 634.
[83] *Cavanagh* v *Ulster Weaving Co Ltd* [1960] AC 145. See also *Paris* v *Stepney Borough Council* [1951] AC 367.
[84] *Brown* v *Rolls-Royce Ltd* [1960] 1 WLR 210.
[85] (1856) 11 Ex 781.
[86] *Morris* v *West Hartlepool Steam Navigation Co Ltd* [1956] AC 552 at 574.

The calculus of risk

What was the likelihood of injury?

5-23   In *Bolton* v *Stone*[87] the plaintiff was struck by a ball hit out of a cricket ground. The ball had gone over a fence that stood some 17 feet above the pitch and almost 80 yards from the crease. It travelled about 20 yards beyond the fence before hitting the plaintiff. Evidence was adduced showing that a ball had only been hit out of the ground six times in the previous 30 years and no one had ever been hit. Armed with this information, the House of Lords held that the likelihood of injury to a person in the plaintiff's position was so slight that the cricket club was not negligent in allowing cricket to be played without having taken additional precautions such as increasing the height of the perimeter fence.

The balancing process is transparent on the facts. In effect, the court acknowledged that a tiny risk of (probably) relatively minor injury[88] did not justify the massive expense that would be entailed in raising the perimeter fence—and just how high would you need to raise it to be *reasonably sure* of guarding against the risk? Lord Oaksey said:

> "an ordinarily careful man does not take precautions against every foreseeable risk. He can, of course, foresee the possibility of many risks, but life would be almost impossible if he were to attempt to take precautions against every risk which he can foresee. He takes precautions against risks which are reasonably likely to happen. Many foreseeable risks are extremely unlikely to happen and cannot be guarded against except by almost complete isolation."[89]

What is the magnitude of harm likely to be suffered?

5-24   In *Paris* v *Stepney Borough Council*[90] a mechanic who was known to his employers to be blind in one eye was set to work in a garage. In the course of his work he struck a bolt on the underside of a vehicle with a hammer. A chip of metal flew into his good eye and this left him completely blind. The defendants showed in evidence that it was not usual practice to supply goggles for work of the kind undertaken. However, the House of Lords held that goggles should have been provided and found the defendants liable. Whereas a two-eyed man risked the loss of one eye (which is serious enough), the plaintiff risked total blindness.

Again, application of the calculus yields an obvious conclusion. When working under a car without goggles it is almost impossible to avoid contamination of the eyes. The *likelihood* of injury was thus very high. Coupled with this, the potential magnitude of harm, to what in any circumstances is a vulnerable and vital organ, was massive. Balanced against this formidable combination was the cost of taking precautions— shall we say sixpence for a pair of goggles. Little wonder the plaintiff recovered damages.

As we have here, it is particularly important to consider the above two factors in combination. The tiny risk in *Bolton* failed to sustain a duty because the magnitude of

---

[87] [1951] AC 850.
[88] Of course, you *could* be killed by a cricket ball at 100 yards, but mild bruising is more likely.
[89] At 863.
[90] [1951] AC 367.

harm was trivial. Consider the same risk profile (an average one escape per five years) but shift the context from a cricket ground to a biological weapons testing facility. Because the potential magnitude of harm has increased, a higher standard of care would be expected and a lower level of risk would be tolerated. In the new context, it is far more likely that liability would be imposed on the defender in the event of an escape causing injury.

Is there a good excuse for the conduct in question?

Reflect on another extreme example. Ostensibly, a motorcyclist speeding through **5–25** Edinburgh at 80 mph will be liable in negligence if he collides with an oncoming lorry. However, the matter is worth further investigation. If it transpires that the man is the chief engineer at a nuclear power plant that is teetering on the brink of criticality, or a bomb disposal officer on the way to answer an emergency call, the court may hesitate to impose liability. That said, if he collides with a troupe of girl guides instead of a lorry the court might not hesitate for long. Of course, if he is merely late for his tea then his fate is sealed.

In *Watt* v *Hertfordshire County Council*[91] a fireman was injured by the movement of a heavy jack while travelling on a lorry which was not specially equipped to carry it. A woman was lying trapped under a vehicle and the jack was urgently required to effect a rescue and save her life. It was held that the defendant had not been negligent because the risk to the plaintiff, although significant, was not so great as to deter an attempt to save a life. This is the ultimate justification for ostensibly negligent conduct. If the same accident had occurred in a commercial enterprise, recovery would probably have been an easy matter. *Daborn* v *Bath Tramways Motor Co*[92] focused on the wartime policy of commandeering left-hand drive vehicles (from which signaling was difficult) to serve as ambulances. An accident occurred, but again it was held that the ends justified the means.

In summary, it should be noted that *Watt* and *Daborn* are exceptions to the general policy of the courts and against the tide of contemporary jurisprudence. A defender, even the emergency services, will need to produce a cogent excuse to justify conduct that is prima facie negligent.

What are the costs and practicalities of taking precautions?

In *Latimer* v *AEC Ltd*[93] a heavy rainstorm flooded the defendant's factory, leaving the **5–26** floor slippery. The defendants swept the floor and threw sawdust down (no less than three tons of it) to make the factory safe. The plaintiff nevertheless slipped on an untreated part of the floor and was injured. He alleged negligence in the defendant's failure to close down the factory. The House of Lords found the defendants not liable. The defendants had done all that was reasonably practicable to reduce the risk, and in any event, on balance, the risk of injury created by a slippery floor was not so great as to justify, much less require, so onerous and expensive a precaution as to close the factory.

Where adequate precautions are either not practicable or simply unavailable, the risks of persevering with the activity have to be weighed against the disadvantages of

---

[91] [1954] 1 WLR 835.
[92] [1946] 2 All ER 333.
[93] [1953] AC 643.

its cessation. In *Withers v Perry Chain Co Ltd*,[94] where the only work available to an employee susceptible to dermatitis involved a risk of contracting the disease, it was held that the employer was not liable. The only alternative open to the employer was to dismiss the plaintiff, but the employer was not obliged to do so to avoid liability.

Calculus of risk: a summary

5–27   In sum, the calculus of risk offers a useful guide to the identification of factors central to the issue of breach of duty. It is not a conclusive formula and its application is more art than science. It is important to give full consideration to all other relevant factors, the wider context of the case and any in point precedent. However, in the final analysis, common sense should prevail.

RES IPSA LOQUITUR

5–28   *Res ipsa loquitur* means "the thing speaks for itself". This maxim expresses a rule of evidence which, in simple terms, may serve to reverse the burden of proof in negligence-based claims.[95] The general rule is that the burden of proof rests on the pursuer, that is, he must prove negligence on the part of the defender on the balance of probabilities. Sometimes, however, the very occurrence of an accident may substantiate the pursuer's averment of negligence on the part of the defender. *Res ipsa loquitur* may apply where there is no obvious explanation for an accident other than the negligence of the defender. In these circumstances it is for the defender to *disprove* negligence, not for the pursuer to prove it.

In *Scott v London and St Katherine Dock Co*,[96] sacks of sugar fell on the plaintiff as he passed under a warehouse loading bay. There was no explanation as to how the accident had occurred. Erle CJ held:

> "Where the thing is shown to be under the management of the defendant, or his servants, and the accident is such as in the ordinary course of things does not happen if those who have the management use proper care, it affords reasonable evidence, in the absence of an explanation by the defendant, that the accident arose from want of care."[97]

The conditions for the application of this principle are as follows:

(a) the thing or activity must be wholly under the control of the defender or his servants;

(b) the accident must be one which would not have happened if proper care had been exercised;

(c) there must be no evidence of the actual cause of the accident.

---

[94] [1961] 1 WLR 1314.
[95] It has been argued that it is misleading to talk of the burden shifting to the defender: *Ng Chun Pui v Lee Cheun Tat*, *The Times*, 25th May 1988 (PC).
[96] (1865) H & C 596.
[97] At 602.

In *Devine* v *Colvilles*[98] a workman was injured after an explosion in a factory. There was no direct evidence of the cause of the explosion, which had originated in an oxygen hose, but the defenders were unable to establish that the explosion could have been caused without negligence on their part. The House of Lords held the defenders liable on the basis that they were at the material time in full control of the hose and that in the ordinary course of things, with proper care and maintenance, hoses do not usually explode. For a more recent application of this principle see *Caledonia North Sea Ltd* v *London Bridge Engineering Ltd*,[99] which concerned the attribution of liability for the Piper Alpha disaster.

DAMAGE

Unless the pursuer has suffered some recognised form of damage, no loss is recoverable. Consider the following scenario: **5–29**

(a) X decides to buy a car;

(b) X asks mechanic Y to check over his intended purchase;

(c) Y fails to notice car is a "cut & shut",[100] and recommends its purchase;

(d) X reconsiders and ultimately buys a different car.

On the facts, there is a duty of care owed by Y to X, and probably a breach of that duty in the delivery of negligent advice. However, the man suffers no damage as a consequence and therefore has no claim in negligence. The range of recoverable damage has gradually extended beyond simple physical injury and now includes, *inter alia*, psychiatric injury and various forms of economic loss (in particular those consequential upon physical injury such as lost wages).

Psychiatric injury and nervous shock

It is possible to recover damages for psychiatric as well as physical injury: "it is now   **5–30** well recognised that an action will lie for injury by shock sustained through the medium of the eye or ear without direct contact."[101] *Rorrison* v *West Lothian College*[102] confirmed that the injury sustained must amount to a recognised psychiatric illness or disorder; ordinary anxiety or distress will not suffice.[103] Psychiatric injury can develop over a period of time, perhaps resulting in what is commonly referred to as a "nervous breakdown", and some of the best examples are to be found in cases of work-related stress.[104] In *Ingram* v *Worcester County Council*[105] the warden of a gipsy site suffered

---

[98] 1969 SC (HL) 67.
[99] Inner House, 17th December 1999: http://www.scotcourts.gov.uk/index1.htm.
[100] The front half of one vehicle welded to the rear half of another—an obvious fault to the trained eye.
[101] *Bourhill* v *Young* 1942 SC(HL) 78.
[102] Outer House, 21st July 1999.
[103] See also *Simpson* v *ICI* 1983 SLT 601.
[104] See, *eg*, *Rorrison* v *West Lothian College*, 21st July 1999: http://www.scotcourts.gov.uk/index1.htm.
[105] Birmingham County Court, 10th January 2000 (unreported).

serious harassment and intimidation at work, but his employer ignored his complaints and requests for help. Eventually, the plaintiff suffered a mental breakdown. He was awarded a record £203,000 in compensation.

A single event or accident can also cause psychiatric injury. Traditionally, lawyers have referred to the injury sustained in such circumstances as "nervous shock", although today the term "Post Traumatic Stress Disorder" may be more appropriate. In these cases, it is necessary to distinguish between primary shock victims, who also sustain physical injury or are in some other way directly involved in the accident and secondary shock victims, who are affected either as a consequence of witnessing the accident or out of concern for the safety of another.[106] The question arose in *Haggerty* v *EE Caledonia*,[107] which concerned the Piper Alpha disaster. The pursuer, who was situated on a supply ship approximately 500 metres from the oil platform, witnessed the incident. Some of the fireballs emanating from the platform came as close as 50 metres to him. His claim to qualify as a primary victim was dismissed. His concern for his own personal safety could not be justified in the circumstances.

Primary victims

5–31   In order to establish liability for the injury sustained by a primary victim it is necessary to prove that injury to the pursuer was reasonably foreseeable in the circumstances.[108] Moreover, once liability is established the victim must be taken as he is found. The eggshell skull rule[109] applies to extend liability to damage sustained as a consequence of some unforeseeable psychological susceptibility.

Secondary victims

5–32   As stated above, secondary victims are those who suffer psychiatric illness as a result of the death, injury or impairment of another. Mindful of the risk of a flood of tenuous claims, the courts have determined that rigorous criteria must be met before the existence of a duty of care to prevent psychiatric injury will be acknowledged. In *Alcock*,[110] which resulted from the Hillsborough football ground disaster, the House of Lords held that a wrongdoer will owe a duty of care to a secondary victim only if:

(a) there is a tie of love and affection between the secondary victim and the primary victim such that it is reasonably foreseeable that the former will suffer nervous shock;

(b) the secondary victim was present at the accident or in its immediate aftermath; and

(c) nervous shock was suffered as a consequence of the secondary victim's perception of the accident with his own unaided senses (that is, he personally heard or saw the accident).

---

[106] See *Alcock et al* v *Chief Constable of South Yorkshire Police* [1991] 4 All ER 907.
[107] [1997] TLR 69.
[108] *Page* v *Smith* [1996] 1 AC 155.
[109] Discussed in more detail at para 5–43.
[110] [1991] 4 All ER 907.

In addition, the pursuer-friendly eggshell skull rule is not applicable in this context. An injury attributed to a particular susceptibility of a secondary victim will normally be deemed unforeseeable. The "tie of love and affection" criterion has been quite strictly applied. There will be a presumption of such where the relationship is spousal or parental, but other family relationships may not suffice *per se*. In *Robertson v Forth Road Bridge Joint Board*[111] the pursuer was a longtime friend and workmate of the primary victim, who was blown off the Forth Road Bridge, but it was held that this was not a sufficient tie of affection. This test does not apply where the secondary victim suffers psychiatric injury as a result of participating in a rescue operation connected to an accident. A duty of care is owed to those attempting a rescue if it is reasonably foreseeable that nervous shock could be suffered as a result of witnessing the aftermath of the accident. It is not necessary to prove a close relationship between rescuer and victim.

The growing judicial recognition of post traumatic stress disorder has unlocked a fast unfolding field. For example, in *Attia v British Gas*,[112] where the plaintiff discovered her house on fire, it was held that it is possible to recover damages for psychiatric injury suffered as a result of witnessing damage to property.

Economic loss

The courts have traditionally been reluctant to hold that a duty of care exists where   **5–33** negligent conduct causes pure economic loss (that is, financial loss not consequential upon physical injury or property damage).[113] To allow recovery in these circumstances would be to open the floodgates to a huge number of claims. Consider a typical motorway accident involving two or three vehicles and caused by the negligence of one driver. It would not be unusual for a queue of vehicles three or four miles long to build up behind the site of the accident. Thousands of people would be delayed in their day to day business and many of them would be able to point to some kind of financial loss sustained as a consequence. This scenario, among many, would generate a potentially enormous liability in damages. The courts have fought shy of permitting such a result by attributing liability only where direct physical damage to person or property is suffered.

In *Dynamco v Holland Hannen & Cubitts (Scotland) Ltd*[114] the defenders negligently damaged a power line and interrupted the pursuer's supply of electricity. As a result of this power failure, Dynamco suffered considerable financial loss. However, recoverability was denied because the loss suffered did not arise directly from damage to Dynamco's property. It is useful to contrast this case with the similar *SCM (UK) Ltd v WJ Whittal & Son Ltd*[115] where power was negligently cut to a factory. In this instance, molten metal solidified in the plaintiff's machines, which were physically damaged as a result. The plaintiff recovered damages in respect of the physical damage to the machines and in respect of the financial loss directly related to that damage—namely the loss of profit on the melt that was interrupted by the failure of the electrical supply. The power cut prevented the processing of four more melts, but

---

[111] 1996 SLT 263.
[112] [1987] 3 All ER 455.
[113] *Allan v Barclay* (1864) 2 M 873.
[114] 1972 SLT 38.
[115] [1970] 3 All ER 245.

the Court of Appeal ruled that loss of profit on those melts was not recoverable. If the power cut had stopped production without damaging the machines no recovery would have been possible. Where there is no "host" claim relating to recoverable physical loss to which a claim for economic loss can attach the latter will perish. Winn J noted: "Apart from the special case of imposition of liability for negligently uttered false statements, there is no liability for the unintentional negligent infliction of any form of economic loss which is not of itself consequential on foreseeable physical injury or damage to property."[116]

As discussed above, the principle established in *Hedley Byrne & Co Ltd* v *Heller & Partners Ltd*,[117] and its subsequent application in a variety of different contexts has breached the rule on the recoverability of pure economic loss. For a good example, see *Martin* v *Bell-Ingram*[118] where a negligent house survey caused substantial financial loss. In *White* v *Jones*[119] a solicitor delayed in carrying out a revision to a will and the testator died without signing the amended version. Beneficiaries of the intended revision sued the solicitor. The House of Lords upheld their claim on *Hedley Byrne* principles.[120] In this context it has also been held that an employer owes a duty of care to a former employee when giving a reference.[121]

In *Junior Books* v *Veitchi & Co*[122] the defenders were nominated subcontractors under a building contract concluded between the pursuers and Oglivie (Builders) Ltd (the main building contractors). The floor laid by the defenders proved to be defective and the pursuers sued in delict to recover damages for the financial loss incurred in relaying the floor. In what is probably the high water mark of *Hedley Byrne* derived jurisprudence, the House of Lords stated that a duty of care could arise where there was a relationship of sufficient *proximity* between the parties. *Inter alia*, this was indicated by the fact that: (1) the defenders were nominated subcontractors; (2) they were specialists in flooring; (3) they knew the pursuers were relying on their skill and experience; and (4) they must have known that if they did their work negligently the resulting defects would at some time need to be put right by the pursuers expending money on remedial measures which would entail the latter suffering economic loss. Lord Roskill held that the relationship between the parties was "almost as close a commercial relationship as it is possible to envisage short of privity of contract."[123]

In *Junior Books* the House of Lords attempted to formulate a general duty of care in respect of pure economic loss resulting from a negligent act. The ruling proved controversial. It was denounced by many commentators and has been sidelined by the English courts. *Junior Books* has, however, been followed in Scotland and should be considered significant authority within its narrow field of application.[124]

In *Anns* v *Merton London Borough Council*[125] a local authority was negligent in the discharge of its building control functions. Economic loss was suffered in the form of

---

[116] At 258.
[117] [1964] At 258. AC 465.
[118] 1986 SC 208.
[119] [1995] 2 WLR 187.
[120] Contrast *Weir* v *Hodge* 1990 SLT 266.
[121] *Spring* v *Guardian Assurance* [1994] 3 All ER 129.
[122] 1982 SC (HL) 244.
[123] At 277.
[124] See, *eg, Comex Houlder Diving Ltd* v *Colne Fishing Co Ltd (No 2)* 1992 SLT 89; *Scott Lithgow Ltd* v *GEC Electrical Products Ltd* 1992 SLT 244.
[125] [1978] AC 728.

the cost of remedying a dangerous defect in a building. It was held that the authority owed a duty of care to the owner and that the loss was recoverable. *Anns* was expressly overruled, however, in *Murphy v Brentwood District Council*,[126] where the local authority approved inadequate foundations for a house. The house was sold subject to the defect for approximately £35,000 less than its potential market value. The loss sustained was recognised as economic loss (no physical damage was suffered) and recoverability was denied on the basis that the authority owed no duty of care to the plaintiff when it approved the plans. Such loss is recoverable in contract but not in delict unless a special relationship of proximity can be established.

In *McFarlane v Tayside Health Board*,[127] as discussed, damages relating to the pain and suffering and associated costs of the unwanted pregnancy (including medical expenses, clothing and loss of earnings), were recoverable, but the costs of the child's upbringing were not recoverable because they amounted to pure economic loss. Lord Hope said:

> "For my part, I would regard these costs as reasonably foreseeable by the wrongdoer. But in the field of economic loss foreseeability is not the only criterion that must be satisfied. There must be a relationship of proximity between the negligence and the loss which is said to have been caused by it and the attachment of liability for the harm must be fair, just and reasonable. The mere fact that it was reasonably foreseeable that the pursuers would have to pay for the costs of rearing their child does not mean that they have incurred a loss of the kind which is recoverable."[128]

CAUSATION

FACTUAL CAUSATION

Proof of duty, breach and recoverable damage will be to no avail unless it can also be shown that the defender's conduct is the factual cause of the pursuer's loss or injury. It is necessary to ask whether the pursuer's injury would have occurred notwithstanding the defender's breach. This is known as the "but for" test and it is for the pursuer to discharge. The question is: would the same damage have been incurred but for the defender's conduct? If the answer is yes, the defender's conduct cannot be deemed a factual cause of the pursuer's injury. If the answer is no, however, the breach will be treated as causal and may sustain a delictual claim against the defender. **5–34**

Barnett v Chelsea & Kensington Hospital Management Committee[129] provides a graphic illustration of the importance of causation. In this case, a nightwatchman attended the casualty department of the defendant's hospital in the early hours of the morning. He spoke to the duty nurse, complaining of vomiting and stomach pain. She consulted a doctor by telephone and he advised the nurse to tell the man to go home and consult his own doctor later in the morning if his symptons persisted. A few hours later the man died of arsenic poisoning. It was held that the doctor's conduct was negligent. In

---

[126] [1990] 2 All ER 908.
[127] 2000 SLT 154.
[128] At 172.
[129] [1969] 1 QB 428.

choosing to triage the patient over the telephone rather than in person the doctor put himself in breach of his duty of care. Again, however, this breach was not deemed to be the active *cause* of death. Evidence was adduced which indicated that the man had imbibed so much arsenic that he was beyond medical assistance by the time he presented at hospital. Even if the man had been examined and treated with all proper care, the great probability was that he would still have died. As in *Kay's Tutor* (discussed above),[130] *damnum* and *injuria* were conspicuous on the facts, but because the doctor's negligence did not *cause* the death, the hospital was found not liable.

LEGAL CAUSATION: *NOVUS ACTUS INTERVENIENS*

5–35 Occasionally, more than one wrongful act or omission will play a part in the sequence of events leading to the loss or injury suffered by the pursuer. If the question of causation is confused by the co-existence of different causal factors it is necessary to isolate the particular act or omission that constitutes the immediate or most direct cause of the harm sustained. This may be regarded as the legal cause of the damage. Delictual liability can be imposed on a wrongdoer only if the chain of causation linking the *damnum* to his *injuria* consists solely of natural and foreseeable consequences of the wrongdoer's breach of duty. Where this causal chain is unforeseeably broken by some new intervening factor (*novus actus interveniens*) the party responsible for the original *injuria* may ultimately avoid liability. To break the chain the *novus actus* must be something outwith the course of things that would ordinarily and naturally be expected to flow from the original act. The test to be applied is that of reasonable foreseeability. Broadly speaking, there are three forms of *novus actus*:

Where the event consists of an act or omission of a third party

5–36 *Wright* v *Lodge*[131] concerned the attribution of liability after a complex traffic accident. When the first defendant's car broke down she negligently failed to take action to remove it from the highway. The car carried three passengers: P1, P2 and P3. The second defendant's lorry then collided with the car, injuring P1 and knocking the car into the opposite carriageway. P2 and P3 were then injured by a collision with a lorry travelling on that carriageway. The court found the first defendant liable for the injury sustained by P1, which was a direct result of her negligence, but not for the injuries suffered by P2 and P3. The direct cause of the injuries sustained by P2 and P3 was the negligent driving of the second defendant. This constituted a *novus actus*, unforeseeably breaking the chain of causation between the first defendant's negligence and the injury suffered by P2 and P3.

Where the event consists of an act or omission of the pursuer

5–37 In *McKew* v *Holland, Hannen & Cubitts (Scotland) Ltd*,[132] the defenders negligently injured the pursuer's left leg. A short time after the accident the pursuer attempted to descend a steep flight of stairs without a handrail and without seeking assistance. Halfway down, his left leg gave way. In a precarious situation, the pursuer took it upon himself to leap to the foot of the stairs. In so doing, he severely injured his right

---

[130] 1987 SLT 577.
[131] [1993] 4 All ER 299.
[132] 1970 SC (HL) 20.

leg. The House of Lords held that the defenders were not liable for injuries to the pursuer's right leg because the pursuer's conduct, in deliberately and unreasonably putting himself in a dangerous situation, constituted a *novus actus*.[133] *Wieland* v *Cyril Lord Carpets Ltd*[134] provides a useful contrast. Again, in this case a previously injured plaintiff suffered new injuries after attempting to descend some steps. The plaintiff was required to wear a surgical collar as a result of her initial injury and, as in *McKew*, this restricted her ability to navigate the steps. The defendants, however, were held liable for the further injuries suffered because the court considered that it was reasonable for the plaintiff to have attempted to descend the steps in the circumstances. It is certainly foreseeable that an injury may restrict a victim's ability to cope with the ordinary vicissitudes of life.

On the occurrence of a natural event

Whereas a windy day in Perthshire is unlikely to break the chain of causation, the **5–38** onset of a tornado or hurricane may well qualify as a *novus actus*. A natural event will only constitute a *novus actus* if it is so rare and extreme in its context as to unforeseeably disturb the sequence of events that would ordinarily be expected to unfold from the original *injuria*.

REMOTENESS

Where all the other essential elements of negligence have been proved, the defender **5–39** may still avoid liability if the pursuer's injury is shown to be too remote from the defender's breach. In *Allan* v *Barclay*[135] Lord Kinloch explained that: "The grand rule on the subject of damages is that none can be claimed except such as to naturally and directly arise out of the wrong done; and such, therefore, as may reasonably be supposed to have been in the contemplation of the wrongdoer."[136]

Unfortunately, this statement, which underpins the modern Scottish authority on remoteness, harbours a fundamental contradiction. Although damages that arise *naturally and directly* from a wrong will usually also be *reasonably foreseeable* consequences of the wrong, this is by no means always the case. It is not unusual for a breach of duty to set in chain a sequence of events that, while directly associated *inter se*, ultimately result in injury or loss that is an entirely unforeseeable consequence of the original breach. The following tests have grown out of the jurisprudence on this matter.

THE *POLEMIS* TEST: DIRECT CONSEQUENCES

In *Re Polemis and Furness, Withy & Co Ltd*[137] stevedores inadvertently knocked a **5–40** timber board into the hold of a ship. The board struck an object and caused a

---

[133] See also *Cutler* v *United Dairies* [1933] 2 KB 297.
[134] [1969] 3 All ER 1006.
[135] (1864) 2 M 873.
[136] At 874.
[137] [1921] 3 KB 560.

spark which in turn ignited petrol vapour in the hold. This caused an explosion and a fire that destroyed the ship. The court acknowledged that the fire could not reasonably have been anticipated, but held that some damage to the vessel was foreseeable. Full damages were awarded on the grounds that the ultimate loss was deemed to be a *direct consequence* of the *foreseeable harm*. Scrutton LJ opined: "... once the act is negligent the fact that its exact operation was not foreseen is immaterial."[138] Bankes LJ took a similar line: "... the anticipations of the persons whose negligent act has produced the damage appear to me to be irrelevant."[139] The *Polemis* test took shape in the statement of Warrington LJ:

> "The presence or absence of reasonable anticipation of damage determines the legal quality of an act as negligent or innocent. If it be thus determined to be negligent, then the question whether the particular damages are recoverable depends only on the question whether they are the *direct consequence* of the act."[140]

In *Kelvin Shipping Co v Canadian Pacific Railway Co*[141] a collision occurred between two ships. The pursuer's ship was thereafter tied up at position X, but slipped its mooring and drifted to position Y. The ship was then moored at position Y, but again it was swept away by the tide. This time it sank in deep water. The defenders admitted responsibility for the initial damage but disputed liability for the loss of the ship. The House of Lords, however, permitted full recovery. Viscount Haldane said: "... the damage is recoverable ... if it is the natural and reasonable result of the negligent act, and it will assume this character if it can be shown to be such a consequence as in the ordinary course of things would flow from the situation which the offending ship has created."[142]

Although dressed in the clothes of a direct and natural consequences test and certainly held up as such in some quarters, Viscount Haldane's statement betrays the same apparent reluctance to disregard the concept of reasonableness that was exhibited by Lord Kinloch in *Allan*.[143]

THE *WAGON MOUND* TEST: REASONABLE FORESEEABILITY

5–41   In an unusually forthright judgment, the Privy Council unreservedly condemned *Polemis* in *Overseas Tankship (UK) Ltd v Morts Dock & Engineering Co Ltd (The Wagon Mound No 1)*.[144] The ship, *The Wagon Mound*, was taking on furnace oil when the appellants' servants negligently allowed oil to spill into the water. Wind and tide carried the oil some 200 yards to the respondent's wharf, where servants of the respondents were repairing a vessel using welding equipment. Experience indicated that welding sparks would not ignite the oil, so the work was allowed to continue. However, a piece of molten metal fell from the wharf and set on fire cotton waste floating on the oil, which

---

[138] At 577.
[139] At 572.
[140] At 574.
[141] 1928 SC (HL) 21.
[142] At 25.
[143] Discussed at para 5–39.
[144] [1961] AC 388.

in turn set the oil alight. The whole wharf was engulfed in flames and extensive damage was suffered.

Making plain its disapproval of *Polemis*, the Privy Council held that, on the question of remoteness of damage, foreseeability is the proper test. Whereas damage to the wharf by oil fouling may have been foreseeable, damage by fire was not, because oil on water (especially this particular type) does not usually ignite. The ignition of the oil occurred only because the metal fragment fell onto combustible waste, which, in the circumstances, was not a reasonably foreseeable event. Viscount Simonds said:

> "... if some limitation must be imposed upon the consequences for which the negligent actor is to be held responsible—and all are agreed that some limitation there must be— why should that test (reasonable foreseeability) be rejected which, since he is judged by what the reasonable man ought to foresee, corresponds with the common conscience of mankind, and a test (the 'direct' consequence test) be substituted which leads to nowhere but the never-ending and insoluble problems of causation."[145]

Cameron v Hamilton's Auction Marts Ltd[146] offers a memorable illustration of the range of this test. Cattle were being delivered to an auction when one cow, apparently in a "visibly excited condition", escaped into a public street. The animal took it upon itself to climb a stairway above the pursuer's shop. It then fell through the floor into the said shop, where in its panic it managed to turn on a tap, causing damage and flooding. Confronted by these facts Sheriff McKechnie QC stated: "*In re Polemis* is not part of the law of Scotland and is inconsistent with the settled principles of that law ... the pursuer must prove that what followed on the negligence averred against the auctioneers was a natural and probable result which was foreseeable by a reasonable man."[147]

If the cow had broken a window or knocked down a person in its bid for freedom, there would have been liability. Moreover, it is likely that the same result would have followed if the cow had entered a proximate building on the ground floor. Sheriff McKechnie, however, was not persuaded that a reasonable man would take account of the possibility that a cow might climb a staircase. Accordingly, liability was denied.

THE NATURE OF FORESEEABILITY

Where at least the *general* type of risk or injury is reasonably foreseeable it may not be **5–42** necessary to anticipate the *specific* nature of the injury or the particular sequence of events that led to it. *Hughes* v *Lord Advocate*[148] settled the issue. In this case, workers left paraffin lamps next to a manhole covered by a tarpaulin. Two boys exploring the site knocked one of the lamps over. This caused an explosion and one of the boys sustained burns and fell into the manhole. Although it was unforeseeable that an explosion would be caused, it was held that it was foreseeable that there was a risk of injury by fire in a general sense and liability was sustained. As Lord Reid put it: "This accident was caused by a known source of danger, but caused in a way which could

---

[145] At 423.
[146] 1955 SLT (Sh Ct) 74.
[147] At 78.
[148] 1963 SC (HL) 31.

not have been foreseen … in my judgment that affords no defence."[149] The law on this point is less clear in England, where prominent cases such as *Doughty* v *Turner Manufacturing Co Ltd*[150] in which a more restrictive approach was endorsed, are difficult to reconcile with *Hughes*.

EGGSHELL SKULL RULE

5–43   Regardless of whether *Polemis* or *Wagon Mound* is preferred, where a pursuer harbours a special sensitivity, which leads to an unforeseeably serious injury, the defender will typically be liable for the full extent of the injury. Known as the "eggshell" or "thin skull" rule, this maxim may apply to any form of weakness or predisposition and essentially dictates that a defender "must take his victim as he finds him". In *McKillen* v *Barclay Curle & Co Ltd*[151] the pursuer fractured a rib and this reactivated dormant tuberculosis. At first instance he recovered damages for both injuries, and on appeal the Inner House confirmed the award. The appellant argued that the reactivation of tuberculosis was not a foreseeable result of the accident. It was held, however, that the doctrine of foreseeability did not apply in the circumstances. Lord President Clyde said:

> "It has always been the law of Scotland … that once a man is negligent and injures another by his negligence he is liable for all damage to the injured man which naturally and directly arises out of the negligence. He must take his victim as he finds him, and if his victim has a weak heart and dies as a result of the injury the negligent man is liable in damages for his death even although a normal man might only in the same circumstances have sustained a relatively trivial injury."[152]

Remoteness: a summary

5–44   Whereas *Polemis* suggests that a defender is liable for all the direct consequences of his negligent behaviour, no matter how unpredictable, extreme or unusual, the *Wagon Mound* test provides that a defender is only responsible for consequences that could reasonably have been anticipated. While the former is based on pursuer-friendly causation, the latter is founded on foreseeability and in marginal cases may favour the defender. The English courts have more or less accepted the *Wagon Mound* test as standard, but in Scotland the position is less clear-cut.

The Scottish courts have oscillated between the two tests and, although a preference for a *Polemis*-style approach has emerged, the picture remains uncertain. The status quo is neatly depicted in *McKillen*,[153] where both tests were respectively dismissed and endorsed by different members of the panel. The majority view took the direct and natural line of Lord Kinloch's *dictum*, and this approach was also adopted by Lord Cameron in *Campbell* v *Moffat (Transport) Ltd*.[154] In *Caledonia North Sea Ltd* v *London Bridge Engineering Ltd*,[155] where the Inner House acknowledged the problem of

---

[149] At 40.
[150] [1964] 1 QB 518.
[151] 1967 SLT 41.
[152] At 42.
[153] 1967 SLT 41.
[154] 1992 SCLR 551.
[155] Inner House, 17th December 1999: http://www.scotcourts.gov.uk/index1.htm.

reconciling *Hughes*, which advocates a looser application of foreseeability, with *Wagon Mound*, it was held that *Hughes* was to be preferred in light of its binding status in Scotland.[156]

It is some consolation to note that outwith the academic realm the debate on remoteness is of little practical consequence. No matter which test is used, the result will generally be the same. In practice, the modern test for breach of duty, and thus base liability in negligence, is itself based on foreseeability and may therefore exclude harm of an unforeseeable nature that might otherwise qualify for recovery under a *Polemis*-style test.

DEFENCES

If all the essential elements of an action are established, a prima facie case can be laid **5–45** against the defender. However, this is only one side of the story. The defender may resort to any of a number of well-established defences.

CONTRIBUTORY NEGLIGENCE

Strictly speaking, it may be argued that a plea of contributory negligence constitutes a **5–46** plea in mitigation rather than a defence, but it is discussed in this context for the sake of convenience. This commonly raised plea involves an assertion that the pursuer has, through his own actions, contributed to the loss or injury suffered. A classic example of contributory negligence is failure to wear a car seat belt.[157] In simple terms, while some degree of responsibility is, by definition, acknowledged by the defender, a plea of contributory negligence maintains that the pursuer is, to a greater or lesser extent, the author of his own misfortune.

Section 1(1) of the Law Reform (Contributory Negligence) Act 1945 provides that:

> "Where any person suffers damage as the result partly of his own fault and partly of the fault of any other person or persons, a claim in respect of that damage shall not be defeated by reason of the fault of the person suffering the damage, but the damages recoverable in respect thereof shall be reduced to such extent as the court thinks just and equitable having regard to the claimant's share in the responsibility for the damage."

Consider the following scenario: a teenage warehouseman suffers a crushed hand when using a forklift truck at work. It transpires that he had not been properly trained to use the forklift and that he was unsupervised. This accident is likely to lead to a claim for damages, *inter alia* for negligence, against the employer. If the employer can adduce evidence suggesting that the pursuer in some way brought the accident on

---

[156] See also *Jolley v Sutton London Borough Council* [1998] 1 WLR 1546 at 1552, per Lord Woolf MR.
[157] See *Froom v Butcher* [1975] 3 All ER 520. Here, Lord Denning suggested that a deduction of 25% should be imposed if wearing a seat belt would have prevented the accident altogether and that damages should be reduced by 15% if the accident would have been made less severe. Since 1983 it has been a criminal offence not to wear a seat belt and the courts may therefore reduce damages still further for failure to wear a seat belt today.

himself, the former may raise a plea of contributory negligence. The court may decide that in all the circumstances, and in the absence of contributory negligence, an award of £10,000 in damages would be appropriate. If the employer is able to argue that the employee was grossly reckless in his behaviour, a substantial deduction of 50 per cent may be obtained. This would result in an award to the worker of £5,000. However, if the employer has evidence of only fairly trivial negligence on the part of the pursuer the court might restrict itself to a nominal reduction of 10 per cent, leaving the worker with £9,000.

The onus is on the defender to raise and prove the issue of contributory negligence. The court will not consider the matter unless called upon to do so. In the event of a well-founded plea, fault is allocated between the parties in proportion to their share of responsibility. The method of apportionment is entirely within the court's discretion and turns on the facts of each case. Contributory negligence is always assessed as a percentage or fraction, and the court will usually settle on a round figure (eg 20%, 25%, 33%, 50%). A 10 per cent reduction is the *de facto* minimum; anything less is usually discounted.[158] It is possible to allocate up to 99 per cent of the blame to either party, but a finding of 100 per cent responsibility would seem to contradict the 1945 Act, which anticipates that the parties will "share in the responsibility" for the damage suffered.

In *Taylor* v *Leslie*[159] the defender drove a car while unlicensed, uninsured and underage. An accident occurred and a passenger in the car was killed. However, on hearing evidence that the deceased had actively encouraged the defender to speed, the court was moved to reduce the damages awarded by 50 per cent. In *Sayers* v *Harlow Urban District Council*[160] S became trapped in a cubicle in a public toilet due to a defective lock. Her calls for help went unanswered so she attempted to escape by climbing out of the cubicle. In so doing she stood on the toilet roll holder, which, unfortunately, almost immediately gave way. She suffered injury and sued the local authority responsible for the toilet. Her own negligence, in choosing a dangerous means of escape, prompted the court to reduce her damages by 25 per cent.

VOLENTI NON FIT INJURIA

5–47 The literal translation of this maxim is "no wrong is done to him who consents". In simple terms, where a person knowingly and voluntarily accepts the risk of an injury, he cannot later expect to be awarded damages if the injury occurs. In *Titchener* v *British Railways Board*[161] a girl intent on a liaison with her boyfriend was able to gain access to a railway line through a hole in a fence for which the defender was responsible. She was injured by a train as she crossed the line. The House of Lords held that no duty of care was owed to the girl. However, the Lords indicated that if such a duty had existed, *volenti* would have been applicable.

In practice, the doctrine of *volenti* is rarely invoked today, at least in comparison with the popular defence of contributory negligence. Furthermore, *volenti* is a pregnable and fragile defence. It is necessary to prove that the pursuer had full knowledge of the risk, that his consent to the risk was freely and voluntarily obtained

---

[158] That said, very occasionally a 5% deduction is imposed in special cases.
[159] 1998 SLT 1248.
[160] [1958] 2 All ER 342.
[161] 1984 SC (HL) 34.

and that the risk was *not* taken for the benefit of another party. These points are underlined in the following case law.

In *Merrington* v *Iron Bridge Metal Works*[162] a fireman suffered injury caused by an explosion in a building. The defence of *volenti* failed because, on choosing to enter the building, the fireman had been unaware of the presence of explosive dust inside. Risk cannot be accepted voluntarily where a person has no knowledge of it. A similar point was made in *Olsen* v *Corry and Gravesend Aviation Ltd*[163] where an inexperienced, apprentice engineer was injured due to a negligent system of starting aircraft engines. It was held that an apprentice could neither appreciate nor have full knowledge of the risk entailed in the operation and a submission based on *volenti* was rejected *in limine*.[164]

In *Neil* v *Harland & Wolff*[165] an employee, this time in full knowledge of the risk he was taking, worked on live wires to prevent the loss of power to a factory. He was electrocuted. This time *volenti* was rejected because, although the employee had knowingly taken the risk, he had done so for his employer's benefit.

Similarly, this defence does not apply in the case of a rescuer who deliberately exposes himself to risk in order to protect the life or property of another. In *Baker* v *TE Hopkins and Son Ltd*[166] a doctor allowed himself to be lowered into a well containing poisonous gases to give assistance to men who had been overcome by the fumes. Unfortunately, the doctor became trapped inside and died. The court held that the doctor had been motivated by the best of intentions and the defence of *volenti* did not bar the claim of his executors. It is useful to contrast *Baker* with *Cutler* v *United Dairies (London) Ltd*[167] where *volenti* was deemed applicable in the case of an attempt to restrain a horse that was posing no real or urgent danger.

In *Bowater* v *Rowley Regis Corporation*[168] an employee was injured by a horse that his employer had ordered him to approach. *Volenti* failed because the employee had only consented because he was in fear of losing his job. For *volenti* to succeed, consent, be it express or implied, must be freely given.

DAMNUM FATALE

A *damnum fatale*, or "Act of God" is some extraordinary happening or unusual accident **5–48** caused by exceptional and unforeseeable natural forces beyond the control of man. A *damnum fatale* offers a complete, albeit fairly narrowly construed, defence against liability. An ordinary natural episode such as a windy day or a rainstorm in Scotland, will not count as a *damnum fatale*. Such events are (entirely) foreseeable and the court will expect precautions to be taken to guard against them. Thus, in *Caledonian Railway* v *Greenock Corporation*[169] rainfall that surpassed previously recorded levels in Greenock did not qualify as a *damnum fatale*. The downpour, which caused flooding that damaged a railway, by no means reached levels unprecedented in Scotland.

---

[162] [1952] 2 All ER 1101.
[163] [1936] 3 All ER 241.
[164] "at the outset of the argument".
[165] (1949) Ll L Rep 515.
[166] [1959] 3 All ER 966.
[167] [1933] 2 KB 297. See also *Sylvester* v *Chapman Ltd* (1935) 79 SJ 777.
[168] [1944] KB 476.
[169] 1917 SC (HL) 56.

Likewise, in *Kerr* v *Earl of Orkney*[170] a newly built dam collapsed after several days of heavy rain. Finding fault in the construction of the dam, the court indicated that a defence of *damnum fatale* would require evidence of an earthquake or something similarly exceptional in the circumstances. Again, a period of heavy rain would not suffice.

BREACH OF STATUTORY DUTY

5–49   The normal sanction for breach of a duty imposed by statute or regulation is criminal liability. However, where breach of statutory duty results in injury to another person, the injured party may in some circumstances have a civil claim in delict. Establishing civil liability for breach of statutory duty can be a somewhat technical exercise and attention to detail is essential. The following conditions must be fulfilled in order to found an action: the breach of duty must give rise to civil liability; the statute or regulation must apply; the duty must be imposed either directly or vicariously on the defender; the duty must be owed to the pursuer; the defender must be in breach of duty; the pursuer must suffer damage; the damage suffered must be of a kind, and inflicted in a way, that the duty was designed to prevent; and the breach must cause the damage.

THE BREACH OF DUTY MUST GIVE RISE TO CIVIL LIABILITY

5–50   At the outset it is necessary to confirm that the breach of the duty actually gives rise to civil liability. Sometimes the Act or regulation in question, in particular modern legislation, gives express guidance on this matter and it is an easy exercise. For example, the Management of Health and Safety at Work Regulations 1992[171] and the Health and Safety at Work etc Act 1974[172] clearly exclude a right of action in civil proceedings. On the other hand, the Sex Discrimination Act 1975,[173] the Race Relations Act 1976[174] and the Consumer Protection Act 1987[175] expressly confer remedies for breach of statutory duty. If the legislation is silent, it is for the court to determine the matter by taking account of the purpose, construction and wording of the provision, and the safety net provided by existing common law remedies.

THE STATUTE OR REGULATION MUST APPLY

5–51   In contrast to delictual duties, which are typically malleable and often susceptible to expansive interpretation and purposive application, statutory duties are highly specific in scope and narrowly construed in application. It is necessary to fit a claim *precisely* within the ambit of a statutory duty in order to ground an action.

---

[170] (1857) 20 D 298.
[171] SI 1992/2051, reg 15.
[172] s 47.
[173] s 66.
[174] s 57.
[175] s 41.

THE DUTY MUST BE IMPOSED EITHER DIRECTLY OR VICARIOUSLY ON THE DEFENDER

It is necessary to ascertain from the legislation that the duty in question is actually **5–52** imposed on the defender. Different duties may be imposed on different parties. For example, the Health and Safety at Work etc Act 1974 imposes duties respectively on employers, employees, the self-employed, manufacturers, importers and suppliers.

THE DUTY MUST BE OWED TO THE PURSUER

Where this is not expressly stated, and it usually *is* in modern legislation, it is a matter **5–53** of construction for the court. Generally speaking, a duty will be owed only to that class of person that the statute or regulation is designed to protect.[176] In *Knapp* v *Railway Executive*[177] an engine driver was injured as the consequence of a breach of statutory duty concerning the maintenance of level crossing gates. However, it was held that the purpose of the statutory duty was to protect road users *not* engine drivers and his claim failed. Similarly, in *Hartley* v *Mayoh & Co*[178] a fireman was electrocuted while fighting a fire at the defendant's factory. His widow sued for breach of statutory duty but the action was unsuccessful. The regulations in question existed only for the protection of persons *employed* at the factory.

THE DEFENDER MUST BE IN BREACH OF DUTY

It is important to remember that statutory duties lack the flexibility of delictual duties. **5–54** In this context the defender will be in breach if he has failed to do *exactly* what was required or if he has done *exactly* what he was prohibited from doing.

THE PURSUER MUST SUFFER DAMAGE

Generally speaking, the damage suffered by the pursuer must amount to personal **5–55** injury or death. Property damage is rarely recoverable under a claim for breach of statutory duty.

THE DAMAGE SUFFERED MUST BE OF A KIND, AND INFLICTED IN A WAY THAT, THE DUTY WAS DESIGNED TO PREVENT

In *Carroll* v *Andrew Barclay and Sons Ltd*[179] a worker was injured when a belt flew out **5–56** of an unfenced part of a machine and hit him on the head. The Factories Act 1937 stipulated that every part of the machine in question should be securely fenced. The court held, however, that the employer was not in breach of the duty: the purpose of the regulation was to keep the worker *out*, not to keep the machine *in*. Although it seems difficult to marry this decision with common sense, *Carroll* was endorsed in the similar *Close* v *Steel Co of Wales*.[180]

---

[176] See *McMullan* v *Lochgelly Iron and Coal Co* 1933 SC (HL) 64.
[177] [1949] 2 All ER 508.
[178] [1954] 1 QB 383.
[179] 1948 SC (HL) 100.
[180] [1962] AC 367.

Gorris v *Scott*[181] offers another graphic illustration of the application of this rule. Here, statutory duties required that animals be fenced-in during transportation on the deck of a ship. The defendant did not supply the required pens and when a storm blew up, sheep belonging to the plaintiff were swept overboard. Understandably perhaps, the plaintiff sued for damages from the defendant for breach of the duty. However, it was held that the plaintiff could not recover for his loss under this particular claim because the object of the duty was to prevent the spread of disease, *not* to prevent animals from being drowned.

THE BREACH MUST CAUSE THE DAMAGE

5–57   As in the case of an ordinary claim in negligence, causation is established by applying the "but for" test. A defender *may* defeat a claim if he can show that the pursuer would have suffered the injury complained of regardless of whether the defender had fulfilled his statutory duty. In *McWilliams* v *Sir William Arrol & Co*[182] there was a statutory duty to provide steel erectors with safety harnesses, but no harnesses were provided. One worker fell to his death. When the matter came to court the defender was able to establish that it was common practice for steel erectors to refuse to wear harnesses and that the deceased, in particular, had never worn a harness in the past. As a consequence, the defender avoided liability.

DEFENCES TO AN ACTION FOR BREACH OF STATUTORY DUTY

5–58   Where the facts of a case permit, the most reliable defence to a claim for breach of statutory duty is contributory negligence. *Volenti* is not normally applicable in this context. In *Wheeler* v *New Merton Board Mills Ltd*[183] a boy employed to clean the blades of a machine chose to do so while the machine was in operation in breach of a statutory duty. After several months of good fortune, his hand was severed. The court held that the boy's claim was *not* defeated by a submission based on the *volenti*. If Parliament had intended to make the defence available it would have been an easy matter to make express provision in the legislation.

---

[181] (1874) LR 9 Ex 125.
[182] 1962 SC (HL) 70.
[183] [1933] 2 KB 669.

SUMMARY

THE NATURE OF DELICTUAL LIABILITY

- Delictual liability arises where injury is suffered as a result of a legal wrong (*damnum injuria datum*).

CAUSATION

- It is important to show a causal connection between the wrong committed (*injuria*) and injury suffered (*damnum*).
- If the chain of causation between the *injuria* and the ultimate *damnum* is broken by a new intervening act the party responsible for the original wrong may avoid liability.

MODES OF DELICTUAL LIABILITY

- Generally, liability in delict is imposed only on the wrongdoer. Where two or more persons are responsible for the wrong (*injuria*) each can be held jointly and severally liable. One person may also be responsible for the acts of another (vicarious liability)—typically, an employer may be held liable for the wrongs of his employees.

VICARIOUS LIABILITY

- To establish the vicarious liability of an employer it is necessary to prove that (a) the wrongdoer has committed a delict; (b) he is an employee of the employer; and (c) that the delict was committed in the course of the wrongdoer's employment.

NEGLIGENCE

- To ground an action in negligence it is necessary to establish (a) duty of care; (b) breach of that duty; and (c) damage. Moreover, it is necessary to prove that the breach caused the damage and that the damage is not deemed remote in the circumstances.

DUTY OF CARE

- The duty of care in negligence is defined by the neighbour principle. You must take reasonable care to avoid acts or omissions which you can reasonably foresee would be likely to injure your neighbour—namely, persons who are so closely and directly affected by your act that you ought reasonably to have them in contemplation.

THE STANDARD OF CARE

- In order to discharge a duty of care the defender must measure up to the standard of care expected of the hypothetical "reasonable man".
- Where a person holds himself out as a professional or as having any special skill he will be judged not by the standard of the reasonable man but by the higher and more exacting standard of the reasonably competent professional in that field or exponent of that particular skill.

THE CALCULUS OF RISK

- In order to identify breach of a duty of care a court may weigh the likelihood of an accident happening, the magnitude of the risk, and the possible seriousness of the consequences if an accident does happen, against the difficulty, expense and any other disadvantage of taking precautions.

RES IPSA LOQUITUR

- Sometimes the very occurrence of an accident may suggest negligence on the part of the defender (*res ipsa loquitur*). In such circumstances it is for the defender to disprove negligence, not for the pursuer to prove it.

DAMAGE

- It is possible to recover damages for psychiatric as well as physical injury. In nervous shock cases it is necessary to distinguish between primary shock victims, who also sustain physical injury or are in some other way directly involved in the accident, and secondary shock victims, who are affected either as a consequence of witnessing the accident or out of concern for the safety of another.
- The courts have traditionally been reluctant to hold that a duty of care exists where negligent conduct causes pure economic loss (*ie* financial loss not consequential upon physical injury or property damage). Such loss is recoverable in contract but not in delict unless a special relationship of proximity can be established.

CAUSATION

- On the issue of causation, the key question is: would the same damage have been incurred but for the defender's conduct?

NOVUS ACTUS INTERVENIENS

- Where the causal chain is unforeseeably broken by some new intervening factor (*novus actus interveniens*) the party responsible for the original *injuria* may ultimately avoid liability. To break the chain the *novus actus* must be something outwith the course of things that would ordinarily and naturally be expected to flow from the original act.

REMOTENESS

- Where all the other essential elements of negligence have been proved, the defender may still avoid liability if the pursuer's injury is shown to be too remote from the defender's breach.
- There are two main tests: *Polemis* (direct and natural consequences) and *Wagon Mound* (on reasonable foreseeability). The English courts have adopted *Wagon Mound* but *Polemis* seems to be preferred in Scotland. The matter is not settled.

EGGSHELL SKULL RULES

- Where a pursuer suffers some special weakness, the defender "must take him as he finds him", and may be liable for the full extent of the injury ultimately suffered. This is known as the "eggshell skull" rule.

DEFENCES

- Once liability is established it is necessary to consider whether a defence is available to the defender. Important defences include contributory negligence and *volenti non fit injuria*.

CONTRIBUTORY NEGLIGENCE

- A plea of contributory negligence amounts to an assertion that the pursuer contributed to the loss or injury sustained by his own actions.

VOLENTI NON FIT INJURIA

- *Volenti non fit injuria* operates to provide a defence to a claim for loss, the risk of which was voluntarily undertaken by the pursuer.

BREACH OF STATUTORY DUTY

- A claim for breach of statutory duty may be made where an applicable duty establishes civil liability between the parties, the damage suffered is of a kind contemplated by the legislation and a causal link between the breach and the damage can be established.

CASE DIGEST

Damnum [see para 5–03]
McFarlane v Tayside Health Board 2000 SLT 154
A husband and wife sought damages from a health board alleging that after the husband's vasectomy they were given negligent advice that they could safely

resume sexual intercourse without contraceptive precautions. The wife became pregnant and after a normal pregnancy gave birth to a healthy child. The question as to whether pregnancy, childbirth and the costs of rearing the child constituted recoverable loss was central to the case. It was held that the wife was entitled to *solatium* for the pain and suffering associated with pregnancy and childbirth because they were physical consequences arising from negligence, and that the claim should extend to the costs of medical expenses, clothing and loss of earnings due to pregnancy and birth. However, the costs of the child's upbringing were not recoverable because the issue was one of pure economic loss and it was not fair, just and reasonable to impose such liability on the defenders in the circumstances

Causation [see paras 5–05, 5–34]

Kay's Tutor v Ayrshire & Arran Health Board 1987 SLT 577

A child suffering from meningitis was negligently given an overdose of penicillin. On recovery the child was found to be deaf. However, the assertion that the overdose had damaged the child's hearing was rejected. Whereas meningitis itself is a recognised and common cause of deafness, the pursuer was unable to point to a single case in which penicillin in any dosage has been found to cause such an injury. Although *damnum* and *injuria* are conspicuous on the facts, the court was compelled to dismiss the action in the absence of any causal link between the two.

Vicarious liability: course of employment [see para 5–14]

Kirby v NCB 1958 SC 514

An explosion injured several miners when one of their number lit a cigarette, contrary to regulation, during a break. It was held that the wrongdoer was acting outwith the course of his employment and no vicarious liability was found. In his judgment, Lord President Clyde offered the following guidance:

> "In the first place, if the master actually authorised the particular act, he is clearly liable for it. Secondly, where the workman does some work he is appointed to do, but does it in a way which his master has not authorised and would not have authorised had he known of it, the master is nevertheless still responsible, for the servant's act is still within the scope of his employment. On the other hand, in the third place, if the servant is employed only to do a particular work or a particular class of work, and he does something outside the scope of that work, the master is not responsible for any mischief the servant may do to a third party. Lastly, if the servant uses his master's time or his master's tools for his own purposes, the master is not responsible."

Negligence [see para 5–15]

Blyth v Birmingham Waterworks Co Ltd (1856) 11 Ex 781

"Negligence is the omission to do something which a reasonable man, guided upon those considerations which ordinarily regulate the conduct of human affairs, would do, or doing something which a prudent and reasonable man would not do." (per Baron Alderson at 784)

Duty of care [see para 5–16]

Donoghue v *Stevenson* 1932 SC (HL) 31

"The rule that you are to love your neighbour becomes in law, you must not injure your neighbour; and the lawyer's question, Who is my neighbour? receives a restricted reply. You must take reasonable care to avoid acts or omissions which you can reasonably foresee would be likely to injure your neighbour. Who, then in law is my neighbour? The answer seems to be—persons who are so closely and directly affected by my act that I ought reasonably to have them in contemplation as being so affected when I am directing my mind to the acts or omissions which are called into question." (per Lord Atkin at 44).

Duty of care [see para 5–17]

Caparo Industries plc v *Dickman* [1990] 2 AC 605

"What emerges is that, in addition to the foreseeability of damage, necessary ingredients in any situation giving rise to a duty of care are that there should exist between the party owing the duty and the party to whom it is owed a relationship characterised by the law as one of "proximity" or "neighbourhood" and that the situation should be one in which the court considers it fair, just and reasonable that the law should impose a duty of a given scope upon the one party for the benefit of the other." (per Lord Bridge at 573).

Duty of care [see para 5–17]

Gibson v *Orr* 1999 SC 420

Floodwater in the River Kelvin caused the Gavell Bridge to collapse. Police officers were directed to the north side of the bridge, which they promptly coned off. The officers proceeded to position their Land Rover vehicle on the north side with its blue light flashing and its headlights illuminated so as to be visible and to give warning to any persons approaching the south side of the bridge. Some time later, and before they had received confirmation that any barrier or warning was in place on the south side of the bridge, the constables withdrew their vehicle. Within a few minutes of their departure, the car in which the pursuer was travelling made its approach from the still unmarked south side and fell into the river. The pursuer suffered injury and sued the police. Rejecting the traditional approach laid down by Lord Atkin in *Donoghue*, Lord Hamilton ruled that the tripartite test expounded in *Caparo Industries plc* v *Dickman* [1990] 2 AC 605 fell to be applied in Scotland in personal injuries actions based on a duty of care as well as in other actions of damages so based.

Negligent misstatement [see para 5–18]

Hedley Byrne & Co Ltd v *Heller & Partners Ltd* [1964] AC 465

Hedley Byrne wanted to ascertain the creditworthiness of a client called Easipower and approached Heller, Easipower's bankers, for a reference. In reply, Heller stated that Easipower was creditworthy, but added a disclaimer to the effect that this statement was made without responsibility on their part. Subsequently, Easipower went into liquidation and Hedley Byrne sued Heller. The action failed due to the disclaimer, but the House of Lords held that, in principle, liability in negligence may extend to negligent misstatement. Lord Reid stipulated that such liability would only arise where there was a "special relationship" between the parties. He explained that a special relationship would exist:

> "where it is plain that the party seeking the information or advice was trusting the other to exercise such a degree of care as the circumstances required, where it was reasonable for him to do that, and where the other gave the information or advice when he knew or ought to have known that the enquirer was relying on him." (At 486.)

Res ipsa loquitur [see para 5–28]
Devine v *Colvilles* 1969 SC (HL) 67

A workman was injured after an explosion in a factory. There was no direct evidence of the cause of the explosion, which had originated in an oxygen hose, but the defenders were unable to establish that the explosion could have been caused without negligence on their part. The House of Lords held the defenders liable on the basis that they were at the material time in full control of the hose and that in the ordinary course of things, with proper care and maintenance, hoses do not usually explode.

Nervous shocks [see paras 5–30, 5–32]
Alcock et al v *Chief Constable of South Yorkshire Police* [1991] 4 All ER 907

The House of Lords held that a wrongdoer will owe a duty of care to a secondary victim of nervous shock only if:

(a) there is a tie of love and affection between the secondary victim and the primary victim such that it is reasonably foreseeable that the former will suffer nervous shock;

(b) the secondary victim was present at the accident or in its immediate aftermath; and

(c) nervous shock was suffered as a consequence of the secondary victim's perception of the accident with his own unaided senses (*ie* he personally heard or saw the accident).

Economic loss [see para 5–33]
Murphy v *Brentwood District Council* [1990] 2 All ER 908

A local authority approved inadequate foundations for a house. The house was sold subject to the defect for approximately £35,000 less than its potential market value. The loss sustained was recognised as economic loss (no physical damage was suffered) and recoverability was denied on the basis that the authority owed no duty of care to the plaintiff when it approved the plans. Such loss is recoverable in contract but not in delict unless a special relationship of proximity can be established.

Remoteness of damage: direct consequences [see para 5–40]
In Re Polemis and Furness, Withy & Co Ltd [1921] 3 KB 560

Stevedores inadvertently knocked a timber board into the hold of a ship. The board struck an object and caused a spark which in turn ignited petrol vapour in the hold. This caused an explosion and a fire that destroyed the ship. The court acknowledged that the fire could not reasonably have been anticipated, but held that some damage to the vessel was foreseeable. Full damages were awarded on the grounds that the ultimate loss was deemed to be a *direct consequence* of the *foreseeable harm*.

Remoteness of damage: foreseeability [see para 5–41]

Overseas Tankship (UK) Ltd v Morts Dock & Engineering Co Ltd (Wagon Mound No 1) [1961] AC 388

The ship, *The Wagon Mound*, was taking on furnace oil when the appellants' servants negligently allowed oil to spill into the water. Wind and tide carried the oil some 200 yards to the respondent's wharf, where servants of the respondents were repairing a vessel using welding equipment. Experience indicated that welding sparks would not ignite the oil, so the work was allowed to continue. However, a piece of molten metal fell from the wharf and set on fire cotton waste floating on the oil, which in turn set the oil alight. The whole wharf was engulfed in flames and extensive damage was suffered. Making plain its disapproval of *Polemis*, the Privy Council held that, on the question of remoteness of damage, foreseeability is the proper test. Whereas damage to the wharf by oil fouling may have been foreseeable, damage by fire was not, because oil on water (especially this particular type) does not usually ignite. The ignition of the oil only occurred because the metal fragment fell onto combustible waste, which, in the circumstances, was not a reasonably foreseeable event.

Contributory negligence [see para 5–46]

Sayers v Harlow Urban District Council [1958] 2 All ER 342

S became trapped in a cubicle in a public toilet due to a defective lock. Her calls for help went unanswered so she attempted to escape by climbing out of the cubicle. In so doing she stood on the toilet roll holder, which almost immediately gave way. She suffered injury and sued the local authority responsible for the toilet. Her own negligence, in choosing a dangerous means of escape, prompted the court to reduce her damages by 25 per cent.

Volenti non fit injuria [see para 5–47]

Merrington v Iron Bridge Metal Works [1952] 2 All ER 1101

A fireman suffered injury caused by an explosion in a building. The defence of *volenti* failed because, on choosing to enter the building, the fireman had been unaware of the presence of explosive dust inside. Risk cannot be accepted voluntarily where a person has no knowledge of it.

Breach of statutory duty [see para 5–57]

McWilliams v Sir William Arrol & Co 1962 SC (HL) 70

There was a statutory duty to provide steel erectors with safety harnesses, but no harnesses were provided. One worker fell to his death. When the matter came to court the defender was able to establish that it was common practice for steel erectors to refuse to wear harnesses and that the deceased, in particular, had never worn a harness in the past. Consequently, the defender avoided liability.

FURTHER READING

Field and Gordon *Elements of Scots Law* (2nd edn, W Green, 1997)
Gloag and Henderson, *The Law of Scotland* (10th edn, W Green, 1995)
McManus and Russell *Delict* (John Wiley & Sons, 1998)
Stewart *A Casebook on Delict* (2nd edn, W Green, 1997)
Stewart *Delict* (3rd edn, W Green, 1998)
Thomson *Delictual Liability* (2nd edn, Butterworths, 1999)
Walker *The Law of Delict in Scotland* (2nd edn, W Green 1993)
Willett and ODonnell *Scottish Business Law* (2nd edn, Blackstone Press, 1996)

6

AGENCY

THE DEFINITION AND NATURE OF AGENCY

Agency is a contractual relationship whereby a party engages someone to act on their **6–01** behalf in transactions with a third party. The person engaged is known as an "agent". The person on whose behalf the agent acts is known as the "principal". The relationship of agency arises in three main areas—commercial transactions, partnership and employment. In some situations, although the terms "agent" and "agency" are not specifically referred to, the law of agency does apply. Certain persons, by the nature of their position, are deemed to be agents. For example, a company director is considered to be an agent of the company of which he is a director, and partners are agents of the partnership, despite the fact that these persons do not refer to themselves as "agents". In other situations, the courts will assess the facts and decide whether the agent/principal relationship truly exists, irrespective of the fact that the parties have given their relationship that name.[1]

CATEGORIES AND TYPES OF AGENT

"GENERAL" AGENTS AND "SPECIAL" AGENTS

One of the primary distinctions in categorising agents is to differentiate "general" **6–02** agents from "special" agents. It has been suggested that a "general" agent:

> "is one who has authority to do some act in the ordinary course of his trade, business or profession, as agent on behalf of his principal, or to act for his principal in all matters or in all matters of a particular trade or business or of a particular nature."[2]

Examples of general agents include company directors, partners and solicitors.

In contrast, the "special" agent is one who is appointed for a particular transaction and whose authority is restricted to that transaction. The implicit feature of special agency is that it is not a continuing relationship. It may well be that the special agent is

---

[1] See, for example, *Powdrill v Murrayhead Ltd* 1997 SLT 1223. See also *Powell v Lloyds Bowmaker Ltd* 1996 SLT (Sh Ct) 117.
[2] Fridman, *The Law of Agency* (6th edn, 1990), p 33.

engaged in a transaction which does not fall within the ordinary course of his business. In theory, third parties dealing with general agents can assume that the agent has the authority ordinarily vested in agents in that particular profession.[3] Third parties dealing with special agents are expected to satisfy themselves as to the authority of the agent.

MERCANTILE AGENTS

6–03 Section 1(1) of the Factors Act 1889[4] states that:

> "the expression 'mercantile agent' shall mean a mercantile agent having in the customary course of business as such agent authority either to sell goods, or to consign goods for the purpose of sale, or to buy goods, or to raise money on the security of goods."

In Scotland, the classification of mercantile agents is further split into brokers and factors.[5] The latter term is not one in common usage in modern commercial parlance in Scotland. It is important to note that the "factor" in its commercial sense is not to be confused with housing or estate factors.

While both a "broker" and a "factor" have as their primary purpose the buying and selling of goods for the principal, the factor is differentiated by the fact that he will be in possession of the principal's goods, and that he normally sells the goods in his own name. The broker, on the other hand, is a mercantile agent who will neither have possession of the goods nor the authority to sell in his own name. In this sense, the broker, much more so than the factor, is a "facilitator" rather than a "primary party".[6] An example of a factor is an auctioneer, while an example of a broker might be an insurance broker, or a stockbroker. Because he does not have possession of the principal's goods the broker does not have a right of lien (right of retention).[7]

Before the mercantile agent can pass possession of the principal's property to a third party he must have either possession of the goods, or documents of title, which he must have acquired in his capacity as a mercantile agent.[8] Moreover, the goods or documents must be in the possession of the mercantile agent with the consent of the owner (the principal).[9]

DEL CREDERE AGENTS

6–04 A "del credere" agent is a mercantile agent who provides the principal with the promise of indemnity if the third party fails to fulfil his obligation to pay the principal. Where, in the course of the agency, goods are supplied for resale, the true relationship may not be that of del credere agency but one simply of sale and return.[10] Given the nature of his undertaking, the del credere agent usually receives a higher commission than would otherwise be the norm. In seeking fulfilment of the obligation to pay, the principal must

---

[3] *Morrison v Statter* (1885) 12 R 1152, per Lord Young at 1154. See para 6–18.
[4] Made applicable to Scotland by the Factors (Scotland) Act 1890.
[5] For the distinction see Lord President Inglis in *Cunningham v Lee* (1874) 2 R 83 at 87.
[6] Stone, *Law of Agency* (1996), p 13.
[7] See para 6–30 for the factor's right of lien see *Glendinning v Hope* 1911 SC (HL) 73.
[8] *Staffs Motor Guarantee Ltd v British Wagon Co Ltd* [1934] 2 KB 305.
[9] *Pearson v Rose and Young Ltd* [1951] 1 KB 275.
[10] *Michelin Tyre Co v Macfarlane* 1917 2 SLT 205 (HL).

look first to the third party. The agent, if he is acting for a disclosed principal, is not a party to the contract and cannot be sued under it. Moreover, all that the del credere agent underwrites is the third party's failure to pay the principal and not in relation to other obligations under the contract. For example, the del credere agent does not warrant to the principal the quality or nature of the third party's performance.[11]

COMMERCIAL AGENTS

The Commercial Agents (Council Directive) Regulations 1993[12] implements Council **6–05** Directive 86/653/EEC dealing with the rights and duties of self-employed commercial agents. A "commercial agent" is defined as:

> "a self-employed intermediary who has continuing authority to negotiate the sale or purchase of goods on behalf of another person, or to negotiate and conclude the sale or purchase of goods on behalf of and in the name of the principal."[13]

A self-employed intermediary includes a company.[14] Anyone who is an agent in his capacity as an employee is excluded from the scope of the directive, as are officers of a company,[15] and partners[16] acting on behalf of their respective organisations.

All that is required of the commercial agent is the authority to negotiate transactions or the authority both to conclude and negotiate on behalf of, and in the name of, the principal[17] on a continuing basis. One-off transactions are excluded from the scope of the Regulations.[18]

The commercial agent must look after the interests of his principal and act dutifully and in good faith.[19] In particular, the commercial agent is required to communicate to his principal all the necessary information available to him; he must make proper efforts to negotiate; and (if appropriate) conclude the transaction he has been instructed to undertake. He must comply with the reasonable instructions of the principal. For his part, the principal must also act dutifully and in good faith in his dealings with the commercial agent.[20] He must provide the agent with all necessary documentation relating to the goods concerned, as well as obtaining all necessary information for the performance of the agency contract. The principal must also inform the commercial agent within a reasonable time of his acceptance or refusal to execute a commercial transaction which the commercial agent has procured.

The Regulations provide extensively for the questions of what, when and how the commercial agent's remuneration and commission is payable.[21] Payment is to be based on any agreement between the parties, or in the absence of any agreement, what is

---

[11] *Thomas Gabriel and Sons* v *Churchill and Sim* [1914] 3 KB 1272.
[12] As amended by the Commercial Agents (Council Directive) (Amendment) Regulations 1993 (SI 1993/3173).
[13] *ibid* reg 2(1). See also *King* v *Tunnock Ltd* 1996 SCLR 742.
[14] Herd, "The Commercial Agents (Council Directive) Regulations 1993" 1994 SLT (News) 357; Schmidt, "The Commercial Agents Regulations—Some Unfinished Business" 1996 SLT (News) 13.
[15] *ibid* reg 2 (1)(i).
[16] reg 2 (1)(ii).
[17] Discussed in Reynolds, "Agency" 1994 JBL 266.
[18] Schmidt, "The Commercial Agents Regulations—Some Unfinished Business" 1996 SLT (News) 13.
[19] reg 3.
[20] reg 4.
[21] regs 6–12.

customary in respect of dealings in those goods (either a particular price or a fixed percentage). Where there is no customary payment in respect of particular goods, the commercial agent is entitled to reasonable payment taking into account all the aspects of the transaction. Commission becomes due to the agent when the principal or the third party executes the contract, or at the time the principal should, according to the contract, have executed the contract. It is mandatory that commission is paid to the agent no later than when the third party has executed his part of the transaction or would have executed it if the principal had fulfilled his obligations.[22] The right to commission is terminated if the transaction is not to be proceeded with through no fault of the principal.

There is a right in the Regulations for either side, on request, to receive a written document setting out the terms of the agency contract.[23] Regulation 17 provides for compensation or indemnity to the agent when the agency is terminated and the agent has provided the principal with substantial benefits arising from his agency. Most likely, this is in situations where the agent introduces continuing business to the principal and the principal continues to benefit. Compensation will be payable for damages sustained resulting from termination of the agreement. Entitlement to compensation is also payable where the agency contract is terminated as a result of the death of the commercial agent.[24] Where the agency is terminated by the principal failing to give notice or by giving shorter notice than the Regulations prescribe, the agent's remedy for the failure to give adequate notice will lie under domestic law of breach of contract; the Regulations do not displace domestic law on this question.[25] Indemnity provides for the agent to be bought out for the goodwill he created and for which the principal continues to derive benefit.[26]

SOLICITORS

6–06 Solicitors are often referred to as "law agents". The solicitor's authority will depend on the nature and type of work entrusted to him by the client. He must carry out the instructions of the person engaging him. In some circumstances it will be possible to infer from what the solicitor actually does that he has the necessary authority from the client and that he has followed instructions.[27] If the solicitor is instructed in a court matter he has the implied authority to take all incidental steps in the litigation process. This has been held to include the taking of an appeal from the sheriff court to the Court of Session,[28] but not authority to defend an appeal taken by the other party to the action.[29] There is some confusion whether, in the absence of instructions, the solicitor has authority to compromise a claim or settle an action.[30] The recent decision of *McKenzie (Carpenters) (in receivership)* v *Mowatt*[31] suggests that the solicitor does possess such implied authority.

A solicitor does not have an implied authority to receive notices on behalf of his

---

[22] reg 10 (2).
[23] reg 13.
[24] reg 17 (8); *King* v *Tunnock Ltd* 1996 SCLR 742 (Notes).
[25] *Roy* v *M R Pearlman Ltd* 1999 SC 459, *cf. Page* v *Combined Shipping and Trading Co Ltd* [1997] 3 All ER 656.
[26] See Schmidt, "The Commercial Agents Regulations—Some Unfinished Business" 1996 SLT (News) 15 at 16–17; *Moore* v *Piretta PTA Ltd* [1999] 1 All ER 174.
[27] *Hopkinson* v *Williams* 1993 SLT 907.
[28] *Riverford Finance Ltd* v *Kelly* 1991 SLT 300.
[29] *Robertson* v *Foulds* (1860) 22 D 714; *Stephen* v *Skinner* (1863) 2 M 287.
[30] *Livingston* v *Johnston* (1830) 8 S 594.
[31] 1991 SLT (Sh Ct) 48.

clients.[32] Nor is there is an implied authority to receive monies lent by his client.[33] However, the solicitor does have implied authority to receive a sum sued for in an action or where property has been sold by the solicitor on the principal's behalf.

Solicitors, in conformity with expectations of their professional body, The Law Society of Scotland, are expected not to act for two or more principals with a conflict of interest. Finally, the solicitor can exercise a lien over the property, files and monies of his client until such times as his professional fees have been met.

AUCTIONEERS

Auctioneers are agents who sell goods, both heritable and moveable, at public auction. **6–07** Auctions may take place in a variety of locations and not just in a salesroom.[34] The auctioneer may, or may not, have physical possession of the property to be auctioned. He may act for a disclosed principal but in many situations the principal is not disclosed. The auctioneer acts uniquely as agent to both parties to the transaction. He does not have the power to sell below the reserve price.[35]

The auctioneer, unlike other agents, has the right to sue for payment of the purchase price even where he has been paid his commission.[36] Similar to other types of agents, the auctioneer can exercise a lien[37] over goods, or the purchase price, to compel payment of their fees or commission.

Where it subsequently transpires that the auctioneer has sold goods or property to which the principal has no title he may be sued by the third party.[38]

ESTATE AGENTS

The primary purpose of estate agents is to find potential purchasers for their principal's **6–08** house or other heritable property. Because of commercial pressures, many engage in other related activities—for example, arranging mortgages and brokering insurance. Notwithstanding that in Scotland many firms of solicitors act additionally as estate agents, there are a substantial number of independent estate agencies. Solicitors acting as estate agents are regulated by the Law Society of Scotland. Other estate agents are regulated by the Estate Agents Act 1979. The Act defines estate agency work as:

> "things done ... pursuant to instructions received from another person who wishes to dispose of or acquire an interest in land—
> (a) for the purpose of, or with a view to, effecting the introduction to the client of a third person who wishes to acquire or, as the case may be, dispose of such an interest; and
> (b) after such an introduction has been effected ... for the purpose of securing the disposal, or as the case may be, the acquisition of that interest."

Estate agents are required to keep their accounts separate from their clients'

---

[32] *Singer v Trustee of the Property of Munro* [1981] 3 All ER 215.
[33] *Peden v Graham* 1907 15 SLT 143.
[34] *McKenzie v Cormack* 1950 SC 183.
[35] *McManus v Fortescue* [1907] 2 KB 1.
[36] *Chelmsford Auctions Ltd v Poole* [1973] 1 All ER 810.
[37] See para 6–30.
[38] *Anderson v Croall and Sons Ltd* (1903) 6 F 153.

accounts,[39] to disclose any personal interest[40] and to disclose to the client how much the client has to pay for their services. Their work is overseen by the Director of Fair Trading, who may issue orders prohibiting "unfit persons" from acting as estate agents, either completely or from engaging in certain aspects of estate agency work.[41]

Estate agents, unlike other agents, are usually not authorised to enter into a binding contract on behalf of their principal. They simply find a buyer and the conclusion of the bargain follows thereon. They may, of course (particularly if they are also solicitors), be specifically authorised to conclude a sale or a purchase of heritable property.[42] The estate agent, like ordinary agent, is liable for breach of fiduciary duty and any failure to exercise the requisite skill and care. The estate agent does not have implied authority to accept a deposit on behalf of his client and if he misappropriates it the principal is not liable for his actions.[43]

The other major piece of legislation regulating the activities of estate agents (including solicitors who act as estate agents) is the Property Misdescriptions Act 1991. As the name implies, the legislation seeks to protect the public from estate agents making false or misleading statements about property. The estate agent who makes a false or misleading statement is guilty of an offence punishable by unlimited fine.[44] An estate agent may make false or misleading statements about outlook, proximity of services and amenities, price, planning permissions, rights of way, measurements, and fixtures and fittings.[45] Statements need not be verbal or written but may include pictures or "any other method of signifying meaning".[46] If the false, or misleading, statement is made by an employee, that employee, as well as the employing estate agent, is criminally liable. Within the Act there is a defence open to the employer of an employee who makes a false or misleading statement. Section 2 allows the estate agent to argue the defence of "due diligence", in that he took all reasonable steps and took all reasonable care in endeavouring to avoid committing the offence. The Act seeks to punish only material misdescriptions; minor errors will not be punished.[47]

THE FORMATION OF THE AGENT/PRINCIPAL RELATIONSHIP

6–09 Agency may be constituted by express appointment, implied appointment, "holding out", ratification, necessity, or it may be created by statute.

AGENCY CREATED BY EXPRESS APPOINTMENT

6–10 As agency is, essentially, a species of contract, it may be constituted expressly, either in writing or orally.[48] Where the agent is expressly appointed in writing, the writing

---

[39] Estate Agents Act 1979, s 14; Estate Agents (Accounts) Regulations 1981 (SI 1981/1520).
[40] Estate Agents Act 1979, s 21.
[41] Estate Agents Act 1979, s 3; Estate Agents (Undesirable Practices) No 2 Order 1991 (SI 1991/1032).
[42] *Spiro* v *Lintern* [1973] 3 All ER 319.
[43] *Sorrell* v *Finch* [1977] AC 728.
[44] Property Misdescriptions Act 1991, s 1.
[45] For a full list see Property Misdescriptions (Specified Matters) Order 1992 (SI 1992/2834).
[46] Property Misdescriptions Act 1991, s 1(5)(c).
[47] *ibid* s 1(5)(a).
[48] See *Robert Barry & Co* v *Doyle* 1998 SLT 1238.

itself may vary in the degree of formality. In certain circumstances, especially in the commercial environment, the written document may be quite formal, regulating in detail the relationship between the principal and the agent. Examples of written documents creating the relationship of agency include powers of attorney, partnership deeds, and letters of mandate. A commercial agent and his principal are entitled to a written document setting out the terms of the relationship.[49]

AGENCY CREATED BY IMPLIED APPOINTMENT

There are many situations where the law implies that the relationship of agency has **6–11** been created. For example, the nature of a person's appointment to a particular post may, by implication, confer the status of agent upon them. A company director on appointment is, by implication, an agent of the company. Likewise a partner, under section 5 of the Partnership Act 1890, is deemed to be an agent of the partnership and his other partners. Agency by implication may also arise where a person is merely an employee holding a senior supervisory, or responsible, position within an organisation and it is reasonable to assume that the authority of an agent is ordinarily accorded to a person in that position. In *MacKenzie* v *Cluny Hill Hydro*[50] a hotel manager was held, by implication, to be an agent of the hotel, and in *Neville* v *C & A Modes Ltd*[51] a shop manager was similarly held to be an agent. However, this question will always be one of degree; employees in lower grades or a purely executive capacity will not ordinarily be deemed to be agents. A railway police inspector,[52] a shop manager,[53] and a gardener[54] have all been held not to be agents by implication of their employment.

AGENCY CREATED BY HOLDING OUT

Agency may be created where a person has "held out" another as his agent. This **6–12** occurs where the party allows someone without objection to represent himself as his agent. The party allowing the representation to take place is debarred from later denying that the person is his agent. In England, this form of agency is known as agency by estoppel. It has been suggested in the English case of *Rama Corporation Ltd* v *Proved Tin and General Investments Ltd*[55] that this form of agency has three essential components—a representation; a reliance on a representation; and an alteration of a party's position resulting from the reliance. The representation made by the principal may take the form of a statement or conduct by the principal. It may arguably amount to a failure by the principal to contradict a statement by the agent. In certain circumstances the fact that the principal has entrusted the agent with certain duties may amount to a representation. The representation must be made to the person who relies upon it or to the public generally.

If agency by holding out is to be created then it must be shown that there was reliance on the representation and, accordingly, if the third party does not know of the

---

[49] Commercial Agents (Council Directive) Regulations 1993 (SI 1993/3053), reg 13.
[50] 1908 SC 200.
[51] 1945 SC 175.
[52] *Mandelston* v *NBRC* 1917 SC 442.
[53] *Neville* v *C and A Modes Ltd* 1945 SC 175.
[54] *Jardine* v *Lang* 1911 2 SLT 494.
[55] [1952] 1 All ER 554, per Slade J at 556.

representation he cannot rely upon it. For the person to rely on the representation the agent must appear to be acting in a manner consistent with his role as an agent. It must, in all the circumstances, be reasonable for the third party to rely upon the representation.[56]

AGENCY BY RATIFICATION

6–13   As suggested earlier, there are some situations where consent is not immediately evident in the relationship between the parties. One such situation is where a person has acted on behalf of another without having the prior authority to do so. This does not preclude the creation of the relationship of agency where the principal ratifies what the person has done. Ratification operates to subsequently endorse the actings of the agent and to confer on the transaction the full validity and effect as if it had been entered into with the full approval of the principal from the outset. The ratification of the principal may be express, implied or deduced from the conduct of the principal. Any act, or statement, or conduct of principal, which displays his intention, will be sufficient. Where the principal does not ratify the actings of the agent then the agent will remain personally liable for his own dealings.

Before agency by ratification can occur, certain conditions must be fulfilled. First, the principal must have been in existence at the time the agent entered into the transaction.[57] This point is of considerable importance in the company law field where those who have promoted companies have entered into transactions, supposedly at the behest of the company they are promoting. Two celebrated company law cases illustrate that if the company does not legally exist at the time of the agent's dealing then it cannot subsequently ratify the pre-incorporation actings of the agent. In both *Kelner v Baxter*[58] and in *Tinnevelly Sugar Refining Company Ltd v Mirrlees, Watson and Yaryan Co Ltd*[59] the company was unable to ratify the contractual dealings of the agent because the company had not been incorporated at the time of the agent's actions.

Second, the principal must have been legally capable of authorising the transaction or act when the agent undertook it.

Third, ratification by the principal must be timeous. A set period may be laid down for ratification or, where no time is laid down, the ratification must take place within a reasonable time. In *Goodall v Bilsland*[60] one finds an example of a fixed time for ratification. A solicitor had lodged an appeal to a Licensing Board on behalf of his principal without the principal's authority. A set time was laid down for the lodging of appeals. Subsequently, the Inner House of the Court of Session held that ratification could not be effected following the expiry of the appeal period and that as a consequence of the solicitor's unauthorised actings the proceedings before the Board were null and void.

Fourth, the principal must be fully aware of all the relevant facts at the time of ratification unless he is prepared to ratify whatever the circumstances.

Fifth, and finally, it is believed (though there are divergent views on this point)[61]

---

[56] *Farquharson Bros v King and Co* [1902] AC 325; *Armagas Ltd v Mundogas SA* [1986] AC 717.
[57] *Lord Advocate v Chung* 1995 SLT 65.
[58] (1866) LR 2 CP 174.
[59] (1894) 21 R 1009. See also Chapter 11.
[60] 1909 SC 1152.
[61] See *Keighley Maxstead and Co v Durant* [1901] AC 110, *cf. Lockhart v Moodie and Co* (1877) 4 R 859; *Stair Memorial Encyclopaedia*, Vol 1, para 625, per Sheriff McEwan.

that before agency can arise by ratification the agent must have claimed to be acting on behalf of a named or disclosed principal.

Where agency arises by ratification it has the effect of creating agency from the time of the agent's actings. A third party who has contracted with an agent whose actings are subsequently ratified cannot withdraw from the contract.[62]

AGENCY BY NECESSITY

Agency by necessity is devoid of prior approval or consent. It occurs where, because **6–14** of some emergency, a person is required to take action on behalf of someone else and that person cannot be contacted. To a certain extent this form of agency is more limited in modern times. Improved communications have lessened the number of occasions where a person cannot get in touch with another. The emergency situation dictates that the agent is required to act without the prior authority of the principal. The relationship that arises in this form of agency is not contractual but is a form of what is known in Scots law as *negotiorum gestio*[63] (the management of affairs). The agent intervenes without authority, in the absence of a contractual relationship, to manage the affairs of someone who is temporarily, or permanently, unable to manage them for himself and where, in all the circumstances, it is reasonable to assume that authority would have been granted prior to the act had the principal had an opportunity to do so. Examples of agency by necessity would be salvors of ships or someone acting on behalf of someone who has become insane or mentally disturbed. The actings of the agent by necessity should be in good faith and in the interest of the person on whose behalf he is acting. Moreover, they should, in all the circumstances, be reasonable and prudent.

AGENCY BY STATUTE

In a few situations and in relation to specific persons, agency can be created by **6–15** statutory provision. For an example of agency created by statute, see the Partnership Act 1890, s 5.

THE AUTHORITY OF AN AGENT

The authority of an agent can be categorised in one of four ways—express authority, **6–16** implied authority, ostensible authority or presumed authority. The first two types of authority—express and implied—are often referred to as the agent's actual authority. The importance of the agent's authority is self evident: it will determine the validity of his actings and affect the relationship between the agent, the principal and the third party.

---

[62] *Bolton Partners* v *Lambert* (1889) 41 Ch D 295.
[63] "Negotiorum gestio is the management of the affairs of one who is absent, or incapacitated from attending to his affairs, spontaneously undertaken without his knowledge, and on the presumption that he would, if aware of all the circumstances, have given a mandate for such interference. An obligation is hence raised by legal construction, to the effect of indemnifying the negotiorum gestor." *Bells Principles* s 540; see also Leslie, "Negotiorum gestio in Scots Law" 1981 SLT (News) 259.

EXPRESS AUTHORITY

6–17 In the simplest scenario, the agent's authority will have been expressly stipulated at the outset in the agreement reached between the principal and the agent. The expression may be oral or in writing. Where the authority is exhibited in writing there is likely to be strict construction of the conferred authority.[64] The extent of that authority may, or may not, be known to the third party at the time he transacts with the agent. However, the third party may rely on the agent's express authority in any subsequent dispute with the principal. In transacting with the agent acting within the scope of his express authority the third party is entitled to hold the contract as concluded between himself and the principal. Where the agent exceeds his express authority and the third party is unable to rely on any other form of authority (or the principal's subsequent ratification), the principal will not be bound by his actings. In these circumstances, the third party's recourse is against the agent for having exceeded his authority.[65] There remains doubt, even in express appointments, as to whether the intention of the agent is to be imputed to the principal.[66]

IMPLIED AUTHORITY

6–18 The actual authority of many agents does not derive solely from their express authority but both from their express authority and from their implied authority. The implied authority may arise from the nature of the appointment, the type of agent appointed or the prevailing circumstances. Implied authority is no less significant than express authority.[67] The agent's implied authority is to do all that is necessary or incidental to his express authority. It is presumed that the principal consents to the agent's implied authority. As has been seen earlier, someone who is a general agent has the implied authority to do all that someone of his particular trade or profession would ordinarily do. The only way the principal can restrict the general agent's authority is to advise the third party of the agent's restricted authority.[68] From the case law, a number of points can be made about the implied authority of an agent: an agent does not have the implied authority to borrow money[69]; an agent does not have the implied authority to facilitate an overdraft on an account he has opened on behalf of the principal[70]; an agent does not necessarily have implied authority to engage a solicitor on the principal's behalf[71]; and salespersons employed by a principal do have an implied authority to take purchase orders on behalf of the principal.[72]

---

[64] See *Midland Bank Ltd v Reckitt* [1933] AC 1; *Jonmenjoy Coondoo v Watson* (1884) 9 App Cas 561; *Jacobs v Morris* [1902] 1 Ch 816.
[65] *J M and J H Robertson v Beatson, MacLeod and Co* 1908 SC 921; see para 6–36.
[66] *Bank of Scotland v Brunswick Developments (1987) Ltd* 1997 SC 226.
[67] See Lord Denning in *Hely-Hutchinson v Braehead Ltd* [1968] 1 QB 549 at 583: quoted in Markesinis and Munday, *An Outline of the Law of Agency* (3rd edn, 1992), p 22.
[68] *Watteau v Fenwick* [1893] 1 QB 346.
[69] *Sinclair, Moorhead and Co v Wallace* (1880) 7 R 874.
[70] *Royal Bank of Scotland v Skinner* 1931 SLT 382.
[71] *J M and J H Robertson v Beatson, McLeod and Co* 1908 SC 921.
[72] *Barry, Ostlere and Shepherd Ltd v Edinburgh Cork Importing Co* 1909 SC 1113.

OSTENSIBLE OR APPARENT AUTHORITY

Ostensible or apparent authority is not authority that is conferred but is taken to exist **6–19** from the actings of the principal and the agent, and the fact that the principal has represented to third parties that the agent is authorised to act on his behalf.[73] In contrast to actual authority (discussed above) ostensible authority is not based on the principal's consent but rather on the principal's conduct. It has been described as:

> "[a] legal relationship between the principal and the contractor created by a represen-
> tation, made by the principal to the contractor, intended to be and in fact acted on by
> the contractor, that the agent has authority to enter on behalf of the principal into a
> contract of a kind within the scope of the 'apparent' authority, so as to render the
> principal liable to perform any obligations imposed on him by such a contract."[74]

The inability of the principal to object to the third party relying on the agent's apparent authority is based on the premise that the principal is personally barred from contending that the agent's authority does not exist.[75] The exception to this is where the principal can show that the third party knew that the agent did not have the authority which he appeared to have.[76] The representation must be made by the principal to the third party and not be a representation by the agent to the third party.[77] Apparent or ostensible authority may arise where the agent was given express authority and this has subsequently been limited or withdrawn. Where this is the case it is incumbent on the principal to notify all those who had dealings with the agent previously and by general notice to all others that the agent's authority has been restricted.

An illustration of the application of ostensible authority is to be found in the leading case of *International Sponge Importers Ltd* v *Watt and Sons*[78] where the agent, though he had no authority to do so, regularly accepted payment by cheque payable in his own name. This conduct was known to the principal. Ultimately, the agent accepted payment in cash and absconded. The principal sought to recover money from the third party. However, the House of Lords accepted that it was reasonable for the third party from the course of earlier dealings to believe that the agent had the authority to accept payment. Consequently, the third party was not liable to the principal for the agent's failure to pay over the money.

In any situation where the third party knows that the agent is acting in his own interest and not that of his principal, he cannot claim that the agent was acting within his ostensible authority.[79]

In assessing whether an agent has acted within his ostensible authority it will always be a question of fact and degree. General agents can be assumed to have all the power and authority ordinarily conferred on someone of that profession. However, as a general proposition, the more unusual the transaction the less likely it is that the

---

[73] See Brown, "Agent's Apparent Authority; Paradigm or Paradox" 1995 JBL 360.
[74] *Freeman and Lockyer* v *Buckhurst Park Properties (Mangal) Ltd* [1964] 1 All ER 630, per Lord Diplock at 644.
[75] See Walker, *Principles of Scottish Private Law* (2nd edn, 1975), p 712.
[76] *Hayman* v *American Cotton Co* (1907) 15 SLT 606.
[77] *British Bata Shoe Co Ltd* v *Double M Shah Ltd* 1980 SC 311; *Armagus Ltd* v *Mundogas SA* [1986] 1 AC 717.
[78] 1911 SC (HL) 57.
[79] *Colvin* v *Dixon* (1867) 5 M 603.

agent has the authority to enter into it and in very unusual circumstances parties are expected to make some inquiry as to the agent's authority.[80]

PRESUMED AUTHORITY

6–20　The authority of the agent in certain circumstances may be presumed. An assumption is made by the law that if the principal had been in a position to be consulted he would have conferred authority on the agent. Agency created by necessity (discussed above) provides a good illustration of the type of scenario where authority may be presumed: the principal is unable to confer authority by consent, nor is the authority implied as implied authority is something which gives efficacy to express authority. The presumption of agency does not arise in other situations.[81] Family relationships do not automatically give rise to the relationship of agency.[82]

THE RELATIONSHIP BETWEEN THE PRINCIPAL AND THE AGENT

6–21　Legal relationships invariably give rise to obligations and rights, and agency is no exception. In the first instance, there are the rights and duties of the agent and the principal. In addition there are the rights and obligations of the third party.

DUTIES OF AN AGENT

6–22　For the most part, the duties incumbent upon the agent will be set out in the agreement between the principal and the agent. Where no contract exists (for example, agency by necessity) or where there are no express provisions between the parties, the agent's duties are implied by law. Even where a contract does exist but is silent on various matters, then these implied duties will apply unless specifically excluded by the express terms.

Duty to obey instructions

6–23　The agent must carry out all lawful and reasonable instructions given to him by the principal. Where he has not been given instructions the agent must use his best judgment and act in the interest of the principal. Where the agent fails to fulfil his principal's instructions he will be personally liable to the principal.[83]

　　Commercial agents within the meaning of the Commercial Agents (Council Directive) Regulations 1993 are required to "comply with reasonable instructions given by [the] principal".[84] Where the instructions are ambiguous the agent will not be liable if he misinterprets them.[85] In many situations, the agent will have been given

---

[80]　*Dornier Gmbh v Cannon* 1991 SC 310.
[81]　*Woodchester Equipment Leasing Ltd v Gindha* 1993 SLT 26.
[82]　*Lord Advocate v Chung* 1995 SLT 65. See also *McCabe v Skipton Building Society* 1994 SLT 1272. See also Chapter 13.
[83]　*Gilmour v Clark* (1853) 15 D 478.
[84]　SI 1993/3053, reg 3(2).
[85]　*Ireland v Livingston* (1872) LR 5 (HL) 395.

only general instructions, and in such a case, he should act in accordance with the general established customs of his profession.[86]

In addition to personal liability where the agent fails to perform the instructions of the principal, he also loses the right to claim the agreed remuneration.[87]

Where the agent exceeds his authority he may also be personally liable to the third party.[88]

Duty to exercise skill and care

Agents must act with skill and care in performance of their obligations to the principal. The requisite care and skill is that of an ordinary prudent man.[89] Where the agent is a member of a particular trade or profession (for example, a solicitor) he is required to exercise the skill and care expected of a member of that profession. Where the professional person acting as an agent exercises reasonable skill and care he will not be liable for errors of judgment. In Scotland, even where the agent takes no payment for his actions (such an agent is known as a mandatory) he is still required to exercise the necessary skill and care.[90] The agent will not be liable for actions he undertakes which transpire not to be in the interests of the principal where he is simply obeying instructions, unless he could reasonably have been expected to render advice to the principal on what instructions should be given. Where the agent is given an absolute discretion by the principal to act in a particular matter, the principal cannot sue the agent for exercising the discretion in a particular way.[91]

6–24

Duty to act in person

The relationship of principal and agent is ordinarily a fiduciary one—that is, one where trust between the parties is of the essence. A requisite feature of the fiduciary nature of the relationship is that the agent acts in person for the principal and does not delegate. There are, however, exceptions to this rule, and the agent will not be acting in breach of trust where: the agreement between the principal and the agent permits delegation; delegation is impliedly authorised from the circumstances of the case and the conduct of the parties; delegation is normal in the particular trade; or, the delegation is minimal, entailing only a minor issue, and does not concern any issue of confidence or trust. Where the agent legitimately delegates, he remains liable for the failings of the person to whom he has delegated. In respect of unauthorised delegation, the agent will be liable to the principal for breach of the agreement. The principal will not be liable for the actions of the sub-agent as no legal relationship arises between them.

6–25

Duty to account and to keep accounts

An agent must account to his principal. The duty to account arises only on the receipt of funds.[92] He must keep separate accounts from his principal.[93] The principal is

6–26

---

[86] *Fearn* v *Gordon and Craig* (1893) 20 R 352 at 358.
[87] *Graham and Co* v *United Turkey Red Co Ltd* 1922 SC 533 at 550.
[88] See para 6–36.
[89] Bell's *Principles* s 221.
[90] *Copland* v *Brogan* 1916 SC 277.
[91] *Glasgow West Housing Association Ltd* v *Siddique* 1998 SLT 1081.
[92] *The Royal Bank of Scotland plc* v *Law* 1996 SLT 83.
[93] cf. *Style Financial Services Ltd* v *Bank of Scotland* 1996 SLT 421.

entitled to any interest earned on money due to the principal.[94] The agent must pay from his own funds any shortfall in money due to the principal even if there is no suggestion of dishonesty.[95] In accounting to the principal, the agent must disclose any discounts he has received, as he is not entitled to retain these without approval. The full benefit of the transactions must be given to the principal.

Duty to act in good faith

6–27 One of the crucial features of agency is that it is a fiduciary relationship. Trust and good faith are of the essence. Whatever the agent does he must do for the benefit of the principal and he must act in good faith. Conflicts of interest must ordinarily be disclosed by the agent to the principal. It is not the case that by acting in his own interests, or for another principal, the agent is automatically in a conflict of interest situation and thus in breach of his fiduciary duty. Any attempt to restrict the agent's activities in this respect requires to be provided for, either expressly or impliedly.[96] Moreover, the fiduciary duty of the agent relates only to his activities in the course of the agency.

The fiduciary nature of agency is evident in three ways. First, the agent is under a duty not to disclose confidential or sensitive information obtained in the course of the agency. Invariably the duty not to disclose will subsist beyond the duration of the agency.[97]

Second, the agent is not entitled to any secret profit from his transactions on behalf of the principal. A secret profit has been described as "any financial advantage which the agent receives over and above what he is entitled to receive from his principal by way of remuneration."[98] It is the non-disclosure of the profits which offends the fiduciary nature of the relationship. If the agent reveals to the principal that he has received payment or benefit over and above the agreed remuneration, and the principal agrees that he may retain it, then naturally the agent may keep the additional sum. Secret profits may take the form of direct or indirect payment, a discount on the purchase price, a bribe or a donation.[99] Discounts or donations must be credited to the principal unless he otherwise agrees. In the event that the agent fails to disclose a secret profit then he is in breach of contract with the principal. The principal may terminate the relationship, dismiss the agent[100] and the agent may lose the right to claim his lawful remuneration for the period he is in breach. He is entitled to payment for the period he is not in breach.[101] In addition to this, the principal may sue the third party paying the secret profit for any damages occasioned by the inducement to the agent. Finally, the principal may refuse to implement the transaction with the third party[102] where the third party has knowledge of the agent's receipt of a secret profit and is involved with the agent's improper conduct. In responding to the discovery of

---

[94] *Brown* v *IRC* 1964 SC (HL) 180.
[95] *Tyler* v *Logan* (1904) 1 F 123.
[96] *Lothian* v *Jenolite Ltd* 1969 SC 111.
[97] *Liverpool Victoria Friendly Society* v *Houston* (1900) 3 F 42.
[98] Fridman, *Law of Agency* (6th edn, 1990), p 162. See also *Solicitors' Estate Agency (Glasgow) Ltd* v *MacTier* 1992 SCLR 804.
[99] *Ronaldson* v *Drummond and Reid* (1881) 8 R 956; *Trans Barwil Agencies (UK) Ltd* v *John S Braid and Co Ltd* 1989 SLT 73.
[100] *Boston Deep Sea Fishing and Ice Co* v *Ansell* (1888) 39 Ch D 339; *Andrews* v *Ramsay* [1903] 2 KB 635; *Sao Paulo Alpargatas SA* v *Standard Chartered Bank Ltd* 1985 SLT 433.
[101] *Graham and Co* v *United Turkey Red Co* 1922 SC 553.
[102] *Logicrose Ltd* v *Southern United Football Club Ltd* [1988] 1 WLR 1256.

the non-disclosure of a secret profit it matters not that the principal has sustained a loss.[103]

Third, the agent must not sell his own goods and property to the principal without the principal's full knowledge and consent.[104] It is also the case that if the agent is intent on purchasing property from the principal then he should disclose this fact to the principal.[105]

RIGHTS OF AN AGENT

Right to remuneration

The most obvious right that an agent would wish to enforce against his principal is the right to remuneration. Payment may take the form of a stipulated amount or a commission. Provision for payment invariably depends on the express or implied terms of the agreement between both parties. Express provision for the amount, quantification and method of payment naturally minimises the potential for ambiguity and dispute.[106] Where no express provision exists as to payment then the normal approach is to look to custom in the particular field of the agency to assess the calculation. For example, a particular scale may be known to apply in certain situations or a professional body may set down a particular rate for the job. Where neither an express provision stipulates the appropriate payment, nor a normal custom applies, the agent will be entitled to payment *"quantum meruit"*—that is, on the basis of how much he has earned.[107]

A dispute may arise as to whether the parties intended that there should be any payment at all to the agent. In such circumstances, the courts will look to the nature of the agency and the relationship of the parties to determine whether payment was intended or not.

Only in circumstances where the agent has earned it, is the principal obliged to make payment to the agent. If it can be shown that the agent has not undertaken what he agreed to do, or brought about what he was employed to do, then the principal may decline to make payment. Disputes of this nature most frequently arise in the sale of property where the seller may feel that the sale has not been brought about by the estate agent's efforts but by his own efforts. Ultimately, the issue is a question of fact and the courts must assess the contribution of the agent.[108] Payment will be appropriate where the agent has brought about a sale but has not effected it.[109] In the normal course of events, if the agent acting for a seller finds the purchaser, he will be entitled to payment. Where the agent finds a putative purchaser but the principal declines to sell, the question of payment will be determined by any agreement and in the absence of any agreement the courts have shown a reluctance to imply a right to any commission.[110] However, there is authority in the Scottish decision of *Dudley Bros* v

6–28

---

[103] *Boardman v Phipps* [1967] 2 AC 46 quote from Court of Appeal decision reported at [1965] 1 All ER 849 at 856, per Lord Denning.

[104] *Armstrong* v *Jackson* [1917] 2 KB 822.

[105] *McPherson's Trs* v *Watt* (1877) 5 R (HL) 9.

[106] *Chris Hart (Business Sales) Ltd* v *Thomas Currie* 1992 SLT 544.

[107] *Kennedy* v *Glass* (1890) 17 R 1085.

[108] *Walker, Fraser and Steele* v *Fraser's Trs* 1910 SC 222.

[109] *Burchell* v *Gowrie Collieries* [1910] AC 614; for a full discussion on the payment of estate agents see Markesinis and Munday, *An Outline of the Law of Agency* (3rd edn, 1992), pp 134–139.

[110] See *Luxor (Eastbourne) Ltd* v *Cooper* [1941] AC 108, *cf. Alpha Trading Ltd* v *Dunnshaw-Patten Ltd* [1981] QB 290; Markesinis and Munday, *An Outline of the Law of Agency* (3rd edn, 1992), p 139.

Barnet[111] for the proposition that, where the agent finds a potential purchaser and the principal refuses to sell, the agent is entitled to sue for damages for the loss of commission.

In assessing the right of the agent to remuneration, it is irrelevant that the principal has not benefited from the actions of the agent. What is important is that the agent has performed what he undertook to do and is not culpable in failing to benefit the principal.[112]

Right of relief against the principal

6–29   An agent has the right to be relieved by the principal of all liabilities, losses and expenditure properly incurred and arising from his performance of his duties on the principal's behalf.[113] The principal need not indemnify the agent who has acted illegally,[114] negligently,[115] or in breach of his fiduciary duties.[116] Where the right to relief is not expressly stipulated in the agreement between the principal and the agent the courts will imply its existence.

The principal need not relieve the agent for liabilities incurred while acting outwith the scope of his authority, nor in respect of liabilities incurred which are the agent's own fault.

Right of lien over the principal's property

6–30   An agent has a right to retain possession of any property of the principal lawfully in his possession until such times as the principal has paid any remuneration or commission due to the agent. This right, known as the agent's right of lien, is exercisable where the principal has failed to relieve the agent in conformity with the agent's right of relief arising under the contract of agency. The agent's right of lien is explained by Lord Kinnear in *Glendinning* v *Hope*[117] where he said:

> "every agent who is required to undertake liabilities or make payments for his principal, and who in the course of his employment comes into possession of property belonging to the principal over which he has power of control or disposal, is entitled, in the first place, to be indemnified for the monies he has expended, or the loss he has incurred, and, in the second place, to retain such properties as come into his hands in his character of agent."

The right of lien simply allows the agent to retain possession of the principal's property. It does not allow the agent to dispose of or sell the property in his possession. Certain types of agent (for example, solicitors, mercantile agents and bankers) are said to have a general lien. This allows them to retain any property of the principal including items other than those to which the debt due to the agent particularly relates. Excepting the small category of types of agents, which are known to have a general lien, all other agents are said to have a special lien. A special lien allows the

---

[111] 1937 SC 632.
[112] See *Chris Hart (Business Sales) Ltd* v *Thomas Currie* 1991 SCLR 613.
[113] *Drummond v Cairns* (1852) 14 D 611; *Stevenson v Duncan* (1842) 5 D 167.
[114] *Re Parker* (1882) 21 Ch D 408.
[115] See *Thacker* v *Hardy* (1878) QBD 685 at 687.
[116] *Robinson v Middleton* (1859) 21 D 1089.
[117] 1911 SC (HL) 73 at 78.

agent to retain property in his possession until such times as the sums due to the agent relating to that particular piece of property have been paid.[118]

In addition to the goods being lawfully in the possession of the agent, it is also the case that the goods must have come into his possession in his capacity as agent. Although it appears to the contrary, there is nothing inconsistent with the agent's right of lien and his obligation to treat the interests of his principal as paramount.[119] In this regard, the agent is perfectly entitled to put his own interests first. The agent will surrender his right of lien if he acts in a manner inconsistent with the existence of a right of lien, or where he parts with possession of the principal's property. Moreover, the right of lien will terminate if the principal discharges his obligations to the principal.

Right to receive work from the principal

For the most part, the agent is not guaranteed work by the principal. In subscribing **6–31** to the agreement he simply takes his chances that work will be forthcoming. However, in certain circumstances, the provision of work may be implied. Where the agency is intended to subsist for a definite period and the agent is to be remunerated by way of commission, there is a suggestion that if the agent has paid for the creation of the agency, then there is an obligation on the part of the principal not to voluntarily discontinue his business so as to deprive the agent of his commission.[120] In circumstances where the agent has not paid for the agency then the agent has a right of recourse if the principal sells, transfers or discontinues the business.[121]

Where an agent is engaged as the sole selling agent, the principal is still allowed to sell goods himself unless the parties to the agency agreement have agreed that he should not.[122]

THE THIRD PARTY'S RIGHTS AND LIABILITIES

The agent's primary role is to act for the principal in transactions with third parties. **6–32** The relationships between the three are affected by the nature of the agent's dealings with the third party. In advising on the question of third party rights and liabilities it is necessary to know the answer to such questions as: did the agent disclose that he was acting on behalf of a principal? Was that principal named? Does the third party think he is dealing with the agent as a principal? Has the agent acted within his authority?

In *Craig and Co Ltd v Blackater*[123] Lord Anderson set out the main rules on the rights and liabilities of third parties dealing with agents. He said:

---

[118] *Scott and Neill v Smith* (1883) 11 R 316.
[119] Fridman, *Law of Agency* (6th edn, 1990), p 187.
[120] *Galbraith v Arethusa Shipping Co* (1896) 23 R 1011; *Ogden v Nelson* [1905] AC 109.
[121] *Patmore and Co v Cannon and Co* (1892) 19 R 1004.
[122] *Bentall v Vicary* [1931] 1 KB 253; *cf. Lothian v Jenolite Ltd* 1969 SC 111.
[123] 1923 SC 472.

"If A contracts as agent for a disclosed principal, A cannot competently sue or be sued with reference to the contract. Again, if A contracts for an undisclosed principal, A may sue and is liable to be sued as a principal, the third party having no knowledge that he is anything but a principal. If, however, A contracts for an undisclosed principal who is subsequently disclosed to the third party, the latter may sue either agent or principal. He cannot, however, sue both. If an action is raised against the third party he may insist that it be at the instance of the disclosed principal."[124]

TRANSACTIONS WHERE THE AGENT ACTS FOR A DISCLOSED PRINCIPAL

6–33   Where the agent discloses that he acts for a principal who actually exists,[125] and names that principal, the effect is that the agent drops from the equation and the direct contract exists between the third party and the principal.[126] The rights and obligations of the principal and the third party proceed independently from any rights and obligations the agent may have to his principal. The agent ordinarily has no interest in the contract, has no liability under it and cannot sue on the basis of it.[127] It matters not that the agent is acting for a foreign principal.[128] However, it is of paramount importance that the agent is acting within his authority actual, apparent or presumed. The principal will not be liable for any actions by the agent, which are outside the scope of the agent's authority.[129] As an exception to this general rule, where the agent can be said to have an interest in the contract (for example, an auctioneer)[130] he may sue for payment of the purchase price. An agent with an interest may, if he wishes, assume personal liability.[131] Personal liability of an agent may also arise as a customary aspect of the trade in which the agent is engaged.[132]

THE AGENT DISCLOSES THAT HE ACTS FOR A PRINCIPAL BUT DOES NOT NAME HIM

6–34   There may be many situations where the agent discloses that he is an agent but declines to name on whose behalf he acts. In law, the position is essentially no different from that above where the agent names the principal. If the agent subsequently refuses to name his principal he will become personally liable to the third party.[133]

---

[124] At 486.
[125] *Tinnevelly Sugar Refining Co Ltd* v *Mirrlees, Watson and Yaryan Co Ltd* (1894) 21 R 1009; and *Cumming* v *Quartztag Ltd* 1981 SLT 205.
[126] *Digby, Brown & Co* v *Lyall* 1995 SLT 932. See also *Catto* v *Lindsay & Kirk* 1995 SCLR 541 (Sh Ct), per Sheriff Principal Risk, *cf. Stirling Park & Co* v *Digby, Brown & Co* 1995 SCLR 375 (Sh Ct).
[127] *McIvor* v *Roy* 1970 SLT (Sh Ct) 58.
[128] *Millar* v *Mitchell* (1860) 22 D 833.
[129] See para 6–36.
[130] *Mackenzie* v *Cormack* 1950 SC 183.
[131] *Brebner* v *Henderson* 1925 SC 643; *Stewart* v *Shannessy* (1900) 2 F 1288.
[132] *Livesey* v *Purdom and Sons* (1894) 21 R 911.
[133] *Gibb* v *Cunningham & Robertson* 1925 SLT 608.

THE AGENT DOES NOT DISCLOSE THAT HE ACTS FOR A PRINCIPAL

If the agent does not disclose that he acts for a principal he runs the risk that the third **6–35** party will hold him personally liable for any defect in performance. As long as the principal remains undisclosed, the agent may be sued or sue on the contract.[134] However, if the agent is acting within the scope of his authority, the principal may identify himself at any time and assume title to sue or may be sued on the contract.[135] In a situation where the principal reveals his identity the third party must elect to sue either the agent or the principal; he cannot sue both, and once he has elected he cannot change his mind.[136] Election to hold one or other of them liable must be clear and unequivocal and can be exhibited in a variety of ways (including conduct)—for example, claiming in the bankruptcy of one and not reserving a claim against the other, or by taking a decree against either.[137] Where an agent has acted for a hitherto undisclosed principal the third party may invoke as a defence in any subsequent action brought by the disclosed principal the facts that he has settled any claim with the agent prior to disclosure. Equally, he may plead that he has set off the debt owed to the principal against debts owed to him by the agent incurred before the disclosure of the principal. One situation where the disclosure of the principal does not exonerate the agent is where goods are sold in the course of business and the seller does not disclose that he acts for a principal. There is an implied term of sale that where the buyer makes known to the seller the purpose for which the goods are sought, there is an implied term in the contract that goods are reasonably fit for that purpose. This applies to a sale "by a person who in the course of a business is acting as agent for another".[138]

THE AGENT ACTING WITHOUT AUTHORITY OR IN EXCESS OF HIS AUTHORITY

Where an agent acts without authority, the principal does not incur any liability, even **6–36** if the agent purports to act on his behalf, unless he subsequently ratifies the agent's actions.[139] If the principal withdraws the authority of the agent it is incumbent on him to ensure that those dealing with the agent know of the change in the agent's authority.

Where that agent exceeds his actual or ostensible authority, the principal is not liable but the agent will be personally liable.

Where the agent's conduct is fraudulent, the agent may be liable in damages to the third party.[140] Even where the agent's actings arise from a mistaken belief as to his authority he will still incur liability to the third party based on the notion that the agent impliedly warrants that he has the necessary authority. This implied warranty does not arise where third parties have the means of judging the agent's authority.

---

[134] *Boyter v Thomson* 1995 SC (HL) 15. However, see *Armour v Duff & Co* 1912 SC 120, where the principal was easily ascertainable.

[135] *Ferrier v Dodds* (1865) 3 M 561.

[136] *David Logan and Sons Ltd v Schuldt* (1903) 10 SLT 598.

[137] *Craig and Co Ltd v Blackater* 1923 SC 472; but not by simply raising proceedings—see *Clarkson Booker Ltd v Andjel* [1964] 2 QB 775.

[138] Sale and Supply of Goods Act 1994, s 14 (5); *Boyter v Thomson* 1995 SC (HL) 15.

[139] See para 6–13.

[140] *Anderson v Croall and Sons Ltd* (1903) 6 F 153.

Moreover, the third party will only be able to utilise the remedy of damages where he has sustained a loss arising out of the agent's actings.[141]

TERMINATION OF AGENCY

TERMINATION BY THE AGENT OR THE PRINCIPAL

6–37 In the simplest scenario, agency will terminate after the expiry of the period for which it was agreed it would last[142] or after the specific transaction which it was created to facilitate, is complete.

Where the agency does not exist for the purposes of one determinate transaction, and the parties have not stipulated a time period for its duration, either the principal or the agent may terminate it at any time by giving notice to the other. If there is a determinate time for the duration of the agency and one party seeks to unilaterally terminate the agreement without just cause, the other may seek damages for breach of contract.

Both parties may mutually agree to terminate the relationship of agency on whatever terms they may agree and without the prospect of any further legal action. Mutual termination may only become effective on notification to third parties. For example, under the Partnership Act 1890, s 36 a retiring partner's authority (as an agent of the firm) is not properly ended until such times as a notice of the retiral is published in the *Edinburgh Gazette*. Notwithstanding the termination of the agency, the principal remains liable to pay the agent any unpaid remuneration and to indemnify the agent in respect of anything arising in the course of the agency which subsequently comes to light after termination of the agreement.

The principal himself may decide to end the relationship between himself and the agent. He remains liable to remunerate and relieve the agent of liabilities arising from the course of the agency. Ordinarily, the agent would complete any transaction in which he is currently engaged at the point of termination by the principal. Following termination, the principal retains the right of access to the agent's files and records, which relate to acts done in the principal's name. Such a right may have been excluded by the parties in drawing up the agency agreement.[143]

In certain situations, the principal cannot terminate the agreement without the agent's consent. In these circumstances, the agent is known as a procurator *in rem suam* (an agent with an interest). He has been given authority by the principal to do something in his own interest and the principal cannot with impunity terminate the agreement before the agent has fulfilled his interest, or agrees to the termination.

The agent himself may seek to terminate the agency but must be careful that he is not committing a breach of contract and thus incurring liability for any damages occasioned by the principal.

---

[141] *Irving* v *Burns* 1915 SC 260.
[142] *Brenan* v *Campbell's Trs* (1898) 25 R 423.
[143] *Yasuda Fire and Marine Insurance Co of Europe* v *Orion Marine Insurance Underwriting Agency* [1995] 2 WLR 49.

FRUSTRATION OF THE AGENCY AGREEMENT

Like similar contractual arrangements, agency may terminate through frustration. **6–38**
Circumstances may intervene, through no fault of either party, which operate to bring
the agency to an end. These circumstances can, most commonly, be summarised under
four headings—death; insanity; bankruptcy; and discontinuance of the business. It
should be noted that frustration of agency might arise also from the supervening
impossibility of performance or the supervening illegality of performance. For
example, the subject-matter of any transaction may have perished or been destroyed.
Moreover, the continuance of the agency may have become impossible because of the
enforced absence of one of the parties. Equally, situations may arise which make either
the agency or its objective illegal. Again, in such circumstances, the agency is said to
be frustrated.

Death of the agent or the principal

Not surprisingly, the death of either party to the agency agreement brings the **6–39**
arrangement to an end. In the case of the agent, the relationship is ended because it
is personal and no longer capable of being fulfilled by that agent. Where there is a
joint agency, the death of one agent may, in certain circumstances, terminate the
entire agreement and end the authority of all agents.[144] The death of the principal
(where it is known to the agent)[145] likewise terminates the agency though the agent
may complete the transaction he is engaged in at the time of death. Again, where
there is more than one principal, the death of one may end the agent's authority to
act.[146]

Insanity of the agent or the principal

The principal's insanity, provided it is permanent, terminates the agency.[147] If the **6–40**
insanity of the principal is temporary then it will not operate to terminate the agency
and the agent will still be entitled to claim remuneration for his actings during the
period of temporary insanity of the principal.[148] In respect of a formally constituted
agency agreement, the supervening mental incapacity of the principal does not
operate to terminate the agency.[149]

Where supervening insanity of the principal occurs and a third party enters into a
transaction unaware of the mental state of the principal, there is support for the
proposition that, as long as the third party is acting in good faith, he is entitled to
regard the agent as still having authority until otherwise notified.[150] There remains the
possibility that a third party contracting with an agent who knows, but conceals, that
his principal is insane may hold the agent personally liable.[151] In circumstances where

---

[144] *Friend* v *Young* [1897] 2 Ch 421.
[145] *Campbell* v *Anderson* (1829) 3 W & S 384.
[146] *Life Association of Scotland* v *Douglas* (1886) 13 R 910.
[147] *Daily Telegraph Co* v *McLaughlin* [1904] AC 776.
[148] *Wink* v *Mortimer* (1849) 11 D 995.
[149] Law Reform (Miscellaneous Provisions) (Scotland) Act 1990, s 71: effective from 1st January 1991 but does not apply retrospectively to these forms of agency prior to that date.
[150] *Pollock* v *Patterson* 10 December 1811, discussed in Marshall, *Scottish Cases on Agency* (1980), p 171.
[151] *Yonge* v *Toynbee* [1910] 1 KB 215.

the agent is insane, the agency terminates because of the agent's incapacity to act on the principal's behalf.

Bankruptcy of the principal or the agent

6–41　Bankruptcy of the principal amounts to legal incapacity of the principal and terminates the agency.[152] Notwithstanding that, the agent may complete the transaction that he is currently engaged in. Although bankruptcy of the agent usually terminates the relationship, there are some circumstances where such a consequence may not ensue.[153] Much will depend on the terms of the agreement between the agent and the principal. The agreement between the parties may provide for termination following the bankruptcy of the agent.

Discontinuance of the principal's business

6–42　Unless the agent can establish that the agency has been expressly or impliedly created for a specified period of time, the principal will be entitled to discontinue his business without the agent having any remedy under breach of contract.[154] If the agent can show that there was agreement that the agency would endure for a specified period he may be able to claim damages for any losses occasioned by the earlier closure of the business.

---

[152] *McKenzie* v *Campbell* (1894) 21 R 904; *Dickson* v *Nicholson* (1855) 17 D 1011.
[153] See, for example, *McCall* v *Australian Meat Co Ltd* (1870) 19 WR 188; *cf. Hudson* v *Grainger* (1821) 5 B 3 Ald 27.
[154] *Patmore and Co* v *Cannon and Co* (1892) 19 R 1004. For other illustrations see *London, Leith, Edinburgh and Glasgow Shipping Co* v *Ferguson* (1850) 13 D 51; *SS "State of California" Co Ltd* v *Moore* (1895) 22 R 562; *Rhodes* v *Forwood* (1876) 1 App Cas 256.

SUMMARY

THE DEFINITION AND NATURE OF AGENCY

- Agency is a contractual relationship whereby a party engages someone to act on their behalf in transactions with a third party. The person engaged is known as an "agent". The person on whose behalf the agent acts is known as the "principal".
- The relationship of agency arises in three main areas—commercial transactions, partnership and employment.

CATEGORIES AND TYPES OF AGENT

- Agents may be "general" agents (an agent who deals with all matters in a particular trade, eg partners or company directors) or they may be "special" agents appointed for a particular transaction.
- Common types of agents include commercial agents, mercantile agents, del credere agents, solicitors, auctioneers and estate agents.

THE FORMATION OF THE AGENT/PRINCIPAL RELATIONSHIP

- Agency may be created by express appointment, implied appointment, where a person is "held out" (represented as) an agent, it may be created by ratification where what a person has done is adopted by the principal, or it may in exceptional circumstances be created out of necessity (eg a stranger intervenes to salvage goods of the principal).

THE AUTHORITY OF AN AGENT

- An agent may have express authority (arising out of what has been agreed between him and the principal either in writing or verbally), or he may have authority, which is implied from his position or implied by law. Alternatively, an agent may have "ostensible authority". Ostensible (or apparent authority) is not authority that is conferred but is taken to exist from the actings of the principal and the agent, and the fact that the principal has represented to third parties that the agent is authorised to act on his behalf.

THE RELATIONSHIP BETWEEN THE PRINCIPAL AND THE AGENT

- An agent has the following duties:
    to obey instructions of the principal
    to exercise skill and care in the performance of his duties
    to act in person

      to account to the principal and to keep separate accounts
      to act in good faith.

- An agent has the following rights:

      the right to remuneration from the principal

      the right to exercise a lien (retain possession) over the principal's goods where the principal has not paid him

      the right to relief from the principal in respect of expenses and outlays he has incurred on the principal's behalf

      in certain circumstances the agent has a right to receive work from the principal, particularly where work is necessary to earn payment.

THE THIRD PARTY'S RIGHTS AND LIABILITIES

- Where the agent discloses that he acts for a principal who actually exists and names that principal the effect is that the agent drops from the equation and the direct contract exists between the third party and the principal.
- There may be many situations where the agent discloses that he is an agent but declines to name on whose behalf he acts. In law the position is essentially no different from that above where the agent names the principal. If the agent subsequently refuses to name his principal he will become personally liable to the third party.
- As long as the principal remains undisclosed, the agent may be sued or sue on the contract. However, if the agent is acting within the scope of his authority, the principal may identify himself at any time and assume title to sue or may be sued on the contract.
- Where an agent acts without authority the principal does not incur any liability even if the agent purports to act on his behalf unless he subsequently ratifies the agent's actings.

TERMINATION OF AGENCY

- The relationship between the agent and principal may be terminated in the following ways:

      at the hands of the agent or principal by giving notice or otherwise

      frustration of the agreement between the agent and the principal

        the death of the agent or principal

        the insanity of the principal or agent

        the bankruptcy of the principal or agent

        discontinuance of the principal's business

CASE DIGEST

Special agent [see para 6–02]
Morrison v *Statter* (1885) 12 R 1152
A shepherd occasionally bought sheep for his master. When the special agent had been instructed to buy three-year-old sheep at a maximum price of 32s but instead bought two-year-old sheep at 48s, the court held that he had no authority to do this. He had special instructions to follow but did not do this.

Ostensible authority [see para 6–19]
Dornier GmbH v *Cannon* 1991 SC 310
This was an action raised for recovery of a sum of money which, the pursuers alleged, was a loan. The defenders asserted that the money was in fact a grant and found upon documents signed by employees of the pursuer. In judgment Lord Cowie said "the more extraordinary the transaction [carried out by the agent], the less likely it is that an agent has authority to enter into it so questions of fact and degree may arise as to the proper limits of the apparent or ostensible authority."

Duty not to make secret profit [see para 6–27]
Solicitors' Estate Agency (Glasgow) Ltd v *MacIver* 1992 SCLR 804
Where an agency received a discount for block advertisements it placed on behalf of clients, it had to account to the clients for the value of the discount.

Breach of fiduciary duty [see para 6–27]
Sao Paulo Alpargatas SA v *Standard Chartered Bank Ltd* 1985 SLT 433
A Brazilian company sold cloth goods by way of bill of exchange to a Scottish Company which following delivery of the goods had gone into receivership. They sued the bank for breach of duty. They claimed the bank had a duty as their agent to collect money for them and to advise of rejection of the Bill of Exchange and the circumstances of the receiving company. The same bank had appointed the receiver to the Scottish company. It was held that the appointment of the receiver had nothing to do with the agency and there was no duty to disclose the appointment of the receiver. An agent only has a duty in respect of matters arising from the course of his agency.

Duty to act in good faith [see para 6–27]
Lothian v *Jenolite Ltd* 1969 SC 111
An agency agreement due to run four years was cancelled after 18 months. The principal asserted that the agent was dealing in goods of competitors. It was held that there is no common law implied condition that the agent will never act for more than one principal. Such a clause could be inserted expressly or by necessary implication of the facts of the case.

Agent entitled to remuneration [see para 6–28]
Chris Hart (Business Sales) v *Thomas Currie* 1992 SLT 544
An agent had been instructed to sell his principal's pub. The agent did this success-fully with the missives conditional on a licence being granted. This did not happen

and the transfer fell. The agent was still entitled to a fee as the missives had been
concluded.

Agent not entitled to remuneration if breached the principal's instructions [see para [6–28]

Graham v *United Turkey Red Co Ltd* 1922 SC 533

An agent had entered into a restrictive covenant whereby he agreed to sell only the
defender's products. He breached agreement and when he sought payment for
the agency period, he was not entitled to payment for the period of the breach.

If no express provision for payment, customary rate should be paid [see para 6–28]

Kennedy v *Glass* (1890) 17 R 1085

Kennedy acted as a broker but was not a proper broker. The court rejected
Kennedy's claim for £250 commission, which he had claimed had been agreed but
held that he was entitled to £50 on account of the time spent by him (*quantum
meruit*).

Reimbursement of expenses properly incurred [see para 6–29]

Drummond v *Cairns* (1852) 14 D 611

Cairns bought shares on behalf of Drummond. When Drummond was asked to
settle the account he refused, and Cairns was forced to sell the shares at a loss.
Drummond had to reimburse Cairns for the difference between the prices.

Agent's right of retention (or lien) [see para 6–30]

Glendinning v *Hope & Co* 1911 SC (HL) 73

Stockbrokers bought shares for a client and subsequently sold them on for him. It
was held that the agent could hold onto the proceeds of sales from earlier transactions for the costs of the latest transaction. The agent has a right of general lien over
any of the principal's property which is in his possession as a result of the agency.

Agent for non-existent principal [see para 6–33]

Cumming v *Quartztag Ltd* 1981 SLT 205

If an "agent" contracts but his principal (company) is not yet in existence, the
principal normally will be unable to enforce the contract. In this case a person had
signed a lease "for and on behalf of a company to be incorporated."

Agent does not incur liability where discloses principal [see para 6–33]

Digby Brown Co v *Lyall* 1995 SLT 932

A letter of obligation granted by a firm of solicitors "on behalf of" their clients, but
signed by them without qualification, was not binding on the firm personally.

Agent expressly incurs liability [see para 6–33]

Stewart v *Shannessy* (1900) 2 F 1288

Where a person signs a contract in his own name, he is prima facie deemed to be a
person contracting personally. A sales manager for a cycle shop and tyre company
appointed persons as agents of the two companies. There was no indication he was
acting as the companies' agent and there was no qualification on the terms of the
appointment.

Agent liable for unnamed principal [see para 6–35]

Ferrier v *Dods* (1865) 3 M 561

An auctioneer who sold an unfit horse was liable for the warranty, as he had sold the horse without disclosing the name of the principal.

Principal undisclosed but reasonably ascertainable [see para 6–35]

Armour v *Duff & Co* 1912 SC 120

Ship chandlers received an order from brokers to deliver stores to a ship. The goods were delivered in the belief that the brokers were the owners of the ship. It was held that an agent is not liable if acting for a disclosed principal or for a principal whose identity is easily ascertainable. In this case the suppliers could have checked the shipping register.

Bankruptcy of the principal [see para 6–41]

McKenzie v *Campbell* (1894) 21 R 904

A solicitor was instructed to defend an accused and paid a sum of money on account. Subsequently, he was sequestrated. It was held that the bankruptcy of the principal will terminate the agency contract and that the agent was bound to account all funds at the date of sequestration.

FURTHER READING

Books

Bowstead, *Bowstead on Agency* (15th edn, Sweet and Maxwell, 1985)

Cusine and Forte, *Scottish Cases and Materials in Commercial Law* (2nd edn, Butterworths, 2000)

Fridman, *Law of Agency*, (6th edn, Butterworths, 1990)

Gloag and Henderson, *The Laws of Scotland* (10th edn, W Green, 1995)

The Laws of Scotland: Stair Memorial Encyclopaedia, (Law Society of Scotland/ Butterworths) Vol 1, pp 247–280, paras 601–700

Markesinis and Munday, *An Outline of the Law of Agency* (3rd edn, Butterworths, 1992)

Marshall, *Scottish Cases on Agency* (W Green, 1980)

O'Donnell, *Agency* (W Green, 1998)

Stone, *Law of Agency* (Cavendish, 1996)

Walker, *Principles of Scottish Private Law* (2nd edn, Clarendon, 1975), Vol 1, pp 701–728

Articles

Brown "Agent's Apparent Authority: Paradigm or Paradox?" 1995 JBL 360

Herd, "The Commercial Agents (Council Directive) Regulations 1993" 1994 SLT (News) 357

Leslie "Negotiorum gestio in Scots Law" 1981 SLT (News) 259

Reynolds, "Agency" 1994 JBL 266

Schmidt, "The Commercial Agents Regulations—Some Unfinished Business" 1996 SLT (News) 13

7   LAND LAW

This chapter deals exclusively with land law. In the first instance it should be recog-   **7–01**
nised that there is a unitary law of property in Scotland meaning that basic concepts
of property law apply to all sorts of property including land. However, various unique
factors including the physical nature of land, its historic value and the special uses to
which it can be put have necessitated the development of certain specialised rules. It
is this mixture of general concepts and specialised rules which makes up the body of
law known as land law.

SOURCES OF LAW

Much of the Scottish law of property is based on Roman law. Feudal law also provided   **7–02**
much substance to the land law of Scotland but its influence was in decline for
centuries prior to the final abolition of the feudal system of landholding at the start of
the third millenium.[1] The Scottish law of property has little in common with English
law or other common law legal systems. Certain decisions of the House of Lords have
tended to adopt certain English notions of property law, or at least a resemblance of
those notions, and this has not facilitated the clear development of Scots law.[2]

REFORM

Major reforms of Scottish land law are likely to take place in the next few years to   **7–03**
implement recommendations of the Scottish Law Commission. These reforms will
begin with the abolition of the feudal system of landholding[3] and are likely to continue
with reform of the law relative to real conditions (legislation due in 2001)[4] and the law

---

[1] Abolition of Feudal Tenure etc (Scotland) Act 2000, ss 1–2 following upon Scottish Law Commission,
Report on Abolition of the Feudal System (Scot Law Com No 168) (February 1999).
[2] *Alvis v Harrison* 1991 SLT 64 (HL); *Sharp v Thomson* 1997 SLT 636 (HL).
[3] Abolition of Feudal Tenure etc (Scotland) Act 2000, ss 1–2 following upon Scottish Law Commission,
Report on Abolition of the Feudal System (Scot Law Com No 168) (February 1999).
[4] Scottish Law Commission, *Discussion Paper on Real Burdens* (No 106) (October 1998).

of the tenement.[5] The legislative competence of the Scottish Parliament extends to enactments relative to land law provided such enactments are not incompatible with Convention rights or Community law.[6] To the extent that this land law comprises "Scots private law" the Parliament's legislative competence includes the passing of enactments relating to matters reserved to the Westminster Parliament provided the law in question relates consistently to reserved matters and otherwise.[7]

PROPERTY

7-04   It is traditionally accepted that the word "property" can refer to two separate matters:

(a) the right of ownership—for clarity the right of property may be referred to as *dominium*, a term derived from Roman law;

(b) the thing, known as the *res*,[8] which is the subject of the right of ownership.

LAND

7-05   In contrast to the term "property", the meaning of the term "land" is generally accepted as varying according to context.[9] It has variously been defined as including[10] or excluding[11] the buildings thereon. More confusing, however, is the occasional use of the term "land" to refer not only to the thing but to certain rights relating to land.[12] This is complicated by the recognition in Scots law of "legal" separate tenements. A legal separate tenement is treated as if it were land itself, as if it were a thing capable of ownership. Today the most important of the incorporeal separate tenements recognised by Scots law is the right to fish for salmon.[13] Separate tenements known as "conventional" or "geographic" separate tenements may be created by a deed when a part of greater lands is split off and sold to another party. The split offs may be vertical or horizontal. Below the ground they include horizontal strata including minerals and coal, mines of silver and gold, petroleum and natural gas. Above ground they include buildings of more than a single storey which are divided up into separate flats.

---

[5] Scottish Law Commission, *Report on the Law of the Tenement* (Scot Law Com No 162) (1998).
[6] Scotland Act 1998, s 29(2)(d). "Convention rights" and "Community law" are defined in the 1998 Act, s 126(1) and (9) respectively.
[7] *ibid* s 29(4).
[8] From which Latin term is derived the expression "real" property and "real estate".
[9] Gordon, *Scottish Land Law* (2nd edn, 1999), para 4–01.
[10] *Glencruitten Trs* v *Love* 1966 SLT (Land Ct) 5 at 6 in the note referring to *Trotter* v *Torrance* (1891) 18 R 848. See also the Interpretation Act 1978, s 5 and Sched 1 and SI 1999/1379, arts 6 and 7 and Sched 1.
[11] *Glasgow City and District Railway* v *MacBrayne* (1883) 10 R 894, per Lord President Inglis at 902.
[12] Such as the right to receive feuduties (an annual payment, formerly dues by a vassal to a feudal superior). See *Presbytery of Ayr and Others, Petitioners* (1842) 4 D 630. *Cf Governors of Cauvin's Hospital, Petitioners* (1842) 4 D 556.
[13] *Stair Memorial Encyclopaedia*, Vol 18, para 10(3).

THINGS

The things or items of property that are the subject of a right of property are classified **7–06** by Scots law in various ways. There are two primary methods of classification, which are derived from Roman law,[14] as follows:

(a) *corporeal* and *incorporeal* property. The former comprises tangible or concrete items such as land whilst the latter extends to intangible items which have no physical presence,[15] such as rights of copyright;

(b) *heritable* and *moveable* property. The distinction is unsatisfactory because the wording is obscure but behind the actual words used there is a basic distinction between immoveable and moveable property based on the nature of the property.[16]

From the interaction of the classification of property in two different ways emerge four separate categories of property: (a) corporeal heritable property; (b) corporeal moveable property; (c) incorporeal heritable property; and (d) incorporeal moveable property. The corporeal heritable property recognised by Scots law includes land[17] and things built or growing on land in so far as they accede to the land.[18] The incorporeal heritable property recognised by Scots law includes the separate tenement of salmon fishing,[19] servitudes,[20] proper liferent, leases,[21] and standard securities.

ACCESSION

Corporeal moveable property which is attached to land may become part of the land **7–07** by accession. The item so attached is known as a "fixture". The classic example is buildings which at one time would have been moveable bricks and cement. When a moveable item is attached to heritage it is then owned by the owner of the heritage to which it is attached.[22] There are three conditions for accession and usually all three must be met before accession takes place. First, there must be some physical connection—usually a physical attachment—between the land and the fixture. Wallpaper pasted on a wall attaches to the wall. Second, the item attached must be subordinate in function to the land or building to which it is attached. Storage heaters attach to the wall of the house in which they are attached as they are intended to heat the house.[23] In some cases this subordination will be sufficient to compensate for a lack

---

[14] Gaius, *Institutes*, II, 12–14; Justinian, *Institutes*, II, ii, 1–3; Erskine, *Inst*, II, ii, 1 and 2.
[15] Erskine, *Inst*, II, ii, 1; Bell, *Commentaries*, II, 1; Bankton, *Institute*, I, iii, 20; *Stair Memorial Encyclopaedia*, Vol 18, para 11.
[16] Gordon, *Scottish Land Law* (2nd edn, 1999), para 1–01.
[17] Erskine, II, ii, 4; Gordon, *Scottish Land Law* (2nd edn, 1999), para 1–03.
[18] Erskine, II, ii, 4; Gordon, *Scottish Land Law* (2nd edn, 1999), para 1–03.
[19] Gordon, *Scottish Land Law* (2nd edn, 1999), para 1–03; *Stair Memorial Encyclopaedia*, Vol 18, para 10(3).
[20] Erskine, II, ii, 5–6; Gordon, *Scottish Land Law* (2nd edn, 1999), para 1–03.
[21] Gordon, *Scottish Land Law* (2nd edn, 1999), para 1–03; *Stair Memorial Encyclopaedia*, Vol 18, para 652.
[22] *Brand's Trs v Brand's Tr* (1876) 3 R (HL) 16.
[23] *Fife Assessor v Hodgson* 1966 SC 30.

of actual attachment: on this basis the front door key of a house is regarded as heritable. Third, the attachment must be more than temporary and usually it is permanent. Where an item has been specially adapted for a particular room, this may indicate an intent that it is to remain there permanently. The converse is also true— where a room has been specially adapted for an item of machinery, such as by the installation of special foundations, this may indicate that the machinery is a fixture.[24] Growing trees, plants and other crops (apart from the instance of industrial growing crops), accede to the ground in which they are planted.[25] Industrial growing crops which require annual seed and labour, however, do not accede and are not heritable.[26] Trees cease to be heritable when they are felled[27] and plants cease to be heritable when put into moveable pots.[28]

REAL RIGHTS AND PERSONAL RIGHTS

7–08   The distinction between real rights and personal rights is not something which is understood by a typical client[29] but it is of primary importance to the Scottish law of property. A real right is absolute in that it prevails against the world at large whilst in general a personal right is enforceable only against a person or a class of persons. In the context of land law, an almost infinite variety of personal rights and obligations may arise in contract. Those which are most frequently encountered include the contractual rights of both seller and purchaser under missives to purchase land[30] and the delictual rights of neighbours arising under the law of nuisance.[31] Parties cannot agree to create any right which they see fit as a real right by entering into an agreement and designating the rights and obligations thereby created as "real rights". As regards land the real rights recognised by Scots law in the modern era include the following:

(a) property (*dominium*);

(b) proper liferent;

(c) servitude;

(d) tenant's right in a lease;

(e) creditor's right in fixed security;

(f) certain public rights such as a public right of way;

---

[24]   *Scottish Discount Ltd* v *Blin* 1985 SC 216.
[25]   *Stewart* v *Stewart's Exrs* (1761) M 5436; *Paul* v *Cuthbertson* (1840) 2 D 1286; *Anderson* v *Ford* (1844) 6 D 1315; Stair, II, i, 34; Erskine, II, i, 14 and 15; Carey Miller, *The Law of Corporeal Moveables in Scotland* (1991), para 3.04; Gordon, *Scottish Land Law* (2nd edn, 1999), para 5–40; *Stair Memorial Encyclopaedia*, Vol 18, paras 12 and 595.
[26]   *Stair Memorial Encyclopaedia*, Vol 18, para 12.
[27]   *Stair Memorial Encyclopaedia*, Vol 18, para 12.
[28]   Stair, II, i, 34; Carey Miller, *The Law of Corporeal Moveables in Scotland* (1991), para 3.04.
[29]   Gretton and Reid, *Conveyancing* (2nd edn, 1999), para 1.08.
[30]   See generally Cusine and Rennie, *Missives* (2nd edn, 1999).
[31]   See generally Whitty, "Nuisance", *Stair Memorial Encyclopaedia*, Vol 14, paras 2001–2168; Gordon, *Scottish Land Law* (2nd edn, 1999), Chap 26.

(g) certain statutory rights; and

(h) tenants at will.

THE MANNER OF CREATION

In relation to the creation of many real rights there is a two-stage process. The first is a **7–09** contractual stage known only to the parties to that contract, the second a stage which almost invariably involves some act which publicises the existence of the right to the general public.[32] For example, when a lease is executed by the landlord and tenant there is a contract of lease but the tenant's right does not become a real right until he takes possession or the lease is recorded in the General Register of Sasines or registered in the Land Register of Scotland (as appropriate). The public act in the second stage of creation of a real right in heritable property operates as the legal equivalent of the delivery of corporeal moveable property. In modern Scots law the public act varies in relation to different real rights. Registration of the deed of creation in a public register, usually the general Register of Sasines or Land Register of Scotland is the most usually encountered form of public act. A right of property, proper liferent, servitudes (both positive and negative), standard security[33] and long leases[34] are among those real rights created by registration of a deed in the General Register of Sasines.[35] Only "interests in land" are registrable in the Land Register of Scotland.[36] This term is defined as meaning "any estate, interest, servitude or other heritable right in and over land, including a heritable security[37] but excluding a lease which is not a long lease". Taking possession of the subject of the right or exercise of the right is another frequently encountered method of creating real rights. Real rights which may be so created include short leases, certain long leases and positive servitudes.[38] For the creation of company charges (standard securities and floating charges granted by limited companies) there is the additional requirement of the registration of the charge within a limited period of time in the charges section of the company file kept by the registrar of companies.[39] The floating charge does not become a real right until it "attaches" or "crystallises".[40]

THE MANNER OF TRANSMISSION

Transmission of property and the creation of derivative real rights is a major branch of **7–10** the law in its own right, known as "conveyancing". Given that about 40 per cent of the business of most firms of solicitors comprises conveyancing its significance is

---

[32] Gordon, *Scottish Land Law* (2nd edn, 1999), para 12–03. For the "publicity principle" in South Africa law, see Van der Merwe and de Waal, "The Law of Things and Servitudes", in Joubert, *The Law of South Africa*, Vols 25 and 27 (1993) paras 7 and 10.

[33] Conveyancing and Feudal Reform (Scotland) Act 1970, s 9.

[34] Registration of Leases (Scotland) Act 1857, s 2; Land Registration (Scotland) Act 1979 ("1979 Act"), ss 2(1)(a)(v) and 28(1).

[35] Johnston, *Prescription* (2000), para 15.10. See also Abolition of Feudal Tenure etc (Scotland) Act 2000, ss 1 and 63.

[36] 1979 Act, s 2; Johnston, *Prescription* (2000), para 15.10.

[37] This term is defined by reference to the Conveyancing and Feudal Reform (Scotland) Act 1970, s 9(8).

[38] Gordon, *Scottish Land Law* (2nd edn, 1999), paras 24–26 *et seq.*

[39] Companies Act 1985, s 410.

[40] Companies Act 1985, s 463(1); Insolvency Act 1986, s 53(7); *Stair Memorial Encyclopaedia*, Vol 18, para 8.

obvious—contrary to the belief of some it is not a rag bag of mere technicalities.[41] A right of heritable property is normally transferred by means of a disposition granted by the existing proprietor. The grantee named in the deed ("the disponee") does not become the owner of the property until the deed is recorded in the General Register of Sasines (or, where appropriate, registered in the Land Register of Scotland). Mere delivery of the disposition is insufficient to transfer ownership of land.[42] A servitude is transferred by a disposition and it cannot be transferred separately from the dominant tenement to which it is attached. As regards the tenant's right in a lease this is transferred by means of a deed known as an assignation which is delivered to the assignee and intimated to the landlord. If the lease is a recorded (or registered lease) the assignation is also recorded in the Sasine register (or registered in the Land Register of Scotland as appropriate).

RIGHT OF PROPERTY

7–11 The right of property, known as *dominium*, is potentially the most extensive power in respect of an item of property. Two or more persons may not hold simultaneously a full and exclusive right of ownership in the same piece of land but this does not preclude the possibility of two people owning property in common. In such a case their ownership is not exclusive. Scots law does not admit that there may be several owners of one item of property some of whom may have better rights than others. Until recently this was obscured by the existence of the feudal system of landholding whereby several parties (superiors and vassals) were regarded as co-owners in one item of land at the same time. The basic theory of this system held that all title to land was derived from the Crown who retained a title as paramount superior. Under the Crown existed mid-superiors each of whom held a right known as *dominium directum* and lastly there was a party (known as a "vassal") who owned the property right known as the *domimium utile*.[43] Only the vassal was entitled to occupy and use the land although the right of superiority conferred several rights on the superior, the most important of which in recent years was to enforce feudal real conditions. Upon the abolition of the feudal system in Scotland superiorities of all types will be extinguished and their rights of enforcement will disappear.

ENTITLEMENTS OF OWNER

7–12 The right of property has been defined by Erskine as "the right of using and disposing of a subject as our own, except in so far as we are restrained by law or paction".[44] A right of property of land confers upon the owner the following entitlements:

---

[41] A measure of the importance of the topic may be assessed from the volume of the highest quality scholarly analysis given to it. See, *eg*, Halliday, *Conveyancing Law and Practice* (2nd edn, 1996); Gretton and Reid, *Conveyancing* (2nd edn, 1999); McDonald, *Conveyancing Manual* (6th edn, 1998); Cusine, *Standard Securities* (1991).

[42] *cf Sharp* v *Thomson* 1997 SLT 636 (HL).

[43] Gordon, *Scottish Land Law* (2nd edn, 1999), para 13–03.

[44] Erskine, *Inst*, II, i, 1.

(a) to use, enjoy and possess the land;

(b) to exclude others from the land;

(c) the right to grant derivative real rights (such as a lease, a proper liferent and standard security).

(d) to alienate the land (transfer it to others).

The right of use, enjoyment and possession in the abstract will permit the owner to use his property in any manner he sees fit. He may build houses or churches, sow and reap crops, or do nothing at all if he pleases. So stated the definition bears little relation to practice. The right of property may be limited by agreement and invariably is restricted by statute where it tends to injure the rights of others.[45] Such limi-tations derogate from the "absolute" nature of the right.[46] So numerous are these limitations that it would be futile to attempt a complete list here. Nevertheless, some of the more common limitations are as follows.

Limitations by agreement

Limitations on use may be merely contractual, as where a builder enters into a **7–13** contractual agreement with another builder that he will not develop a particular plot of ground for a period of years. Real conditions may impose limitations on use. For example, a servient proprietor may be subject to an obligation to use his property for a specific use only. The grant of any derivative real right will almost invariably create a limitation on use. For example, where a servitude is granted the servient proprietor will be precluded from carrying out any activity which is inconsistent with the free and full use of the servitude. For example, where a servient proprietor has granted a servitude of access he cannot dig a trench across the access route and make the taking of access impossible.

Statutory limitations

Statutory limitations are very commonly encountered in practice. For example, **7–14** planning permission is required for any significant building work and for certain changes of use. For the purposes of planning law there are various defined types of use, known as Use Classes, and a change of use within a Use Class does not require planning permission.[47] The obtaining of planning permission does not absolve the proprietor from the requirement of obtaining other statutory permissions which are required under other statutes. For example, construction or demolition of many types of building requires a building warrant.[48] Use of land as a caravan site requires permission.[49] The right of destruction may be limited by statute. For example, demolition of a building within a conservation area requires permission.[50] Outwith a conservation area a proprietor must obtain permission to demolish a listed building[51]

---

[45] Bell, *Principles*, s 939.
[46] Bell, *Principles* s 939; *Stair Memorial Encyclopaedia*, Vol 18, para 195.
[47] Town and Country Planning (Use Classes) (Scotland) Order 1997 (SI 1997/3061) (as amended).
[48] Building (Scotland) Act 1959, s 6(1); Gretton and Reid, *Conveyancing* (2nd edn, 1999), paras 4.23–4.28.
[49] Caravan Sites and Control of Development Act 1960, s 1.
[50] Planning (Listed Buildings and Conservation Areas) (Scotland) Act 1997, ss 66–68.
[51] *ibid* s 6.

or an ancient monument.[52] In special cases statute may restrict the right of a proprietor to carry out certain legal acts. For example, a lease of a vacant croft granted by a proprietor will be null and void unless the proprietor obtains the written consent of the Crofters' Commission or failing such consent, the consent of the Scottish Ministers.[53]

Common law limitations

7–15 Nuisance may be defined as use of property in such a manner as to occasion material and intolerable interference with the enjoyment or use by another party of his land or property.[54] Nuisance may be committed in an infinite variety of ways and what constitutes a nuisance in any one case may be a matter of circumstances. Commonly encountered examples of nuisance include the emission of noxious fumes or smoke which damage buildings, vegetation or animals,[55] the escape of sewage into a neighbouring building,[56] the generation of dust destroying food in a larder[57] and the emission of light which scares away fish in a neighbouring river.[58] The question is to be determined from the point of view of the victim of the harm rather than from the point of view of the alleged wrongdoer. This means that the wrongdoer's use of the land need not be unusual.[59] The matter will be judged by reference to the standards of ordinary inhabitants of the locality and not by reference to persons who are overly sensitive.[60] In deciding what is a nuisance the courts will take into account various factors including the nature of the locality of the area. It is a defence to an action of nuisance to show that the party complaining has consented expressly or impliedly to the nuisance.[61] The right to object to a nuisance may also be lost by the expiry of the 20-year period of negative prescription.[62] It is no defence to an action that the defender will suffer loss if he has to desist from the activity complained of[63] or that the public is benefited by the activity.[64]

Limitations on extent—boundaries

7–16 A proprietor of land may not exercise any rights of property outwith his boundaries although he may be entitled to exercise servitudes over the land of other parties. A proprietor of land may seek interdict to prevent encroachment or trespass on his land or obtain damages where interdict is not available. Trespass is transient intrusion into the land of another as may be occasioned by straying animals. Where the intrusion is permanent or semi-permanent it is classified as encroachment, as may be the case if a party erects a building partly on the land of his neighbour. In respect of both of these matters it is vital to determine the line of the boundaries of the property in question.

---

[52] Ancient Monuments and Archaeological Areas Act 1979, s 2.
[53] Crofters (Scotland) Act 1993, s 23(3); Scotland Act 1998, s 63.
[54] *Watt v Jamieson* 1954 SC 56, per Lord President Cooper at 57–58.
[55] *Chalmers v William Dixon Ltd* (1876) 3 R 461.
[56] *RHM Bakeries (Scotland) Ltd v Strathclyde Regional Council* 1973 SLT 214.
[57] *Ireland v Smith* (1895) 33 SLR 156.
[58] *Stonehaven and District Angling Association v Stevenson Recreation Ground Trs and Stonehaven Tennis Club*, Stonehaven Sheriff Court, 17th January 1997, unreported.
[59] *Maguire v Charles McNeil Ltd* 1922 SC 174.
[60] *ibid.*
[61] *Hill v Dixon* (1850) 12 D 508.
[62] Prescription and Limitation (Scotland) Act 1973, s 8.
[63] *Shotts Iron Co v Inglis* (1882) 9 R (HL) 78.
[64] *Duke of Buccleuch v Cowan* (1866) 5 M 214.

These will be found by a construction of the terms of the titles. This is a relatively simple task in relation to titles registered in the Land Register of Scotland because that system of registration is a map-based system. A plan based on the Ordnance Survey map showing the boundaries of each interest in land is attached to the relevant Land Certificate. Many titles recorded in the Sasine register also have plans attached to them but these may be declared to be "demonstrative", meaning the plan is not guaranteed to be accurate. Many Sasine titles contain a verbal description of the property which is of a general nature and may not define the exact line of the boundaries. In such cases the law relies on certain presumptions. The most important of these relate to roads. Where a property is stated to be "bounded by" a road the boundary is presumed to be the mid-line of the road if the road is a public road[65] and the near edge of the road where it is a private road.[66] These presumptions are rebuttable by contrary provisions in the titles.[67] As regards horizontal boundaries the normal rule is that a proprietor owns the minerals below his ground and the airspace above, consonant with the maxim recognising the extent of ownership as being *a coelo usque ad centrum*. He may therefore prevent encroachments into airspace by machines such as tower cranes.[68] The general rule of vertical ownership is varied where minerals under a site are held on a separate title or where flats on different storeys within a single building are owned by different owners. In the latter case the boundary above and below a tenement flat is presumed to be the mid-line of the joists.[69] Again this may be altered by alternative provision in the titles.

CO-OWNERSHIP

More than one person may have a right of property in the same item of heritable   **7–17** property as an undivided whole. This is known as *pro indiviso* or undivided ownership and may also be referred to as co-ownership. In this form of ownership the individual parts of the item owned are not individually attributed. Thus, where two parties own a two bedroom house on a *pro indiviso* basis they each do not have the exclusive ownership in one bedroom: rather each bedroom (and all the other parts of the house) are owned in common. It is equally possible for the derivative real rights to be held on a *pro indiviso* basis. For example, unless it is otherwise excluded a tenant's right in a lease may be held by two or more tenants. For simplicity's sake, the comments in the following paragraphs will be limited to the right of ownership.

Types of co-ownership

The most commonly encountered forms of co-ownership in recent years are joint property   **7–18** and common property. The main distinctions between joint and common property are:

(a) Common property is much more frequently encountered than joint property. Joint property may exist only in limited circumstances—these are (i) trust ownership and (ii) ownership by unincorporated associations.

---

[65] *Mags of Ayr* v *Dobbie* (1898) 25 R 1184.
[66] *Argyllshire Commissioners* v *Campbell* (1885) 12 R 1255.
[67] *Houston* v *Barr* 1911 SC 134.
[68] *Brown* v *Lee Construction Ltd* 1977 SLT (Notes) 61.
[69] Bell, *Principles*, s 1086; *Dickson* v *Morton* (1824) 3 S 310.

(b) In common property each of the co-owners has a share in the *pro indiviso* (as undivided) whole.[70] The undivided shares held by each of the co-owners need not necessarily be equal.

(c) In common property the general rule is that each of the co-proprietors may carry out certain legal acts in relation to their separate share. Thus each of them may sell, bequeath, [71] dispone (gratuitously or for a consideration) their share[72] or sub-divide into smaller *pro indiviso* shares[73] their own share or grant a right of security over it without the consent of any of the other proprietors. A *pro indiviso* proprietor cannot carry out legal acts in relation to the shares of others unless authority has been delegated to him.[74] A co-proprietor, however, cannot contract with himself. On this basis it has been held that co-proprietors even if they all act together cannot grant a lease to one of their own number.[75] There are certain limitations arising from the special statutory regulation of matrimonial homes.[76]

(d) In joint property there are no separate shares. Instead, the title to the property is held by the trustees for the time being or, as the case may be, by the members of the unincorporated association.[77] A trustee may not grant a security over property in joint ownership in respect of his private debts. Upon resignation or death of a joint owner the right of property will accresce automatically to the remaining trustees or members of the association.

(e) The management of joint property is dealt with by rules relative to trust property whilst the details of the applicable rules of common property are outlined below.

Management and use of common property

7–19 The rules for management of common property are surprisingly unclear[78] but the generally accepted view is that the consent of all co-proprietors must be obtained in respect of acts of management with the result that any one co-owner has a veto. Where deadlock occurs any of the co-proprietors may apply for judicial regulation[79] or the appointment of a judicial factor.[80] Subject to contrary agreement between the co-owners and subject to the special rules relative to "matrimonial homes"[81] the use of common property is governed by the following:

---

[70] *Eunson* v *The Braer Corporation* 1999 SLT 1405.
[71] Provided always there is no extant survivorship destination which the parties are contractually bound not to evacuate. This obligation may arise expressly or impliedly, albeit the latter is much more common: see *Perrett's Trs* v *Perrett* 1909 SC 522; 1909 1 SLT 302; *Brown's Trs* v *Brown* 1943 SC 488; 1944 SLT 215; *Hay's Tr* v *Hay's Trs* 1951 SC 329; 1951 SLT 170. See generally Gretton, "Destinations" (1989) 34 JLSS 299.
[72] Bell, *Principles*, s 1073. This is not affected by an extant survivorship destination: see *Steele* v *Caldwell* 1979 SLT 228 (OH); *Smith* v *Mackintosh* 1989 SLT 148; 1989 SCLR 83.
[73] *Menzies* v *Macdonald* (1854) 16 D 827; *Stair Memorial Encyclopaedia*, Vol 18, para 28.
[74] For an example of authority given by all co-proprietors to one co-proprietor to lease the common property, see *Grozier* v *Downie* (1871) 9 M 826.
[75] *Barclay* v *Penman* 1984 SLT 376; *Clydesdale Bank plc* v *Davidson* 1996 SLT 437.
[76] See para 7–19.
[77] *Stair Memorial Encyclopaedia*, Vol 18, para 20.
[78] Bell, *Principles*, ss 1072, 1075 and 1077.
[79] *Stair Memorial Encyclopaedia*, Vol 18, paras 23 and 30.
[80] *ibid* Vol 18, paras 23 and 31.
[81] See note 85.

(a) Each common proprietor is entitled to use every part of the item which is subject to common ownership.[82] No common owner may take exclusive possession of the whole or any part of that property without the consent of the other co-proprietors.[83]

(b) Each co-owner may make only "ordinary" use of the property.[84] What amounts to an ordinary use may depend both on the nature of the property in question and on the recent history of use. It remains open to the parties to define "ordinary" and permitted uses by means of a real condition in a deed of declaration of conditions affecting all the shares. "Ordinary" use of a "matrimonial home"[85] commonly owned by a husband and wife or matrimonial homes owned by the spouses in common with one or more third parties clearly includes the occupancy of that property by either of the spouses for residential purposes. Under statutory provision either spouse may apply to the court for an order to regulate the exercise of occupancy rights.[86] In suitable cases the court may exclude the other spouse from the matrimonial home.[87]

(c) No co-proprietor may obtain an excessive benefit at the expense of the other co-proprietors. What amounts to "excessive" benefit may depend on the nature of the property, the total number of co-proprietors and the size of share held by the party alleged to be taking the excessive benefit.

(d) A co-owner may communicate his right of use to third parties[88] although he may not create a lease conferring exclusive possession of the whole subjects on the grantee.

Alterations, improvements and repairs

Subject to contrary agreement by means of real conditions the issue of alterations, **7–20** improvements and repairs is governed by the following principles:

(a) Each common proprietor has a right to veto the carrying out of any alterations to the common property.[89]

---

[82] Erskine, *Inst*, II, vi, 53.
[83] *Bailey* v *Scott* (1860) 22 D 1105, per Lord Benholme at 1109. A similar rule exists in South Africa: see *Swart* v *Taljaard* (1860) 3S 35.
[84] Bell, *Principles*, s 1075.
[85] This is defined in the Matrimonial Homes (Family Protection) (Scotland) Act 1981 ("1981 Act"), s 22, as amended by the Law Reform (Miscellaneous Provisions) (Scotland) Act 1985, s 13(10). The term means any house, caravan, houseboat or other structure which has been provided or has been made available by one or both of the spouses as, or has become a family residence. It includes any garden or other ground or building attached to, and usually occupied with, or otherwise required for the amenity or convenience of, the house, caravan, houseboat or other structure. Excluded from the definition is a residence provided or made available by one spouse for that spouse to reside in, whether with any child of the family or not, separately from the other spouse.
[86] 1981 Act, s 3(1)(d).
[87] 1981 Act, s 4, as amended by the Law Reform (Miscellaneous Provisions) (Scotland) Act 1985, s 13(5). See *Stair Memorial Encyclopaedia*, Vol 18, paras 863 and 864.
[88] *George Watson's Hospital Governors* v *Cormack* (1883) 11 R 320, per Lord McLaren at 323 (affd (1883) 11 R 320 (IH)).
[89] Bell, *Principles*, s 1075; *Anderson* v *Dalrymple* (1709) M 12831; *Reid* v *Nicol* (1799) M "Property", App No 1; *Taylor* v *Dunlop* (1872) 11 M 25.

(b) An exception to the requirement of unanimity exists in relation to necessary repairs. A single co-proprietor may instruct necessary repairs without the consent of his co-proprietors[90] and probably also without consulting with them in advance.[91] The instructing party may then recover a proportion of the cost from his co-proprietors conform to the size of their respective shares.[92]

(c) A statutory removal of the common law veto relative to repairs, alterations and improvements exists where the co-owned property comprises a "matrimonial home".[93]

Division and sale

7–21   Each co-owner in common property is entitled to apply to the court to have the property divided proportionately amongst all the co-owners or, if such physical division is impracticable, to have the entire property sold and the proceeds divided.[94] Subject to the exceptional cases noted below,[95] the entitlement of each co-proprietor to a division and sale is absolute.[96] Only where property is indivisible will the court order it to be sold. Property will be considered indivisible if it is impossible to divide the property in such a manner as to give each co-proprietor a *pro rata* share or if such a division can be carried out only by adversely affecting the value of the whole property.[97] The method of sale may be by public roup or by private bargain,[98] the latter being more common in modern practice. The absolute right of a *pro indiviso* proprietor to obtain a division and sale in respect of the common property may be limited in various ways as follows:

(a) The right may be excluded by contract but this will not bind singular successors.

(b) In appropriate circumstances a co-proprietor may be personally barred from insisting on division and sale.[99]

(c) Limitations may arise from the nature of the property. Indivisible property includes essential access areas owned in common such as stair cases in tenements, common access roads serving modern developments and shared gardens.[100]

---

[90] Bell, *Principles*, s 1075, approved in *Deans v Woolfson* 1922 SC 221; 1922 SLT 165. *Cf Murray v Johnstone* (1896) 23 R 981, per Lord Moncreiff at 990.
[91] *Rennie v McGill* (1885) 1 Sh Ct Rep 158. *Cf Homecare Contracts (Scotland) Ltd v Scottish Midland Co-operative Society Ltd* 1999 GWD 23–1111 (Sh Ct).
[92] *Rennie v McGill* (1885) 1 Sh Ct Rep 158; *Miller v Crichton* (1893) 1 SLT 262 (OH); Gloag, *The Law of Contract* (2nd edn, 1929), p 323.
[93] As defined in statute: see note 85.
[94] Craig, *Jus Feudale*, II, 8, 35, 41; Stair, I, vii, 15; Bankton, I, viii, 36, 40; Erskine, *Inst*, III, iii, 56; Bell, *Principles*, ss 1079–1082.
[95] See subparagraphs (a) to (d) in this paragraph.
[96] *Upper Crathes Fishing Ltd v Bailey's Exrs* 1991 SCLR 151; 1991 SLT 747.
[97] See *Thom v MacBeath* (1875) 3 R 161.
[98] *Campbells v Murray* 1972 SC 310; 1972 SLT 249.
[99] *Upper Crathes Fishing Ltd v Bailey's Exrs* 1991 SCLR 151 at 152, 1991 SLT 747 at 749 (per Lord President Hope).
[100] *Grant v Heriot's Trust* (1906) 8 F 647, per Lord McLaren at 665; *Stair Memorial Encyclopaedia*, Vol 18, para 26.

(d) Where the co-owned property comprises a "matrimonial home"[101] co-owned by a husband and wife statutory rules limit, but do not wholly exclude, the right of each of the spouses to apply for a division and sale.

Legal proceedings—title to sue

The general rule is that legal proceedings affecting one *pro indiviso* share only must be **7–22** raised by the owner of that share and a co-proprietor has no title to raise legal proceedings in respect of matters affecting only another share.[102] Actions relating to the whole common property must be raised by all the owners acting together.

TIMESHARES

Timeshares usually involve various people having the right to the exclusive use of **7–23** land or salmon fishings for fixed periods of time. They do not usually involve co-ownership of any sort. The most commonly encountered method of creating a timeshare in Scotland is for the real right of property in the item subject to the timeshare to be held by a trustee and for the persons purchasing timeshares to be beneficiaries of that trust.

LIFERENTS

Liferent is the right to the use or income of property for the duration of the lifetime of **7–24** the holder or some shorter period as determined in the deed of constitution. It may affect both moveables[103] and heritage but the former will not be discussed further here. It should be noted, however, that it is common for liferents which affect a domestic house to affect the furniture in that house as well.[104] The essence of the right is that the liferenter will not destroy or waste the substance of the subject. The liferenter is therefore entitled to enjoy the fruits of the subject but not anything which is part of its capital. An exception is made in cases where a liferent is created over mineral workings. In such a case the liferenter may extract the minerals even though this diminishes the extent of the estate by so doing.

PROPER AND IMPROPER LIFERENTS

Two types of liferent are recognised in Scotland—proper and improper.[105] Improper **7–25** liferents are sometimes termed "beneficiary" liferents.[106]

---

[101] As defined in statute: see note 85.
[102] *Eunson* v *The Braer Corporation* 1999 SLT 1405.
[103] *Stair Memorial Encyclopaedia*, Vol 18, para 534(2).
[104] *Cochran* v *Cochran* (1755) M 8280; Bell's *Illustrations*, Vol 2, p 141.
[105] Gordon, *Scottish Land Law* (2nd edn, 1999), para 17–02.
[106] See, *eg*, Gordon, *Scottish Land Law* (2nd edn, 1999), para 17–02.

(a) Proper liferent is one of the real rights recognised by Scots law.[107] A proper liferent may be constituted either by a grant in liferent or by reservation of a liferent in a grant of fee.

(b) Improper liferent is merely the beneficial interest under a trust and the beneficiary has no real right in the land. The real right of ownership rests with the trustees[108] who hold the property for two classes of beneficiary: the liferenter and the fiar. It follows that an improper liferent may be constituted only by the creation of a trust.

Alimentary liferents

7–26 An alimentary liferent is a special category of improper liferent which is intended to provide for the maintenance of the liferenter in a manner which also protects the liferenter from his or her own improvidence. A proper liferent may not be created as an alimentary liferent.[109] No person may create an alimentary liferent of his own property in his own favour.[110] In relation to such a liferent there are two main limitations which secure protection for the liferenter. First, the liferented subjects may not be attached by the liferenter's creditors (except creditors for alimentary debts[111]). Second, the beneficiary may not assign, terminate or vary the alimentary liferent except with the court's approval.[112] In an alimentary liferent the trustees must be independent from the beneficiary.[113]

RIGHTS AND OBLIGATIONS

7–27 In a proper liferent the liferenter has a right to grant servitudes[114] or leases which have an endurance equal to or less than the liferent itself but may grant rights extending beyond this duration only with the consent of the fiar. Liferenters bear the annual and ordinary burdens on the subjects such as taxes, ordinary repairs and fire insurance premiums. They are not liable for ordinary wear and tear.

LEASES

7–28 A lease is a grant of land by one person (known as "the landlord" or "the lessor") to another person (known as "the tenant" or "the lessee") for a specified period of time

---

[107] *Stair Memorial Encyclopaedia*, Vol 18, paras 5(3) and 74. Abolition of Feudal Tenure etc (Scotland) Act 2000, s 63.
[108] *ibid.*
[109] *Forbes's Trs v Tennant* 1926 SC 294; Gordon, *Scottish Land Law* (2nd edn, 1999), para 17–32.
[110] The rule for men arises from the common law: see, *eg, Ker's Tr v Justice* (1866) 5 M 4; *Ord Ruthven* v *Drummond* 1908 SC 1154. For women, the exceptional cases in which such a device was permitted at common law have been removed by statute in so far as the contract is entered into after 24th July 1984: see the Law Reform (Husband and Wife) (Scotland) Act 1984, s 5(1)(b).
[111] *Earl of Buchan* v *His Creditors* (1835) 13 S 1112; *Lord Ruthven* v *Pulford & Sons* 1909 SC 951; *Maitland* v *Maitland* 1912 1 SLT 350.
[112] Gordon, *Scottish Land Law* (2nd edn, 1999), paras 17–01 and 17–32; Trusts (Scotland) Act 1961, s 1(4). See Chapter 15.
[113] *McCallum v McCulloch's Trs* (1904) 7 F 337.
[114] *Stair Memorial Encyclopaedia*, Vol 18, para 449.

in return for the payment of a rent. For the landlord it enables him to arrange for the use of land which he cannot use personally or does not want to use personally. It may be a form of investment in which the rent represents the return. For the tenant it provides a way of securing the use of land without the capital outlay involved in an outright purchase. Sometimes, however, in addition to the rent a lump sum at the start of the lease is to be paid by the tenant. This is known as a "premium" or "grassum". In relation to "ground" leases—long leases granted for development purposes—the tenant usually pays a large premium at entry but thereafter is required to pay only a nominal annual rent. Leases are now widely used for residential, commercial or agricultural purposes in Scotland.

LEGAL ESSENTIALS OF A LEASE

There are four essentials to constitute a lease: two identified parties; an identified property; a rent; and a term or period of endurance. **7–29**

Parties

A lease is fundamentally a contract between a landlord and a tenant. No one may contract with himself.[115] As a result there must be two parties before there is a lease— the landlord and tenant. It is possible, however, to have a lease between one party acting in two capacities such as an individual on the one hand and the same party acting as a trustee on the other hand. Common proprietors may not grant a lease to one of their number.[116] In general a proprietor of land is free to decide whether or not to grant a lease. Nevertheless in rare cases a proprietor may be obliged to grant a lease in terms of statute. For example, where a croft is vacant the proprietor may be obliged by the Crofters' Commission to submit letting proposals and where this is not done timeously the Commission may proceed to do so themselves. Any lease granted by the Commission in terms of this provision shall have effect in all respects as if it had been granted by the landlord.[117] **7–30**

Property

A lease must have an item of heritable property as its subject. Any lease must properly identify the property which is subject to the lease. Broadly speaking, if a property or interest in land can be sold it can also be leased. Two rights, however, may be leased separately from the land over which the right is exercised even though they cannot be sold separately. These are rights to fish for fish other than salmon and rights to shoot game over land. **7–31**

Rent

A lease must have a rent. A party who is permitted to occupy ground without payment of a rent may be entitled to do so by some other form of contractual licence but it is not a lease. The rent, however, need not be money and it may consist of services. If the services are rendered as part of a contract of employment the services may not be a rent and the whole arrangement may not be a lease. For example, a **7–32**

---

[115] *Kildrummy Estates (Jersey) Ltd* v *IRC* 1991 SC 1.
[116] *Clydesdale Bank plc* v *Davidson* 1998 SC (HL) 51.
[117] Crofters (Scotland) Act 1993, s 23(5).

caretaker may be provided with a flat as part of his contract of employment. This is a service occupancy which is part of the contract of employment and is not a lease. Rent is usually a fixed sum of money per month or per annum depending on the length of the lease. In long leases there is usually extensive provision for review of rent to prevent the landlord's return being outstripped by inflation. In other cases the level of rent may be determined by reference to a formula, as is the case in leases of many retail premises where the rent increases where the turnover of the tenant increases.[118]

Term

7-33   There must be a term to a lease. Where parties have agreed to a lease but no period is specified the law will imply a term. This implied term will be year to year or the shortest term consistent with the tenancy. The period of occupation need not be continuous throughout the whole term. A lease may be granted of a holiday home for two weeks in July for a total period of 10 years. A tenant cannot grant a sub-lease for a period longer than his own lease.

CONSTITUTION OF A LEASE

7-34   With one exception, a lease should be in writing.[119] The exception is where the lease is for less than one year. Defects in the constitution of a lease may be cured by the conduct of the parties such as where the tenant takes occupation and pays rent. It is always prudent for the parties to reduce their agreement to writing even if writing is not required. Nevertheless, where a written lease is not required neither party can demand that the other party enters into a written agreement except where this right is conferred by statute. There is special statutory provision permitting either party to an agricultural tenancy to require that the other enters into a written lease with certain minimum contents.[120]

REAL RIGHT

7-35   A lease is essentially a personal contract between the original landlord and the original tenant. Where assignation is permitted there may be a substitution of a new tenant. The converse case is that of a new landlord which occurs when the landlord's interest is purchased. The new owner is bound by the lease provided it is a real right. The old Scottish statute known as the Leases Act 1449 provides that where a property which is subject to a lease is sold by the landlord or is otherwise transferred to a new owner then the new owner is bound by the lease. As a result the tenant can continue in occupation despite the sale. In legal terms this means that the tenant under the lease obtains not only a contractual right but a real right—a right enforceable against the whole world. In particular the lease is enforceable against a heritable creditor holding a standard security over the landlord's interest unless that creditor's right was established prior to the creation of the lease and he did not consent to the grant of the lease.[121] Not all leases may be converted into real rights. Where a lease cannot be

---

[118] See, *eg, Smyth* v *Caledonia Racing (1984) Ltd* 1987 GWD 16–612.
[119] Requirements of Writing (Scotland) Act 1995, ss 1 and 2.
[120] Agricultural Holdings (Scotland) Act 1991, s 4(1)(a).
[121] *Trade Development Bank* v *Warriner and Mason (Scotland) Ltd* 1980 SC 74.

converted into a real right it remains as a contract. To be created as a real right a lease must comply with the following:

(a) it must be of heritage (*ie* land or a fixture). It is doubtful whether a real right of lease may exist in relation to something like an advertising hoarding or a static wheelbarrow stall in a retail complex. Arrangements to use such items are probably some form of contractual licence. Statute has confirmed that the right to freshwater fishing may be created as a real right if granted for a period of not less than one year[122];

(b) there must be a rent. An arrangement for rent-free accommodation cannot be a real right.[123] In rare cases the right to receive the rent under a lease may be assigned to a third party separately from the landlord's other interests under the lease;

(c) there must be a term date. Leases for a perpetual period cannot be created as real rights. In terms of the legislation abolishing the feudal system a maximum duration of 175 years will be imposed on leases granted after the date of the legislation.[124] It is a condition of all leases granted after 1st September 1974 for a period of more than 20 years that the subjects of lease shall not be used as a private dwelling house[125]; and

(d) the tenant must have entered into possession. Where the lease is for a period of over 20 years (conveniently known as a "long lease") the tenant has the alternative of registering the lease to make it a real right and this is deemed to have the same effect as possession.[126] Under the new land registration system registration of a long lease is obligatory to obtain a real right in respect of a registered interest.[127] Possession is insufficient in such cases.

VARIOUS ASPECTS OF LEASES

A lease is a very flexible device. In general parties to a lease are free to include in that **7–36** lease whatever terms they wish provided they contain the four essentials of (a) parties (b) subjects (c) duration, and (d) rent. A specialty exists in relation to leases of agricultural tenancies, where either party may require the other enter into a lease containing, in addition to these four essentials, provisions for insurance of buildings and harvested crops.[128] Certain statutes also import obligations on the parties regardless of what is stated in the lease. For example, whatever the landlord and tenant may agree all crofts are subject to the statutory conditions listed in the relevant legislation[129] and agreements which deprive a crofter of his statutory rights are void unless the

---

[122] Freshwater and Salmon Fisheries (Scotland) Act 1976, s 4.
[123] *Wallace* v *Simmers* 1960 SC 255.
[124] Abolition of Feudal Tenure etc (Scotland) Act 2000, s 65. Scottish Law Commission, *Report on Abolition of the Feudal System* (Scot Law Com No 168) (December 1998), cl 61 of draft Bill.
[125] Land Tenure Reform (Scotland) Act 1974, s 8, as amended.
[126] Registration of Leases (Scotland) Act 1857, s 15, as amended by the Land Tenure Reform (Scotland) Act 1974, ss 8–10 and Sched 6.
[127] Land Registration (Scotland) Act 1979, s 2.
[128] Agricultural Holdings (Scotland) Act 1991, s 4 and Sched 1.
[129] Crofters (Scotland) Act 1993, s 5 and Sched 2.

agreement is approved by the Land Court.[130] For example, an agreement prohibiting a crofter from locating a caravan on his croft has been held void on the basis that it was unreasonable as it restricted the crofter's right to use the croft for a subsidiary or auxiliary use. In relation to residential leases for less than seven years granted on or after 3rd July 1962 there is a legally implied obligation on the landlord to keep in repair the structure and installations in the house.[131] Agreements to contract out of this obligation are void unless they are determined by the sheriff to be reasonable.[132] There are no reported instances of this having occurred.[133] In general, however, one must consult the lease to determine the obligations and rights of the landlord and tenant in any particular case. With this caveat in mind it is useful to outline certain commonly encountered aspects of leases.

Tacit relocation

7–37   A lease is not ended by the arrival of the term date (known as the "ish date") unless either (a) due notice of termination is given by the landlord to the tenant, or (b) the circumstances show that the parties regard the lease as ended. If due notice is not given, the lease is held to be renewed by the tacit consent of the parties. This is known as "tacit relocation". The lease is renewed from year to year if the original lease was for a year or more. The lease is renewed for the same term if the original lease was for less than a year. Tacit relocation will not operate if the parties have negotiated a new lease[134] or if the terms of the lease itself exclude tacit relocation.[135] There are special statutory rules for agricultural holdings[136] and crofts which are given special statutory protection. By and large these leases are continued perpetually by statute despite any term date stated in the written lease.

Assignation

7–38   The effect of assignation (otherwise "assignment") is normally to substitute a new tenant for the former one. The general rule at common law is that a lease is not assignable by the tenant either during his life or on his death because of the legal rule known as *delectus personae*. This means that the landlord has made a special choice of a person with whom he wishes to contract. There are exceptions to this common law rule where the assignation is involuntary such as where the tenant is rendered insolvent and a trustee in bankruptcy is appointed to his estate. Despite the common law rule the lease itself may permit assignation. Conversely it may expressly reinforce the common law rule by excluding assignation altogether. A common form of words used in a lease is that the tenant is given right to assign "with the express consent of the landlord". This leaves unfettered the discretion of the landlord to accept or reject a new tenant.[137] There is no implied requirement in Scotland that a landlord must act reasonably in granting consent. This may be compared with the position in England where statute implies a provision into a lease that "the landlord's consent will not be

---

[130] Crofters (Scotland) Act 1993, s 5(3) and Sched 2, para 9.
[131] Housing (Scotland) Act 1987, Sched 10, para 3.
[132] *ibid* Sched 10, para 5.
[133] Robson and Halliday, *Residential Tenancies* (2nd edn, 1998) para 3–51.
[134] *McFarlane v Mitchell* (1900) 2F 901.
[135] *MacDougall v Guidi* 1992 SCLR 167 (Sh Ct).
[136] Agricultural Holdings (Scotland) Act 1991, s 3.
[137] *Lousada & Co Ltd v JE Lessel (Properties) Ltd* 1990 SC 178.

unreasonably withheld" in respect of assignation.[138] Such wording may be expressly contained in a Scottish lease and, particularly in a commercial context, a tenant's solicitor would be wise to ensure that such words are revised into the draft lease if this is commercially negotiable. Where assignation is permitted, the original tenant's right comes to an end when the assignee completes his right to the lease. This will include intimation (notice) to the landlord. With the acceptance of the new tenant by the landlord, the former tenant is normally free of all obligations in the lease—other than those which accrued before the landlord was notified of the assignment. Where assignation is not permitted, a purported assignation will be ineffective and, provided the lease is suitably drafted, may involve forfeiture of the tenant's interest.

Sub-letting

By sub-leasing, the tenant carves a sub-lease out of his own lease. The tenant's lease **7–39** then becomes known as the "head lease". This is a term which originates in England but it is now commonly used in Scotland. The sub-lease must be for a term which is no longer than the tenant's lease. The existing tenant remains the tenant of his existing landlord but, in addition, becomes landlord in respect of the tenant. The existing tenant therefore continues to be liable to his landlord for all his obligations under the lease. The head landlord, notwithstanding the continuing relationship with his tenant, is likely to want to control sub-letting in much the same way as he will want to control assignation. Nevertheless, under sub-letting the landlord has the continuing liability and covenant of the existing tenant and may be willing to permit sub-letting where he would not be willing to permit assignation. The general rule at common law is that where assignation is excluded so is sub-letting. Despite this the terms of the lease may make their own provisions about sub-letting. In a sub-let the original lease remains in full effect. The sub-letting creates a new lease to which the law of leases also applies. There is no contractual relationship between the head landlord and the sub-tenant unless the former is joined as a party to the sub-lease. The mere fact that the head landlord consents to the granting of the sub-lease does not make him a party to the sub-lease.

Death of the tenant

A lease does not come to an end on the death of a tenant unless granted only for the **7–40** original tenant's lifetime. In some particular cases succession is regulated or excluded by statute, as is the case with the special rules for crofts and agricultural tenants. The lease itself may provide for succession to someone other than the tenant's successor at law. A power to assign in a lease will include a power to bequeath on death—it is simply a form of assignation. Sometimes the power to bequeath will be expressly dealt with in the lease. In the case of a lease of a private dwelling house protected by the Rent (Scotland) Act 1984[139] a statutory right of succession is given to the tenant's spouse, failing whom to any one member of the tenant's family who has been residing with him or her for six months preceding the tenant's death. This is known as a statutory tenancy and that tenancy may pass in turn to a second successor in the same way. The Housing (Scotland) Act 1988 has further restricted this.[140] A first succession is now limited to the tenant's spouse or a member of the tenant's family who has been

---

[138] Landlord and Tenant Act 1927, s 19.
[139] s 3 and Sched.1.
[140] s 46 and Sched 6; Robson and Halliday, *Residential Tenancies* (2nd edn, 1998), para 9–07.

in residence with the deceased for a two-year qualifying period. Such successors acquire a statutory assured tenancy. Succession to the statutory assured tenancy is also limited in a similar manner. Similar statutory provision is made for succession to a tenancy of a council house or flat.[141]

Breaks in the lease

7–41 Instead of providing for a single unbroken definite term, a lease may provide for an option for either party to break the lease at prescribed intervals. It may also provide for renewal at the end of the term. Such arrangements can be of advantage to both tenant and landlord. In a rising market a landlord can negotiate better terms. In a failing market a tenant may escape from an unduly burdensome lease. The arrangements are common in mining leases. They are encountered in commercial leases where a rent review clause is more common although the two may be linked. This would occur where a tenant is given an opportunity to break the lease if the new revised rent is too high for his business to support.

Resumption by the landlord

7–42 Where a landlord exercises his option under a break clause in a lease he resumes the land which is leased. Quite apart from a break clause, a lease may make express provision for resumption in special circumstances. For example, a landlord may make a provision that he can resume a field if he obtains planning permission allowing the field to be developed. There are detailed statutory provisions which regulate the resumption of agricultural tenancies[142] and crofts.[143]

Renunciation by the tenant

7–43 A lease may provide for renunciation (surrender) by the tenant in specified circumstances. In the absence of such a provision a tenant cannot renounce a lease, however burdensome, without the consent of the landlord. Where a landlord does consent to a renunciation sought by the tenant the landlord will usually do so on terms which require a payment from the tenant to compensate the landlord for loss of rent and oblige the tenant to reinstate the property. Where the renunciation is sought by the landlord the tenant will seek payment in compensation for the loss of the use of the property for the remainder of the lease.

Irritancy

7–44 "Irritancy" is a peculiar expression which denotes the bringing to an end of the legal relationship between the landlord and tenant. The tenant's right to the lease and to possession is extinguished. There are two types of irritancy provisions as follows: legal and conventional.

Legal irritancies

7–45 At common law there is an implied irritancy if a tenant does not pay his rent for two years. This is not much use in practice as very few landlords can afford to wait

---

[141] Housing (Scotland) Act 1987, s 52.
[142] Agricultural Holdings (Scotland) Act 1991, s 21(7) and ss 31 and 58; Gill, *Agricultural Holdings* (3rd edn, 1997), Chap 13.
[143] Crofters (Scotland) Act 1993, ss 20–21.

two years in cases of non-payment of rent. Under the agricultural holdings legislation there is an irritancy when rent is not paid for six months.[144] A crofter may also be removed for non-payment of rent for one year[145] or for breach of any of the statutory conditions.[146]

Conventional irritancies

These are expressly provided for in the lease. They may be used to support any **7–46** condition in the lease which the parties agree to be suitable for protection in this way. This includes non-payment of rent, failure to repair, assignation without landlord's consent or bankruptcy of the tenant. To secure irritancy of the lease the landlord usually proceeds to obtain a court decree confirming that the lease has been irritated. He can then show this decree to a new tenant to whom he wishes to re-lease the premises. Legal irritancies may be purged at any time before decree—the tenant may remedy the fault and avoid losing his lease. Conventional irritancies are enforceable according to their terms and are not purgeable as of right. They may be purged at common law if there is oppression on the part of the landlord but this is difficult to establish.[147] The effect of this common law rule undermined the value of the tenant's interest in a lease so the law was changed by statute. In the Law Reform (Miscellaneous Provisions) (Scotland) Act 1985, ss 4–7 there is provision that:

(a) for non-payment of money the landlord must serve a notice on the tenant giving at least 14 days' notice before irritancy;

(b) for other conditions (such as the obligation to carry out repairs) such notice is required as would be given by a reasonable landlord and the landlord may rely on the provision only if, in all the circumstances, a reasonable landlord would do so.

At the end of the notice period if the breach has not been purged, the landlord may irritate the lease. The decision to irritate the lease upon the tenant's default rests entirely with the landlord. If the market is strong and a new tenant is available he will take advantage of the situation. If the market is weak he may prefer to use another remedy such as suing for the rent from the existing tenant. What an irritancy clause will not allow a tenant to do is to unburden himself of an unwelcome lease by provoking the landlord into irritating the lease. Enforcement of an irritancy usually results in the loss of all real rights deriving from the lease such as standard securities created over the lease and will not normally give rise to a claim by the tenant against the landlord for unjustified enrichment.[148] Parties are free to contract to contrary effect in the lease on both these matters but, usually, only the first point receives attention with the heritable creditor being given a certain limited period of time to dispose of the tenant's interest in the lease provided, in the meantime, he undertakes the tenant's obligations in the lease.

---

[144] Agricultural Holdings (Scotland) Act 1991, s 20.
[145] Crofters (Scotland) Act 1993, ss 5(2)(a) and 26(1)(a).
[146] *ibid* ss 5(2)(b) and 26(1)(b).
[147] *Dorchester Studios (Glasgow) Ltd* v *Stone* 1975 SC (HL) 66; *HMV Fields Properties Ltd* v *Skirt and Slack Centre of London* 1982 SLT 477.
[148] *Dollar Land (Cumbernauld) Ltd* v *CIN Properties Ltd* 1988 SC (HL) 90.

Statutory security of tenure

7–47   In some situations the rights of tenants has been increased very considerably by special legislation. The tenants for whom such legislation has been enacted include those who occupy: (1) dwelling houses[149]; (2) shops[150]; and (3) agricultural tenancies[151] and crofts.[152] These provisions are too detailed to be covered in detail in this chapter and reference may be made to the specialist texts noted in the footnotes.

Conversion to ownership

7–48   There is no general legislation presently in force in Scotland which allows a tenant to convert his lease into ownership. If a tenant wishes to obtain a property right in the property subject to his lease he must buy the right from his landlord. He cannot compel his landlord to sell. There are three particular exceptions to this general rule. These are tenants who are public sector tenants holding secure tenancies, [153] tenants who are crofters[154] and tenants who hold under a customary form of tenure known as a "tenancy at will".[155] In all these limited cases the tenant has a right to acquire the interest of his landlord at a price which, failing agreement, is fixed by a statutory formula.

Possession

7–49   The landlord's primary obligation is to give his tenant possession of the subjects let. The tenant has a converse obligation to take possession of the subjects let. The nature of possession will depend on the subjects of lease. For example, a much lesser degree of possession is required for a shooting lease of a field than a lease of the same field for grazing purposes. Once possession has been taken, the landlord is obliged to maintain the tenant in undisturbed possession for the duration of the lease. If the landlord grants "warrandice" to the tenant this is a warranty that nothing has been done in the past and nothing will be done in the future by anyone to disturb possession. Mere business competition by the landlord or another tenant of the landlord is not disturbance which will found a claim for breach of warrandice. It is possible that the tenant may wish to bolster his position in relation to protection of his business by obtaining an assurance that the landlord (and his tenants) will not set up in the same business as the original tenant. This is a restrictive covenant and will be strictly construed by the courts. They are common in relation to what are known as "anchor tenants" or specialist shops in retail arcades. The converse of the landlord's obligation to give possession is the tenant's obligation to take possession. The tenant is obliged to continue in possession throughout the currency of the lease. In the absence of special stipulation the obligation of the tenant to occupy the subjects of lease will not constitute an obligation to trade from the subjects. Such express obligations—known

---

[149] Housing (Scotland) Act 1987 and Housing (Scotland) Act 1988; Robson and Halliday, *Residential Tenancies* (2nd edn, 1998).

[150] Tenancy of Shops (Scotland) Act 1949, as amended by the Tenancy of Shops (Scotland) Act 1964; McAllister, *Scottish Law of Leases* (2nd edn, 1995), Chap 8; *McMahon v Associated Rentals Ltd* 1987 SLT (Sh Ct) 94.

[151] Agricultural Holdings (Scotland) Act 1991; Gill, *Agricultural Holdings* (3rd edn, 1997).

[152] Crofters (Scotland) Act 1993; Agnew, *Crofting Law* (2000).

[153] Housing (Scotland) Act 1987, Pt III, ss 61–84.

[154] Crofters (Scotland) Act 1993, ss 12–19,

[155] Land Registration (Scotland) Act 1979, s 20.

as "keep open clauses"—are common in leases of retail subjects.[156] Such provisions are particularly useful where the lease relates to an important unit in a retail centre which would suffer considerable loss of prestige if a major tenant shut up shop and left. Similar provisions are found in agricultural leases where the obligation to farm continuously is designed to retain the value of the land.

Use of the subjects

A tenant has two duties in this regard: (a) to use the premises in a reasonable manner so as not to cause deterioration. For example, under an agricultural lease, a tenant will be expected to cultivate the land in accordance with the rules of good husbandry[157]; and (b) to use the premises for the purposes for which they were let and for that purposes only. Many leases expressly exclude particular uses such as the sale of alcoholic liquor.[158] The lease may allow for a change in the use with the landlord's consent. The landlord will obviously want to control this so as to maintain the value of the leased subjects. A lease will sometimes permit a change of use within a limited class of uses.

7–50

Rent

One of the primary obligations of the tenant is to pay the rent on the due date.[159] Correspondingly, one of the primary rights of the landlord is to receive the rent. As noticed before, rent is not always money. The lease may provide for rent to be in the form of certain services to be rendered by the tenant. An obligation on a tenant to maintain his mother (the landlord) and supply her with necessaries was sufficient to satisfy the requisites of a fixed rent.[160] Subject to statutory control, the parties may set their own rent. Because of inflation, it is common in a commercial lease for there to be a rent review provision. During wartime or periods of high inflation governments have sometimes resorted to general limitations on rent increases in an attempt to control the general economy. None of these general provisions are in force now. There are statutory restrictions limiting the increase of rents in relation to agricultural tenancies[161] and crofts.[162] There is now only limited statutory provision to control rents in residential tenancies which are protected tenancies or short assured tenancies.[163]

7–51

Repairs

There are a number of aspects of leases relating to repairs as follows:

7–52

   (a) At common law, the tenant is entitled to take possession of subjects which are reasonably fit for the purpose for which they are let.[164] The common law obligation of the landlord is sometimes circumvented by a clause in the lease

---

[156] See, eg, Cooperative Wholesale Society Ltd v Saxone Ltd 1997 SLT 1052.
[157] McCulloch v Grierson (1862) 1 M 53; Agriculture (Scotland) Act 1948, s 26 and Sched 6.
[158] See, eg, Crofters (Scotland) Act 1993, Sched 2, "The Statutory Conditions", para 12.
[159] See, eg, ibid para 1.
[160] Farquhar v Farquhar 1924 SLCR 19 at 22.
[161] Agricultural Holdings (Scotland) Act 1991, s 13.
[162] Crofters (Scotland) Act 1993, s 6.
[163] Rent (Scotland) Act 1984, s 46; Housing (Scotland) Act 1988, ss 24 and 34; Robson and Halliday, *Residential Tenancies* (2nd edn, 1998), Chapter 4.
[164] See, eg, Glebe Sugar Refining Co v Paterson (1900) 7 SLT 374 L; and McGonigal v Pickard 1964 SLT 526.

requiring the tenant to accept the premises as fit for occupation. In such circumstances it is vital that the tenant obtain a survey making it clear to him exactly what is the condition of the property he is taking on.

(b) At common law there is an obligation in what are known as "urban" leases which falls on the landlord to keep the property in a tenantable and habitable condition during the currency of the lease. In this context the term "urban" is a generic term which has no precise meaning. It generally means leases relating to buildings used for purposes other than agricultural uses. At common law it did include houses used for residential property. This obligation is basically an obligation to keep the premises in a wind and water tight condition. The landlord is only liable once the condition of the premises is drawn to his attention and the landlord fails to act. In this regard a landlord is not liable for any of the following: an act of God; an act of a third party such as a neighbour; and damage caused by the tenant's own negligence.

Residential leases

7–53   The common law position relating to urban leases has been fortified by statutory provisions to some extent. The statutory provisions do not relate to all urban leases but only to leases of houses. The landlord has only a limited freedom to contract out of these statutory provisions by putting a contrary statement in a lease. Under the Housing (Scotland) Act 1987, as amended by the Housing (Scotland) Act 1988, there are two provisions as follows: (a) where the letting of a dwelling house is for less than three years at a low rent (this level is set from time to time by the Secretary of State by statutory instrument[165]) then the landlord is obliged to ensure that the house is reasonably fit for habitation at the outset and the landlord is obliged to maintain the house in this condition throughout the let[166]; and (b) where the letting of a dwelling house is for less than seven years the landlord is obliged to keep the premises and installations and common parts in repair and tenantable order.[167]

Commercial leases

7–54   The common law repairing obligation falling upon the landlord is frequently contracted out of in leases relative to commercial property. These are generally known as "commercial leases". These leases are also known as "full repairing and insuring leases" or "FRI" leases for short. The reference to repairs indicates that the full burden of repairing is transferred to the tenant. One particular type of defect in property which has caused difficulty in this context is the "latent" defect. This is a defect which is hidden at the time the lease is granted and is not known either to the landlord or the tenant. This tends to be most relevant in the context of new buildings where some fault in the construction is not apparent at the grant of the lease. In Scotland only very clear wording in a lease will place an obligation on a tenant to remedy this type of defect. If there is no provision in the lease for latent defects the liability of repair falls on the landlord subject to one exception. The exceptional case is where the premises are destroyed totally or rendered wholly unusable by latent defect. In such a case the

---

[165] Landlord's Repairing Obligations (Specified Rent) (Scotland) (No 2) Order 1988 (SI 1988/2155).
[166] Housing (Scotland) Act 1987, Sched 10, para 1(2).
[167] *ibid* Sched 10, para 3.

common law provides that the legal doctrine known as *rei interitus* will terminate the lease.[168] It is common for parties to FRI leases to contract out of the application of the doctrine of *rei interitus* but where this is done particular attention should be given to the obligations relative to reinstatement and insurance.

Rural leases

At common law there were obligations on the landlord and tenant in relation to buildings and fences in the following regard: (a) the landlord had to put buildings and fences in repair at entry; (b) the landlord had to effect extraordinary repairs arising from natural decay; (c) the tenant had liability for ordinary maintenance and repairs; and (d) the tenant was required to leave the subjects in the same condition as when he entered into possession, fair wear and tear excepted. These common law provisions may be varied in a lease. The common law provisions are largely restated and amplified for the benefit of the tenant in the agricultural holdings legislation.[169] These statutory provisions cannot generally be contracted out of in a lease. There is some provision to contract out of the agricultural holdings provisions in what is known as a post-lease agreement, which is an agreement entered into after the lease has been entered into.[170]

7–55

Fixtures

In many situations the issue of what happens where the tenant has made additions to the property ("fixtures") will be dealt with in the lease. In the absence of provision in the lease the rule is that such fixtures will belong to the landlord unless (a) they are trade fixtures, in which case they may be removed by the tenant at the end of the lease,[171] or (b) there is special statutory provision. For example, at the end of his lease the tenant in an agricultural lease is entitled to remove certain fixtures and buildings improvements.[172]

7–56

Compensation for improvements

The tenant is not under any obligation to improve the subjects let unless there is a specific obligation to do so in the lease. In the absence of agreement, the common law makes no provision for compensation to a tenant in respect of improvements which he makes to the subjects. He is presumed to make them for his own advantage during the tenancy. This common law position is sometimes reinforced by a general statement in leases to the effect that the tenant will not be entitled to any compensation for improvements. This discouragement to a tenant making improvements has been removed as a matter of public policy in respect of rural leases. There are a number of instances where a statutory right to compensation has been given to the tenant where the common law makes no provision. The most well known of these are contained in the agricultural holdings legislation[173] and the crofting legislation.[174] These statutory rights cannot generally be contracted out of in a lease. Whilst the common law gave

7–57

---

[168] *Cantors Properties (Scotland)* v *Swears & Wells* 1978 SC 310.
[169] Agricultural Holdings (Scotland) Act 1991, s 5.
[170] *ibid* s 5(3).
[171] *Cliffplant Ltd* v *Kinnaird* 1982 SLT 2.
[172] Agricultural Holdings (Scotland) Act 1991, s 18.
[173] *ibid* ss 33–42.
[174] Crofters (Scotland) Act 1993, ss 30–33.

the tenant no compensation for improvements, neither did it generally allow the tenant to increase the rent during the currency of the lease in respect of improvements which the tenant had made. The landlord could, however, increase the rent if there was a break in the lease and he would inevitably try to rent the tenant on his improvements in these circumstances. In modern commercial leases there is usually an express statement that in relation to rent review the increase in the value of the premises caused by any improvements carried out by the tenant will be disregarded except where they have been carried out in the implement of an express obligation to the landlord.

Insurance

7–58 There is no general common law provision requiring either the landlord or the tenant to maintain insurance in respect of the subjects of lease. This position is usually altered in modern leases. In commercial leases the landlord will either require the tenant to maintain this insurance at the tenant's cost or alternatively he will maintain the insurance himself and provide that the costs may be recovered from the tenant. There are special statutory provisions for insurance of buildings and harvested crops in relation to agricultural holdings.[175]

Remedies for contravention of the terms of the lease

7–59 Different remedies are available to the landlord and the tenant.

Landlord

7–60 The landlord has the following remedies.

(a) The landlord may obtain interdict where damage by the tenant is threatened or to prevent future damage. Interdict is used to prevent the tenant from doing something. It is therefore a "negative" remedy. There is considerable difficulty in obtaining interdict to make the tenant do something. For example, if a tenant is under an obligation in a lease to continue to trade, it is not possible to obtain an interdict to stop the tenant from breaching this obligation—that would be asking the court to require the tenant to trade, which is a positive remedy.

(b) Specific implement where the tenant has failed to carry out a positive obligation in the lease.

(c) Where specific implement or interdict will not wholly restore the position the landlord may be entitled to interdict and, in appropriate cases, to irritancy.

(d) The landlord will have all the general remedies available to a creditor for recovery of debt. He has in addition one special remedy known as the landlord's hypothec. This is a remedy for non-payment of rent but extends only to the current year. It enables the landlord to take possession of moveable items of the tenant on the leased subjects and to sell them to recover the rent.[176]

---

[175] Agricultural Holdings (Scotland) Act 1991, Sched 1, paras 5 and 6.
[176] *Scottish & Newcastle Breweries Ltd* v *City of Edinburgh District Council* 1979 SLT (Notes) 11.

This action involves the use of sheriff officers and is consequently fairly expensive and relatively rarely used.

(e) An action of removing: when all else fails the landlord may attempt to remove his tenant. There are strict statutory controls over such action, particularly where there is a form of security of tenure.

Tenant

The remedies generally available to the tenant include interdict, specific implement **7–61** and damages. Two particular remedies in addition should be noticed: (a) the tenant may be entitled to a reduction in the rent where the landlord is in material breach of the lease; (b) the tenant may be entitled to abandon the lease on the ground that the landlord is in material breach of the lease. A lease will frequently expressly exclude these two additional remedies.

Arbitration

In an attempt to reduce the cost of enforcement of lease, many leases require reference **7–62** to arbitration before court procedure is invoked. Such arbitration is widely used in agricultural leases, where it is required by statute. It has to be said, however, that many arbitrations are as long as and as costly as court proceedings.

LAND OBLIGATIONS

Some of the most important restrictions on the use of land may be described as "land **7–63** obligations". This is a term which is not found at common law but was originally first used in Scotland as part of a statute enacted in 1970.[177] The term was borrowed from English law. The expression describes a family or group of various rights affecting land. The term "land obligation" is defined in statute[178] as an obligation which: (a) relates to land—the term "land" includes buildings on land; (b) is enforceable by a proprietor of an "interest in land" (another defined term) by virtue of his being such a proprietor and by his successors in title; and (c) is binding upon a proprietor of another interest in that land or of an interest in another land by virtue of being such proprietor and upon his successors in title. The term "interest in land" means any estate or interest in land which is capable of being owned or held as a separate interest and to which a title may be recorded in the Register of Sasines or Land Register of Scotland. The land burdened by the land obligation is known as the "burdened land" or "burdened tenement" or "servient tenement". The land benefited by the obligation is known as the "benefited land" or "benefited tenement" or "dominant tenement".

The sort of obligations included in the definition of "land obligation" are as follows:

(a) Restrictions in "long leases" (which endure for 20 years or more) enforceable by the landlord against the tenant—it does not include restrictions in short

---

[177] Conveyancing and Feudal Reform (Scotland) Act 1970.
[178] *ibid* ss 1 and 2. These definitions will be altered to substitute "land, or a real right in land" for the term "interest in land" in terms of the Abolition of Feudal Tenure etc (Scotland) Act 2000, s 74 and Sched 10, para 32.

leases (endurance of under 20 years) as these leases cannot be recorded in the General Register of Sasines or registered in the Land Register of Scotland (dealt with in the context of leases, which are examined above).

(b) Restrictions in a feudal grant enforceable by a superior against the vassal. This type of right is known as a "feudal real burden". It will become incompetent to create these restrictions after the abolition of the feudal system of landholding and existing feudal real burdens will cease to be enforceable as such.[179]

(c) Servitudes. These are an important sub-class of rights such as a private right of way affecting one piece of land and benefiting a neighbouring piece of land.[180]

(d) Rights created in a deed of conditions or created in a disposition enforceable by one neighbouring proprietor against another. This type of right is known as a "real burden".[181]

(e) Rights of common interest—such as the rights of one tenement flat owner enforceable against another tenement flat owner.[182]

The term "land obligation" does not include public rights of way as these benefit not a piece of land but the general public.[183]

SERVITUDES

7–64 A servitude is a burden on one piece of land ("the servient or burdened tenement") in favour of another piece of land ("the dominant or benefited tenement"). The term servitude is largely synonymous with the term "easement" which is used in England. Servitudes are rights which "run with the land" in that they continue to bind the burdened land even though it changes hands and the owner and his successors in title are bound. They also benefit the original owner of the benefited tenement and his successors in title. Following Roman law, servitudes may be divided into "rural" and "urban" servitudes. The former relate to buildings and the latter relate to undeveloped land. The distinction has no practical use today.

Difference from other rights

7–65 Where servitudes differ from real burdens is that at common law real burdens are enforceable only against the party who is the proprietor of the servient tenement. Servitudes, by contrast, are enforceable against this party and, in addition, are enforceable against the whole world. Thus, if a party is entitled to a servitude of access he can obtain a legal remedy if it is blocked by the proprietor of the servient tenement, his tenants, or members of the general public. Servitudes of access differ from public

---

[179] Abolition of Feudal Tenure etc (Scotland) Act 2000, Pt 4. Scottish Law Commission, *Report on Abolition of the Feudal System* (Scot Law Com No 168) (February 1999).
[180] See paras 7–64 *et seq.*
[181] See paras 7–80 *et seq.*
[182] See paras 7–90 *et seq.*
[183] See paras 7–102 to 7–104.

rights of way. A servitude of access is a form of a private right of way. It cannot be enforced by the general public as a public right of way can.[184] Servitudes differ from leases in that a rent is not usually charged in return for a servitude although some deeds of servitude provide for this.[185]

Occurrence

7–66

Where a person is making a grant of lands he will often want to grant and reserve servitudes. For example: (a) Where a person owns a tenement of flats and is selling one of the flats, he will want to grant the right of access through the central stairwell to each flat. He may also wish to reserve servitude rights to run service media through the flat sold off for the benefit of the remaining flats. (b) Where a building firm is selling houses in a development, the firm usually imposes negative servitudes to prevent the house owner building an additional house in the garden. (c) Where a farmer is selling off a cottage he may grant a servitude right to a private water supply and a septic tank. From these examples, the essentials of servitude rights may be observed. These are as follows:

(a) No one can have a servitude over his own land. A servitude is a burden over someone else's land in favour of land owned by the "benefited" party.

(b) The "burdened property" and the "benefited property" are usually neighbouring properties but they do not require to be adjacent. They do, however, require to be sufficiently close so that the owner of the dominant tenement has an interest to enforce the servitude.

(c) Only the owner of the servient land and not a tenant of that land may grant a servitude.[186] Similarly only the owner of the dominant land and not the tenant of that land may acquire a servitude.

(d) A servitude can affect only heritable property. No one can have a servitude over moveables. In a servitude of pasturage the right burdens the ground over which the cattle graze. It does not burden the grass itself when it is cut off from the ground as that grass, when separate from the ground, is moveable.

Content

7–67

If the activity permitted by a right does not fall within the activity permitted by one of the recognised class of servitudes the right is not a servitude. The most commonly encountered servitude is a right of way benefiting one plot of ground and burdening another plot of ground.

Positive rights

7–68

Servitudes, however, are not restricted to rights of way and comprise a class of rights including the following positive rights:

---

[184] *Thomson v Murdoch* (1862) 24 D 975.
[185] See, *eg*, *Stewart v Steuart* (1877) 4 R 981.
[186] *Safeway Food Stores Ltd v Wellington Motor Co (Ayr) Ltd* 1976 SLT 53.

(a) Rights of way, including pedestrian and vehicular traffic.[187] Such rights of way may also extend to rights for boats over canals[188] and rights for planes to fly over land and inspect pipelines. The rights may be exerciseable over man-made structures such as bridges and pedestrian walkways.

(b) Rights to put drains or pipes in or over the ground to carry water, sewage, oil, gas and similar substances.

(c) Rights of pasturage for sheep and cattle.[189] This does not include a right to cut hay or to plant crops.

(d) Rights to obtain fuel in the form of peat or turf from the servient tenement.[190]

(e) Rights to obtain building materials from the servient tenement.[191] This may extend to the extraction of sand, gravel, slate or stone. This right is now rarely used and in most cases where a party obtains a right to extract minerals from the land of another party his right will be constituted by means of a lease.

(f) A right to bleach linen on the servient tenement.[192] This is very rarely used these days since the invention of modern washing machines. It is still frequently encountered in old title deeds in urban areas.

(g) A right of lateral and vertical support which is found in buildings and mineral strata.

All of the above are known as "positive" servitudes as they enable the holder of the right to carry on positive activity on the servient tenement. The owner of the servient tenement is obliged to submit to such activity. He must not put up obstacles to the exercise of a right of way, although in rural areas an unlocked gate is probably allowed in most cases.[193] The owner of the servient tenement is not obliged to do anything. For example, where a servitude or access is taken over a road, the owner of the road is not obliged to repair or maintain the road. Similarly, where a cottage owner has a private water supply system which runs through a field, if the pipe bursts because of frost, the owner of the field is not obliged to repair the pipe; that is the responsibility of the cottage. By contrast, if the owner of the field causes damage to the pipe by some negligent act such as by ploughing the field and ripping up the pipe he will be obliged to repair the damage he has done. The one possible exception to the rule may exist in relation to the obligation to provide support. This appears to place a positive obligation on the servient proprietor to do something, that is, provide support.[194] This has led to the view that the obligation to provide support is really not a servitude at all but is a right of common interest.[195]

---

[187] *Alvis v Harrison* 1991 SLT 64 (HL).
[188] *Tennant v Napier Smith's Trs* (1888) 15 R 671.
[189] *Fearnan Partnership v Grindlay* 1988 SLT 817.
[190] *Watson v Sinclair* 1966 SLT (Sh Ct) 77.
[191] *Aikman v Duke of Hamilton and Brandon* (1832) 6 W & Sh 64.
[192] *Sinclair v Mags of Dysart* (1779) M 14519; (1780) 2 Pat App 554.
[193] *Wood v Robertson* 9th Mar 1809, FC.
[194] *Dalton v Angus* (1881) 6 App Cas 740.
[195] See paras 7–90 *et seq.*

Negative rights

There are, in addition, a number of rights known as "negative servitudes" because **7–69** they enable the holder of the right to prevent activity on the servient tenement. The recognised negative servitudes include:

(a) a right to prevent building on the servient tenement[196];

(b) a right to prevent obstruction of a view.[197]

In negative servitudes the servient proprietor is obliged to refrain from some form of activity. In both cases of the recognised servitudes that activity relates to building. Reforms presently being considered by the Scottish Law Commission may result in the prohibition of the creation of negative servitudes after the enactment of the relevant legislation. Instead the prohibition of building will be achieved by means of a real burden or condition.[198]

Additional or new rights

It remains an open question as to whether additional rights may be added to the lists **7–70** set out above and recognised as servitudes at common law. In case law there has been some debate as to whether a right to play golf on adjacent land can be recognised as a servitude.[199] It has been confirmed that a right to play curling cannot be recognised as a servitude because servitudes generally are exerciseable all year round and curling on an outdoor loch is capable of exercise only in winter.[200] Recently it has been held that a right to put in an electricity line cannot be a servitude but the case in question has been criticised as not giving enough regard to developments in modern social conditions.[201] There remains some doubt as to whether the right to park a vehicle on adjacent land can be a servitude.[202] Reforms presently being considered by the Scottish Law Commission may result in a limited extension or abandonment of the recognised categories of servitudes with the result that a much wider class of positive activity may be carried out on a servient tenement by a dominant proprietor in terms of a servitude.[203]

Methods of constitution

There are various methods by which a servitude can be constituted. It should be noted that servitudes may arise in ways other than creation by means of a deed. In this **7–71** regard servitudes differ from real burdens. The means of creation include the following.

---

[196] *Braid Hills Hotel Co v Manuels* 1909 SC 120.
[197] *Banks & Co v Walker* (1874) 1 R 981.
[198] Scottish Law Commission, *Discussion Paper on Real Burdens* (No 106) (October 1998).
[199] *Mags of Earlsferry v Malcolm* (1829) 7 S 755; (1832) 11 S 74.
[200] *Harvey v Lindsay* (1853) 15 D 768.
[201] *Neill v Scobbie* 1993 GWD 8–572.
[202] See *Stewart Pott & Co v Brown Brothers* (1878) 6 R 35; *Ayr Burgh Council v British Transport Commission* 1955 SLT 219; *Murrayfield Ice Rink Ltd v The Scottish Rugby Union* 1973 SLT 99.
[203] Scottish Law Commission, *Discussion Paper on Real Burdens* (No 106) (October 1998).

Creation in a deed

7-72 Servitudes may be created in a variety of deeds as follows:

(a) A deed which forms part of the title of the burdened land. This is known as express reservation as the servitude is usually reserved when the burdened land is first split off from a larger estate. Usually a deed conveys a piece of ground and then proceeds to reserve from the land a list of servitude rights such as access, the right to use drains and a septic tank, etc. There may, however, be a separate deed of servitude or a deed of conditions.[204] This is usually the case when additional rights are required to service a new development on a site.

(b) A deed which forms part of the title of the benefited land. This is usually an express grant.

(c) A deed which is unrecorded and is not part of the recorded title deeds of any land.

Reforms presently being considered by the Scottish Law Commission may result in a requirement that a servitude shall be constituted by a deed only if the deed is recorded (or registered as appropriate) in the title of both the dominant and servient tenement.[205]

Where a servitude is created by a deed (whether by grant or reservation) then it is important to read the deed. The reason is that the terms of the deed will govern the extent of the right. This may be illustrated by reference to a servitude of access. The deed may place a number of conditions on the access right as follows.

(a) The right may be limited to vehicular access with lorries of a maximum width and weight.

(b) Traffic may have a speed limit placed on it and there may be single direction traffic where appropriate.

(c) The purpose of the access may be limited to particular businesses such as agriculture or horticulture. Alternatively, the servitude may expressly permit the road to be used for whatever purpose the holder of the servitude wishes including all future development of the dominant tenement. If a servitude is expressly limited to one purpose it cannot be used for anything else.[206] If the deed of servitude grants a general right of access without specifying any purpose for which it may be used it is now accepted that the access right may be used for any lawful purpose to which the dominant tenement may be put.[207]

---

[204] In terms of the Conveyancing (Scotland) Act 1874, s 32, as amended by the Land Registration (Scotland) Act 1979, s 17.
[205] Scottish Law Commission, *Discussion Paper on Real Burdens* (No 106) (October 1998).
[206] *Cronin v Sutherland* (1899) 2 F 217.
[207] *Alvis v Harrison* 1991 SLT 64 (HL).

(d) The owner of the servient tenement may reserve the right to install traffic calming measures such as speed humps or signs and lights.

(e) The owner of the servient tenement may reserve the right to re-route the servitude if he wishes to develop the land at a future date.

(f) The owner of the servient tenement may reserve the right to install pipes and wires underneath the road.

(g) The owner of the servient tenement may reserve the right to terminate the servitude if the holder of the servitude does not comply with the conditions of grant. This is very like an irritancy clause.[208]

Implied grant and reservation

Sometimes the title deeds are totally silent about servitudes benefiting a plot of **7–73** ground. This can lead to problems where rights are needed to make the site usable. For example, a plot of ground may be landlocked to the extent that it is totally enclosed by land owned by someone else. How can the owner obtain access to the landlocked plot? The law may intervene to grant access rights and other servitude rights to make the plot of ground usable by virtue of the doctrines of implied grant and implied reservation.[209] Broadly speaking, these legal doctrines are resorted to only when someone has made a mistake in the conveyancing process.[210] Generally speaking the law is less inclined to recognise a servitude claimed to be reserved by implication than one granted by implication as the former attempts to reserve something out of the land conveyed away and this is regarded as giving with one hand and taking with the other. Technically this is known as derogating from the grant and is disapproved.[211]

Use for the prescriptive period

A servitude may be constituted without any deed if there has been continuous use **7–74** openly, peaceably and without judicial interruption for a period of 20 years.[212] Thus, if a party who owns the neighbouring farm walks across another party's field along a definite route for 20 years every morning that party may acquire a servitude of access over the other party's field. Such a servitude will not be noted in the title deeds of any property. This has the practical consequence that a purchaser should always go to see a property if he wants to find out all the burdens affecting it. In relation to a servitude acquired by usage the measure of the right is the actual use during the 20 years.[213] As a result if a party walks over his neighbour's land for 20 years he may acquire a pedestrian right of access—he will not acquire a servitude right of access for vehicles.

Creation by statute

It is theoretically possible for a servitude to be created by statutory provision. This is **7–75** rare but it is found in some statutes relative to public works such as railways and bridges.

---

[208] For irritancy clauses in leases, see paras 7–44 *et seq*.
[209] *Ewart* v *Cochrane* (1861) 23 D (HL) 3.
[210] See, *eg*, *Moffat* v *Milne* 1993 GWD 8–572.
[211] *Wheeldon* v *Burrows* (1879) LR 12 ChD 31.
[212] Prescription and Limitation (Scotland) Act 1973, s 3.
[213] *Carstairs* v *Spence* 1924 SC 380.

Clarity and precision of words

7–76 To create a servitude in a deed it is important to use words which are clear and precise. A number of rules in this regard may be identified.

Just like real burdens, no special technical words are required to create a servitude but it has to be clearly shown that the right is intended to affect the property and the successive owners of the property, not just the original grantee and his heirs. It is obviously easier to come to the conclusion that a right is a servitude if the deed expressly states that the obligation concerned is a "servitude" and uses that very word. If that word is not used the courts will look at the nature of the right for guidance. If the right created in the deed purports to permit activity falling within the activities which are recognised in the general law as servitudes then the right in the deed will be treated as a servitude. So, if a deed grants a right to drive a car across a road but does not use the word "servitude" it is likely that the right is still a servitude because access is a recognised servitude. Conversely, if the deed purports to allow the grantee to do something which is beyond the recognised servitudes (such as a right to play bagpipes on an adjacent field on the anniversary of the Battle of Bannockburn) this will not be regarded as a servitude.

Just like the law in relation to real burdens, precision must be employed in drafting servitudes because the words used will be strictly construed by the courts. The words are construed *contra proferentem* (against the interests of the party relying on them). There is, however, a slightly more lax approach with servitudes than real burdens because servitudes are rights which are generally recognised by the law. As a result some general phrases constituting servitudes may be upheld where they would fail if the right were a real burden.[214]

Enforcement

7–77 A person wishing to enforce a servitude must have (a) a title to enforce, and (b) an interest to enforce. In this regard the law is similar to the law relating to real burdens. In relation to a servitude, however, it is generally accepted that a close location of the dominant and servient tenements is sufficient to show interest to enforce on the part of the proprietor of the dominant tenement. Only he (and not a tenant of the dominant proprietor) has a title to enforce a servitude.

Remedies

7–78 The remedies available to a party wishing to enforce a servitude are as follows: a personal action against the burdened proprietor for specific implement, interdict or damages.

Exercise

7–79 Unless there is contrary provision in a deed, the exercise of every servitude is governed by three implied rules as follows.

(a) The servitude can be used only for the dominant tenement.[215] This means that a servitude may be exercised only for the plot of land described as the dominant

---

[214] *McLean v Marwhirn Developments Ltd* 1976 SLT (Notes) 47; *Axis West Developments Ltd v Chartwell Land Investments Ltd* 1999 SLT 1416 (HL).
[215] *Irvine Knitters Ltd v North Ayrshire Co-operative Society Ltd* 1978 SC 109.

tenement. If the dominant proprietor buys the adjacent field he cannot take access to the new field by the servitude of access which existed for the old and existing field. This is a problem in relation to what is known as "site assembly" where a developer is acquiring different plots of ground to build up a viable site but the servitude of access benefits only one part of his intended site.

(b) *The servitude must be exercised* civiliter, *which means that it must be exercised only in such manner as is least burdensome to the servient tenement.* This rule means different things in different contexts. If a property owner acquires a servitude upon a road running through an established residential area for the purpose of taking access to his house he will not be able to abuse this right by driving a muddy tractor along the road and causing damage to the tarmac on the road. By contrast, if the lane over which access is taken is a farm lane the driving of a tractor would be perfectly acceptable even if some mud were left on the road, unless this were excessive in amount.

(c) *The servitude must be exercised in such manner as will not increase the burden on the servient tenement beyond that which was originally anticipated.* If a property owner grants a servitude to a neighbouring proprietor to allow him to take access to a new cottage he is building, it would not be permissible for the neighbour to demolish the cottage and, instead, mine the minerals under the site and cart the material in large lorries along the lane. If, however, the servitude was originally granted for the purposes of taking access to an existing quarry it would not be an increase in the burden to take access by means of quarry trucks.[216]

REAL BURDENS

Real burdens are otherwise known as "real conditions" and as "obligations which run with the lands". This terminology simply means that the obligations continue to bind the burdened land even though it changes hands and the owner and his successors in title are bound. They also benefit the original owner of the benefited tenement and his successors in title.

7–80

Occurrence

Where a person is making a grant of lands he will often want to impose conditions in the title. For example:

7–81

(a) Where a person owns a tenement of flats and is selling one of the flats, he will want to impose conditions concerning payment for mutual repairs in relation to common parts such as the roof etc. This is a positive obligation falling on the servient proprietor. In terms of the obligation the servient owner is required to do something.

(b) Where a building firm is selling houses in a development, the firm usually imposes conditions to preserve the amenity of the housing development. A common example is a restriction declaring that the houses cannot be used for industrial or business purposes. This is a negative obligation and the servient owner is required to desist from some activity.

---

[216] *Lovie v Kirkmyres Sand & Gravel Ltd*, Peterhead Sheriff Court (case ref A572/90), 9th Jan, 9th and 24th Oct and 5th Nov 1991, unreported.

(c) Where a person wishes to sell off a plot of ground and retain the development potential of his remaining ground he may retain the right to put a road and service media through the plot sold off.[217] This type of reservation permits the dominant proprietor to do something and the servient owner is bound to submit to it. This form of right is frequently coupled with a servitude permitting the dominant proprietor to use the road or the service media after they have been built.

Content

7–82 Not every obligation can be constituted as a real burden. The principal rule is that the obligation sought to be imposed must relate to land or the buildings thereon or the use of land or buildings.[218] For example, it is competent to have a real burden requiring the owner of a plot of land to wash the windows in his house regularly. Such an obligation relates to the use of buildings. It is not competent to impose a real burden requiring the owner of land to wash himself every day. That obligation relates to the body of the owner and not the land which he occupies. There are, however, cases where the distinction is not so clear cut. It is probably impossible to impose an obligation by means of a real condition that the owner of a plot of ground will not read books or play music because this relates to his personal behaviour, but it would be possible to impose an obligation that the owner will not play music in such a manner as will annoy neighbours. Thus it may be possible to impose an obligation not to play the bagpipes in a tenemental flat. The reason for the justification is that this sort of restriction protects the amenity of the neighbouring flats.

In addition to this general limitation there are a number of more detailed restrictions. These more detailed restrictions were identified by Lord Corehouse, giving the opinion of the Court, in *Tailors of Aberdeen* v *Coutts*.[219] This confirmed that a real burden must comply with the following:

(a) It must not be contrary to law. For example, a real burden cannot require a proprietor to do something which is illegal. A landowner cannot be required to carry out activities which would amount to a criminal offence.

(b) It must not be contrary to public policy. In this context, restrictions which purport to create trade monopolies which impede the commerce of land are treated as contrary to public policy.[220] It is difficult to say with certainty exactly what this means. The rule does not preclude simple restrictions which prevent the use of property for something like a public house or industrial purposes, where such restrictions are imposed to protect the amenity of surrounding subjects. It may, however, render invalid a restriction against the use of a plot of ground for a public house where the purpose of the restriction is not to enhance amenity but merely to protect the trade of another public house next door.

(c) It must not be "vexatious" or "useless". Generally, an obligation which is imposed for no real benefit and is simply imposed to make life miserable for

---

[217] *B and C Group Management Ltd, Haren & Wood, Petitioners*, Lord Cullen, OH, 4th Dec 1992, unreported.
[218] *Earl of Zetland* v *Hislop* (1882) 9 R (HL) 40; *Stair Memorial Encyclopaedia*, Vol 18, para 391.
[219] (1840) 1 Rob App 296.
[220] *Aberdeen Varieties Ltd* v *James F Donald (Aberdeen Cinemas) Ltd* 1940 SC (HL) 52; 1939 SC 788.

the owner will not be enforced. For example, an obligation which requires a proprietor to paint his house a different colour every day will probably fail by virtue of this rule.

(d) It is sometimes said that a real burden must not be "inconsistent with the nature of the species of property". This phrase may seem almost unintelligible. What it means, however, is that a real burden must not preclude the exercise of legal transactions or deprive the owners of certain inherent rights of ownership. For example, a real condition cannot remove the right of a proprietor to sell land, lease it or grant securities over it. It is possible to limit (rather than remove totally) the exercise of these rights by means of real condition. Thus, rights known as rights of pre-emption are competent.[221] Under such a right it is declared that the proprietor shall not have a right to sell unless he first offers the subjects for sale to the dominant proprietor.

Document of constitution

All real burdens must be created in a deed which forms part of the title of the **7–83** burdened land. These rights cannot arise by use alone even if that use continues for the prescriptive period of 20 years. This is a point of distinction with servitudes. Writing is required to constitute a real condition and the deed must be recorded in the General Register of Sasines or the Land Register of Scotland. A real burden is usually created in a deed conveying the servient land, known as a disposition. These real burdens are also created in deeds which do not transfer land and are known as deeds of conditions.[222] Deeds of conditions are common in modern developments. These deeds are recorded in the General Register of Sasines or the Land Register of Scotland. In terms of reforms presently being considered by the Scottish Law Commission it will probably be necessary to record (or register as appropriate) the deed of constitution in the titles of both the dominant and servient tenement.[223] These reforms may also relax to some extent the following rules which presently govern the manner in which real burdens are to be expressed. The full text of the real burden must be included in the deed which is registered or recorded. It is not competent to refer to an unrecorded deed for greater detail. If the full text of the restriction is not set out in the recorded or registered deed the purported real condition will be invalid. Thus an obligation to comply with a statute or Act of Parliament cannot be created a real burden if all the draftsman does is to refer to the statute.[224] The full text of the statutory provision must be incorporated into the deed. Similarly, it is not competent to refer to an unrecorded list of estate conditions which can be examined at the office of the estate factor. These conditions should be added as a schedule to the deed.

Clarity and precision of words

To create a real burden it is important to use words which are clear and precise. A **7–84** number of rules in this regard may be identified:

No special technical words are required but it has to be clearly shown that the obligation is intended to affect the property and the successive owners of the property

---

[221] See, *eg, Mathieson v Tinney* 1989 SLT 535.
[222] Conveyancing (Scotland) Act 1874, s 32, as amended by the Land Registration (Scotland) Act 1979, s 17.
[223] Scottish Law Commission, *Discussion Paper on Real Burdens* (No 106) (October 1998).
[224] *Aberdeen Varieties Ltd v James F Donald (Aberdeen Cinemas) Ltd* 1940 SC (HL) 52; 1939 SC 788.

and not just the original grantee and his heirs. It is obviously easier to come to the conclusion that an obligation is a real burden if the deed expressly states that the obligation concerned is a "real burden" or a "real condition" and uses those exact words. If those words are not used the courts will look at the nature of the obligation for guidance. If the obligation is capable of performance by a single act (such as an obligation to erect a fence or a house) it is likely to be regarded as not a real burden but simply a contractual obligation affecting the original grantee. Conversely, an obligation to maintain a fence or a house is an obligation which requires repeated acts or a series of acts over time and this is likely to be regarded as a real burden.

Precision must be employed in drafting real burdens because the words used will be strictly construed by the courts. Another way of stating this is that real burdens are construed *contra proferentem*—in other words, they are construed against the interests of the party wishing to rely on them. This results from a presumption in Scots law that land should be free from restrictions. So if there is an ambiguity it is resolved always in favour of freedom.

Presumption in favour of freedom

7–85   There are a number of aspects of this rule as follow:

(a) The land burdened must be exactly defined.[225]

(b) Where the burden relates to the paying of a sum of money, it must be a definite amount and it must be payable to an identified creditor. This rule has led to some debate. It is common in tenemental situations to find provisions burdening each flat with a share of the costs of repairs of the common parts such as the roof. For example, if there are six flats in a tenement it is common for each share to be a one-sixth share. It is generally accepted that such a precise division is enforceable. By contrast, an obligation which states that each flat owner will be liable for "an equitable share" or "a fair share" or some other share calculated by another equally vague phraseology is generally regarded as too vague for enforcement.

(c) Words will be given their normal meaning and not an over-extended or benevolent meaning. For example, an obligation to build a house or a building will not be construed as an obligation to maintain the house in all time coming.[226]

Enforcement

7–86   A person wishing to enforce a real burden must have a title to enforce and an interest to enforce.

Title to enforce

7–87   The proprietor for the time being of the dominant tenement (the benefited property) has a title to enforce a real burden. This means that the original creator of the burden and his successors in title, as owners of the dominant tenement, have a title to enforce the burden. An exceptional case sometimes permits neighbouring proprietors to enforce a

---

[225] *Anderson* v *Dickie* 1915 SC (HL) 74.
[226] *Kemp* v *Mags of Largs* 1939 SC (HL) 6; *Peter Walker and Son (Edinburgh)* v *Church of Scotland General Trustees* 1967 SLT 297.

title restriction in a deed to which they were not a party. This is known in Scotland as the rule of the *jus quaesitum tertio*—the rule of third party rights. The right may be granted expressly to third parties such as neighbours. This is common in deeds of conditions. If there is no express grant of the right to third parties it may be granted by implication. Such an implication arises where a proprietor dispones off a series of plots of ground in similar terms in one neighbourhood. If the terms of the dispositions are sufficiently similar, this is regarded as sufficient to give rise to an implication that the neighbours can enforce the right amongst themselves for the benefit of the neighbourhood.[227]

Interest to enforce

A party wishing to enforce a real burden must show that he has an interest to enforce **7–88** it. This interest must relate to the land and not merely to the personal circumstances of the owner for the time being.

Remedies

The remedies available to a party wishing to enforce a real burden or condition include **7–89** a personal action against the burdened proprietor for specific implement, interdict or damages.

COMMON INTEREST

Common interest is a form of right which arises by implication of law. It is not usually **7–90** created by provision in a deed.[228] The most commonly encountered situation in which rights of common interest exist is tenemental buildings. Each proprietor of the various flats has a right of common interest in those parts of the building which he does not own. In this context common interest includes the following rights:

(a) *The right to support.* The lower flats must bear the weight of the upper flats. A lower flat owner may be restrained by interdict from carrying out building operations which would prejudice the support of the upper flats.[229]

(b) *The right to shelter.* The owner of the roof must maintain it in a wind and water tight condition and not allow water ingress.[230] As this places a considerable burden on upper flat proprietors, the obligation is commonly varied in deeds of conditions.

(c) *The right to light.* This exists in respect of any garden ground attached to the tenement.[231]

Common interest may also exist in other contexts. Where boundary walls or mutual gables are owned by neighbours up to the mid-line, each has a common interest in the other half of the wall entitling them to support by the other half of the wall.[232]

---

[227] *Hislop* v *MacRitchie's Trs* (1881) 8 R (HL) 95.
[228] *cf Fearnan Partnership* v *Grindlay* 1992 SLT 460, per Lord Jauncey at 463. Future legislative reform may remove this possibility altogether.
[229] *Fergusson* v *Marjoribanks*, 12th Nov 1816, FC.
[230] *Luke* v *Dundass* (1695) 4 Brown's Supp 258.
[231] *Heron* v *Gray* (1880) 8 R 155.
[232] *Crisp* v *McCutcheon* 1963 SLT (Sh Ct) 4.

Where private gardens serving two or more properties are in common ownership (such as an ornamental square surrounded by houses) there is a view that each of the co-proprietors has a right of common interest in the garden.[233]

Common interest rights apply in the absence of express regulation to the contrary in the form of real conditions. The right is a form of legally implied real condition which is enforceable against the proprietor of the burdened tenement by the benefited proprietor. No liability falls on tenants in the burdened tenement, nor can the obligation be enforced by tenants in the benefited tenement.

LAND OBLIGATIONS—EXTINCTION, VARIATION AND DISCHARGE

7-91 Land obligations of all sorts may be discharged in various ways which include:

- express discharge;
- prescription;
- consolidation;
- compulsory purchase;
- variation and discharge by the Lands Tribunal.

EXPRESS DISCHARGE

7-92 The person entitled to enforce a land obligation has a right to grant a discharge of the land obligation. Thus a party entitled to enforce a servitude or a real burden may discharge it. A common example of when a minute of waiver is sought is where the titles of the servient tenement prohibit the use of the subjects for the sale of alcohol and the purchaser of the property wishes to convert it into a public house. The discharge should be executed in the same manner as a formal deed of servitude. Usually a sum of money is expected in exchange for an express discharge although the introduction of the Lands Tribunal's jurisdiction (introduced in 1970) has tended to keep the amount within reasonable bounds. Once the deed of discharge is granted it should be registered in the General Register of Sasines or the Land Register of Scotland and it then becomes binding upon the granter of the discharge and his successors in title in the dominant tenement.[234]

PRESCRIPTION

7-93 A failure to enforce or exercise a land obligation for a period of 20 years will render the land obligation unenforceable. This gives rise to practical problems as it is difficult

---

[233] *Grant* v *Heriot's Trust* (1906) 8 F 647.
[234] Land Registration (Scotland) Act 1979, s 18. Additional requirements as to recording may be added by the legislation relative to reform of the law of real burdens.

to prove that no one has exercised a servitude right of way for 20 years. The matter is even more difficult if the servitude in question is a right of drainage by means of an underground drain. Unless the drain has been wholly wrecked, it is often impossible to show that it has not been used for 20 years. As a result, the law of prescription is rarely resorted to in practice.

CONSOLIDATION

At common law a land obligation will be extinguished if the dominant and servient **7–94** tenements come into single ownership. There is some doubt as to whether the land obligation is re-established when the ownership of the two plots is split at a later date. The safest course is to re-grant the land obligation if it is intended to re-establish the right. This rule may be altered to some extent in terms of the anticipated legislation relative to the reform of the law of real burdens.

COMPULSORY PURCHASE

Land obligations affecting a plot of ground are extinguished when the plot of ground **7–95** which they affect is compulsorily purchased.

VARIATION AND DISCHARGE BY LANDS TRIBUNAL

Since 1970 the Lands Tribunal for Scotland has been empowered on application by the **7–96** servient proprietor to grant an order varying or discharging land obligations.[235] The term "discharge" means that the obligation is removed in full. "Variation" means that only part of the obligation is removed or that the obligation is altered in some way. The order takes effect on an extract thereof being registered in the General Register of Sasines or the Land Register of Scotland and is binding on all parties having interest. The jurisdiction and powers of the Lands Tribunal in relation to the discharge and variation of land obligations may be altered in terms of legislation to implement reforms presently being considered by the Scottish Law Commission.[236]

Excluded land obligations
                                                                                                              7–97
The Lands Tribunal can vary or discharge most land obligations but certain excluded land obligations cannot be varied or discharged. These include[237]:

(a) obligations to work minerals,

(b) obligations imposed on behalf of the Crown to protect any royal park, garden or palace,

(c) obligations imposed for naval, military or air force purposes,

(d) obligations imposed in any agricultural tenancy or croft.

Land obligations cannot be varied within two years of their creation.[238]

---

[235] Convevancing and Feudal Reform (Scotland) Act 1970 ("1970 Act").
[236] Scottish Law Commission, *Discussion Paper on Real Burdens* (No 106) (October 1998).
[237] 1970 Act, Sched 1.
[238] *ibid* s 2(5).

Grounds for variation or discharge

7–98   The Tribunal may exercise its power to vary or discharge only where it is satisfied in all the circumstances that one or other of three grounds for waiver set out in the statute has been established. Any one of the grounds is sufficient, but even if one ground is established there remains a discretion on the part of the Lands Tribunal to vary or discharge or not. The three statutory grounds for waiver are as follows[239]:

(a) that by reason of changes in the character of the servient tenement or the neighbourhood thereof or other circumstances which the Tribunal may deem material, the obligation is or has become unreasonable or inappropriate;

(b) that the obligation is unduly burdensome compared to any benefit resulting or which would result from its performance;

(c) that the existence of the obligation impedes some reasonable use of the servient tenement.

Comment on the three grounds

7–99   *(a) Obligation unreasonable or inappropriate in the light of changes.* There are two parts to this ground. First, there may be changes in the affected land. This ground has been interpreted as covering cases where the land has become useless for the purpose or purposes which the obligation was designed to support. For example, if the land obligation imposes a duty on the proprietor to build a factory within two years and the land has become permanently flooded the obligation may be discharged. Second, there may be changes in the neighbourhood. If there is an obligation to maintain a house on the plot of ground and not to build any factory or office on that plot there may be a ground for variation if a large proportion of properties in the neighbourhood have already been converted into factories. Defining exactly what the neighbourhood is may be a difficult question and the answer to that question differs from area to area, in rural areas it may be a whole village but in a town it may be limited to a housing estate and in a city it may be limited to one single square.[240]

(b) Obligation unduly burdensome. The Tribunal is required to balance the interests of the burdened and benefited proprietors. The interests concerned, however, are not the personal circumstances of the parties but their interests in the maintenance or variation of the obligation as a permanent burden on the land.[241] This ground is frequently resorted to where the applicant wishes to change the existing use of the land burdened by the obligation. An example is where a developer wishes to build a housing development on a plot of ground. He finds that this plan is frustrated because the neighbour has a servitude of drainage running right through the site. If the developer can show that he can provide suitable alternative drainage or that the drain is never really used and closing up the drain would not prejudice the neighbour, the existing obligation may be regarded as unduly burdensome.

(c) Obligation impeding reasonable use. This is the provision most commonly relied on. It looks to the future and attempts to see what the proprietor of the servient tenement

---

[239] 1970 Act, s 1(3).
[240] See, *eg, Main* v *Doune* 1972 SLT (Lands Tr) 14.
[241] *Stoddart* v *Glendinning* 1993 SLT (Lands Tr) 12.

wishes to do with the ground: if the new use is reasonable and it is impeded by the existing obligation then the ground is established. In assessing whether a proposed use is reasonable the fact that planning permission or another statutory licence (such as under the Licensing (Scotland) Acts) has been obtained will be a favourable factor. But the obtaining of such a licence or consent is not conclusive. Where, however, the land obligations are imposed and are enforceable by a local authority as a form of planning control, the fact that planning permission for a development has been obtained will be given considerable weight.[242]

Compensation

In exchange for the Lands Tribunal granting a variation or discharge, the servient proprietor may be directed to pay compensation to the dominant proprietor. This compensation may be paid under one of two alternative heads of claim.[243] These are either: (a) a sum to compensate for any substantial loss or disadvantage resulting from the order. The loss or disadvantage must be substantial but there is no minimum sum for compensation. On more than one occasion no compensation whatsoever has been awarded. It is possible, however, that where there is a very substantial loss or disadvantage this might be a reason for refusing a variation or discharge; or (b) a sum to make up for any substantial loss or disadvantage resulting from the order or a sum to make up for any effect which the land obligation produced, at the time when it was first imposed, in reducing the consideration paid for the servient tenement. A common situation is where land is sold off by a proprietor to a church on the basis that it will be permanently used for religious purposes. This obligation is inserted in the titles by means of a land obligation. The price for the land is substantially less than would have been obtained if the land were sold on the open market. Years later the church closes and the purchaser wishes to develop the land for a public house. The party entitled to enforce the land obligation is unwilling to discharge the land obligation without payment of a sum of money in exchange. That party is entitled to receive some compensation given the original reduced consideration for the plot. There is no ground upon which the person entitled to enforce the land obligation is entitled to a share of the development value of land. So, if a party entitled to enforce a real condition wishes to grant a minute of waiver only in exchange for a share of the increased development value of the land, his claim for compensation will be rejected by the Lands Tribunal.[244]

7–100

Substitute provisions

The Lands Tribunal has a power to impose substitute land obligations as appear to the Lands Tribunal to be reasonable as a result of the variation or discharge of the original burden provided these are accepted by the servient proprietor.[245] This power has been used in a number of cases to allow variations which might otherwise not have been granted—for example, by permitting building subject to conditions such as screening by trees to protect privacy.[246]

7–101

---

[242] *British Bakeries (Scotland) Ltd* v *City of Edinburgh District Council* 1990 SLT (Lands Tr) 33 at 34 (HL).
[243] 1970 Act, s 1(4).
[244] *Keith* v *Texaco Ltd*, 1977 SLT (Lands Tr) 16.
[245] 1970 Act, s 1(5).
[246] See, *eg*, *Crombie* v *George Heriot's Trust* 1972 SLT (Lands Tr) 40.

PUBLIC RIGHTS OF WAY

7–102 Public rights of way are rights enforceable by members of the general public to take access along a definite route across land. Members of the general public may include limited companies and local authorities. The right differs from a servitude because a member of the general public does not need to own a piece of ground comprising a dominant tenement to give him a title to enforce the right of way.[247] Public rights of way can be vehicular or pedestrian. If the public right of way is constituted by a deed then the terms of the deed will decide the issue. Most public rights of way, however, are not constituted by deeds but by use of the right of way for the prescriptive period for 20 years.[248] In such cases the measure of the right is the extent of the use over the past 20 years. Accordingly, if the public have used the right only for pedestrian purposes the right will never be established for the purposes of vehicles. The fact that a road is shown on a map or the Ordnance Survey map in no way indicates that the road is open to the public and does not indicate that the road is subject to a public right of way.

Essentials

7–103 The following are essentials of public rights of way[249]:

(a) It must lead from one public place to another. A public place is not necessarily a place owned by a public authority but is a place to which the public as a matter of fact have resort. For example, a public road is a public place[250] but a sub-post office located within a private house is probably not a public place.[251] The public right of way does not require to lead from one public road to another public road.

(b) There must be a definite route for a public right of way.[252] It is not essential that the route is marked out on the ground. It is not necessary that a public right of way go in a straight line or by the most convenient route. No right of way is acquired by merely strolling or walking at random over private property.

Extinction

7–104 Public rights of way are usually extinguished by non-use for 20 years.[253] There are, however, powers under statute by which public rights of way can be stopped up.[254] Public rights of way are not land obligations and cannot be varied or discharged upon application to the Lands Tribunal.

PUBLIC NAVIGATION

7–105 The public have certain limited rights of navigation of non-tidal rivers.[255] The right of navigation does not require to be taken over a route between two public places. Unlike

---

[247] *Thomson* v *Murdoch* (1862) 24 D 975.
[248] Prescription and Limitation (Scotland) Act 1973, s 3(3).
[249] *Rhins District Committee of Wigtownshire County Council* v *Cuninghame* 1917 2 SLT 169.
[250] *Darrie* v *Drummond* (1865) 3 M 496.
[251] *Love-Lee* v *Cameron* 1991 SCLR 61.
[252] *Mackintosh* v *Moir* (1871) 9 M 574; (1872) 10 M 29, 517.
[253] Prescription and Limitation (Scotland) Act 1973, s 8.
[254] See, *eg*, Countryside (Scotland) Act 1967, s 34(1).
[255] *Will's Trs* v *Cairngorm Canoeing and Sailing School Ltd* 1976 SC (HL) 30; 1976 SLT 162.

a servitude or a public right of way, it is not extinguished by non-use for the period of long negative prescription.[256] The measure of the public right is the physical capacity of the river and is not limited by evidence of past user.[257]

Foreshore, seabed and territorial sea

The general public have rights to navigate and fish for white fish in the territorial sea[258] **7–106** and to recreate on the foreshore.[259]

STATUTORY RIGHTS

A variety of statutes create rights which have certain of the characteristics of real **7–107** rights. Other statutes confer power on the courts or certain parties to create rights which have a similar nature. Whilst each statute must be considered for its terms the following frequently exercised rights may be noted:

(a) Fishermen have statutory rights to use the foreshore and the land above the foreshore.[260]

(b) A telecommunications operator has limited rights to carry out works in lands owned by third parties.[261]

(c) Electricity companies have limited rights to carry out works in lands owned by third parties.[262]

(d) "Non-entitled" spouses (those having no formal legal entitlement such as ownership) have limited rights to occupy a matrimonial home.[263]

TENANCIES AT WILL

The term "tenancy at will" is applied to a form of title to occupy land which exists in **7–108** some villages in some areas of Scotland such as the north-east, the Highlands and certain parts of Lanarkshire such as Leadhills.[264] Under the arrangement the occupier (otherwise known as "the tenant at will") builds a house on ground provided by the landowner. The occupier is required to pay rent and may be removed only on failure to do so. This right is something other than a lease. Statute confers on the tenant at will the right to acquire his landlord's interest upon payment of compensation determined either by agreement or by the application of a statutory mechanism.[265]

---

[256] *Will's Trs* v *Cairngorm Canoeing and Sailing School Ltd* 1976 SC (HL) 30; 1976 SLT 162; *Stair Memorial Encyclopaedia*, Vol 18, paras 497 and 523.
[257] *Will's Trs* v *Cairngorm Canoeing and Sailing School Ltd* 1976 SC (HL) 30 at 169; 1976 SLT 162 at 216 (per Lord Fraser).
[258] *Nicol* v *Blaikie* (1859) 22 D 335.
[259] *Scott* v *Mags of Dundee* (1886) 14 R 191.
[260] Gordon, *Scottish Land Law* (2nd edn, 1999), para 8–08.
[261] Telecommunications Act 1984, Sched 2, paras 2, 3 and 5.
[262] Electricity Act 1989, Sched 4, para 6 and Sched 5, para 1.
[263] Matrimonial Homes (Family Protection) (Scotland) Act 1981, s 6, as amended.
[264] Gordon, *Scottish Land Law* (2nd edn, 1999), para 19–16.
[265] Land Registration (Scotland) Act 1979, s 22(3).

SECURITIES OVER LAND

7–109 A debt is a personal obligation owed by the debtor to the creditor and may be enforced by a personal action in the normal way. A heritable security improves the position of the creditor by conferring upon him additional remedies (such as the right to sell the security subjects) and an advantageous position in a situation where the debtor becomes insolvent.[266]

Standard securities did not exist at common law and are creatures of statute.[267] A standard security is a multi-purpose form of security which can secure both obligations to pay money and obligations *ad factum praestandum* (obligations to do something).[268] The debt may be a present, future or contingent debt.[269] The debt secured may be the debt of the granter of the security or of a third party.[270] The security may be for a fixed amount, an amount calculated according to a statutory formula,[271] or, as is more common in practice, for all sums due or to become due.[272] A standard security may create a security only over heritage, or more precisely only over an "interest in land". In terms of the Abolition of Feudal Tenure etc (Scotland) Act 2000, this term will be deleted and replaced with the expression "land or real right in land". Since 29th November 1970 the standard security has been the only kind of fixed security which may be created over an "interest in land".[273] For the purposes of the 1970 Act, an "interest in land" is defined as meaning "any estate or interest in land ... which is capable of being owned or held as a separate interest and to which a title may be recorded in the Register of Sasines".[274] A standard security may be constituted over a right of property, a proper liferent, a standard security,[275] a long lease[276] and a servitude but not separately from the dominant tenement.[277] It may not be created over a short lease.[278]

FORMS OF STANDARD SECURITY

7–110 The deed creating the standard security must be in one of the two prescribed forms, A and B, set out in Schedule 2 to the 1970 Act.[279] Precise adherence to the actual words

---

[266] Styles, "Rights in Security" in Forte (ed), *Scots Commercial Law* (1997), Chap 6.
[267] Conveyancing and Feudal Reform (Scotland) Act 1970 ("1970 Act").
[268] 1970 Act, s 9(8)(c): definition of "debt". Many of the remedies afforded to a creditor are not well suited to a standard security in respect of the latter type of obligation.
[269] An example of a security for a contingent debt is a discount standard security in terms of the Housing (Scotland) Act 1987, ss 72 and 73. See Cusine, *Standard Securities* (1991), paras 4.41 and 10.06; Gretton and Reid, *Conveyancing* (2nd edn, 1999), para 30.12.
[270] Gretton and Reid, *Conveyancing* (2nd edn, 1999), para 20.05.
[271] See, *eg*, Housing (Scotland) Act 1987, s 72(3).
[272] Gretton and Reid, *Conveyancing* (2nd edn, 1999), para 20.05.
[273] 1970 Act, s 9(3). For older forms of security, see Gretton and Reid, *Conveyancing* (2nd edn, 1999), paras 20.01–20.03.
[274] 1970 Act, ss 9(8)(b) and 30(1).
[275] Cusine, *Standard Securities* (1991), para 4.03; Gretton and Reid, *Conveyancing* (2nd edn, 1999), para 20.16.
[276] These are generally leases for a period exceeding 20 years—Registration of Leases (Scotland) Act 1857, s 1. See, *eg*, *Trade Development Bank v Warriner and Mason (Scotland) Ltd* 1980 SC 74; 1980 SLT 223.
[277] Halliday, *Conveyancing Law and Practice* (2nd edn, 1996), Vol 2, para 51–05(3); Cusine and Paisley, *Servitudes* (1998), para 1.24.
[278] A lease of a period up to and including 20 years.
[279] 1970 Act, s 9(2) and Sched 2.

of the prescribed forms is not absolutely essential.[280] Unfortunately the degree of permitted deviation is not made clear in the statute.[281] It is likely, however, that the words "standard security" will be regarded as essential in any clause of grant of a deed which purports to be a standard security. Form A is a combined personal obligation to repay the debt and a grant of security. Form B is a grant of security used where the personal obligation to repay is constituted in a separate deed. Form B is used more frequently in commercial situations[282] because the loan contract is not recorded in any public register and the parties may retain a degree of confidentiality about their dealings.[283]

Standard conditions

The 1970 Act, Schedule 3 sets out standard conditions which are automatically **7–111** imported into any standard security unless altered or varied.[284] Broadly speaking the statutory standard conditions can be divided into two classes according to function. These are: the maintenance of the value of the security subjects prior to enforcement of the security; and the realisation of the value of the security subjects upon enforcement of the security and the freeing of the creditor of expenses.

Maintenance of value

Into the first class fall standard conditions 1–6, which contain the practical obligations **7–112** on the proprietor to maintain the security subjects and to refrain from activity which might destroy it. They also require the proprietor to comply with certain legal obligations such as title conditions and to refrain from exercising certain legal powers (such as the granting of leases) which might diminish the value of the security subjects. Standard condition 1 places obligations on the debtor to maintain and repair the security subjects and to permit the creditor to enter upon the security subjects to examine their condition. Standard condition 2 obliges the debtor to complete as soon as practicable any uncompleted buildings and not to demolish or alter any existing buildings without the consent of the creditor. The debtor is also required to obtain any statutory consent or licence appropriate to such alterations and to exhibit them to the creditor. Standard condition 3 obliges the debtor to comply with all title conditions and any requirement imposed on him by virtue of any enactment. Standard condition 4 relates to notices or orders received by the debtor under the Town and Country Planning (Scotland) legislation. It obliges the debtor to give the creditor a copy of such notice within 14 days of receipt a copy of such notice. The debtor is also obliged to join with the creditor in objecting to any such notice if required by the creditor. Standard condition 5 obliges the debtor to insure the security subjects or to permit the creditor to insure it in the names of the creditor and the debtor to the extent of the "market value" thereof. Frequently this is varied to require the debtor to insure for the

---

[280] *ibid* s 53(1); Halliday, *Conveyancing Law and Practice* (2nd edn, 1997), Vol 2, para 52–31; Gretton and Reid, *Conveyancing* (2nd edn, 1999), para 20–03.

[281] *Royal Bank of Scotland* v *William and George Marshall*, Sheriff Gerald Gordon QC, Glasgow Sheriff Court, 5th June 1996, unreported; Begg, *The Conveyancing Code* (1879), p 48; Cusine, *Standard Securities* (1991), paras 4.36 and 8.10.

[282] Gretton and Reid, *Conveyancing* (2nd edn, 1999), para 20.03.

[283] Paisley, "Development Sites, Interdicts and the Risks of Adverse Title Conditions" (1997) SLPQ 249–273 at 267.

[284] 1970 Act, s 11(2).

reinstatement value. Standard condition 6 prohibits the granting of a lease by the proprietor of the security subjects without the consent of the heritable creditor. After the creation of the standard security if the proprietor of the security subjects grants a lease without the consent of the heritable creditor that lease may be reduced by the heritable creditor.[285]

Realisation of value

7–113 Into the second class fall the various remedies available to the creditor such as power of sale, power of lease, power to maintain the security subjects, etc. These are contained in standard conditions 7–11. Standard condition 12 makes provision for the securing of expenses incurred by the creditor in relation to a number of matters including creation and realisation of the standard security. Standard condition 7 confers on the creditor a general power to perform obligations on the failure of the debtor and to charge the debtor for the costs in so doing. Standard condition 8 entitles the creditor to call up the security in conformity with the statutory procedure in appropriate cases. Standard condition 9 states the circumstances in which a debtor will be in default. They include: (a) where a calling-up notice has been served in respect of the security subjects and not complied with; (b) where there has been a failure to comply with any other requirement arising out of the security; and (c) where the proprietor of the security subjects has become insolvent. Standard condition 10 lists some of the rights of the creditor on default. These will be examined more fully later. Standard condition 11 governs the exercise by the debtor of a right of redemption. Standard condition 12 renders the debtor personally liable to the creditor for the whole expenses of the preparation and execution of the standard security and any variation, restriction and discharge thereof and the recording dues of any deeds, all expenses reasonably incurred in calling up the security and exercising the powers conferred on the creditor in the security.

Variation of the standard conditions

7–114 The parties are free to vary, supplement or exclude this statutory code of standard conditions as they wish except in certain respects. To protect borrowers certain standard conditions are declared to be incapable of variation. The statutory standard conditions relative to sale and foreclosure of the subjects may not be varied[286] nor may any other standard condition be varied to conflict with these standard conditions in their unvaried form and any such purported variation is void and unenforceable.[287]

Ranking

7–115 Where more than one security is granted over the same property the issue of ranking arises. The starting position is the common law rule that in a competition between standard securities an earlier recording date gives a priority of ranking.[288] The debtor and creditors may make such alternative provision as to ranking as they think fit by means of a ranking agreement.[289]

---

[285] *Trade Development Bank* v *Warriner and Mason (Scotland) Ltd* 1980 SC 74; *Trade Development Bank* v *David W Haig (Bellshill) Ltd* 1983 SLT 510; *Trade Development Bank* v *Crittall Windows Ltd* 1983 SLT 510.
[286] 1970 Act, s 11(3).
[287] *ibid* s 11(4)(b).
[288] Gretton and Reid, *Conveyancing* (2nd edn, 1999), para 20.21.
[289] 1970 Act, s 13(3)(b).

Default

A debtor will be deemed to be in default in three situations. As noted before, these are: **7–116**
(a) where a calling-up notice has been served but not complied with; (b) where there
has been a failure to comply with any other requirement arising out of the security;
and (c) where the proprietor of the security subjects becomes insolvent.[290] Where a
debtor is in default a court has no option but to grant warrant to the creditor to exercise
the remedies in standard condition 10. The remedies open to a creditor on the debtor's
default are varied but many of these remedies are rarely encountered in practice and
are of theoretical interest only. In the vast majority of cases the creditor will simply
wish to enter into possession and sell.[291] The creditor's primary remedy is the power
to sell the security subjects.[292] The creditor may obtain a power of sale by three
different routes. These are (a) calling up; (b) notice of default; and (c) section 24
warrant.

Other remedies

The creditor's other remedies include: **7–117**

(a) once possession has been obtained, the power to let the security subjects[293];

(b) once possession has been obtained, the right to uplift rents in any extant leases
of the security subjects[294];

(c) the power to effect repairs to the security subjects[295];

(d) the power to apply to the court for a decree of foreclosure.[296] This is a remedy
which is not frequently exercised.[297] The remedy of foreclosure enables a
creditor who has failed to find a purchaser for the security subjects at a price
sufficient to cover the amount due to the creditor to take title to the security
subjects rather than sell them at a lower price. This vests the security subjects
in the creditor—he becomes the proprietor in place of the proprietor granting
the security[298];

(e) remedies available to the debtor arising from the contract of loan.[299]

Redemption

The debtor or the proprietor of the security subjects each have a right to redeem the **7–118**
standard security upon giving two months' notice in a statutory form.[300] This right is
subject to "any agreement to the contrary".[301]

---

[290] 1970 Act, Sched 3, SC 9(1).
[291] Gretton and Reid, *Conveyancing* (2nd edn, 1999), para 20.28.
[292] 1970 Act, Sched 3, SC 10(2).
[293] *ibid* SC 10(4).
[294] *ibid* SC 10(5).
[295] *ibid* SC 10(6).
[296] 1970 Act, s 28 and Sched 3, SC 10(7).
[297] It is stated to be "extremely rare" in Gretton and Reid, *Conveyancing* (2nd edn, 1999), para 20.31.
[298] Gretton and Reid, *Conveyancing* (2nd edn, 1999), para 20.31.
[299] 1970 Act, s 20(1).
[300] *ibid* s 18(1), Sched 3, SC 11 and Sched 5, Form A.
[301] *ibid* s 18(1); Redemption of Standard Securities (Scotland) Act 1971, s 1.

Discharge

7–119 A standard security may be discharged by the recording of a discharge in statutory form granted by the creditor.[302] Where a discharge by the creditor cannot be obtained due to the death or absence of the creditor or any other cause a standard security may be discharged by the recording of a certificate in statutory form confirming either that the redemption sums have been consigned or that the court has declared that the whole obligations under the contract to which the security relates have been performed.[303]

FLOATING CHARGES

7–120 A floating charge is a method of obtaining security over both heritage and moveables. It is a creature of statute but there is no comprehensive statutory definition of what a floating charge is.[304] This may cause some difficulty in determining whether some forms of security used outwith the UK would be regarded as a floating charge.[305] It is not essential for the constitution of a Scottish floating charge that the deed creating the charge uses the term "floating charge"[306] although this is clearly desirable to avoid confusion. Until the floating charge attaches the statutory provisions clearly imply that the company is to be free to dispose of the assets covered by the charge without the consent of the holder of the floating charge.[307] For a purchaser of land it is therefore essential that he is able to determine that the charge has not attached or crystallised. As crystallisation may occur without a public act, the best that can be done in practice is for a warranty or certificate of non-crystallisation to be obtained, usually from the creditor in the floating charge. This is generally known as a "letter of non-crystallisation". There is no statutory form of such letter.

Attachment

7–121 A floating charge is not a fixed charge when it is created but it becomes a fixed charge when it "attaches" or "crystallises".[308] The only mechanism for enforcing the floating charge is through the appointment of a receiver to gather in the assets, convert them into cash and distribute the money realised.[309] It is the receiver and not the charge-holder who has various powers to realise the value of the assets subject to the security even though the receiver has no real right in those assets.[310] A floating charge attaches when the company goes into liquidation[311] or a receiver is appointed to the company

---

[302] 1970 Act, s 17 and Sched 4, Form F.

[303] *ibid* s 18(2)–(4) and Sched 5, Form D. Cusine, *Standard Securities* (1991), para 10.05.

[304] The nearest approximation to such a statement is in the Companies Act 1985, s 462. See *Stair Memorial Encyclopaedia*, Vol 4, para 652.

[305] *Stair Memorial Encyclopaedia*, Vol 4, para 652.

[306] *ibid*.

[307] *ibid*.

[308] The two terms have identical meanings. The first term is used in the statute but the latter is widely used. See *Stair Memorial Encyclopaedia*, Vol 4, para 659; Gretton and Reid, *Conveyancing* (2nd edn, 1999), para 28.09.

[309] Insolvency Act 1986, s 60; *Myles J Callaghan Ltd v City of Glasgow District Council* 1987 SCLR 627; 1988 SLT 227. Gretton and Reid, *Conveyancing* (2nd edn, 1999), para 29.06.

[310] Gretton and Reid, *Conveyancing* (2nd edn, 1999), para 29.06.

[311] Companies Act 1985, s 463(1) prospectively amended by the Companies Act 1989, s 140(1) from a day to be appointed under s 215(2). See *Stair Memorial Encyclopaedia*, Vol 4, para 659.

under the floating charge.[312] It is competent for the parties to a floating charge to provide that the creditor may appoint a receiver on any ground specified in the instrument creating the charge under which the appointment was made. Not all property to which the company has title is attached by the floating charge on the appointment of a receiver. Excluded property extends to property held by the company subject to a valid trust in favour of a third party[313] and property held by the company subject to a beneficial interest in favour of a purchaser holding a delivered disposition as yet unrecorded.[314]

Ranking of floating charges

Irrespective of any ranking provisions contained in a floating charge a floating charge will always rank after a fixed security arising by operation of law.[315] A floating charge may contain ranking provisions.[316] In the absence of express restrictive provisions or ranking provisions the following rules apply[317]:

7–122

(a) a fixed security the right to which has been constituted as a real right before the floating charge has attached has priority of ranking over the floating charge;

(b) floating charges rank with one another according to the time of their registration in the Charges register; and

(c) floating charges which have been received by the Registrar of Companies for registration by the same postal delivery rank with one another equally.

Functions and powers of the receiver

The principal function of the receiver is to seek enforcement of the obligation secured by the floating charge. To do this he will usually realise the assets of the company to the extent required and distribute the money received in accordance with the statutory order of ranking. In carrying out his functions a receiver is deemed to be the agent of the company in relation to the property attached by the floating charge.[318] In relation to the property attached by the floating charge a receiver has all the powers given to him in the instrument creating the floating charge[319] and, in addition, so far as they are not inconsistent with any provision of the floating charge, the powers conferred upon him by statute.[320]

7–123

---

[312] Insolvency Act 1986, ss 53(7) and 54(6); *Forth & Clyde Construction Co Ltd v Trinity Timber & Plywood Co Ltd* 1984 SC 1, per Lord President Emslie at 10; *National Commercial Bank of Scotland Ltd v Telford Grier Mackay & Co Ltd Liquidators* 1969 SC 181.

[313] *Tay Valley Joinery Ltd v C F Financial Services Ltd* 1987 SCLR 117; 1987 SLT 207. For difficulties with the case, see Reid, "Trusts and Floating Charges", 1987 SLT (News) 113. See also *Stair Memorial Encyclopaedia*, Vol 4, para 660.

[314] *Sharp v Thomson* 1997 SC (HL) 66; 1997 SLT 636; 1997 SCLR 328. For difficulties with this case, see Styles, "Rights in Security" in Forte (ed), *Scots Commercial Law* (1997), p 196; Gretton and Reid, *Conveyancing* (2nd edn, 1999), paras 11.31 and 28.09.

[315] Companies Act 1985, s 464(2).

[316] *ibid* s 464(1), (1A) (respectively amended and added by the Companies Act 1989, s 140(3), (4)). The provisions of the 1989 Act, ss 140 and 178 come into force on a day to be appointed under s 215(2). See *Stair Memorial Encyclopaedia*, Vol 4, para 664.

[317] Companies Act 1985, s 464(4)(a)–(c).

[318] Insolvency Act 1986, s 57(1); *Stair Memorial Encyclopaedia*, Vol 4, para 676.

[319] *ibid* s 55(1).

[320] *ibid* s 55(2) and Sched 2.

SUMMARY

THE CONCEPTS

- Land law is a branch of the general law of property which relates to "heritable" property. The land is the thing which is subject to the right. Moveable property may become heritable by being fixed to the land.
- Real rights are enforceable against the world whilst personal rights are enforceable only against a limited class of persons, such as the party who has undertaken a contractual obligation. There is usually a two-stage process in the creation of real rights, the first being private and the second requiring some form of publicity.

RIGHT OF PROPERTY

- The right of property is the most extensive real right. It may be restricted in various ways—by agreement, statute and common law.
- Co-ownership occurs where more than one party owns a property.
- Joint and common property are distinguisable—the former relating to the title of clubs and trusts.
- Special rules relate to the exercise of the rights of common ownership. Division and sale may end common ownership.

LIFERENTS

- A liferent is a limited real right which entitles the liferenter to use the property for his lifetime. The owner of the property is known as the "fiar". His right is one of ownership but it is limited by the liferent.
- Liferents may be classified as proper and improper, legal and conventional.
- A special form of liferent is an alimentary liferent which is linked to the maintenance of the liferenter.

LEASES

- A lease is probably the most frequently encountered derivative real right. All leases are contracts and only some qualify as real rights.
- Leases have a term date but may be continued by tacit relocation.
- There may be limits on the assignation of the lease by the tenant and on sub-letting.
- Provisions in the lease may create special terms relative to a variety of matters including breaks in the lease, resumption, renunciation and irritancy.
- Some types of lease attract security of tenure.
- The tenant's main interest in a lease is generally to obtain possession in exchange for payment of rent.
- In commercial leases, the landlord will wish the tenant to pay for insurance and repairs but he is constrained in imposing these provisions in residential leases.

LAND OBLIGATIONS

- Land obligations is a generic name for servitudes, real burdens and common interest. They may be varied and discharged by the Lands Tribunal.

SERVITUDES

- A servitude is a burden on a piece of land in favour of another. The most commonly encountered servitude is a private right of way to a plot of land.
- Servitudes are real rights enforceable against the rest of the world by the owner of the dominant tenement.
- There is a limited class of rights which may be created as a servitude.
- Servitudes may be positive or negative.
- There are various methods of creation of servitudes and the most common are express creation by a deed and creation by exercise for the prescriptive period.

REAL BURDENS

- Real burdens are limitations on the use of land. They are also known as real conditions.
- Real burdens are enforceable by one landowner against another. They may be created by express grant or reservation only.
- The deed should be clearly expressed as there is a presumption in favour of freedom.
- Title and interest are needed to enforce.

COMMON INTEREST

- Common interest arises by implication of law. It is a restriction on one property enforceable by the owner of another. It comprises a number of types of rights but is most commonly encountered in a tenemental situation where it imposes repairing obligations.

PUBLIC RIGHTS OF WAY

- These enable the public to pass from one public place to another. They are usually created by prescriptive exercise for 20 years. They may be extinguished by non-use.
- Similar rights on rivers are public rights of navigation but they do not require to lead from one public place to another.

STATUTORY RIGHTS

- Various statutory rights affect land and each statute must be considered for its own terms. They include the rights of fishermen and occupancy rights for spouses.

TENANCIES AT WILL

• These are a customary form of landholding which, to a certain extent, resemble a lease. The tenants have certain statutory rights.

SECURITIES

• The primary form of security over land is a standard security although a floating charge may also affect land owned by companies. There are two statutory forms of standard securities but no form for a floating charge.
• Standard securities are regulated by standard conditions. These may be amended by agreement.
• Securities may be governed by ranking agreements.
• When a debtor is in default a holder of a standard security has various remedies, chief of which is the power to sell.
• The creditor in a floating charge may appoint a receiver who realises the assets of the company.

CASE DIGEST

Lease—landlord's implied warranty of fitness for purpose [see para 7-52]
  Glebe Sugar Refining Co v Paterson (1900) 7 SLT 374
A warehouse collapsed one month after entry. The tenant sued the landlord on the ground that it was not fit for the purpose. It was held on the facts that the tenant had overloaded it and there was not any liability on the part of the landlord. In short, the warehouse was fit for the purpose for which it was let but the tenant had abused the warehouse.

Lease—landlord's implied warranty of fitness for purpose [see para 7-52]
  McGonigal v Pickard 1964 SLT 526
The floor of premises collapsed as a result of deterioration caused by dampness, precipitating the tenant and the bed upon which she was lying into the basement. It was held that the landlord was not liable. The collapse was due to an exceptional encroachment of water due to a cause other than the ordinary attacks of the elements.

Servitude expressly limited to one purpose [see para 7–72]
  Cronin v Sutherland (1899) 2 F 217
It was held that a right of passage for the "purpose of entry to cart fuel and manure" did not include transporting out the contents of an ashpit (old fashioned toilet).

Servitude may be created by general phrase in deed [see para 7–76]
  McLean v *Marwhirn Developments Ltd* 1976 SLT (Notes) 47
The court upheld a reservation of all existing pipes, connections, sewers, etc as sufficient to constitute a servitude of drainage even although there was no specification as to the route or location of the pipes.

Real condition—land burdened to be precisely defined [see para 7–85]
  Anderson v *Dickie* 1915 SC (HL) 74
A deed imposed a restriction on the type of building that could be built on "the lawn between the ground feued to [a named party] and the present mansion house of Eastwood Park". It was held that this was not a sufficiently detailed description to create a real burden as the land described might cease to be a lawn at any time and it would then be impossible to locate the area in question.

Real condition—obligation to build does not include obligation to maintain [see para 7–85]
  Kemp v *Mags of Largs* 1939 SC (HL) 6
The obligation was to use a piece of ground in all time coming for a pier and harbour. It was held that this did not imply a prohibition against using the ground for other purposes as well. As a result, the feuar was entitled to build a dance hall and amusement arcade in addition to the pier.

FURTHER READING

Agnew, *Crofting Law* (T&T Clark, 2000)
Cusine and Paisley, *Servitudes and Rights of Way* (W Green, 1998)
Gloag and Henderson, *The Law of Scotland* (10th edn, W Green, 1995), Part VI
Gordon, *Scottish Land Law* (2nd edn, W Green, 1999)
The Laws of Scotland: Stair Memorial Encyclopaedia (Law Society of Scotland/ Butterworths), Vol 18

8 PROPERTY AND GOODS

OVERVIEW

Various legal rights pertain to the ownership of property and goods and govern their transfer and use.[1] Relevant aspects include general classifications of property, intellectual property, rights in security and cautionary obligations, diligence, the sale and supply of goods, insurance and negotiable instruments.

8–01

PROPERTY RIGHTS

The term "property" itself, can be somewhat confusing. This stems from the fact that it may be used to denote both a particular item or thing itself or may refer to the legal ownership of the thing. Hence, it can be said that a person has property in a particular property.

8–02

In terms of rights over an item, the right of property is the most extensive that can be held. This has been defined as "the right of using and disposing of a thing as our own".[2] Thus, two parties cannot have the same full right of property in an item simultaneously.[3] Subject to the existence of inferior rights that others may have in respect of the item, the right of property is exclusive and others may be prevented from interfering with it.[4]

When using the term "property" to denote the subject of ownership itself, property can be classified in different ways:

- Heritable and moveable property

- Corporeal and incorporeal property

- Fungible and non-fungible property.

---

[1]   Heritable property is dealt with in Chapter 7.
[2]   Erskine, *Inst* II, ii, 1.
[3]   Erskine, *Inst* II, i.
[4]   *eg* restrictions on rights of landownership—see Chapter 7.

As its name would suggest, moveable property refers to property which is inherently capable of motion. All property which is not heritable is by definition moveable property. This chapter is not concerned with the law relating to heritable property as this has been dealt with in detail elsewhere in the text.[5]

Moveable property can be further divided into corporeal and incorporeal moveable property. Corporeal property is tangible property, which includes furniture, cars, food and money. By contrast, incorporeal property is intangible in nature, including intellectual property rights, shares in a company and a right under an insurance policy.

A further classification is that property can be either fungible and non-fungible. Fungible property is non-specific in the sense that it can be weighed out or measured and replaced by an equivalent quantity—for example, firewood or money. Fungible goods are non-specific. On the other hand, non-fungible property is that which is unique and cannot be replaced by an equivalent. An example of a non-fungible item may be a particular classic car or antique painting.

POSSESSION

8–03   Any discussion of this area of law inevitably conjures up the well-worn phrase, "possession is nine-tenths the law". While this saying by no means paints a true picture of the law relating to property in goods, nonetheless it is not without some foundation. A person who is in possession of a good will be presumed to be the true owner in the absence of any conflicting evidence to the contrary.[6] Any person seeking to challenge the possessor's right to the thing must establish his right of ownership and prove that his possession was not lost in such a fashion as to pass title of the goods on to another party.[7]

What amounts to possession would, at first glance, appear to be self-evident. In fact there has been a great deal of debate amongst legal jurists as to the nature of possession. The classic definition was given by Stair when he identified two elements to possession : "to possession there must be an act of the body which is the detention and holding; and an act of the mind which is the inclination or affection to make use of the thing detained".[8]

Obviously the physical element of possession will vary according to the type of property concerned—if one compares a house to a sum of money, the nature of the physical holding of the property of each would obviously differ. The mental element required is the intention to hold on to the thing for one's own benefit.[9] This is generally presumed from the fact that the property is in a party's custody. It is for other parties to dispute that the holder of the thing is not in fact in possession.

Where there is no such mental intention, then there may be what can be termed "custody" of the item but no possession. For example, if an employee holds property on behalf of his employer, the employee merely has custody of the property and not possession.[10] Conversely, it is not necessary that a person has a

---

[5] See Chapter 7.
[6] *Scott* v *Elliot* (1672) Mor 12727; Stair II, i, 42; IV, xxx, 9.
[7] *Russel* v *Campbell* (1699) 4 Brown's Supp 468; *Prangnell-O'Neil* v *Skiffington* 1984 SLT 282.
[8] Stair II, i, 17.
[9] Known as *"animus possidendi"*—literally the intention to possess.
[10] Stair II, i, 17; *Barnton Hotel Co* v *Cook* (1899) 1 F 1190.

legal right to hold goods for possession to occur: a thief is said to have possession of stolen goods as he both physically holds the goods and intends to hold them for his own benefit.

Possession can be either natural or civil.[11] Natural possession arises where a party has actual physical possession of the item.[12] Civil possession arises where a party does not physically hold an item, but it is held by another party on his behalf. For example, an employer may possess goods which are in the custody of his servants and a landlord may possess a house, although it is resided in by his tenant.[13]

Possession is also "exclusive" in the sense that two or more persons cannot each have full possession of the item simultaneously. There can, however, be what is known as concurrent possession, in which two or more parties hold rights of possession which do not conflict with another—that is their rights of possession are for different purposes. A landlord and a tenant, for example, may both possess a house for their distinct, respective interests.

INTELLECTUAL PROPERTY RIGHTS

In general terms, these relate to rights which arise over original and creative works, **8–04** and which grant the author or inventor certain benefits in relation to their creation. Such intangible property rights amount to incorporeal moveable property.

This section does not attempt an all-encompassing discussion of this topical, at times complex and fluid, area of the law; rather it discusses the main legal provisions relating to some of the main forms of property rights which arise under the umbrella term "intellectual property"—trademarks, patents and copyright.[14]

TRADE MARKS

Introduction

Trade marks can be defined as "any sign capable of being represented graphically **8–05** which is capable of distinguishing goods or services of one undertaking from those of other undertakings" and "may, in particular, consist of words (including personal names), designs, letters, numerals, or the shape of goods or their packaging".[15] The main purpose of the trade mark is to enable the consumer to readily identify a particular company associated with the mark and distinguish between products offered by different companies. For example, the pound sign trade mark on Parlaphone records makes their products instantly recognisable, as does the "Fender" logo on Fender guitars and amplifiers.

As distinct from the law relating to the protection of trade names which remains governed by the common law, the protection of trade marks is underpinned by statute.

---

[11] Erskine, *Inst* II, i, 20.
[12] Or, in relation to heritable property such as land, if he cultivates that land; or, in relation to a house, if he occupies it—see Chapter 7.
[13] *Mitchell's Trs* v *Gladstone* (1894) 21 R 586.
[14] Given space constraints, there is no discussion of the law relating to design.
[15] Trade Marks Act 1994, s 1(1); hereinafter cited as "TMA".

It should be noted, however, that common law protection in relation to trade marks has remained.[16] Legislation was first introduced in this area by way of the Trade Marks Registration Act 1875. The relevant provisions have been amended over the years and are now embodied in the Trade Marks Act 1994 which, taking account of provisions of European law,[17] came into force on 31st October 1994.[18]

Protection

8–06　In fundamental terms, protection under the Act is effected by registration of the trade mark with the Register of Trade Marks. Registration covers an initial 10-year period (from when the application was made) although this can be renewed thereafter for successive periods of 10 years.[19] Prior to the registration being granted, the registrar is bound to publish details of the application and within a three-month period third parties may bring forth notice of any opposition to the registration.[20]

Once a mark is registered, the user gains the exclusive right to use that mark. Registration of the mark must be sought, however, in relation to particular categories of goods or services for which protection is sought—that is the statutory protection is available only in relation to the particular category the mark is registered in. There are eight categories of service and some 32 categories of goods. Certain trade marks may, of course, be associated with goods and services from a number of categories. In these situations, a multiple application may be sought, but payment must be made for each category within which protection is sought.[21]

Refusal of registration

8–07　Registration of the trade mark may be refused on a number of grounds which can be divided into two distinct categories: "absolute grounds"[22] or "relative grounds".[23]

Absolute grounds

8–08　Absolute grounds are intrinsic to the trade mark itself. Absolute grounds include those where the mark: does not exhibit its own distinctive character[24]; comprises purely of characteristics of the goods or services such as their nature, quantity, quality, purpose, value or origin[25]; or consists exclusively of signs which have become customary in the particular trade in question.[26] In addition, the trade mark may be refused when it is deemed contrary to public policy or an affront to accepted moral standards.[27] Refusal may also occur if the application is deemed to have been made in bad faith or it is likely that the trade mark will deceive the public in some way.[28]

---

[16]　TMA, s 2.
[17]　The EC Directive to Approximate the Laws of Member States Relating to Trade Marks (89/104/EEC).
[18]　Replacing the Trade Marks Act 1938.
[19]　TMA ss 42 and 43.
[20]　*ibid* s 38(2).
[21]　*ibid* s 32(4).
[22]　*ibid* s 3.
[23]　*ibid* ss 5–8.
[24]　*ibid* s 3(1)(b).
[25]　*ibid* s 3(1)(c).
[26]　*ibid* s 3(3).
[27]　*ibid* s 3(3).
[28]　*ibid* s 3(6).

Relative grounds

In general terms, relative grounds apply to situations where the trade mark conflicts **8–09** with a previously registered mark. The most concrete grounds for refusal will arise where a trade mark is identical to an earlier mark and the later mark relates to the same goods or services protected by the earlier mark.[29] In addition, refusal will occur where a later mark is identical to an earlier mark and relates to *similar* goods and services, or where the later mark is *similar* to the earlier mark and relates to similar goods and services where the later mark is likely to confuse the public[30]; or where a later mark is similar or identical to an earlier mark and although the goods and services it relates to are not similar, the earlier trade mark has a renowned reputation and use of the trade mark would take advantage of or be prejudicial to the holder of the earlier trade mark.[31]

Assignation of the trade mark

A trade mark is incorporeal property. Hence it may be assigned either in whole or in **8–10** part.[32] Any such assignation must be in writing and signed by the assignor (or his agent).[33]

Unregistered trade marks

Although, apart from under statute, there can be no right of property in a trade mark,[34] **8–11** at common law a trader has a right to use a particular name or trade mark and can prevent other parties from making use of that name or mark.[35] Hence, where a firm has failed to register a trade mark, protection can still be found by reference to the common law. Such common law rights are protected by what is known as an action for "passing off". The main remedy sought in such an action is one of interdict to stop the other party's use of the trade mark. Damages stemming from the misuse of the trade mark may also be payable. It is of no consequence that the abuser was unaware of the existence of the prior trade mark[36]; nor that the public have in fact not been deceived.[37] All that need be proven is that the public are likely to become confused, hence the abuser may well profit from the goodwill and reputation of the prior user of the trade mark.[38]

PATENTS

The right to grant patents is exercised by the Crown under the Royal Prerogative.[39] In **8–12** basic terms, patents grant the creator of an invention a monopoly in respect of

---

[29] *ibid* s 5(1).
[30] *ibid* s 5(2).
[31] *ibid* s 5(3).
[32] *ibid* s 24(2).
[33] *ibid* s 24(3).
[34] *Kinnel & Co v Ballantine & Sons* 1910 SC 246.
[35] *Williamson v Meikle* 1909 SC 1272.
[36] *Singer Machine Manufacturers v Wilson* (1877) 3 App Cas 376.
[37] *Kinnel & Co v Ballantine & Sons* 1910 SC 246.
[38] See, *eg Haig & Co v Forth Blending Co* 1954 SC 35; *Reckitt & Colman Products Ltd v Borden Inc* [1990] 1 All ER 873.
[39] Residual powers of the Crown—see Chapter 2.

manufacture and use of the invention. Such rights have been recognised in the UK for centuries, although they have been varied in certain respects over the years.[40] The current law is set out in the Patents Act 1977 ("PA") and the Patents Rules 1990.[41] The current statutory provisions take into account provisions of European Community law which impact upon this area.[42]

Granting patents

8–13 As has been stated, patents are granted in respect of inventions. Although the term "invention" is not defined in the Act, an invention must be new, involve an inventive step and be capable of industrial or agricultural application.[43] To satisfy the requirement of newness, the invention must not form part of the existing "state of the art"—that is the invention must not have been available to the public in the UK or elsewhere in any form prior to the application being made.[44] Determining whether an inventive step has taken place or not, may not always be an easy task. The test of innovation that the Act prescribes is that the inventive step should be one which would not be obvious to an expert in the field.[45]

Various analyses of this test have undertaken by the courts. A useful list of steps to be taken in determining whether an advancement was obvious to an expert in the field was set out by Oliver LJ in *Windsurfing International Inc* v *Tabur Marine (GB) Ltd*[46]:

(a) Identify the inventive concept embodied in the patent.

(b) Ascertain from a normally skilled expert in the field what was the common general knowledge of state of the art.

(c) Identify the differences (if any) between the state of the art and the alleged invention.

(d) Decide whether those differences, viewed without any knowledge of the alleged invention, constituted steps that would have been obvious to the skilled man or whether they required any degree of invention.[47]

Generally speaking, an invention is capable of industrial action if it can be used in any form of industry.[48] This includes agriculture but methods of treatment or diagnosis practised on either humans or animals are not capable of industrial application. This stems from the fact that such medical matters are too important in the sense of sustaining life to be the subject of a monopoly.

---

[40] The English Statute of Monopolies 21 Jac 1, c 3, extended to Scotland at the Union of Parliaments.
[41] SI 1990/2384, as amended.
[42] The Convention for the European Patent for the Common Market, the Convention on the Grant of European Patents and the Patent Co-operation Treaty, 1970.
[43] PA, s 1(1).
[44] s 2.
[45] s 3.
[46] [1985] RPC 59 at 73–74. Although this case is related to patents under the 1949 Patents Act, subsequent case law has deemed it as a useful test for patents under the 1977 Act.
[47] See also *Hallen Co v Brabantia (UK) Ltd* [1991] RPC 195; *Shoketsu Kinzoku Kogyo KK's Patent* [1992] FSR 184.
[48] PA, s 4. This includes agriculture, but methods of treatment or diagnosis practised on either humans or animals are not capable of industrial application.

Exemptions

Certain manifestations of originality are not treated as inventions for the purposes of **8–14** the Act. Such matters as discoveries, scientific theories or mathematical methods, literary or other works are exempted on the basis that they are deemed better protected under the laws of copyright.[49] Likewise, patents will not be granted in respect of inventions which would be "generally considered to encourage offensive, immoral or anti-social behaviour" or for certain processes in respect of the production of animals or plants.[50]

The patent

A patent application should be made by the inventor to the Comptroller-General of **8–15** Patents, Designs and Trade Marks at the Patent Office in London. The granting of the patent grants the inventor a monopoly on manufacture and use of the invention for a 20-year period.[51] The patent itself is treated as incorporeal moveable property.[52] In common with other property, the patent may pass on succession, can be sold or licensed to another, and can legitimately be offered as security in respect of a loan.[53]

Either the court or the comptroller may, on the application, revoke the patent on a number of specified grounds, including: that the patent was not patentable; that the patent holder was in fact not the only person entitled to it; that the specification of the invention did not disclose the nature of the invention in sufficient detail.[54]

A person may infringe a patent in a number of different ways—for example, if, without the consent of the holder of the patent, he manufactures, disposes of or offers to so dispose, uses or imports the invention or keeps it; or, where the invention is a process, uses or offers to use the process in the UK or disposes of, uses, imports or keeps any product obtained directly by the process.[55]

If the patent is so infringed, the patent holder may seek an interdict to bring violation of the patent to an end.[56] In addition to the right of interdict, the patent holder may be entitled to damages in respect of losses resulting from the violation, except where the violator can show that he was not aware of and had no reasonable grounds to believe in the patent's existence.[57] In lieu of damages, the patent holder may be entitled to a share of the profits made in respect of the patented product by the violator.[58]

COPYRIGHT

Introduction

The law relating to copyright is now set out in the Copyright, Designs and Patents Act **8–16** 1988 ("CDPA"). Copyright is a right of incorporeal moveable property which exists in a "copyright work".[59]

---

[49] *ibid* s 1(2).
[50] *ibid* s 1(3)(a). The latter exception relates largely to the genetic engineering of animals and plants.
[51] *ibid* s 25.
[52] *ibid* s 31(2).
[53] *ibid* s 31(3).
[54] *ibid* s 72.
[55] *ibid* s 60.
[56] *ibid* s 61.
[57] See *British Thomson-Houston Co v Charlesworth, Peebles & Co* 1923 SC 599.
[58] PA, s 61(2).
[59] CDPA, s 1(2).

The types of work in which copyright may exist are set out in section 1(1) of the Act:

(a) original literary, dramatic, musical or artistic works

(b) sound recording, films, broadcasts or cable programmes

(c) the typographical arrangement of published editions.

A fundamental principle is that no copyright can exist in a work—for example, a song or a dramatic idea—until that work is expressed in writing or otherwise. An idea rolling around in one's mind, even if communicated verbally to another party, is not capable of being protected by copyright. The key point is that it is not so much the idea itself which is protected; rather it is the expression of that idea which is protected. Indeed, the reference to originality refers to the way in which a particular idea is expressed; the idea itself need not be an original one.[60]

Unlike the situation pertaining to patents, protection of copyright arises without the need for any sort of registration of the work. While this is useful in the sense that a copyright can arise automatically, the absence of any registration begs the question as to how the copyright can be proven. The author needs to produce an original and preferably dated evidence of the creation of the work and proof of its authorship.

A literary work is any work, other than a dramatic or musical work, which is written, spoken or sung. Under the Act, literary works include tables, compilations and, importantly, computer programs. Given the high-tech nature of modern life, the inclusion of the latter is obviously of the utmost importance.[61] The term "literary" should not be taken to indicate any real literary merit—the key facet of the work is that it must be original. For example, copyright may exist in instructions for a video recorder or in the layout of a football coupon.

Copyright in literary, dramatic or artistic work expires at the end of 50 years from the end of the calendar year in which the author has died.[62] Similarly, copyright in sound or film recordings expire at the end of 50 years after the end of the calendar year in which they have been created (or, if released before the end of the calendar year in which it was made, 50 years after the release).[63] Similar 50-year copyright periods pertain to broadcasts and programmes.[64] Generally speaking, copyright exists for a 25-year period in relation to typological arrangements of published editions (that is the arrangement of text on a page).[65]

Ownership of the copyright

8–17   Generally speaking, the owner of the copyright is the creator of the work.[66] As may often be the case, however, where the work has been created by the author in the

---

[60] *Harpers* v *Barry, Henry & Co* (1892) 20 R 133.
[61] The inclusion of computer programs resulted from the Copyright (Computer Software) Amendment Act 1985, although the courts had already expressed the view that a computer program ought to be viewed as a literary work: *Thrustcode* v *WW Computing Ltd* [1983] FSR 502.
[62] CDPA, s 46(2).
[63] *ibid* s 13(1).
[64] *ibid* s 14(1).
[65] *ibid* s 15.
[66] *ibid* s 9(1).

course of his employment, the employer will be the owner of the copyright subject to any agreement to the contrary.[67] As copyright is viewed as incorporeal moveable property it may be sold, transmitted by operation of law (for example, by the rules of succession) or assigned.[68]

Copyright protection

A copyrighted work is protected in the sense that certain acts in respect of that work cannot be undertaken by other parties. As would be expected, the main restriction is **8–18** on copying the work. Depending on the nature of the work, copying may arise by different means. In the case of a literary, dramatic, musical or artistic work, copying includes reproducing the work in any material form and storing it in electronic form.[69] The second offence is the issuing of copies of the work to the UK public when the work had not previously been put in circulation.[70] In the case of sound recordings and films, the issuing of copies extends to the renting of copies to the public. Other infringements include: the performance, showing or playing of a literary, dramatic or musical work in public, which includes the delivery of lectures, addresses, speeches and sermons[71]; broadcasting the work or including it in a cable service; adapting works and transferring non-literary works into literary works and vice versa.[72]

There are also certain "secondary" offences—for example, where a party imports "pirate copies" of works into the UK for commercial use and where a person possesses or sells pirate copies in the course of a business.[73]

It should be noted that in cases where an amount of flexibility is deemed appropriate, some of the above kind of acts will be permitted. These situations include "fair dealing" with certain copyrighted work for research or private study purposes,[74] or for the purpose of criticism or review and the reporting of topical events.[75] Permitted acts may also be undertaken by seats of learning such as schools and universities,[76] libraries[77] and public bodies in respect of parliamentary and judicial proceedings. Many of these areas are the subject of detailed regulations relating to permitted use.

Remedies

If infringement of the copyright takes place then the owner of the copyright may raise **8–19** an action of interdict in order to bring the infringement to an end, claim damages for losses incurred resulting from the infringement or seek payment of profits made in respect of the copyrighted works by the infringer.[78] In an action for damages, it will be a valid defence that the infringer did not believe and had no reasonable grounds for believing that the work was copyrighted.[79]

---

[67] *ibid* s 11.
[68] *ibid* s 90(1).
[69] *ibid* s 57.
[70] *ibid* s 58 (as amended).
[71] *ibid* s 19.
[72] *ibid* s 21.
[73] *ibid* ss 22, 23.
[74] *ibid* s 29(1).
[75] *ibid* s 30(1).
[76] *ibid* ss 32, 34–36.
[77] *ibid* ss 37–43.
[78] *ibid* ss 96, 97.
[79] *ibid* s 97(1).

Additionally, the court may order that "pirate copies" of works (and equipment designed to copy works) are delivered to the owner of the copyright or destroyed.[80]

Moral rights

8–20   Moral (non-economic) rights relate to situations where the copyright in a work no longer belongs to the original author. Where an author no longer holds the copyright in his work, he is nonetheless entitled to assert moral rights over the work as to how it is represented to the public.[81]

There are four basic moral rights: "the paternity right", a right to be named as the author of the work[82]; "the integrity", the right to prevent derogatory treatment (for example, to prevent a musical or dramatic work being cut or mutilated in some form which would have some adverse bearing on the author's professional reputation)[83]; the right to prevent oneself being falsely attributed with the authorship of the work[84]; and a right to privacy in respect of photographs or films which were shot for private purposes.[85]

RIGHTS IN SECURITY

INTRODUCTION

8–21   A common problem with lending money to another is being left out of pocket when the other party fails to pay back what is owed. Seeking repayment of the debt through the civil courts may be costly and time-consuming. In any case, if the debtor is sequestrated or is wound up (in the case of companies) then it may be that there will be insufficient assets to repay the debt when there is a myriad of competing claims for payment from other creditors.

REAL RIGHTS IN SECURITY

8–22   Such problems in relation to non-payment of a debt can be alleviated by the creation of a right in security. Certain rights in security are "real" in nature in that the creditor holds a right over certain property of the debtor (either heritable or movable) which can be exercised in the event that the debtor fails to make payment of the debt.[86] Generally speaking, where the debtor fails to make payment, the right allows the creditor to seize and sell the property in question and the proceeds are used to meet the outstanding balance owed. Such a real right in the property cannot generally be defeated by the claims of others.

Real rights in security can be contrasted to those rights in security which are personal in nature. Such rights, termed as "cautionary obligations" grant creditors the

---

[80] *ibid* ss 99, 114. Copyright holders also have limited rights to take possession of such pirate works prior to seeking a court decree: s 100, as amended.

[81] Such moral rights originate from the Convention for the Protection of Literary and Artistic Works (Berne, 9th September 1886; 77 BFSP 22; C 5167) ("the Berne Convention").

[82] CDPA, s 77.

[83] *ibid* s 80.

[84] *ibid* s 84.

[85] *ibid* s 85.

[86] Known as a *"jura in rei"*.

right to make a claim from a third party to pay the outstanding debt in the event of non-payment by the debtor. Cautionary obligations are dealt with later in this chapter.

The general rule which governs the establishment of real rights in security is that in order for such a right to be effective, delivery of the goods (or its equivalent) from the debtor to the creditor must occur before such a right can arise.[87] In the absence of delivery, the lender is bestowed with a mere personal right to the debt and no real right in the property itself.

SECURITY WITHOUT DELIVERY

There are certain exceptions to this general rule regarding delivery of the property, however, which have arisen either under statute or have developed under the common law—the most notable being "hypothecs" and "floating charges". **8–23**

Hypothecs

The common law bestows upon a creditor a right in security, notwithstanding that the debtor's property has not been delivered to him, in a small category of cases. Such rights are known as hypothecs and can be created in any one of two ways: those created by contracts—"conventional" hypothecs; and those which arise by operation of the general law—"legal" hypothecs. **8–24**

Conventional hypothecs

Conventional hypothecs arise by express provision in a contract. In modern times, these are rarely encountered and only occur in relation to bonds of bottomry and bonds of *respondentia* in the context of maritime law. Such bonds are rights in security which have been granted by a ship's master when in an emergency situation funds require to be raised to complete a voyage. A bond of bottomry is a security over the ship itself, whereas the bond in *respondentia* relates to security over the ship's cargo.[88] **8–25**

Legal hypothecs

The bulk of hypothecs, however, arise by implication of the law. Doubtless the one which may strike fear into the student readers of this book is the landlord's hypothec. A landlord has a hypothec for rent over certain moveable property brought into the landlord's premises by the tenant, known as the *"invecta et illata"* (literally "things brought in and carried in"). The hypothec extends to goods purchased by the tenant on hire purchase but not to certain exempted items such as the tenant's money and articles of clothing or goods which belong to third parties.[89] **8–26**

The hypothec is a security in relation to one year's rent only, not prior arrears.[90] If the landlord wishes to realise the security and take possession of the assets he must raise an action of "sequestration for rent" in the sheriff court, which must take place

---

[87] This is expressed by the Roman law maxim, *traditionibus, non nudis pactis, dominia rerum transferuntur*—literally "by delivery, not by mere agreements, are real rights in property transferred". In relation to heritable property, where the actual delivery of property is impossible, the equivalent of delivery is to register the security deed in the Register of Sasines or Land Register—see Chapter 7.
[88] Bell, *Principles*, s 456; *Dymond v Scott* (1877) 5 R 196.
[89] Bell, *Principles*, s 1276. The category of items exempted was extended by s 16 of the Debtors (Scotland) Act 1987—see para 8–54.
[90] *Young v Welsh* (1833) 12 S 233.

within three months of the last date of payment. If a decree in this respect is subsequently granted by the court, the landlord may instruct sheriff officers to enter into the property, take an inventory of the goods and, in due course, sell them. The landlord's hypothec can only be exercised in relation to urban properties or agricultural holdings of no more than two acres in size.[91]

In a similar fashion to the landlord's hypothec, a feudal superior has a hypothec over the assets of a vassal in respect of unpaid feuduties.[92] This right is now rarely enforced.

Solicitor's hypothec

8–27   A solicitor may hold a hypothec in relation to expenses incurred in a court action over costs awarded to the client[93] and also any property recovered as a consequence of the court action.[94]

Maritime hypothecs

8–28   Commonly referred to as "liens",[95] these rights in security are in fact hypothecs as, unlike the case with liens, assets are not in the possession of the holder of the security. Maritime hypothecs bestow rights in security over a ship, for example to seamen in respect of unpaid wages[96] and the ship's master in respect of expenses he properly incurs.[97]

Floating charges[98]

8–29   An important statutory exception to the rule that delivery was necessary to create a valid security was introduced by the Companies (Floating Charges) (Scotland) Act 1961. Floating charges are rights in security which are available only to registered companies and industrial and provident societies.[99] The name "floating charge" derives from the fact that the charge does not attach to any particular property belonging to the company; rather, the charge floats above the assets of the company until a certain event (for example, non-payment of an instalment or the winding up of the company) has the effect that the charge "crystallises", meaning that it attaches to the assets. The major benefit of the floating charge is that the debtor is free to deal in the assets until such a time as the charge crystallises.

SECURITIES REQUIRING DELIVERY

Heritable securities

8–30   Security over heritable property is now effected by the creation of a "standard security" under the provisions of the Conveyancing and Feudal Reform (Scotland) Act

---

[91] Hypothec (Abolition) (Scotland) Act 1880, s 1.
[92] See Chapter 7.
[93] It is a general rule of civil court practice in Scotland that the loser will pay the winning party's costs incurred in participating in the litigation.
[94] By virtue of the Solicitors (Scotland) Act 1980, s 62(1).
[95] See para 8–35.
[96] See the Merchant Shipping Act 1995, s 39.
[97] *ibid* s 40.
[98] The law relating to floating charges is discussed in greater detail in Chapter 11.
[99] The relevant legislation is now the Companies Act 1985, Pt XVIII. The statutory intervention served to bring Scottish law into line with English law, where floating charges were already possible at common law.

1970. The equivalent of delivery in the case of heritage is the registration of the security with either the Register of Sasines or the Land Register. The vast majority of home owners finance the purchase of their home by means of borrowing money from a bank or building society subject to the granting of a standard security[100] (colloquially known as a "mortgage") over their property in favour of the lender.[101]

Security over moveables

A security over moveable property may be created either by an express provision in a **8–31** contract or may arise by implication of the general law.

Security over moveables arising from contract

The simplest form of security, in this sense, is known as "pledge", where corporeal **8–32** moveable property is delivered to the lender as security for a debt. The person who owns the property is known as the "pledger" and the lender who obtains the security is known as the "pledgee". When the debt is paid, the pledgee is bound to return the property to the pledger. If there is no delivery, then the general common law rule applies and no security will be constituted.

A relic of the past, which has recently made a return to city high streets, is the pawnbroker, where those in need of immediate cash "pawn" their goods in return for payment, with the goods being retained until repayment is made. If repayment is not made within the agreed time limit, the goods may then be sold by the pawnbroker. Pawnbroking is in fact a special form of pledge which is extensively regulated under the Consumer Credit Act 1974.

Forms of delivery

Despite the requirement for delivery, it is not always delivery in its true sense that is **8–33** required. Indeed, it may not always be possible or practicable to effect delivery in relation to bulkier items. Delivery may be actual, symbolic or constructive.

Actual delivery relates to the physical delivery of the assets and also occurs where the goods are confined to a particular place and absolute control over that place is transferred to the pledgee. In *West Lothian Oil Co v Mair*,[102] a creditor loaned money to the debtor on the security of a number of barrels belonging to the debtor. The barrels were placed in a yard enclosed by a fence, the key to which was given to the creditor. The court held that a valid security had been created.

The main instance of *symbolic* delivery occurs where goods are shipped and a bill of lading is transferred (either in respect of a sale or pledge). The transfer of the bill of lading is deemed as the equivalent of delivery of the goods.[103] Other attempts at symbolic delivery have not in the main been successful.[104]

Constructive delivery occurs where goods are in storage and delivery is effected by serving the store keeper with a notice directing him to deliver the goods to the pledgee instead of to the owner. *HD Pochin & Company v Robinows & Majoribanks*[105] sets out a

---

[100] The law relating to standard securities is discussed in more detail in Chapter 7.
[101] "Mortgage" is not a term of Scots law.
[102] (1892) 20 R 64.
[103] See *Hayman & Son v McLintock* 1907 SC 936.
[104] See *Paul v Cuthbertson* (1840) 2 D 1286 (symbolic delivery of trees by cutting and removing a few of them); *Stiven v Cowan* (1878) 15 SLR 422 (attempt to effect symbolic delivery of machinery in a mill).
[105] (1869) 7 M 622.

number of criteria for the valid creation of a security in such instances : the goods must be in the hands of a bona fide independent third party, not the debtor or his agent; the holder of the goods must be informed that he holds the goods on behalf of the pledgee; the goods must be ascertained and identifiable; and the debtor must have no enduring right to dispose of the goods.

Security over incorporeal moveable property

8–34 Incorporeal moveable property such as shares and insurance policies are often the subject of security for debts. If a valid security is to be created over, for example, an insurance policy, there needs to be some written assignation of the policy to the lender, which must be followed by intimation of the assignation to the insurance company. The intimation to the insurance company is treated as the equivalent of delivery. The mere transfer of the policy to the lender[106] or mere assignation[107] would not be sufficient to create a valid security.

In relation to securities over company shares, again no valid security right can be constituted by the mere transfer of the share certificate. In order to create an effective security the shares need to be transferred to the creditor and the transfer registered by the company in question.[108] Such a transfer would be made subject to the stipulation that the shares would be transferred back to the debtor when the debt is paid. In light of the expenses involved in the process of registration of shares, it may be that the creditor is happy to take receipt of share certificates and a stock transfer form signed by the debtor. At any time in the future, the creditor can complete the security by sending the transfer form to the company for registration.[109]

Securities over moveables arising from possession—liens

8–35 Lien arises in circumstances where a creditor has possession of goods belonging to his debtor. The creditor has a right to retain these goods until the debt is paid to him.

A lien may be *special* or *general*. A special lien is a right to retain an item until a debt is met on a contract through which the creditor has gained possession of that asset.[110] For example, if a car is placed in a garage for repairs and payment is not made by the car owner in respect of those repairs, then the garage will have a special lien over the car and be able to retain the car until the debt is paid.

A general lien, by contrast, allows the creditor to retain possession of a debtor's item until general debts arising from a contract or course of dealing have been met. The item in question need not be connected with these contracts. Whether or not a general lien exists will depend on the usage of the particular trade concerned. Some established general liens include those of the factor, the banker, the solicitor and the innkeeper.

Factor's lien

8–36 A factor[111] has a general right of lien over all goods, bills, money or documents

---

[106] *Christie v Ruxton* (1862) 24 D 1182.
[107] *Gallemos Ltd (in receivership) v Barratt Falkirk Ltd* 1990 SLT 98.
[108] Bankruptcy (Scotland) Act 1985, s 36(3).
[109] It should be noted that in such a situation, the creditor may be at risk in the sense that in the absence of registration to create a real right, the shares may potentially be arrested by another creditor or transferred to another party. For general information on the transfer of shares in companies, see Chapter 11.
[110] Bell, *Commentaries*, ii, 92.
[111] See Chapter 6.

belonging to his principal which he (the factor) has taken possession of in the course of his employment.[112] The right of lien extends to any advances he has made to the principal, his salary and commission, and any costs and liabilities incurred on behalf of the principal.[113]

Banker's lien

A banker has a general lien over negotiable instruments (including cheques) which **8–37** belong to customers, in so far as they have come into the possession of the bank in the course of banking business, rather than merely being deposited with the bank for safe-keeping.[114]

The lien can be applied in relation to any balance due by the customer.[115]

Solicitor's lien

A solicitor holds a general lien over all of his client's papers which are in his (the **8–38** solicitor's) possession. Such documents would include title deeds, share certificates and contracts. The lien can be applied in respect of any unpaid bills, expenses or advances made in the ordinary course of the solicitor's business (for example, in respect of counsel's fees).[116] The lien would not generally be applicable to advances made to the client himself.[117]

Innkeeper's lien

An innkeeper holds a lien over the luggage of a guest in respect of any unpaid bill.[118] **8–39** The lien may be exercised even though the luggage does not belong to the guest.[119] The innkeeper may not detain the guest, nor can he seek to exercise the lien over clothes the guest is wearing.[120]

Unlike other forms of lien, the innkeeper can gain the right to sell the property in his possession to make good his debt. If luggage has been left at the inn for a six-week period within which the bill has not been paid, the innkeeper has a statutory right to sell the goods and take the debt from the proceeds. Any surplus on the sale must be accounted to the guest.[121]

CAUTIONARY OBLIGATIONS

INTRODUCTION

A cautionary obligation (pronounced "kay-shun-ary") can be defined as "an accessory **8–40** obligation or engagement, as surety for another, that the principal obligant shall pay

---

[112] Bell, *Principles*, s 1445.
[113] *Glendinning* v *Hope* 1911 SC (HL) 73.
[114] *Brandao* v *Barnet* (1846) 12 Cl & F 787.
[115] Bell's *Principles*, s 1445.
[116] Bell's *Principles*, s 1438.
[117] *Christie* v *Ruxton* (1862) 24 D 1182.
[118] Bell's *Principles*, s 1428.
[119] *Bermans and Nathans Ltd* v *Weibye* 1983 SC 67.
[120] *Sunbolf* v *Alford* (1838) 3 M & W 248.
[121] Innkeepers Act 1878, s 1.

the debt or perform the act for which he has engaged, otherwise the cautioner shall pay the debt or fulfil the obligation".[122]

In plain terms, this means that one party guarantees that another will pay a debt due or carry out some act and, in the event that the latter party does not fulfil his obligations, the first party will become liable for those obligations.

Caution is a personal right (*jus in personam*) rather than a real right. This has the result that the creditor has no better right to the cautioner's assets than any other creditor in the instance of the cautioner's insolvency. In this sense, therefore, cautionary obligations are not as useful to creditors as real rights in security. Nonetheless they remain common in a number of commercial situations—for instance, where a bank seeks some form of security from a director where a new company seeks to borrow money,[123] or, similarly, where a bank requires the guarantee of a parent when a student opens a bank account.

Caution may also arise where the creditor is not in fact a party to the contract of caution. In such a situation, the cautioner undertakes to guarantee all of another party's debts to future, unspecified third parties. If a third party seeks compensation from the cautioner in respect of unpaid debts, then he must illustrate that he in fact relied upon the guarantee when entering into the contract with the debtor.[124] As a general point, it should be noted that such guarantees arise in respect of financial debts rather than other forms of obligations of the debtor.

One would rarely stumble upon use of the word "caution" in this context nowadays. Modern vernacular has seen "caution" replaced with the term "guarantee". "Caution" is still referred to, however, where a pursuer raising an action in the civil courts is required to lodge funds into court of sufficient amount to cover both the court's and the defender's expenses. This is known as "lodging caution".

FORM OF GUARANTEE

8–41   As with many contractual documents, there is nothing to prohibit parties from entering into the agreement orally. Problems with proof may well ensue, however, and in the interests of good commercial practice it is preferable that the agreement be in writing.[125] Indeed, if the guarantee is gratuitous (that is where no payment is made in respect of the guarantee) and not given in the course of business, the agreement must be in written form.[126]

As a general rule, the guarantee cannot outweigh the principal debt.[127] It is common practice, however, to word guarantees in such a fashion as to encompass interest on the debt and expenses associated with the debt collection.[128] It is generally prudent

---

[122] Bell's *Principles*, s 245.
[123] Given the fact that a company exhibits a separate legal persona, directors are not liable for company debts beyond their investment in the company—see Chapter 11.
[124] *Fortune v Young* 1918 SC 1.
[125] If not in writing the agreement may be evidenced by parole evidence or inferred by the actings of the parties.
[126] Requirements of Writing (Scotland) Act 1995, s 1(2)(a)(ii).
[127] See, *eg, Jackson v McIver* (1875) 2 R 882 where a debt of £300 was secured by a cautionary obligation which took the form of a blank promissory note and the debtor's agent later filled in the amount as £2,000.
[128] *Moschi v Lep Air Services* [1973] AC 331.

that cautioners ensure that their guarantee is only effective in respect of debts arising from particular contracts which the debtor may enter into.

If there are a number of cautioners providing guarantees in respect of the debtor's contracts, then one cautioner must take care to avoid "joint and several liability" (that is where each cautioner becomes liable for the whole debt). If a cautioner is held liable for more than his share, he will be entitled to pro rata relief from the co-cautioners.[129]

A cautionary obligation is an ancillary contract. This means that the guarantee does not stand on its own feet; it is dependent on the principal debt. When the debt is extinguished, in a like fashion so is the cautionary obligation. Similarly, if a debt is rendered unenforceable or is an illegal agreement, then the guarantee will also be unenforceable.[130]

RIGHT OF RELIEF AGAINST THE DEBTOR

When payment of the debt is made by the cautioner, he is entitled to seek relief from   **8–42**
the original debtor.[131] This in itself may be of little value as, if the debtor was unable to pay the debt to the creditor, there may be little scope for the debt being paid to the cautioner. In addition, where a debtor is sequestrated (or is liquidated, if the debtor is a registered company) then no right of relief arises. The right of relief prescribes after a five-year period.[132]

It should be noted, however, that on payment of the debt the cautioner has a right to have the debt assigned to him, which importantly includes the right to have any securities held in respect of that debt assigned to him.[133] This may serve to grant the cautioner a prior right of recovery of debt over the debtor's other creditors.

MISREPRESENTATION AND CONCEALMENT

Cautionary agreements are not contracts *uberrimae fidei* (that is, of the utmost good   **8–43**
faith). The consequence of this is that the parties are "at arm's length" and hence are not subject to a general duty to disclose facts which are relevant to the contract.[134] The debtor is under an obligation, however, not to misrepresent facts which the cautioner has relied upon in entering into the contract. It does not follow from this, however, that the cautioner's liability in respect of the guarantees given to creditors is extinguished.[135] If such misrepresentation has taken place, the cautioner has a right to claim damages in respect of losses incurred. This right may be of little value, however, against a debtor unable to pay his debts.

An exception to this rule may be possible on the limited grounds that given the proximity of the relationship between the debtor and the cautioner, the debtor has exerted undue influence on the cautioner to compel him to provide a guarantee.[136] In

---

[129] *Marshall v Pennycook* 1908 SC 276.
[130] *Garrad v James* [1925] 1 Ch 616.
[131] *Smithy's Place Ltd v Blackadder and McMonagle* 1991 SLT 790.
[132] *ibid.*
[133] *Scott v Young* 1909 1 SLT 47 (OH).
[134] Compare, for example, the duty of disclosure inherent in insurance contracts—see para 8–115.
[135] *Young v Clydesdale Bank Ltd* (1889) 17 R 231.
[136] See *Smith v Bank of Scotland* 1997 GWD 21–1004 (HL). See also Gretton, *Sexually Transmitted Debt* 1997 SLT (News) 195.

such a case, for example, if a spouse acts as a guarantor for the other spouse's debts, it would seem prudent for the creditor (for example, a bank) to ensure that independent advice has been made available to the cautioner.

The actions of the creditor himself may, however, serve to render the cautionary obligation void. While it is a well established rule of the common law that a creditor is under no general obligation to disclose information regarding the debts of the principal debtor to the cautioner,[137] any actual misrepresentation to the cautioner concerning the status of the debtor will allow the cautioner to resile the contract. This rule applies even if the misrepresentation was innocent.[138]

DISCHARGE OF THE GUARANTEE

8–44 As has been noted above, the guarantee is discharged at the time the principal debt is paid. Additionally, if the creditor discharges the debtor for liability in respect of the debt without the cautioner's consent then the cautioner will similarly be discharged of the debt.[139]

When the debt is discharged by the incidence of the debtor's bankruptcy, however, the cautioner will remain liable.[140] The death of the debtor will serve to prevent any further liability under the guarantee, although the cautioner will remain liable in respect of debts which have incurred up to the time of death and are covered by the guarantee.[141] The death of the cautioner has the effect that liability transfers to his estate.

If there are a number of cautioners in respect of one debtor, and one of the cautioners is discharged by the creditor without the consent of other cautioners who remain undischarged, the law provides that the other cautioners are automatically discharged, unless expressly the contrary is provided for in the cautionary agreement.[142]

The creditor is bound to do nothing which may add to the liability of the cautioner.[143] An example of such might be where the debtor is granted more time to pay.[144] Commercial practice would tend to ensure the presence of a clause in the guarantee contract allowing the creditor to grant the debtor additional time to pay.

The cautioner's liability will prescribe after a five-year period after the date on which the debtor defaulted on a payment.[145]

---

[137] See the recent case of *Smith v Bank of Scotland* 1996 SLT 392.
[138] *Royal Bank of Scotland v Ranken* (1884) 6 D 1418.
[139] Bell's *Principles*, s 260.
[140] Bankruptcy (Scotland) Act 1985, s 60.
[141] *Woodfield Finance Trust (Glasgow) Ltd v Morgan* 1958 SLT (Sh Ct) 14.
[142] Mercantile Law Amendment (Scotland) Act 1856, s 9.
[143] *Lord Advocate v Maritime Fruit Carriers Co Ltd* 1983 SLT 357 (OH).
[144] Bell's *Principles*, s 262.
[145] Prescription and Limitation (Scotland) Act 1973, s 6 and Sched 1, para 1(g).

DILIGENCE

INTRODUCTION

While a primary function of the civil courts is to grant remedies for the non-payment   **8–45**
of debts, such decrees are of scant use to a creditor if he is unable to enforce them. To
assist in the enforcement of court decrees and the payments of debts due to creditors,
various forms of what is termed as "diligence" may be employed. In basic terms,
diligence involves the requisitioning of assets of a debtor and appropriating them in
some way to make good his debt.

Of course, in many cases a creditor does not need to resort to diligence; the debtor
may make immediate payment of the debt following the court decree. In other cases
debtors may be more unable rather than unwilling to make immediate payment of
their debt. In order to avoid the unnecessary deployment of diligence in such
instances, Part 1 of the Debtors (Scotland) Act 1987 ("DSA")[146] introduced two new
court orders: the "time to pay direction" and the "time to pay order".

A time to pay direction may be issued by the court after decree has been granted
against a debtor for payment. Such a direction may be issued where the debtor seeks
sanction from the court that either the sum be payable in instalments or the full debt
be payable at some future specified date. Only in the event that the debtor fails to
comply with the order will the creditor be entitled to resort to diligence.

A time to pay order, by contrast, can only be sought after diligence has already been
commenced against the debtor. If such an order is granted (along the same lines as a
time to pay direction) the creditor will be required to suspend diligence proceedings
until such a time as the debtor fails to act in accordance with the order.

Many different species of diligence can be deployed by unpaid creditors. The most
widely used processes are arrestment, diligence against earnings, poinding and
inhibition. Others, less widely employed today, include adjudication, poinding of the
ground, civil imprisonment and the landlord's hypothec.

As a general point, diligence procedures are carried out by officers of the court
rather than by the creditor himself. Such officers are known as "Messengers at Arms"
in respect of decrees of the Court of Session and "sheriff officers" in respect of sheriff
court decrees. Given that the majority of debts are sought through the sheriff court,
further references to these debt enforcement officials will be made to sheriff officers,
although the reader should note that for all intents and purposes the powers of the
sheriff officer and his Court of Session equivalent are identical.

ARRESTMENT

Arrestment is a process by which the creditor "attaches" to assets which belong to the   **8–46**
debtor but which are in the hands of a third party.[147] The effect of the arrestment is to
effectively freeze the assets, in the sense that neither the third party nor the debtor is
entitled to dispose of them. If the third party (known as the "arrestee") disposes of the

---

[146] Based largely on the *Report on Diligence and Debtor Protection* (Scot Law Com No 95) (November 1995).
[147] Stewart, *Diligence* (1898) p 105.

goods in contravention of the arrestment, he will find himself in contempt of court and subject to criminal sanction.[148]

The effect of the arrestment is that the assets must remain in the hands of the arrestee until the debtor signs a mandate empowering the arrestee to hand the assets over to the creditor, or the creditor raises an action of "furthcoming", which allows the goods either to pass to the creditor or to be sold without the debtor's consent.[149]

Arrestment on the dependence

8–47   Arrestment on the dependence (or "in security") contrasts with other forms of diligence in that it is applied to the assets of a debtor prior to a court decree being granted against him. It is generally only available in respect of a current debt as opposed to future debts, although it may be applied in respect of the latter where the debtor is deemed to be on the verge of insolvency ("*vergens ad inopiam*") or may be considering absconding ("*in meditatione fugae*").[150] Arrestment on the dependence is not an automatic remedy and the right must be granted by the appropriate court in which the debt is to be sought. As a final brake on the use of this type of diligence, certain assets—for example, earnings and pensions—cannot be arrested on the dependence.[151]

Arrestment in execution

8–48   Arrestment may also be sought after decree has been granted by the court—the right, known as "arrestment in execution", arises automatically.[152] A similar right of arrestment may arise where a contract, lease or bond states that the document in question is to be registered in the Books of Council and Session or sheriff court books for preservation and execution.[153] Similarly, arrestment may follow a bill of exchange[154] executed in the presence of a notary public[155] or where a summary warrant for the recovery of taxes has been obtained from a sheriff.[156]

Actions of furthcoming

8–49   Although arrestment of assets may well inconvenience the debtor (and in some cases, the arrestee), the mere freezing of assets will by itself provide cold comfort to a creditor who remains to be paid. Following the arrestment, if the debtor fails to instruct the arrestee to hand over the assets to the creditor in respect of the debt due, then the creditor may apply to the court for an action of furthcoming. In such an action the creditor specifies to the court the action he wishes to be taken in respect of the assets. If the assets are cash, he will probably ask that his debt plus any interest and associated costs be paid directly to him from these funds; if the assets are in some form other than cash, the creditor will normally request that the goods be sold and monies

---

[148] Stair, III, i, 25–26.
[149] This is discussed in more detail at para 8–49. See *Lord Advocate* v *Royal Bank of Scotland* 1977 SC 155.
[150] See *Gillanders* v *Gillanders* 1966 SC 54; *Brash* v *Brash* 1966 SC 56.
[151] Law Reform (Miscellaneous Provisions) (Scotland) Act 1966, s 1.
[152] Subject to time to pay directions.
[153] By virtue of the Writs Execution (Scotland) Act 1887. For example, the decision ("award") of an arbiter in arbitration proceedings is often rendered legally binding by being lodged in court books in this fashion.
[154] See para 8–128 for a discussion of bills of exchanges.
[155] Most solicitors also qualify as notary publics, which allows them to undertake such functions as receiving statements under oath and the drawing up of wills for blind persons.
[156] DSA, s 87.

due to him be met from the proceeds.[157] Sales are generally carried out by warrant sale.[158]

An arrestment will generally take precedence over subsequent arrestments of the same assets.[159] If two arrestments are served on the same day they will rank *pari pasu* (equally). If there are competing claims in respect of the same assets, however, then an action of "multiplepoinding" may be sought by a subsequent creditor to ensure that he receives at least a measure of payment from what may be a limited pot of debtor's funds or assets.

Subjects arrestable

While it is common for debtor's funds in a bank or building society account to be the subject of the arrestment order, many other assets are arrestable, such as any corporeal moveable property in the hands of an independent third party (for example, a car for repair at a garage),[160] and incorporeal moveables such as company shares,[161] insurance policies,[162] and interests in a trust estate.[163] The debtor's earnings were formally arrestable but are now subject to separate diligence procedures.[164]

8–50

Certain items are not arrestable—for example, items which are alimentary in nature (to feed and clothe children)[165]—except in situations where the creditor has in fact been supplying such items to the debtor. Certain other items relating to the debtor's trade or profession and those deemed necessary for the well-being of the debtor and his family are also exempt.[166]

Finally, it should be noted that there are special rules relating to the arrestment of ships, provided by section 47 of the Administration of Justice Act 1956. These rules have placed certain limits on the hitherto general common law right to arrest ships in a similar manner to other moveable property.

Arrestments will "prescribe" (be nullified) after a three-year period has passed, except that where arrestment has been made in relation to a future or contingent debt, the three-year period will run from the date the debt becomes due.[167] If goods can be proven to belong to the arrestee, then the arrestment will be "loosed" or recalled by the court, which essentially extinguishes the diligence.[168] An arrestment may also be loosed if it can be proved that the goods are not arrestable[169] or the arrestment is excessive or oppressive in some way.[170]

---

[157] Summary Cause Rules, r 64.
[158] Discussed below in relation to poinding at para 8–54.
[159] *Hertz v Itzig* (1865) 3 M 813. Arrestments executed within 60 days of the apparent insolvency of a debtor or four months thereafter are ranked *pari pasu* (equally): Bankruptcy (Scotland) Act 1985, Sched 7, para 24. See Chapter 9.
[160] *Inglis v Robertson & Baxter* (1898) 25 R (HL) 70.
[161] *American Mortgage Co v Sidway* 1908 SC 500.
[162] *Bankhardt's Trs v Scottish Amicable* (1871) 9 M 443.
[163] *Learmont v Shearer* (1866) 4 M 540.
[164] See para 8–51.
[165] *Cuthbert v Cuthberts' Trs* 1908 SC 967.
[166] Set out in the DSA, s 16. See also para 8–54.
[167] Debtors (Scotland) Act 1838, s 22 (as amended).
[168] *Laing v Barclay, Curle & Co* 1908 SC (HL) 1.
[169] *Lord Ruthven v Drummond* 1908 SC 1154.
[170] *Magistrates of Dundee v Taylor* (1863) 1 M 701; *Svesnka Petroleum AB v HOR Ltd* 1986 SLT 513.

DILIGENCE AGAINST EARNINGS

8–51   Given the difficulties of tracking down assets of debtors, one of the most useful forms of arrestment has been to freeze the debtor's wages at source. Concerns relating to the high level of expenses involved in repeated arrestments of earnings, however, paved the way for a new, more accessible form of diligence—diligence against earnings—which was introduced by the Debtors (Scotland) Act 1987.

There are in fact three distinct types of diligence under this broad heading, which will be applicable in different circumstances: an earnings arrestment, appropriate in respect of general debts and court fines; a maintenance arrestment, which is applicable in respect of payments for the maintenance of children; and a conjoined arrestment order relating to two or more debts owed to different creditors against the same earnings.[171]

The term "earnings" is widely defined so as to include the normal wages or salary of the debtor as well as any fees, bonuses, commissions, pensions and annuities for previous services, statutory sick pay and compensation for loss of earnings.[172]

The arrestment of earnings may follow a court decree or on a summary warrant for recovery of taxes.[173] The right does not arise automatically; rather the debtor must first be served with a charge to pay the debt within 14 days.[174] If the debt is not paid within the specified time, a schedule of arrestment is served on the employer by sheriff officers. This stipulates that the employer must pay a statutorily prescribed proportion of the debtor's earnings to the creditor.[175] The arrestment will continue until either the debt is paid, the debtor leaves the employment of the employer, the arrestment is recalled, or the debtor is sequestrated.[176]

In addition to being a millstone around the neck of the debtor, the arrestment may well cause inconvenience to the employer. Nonetheless, the employer will be rendered liable to the creditor (for the amount he should have deducted) if he fails to act in accordance with the arrestment order. However, for his troubles, the employer is entitled to be compensated—the princely sum of 50p is payable from the debtor's funds to the employer per payment of the arrested amount.[177]

POINDING

Introduction

8–52   This form of diligence is aimed at assets which are in the possession of the debtor himself. In common with arrestment on execution, poinding (pronounced "pinding") normally follows a court decree, although in a like fashion it may arise in other ways—for example, following from a deed registered in the Books of Council and Session or the sheriff court.[178] Unlike arrestment, however, poinding can never be executed on the dependence.

---

[171] DSA, s 46 (as amended).
[172] *ibid* s 73(2).
[173] *ibid* s 87.
[174] *ibid* s 90; 28 days if the debtor resides outwith the UK (or his whereabouts are unknown).
[175] The statutory amounts are set out in the DSA, s 58(1).
[176] *ibid* s 72.
[177] *ibid* s 71.
[178] *ibid* s 87.

Poinding process

The poinding process is commenced by a charge for payment being served by sheriff **8–53** officers at the debtor's home or place of business, either in person or by recorded delivery.[179] In the event that the debtor's address is unknown, or if the debtor is abroad, recorded delivery must be attempted and an advert placed in an appropriate newspaper in the last known area of residence.

After the charge is served on the debtor, he has 14 days within which to pay the debt.[180] The 14-day period is known as the "*induciae*". If payment is not made within the period of the *induciae*, the sheriff officers may return with a warrant to poind goods belonging to the debtor and again request payment. If payment is not duly made, then the sheriff officers will proceed with poinding the goods in the possession of the debtor by the drawing up of a schedule of poindable assets and their estimated values.[181] The goods are not taken away at this point and are left in the hands of the debtor. The debtor is bound, however, not to dispose of the goods at this stage.[182]

Warrant sales

A further 14-day period follows, within which any of the goods may be redeemed by **8–54** the debtor by paying the value as set by the sheriff officers.[183] An application by the creditor can then be made to the court that a warrant sale be held in respect of the goods. Such sales are generally held by public auction at an auction house specified by the court. In rare cases, the sale may be held in the debtor's or another's dwelling house if consent by the debtor or the occupier (if he is not the debtor) has been given.[184]

In situations where the proceeds of the sale have not resulted in sufficient funds for the debt to be paid to the creditor, any unsold items become the property of the creditor.[185] Any proceeds remaining from the sale after the debt has been paid and associated expenses of the sale have been met, will be returned to the debtor.[186]

Generally speaking, any corporeal property which is of any financial value is capable of being poinded. As is the case with arrestment, certain items cannot be poinded. A detailed list is set out in section 16 of the Debtors (Scotland) Act 1987, including clothing, tools of trade, medical equipment, toys and education equipment, food and basic furniture.

Law reform

Poinding has long been attacked by opponents who claim that it is a draconian, **8–55** outdated measure which has no place in modern society. This probably stems from the fact that it seems far more unpalatable to witness goods being physically removed from a home, than to accept the less visible process of arrestment. Whatever the merits of this argument, it can hardly be contended that poinding has been a particularly effective method by which creditors have been able to recover their debts. The twin

---

[179] Execution of Diligence (Scotland) Act 1926.
[180] If the debtor is abroad or his address is unknown, he has 28 days: DSA, s 30(3).
[181] DSA, s 20(5).
[182] *ibid* s 29.
[183] *ibid* s 21(4).
[184] *ibid* ss 30–32.
[185] If the sale takes place in the home of the debtor, the creditor is bound to uplift the goods, otherwise ownership will return to the debtor.
[186] DSA, s 38.

ingredients of public indignation and strong community spirit have combined to make public protests at warrant sales common with the result that sheriff officers' tasks in this respect have been difficult and at times impossible to carry out. Furthermore, debtors may often claim that goods in their possession belong to third parties and thus cannot be poinded. In any case, the 14-day *induciae* period often affords debtors a window of opportunity within which to remove assets from their homes, which thus largely defeats the purpose of the poinding order.

A recent Scottish Law Commission consultation paper has tackled many of these issues.[187] Although falling short of recommending the abolition of poinding, the paper sets out a number of reforms relating to issues such as reviewing and clarifying those assets which are poindable and those which are exempt; avoidance of warrant sales where it is unlikely that the sale will result in sufficient funds to pay any significant part of the debt; and measures to make time to pay directions and orders more accessible to debtors.[188]

INHIBITIONS

8–56 Diligence is not merely applicable over the debtor's moveable property—inhibition is a highly effective type of diligence that can be employed in respect of heritable property. Broadly speaking, inhibition prohibits the sale by the debtor of heritable property, or the use of that property in a manner which contravenes the purpose of the inhibition (for example, to grant a security over the property).

A third party who attempts to purchase heritable property which is subject to an existing inhibition order will find their contract voidable at the instance of the creditor.[189] In a similar fashion to arrestment and poinding, an inhibition may be obtained following a court decree, registered bond or protested bill of exchange. In common with arrestment, an inhibition may be granted on the dependence, prior to a court action being raised in respect of the debt. Again, an inhibition will normally only be granted in respect of a future debt when the debtor is deemed to be *vergens ad inopiam* (on the verge of insolvency) or *in meditatione fugae* (considering absconding).[190]

The inhibition must be served on the debtor and notice of the inhibition registered in the Register of Inhibitions and Adjudications, which serves to protect would-be purchasers of the property. Without registration, the inhibition is not valid.[191]

Unlike arrestment and poinding, inhibition is purely a negative remedy and cannot be followed by some other action which seeks to effect the sale of the property to make good the debt or transfer the property to the creditor. Inhibition proceedings merely serve to "tie-up" the property.

If the debt to which the inhibition relates has been paid, the creditor is bound, at the expense of the debtor, to record a discharge of the inhibition in the Register, which serves as notice to third parties that the inhibition is no longer in effect. Similarly, if the

---

[187] *Discussion Paper on Poinding and Sale: Effective Enforcement and Debtor Protection* (Scot Law Com No 110) (November 1999).
[188] At the time of writing, a Private Member's bill is travelling through the Scottish Parliamentary process which seeks to abolish poinding and warrant sales. The bill is not supported by the Scottish Executive, although they have indicated plans to bring in their own provisions to this effect in the near future.
[189] *Lennox v Robertson* (1790) Hume 243. See Chapter 4 for a discussion of voidable contracts.
[190] *Wilson v Wilson* 1981 SLT 101.
[191] Titles to Land Consolidation (Scotland) Act 1868, ss 44 and 155.

inhibition has been granted on the dependence and the court subsequently finds that the defender is not in fact liable for the debt, then the court will grant an order that the inhibition be recalled by the Keeper of the Register.[192] If the inhibition is deemed to be excessive or oppressive, then the debtor may seek recall of the inhibition by the court.[193] In any event, an inhibition will prescribe after a five-year period from the date of registration.[194]

OTHER FORMS OF DILIGENCE

The following outlined forms of diligence, although still legally valid, are in the main rarely encountered in practice.   **8–57**

Adjudication

Adjudication is a form of diligence over heritable property which is similar in nature to the inhibition. Provided for by the Adjudications Act 1672, adjudications can only be granted in the Court of Session by the raising of a summons of adjudication.[195] Such a summons is registered in the Register of Inhibitions and Adjudications, which has the effect of making the relevant property "litigious"—this means that the debtor is not free to transfer the property and, significantly, any other party who purchases the property becomes liable for the debt. This makes the sale of such property an unlikely prospect.   **8–58**

Once a decree of adjudication has been obtained, this has the effect of transferring the property to the creditor, who may assume title by registration of the decree in the Register of Sasines or the Land Register.[196] What follows is a 10-year period—known as "the legal"—within which the debtor is entitled to pay the debt and have the property transferred back to him. At the expiry of the legal, if the debt has not been paid, the creditor can raise a court action granting himself irredeemable title to the property.

Adjudication can on occasion be granted in respect of future debts, but only where the debtor is deemed to be on the verge of insolvency or if he has been the subject of adjudication proceedings in the past.

Poinding of the ground

This rarely employed form of diligence in fact attaches to a debtor's moveable property on land rather than the "ground" itself. It is available to those parties who have some sort of property right over heritable property—for example, a superior claiming feuduty,[197] or someone with a standard security (in colloquial terms a "mortgage") over heritable property.[198] In basic terms, this form of diligence attaches to moveable property belonging to the owner or tenant of the property much in the same way as general poinding does.   **8–59**

---

[192] *Barbour's Trs* v *Davidson* (1878) 15 SLR 438.
[193] *Mackintosh* v *Miller* (1864) 2 M 452.
[194] Conveyancing (Scotland) Act 1924, s 44(3)(a).
[195] Sheriff Courts (Scotland) Act 1907, s 5(4).
[196] For a discussion of these registers, see Chapter 7.
[197] See Chapter 7.
[198] See Chapter 7.

Maills and duties

8-60   In modern terms, "maills (money) and duties" relates to rent payable by a tenant to a landlord. It was previously commonplace that tenants provided services to landlords in addition to rent—hence the reference to "duties". This form of diligence allows a creditor with a security over heritable property to attach to the rent payable by tenants in respect of the property to the landlord, to whom the rent would otherwise be payable.[199] The rarity of this form of diligence is to a great extent derived from the fact that the general terms of standard securities[200] tend to bestow such powers in any case.

Civil imprisonment

8-61   Civil imprisonment is in fact a species of diligence in the sense that the diligence attaches to the *person* rather than the property of the debtor. Imprisonment for the failure to pay one's debts is not common in modern times. Indeed the practice (save some notable exceptions) was largely abolished by the Debtors (Scotland) Act 1880. Civil imprisonment does remain possible where the non-paying debtor is held in contempt of court,[201] or wilfully refuses to pay debts relating to aliment (maintenance of one's spouse and children) when he in fact has the funds to make such payments.[202]

SALE OF GOODS

8-62   The law relating to contracts for the sale of goods—unlike that relating to contract in general—is largely underpinned by statute. The first legislation which sought to govern this area of law was the Sale of Goods Act 1893. The 1893 Act was subsequently amended in 1973 by the Supply of Goods (Implied Terms) Act ("SOGITA") and in 1979 the Sale of Goods Act ("SOGA") served to consolidate much of the existing law in relation to sale of goods into one piece of legislation.[203] This remains the dominant piece of legislation and provides the main legal backdrop to the sale of goods. The Act does not cover all legal aspects relating to the sale of goods, however. Indeed, the 1979 Act stipulates that the common law will apply in so far as it is consistent with the legislation.[204] The law has remained fluid in this area and has subsequently been amended by the provisions of the Sale and Supply of Goods Act 1994 ("SSGA") and the Sale of Goods (Amendment) Act 1995.

THE NEED FOR LEGISLATION

8-63   The importance of the law which underpins the sale of goods cannot be overestimated. The sale of goods is by far and away the most common commercial transaction and

---

[199] Governed by the Heritable Securities (Scotland) Act 1894.
[200] See Chapter 7.
[201] Debtors (Scotland) Act 1880, s 4.
[202] Civil Imprisonment (Scotland) Act 1882, s 4.
[203] All references in the section are to this Act unless stated otherwise.
[204] A number of other Acts provide input to this area of law, including the Consumer Credit Act 1974, the Unfair Contract Terms Act 1977 and the Agriculture Act 1970.

encompasses a multiplicity of different situations, from the simple buying of a pint of milk in a newsagent, to purchasing a car, to huge commercial transactions for the supply of raw materials.

Although the legislation has been amended to varying degrees throughout the years, its primary function—to provide protection for the buyers of goods—has remained the same. At the heart of the English common law relating to the sale of goods is the old Roman law maxim of *caveat emptor*—"let the buyer beware". Operation of this rule afforded unsuspecting buyers with little protection in that the onus was placed firmly upon their shoulders to root out any defects or problems with a product or good before entering into the contract of sale. In the absence of any misrepresentation on the part of the seller, the buyer would be afforded no remedy under the common law if the good proved to be defective. It is interesting that this has never been the position under Scots common law, which did provide certain protection for unsuspecting buyers: a contract for the sale of goods in Scotland is a contract *bona fide* (of good faith) at common law, which had the effect of obliging sellers to ensure their products were price worthy.

Much of the law relating to the sale of goods has now been standardised throughout the UK and the overall effect of the Act has been to import many principles of English common law into Scots law.

WHAT IS A SALE OF GOODS?

The Sale of Goods Act 1979 and its amending legislation applies primarily to sales of goods. Obviously, one of the most fundamental questions is to determine when such a contract exists. By definition there must be a contract of sale and that sale must relate to "goods" before the legislation will be applicable.

8–64

What is a sale?

A sale is defined in the 1979 Act[205] as "a contract in which the seller transfers or agrees to transfer the property in goods to the buyer for a money consideration, called the price".

8–65

A contract of sale may be "absolute" or "conditional".[206] When the seller is in the position to transfer the goods immediately (that is he is willing and able to effect transfer) there is a sale. If some sort of condition must be fulfilled or some act must be carried out before the sale can take place, then there will merely be an agreement to sell.[207] An agreement to sell must be distinguished from a sale, as the legal rights bestowed upon the buyer will be different in each situation. In a sale, property in the goods passes to the buyer, who thus acquires a real right over those goods. In an agreement to sell, the buyer merely holds a personal right against the seller in relation to the contract. The transfer of ownership is discussed in detail below.[208]

Given that the consideration central to an exchange or barter is other than in monetary terms, such a contract is not a sale and accordingly is outwith the scope of the SOGA. A barter was formerly governed by the general law of contract.[209] Section 6

---

[205] s 2.
[206] s 2(3).
[207] s 2(5).
[208] At para 8–79.
[209] *Urquhart* v *Wylie* 1953 SLT (Sh Ct) 87; *Widenmeyer* v *Burn Stewart & Co Ltd* 1967 SLT 129.

of the SSGA has introduced new implied terms into these contracts in a similar fashion to those applicable to sale of goods set out in the SOGA. It seems likely, however, that part-exchanges of goods, in return for cash, do amount to sales of goods.[210] This is important in the sense that in many commercial sales situations (for example, car purchasing), part-exchange is a common method by which payment is made.

It is also necessary to distinguish a sale from a contract for the supply of services, although admittedly there may be a fine line between the two. The question to be asked is this: in reality, what is the buyer actually paying for—a particular good or the craftsman's skill? It is, of course, common for both elements to be present. For example, if a new kitchen is purchased, the buyer is likely to be paying for both the appliances and units and also for the craftsman's skill in fitting the kitchen. Prior to the SSGA, one had to look to whichever element was stronger. If the service element was stronger, then the common law would apply; if the goods element was stronger, the SOGA applied. Under the SSGA, where the contract exhibits elements of both sale of goods and supply of services, the former will be subject to the relevant statutory provisions and the service element subject to the common law.

Other contracts which resemble sale, such as hire purchase[211] or buying goods with trading stamps, are also underpinned by a number of similar implied terms by virtue of the relevant statutes.[212]

What are goods?

8–66   Section 61(1) of the 1979 Act refers to goods as "all corporeal moveables except money; and in particular "goods" includes emblements, industrial growing crops, and things attached to or forming part of the land which are agreed to be severed before sale or under a contract of sale".[213] Notable absentees from the statutory provisions are contracts for the sale of heritable property, and also incorporeal (that is intangible) property such as shares, intellectual property rights and rights under insurance policies.[214]

How is the price determined?

8–67   Generally speaking, the price of the goods will be specified in the contract. If, for any reason, the price is not so fixed, the buyer will be bound to pay a reasonable price for the goods. What will amount to a reasonable price will normally be the market price, but this may vary according to the particular circumstances of the case. In *Stuart* v *Kennedy*,[215] some confusion between the seller and buyer existed over how the price of the goods was to be set. The court ruled that a reasonable price should be the market price.[216] In *Glynwed Distribution Ltd* v *S Koronka & Co*[217] however, G delivered "hot-rolled steel" to K. K thought that the steel they had taken delivery of was "British

---

[210] *Sneddon* v *Durrant* 1982 SLT (Sh Ct) 39.

[211] Discussed below at para 8–110.

[212] Supply of Goods (Implied Terms) Act 1973 and the Trading Stamps Act 1964.

[213] For property definitions, see Chapter 7.

[214] Although money is generally exempt from the statutory provisions it may be considered to be a good if it is not treated as currency: see *Moss* v *Hancock* [1899] 2 QB 11, where a gold coin was held to be a good.

[215] (1885) 13 R 221.

[216] See also *Wilson* v *Marquis of Breadalbane* (1859) 13 R 221.

[217] 1977 SLT 65.

Steel" priced at £103.50 per tonne; whereas G thought that they had delivered "foreign steel" at £149.00 per tonne. The court ruled that a reasonable price need not be a market price and fixed a price of £135.00 per tonne, which was "fair and just to both parties" in the circumstances.[218]

CAPACITY

Section 3 of the SOGA stipulates that capacity to buy and sell goods is regulated by the general law relating to capacity to contract. These general rules are set out elsewhere.[219]   **8–68**

FORMALITIES

The SOGA does not stipulate any formalities to be observed in relation to the form the contract of sale must take. The contract can be in writing, be made verbally or by a combination of these.[220] In common with other contracts, the terms of the contract may also be implied by the course of dealing between the parties or from an established custom of trade.   **8–69**

TIME

Section 10 of the SOGA states that unless the contrary is provided for, time of payment shall not be of the essence of the contract. The result of this is that, generally speaking, failure to make a timeous payment will not render the seller with the right to rescind the contract.   **8–70**

IMPLIED TERMS

The following are default terms which are implied in contracts of sale. Each of the implied terms is subject to a strict liability, which means that it is no defence for a seller to argue that all due diligence had been exercised to avoid contravention of the term.   **8–71**

Title

Under section 12(1), the seller must have the right to sell the goods. The seller must therefore either own the goods or have authority from the owner to sell the goods. Any attempt by the seller to contract out of this implied term is rendered void.[221] This rule is of the utmost importance in the sense that where a party sells goods to which he has no good title, the buyer in a like fashion does not gain good title.[222] This is a reflection of the Latin rule *nemo dat quod non habet* ("no one gives what he does not have").[223]   **8–72**

Section 12(2) further provides that "(a) the goods are free, and will remain free until the time when the property is to pass, from any charge or encumbrance not disclosed

---

[218] See also *MacDonald* v *Clark* 1927 SN 6.
[219] See Chapter 4.
[220] SOGA, s 61(1)
[221] Unfair Contract Terms Act 1977, s 20(1).
[222] SOGA, s 21(1).
[223] Under SOGA, s 12(2). There are exceptions to this rule, however, discussed at para 8–83.

or known to the buyer before the contract is made". This relates to the situation where a third party has some sort of right over the seller's goods—for example, a right of lien over the goods by an unpaid creditor.[224] Additionally, "(b) the buyer will enjoy quiet possession of the goods except so far as it may be disturbed by the owner or other person entitled to the benefit of any charge or encumbrance so disclosed or known". In *Niblett Ltd* v *Confectioners Materials Co*[225] the buyers of a quantity of tins found that labels on the tins were in breach of copyright.[226] The labels required to be replaced and the buyers successfully brought an action on the grounds that this amounted to an invasion of their right to "quiet possession" of the goods.[227]

Subsections (3) to (5) govern situations where the seller only intends to sell what limited title he has in the goods to the buyer. In such a case, it is an implied term of the contract that the seller informs the buyer of all charges and encumbrances known to him. It is further implied that the buyer's quiet possession shall not be disturbed, except to the extent of any charges or encumbrances made known to the buyer when the contract was formed.

Description

8–73   In a sale of goods, there is an implied term that the goods will comply with their description. If the sale is one by sample (that is where a sample is forwarded for inspection prior to the sale being made) then the goods must comply with both the sample and the description.[228] It is clear that where a buyer does not see goods prior to purchase and relies upon a description, this will amount to a sale by description. The 1973 Act made provision, however, that even where goods on display are self-selected by a buyer, this may nonetheless amount to a sale by description. For example, if a buyer self-selects packaged goods, the contents of which can only be ascertained after opening the packet, he relies upon the description on the packet. Further, in *Grant* v *Australian Knitting Mills Ltd*,[229] G bought a pair of woollen under-pants across the shop counter. The sale of the pants was held to be a sale by description because, although the goods were sold as a specific item, they were also sold by reference to a description.

Over the years there has been a great deal of judicial discussion in relation to what the term "description" denotes. In particular, does description merely relate to the identity of the goods or should the term be construed in a wider sense to encompass particular characteristics of those goods? This is a fluid area of the law and over time case law has moved from a more liberal interpretation of description to a more restrictive viewpoint. Hence, where the complaint actually relates to the qualitative characteristics of the goods, reliance cannot be placed upon section 13.

In *Ashington Piggeries Ltd* v *Christopher Hill Ltd*,[230] H sold A mink food. The food, however, was found to be contaminated with a substance which was highly toxic to mink. The buyers, *inter alia*, claimed for damages for the death and injury of the mink

---

[224] See para 8–35.
[225] [1921] 3 KB 387.
[226] See plara 8–16.
[227] See also *McDonald* v *Provan (of Scotland Street) Ltd* 1960 SLT 231 (OH); *Microbeads AG* v *Vinhurst Road Markings Ltd* [1975] 1 WLR 218.
[228] SOGA, s 13(2).
[229] [1936] AC 85.
[230] [1972] AC 441.

which ensued from their consumption of the food on the basis that the goods did not correspond with the description of the goods, under section 13 of the 1893 Act. The court held, however, that "the defect in the meal was a matter of quality or condition rather than description".[231]

Satisfactory quality

The starting point of section 14 is the English common law rule of *caveat emptor* ("let **8-74** the buyer beware") which places the onus on the buyer to ensure that goods he buys are of a reasonable quality and fit for any specific purpose required. This doctrine can be starkly contrasted with the Scottish common law principle that a sale of goods was a contract *bona fide* (that is one of good faith), which meant that the seller was duty bound to supply goods which were worthy of the price.

In any case, section 14 proceeds to water down strict application of *caveat emptor* in that it provides that the doctrine will not apply in certain prescribed ways. The caveats to this rule are that goods sold will be of satisfactory quality, fit for their purpose and in accordance with terms incorporated into the contract by usage.

Section 14(2) prescribes that goods should be of "satisfactory quality". Prior to the 1995 Act, the applicable term had been "merchantable quality". This term, however, was somewhat unclear and outdated. In particular, it had been argued that the old term focused exclusively on the usability of goods and did not take account of a number of issues which were of importance to consumers, such as appearance, freedom from minor defects, durability and safety.[232]

A case which illustrates the difficulty with the application of the old merchantable quality rule is *Millars of Falkirk Ltd v Turpie*,[233] where a buyer of a car could not reject a car on the grounds of repeated minor faults; despite the glitches the car was nonetheless roadworthy and hence of merchantable quality.

Under the amended section 14(2A), goods must be of a standard "that a reasonable person would regard as satisfactory, taking account of any description of the goods, the price (if relevant) and all other relevant circumstances". This means that if goods are advertised as "seconds", are out of date, or are sold in a sale, it may have some bearing on the quality that could be expected. Interpretation of the term "satisfactory" quality is aided by section 12(2B). This subsection sets out a non-exhaustive list of factors which will be relevant in determining whether goods are of a satisfactory quality:

(a) fitness for the purpose for which goods of the kind sold are commonly supplied;

(b) appearance and finish;

(c) freedom from minor defects;

(d) safety; and

(e) durability.

---

[231] per Lord Wilberforce at 489. This was approved in the Scottish case of *Border Harvesters Ltd v Edwards Engineering (Perth) Ltd* 1985 SLT 128 (OH). Compare this with the earlier, more liberal, interpretation of description in the English case of *Varley v Whipp* [1900] 1 QB 513.
[232] See *Report on Sale and Supply of Goods* (Law Com No 160; Scot Law Com No 104; Cm 137) (1987).
[233] 1976 SLT (Notes) 66.

Section 14(2C) states that the implied term does not extend to any matter making the quality of the goods unsatisfactory: which is specifically drawn to the buyer's attention before the contract is made; where the buyer examines the goods before the contract is made, which that examination ought to reveal; or, in the case of a sale by sample, which would have been apparent on reasonable examination of the sample.[234]

Fitness for the purpose

8–75   As noted above, one measure of the satisfactory quality of a good is the extent to which it is fit for its general purposes. Section 14(3) includes the additional provision, however, that where the buyer, either expressly or by implication, makes known to the seller any particular purpose for which the goods are to be bought, there is an implied term that the goods are reasonably fit for this purpose regardless if it falls within the normal use of such goods.

In relation to goods that have only one primary purpose, there is no need for the buyer to intimate this use to the seller. In such a case the seller is deemed to have implied knowledge of this use. For example, in *Priest v Last*,[235] a buyer who was scalded after using a hot-water bottle in the normal way was able to sue the seller on the basis that the bottle was unfit for the purpose. The seller was deemed to know the purpose by implication.[236]

The section comes into its own, however, where more than one use is possible and the buyer either expressly or by implication indicates that a particular use is required. In *Jacobs v Scott & Co*[237] J agreed to purchase a quantity of "No. 1 export hay" from S. This was to allow J to carry out a contract with T to provide a quantity of "best Canadian Timothy hay". S, who was aware that the hay he provided to J was to be used in J's contract with T, provided hay which was a mix of Timothy hay and other grasses. This was not acceptable to T. In an action brought by J against S, the court ruled that S had knowledge of the purpose for which the hay was required and, as the hay did not fit that purpose, S was entitled to bring an action for damages accordingly.

A further relevant case is *McCallum v Mason*[238] where McC, believing his tomato plants to be poorly, consulted M, a dealer in fertilisers. M sold McC a bag of his own brand of fertiliser mixed in with magnesium sulphate. McC applied this to his plants, which duly died. The following year McC again applied the mixture to his plants, again with the result that they died. After analysing the mixture it was discovered that the mixture contained sodium chlorate, a weedkiller, instead of magnesium sulphate. McC brought an action for damages against M in respect of all the plants destroyed on the basis that the mixture did not fit the purpose specified. It was held that McC was entitled to damages in respect of the first crop only, as McC had not disclosed his intention to use the mixture on the second crop of plants.

Equally, where a buyer has special needs which goods must be compatible with, these must be made known to the seller before the section will apply. In *Griffiths v Peter Conway*,[239] a woman with particularly sensitive skin bought a coat which

---

[234] See, *eg Bartlett v Sydney Marcus* [1965] 1 WLR 1013.
[235] [1903] 2 KB 148.
[236] There is an overlap in the grounds for a claim here—an action on the ground that the goods are not of satisfactory quality would also be possible.
[237] (1899) 2 F (HL) 70.
[238] 1956 SC 50.
[239] [1939] 1 All ER 685.

aggravated her condition. As the seller had been unaware of this condition, the buyer could not claim that the goods were not fit for their purpose.

This implied term will not apply where circumstances show that the buyer does not rely on the skill or judgement of the seller, or where it is unreasonable for the buyer to rely on the seller's skill and judgement. It is generally for the seller to prove that the buyer did not rely on the seller's skill. In *Grant v Australian Knitting Mills,* it was stated that "... the reliance will in general be inferred from the fact that a buyer goes to the shop in confidence that the tradesman has selected his stock with skill and judgement."[240]

If a buyer has more expertise than the seller then it would clearly be unreasonable for him to rely on the seller's advice. In *Teheran-Europe v St Belton,*[241] a buyer could not reasonably rely on the seller's advice that certain tractors purchased for export to Persia conformed to Persian law when it was revealed that the buyer had a far more detailed knowledge of Persian law than the seller.

An important point about section 14 is that liability is strict and it is of no consequence that the seller has done all that is reasonable to avoid breach of the provision. A case which illustrates this point is *Frost v Aylesbury Dairy Co Ltd,*[242] in which milk carrying the typhoid virus was sold to F. His wife consumed the milk and consequently she died. It was no defence that the dairy could not reasonably have discovered the presence of the virus in the milk.

Usage

It should be noted that an implied term as to quality or fitness may become part of a contract of sale by usage.[243]   8–76

Sale by sample

A sale will only be a sale by sample if there is either express or implied agreement to this effect between the parties.[244] The mere fact that a sample is displayed and a sale results does not itself render the contract a sale by sample. There are two implied terms that relate to such a sale[245]: first, the bulk will correspond to the sample in quality; and second, the goods will be free from any defect, making them unsatisfactory, which would not be apparent on reasonable examination of the sample.[246]   8–77

Contracting out

As noted above, it is not possible to contract out of the provisions of section 12 in any sale.[247] It is not possible to contract out of the implied terms of s 13 to 15 in consumer sales (that is where one party sells in the course of a business, the other party is a consumer and the goods are of a type ordinarily supplied for private use and consumption).[248] In commercial contracts (where both parties are commercial   8–78

---

[240] [1936] AC 35.
[241] [1968] 2 QB 545.
[242] [1905] 1 KB 608 (CA).
[243] SOGA, s 14(4) (as amended).
[244] SOGA, s 15(1).
[245] SOGA, s 15(2) (as amended).
[246] See *Godley v Perry* [1960] 1 WLR 9.
[247] Unfair Contract Terms Act 1977, s 20(1).
[248] *ibid* s 20(2).

concerns), it is possible to contract out of the terms of sections 13 to 15, if it is fair and reasonable to do so.[249]

The onus of proof that it is fair and reasonable to contract out lies with the party seeking to enforce the contracting-out clause. In determining whether it is fair and reasonable in the circumstances, the court shall take account of the provisions of Schedule 2 to the Unfair Contract Terms Act 1977, which include the following matters: the relative bargaining strengths of the parties; whether the buyer was given an inducement such as a discount to accept the contracting out; whether the buyer knew or should have known about the exclusion clause; and whether the goods were adapted or manufactured in a particular manner specified by the buyer.

THE PASSING OF PROPERTY AND RISK

8–79   Under Scottish common law, property in goods passed at the time of delivery (or its equivalent). The 1893 Act, however, has brought into force rather complex rules of the English common law of corporeal moveables into Scots law. Under the rules it should be noted that neither delivery nor payment are necessarily crucial factors in determining when property in goods passes.

The passing of property in the goods is important in that it vests in the buyer a real right in the goods even when they are not in his possession. In the event of the seller's insolvency, for example, goods belonging to the buyer but still in the possession of the seller would be recoverable by the buyer. The other side of the coin, however, is that in the case of damage or destruction of the goods, the loss will fall to whatever party is the owner of the goods as risk passes with ownership unless the contrary is agreed.[250]

Prior to examining the various rules governing the passing of goods in detail, the consideration of a number of definitions relating to different types of good is necessary. Section 5 of the Act classifies goods into either "existing goods" or "future goods". Existing goods are goods the seller owns or has in his possession at the time of the contract. Future goods are those that the seller must either manufacture or acquire from a third party after the contract has been formed.

There is a further differential to be made between specific and unascertained goods. Section 61 of the Act defines specific goods as goods which are identified and agreed upon at the time the contract is made—for example, a contract to purchase a particular vehicle. By contrast, unascertained goods are those which are not identified and agreed upon at the time the contract is made. This lack of identification can arise in different ways: where the goods are part of a bulk of goods which the buyer is aware of, but his particular goods have not yet been identified, or where goods are generic and part of a bulk that the buyer is not aware of.

Rules relating to passing of property

8–80   The default rules regulating the passing of property in goods are set out in sections 16, 17 and 18. By virtue of section 16, a buyer of unascertained goods does not become the owner of the goods until they are ascertained. Strict application of this rule can be seen

---

[249] Under the Unfair Contract Terms Act 1977, s 20(4). It should be noted that both sections 12 and 13 are applicable in private sales where neither party is a commercial concern.
[250] See para 8–81.

in the case of *Hayman & Son* v *McLintock*,[251] where a firm of flour merchants sold consignments of flour to two purchasers. After the sale, the sacks were kept as a part of bulk in their warehouse and were not separated from the bulk nor labelled as being the property of the buyers. After the sequestration of the flour merchants, the court upheld the trustee in sequestration's claim to all the bags of flour on the basis that, as the flour remained unascertained, ownership did not pass to the buyers notwithstanding payment.

In light of the inherent unfairness engendered by strict application of the rule in *Hayman* the law has since been reformed to provide that in the absence of any agreement to the contrary, a pre-paying buyer from an identifiable bulk will become the owner of the goods when payment is made.[252]

Where goods are specific, or are ascertained, ownership will pass when the parties intend it to pass.[253] Where such intention is not expressed or cannot be inferred from the actings of the parties, section 18 provides that one of five rules will apply in determining when ownership passes.[254]

Rule 1: Where there is an unconditional contract for the sale of specific goods in a "deliverable state", ownership will pass to the buyer at the time the contract is made. In such a case, ownership will pass regardless of whether the goods have been delivered to the buyer or whether the buyer has paid for the goods. The term "deliverable state" denotes that the goods are in a state that the buyer would be bound under the terms of the contract to take delivery.

A classic case is *Tarling* v *Baxter*,[255] in which B purchased a haystack from T, but it was destroyed by fire before he could take delivery of it. A question arose as to the ownership of the haystack. As the haystack was in a deliverable state when it was destroyed it thus belonged to T. The loss of the haystack therefore fell with T, as the maxim *res perit domini* applies—"a thing perishes at the owner's loss".[256]

Rule 2 relates to conditional sales: "where there is a contract for the sale of specific goods and the seller is bound to do something to the goods for the purpose of putting them into a deliverable state, the property does not pass until the thing is done and the buyer has notice that it has been done". In *Brown Brothers* v *Carron Co*,[257] C bought a crane subject to it being modified by B. C subsequently decided not to buy the crane, at which time the modifications had not yet been made. The court held that property in the crane had not passed to C and hence B could only sue for damages and not the contract price.[258]

Similarly, in *rule 3*: where there is a contract for the sale of specific goods in a deliverable state and the seller is bound to weigh, measure or otherwise test the goods in order to calculate the price, ownership passes to the buyer only when this is done. It

---

[251] 1907 SC 936.
[252] SOGA, s 20A.
[253] *ibid* s 7.
[254] See *Woodburn* v *Andrew Motherwell Ltd* 1917 SC 533 where intention was inferred from the conduct of the parties. "The rules in section 18 are merely intended to be a guide in ascertaining the intention of the parties … if the intention of the parties is quite plain … then the rules of section 18 do not come into play at all": per Lord President at 538.
[255] (1827) 6 B&C 360.
[256] See para 8–81. See also *Gowans (Cockburn's Trustee)* v *Bowie & Sons* (1910) 2 SLT 17 (OH); *Munro* v *Balnagown Estates Co Ltd* 1949 SC 49.
[257] (1898) 6 SLT 231.
[258] s 49(1).

has been held that rule 3 applies only where it is the seller who carries out the testing; if this is to be undertaken by a third party, then unless there was any stipulation between the parties to the contrary, property would pass in accordance with rules 1 and 2.[259]

Rule 4 relates to situations of sale and return. Where goods are delivered to the buyer on approval or on sale and return or other similar terms, the property in the goods passes to the buyer: (a) when he signifies his approval or acceptance to the seller or does any other act adopting the transaction; (b) if he does not signify his approval or acceptance to the seller, but retains the goods without giving notice of rejection then, if a time has been fixed for the return of the goods, on the expiration of that time and, if no time has been fixed, beyond a reasonable time.

Approval or acceptance may be expressed by keeping the goods and sending off payment or may arise by implication if, for instance, the buyer carries out some sort of act which adopts the goods such as selling, hiring, pawning or using the goods in some way.

What will amount to a reasonable time (in terms of keeping the goods without rejecting them) will depend on the circumstances of the case. In *Poole* v *Smith's Car Sales (Balham) Ltd*[260] P left a car with a dealer, S, in August 1960, so that he could try to sell the car, with a set amount being returned to P. By November, P had received neither the car nor the amount. By the end of November S returned the car to P in a damaged state. It was held in this case, however, that the period which had lapsed amounted to a "reasonable time" and hence property in the car had passed to S and he was liable for the contract price of the car.

Rule 5: In a contract for the sale of unascertained or future goods, ownership transfers to the buyer when such goods, complying with the contract description, are "unconditionally appropriated" to the contract in a deliverable state. The appropriation of the goods may be by the seller with the buyer's consent or by the buyer with the seller's consent. Consent may be express or implied by the conduct of the parties and may be given either before or after the goods have been appropriated.

Goods are unconditionally appropriated to the contract when they are "irrevocably earmarked" for use in that contract.[261] In the aforementioned case of *Hayman & Son* v *McLintock*,[262] the sacks of flour which were part of a bulk in a warehouse were not specifically set aside or earmarked for the buyer, therefore property in the flour did not pass. By contrast, in *Warder's Import and Export Co* v *Norwood & Sons Ltd*[263] there was a contract for the purchase of 600 cartons of kidneys held in a coldstore. When the purchaser's carrier arrived to take delivery, he found the cartons stacked up on the street outside the coldstore. The carrier handed over a delivery note and began loading at 8 am. By the time he had finished loading, some four hours later, the kidneys had thawed out and were unfit for human consumption. The court held that property did not pass when the contract was made as the kidneys were still unascertained. When the delivery note was handed over and the carrier began loading, this

---

[259] *Nanka-Bruce* v *Commonwealth Trust Ltd* [1926] AC 77 (PC).
[260] [1962] 1 WLR 774.
[261] See *Carlos Federspiel & Co* v *Charles Twigg & Co Ltd* [1957] 1 Lloyd's Rep 240, per Pearson J at 256.
[262] 1907 SC 936.
[263] [1968] 2 QB 663.

amounted to the unconditional appropriation of the goods and hence property and risk passed to the buyer at this time.

Rule 5(2) further stipulates that where the seller places the goods in the hands of a carrier for transmission to the buyer, this is deemed to be unconditional appropriation unless he reserves the right to dispose of the goods.

Transfer of risk

Unless the parties agree otherwise, risk (that is the bearing of loss should goods be **8–81** damaged) walks hand in hand with ownership.[264] When property in the goods passes to the buyer, risk also passes. A notable exception to this rule occurs where delivery is delayed because of the fault of one of the parties. The party responsible for the delay will become liable for any damage to the goods resulting from the delay.

Retention of title clauses

An unpaid seller may transfer goods to a buyer on credit whilst retaining title to these **8–82** goods.[265] Indeed, it has become very common in commercial contracts for sellers to include "retention of title" clauses in their contracts of sale. There are a number of different species of such clauses. A "price-only" clause is the most straightforward in the sense that the seller retains title to the goods thereunder subject to the price of these goods being paid. When payment is made, property in the goods passes. The efficacy of this type of clause has never really been in question as this merely represents a conditional sale.[266]

Other clauses seek to retain title to goods until "all sums" owed to the seller from the contract in question and any other contracts have been made. Such clauses were initially given short shrift by the Court of Session in *Emerald Stainless Steel Ltd* v *South Side Distribution Ltd*[267] and *Deutz Engines Ltd* v *Terex Ltd*.[268] In both cases, Lord Ross held that the clauses were ineffective as they represented no more than an attempt to create a security over moveable property without possession of the goods.[269]

The decisions in *Emerald Steel* and *Deutz Engines* were overruled, however, by the House of Lords in *Armour & Another* v *Thyssen Edelstahlwerke AG*,[270] in which Lord Kerr stated that "the parties clearly expressed ... their intention that the property in the steel should not pass ... until all debts ... had been paid. In my opinion there are no grounds for refusing to give effect to that intention". In view of this decision, "all sums" clauses are commonly employed by sellers where goods are often sold on credit to the same buyer. In the event of the buyer's bankruptcy or insolvency (if the buyer is a company), the seller can reclaim the goods from the permanent trustee or liquidator.

Third parties who purchase in good faith from an original buyer goods which are the subject of a retention of title clause, do receive good title to those goods and may fend off any claims from the original seller.[271]

---

[264] SOGA, s 20.
[265] *ibid* s 19.
[266] See *Archivent Sales and Development Ltd* v *Strathclyde Regional Council* 1985 SLT 154.
[267] 1982 SC 61.
[268] 1984 SLT 273.
[269] See para 8–22.
[270] 1990 SLT 891.
[271] SOGA, s 25(1). Claims by sellers to the proceeds of any sub-sales of these goods have proven problematic: see Gretton and Reid, "Romalpa Clauses: The Current Position", 1985 SLT 329; Gretton and Reid, "All Sums Retention of Title", 1989 SLT (News) 185; Clark," "All Sums Retention of Title", 1991 SLT (News) 155.

TRANSFER OF TITLE

8–83   As a general rule, where a party sells goods to which he has no good title, the buyer does not gain good title.[272] This is a reflection of the Latin rule *nemo dat quod non habet* ("no one gives what he does not have"). A third party, therefore, who in fact is the true owner of the goods, can successfully bring an action against the buyer to have the goods returned to him, which would render the buyer with merely a personal action for damages against the seller.[273]

There are, however, certain exceptions to this rule. The true owner may be personally barred from "denying the seller's authority to sell". This would occur when a seller sells goods under a voidable title,[274] and when the true owner has "held out" the seller as the true owner—for example, where the owner has failed to take appropriate steps in rescinding a contract which he entered into and sold goods on the basis of the fraud of the buyer, who has since sold the goods on. Furthermore, the owner must take reasonable steps to bring the reccission to the attention of any third party who seeks to purchase the goods from the original buyer. In *MacLeod* v *Kerr*,[275] G bought a car from K using a forged cheque and subsequently sold the goods on to a third party who bought the car in good faith. The third party obtained good title to the car, as G had not rescinded the initial contract of sale when the sale to the third party took place.

If property in goods has passed from the seller to the buyer but the seller remains in possession of the goods, by virtue of section 24, a third party may acquire good title to these goods provided both that the seller's possession was with the express or implied consent of the buyer and that the third party had no knowledge of the sale to the original buyer.

Similarly, as noted above, a third party who purchases goods which remain the property of another party (not being the currrent seller) under a retention of title clause, will gain good title to the goods.[276]

PERFORMANCE OF THE CONTRACT

8–84   The fundamental principle here is that the seller is under a duty to deliver the goods and the buyer is under a duty to accept and pay for the goods.[277] The duties of the buyer and seller are "concurrent" in the sense that the seller can only compel the buyer to carry out his side of the contract when he (the seller) is ready and willing to carry out his part of the bargain, and vice versa.[278]

Seller's duty to deliver

8–85   Delivery is defined as "the voluntary transfer of possession of the goods from one person to another".[279] Whether it is for the buyer or the seller to take possession of the

---

[272] SOGA, s 21(1).
[273] Under SOGA, s 12(2).
[274] See Chapter 4.
[275] 1965 SC 253.
[276] SOGA, s 25(1).
[277] *ibid* s 27.
[278] *ibid* s 28.
[279] *ibid* s 61(1).

goods is a matter to be determined by the express or implied terms of the contract.[280] Except where provision is made to the contrary, the place of delivery shall be the seller's place of business (or residence); except that in the sale of specific goods which, to the knowledge of the parties when the contract was made, are in some other place, then that place is the place of delivery.[281] If the seller is bound under the terms of the contract to deliver the goods to the buyer and no time is fixed for when delivery should take place, delivery shall take place within a reasonable time.[282] Where goods are held by a third party, there is no delivery to the buyer until the third party acknowledges that he holds the goods on behalf of the buyer.[283] Delivery should be made by the seller at a reasonable hour and all expenses relating to delivery are to be borne by the seller unless the contrary is agreed by the parties.[284]

Particular problems may arise when the seller delivers the wrong quantity of goods. If too small a quantity is delivered and the shortfall is material, then the seller may reject the goods, or he may accept and pay for the goods on a *pro rata* basis.[285] If the seller delivers too large a quantity and the excess is material, then again the buyer may reject the goods outright, or he may accept only the contracted amount and reject any surplus or he may accept all of the goods delivered and pay for the goods on a *pro rata* basis.[286]

Unless provision is made to the contrary, the seller is bound to deliver the whole consignment of the goods; the buyer is not bound to accept delivery of instalments.[287] If, however, the contract does make provision for delivery of the goods in instalments, it will fall to the courts to determine, in all the circumstances of the case, whether breach of the contract by either party in relation to delivery of one instalment shall entitle the innocent party to treat the whole contract as repudiated.[288]

Where the seller is required to deliver the goods to the buyer, then delivery of the goods to a carrier will amount to prima facie delivery of the goods to the buyer.[289] The seller must arrange a reasonable contract in this respect with the carrier. For example, if the goods are perishable, the seller must ensure that delivery be speedy.[290]

Buyer's duty to accept

Where the seller is willing and able to deliver the goods and requests the buyer to take **8–86** delivery within a reasonable time, the buyer will be responsible for the costs of storage of the items.[291]

When goods which the buyer has not previously examined are delivered to the buyer, he will not be deemed to have accepted these until he has had a reasonable opportunity to ensure that they conform to the contract.[292]

---

[280] *ibid* s 29(1).
[281] *ibid* s 29(2).
[282] *ibid* s 29(3).
[283] *ibid* s 29(4).
[284] *ibid* s 29(5), (6).
[285] *ibid* s 30(1).
[286] *ibid* s 30(2).
[287] *ibid* s 31.
[288] *ibid* s 31(2); see *Warinco AG* v *Samor SPA* [1977] 2 Lloyd's Rep 582.
[289] *ibid* s 32(1).
[290] *ibid* s 32.
[291] *ibid* s 37.
[292] *ibid* s 34.

Section 35 governs the time at which the buyer is deemed to have accepted the goods, with the effect that he may no longer reject them. The relevant provisions have been amended by the Sale and Supply of Goods Act 1994 to afford buyers more protection—the buyer is deemed to have accepted goods when he intimates to the seller that he has accepted them, except where the buyer has as yet had no reasonable opportunity to examine the goods; or when, after delivery of the goods, he does any act in relation to them inconsistent with the ownership of the seller (for example, selling or consuming the goods).[293] Importantly, in a consumer contract the right to reject cannot be waived or excluded (for example, by signing a delivery note).[294]

The buyer is also deemed to have accepted goods within a reasonable time if he fails to intimate rejection of the goods to the seller.[295] Reasonable time must now encompass an opportunity for the buyer to inspect the goods. In addition, the buyer is not deemed to have accepted goods merely because he has either asked for or accepted an offer by the seller to repair the goods. If the buyer legitimately intimates rejection of the goods to the seller, then he is under no obligation to transfer these to the seller.[296]

A buyer may have a partial right of rejection in respect of the goods. Section 35A sets out the proposition that the buyer may accept those goods which conform to the contract and reject the remainder.

RIGHTS OF THE UNPAID SELLER OVER THE GOODS

8–87 These rights are "real" in the sense that they can be exercised over the goods themselves. There are three real remedies available to the unpaid seller: the right of "lien"; "stoppage in transit"; and the right of resale.

Lien

8–88 An unpaid seller who remains in possession of goods holds a right to retain possession until he receives payment. The seller holds this right even where property in the goods has passed to the buyer.[297] The right of lien also extends to an undelivered part of goods when payment remains due for those already supplied.[298] The seller will lose his right of lien when he allows a carrier to take possession of the goods for delivery to the buyer.[299]

Stoppage in transit

8–89 In the event of the buyer's insolvency, the seller may resume possession of goods that are already in transit—that is where a carrier is delivering the goods to the buyer and the buyer has not yet taken delivery of the goods.[300] The goods must be in the possession of an independent carrier. If, for example, goods are being transported to

---

[293] *ibid* s 35(1).
[294] Previously, signing an acceptance note could act as a bar against rejecting goods in the future: *Mechans Ltd* v *Highland Marine Charters Ltd* 1964 SC 48. See also Law Commission's *Report on Sale and Supply of Goods* (Law Com No 160; Scot Law Com No 104; Cm 137), (1987), para 5.20.
[295] SOGA, s 35(4).
[296] *ibid* s 35(6).
[297] *ibid* s 41. This is an illustration of a special lien—see para 8–35.
[298] *ibid* s 42.
[299] *ibid* s 43(1).
[300] *ibid* s 44.

the buyer in the seller's own vehicle, then the goods are deemed to have remained in the seller's possession and he may exercise a right of lien at this time.

The seller may either intercept the goods personally and take the goods back to his premises or issue notice to the carrier that the transit is to be "stopped",[301] in which case the carrier is bound to follow the instructions of the seller.[302]

If the goods are deemed to have been delivered to the buyer, then the seller cannot exercise his right of stoppage at this stage.[303] This may occur where the carrier has reached his destination and has informed the buyer that he is holding the goods on the buyer's behalf. In *Muir v Rankin*,[304] goods were sent by the seller to the buyer by rail. The seller subsequently discovered that the buyer had become insolvent and attempted to "stop" the goods in transit. The goods had already been delivered to their final destination (a railway station), however, and the buyer had signed the delivery book at the station. Transit was therefore at an end and the seller could not exercise stoppage in transit.

Resale

As mere late payment does not amount to material breach of the contract,[305] the resale **8–90** of the goods by an unpaid seller must be approached with caution. An unpaid seller who has exercised his right of lien or stoppage in transit may resell goods where the goods are perishable, where reasonable notice of his intention to resell the goods has been intimated to the buyer, where the buyer has been advised that the price must be paid within a certain time and no payment has been received, or where there is an express term in the contract sanctioning resale.[306] In the case of perishable goods, the seller may resell goods without providing notice to the buyer in so far as the buyer has already been given a reasonable time to pay for the goods. Any third party who purchases the goods as resold, obtains good title and can defeat the claims of the original buyer.[307]

Any losses incurred by the seller in the course of the resale may be claimed from the original buyer. This would encompass the difference between the sale price under the original contract and the price obtained in the resale and may also include storage and advertising costs.[308]

SELLER'S PERSONAL REMEDIES FOR BREACH OF CONTRACT

An action for the price

Where property in the goods has passed to the buyer and he wrongfully neglects or **8–91** refuses to pay the contract price, the seller is entitled to raise an action for the price.[309] Additionally, where the contract provides a date for payment of the price, and the

---

[301] *ibid* s 46(1).
[302] Otherwise the carrier may be liable in damages to the seller: *Mechan & Sons Ltd v North Eastern Railway Co* 1911 SC 1348.
[303] SOGA, s 45(1).
[304] (1905) 13 SLT 60.
[305] SOGA, s 10, unless the parties agree to the contrary.
[306] *ibid* s 44.
[307] *ibid* s 48(2).
[308] See *Ward v Bignall* [1967] 2 All ER 449.
[309] SOGA, s 49.

buyer has failed to make payment timeously, the seller may raise an action for the price regardless of whether property in the goods has passed to the buyer or not. The Act does not interfere with the seller's common law right to obtain interest.[310]

Damages for non-acceptance

8–92   An unpaid seller may also claim damages in respect of a buyer's non-acceptance of the goods and refusal to make payment of the price.[311] The damages awarded are those arising directly and naturally from the breach. This would normally be measured by the difference between the contract price and (if there is a market for the goods) the market price of the goods when the goods ought to have been accepted; or, where there is no time stipulated in the contract for acceptance of the goods, the market price at the time the buyer intimated refusal to accept the goods. The seller may also claim a reasonable charge for storage of the goods.[312]

BUYER'S PERSONAL REMEDIES FOR BREACH OF CONTRACT

Damages for non-delivery

8–93   If the seller wrongly neglects or refuses to deliver the goods, then the buyer may bring an action for damages.[313] The amount of damages is measured by reference to that which has arisen naturally from the seller's breach. This would normally be measured by the difference between the contract price and the market price at the time the goods ought to have been delivered, where there is a date fixed for delivery; otherwise, at the time when the seller intimated refusal to deliver.

Specific performance

8–94   Section 52 provides that in relation to specific goods, the buyer may seek specific performance—that is that the seller deliver the goods. This remedy follows the English common law remedy of specific performance in the sense that the court will only grant the remedy if the buyer has sound reasons for seeking this in preference to a claim for damages. Accordingly, the buyer must show that he cannot obtain goods of the same kind elsewhere.[314]

Rejection of goods and damages

8–95   Whereas sections 51 and 52 relate to situations where the seller has failed to deliver goods, other instances of contractual breach by the seller are covered by section 15B and the common law rules relating to breach of contract. Under section 15B, if there is a breach of contract then the buyer may claim damages. If the breach is material, this will allow the buyer both to claim damages and to reject the goods. Where the contract is a consumer contract, a breach of any of the implied terms under sections 13, 14 and 15 will amount to a material breach and allow the consumer to reject the goods and claim damages.

---

[310] See Chapter 4.
[311] SOGA, s 50.
[312] *ibid* s 37.
[313] *ibid* s 51.
[314] This remedy does not prejudice the buyer's right to pursue the Scottish common law remedy of specific implement which, regarded as the primary remedy in Scotland, would be granted automatically.

Damages are generally measured as the estimated loss directly and naturally arising, in the ordinary course of events, from the breach.[315]

UNSOLICITED GOODS

Those who receive unsolicited goods are protected by the provisions of the Unsolicited Goods and Services Act 1971. If the recipient has held the goods for a six-month period, the goods become his property. Alternatively, if the recipient gives the owner 30 days' notice in writing of the fact that he has received the goods and that they can be collected from him at a designated place and time, if the seller fails to respond, the recipient becomes the owner of the goods.

8–96

CONSUMER SAFETY

As has been stated above, section 14 of the Sale of Goods Act 1979 provides buyers who are injured as a consequence of using goods in the normal manner with a remedy against the seller. Given the lack of any contractual relationship, this remedy is of no value to third parties who are injured by the use of a defective product purchased by another. Previously, the only remedy that such individuals would have against either the seller or the manufacturer would be a right to claim damages in respect of their injuries and other losses under the common law of delict.[316]

8–97

The legal landscape was altered significantly, however, by the advent of the Consumer Protection Act 1987 ("CPA"), which introduced a new statutory ground of claim against manufacturers by those consumers injured as a result of the use of a defective product.[317]

The principal advantage of the new statutory remedy is that, unlike the situation under the common law, the consumer does not have to establish that the manufacturer had been negligent; liability is strict (subject to certain defences).[318]

In general terms, in order to bring a claim, the pursuer must illustrate that:

- the product contained a defect

- the pursuer suffered damage

- the damage was caused by the defect

- the defender was a producer, own brander, or importer of the good.

Producers

Section 1(2)(a) defines a producer in wide terms, including:

8–98

(a) the manufacturer of a finished product or of a component;

---

[315] SOGA, s 53A(1).
[316] As established in *Donoghue* v *Stevenson* 1932 SC (HL) 31—see Chapter 5.
[317] Implementing the EC Product Liability Directive—EC Council Directive 85/374 ([1985] OJ L210/29).
[318] Discussed at para 8–102.

(b) any person who "won or abstracted" the product, where the goods have not been manufactured;

(c) any person responsible for an industrial or other process to which any essential characteristic of the product is attributable.

Although the seller or supplier of the product is not the primary subject of liability under the Act, such a person may incur liability if he fails to identify the producer or importer when requested to do so.[319]

Furthermore, a person may be deemed to be a "producer" of a defective product if that person claims to be a producer by placing his name or trade mark on the product.[320] This stipulation serves to cover "own branders"—for example, super-markets who market their own range of products—on the basis that they have represented themselves as producers of the product. The "own brander" can evade liability, however, if the product is labelled in such a way as to reveal the name of the real manufacturer.

Damage

8–99   The damage that the Act guards against is death, personal injury and damage to property. Personal injury extends to diseases and physical and mental impairments.[321] Claims for property damage, however, are limited in the sense that awards of damages below the value of £275 will not be made by the courts.[322] Pure economic loss (that is financial loss not directly caused by the defect in the product) is also not recoverable.[323] Significantly, claims can only be made in relation to damage to private property— damage to business or public property is not recoverable.[324]

Products

8–100   A product is defined by section 1(2) as "any goods or electricity". Expressly included in the definition are components and raw materials which are incorporated into products. Additionally, goods include "substances, growing crops and things comprised on land by virtue of being attached to it and any ship, aircraft or vehicle".[325]

Heritable property, such as buildings, are not themselves included, although claims may be made in respect of damage to buildings or injury caused by products which are incorporated into the property. There is no liability in respect of agricultural produce or game unless it has undergone some type of industrial process.[326]

Defects

8–101   Goods do not require to be absolutely risk free. By virtue of section 3, a product will be defective if the safety of the product is not that which consumers would *reason-ably* expect,[327] taking into account a number of factors including the marketing and

---

[319] CPA, s 2(3).
[320] *ibid* s 2(2)(b).
[321] *ibid* s 45(1).
[322] *ibid* s 5(4).
[323] *ibid* s 5(2). This reflects the general position in the common law of delict—see Chapter 5.
[324] *ibid* s 5(3).
[325] *ibid* s 45(1).
[326] *ibid* s 2(4).
[327] *ibid* s 3(1).

presentation of the product (including warnings and instructions), the use to which it might reasonably be put, the time of supply and the state of the art at that time.[328]

Defences

The Act makes provision for strict liability, which has the effect that a producer cannot claim that he exercised all due diligence in ensuring that the product was not defective. There are, however, a number of defences available to the producer and liability will not lie where he can show that: **8–102**

(a) the defect has arisen out of compliance with either domestic legislation or a provision of EC law;

(b) the person was not at any time the supplier of the product (covering the situation where the manufacturer's goods are stolen);

(c) the supply was not in the course of business (for example, goods sold at a charitable event would not be covered by the Act);

(d) the defect did not exist in the product at the time it was supplied (covering situations where damage to the product has occurred further down the distribution chain);

(e) the state of scientific and technical knowledge at the time of supply of the product was not such that the producer could have been able to detect the defect;

(f) the defect was in a product in which the product in question comprised and was wholly attributable to the design of the product it so comprised;

(g) more than 10 years have elapsed since the product was first supplied.[329]

It is in defence (e) where there is most likelihood that grey areas will abound. One particular criticism of this defence is that it does not take into account subjective criteria, such as the particular knowledge as to possible defects that a particular producer has. Rather, the defence is judged by reference to an objective evaluation of the recognised "state of the art" in the industry that the defender is deemed to have knowledge of. Thus, if other producers of similar products would not be expected to detect the defect then the producer of the defective product in question will not be liable. The result of this approach is that smaller producers are deemed to have the same knowledge as larger, better resourced organisations.[330]

Criminal sanctions

Part II of the Consumer Protection Act 1987 sets out a criminal liability for producers who provide unsafe goods.[331] It is a defence, however, if the accused producer can prove that he reasonably believed that the goods would not be used or consumed in **8–103**

---

[328] *ibid* s 3(2).
[329] *ibid* s 4(1).
[330] See Case C-300/95, *EC Commission* v *United Kingdom*, discussed in Forte (ed), *Scots Commercial Law* (1997), p 63.
[331] CPA, s 10.

the UK; or that he neither knew nor had reasonable grounds to believe that the goods failed to comply with a safety requirement; or that the goods were purposely offered for sale in an imperfect state.[332]

Failure to conform to safety regulations set out by the Secretary of State[333] may result in initial warnings and subsequent suspensions served on those who act in contravention.[334] Enforcement agencies are also empowered to enter the premises of those who act in contravention of the safety provisions and to seize those goods which do not meet the required standards.[335]

MISLEADING TRADE DESCRIPTIONS

Trade Descriptions Act 1968

8–104 One of the main pieces of legislation relevant to this area of law is the Trade Descriptions Act 1968 ("TDA"). Breach of provisions of the TDA may result in a criminal prosecution. Section 1 of the Act sets out the fundamental provision that it is an offence to apply a "false trade description" to goods which are sold in the course of a business. It is further an offence to supply (or offer to supply) goods which have a false trade description attributed to them. A key facet of the offences is that they are characterised by strict liability. Unlike common law criminal offences, no relevant *mens rea* ("state of mind") such as intention or recklessness must be proven.[336]

A "trade description" is defined widely by the 1968 Act as any indication, direct or indirect, of a wide variety of matters relating to goods—for example, quantity, size, method of manufacture or process (for example, free-range eggs), fitness for purpose, composition, approval by any person, history including previous ownership (*eg* in relation to second hand cars, stipulating "one previous owner" and "12,000 miles").

Although liability is strict, those in contravention of the legislation can make use of a "due diligence" defence which will allow the defender to evade liability.[337] There are two strands to this defence, both of which must be present before the defence will apply. The first branch states that for the defence to be available, the accused must show that the offence was committed "due to a mistake or reliance on information supplied by him or to the act or default of another person". For example, this defence allows companies to escape liability for acts committed by their employees on the basis that the "other person" is the employee. For instance, in *Tesco Supermarkets Ltd* v *Nattrass*,[338] Tesco was able to evade liability for contravention of the Act, amongst other things, on the basis that the offence was carried out by another person—a shop manager. It should be noted that when an employee or officer is of a sufficient status in a company to be held to be acting as the company's *alter ego*, then the defence will not be available.[339]

The second branch of the defence is that the accused must prove that, in addition to

---

[332] *ibid* s 10(4).
[333] Crafted in consultation with the Health and Safety Commission: *ibid* s 11(5).
[334] *ibid* ss 13 and 14.
[335] *ibid* s 17.
[336] See Chapter 14.
[337] TDA, s 24.
[338] [1972] AC 153.
[339] This issue of corporate crime is a difficult and, particularly in Scotland, an underdeveloped area of the law—see *Clydesdale* v *Co-op Society* 1937 JC 17; *Purcell Meats (Scotland) Ltd* v *McLeod* 1987 SLT 528.

the intervention by "another person", he took all reasonable precautions and "due diligence" to avoid the offence being committed. In the *Tesco* case, it was sufficient that Tesco had policies and practices in place intended to avoid commission of the offence.

Tesco Supermarkets can be compared to *Ford* v *Guild*,[340] where it was held that the defence did not apply. In this case, a car dealer was charged with supplying a vehicle to which a false trade description had been applied. The mileage as stated on the car's mileometer was 32,257 miles, whereas the actual mileage of the car was in excess of 72,000 miles. The dealer offered the defence to the charge that the mileage was obtained from the previous owner, Dalrymple, who had in turn provided information as to the person from whom he had bought the car. It transpired that the information related to a fictitious person. The car dealer was found guilty as, although it was not disputed that they had relied on the advice of another person (Dalrymple), they had not exercised all due diligence by checking out the details he provided to them.

Consumer Protection Act 1987, Part III

It is a criminal offence for a person in the course of a business to provide misleading information to consumers about the prices at which goods, services, accommodation or other facilities may be available.[341] The provisions therefore relate not only to shops but also to hotels, restaurants, and those who offer services in the course of business. Indeed, the Act specifically provides that "services and facilities" encompasses credit, banking and insurance services; foreign currency exchanges; electricity supply; off-road and caravan parking facilities; and, as a general catch-all, "the provision of services".[342]   **8–105**

This information may be verbal or made in writing. The test is an objective one, although certain guidance is given in the Consumer Protection Act 1987 as to what will amount to a misleading statement. An understatement of the price will amount to misleading information; as will be the case if the price fails to include additional charges (for example, a service charge) or provide all relevant information that may have a bearing on the price.[343]

Those whose businesses are subject to the relevant provisions can refer to a Code of Practice which is designed to provide practical guidance on best practice and the avoidance of prosecution.[344] The code is not legally binding, although failure to adhere to its provisions may be used as evidence in a subsequent prosecution.

The Consumer Protection Act 1987 sets out various defences available to those who contravene the provisions. The main general defence mirrors that available in respect of contravention of the Trade Descritpions Act 1968—that the offence was committed either by or upon the reliance of another person, and all "due diligence" had been exercised in avoiding commission of the offence.[345] Other specific defences are also available: that the accused had acted in accordance with the Code of Practice[346]; that

---

[340] 1990 SLT 502.
[341] CPA, s 20(1).
[342] *ibid* s 20.
[343] *ibid* s 21.
[344] Consumer Protection (Code of Practice for Traders on Price Indications) Approval Order 1988 (SI 1988/2078).
[345] CPA, s 39.
[346] *ibid* s 25(2).

information has been published in newspaper articles as opposed to adverts (and therefore is not subject to the CPA's provisions)[347]; that a publisher of a newspaper did not know and had no reasonable grounds for suspecting that adverts in the newspaper were misleading[348]; that in the case of a supplier, the product was advertised in the reasonable belief that those who sold the goods would comply with a price recommended by him.[349]

HIRE OF GOODS

8–106   The fundamental difference between a sale of goods and a hire of goods is that in the latter there is no intention to transfer ownership of the goods from the lessor. The purpose of the contract of hire is to transfer possession of the property from one party (the "lessor") to the other party (the "hirer"), who is able to make use of the goods whilst in his possession. At the end of the period of hire, possession of the goods reverts back to the lessor. The law relating to hire in Scotland is derived from a mixed bag of statutory provisions and the common law. The most salient statutory provisions are the Supply of Goods and Services Act 1982 ("SGSA"), the Consumer Credit Act 1974 ("CCA"), the Unfair Contract Terms Act 1977 ("UCTA") and the Unfair Terms in Consumer Contracts Regulations 1994 ("UTCCR").[350]

The bulk of contracts of hire are regulated by the Consumer Credit Act 1974. The statutory terms cannot be contracted out of but they apply only to certain hire agreements known as "consumer hire agreements". A consumer hire agreement is one where the hirer is a consumer. "Consumer" is interpreted in a somewhat creative fashion, however, in that in this context the term encompasses not only private individuals but also sole traders and partnerships (although not limited companies).[351] The term of hire must not be less than three months and payments of the hirer should not amount to more than £15,000.[352]

If the hire agreement is deemed a consumer hire agreement, then the consumer is entitled to various forms of statutory protection. Adverts and quotations must disclose the "true" costs of the hire.[353] The terms and conditions of the hire agreement must be in writing and set out in an appropriate manner.[354] Copies must be available to the hirer and both parties' rights under the agreement must be made explicit.[355] If the requisite information has not been disclosed or the contract is not in the proper form, the hire agreement is deemed to have been improperly executed, which has the effect that its terms can only be enforced by the lessor (for example, to repossess goods from the hirer) by obtaining an order from the sheriff court.[356]

---

[347] *ibid* s 24(2).
[348] *ibid* s 24(3).
[349] *ibid* s 24(4).
[350] SI 1994/3159.
[351] CCA, s 189(1).
[352] *ibid* s 15.
[353] *ibid* ss 44 and 52.
[354] As determined by regulations crafted by the Secretary of State for Trade and Industry.
[355] CCA, s 63.
[356] *ibid* ss 65 and 189(1).

Prior to the hire agreement taking effect, the hirer may be entitled to a "cooling off period" of five clear days after signing the agreement within which he may change his mind and cancel the hire. This provision is only of effect, however, where face to face negotiations have preceded the signing of the agreement and the hirer has signed the agreement in a place other than the hirer's business premises.[357] If the hirer wishes to cancel the agreement, he should intimate this in writing to the lessor. The effect of the cancellation is to free the hirer from any further obligations; goods must be returned to the lessor and any hire payments made returned to the hirer.[358]

IMPLIED TERMS

Various terms are incorporated into hire contracts by the Supply of Goods and Services Act 1982. In many senses these terms mirror the implied terms that the Sale and Supply of Goods Act 1994 implies into contracts for the sale of goods. Thus, the lessor warrants that he has good title to the goods,[359] that the hirer will enjoy "quiet possession" of the goods,[360] that the goods conform to the description,[361] that where the goods have been hired by sample, that the sample conforms to the bulk,[362] and that the goods are of satisfactory quality and are fit for their purpose.[363]
    8-107

In common with sales of goods, the implied terms relating to quality and fitness are to be measured against a reasonable standard, taking into account such issues as hire costs and how the goods have been described. Again, in common with sales of goods, no claim in respect of defective goods can be made where goods have been examined by the hirer and such examination ought to have revealed the defects.[364]

Under the common law, the goods should be in adequate order to be used by the hirer for the life of the agreement.[365] If repairs are required, however, the costs of these will fall to the lessor except to the extent that damage to the goods has been the fault of the hirer. In a like fashion to contracts for the sale of goods, a lessor may incur strict liability under the Consumer Protection Act 1987 where defective goods hired[366] cause personal injury or damage to property.[367] A lessor who supplies goods which breach safety regulations laid down by the Secretary of State may also incur criminal and civil liability in the same way as a seller under the 1987 Act.[368]

Contracts of hire are also subject to the Unfair Contract Terms Act 1977.[369] As a result, the lessor is unable to contract out of the provisions relating to liability for personal death or injury resulting from the use of hired goods.[370] Clauses seeking

---

[357] CCA, s 68.
[358] *ibid* ss 67–73.
[359] SGSA, s 11H(1)(a).
[360] *ibid* s 11H(2); subject to the lessor's right to repossess goods where the hirer is in default—see para 8–109.
[361] *ibid* s 11I.
[362] *ibid* s 11K.
[363] *ibid* s 11J.
[364] *ibid* ss 11J (2)–(4).
[365] Bell's *Commentaries* i, 482.
[366] CPA, s 3—see para 8–101 for a discussion of defects.
[367] *ibid* s 2(1). Damage to business property cannot be claimed. In common with a sale, the lessor can avoid paying damages if he identifies the manufacturer.
[368] *ibid* s 12 and 41.
[369] UCTA, s 15(2)(a).
[370] *ibid* s 16(1)(a).

exclusion or limitation in respect of the lessor's liability for breach of duties will be enforceable only to the extent that they are "fair and reasonable".[371]

Further consumer protection is available in the guise of the terms of the Unfair Terms in Consumer Contracts Regulations 1994.[372] Under the UTCCR, any consumer hire agreement which has not been individually negotiated requires to meet the Regulations' test of fairness. In the same fashion as contracts of sale, such agreements may be nullified by the courts where the contract is one-sided and has not been made in good faith.[373]

HIRER'S LIABILITY

8–108   At common law, the hirer is bound to pay his charges as set out in the agreement, or, if there is no agreement as to the charge, a reasonable amount. If goods are faulty or defective, then the hirer has a right at common law to make reduced payments which reflect the limited enjoyment he is receiving from use of the goods.[374] The hirer is expected to take reasonable care in respect of the goods. This would not render the hirer liable for general "wear and tear" except perhaps in the case where he "overuses" the goods.[375]

TERMINATION OF THE AGREEMENT

8–109   There are detailed provisions relating to termination of the hire agreement set out in the Consumer Credit Act 1974. The hirer has a general right to terminate the agreement ahead of any agreed hire period.[376] The right will only exist after the first 18-month period of the agreement has elapsed.[377] Generally speaking, notice will depend on how often payments are due under the contract—if payments are made every month by the hirer, then the minimum notice will be one month. If the contract exceeds £900 a year, the notice provisions of the CCA are excluded. If the hire agreement does not fall under the auspices of the CCA provisions, then the common law will dictate that the hirer must provide the notice provided for in the contract, or if no notice is specified, he may provide reasonable notice.

The lessor may also terminate the agreement in circumstances where the hirer is in breach of the agreement. Prior to termination, the lessor must serve the hirer with a default notice set out in a statutory form, giving the hirer an opportunity to remedy his default.[378] If the hirer does not comply with the notice, then the lessor may take steps to recover his goods within seven days.[379] This may require a court order if the hirer does not consent to the lessor entering his premises.[380]

The hirer may be entitled to some financial compensation when the lessor

---

[371] *ibid* s 16(1)(b).
[372] SI 1994/3159.
[373] UTCCR, reg 4.1.
[374] Bell's *Principles*, s 143.
[375] See *Seton* v *Paterson* (1880) 8 R 236.
[376] CCA, s 101(7).
[377] Unless the parties dictate otherwise.
[378] CCA, ss 87–89.
[379] Where the court deems it just, it may extend the seven-day period.
[380] CCA, s 92.

repossesses the goods if the court deems it just given the payments that the hirer has already made.

HIRE PURCHASE

A hire-purchase agreement differs from a hire in the sense that it affords the oppor- **8–110** tunity for property in the goods to pass to the hirer. Hire-purchase agreements are in essence forms of credit under which the costs of purchasing goods are spread over a period of time by means of regular hire payments followed by an option to purchase by the payment of an additional sum laid down in the contract. Hire-purchase agreements are covered by the Consumer Credit Act 1974 if the value of payments to be made do not exceed £15,000 and the hirer is either an individual, partnership, unincorporated club, society or charitable body. Incorporated companies are excluded.

In common with other consumer credit agreements, certain statutory protection exists under the CCA for the hirer—the hirer is entitled to receive certain prescribed information regarding the agreement in adverts and quotations, full disclosure of each parties' rights must be made in the agreement and this agreement must be in writing and in an approved form.[381] If the agreement is not in the correct form, it will be deemed improperly executed and enforceable only through application to the sheriff court.[382]

In addition, hirers are protected in the sense that similar statutory terms to those applicable to contracts of sale and contracts of hire are implied into hire-purchase contracts by the Supply of Goods (Implied Terms) Act 1973 ("SOGITA"): that is that the hirer enjoys quiet possession of the goods; that the lessor has a right to sell the goods when the relevant conditions allowing the sale have been fulfilled; that the goods correspond with the description (if hired by description) and that they are of satisfactory quality.[383] Any attempt to contract out of the implied terms relating to description and quality will be rendered void in relation to a consumer contract.[384] In other contracts the contracting out must be "fair and reasonable".[385] A breach of any of the implied terms in a consumer contract is treated as material and will bestow upon the hirer a general right to reject the goods and claim damages.[386]

Termination

In contracts regulated by the Consumer Credit Act 1974, the hirer may terminate the **8–111** contract at any time before final payment is due.[387] Generally, if the hirer has paid less than 50 per cent of the total amount payable for the goods, he must compensate the lessor up to this value. This value may be varied by the court, however, to take account of actual losses of the lessor.[388]

For contracts governed by the CCA, in a similar fashion to hire agreements, the hirer must be given seven days' notice by the lessor before the contract can be terminated.

---

[381] *ibid* ss 60 and 61.
[382] *ibid* s 61.
[383] SOGITA, ss 8–10.
[384] UCTA, s 25(1).
[385] *ibid* s 20; discussed in more detail in relation to hire contracts at para 8–107.
[386] SOGITA, s 12A.
[387] CCA, s 99.
[388] CCA, s 100(3) and (4).

If the hirer has paid more than 30 per cent of the value of the goods, however, they become protected in the sense that a court order is required by the lessor before he can repossess the goods. In such a case the lessor needs to petition the court for a "return order" for the goods to be returned to him.

In order to guard against inequities that might arise when hirers have already made significant payments in respect of goods that the lessor seeks to repossess, the court may issue a "time order" under which the court can make orders to reschedule payments if it deems it just to do so.[389] Additionally, a court may issue a "transfer order" under which some goods may be transferred to the lessor and others kept by the hirer in view of the payments he has already made in their respect.

INSURANCE

INTRODUCTION

8–112 The insurance industry is a vibrant and dynamic sphere of business. Indeed, there are very few aspects to modern life where insurance does not have its part to play—for example, insurance can help protect against the repercussions of theft of possessions, car accidents, accidents at work, risk in carriage of goods, inability to make mortgage and credit card payments, and death itself. Given the prevalence and importance of insurance, it may be of some surprise that this is not an area of law regulated by any great measure of legislation; insurance contracts are largely underpinned by the common law, although certain statutory provisions are of some import.[390]

In basic terms, insurance contracts are intrinsically concerned with providing safeguards in the event of some sort of misfortune. Valuable rights accrue under an insurance policy, thus having the effect that an insurance policy can itself be viewed as incorporeal moveable property.

Although there is no statutory definition, in legal terms an insurance contract can be said to arise where one person (known as the "insurer") in return for a payment (known as a "premium") agrees to take on the financial or other consequences (known as "risk") which result from an uncertain event that may befall either the person paying the premium ("the insured") or that person's property at or before a specified time, which may result in the insurer making a monetary payment or granting some other sort of compensation to the insured.

THE LEGAL BACKDROP TO INSURANCE CONTRACTS

8–113 As has been stated, insurance contracts are primarily regulated by the common law. The Marine Insurance Act 1906 is of some importance, however, in that it served to codify and recast much of the common law relating to marine insurance. Although other forms of insurance were not tackled by the Act, the courts have tended through time to interpret other forms of insurance with reference to standard marine insurance

---

[389] *ibid* s 129.
[390] Including the Marine Insurance Act 1906 ("MIA"), the Insurance Brokers (Registration) Act 1977, the Insurance Companies Act 1982 and the Financial Services Act 1986.

contracts. As such, therefore, the law relating to marine insurance has had a significant impact on the development of insurance law in general.[391]

Significantly, insurance contracts are not subject to the protective measures set out in the Unfair Contract Terms Act 1977.[392] Protection is provided for insurers, however, in the form of self-regulatory guidelines and codes of practice issued by the insurance industry. The majority of insurers belong to the Association of British Insurers, a regulatory body which issues guidelines that members are bound to follow: The "Statement of General Insurance Practice" (dealing with indemnity cover for losses to property) and the "Statement of Long-Term Insurance Practice" (in respect of life cover). These guidelines are far-reaching and in fact provide more stringent controls on insurers than is provided by the general law. In particular, the guidelines stipulate that in relation to situations where the insured is a private individual, the insurance companies agree to waive certain legal rights. Where insured parties are themselves commercial concerns, insurance companies are entitled to enforce the full extent of their legal rights.[393]

The Insurance Companies Act 1982 provides the general regulatory framework for the insurance industry. In plain terms, the Act in effect delegates control of the industry to the Department of Trade and Industry (DTI). Any person seeking to engage in insurance services in the UK must first be granted authorisation by the DTI, which requires to be satisfied both that the individuals running the organisation are proper and fit persons for that purpose and that the business will be run in an efficient and effective manner. The DTI then assumes a monitoring role to ensure, *inter alia*, that insurance organisations remain solvent to a specified degree to ensure that insurers can meet policy claims from insured parties.[394]

In the event that insurers cannot meet policy claims from insured parties, all is not lost for uncompensated parties in the sense that the Policyholders Protection Board, a body set up under the auspices of the Secretary of State for Trade and Industry,[395] may indemnify or otherwise assist policyholders who have been adversely affected by the insurance companies' inability to pay out claims.

Complaints relating to the conduct of insurance companies in relation to policy claims or issues relating to the marketing or administration of claims are handled by the Insurance Ombudsman Bureau, an investigative body established in 1981, of which the vast majority of insurance companies are members. In relation to issues relating to life insurance and investment issues, complaints are handled by an equivalent body, the Personal Investment Authority Ombudsman, created in 1994.

FORMATION AND TERMS OF THE INSURANCE CONTRACT

The general view in relation to insurance contracts is that they need not be in writing and, subject to proof, may be constituted orally.[396] Generally speaking, insurance

8–114

---

[391] See, *eg*, *Thomson v Weems* (1884) 9 App Cas 671, per Lord Blackburn at 684.

[392] UCTA, s 15(3)(a)(i).

[393] The main rights waived are discussed at para 8–118.

[394] Insurance Brokers (*ie* intermediaries) are regulated by the Insurance Brokers (Registration) Act 1977 and the Financial Services Act 1986.

[395] Under the Policyholders Protection Act 1975 (as amended).

[396] Bell, *Commentaries*, i, 653; *Christie v North British Insurance Co* (1825) 3 S 519 and *Parker & Co (Sandbank) Ltd v Western Assurance Co* 1925 SLT 131. However, a marine insurance contract is inadmissible in evidence if it is not in writing: MIA, s 22.

contracts are formed on standardised contracts that set out the terms upon which the insurance company is offering insurance, and which require to be completed by those seeking insurance by filling in the form with relevant details. In legal terms, the completion and posting of an insurance form to the insurer represents an offer which the insurance company is then free to accept or reject. It many cases, of course, the insurer will issue a conditional acceptance (which is effectively a counter offer) and issue insurance subject to clarification of any moot points and receipt of a premium or deposit.

Many agreements are, of course, initially entered into over the telephone, prior to any written agreement. Difficulty may arise here in the sense that a question can be posed as to whether consensus has been reached over the contract terms, because the insured may not be aware of the insurer's standard contract terms. This problem can be alleviated by holding that the telephone call has been sufficient to reach agreement on the essential elements of the contract: subject-matter, risk, premium, duration and sum insured.[397]

In some cases, in the first instance the insurer issues a "cover note" to an insured person. A cover note is a temporary contract of insurance which is issued pending the issue of the insurance policy. These are most prevalent where there is a legal requirement for insurance—for example, in the motor industry. The cover note, which will generally make reference to the insurer's standard conditions of insurance, represents evidence of the insurance concerned.

Implied terms at common law

8–115   An insurance contract is a contract *uberrimae fide*—that is one of the utmost good faith.[398] The insurance contract can be contrasted with other commercial contracts where parties are at "arm's length"—what this means is that although parties are under an obligation not to misrepresent any relevant facts to the other parties, there is no general duty to disclose information relevant to the contract. Insurance contracts, however, as contracts, *uberrimae fide*, are characterised by a duty of disclosure, and as such both the insured and the insurer are duty bound to observe this principle. Obviously, as in common with other contracts, any questions asked on the proposal form must be answered truthfully.[399] Given the trust inherent in the contract, the duty of disclosure is taken further, however, and extends to every material circumstance which the insured party is aware of.[400] The insurer is similarly bound to disclose all information known to him but not known to the insured which has the effect of reducing the risk.[401]

The duty of trust inherent in the contract means that the insured cannot wallow in his own ignorance; rather he is under an obligation to disclose any information that a small measure of research or common sense would have revealed and where that information would have been material to the insurer.[402] In *McPhee v Royal Insurance Co*

---

[397] Or see the analysis of the court in *General Accident Insurance Corp v Cronk* (1901) 17 TLR 233.
[398] See *Life Association of Scotland v Foster* (1873) 11 M 351.
[399] See *The Spathari* 1925 SC (HL) 6, where the Greek ownership of a ship was hidden.
[400] MIA, s 18(1).
[401] *Banque Financière de la Cité SA v Westgate Insurance Co* [1990] 1 QB 665 (CA).
[402] *McPhee v Royal Insurance Co Ltd* 1979 SC 304.

Ltd[403] the insured had provided incorrect dimensions of his boat, the dimensions being ascertained by telephoning the previous owner rather than by taking them himself. When the boat was subsequently destroyed, the insurance claim failed, *inter alia*, on the basis that the insured had not taken all due care and attention in providing accurate information, which in turn caused the insurer to be misled in a material sense. In addition to making reasonable efforts to uncover relevant information, the insured is deemed to be aware of issues of common knowledge in his particular business sphere.[404]

Information is deemed material if knowledge of that information would have a bearing on the insurer's risk. There is some discrepancy in Scotland as to how this test is gauged. In relation to life insurance it has been held that in judging whether or not information may in this sense be material, the test is that of a reasonable insured—that is would a reasonable insured person have deemed that information to be such as would affect his risk under the policy?[405] This can be contrasted with the position relating to indemnity contracts, where the test appears to be what the reasonable *insurer* would deem to be material.[406]

General matters, which may be deemed material, include previous convictions,[407] the occupation of the insured, general states of health, dangerous leisure activities, and previous claims. Certain matters not normally deemed to be material include those which actually diminish the insurer's risk, those facts which are common knowledge and those which are not relevant to the claim.

Duration of the duty to disclose

Once the contract has been entered into, generally speaking there is no continuing duty to disclose material facts.[408] Many insurance policies will dictate, however, that a material change in circumstances must be disclosed to the insurer, else the policy will fail. Similarly, if the insurance contract is renewed, the duty to disclose occurs again as each renewal is treated as a new contract.[409] **8–116**

Disclosure to insurance agents and brokers

Where disclosure is made through some form of intermediary, such as an insurance broker, the law is somewhat unclear as to whether such disclosure of a material matter amounts to disclosure to the insurers. Case law has suggested that if the broker can be deemed to have acted as the insurer's agent then a subsequent failure by the broker to pass on the information to the insurer will not render the policy void. This is on the basis that what is known to the agent is deemed to be known by his principal.[410] If, on the other hand, the broker is deemed to have been acting as agent for the insured, then a failure to pass on any material information to the insurer will render the policy void. **8–117**

---

[403] 1979 SC 304.
[404] MIA, s 18(1).
[405] *Life Association of Scotland v Foster* (1873) 11 M 351.
[406] *Hooper v Royal London General Insurance Co Ltd* 1993 SLT 679.
[407] *Hooper v Royal London General Insurance Co Ltd* 1993 SLT 679; unless convictions are "spent" under the Rehabilitation of Offenders Act 1974.
[408] *Banque Financière de la Cité SA v Westgate Insurance Co* [1990] 1 QB 665 (CA).
[409] See *Lambert v Co-operative Insurance Society Ltd* [1975] 2 Lloyd's Rep 485.
[410] *Stockton v Mason* [1978] 2 Lloyd's Rep 38; *Woolcot v Excess Insurance Co Ltd (No 2)* [1979] 1 Lloyd's Rep 210. See Chapter 6.

The following two cases assist in distinguishing between these two scenarios. In *Bawden v London, Edinburgh and Glasgow Assurance Co*[411] an insured party with one eye had disclosed information to an agent in good faith and with no intention to defraud. When the agent subsequently misrepresented facts to the insurance company (the insurance form stated that the insured party had no physical infirmity), he was deemed to be acting as agent for the insurance company and not the insured. The insurance company was therefore liable on the policy. By contrast, in *Newsholme Brothers v Road Transport and General Insurance Co Ltd*[412] an agent inserted false information on the insurance form. The insured party was aware of the inaccuracies, but signed the policy anyway. In this instance it was held that, given the facts, the broker had acted as agent for the insured and thus the insurance policy was void.

WARRANTIES

8–118   In plain terms, a warrant is a form of promise by an insured party that either a previous act has taken place or will take place and continue to take place in the future (or not take place as the case may be); or that a particular state of affairs endures. It is probably easier to explain what this means by example—for instance, in relation to car insurance, the insured may stipulate that the car will be kept overnight locked up in a garage and not parked in the street. Similarly, an insured may warrant that he is of a particular profession and has not previously been involved in an accident. In a life insurance policy, the insured may warrant that he is of sound health and that he does not and will not in the future take part in hobbies which could be considered dangerous.

No special form of words is required to create a warranty but it is in practice commonplace to use the term "warranty". What is necessary is that it is made clear that breach of the term will result in the policy being void. It is possible, although not common, in commercial insurance contracts to state that every item of information provided by the insured in the insurance proposal is to be treated as a warranty. This is achieved through a "basis of contract clause". This has the effect that any information provided by the insured that is revealed to be false will render the insurance policy void, even if such information could not *per se* be deemed to be material.[413] From the date of breach of the warranty, the insurer will incur no liability in respect of the policy.[414] The insurer will be responsible, however, in respect of contractual claims arising from incidents prior to the breach of warranty.[415]

Under the terms of the common law, it is of no consequence that there is no causal link between the breach of the warranty and the loss suffered by the insurer. In *Jones and James v Provisional Insurance Co Ltd*[416] an insurance policy contained the warranty that Jones' vehicle was to be kept in an efficient condition. This was not done and the vehicle was subsequently stolen. The insurer was not liable on the basis that the warranty had been breached, even though it could not be argued that the breach of

---

[411] [1892] 2 QB 534.
[412] [1929] 2 KB 356.
[413] *Unipac (Scotland) Ltd v Aegon Insurance Co (UK) Ltd* 1996 SLT 1197; *Dawsons Ltd v Bonnin* 1922 SC (HL) 156.
[414] MIA, s 33(3).
[415] *ibid*.
[416] [1929] 35 Ll L Rep 135.

warranty had caused the loss. It should be noted, however, that under the direction of self-regulating codes of the insurance industry, insurance companies accept that unless fraud is involved they will not refuse to pay claims where no causal link exists between a breach of warranty and the loss suffered.[417] In any case, it is possible for the insurer to waive the breach of warranty and allow the policy to remain valid.[418]

INTERPRETING INSURANCE CONTRACTS

The general rule in relation to insurance contracts is that any words used in the **8–119** contract will be given their common normal meaning unless a contrary meaning is expressly provided for.[419] This general proposition is augmented by the *contra preferentem* rule, which stipulates that any ambiguity in the insurance contract should be construed against the party seeking to rely upon the ambiguous clause (such a party is known as the *"proferens"* and is most likely to be the insurance company).[420]

PROXIMATE CAUSE

In order to make a valid claim under the insurance contract, the insured must illustrate **8–120** that any loss or damage is the result of an insured peril (that is a cause of damage covered in the policy). When loss or damage results from any other cause which is not insured against under the policy, the insurer is not liable.[421] At first, this rule may appear clear cut. Problems may arise, however, where it is difficult to determine the cause of the loss or damage. In particular, there may be instances where there is more than one cause of the loss. In such a situation the court would need to determine what the proximate (dominant) cause of the loss was. If the proximate cause is an insured peril then a claim will be valid; if this is not the case, the claim will fail.

In *Leyland Shipping Co Ltd* v *Norwich Union Fire Insurance Society*,[422] a marine insurance policy relating to a ship expressly excluded liability for damage caused by wartime hostilities. The ship was torpedoed and towed to a port, but amidst concerns that she might sink and block the harbour, the ship was required to anchor outside the harbour. At low tide the ship became grounded, took in water and sank. In a claim by the insured party in respect of the loss of the vessel, the court ruled that the proximate cause of the sinking was in fact the torpedo damage and not the grounding of the ship; hence no claim could be made, as war damage was not an insured peril.[423]

INSURABLE INTEREST

It has long been a principle of insurance law that before a valid insurance claim can be **8–121** made, the insured requires to hold an insurable interest in the subject of the

---

[417] See the Association of British Insurers' Guidelines, "Statement of General Insurance Practice" and "Statement of Long-Term Insurance Practice".
[418] MIA, s 34(3).
[419] *Scragg* v *UK Temperance and General Provident Institution* [1976] 2 Lloyd's Rep 227.
[420] *Kennedy* v *Smith and Ansvar Insurance Co Ltd* 1976 SLT 110.
[421] MIA, s 55(1).
[422] [1918] AC 350 (HL).
[423] See also *Wayne Tank and Pump Co Ltd* v *Employers' Liability Assurance Corpn Ltd* [1974] QB 57 (CA), where there were two causes of the loss (one an insured peril and the other excluded) and it was not possible to determine which was the proximate cause. In this case, no claim could be made.

insurance.[424] The most obvious interest is that the insured is the owner of the subject of the insurance.[425] The insurable interest may be one which falls short of full ownership, however, such as that of a lessee (one who leases property) or the holder of a right in security in property.[426] Particular problems may arise in relation to property which is owned by registered companies. Even though he may hold all of the shares in a company, a shareholder has himself no insurable interest in company property. This is because the company, as a separate legal entity, owns property in its own name. Any such insurance, therefore, must be in the company's name.[427]

In the context of life insurance, it is possible to hold an insurable interest in the life of another. The interest must be pecuniary (financial) in nature—in the sense that one party benefits financially from the continued existence of another. So, for example, an employee may have an insurable interest in his employer's life,[428] a creditor may have an interest (up to the amount of his debt) in the life of his debtor,[429] and those with an obligation to provide aliment—that is husband and wife—each have an insurable interest in the other's life.[430]

INDEMNITY AND SUBROGATION

Indemnity

8–122   It is a general principle of indemnity insurance contracts that parties are to be put in the position in which they would have been had the loss not occurred. This has the effect that compensation with regard to destroyed property will be made commensurate to what the goods were in fact worth rather than what the goods were insured for.[431] It should be noted that this principle can be amended by making express provision to the contrary in various forms, including: the "agreed value policy", which stipulates that an agreed sum will be paid out in respect of the loss of assets which are difficult to value in advance; a "reinstatement value policy" where the insurer pays out a sum sufficient to replace the property in the condition it was in before loss occurred; "excess" clauses, a common feature of insurance contracts, which stipulate that the insured must meet a certain amount of the claim. (This is designed to discourage a careless disposition on the part of the insured in relation to the property.)

Subrogation

8–123   Subrogation arises by operation of the common law in situations where it is possible for the insured party to make a claim for loss from both the insurer and a third party who has in some way been at fault for the damage. This is common in the case of car accidents: if X's car is damaged as a result of a car crash with Y and Y was at fault, then X would have a claim for damages for losses caused by Y's negligence. Similarly, X

---

[424] *eg*, under the Life Assurance Act 1774.
[425] *Arif* v *Excess Insurance Group Ltd* 1987 SLT 473.
[426] *Fehilly* v *General Accident Fire and Life Assurance Corp* 1983 SLT 141.
[427] *Macaura* v *Northern Assurance Co Ltd* [1925] AC 619; *Mitchell* v *Scottish Eagle Insurance* 1997 SLT 793; *Cowan* v *Jeffrey Associates* 1998 SC 496.
[428] *Hebdon* v *West* (1863) 3 B & S 579.
[429] *Lindsay* v *Barncotte* (1851) 13 D 718.
[430] *Wight* v *Brown* (1849) 11 D 459.
[431] *Hercules Insurance Co* v *Hunter* (1836) 14 S 1137.

could also seek indemnity for the damage from his insurance company. It is clearly inequitable for the insured to be able to recover monies in respect of the loss twice. Subrogation allows the insurer to indemnify the insured and then step into the insured's position to recover its losses from the other third party.[432]

ASSIGNATION OF POLICY

There is a presumption that an insurance policy is assignable unless there is a stipulation to the contrary. The mere transfer of the subject of the policy does not, however, amount to assignation[433]; the assignation must be in writing and intimation to this effect must be made to the insurance company.[434]   **8–124**

Assignation occurs mainly in the context of life insurance (or "life assurance", where a payment is guaranteed by the insurer if the insured does not die within the life of the policy), where the rights arising from a policy are transferred to a third party (known as the "assignee"). The assignee may sue the insurance company under the policy in his own name[435]; however, the insurance company may make use of any defence which would be relevant in respect of the original insured party. Thus, if false statements were made on the proposal by the insured party, this may act as a bar to the assignee making a claim.[436]

BANKRUPTCY OF POLICY HOLDER

Under the common law, generally speaking, when the policy holder becomes bankrupt any sum due under the insurance passes to the trustee in sequestration.[437] A statutory exception to this rule exists, however, in relation to cases where the insurance serves to protect against liability arising from injury to third parties. Where   **8–125** an insured party has become bankrupt,[438] his rights under the policy will transfer to the person who has been injured, whether the injury occurred prior to or after the bankruptcy.[439]

ADDITIONAL COMMENTS

The above discussion has been confined to some of the basic legal provisions relating to insurance contracts generally. There are various detailed provisions which relate to particular species of insurance, such as life insurance, motor insurance, maritime insurance and fire insurance. A discussion of these can be found in some of the reading   **8–126** listed at the end of this chapter.

---

[432] The insurer must make good the insured's claim before subrogation can take place: *Page* v *Scottish Insurance Corp* (1929) 33 Ll L Rep 134.

[433] MIA, s 50.

[434] Transmission of Moveable Property (Scotland) Act 1862.

[435] Policies of Assurance Act 1867, s 1.

[436] *Scottish Equitable* v *Buist* (1877) 4 R 1076.

[437] See Chapter 9.

[438] Or has made a composition with his creditors or, in the case of a company, entered into receivership, winding-up or a voluntary arrangement (see Chapter 11).

[439] Third Parties (Rights against Insurers) Act 1930 (as amended).

NEGOTIABLE INSTRUMENTS

The term negotiable instruments refers to various methods by which payment of a debt can be made without recourse to cash or modern forms of electronic transfer of funds. The law relating to these forms of payment—bills of exchange, cheques and promissory notes—is underpinned by the Bills of Exchange Act 1882 ("BOEA").[440] These forms of payment can themselves be categorised as incorporeal moveable
8–127 property.

BILLS OF EXCHANGE

The primary form of negotiable instrument is the bill of exchange, which can be defined as "an unconditional order in writing, addressed by one person to another, signed by the person giving it, requiring the person to whom it is addressed to pay on demand or at a fixed or determinable future time a sum certain in money, or to the order of a specified person or to bearer".[441]
8–128   Bills of exchange developed out of the customary European trade laws as a way to facilitate payment of cross-border debts. If, for example, merchant A in Edinburgh owed a debt to a merchant B in Paris and merchant A was himself owed money by another merchant C in Paris, then he could make payment to merchant B by transferring the right to claim payment of his debt from merchant C. To carry this out, he would send instructions to merchant B to make payment of the debt to merchant C.

This method of payment remains a mystery to the majority of members of the public because in the main their use is confined to the context of international trade. In fact, since the advent of bank accounts, bills of exchange are far less widely employed and are to a great extent obsolete in the context of domestic trade. It should be noted that the vast majority of the public do in fact make use of a special form of bill of exchange in the form of cheques.

Negotiability

The concept of negotiability is of particular import as it relates to the fact that the bill (and thus the right to receive payment of the debt) "stands on its own feet" and may be transferred from one party to another much in the same way as cash. This sets the bill of exchange apart from other forms of incorporeal moveable property such as insurance policies—benefits thereunder can be assigned only when accompanied by
8–129 intimation of the assignment to the insurance company. In addition, the assignee gains no better right to payment from the insurance company than the cedent (the party who assigned the policy) had. Thus, if the policy was voidable on the basis of a breach of warranty of the policy holder, the policy is also voidable in the hands of the assignee.

Negotiable instruments, however, require no such assignation or intimation to the debtor. The document may be payable to the "bearer" (whomsoever that may be at any given time), and the mere physical transfer of the document is normally sufficient to give the transferee good title to the debt. If payment is made to a specified person

---

[440] More recent amendments in relation to cheques include the Cheques Act 1957 and the Cheques Act 1992.
[441] BOEA, s 3.

(known as a "payee") then he may transfer it to another party by indorsing (signing) the bill and delivering it to that other party.[442] Additionally, provided that the transferee takes the document in good faith, he will gain good title; it is of no consequence that the transferor himself did not hold good title.

Terms relating to bills

The terminology relating to bills of exchange can be confusing at times. The person who instructs the bill is known as the "drawer". The instruction is known as the "order", with the process of seeking payment of a debt in this fashion being termed "drawing the bill" on the person from whom payment is sought—the "drawee". (although when he accepts the bill[443] he becomes known as the "acceptor"). The party to whom payment should be made is known as the "payee", although he is free to transfer the bill to another and thus would no longer be entitled to payment. If a bill is   8–130
merely made out to "bearer", then that will be whomsoever has the bill in his possession and is seeking payment.[444]

Unconditional nature of bill

The bill must be unconditional in the sense that no conditions are attached to the right to obtain payment—the amount payable must be readily identifiable and at a fixed or determinable time. If this is not the case, then the document cannot be viewed as a Bill of Exchange.

Indorsement

When a bill is payable to a specified "payee", he may transfer the bill by signing his   8–131
name on the bill (known as "indorsement") and delivering the bill to another party. If the payee seeks to transfer the bill to a specific person, say "John Doe", then this can be denoted by adding the words "pay John Doe" and delivering the bill to that person. This can be termed as a special indorsement and has the effect that the bill can only be transferred to that specific person, although the indorsee may in turn transfer the bill to another. The negotiability of the bill can be limited by the payee if he indorses the   8–132
bill, "pay John Doe only". This has the effect that if the bill is transferred by John Doe to another then that person will only obtain as good a title to the bill as John Doe had.

Bills made to bearer can be transferred without the requirement of any signatures.[445] If a bill payable to order (to a specified payee) is transferred without indorsement then it becomes a bill to bearer and is treated as such.[446] A bearer bill is risky in the sense that if it is stolen the thief may be able to obtain payment and the victim of the theft would be unable to take payment. A recipient of a "blank indorsed bill" can gain some protection by inserting his own name where it should have been inserted by the indorser with the effect that the bill becomes a special indorsement.[447]

The indorser of the bill becomes liable to the indorsee in the event that the bill is not honoured. Given the fact that the bill stands on its own, it is of no consequence in

---

[442] See para 8–132.
[443] See para 8–133.
[444] BOEA, s 31(2).
[445] *ibid* s 31(2).
[446] *ibid* s 34(1)

terms of the indorser's liability that previous indorsers' signatures were forged or irregular in some way,[448] or that he did not have a valid title to the bill in any case.[449]

Liability for the debt

A drawee can only become liable on a bill from the time that he accepts it. If the bill is to be paid on demand then the drawee must make immediate payment. If he fails to do so then the bill is "dishonoured" and the drawer becomes liable. It usual, however, for the bill to be payable at some future specified date known as a "maturity date" which means that the drawee must "accept" the bill. Acceptance is generally denoted **8–133**   by the drawee signing his name on the bill, along with the words "accepted", at which point the drawee becomes known as the "acceptor". At the time of acceptance, the drawee becomes the principal debtor under the bill.

To summarise the strands of liability for the debt set out on the bill:

- *before acceptance by the drawee*—the drawer is the principal debtor, then any indorsers, who are liable among themselves in the order in which their names appear on the bill

- *after the bill has been accepted by the drawee*—the drawee is the principal debtor, then the drawer, then the indorsers in the order in which their names appear on the bill.

It should be noted that the above sets out how liability is regulated as between the potentially liable parties; the holder of the bill is entitled to demand payment from any of the parties who may be held liable on the bill.

The holder

When a bill is transferred by a payee to another by indorsement and delivery (or delivery if the payee is "bearer"), that person is known as the "holder". The holder is entitled to present the bill to the acceptor for payment.[450] Any holder is entitled to sue for payment but if there is some defect in the title then the holder may find it impossible to assert his claim. In order for the bill to stand on its own and the holder **8–134**   to gain good title to the debt notwithstanding any defect in his title, the holder must be both a "holder for value" and a "holder in due course".

A holder for value is one who has made payment for the bill.[451] This stems from the fact that the English common law rule of contract requires some form of consideration or payment. Although not a rule which is part of Scots common law,[452] under the Bills of Exchange Act 1882, consideration would also be required in Scotland for the holder to gain the valuable rights in respect of enforcement of the bill.[453]

A holder in due course is one who holds in the following circumstances: the bill is prima facie regular and complete in that it appears to have been properly executed[454]; the debt under the bill is not overdue[455]; the bill has been acquired by the holder in

---

[447] *ibid* s 34(4).
[448] *ibid* s 52(2)(b).
[449] *ibid* s 52(2)(c).
[450] *ibid* s 45(3).
[451] *ibid* s 27(1) and (2).
[452] See Chapter 4.

good faith[456]; and the holder was unaware of any previous dishonour of the bill or any defect in the title of the previous holder (or indorser) who transferred the bill to him.[457]

Dishonour of bill

If the bill is dishonoured by the acceptor then the holder may claim against the drawer, who himself has a right of relief against the acceptor.[458] The holder has an option of claiming against the party who transferred the bill to him (the indorser), who in turn may claim against the acceptor, or the drawer or the person who transferred the bill to him. If a bill is dishonoured either for acceptance or for payment, the holder may have the bill "noted and protested" before a notary public, which has the effect that it allows the holder to exercise diligence proceedings such as arrestment or poinding[459] in an effort to obtain payment.

8–135

Forgeries and alterations

The forgery of a signature has the effect that the person whose signature has been forged is free from liability.[460] The holder in due course cannot enforce the bill against that person, although an acceptor cannot refuse to pay a bill on the basis that the drawer's signature has been forged.[461] Again, where the payee is fictitious the holder is protected as such a bill can be presented for payment as a "bearer bill".[462]

Where the terms of a bill are altered to a material extent, without the consent of all parties to it, the bill becomes voidable. The party who altered the bill and any other party who knew of the alteration and took no steps to disclose this, will be liable on the bill. A holder in due course, unaware of the alteration (and where such alteration is not readily noticeable), will be able make a claim in respect of the bill.[463] Immaterial alterations have no effect on the validity of the bill.[464]

8–136

Discharge

As logic would dictate, bills are discharged when they are paid by the drawee (in the case of bills payable on demand) or the acceptor. If the acceptor becomes the holder, then the bill is also discharged.[465] A holder may also renounce his right to enforce payment (this must be done in writing[466]) or cancel the bill.[467] In any case, a bill of exchange will prescribe after five years.[468]

8–137

---

[453] The fact that value has been given for the bill is, however, assumed: *Law v Humphrey* (1875) 3 R 1192 at 1193; BOEA, s 30(1).
[454] BOEA, s 29(1).
[455] *ibid* s 36(2).
[456] *ibid* s 90(1). It is a rebuttable presumption that the holder took in good faith: *ibid* s 30(2).
[457] *ibid* ss 36(5) and 125(4).
[458] *ibid* s 57(1).
[459] See para 8–45.
[460] BOEA, s 24.
[461] *ibid* s 54(2).
[462] *ibid* s 7(3).
[463] *ibid* s 64(1).
[464] Immaterial alterations include: the insertion of a date (*ibid* s 12); the conversion of a blank indorsement into a special indorsement (*ibid* s 34(4)); crossing a cheque *ibid* (s 77).
[465] *ibid* s 61.

CHEQUES AND PROMISSORY NOTES

Special forms of bills of exchange include cheques and promissory notes. A cheque is a particular form of bill which is payable on demand (although some may be post-dated). The drawer is the person who writes the cheque, the drawee is the bank, and the payee the person to whom the money is paid.

8–138

A promissory note is an unconditional assurance by one party to another that at a given time he will pay a fixed fee to a designated party (or such other party as the designated party stipulates).

---

[466] *ibid* s 62.

[467] *ibid* s 63(1).

[468] Prescription and Limitation (Scotland) Act 1973, s 6(1) and Sched 1, para 1(e).

SUMMARY

PROPERTY—OVERVIEW

- The term "property" may be used to refer to an item itself or ownership of that item.
- Moveable property may be corporeal (tangible) or non-corporeal (intangible), fungible (generic) or non-fungible (unique).
- A party in possession has a rebuttable presumption of ownership.

INTELLECTUAL PROPERTY RIGHTS

- Intellectual property rights are treated as incorporeal moveables. Some of the main rights include trade marks, patents and copyright.
- A trade mark is a mark which distinguishes a product from that of other manufacturers. Trade mark protection is provided under the Trade Mark Acts and also the common law.
- Patents are granted in respect of inventions. They bestow a monopoly right in respect of the invention on the patent holder.
- Certain creative works can be protected through copyright. Generally speaking, the copyright holder is granted exclusive rights to copy and make use of the work.

RIGHTS IN SECURITY

- A right in security is a real right held over property as collateral for a debt.
- The general rule of Scots law is that a security requires delivery (or its equivalent) of the subject of the security to the creditor.
- There are instances where security can be effected over moveables without delivery—hypothecs and floating charges. Most hypothecs arise by implication and allow a creditor to retain the property of a debtor. Floating charges are creatures of statute available primarily to limited companies and allow securities to be granted over their assets.
- Security over heritable property is effected by a standard security.
- There are various forms of security over moveables where delivery (or its equivalent) is required: assignation and intimation (incorporeal moveables); pledge, lien (corporeal moveables).

CAUTIONARY OBLIGATIONS

- A cautionary obligation is a guarantee that one party grants to another in respect of the debts of a third. This is a personal right rather than a real right.

DILIGENCE

- The term diligence is used to refer to various procedures which can be employed to "attach" the assets of another to enforce payment of a debt, usually after a court decree in respect of that debt, has been granted. The main forms are arrestment, diligence against earnings, poinding and inhibition.

- An arrestment order "freezes" moveable property of the debtor which is in the hands of a third party. An action of "furthcoming" is necessary to facilitate any necessary sale of the debtor's assets and the transfer of funds to the creditor.
- An order for diligence against earnings allows a creditor to "attach" a debtor's earnings in pursuance of a debt.
- A poinding order attaches to assets of the debtor in his possession. A creditor can apply to have such assets sold by way of a "warrant sale" and to receive payment from the proceeds.
- An inhibition is a form of diligence which can be exercised over heritable property. The inhibition order prevents the property from being sold or having a security granted over it.
- Other rarely employed forms of diligence include adjudication, poinding of the ground, maills and duties, and civil imprisonment.

SALE OF GOODS

- The term "goods" encompasses corporeal moveables but not incorporeal moveables or heritable property.
- Every sale of goods has a number of implied contractual terms. These include: the seller has good title to the goods sold; the goods correspond with their description; the goods are of satisfactory quality and the goods are fit for their purpose. There are stringent restrictions on the ability to contract out of these terms.
- When ownership of goods passes to the buyer he gains a real right in the goods.
- In the absence of express agreement, there are somewhat complex rules which govern the transfer of goods from the seller to the buyer. The result of these rules can be that on occasion ownership passes independently of payment or delivery.
- Generally speaking, risk of damage to goods passes at the time ownership passes.
- An unpaid seller has certain "real rights" over goods including "lien", "stoppage in transit" and "resale".
- Both parties may seek personal remedies for breach of contract against the other side. A seller may bring an action for the price, or sue for damages for non-acceptance. A buyer may claim damages for non-delivery, may seek specific performance of the contract or may reject the goods and claim damages.
- Manufacturers of defective goods may be liable in damages for losses caused by use of those goods under consumer protection legislation. Manufacturers of unsafe goods may also be subject to criminal sanctions.
- Those who apply false trade descriptions to goods may be held criminally liable.

HIRE OF GOODS

- A hire of goods occurs where one party transfers possession of goods to another party for a designated time in exchange for payment.
- "Consumer hire agreements" are protected under various pieces of legislation. A

consumer hire agreement is one where the term of hire must is not less than three months and payments of the hirer amount to no more than £15,000.

- To protect consumers, consumer hire agreements must be in a prescribed form and similar terms to those implied in contracts of sale apply.
- A hire purchase is a form of hire with a view to the hirer making a final payment and becoming the owner of the goods.

INSURANCE

- An insurance contract is one where one person ("the insurer") in return for payment agrees to take on the risk which may result from future events which may befall a person ("the insured") or his property.
- Insurance contracts are *uberrimae fidei* (of the utmost good faith) and characterised by a duty on the parties to disclose all relevant information. Insured parties must disclose all facts which would be material to the insured party's risk.
- Warranties are assurances given by insured parties to insurers that certain circumstances exist or that certain acts will take place in the future.
- Insured parties must hold an insurable (a financial) interest in the subject of the insurance.

NEGOTIABLE INSTRUMENTS

- A negotiable instrument is a method of payment by which one party agrees to pay another a fixed sum of money at a set time.
- The main form of negotiable instrument is the bill of exchange.
- Bills are negotiable in the sense that they can be transferred between parties and in a similar fashion to money, "stand on their own"—a party who obtains a bill in good faith will generally gain good title notwithstanding that the party who transferred the bill did not have good title.
- Somewhat complex legal provisions govern the various liabilities of the parties to the bill—after the bill has been accepted by a debtor, he (known as the "acceptor") becomes the principal debtor. If he fails to make payment, the next party liable is the party who drew up the bill ("the drawer"), then parties who have transferred the bill (known as "indorsees"), who become liable in the order that they transferred.

CASE DIGEST

IT Law: whether an advancement has been made in respect of patent application [see para 8–13]

Windsurfing International Inc v Tabur Marine (GB) Ltd [1985] RPC 59

A useful list of steps to be taken in determining in respect of a patent application whether an advancement was obvious to an expert in the field was set out by Oliver LJ at 73–74:

(a) Identify the inventive concept embodied in the patent.

(b) Ascertain from a normally skilled expert in the field what was the common general knowledge of state of the art.

(c) Identify the differences (if any) between the state of the art and the alleged invention.

(d) Decide whether those differences, viewed without any knowledge of the alleged invention, constituted steps that would have been obvious to the skilled man or whether they required any degree of invention.

Rights in security: equivalent to delivery [see para 8–33]
  West Lothian Oil Co v *Mair* (1892) 20 R 64
When a creditor loaned money to the debtor on the security of a number of barrels belonging to the debtor, the barrels were placed in a yard enclosed by a fence, the key to which was given to the creditor. The court held that a valid security had been created as giving sole control over access to the yard was equivalent to delivery of the barrels.

Sale of goods: if no price set in a contract of sale, court can set a fair price which need not be the market price [see para 8–67]
  Glynwed Distribution Ltd v *S Korona & Co* 1977 SLT 65
When G delivered steel to K and confusion ensued about the price, the court ruled that a reasonable price need not be a market price but a price which was "fair and just to both parties" in the circumstances.

Restrictive interpretation on what is denoted by the description of goods [see para 8–73]
  Ashington Piggeries Ltd v *Christopher Hill Ltd* [1972] AC 441
Mink food contaminated with a toxic substance was held to conform to the description. The court held that "the defect in the meal was a matter of quality or condition rather than description".

Not fit for the purpose—seller deemed to know purpose by implication [see para 8–75]
  Priest v *Last* [1903] 2 KB 148
A buyer who was scalded after using a hot-water bottle in the normal way was able to sue the seller on the basis that the bottle was unfit for the purpose. The seller was deemed to know the purpose by implication.

A buyer of unascertained goods does not become the owner of those goods until they are ascertained [see para 8–80]
  Hayman v *McLintock* 1907 SC 936
A firm of flour merchants sold consignments of flour to two purchasers. After the sale, the sacks were kept as a part of bulk in their warehouse and were not separated from the bulk nor labelled as being the property of the buyers. As the flour remained unascertained, ownership did not pass to the buyers notwithstanding payment.

When goods are unconditionally appropriated to the contract, ownership and risk pass to the buyer [see para 8–80]

Warder's Import and Export Co v *Norwood & Sons Ltd* [1968] 2 QB 663

In this case there was a contract for the purchase of kidneys from a coldstore. The kidneys melted in the time it took the buyer's carrier to load the kidneys for carriage. When the delivery note was handed over and the carrier began loading, this amounted to the unconditional appropriation of the goods, and hence property and risk passed to the buyer at this stage.

Parties may determine when ownership passes, including stipulating that ownership will only pass when "all sums" owing by the buyer are paid to the seller [see para 8–82]

Armour & Another v *Thyssen Edelstahlwerke AG* 1990 SLT 891

Lord Kerr stated that "the parties clearly expressed ... their intention that the property in the steel should not pass ... until all debts ... had been paid. In my opinion there are no grounds for refusing to give effect to that intention".

Where a party gains a voidable title to goods, any person who obtains those goods in good faith gains good title [see para 8–83]

MacLeod v *Kerr* 1965 SC 253

G bought a car from K using a forged cheque and subsequently sold the goods on to a third party who bought the car in good faith. The third party obtained good title to the car, as G had not rescinded the initial contract of sale when the sale to the third party took place.

Stoppage in transit can only be exercised by the seller before goods reach the buyer [see para 8–89]

Muir v *Rankin* (1905) 13 SLT 60

Goods were sent by the seller to the buyer by rail. The seller subsequently attempted to "stop" the goods in transit. The goods had already been delivered to their final destination (a railway station), however, and the buyer had signed the delivery book at the station. Transit was therefore at an end and the seller could not exercise stoppage in transit.

Breach of the Trade Descriptions Act 1968 can be defended on the basis that all due diligence was taken and the offence was committed by or on the advice of another person [see para 8–104]

Tesco Supermarkets Ltd v *Nattrass* [1972] AC 153

Tesco was able to evade liability for contravention of the Act on the basis that the offence of permitting an employee to price goods wrongly was carried out by another person—a shop manager—and that all due diligence to avoid the offence had been exercised by the company

Insurance: insured parties are obliged to provide material information that a small measure of research or common sense would have revealed [see para 8–115]

McPhee v *Royal Insurance Co Ltd* 1979 SC 304

The insured had provided incorrect dimensions of his boat, the dimensions being ascertained by telephoning the previous owner rather than by taking them himself. When the boat was subsequently destroyed, the insurance claim failed as the insured had not taken all due care and attention in providing accurate information, which in turn caused the insurer to be misled in a material sense.

It is the proximate (dominant) cause that is relevant in determining whether a claim can be made under the policy [see para 8–120]

Leyland Shipping Co Ltd v *Norwich Union Fire Insurance Society* [1918] AC 350 (HL) A marine insurance policy relating to a ship expressly excluded liability for damage caused by wartime hostilities. The ship was torpedoed and later anchored outside the harbour. At low tide the ship became grounded and sank. The court ruled that the proximate cause of the sinking was the torpedo damage and not the grounding of the ship, and hence no claim could be made.

FURTHER READING

Atiyah, *The Sale of Goods* (9th edn, Pitman, 1995)

Birds, *Modern Insurance Law* (4th edn, Sweet & Maxwell, 1998)

Cusine and Forte, *Scottish Cases in Commercial Law* (2nd edn, Butterworths, 1998)

Ervine, *Consumer Law in Scotland* (W Green, 1995)

Forte (ed), *Scots Commercial Law* (Butterworths, 1997), Chapters, 2, 4, 5, 6 and 10

Gloag and Henderson, *The Law of Scotland* (10th edn, W Green, 1995) Chapters 16–20, 23, 24, 36–39 and 54

Goode, *Consumer Credit Law* (Butterworths, 1989)

Hart and Fazzani, *Intellectual Property Law* (MacMillan, 1997)

The Laws of Scotland: Stair Memorial Encyclopaedia (Law Society of Scotland/ Butterworths), Vol 20: "Rights in Security over Moveables"; Vol 18: "Property, I General Law"; Vol 3: "Cautionary Obligations and Representations as to Credit"; Vol 20: "Sale and Exchange"; Vol 6: "Consumer Protection"; Vol 5: "Consumer Credit"; Vol 4: "Commercial Paper: Negotiable Instruments"

Marshall, *Scots Mercantile Law* (3rd edn, W Green 1997), Chapters 4–8

Miller, *Corporeal Moveables in Scots Law* (W Green, 1991)

Reid *et al*, *The Law of Property in Scotland* (Butterworths, 1999)

Wilson, *The Scottish Law of Debt* (2nd edn, W Green, 1991)

9 PERSONAL INSOLVENCY

OVERVIEW

Personal insolvency[1]—not having enough money to meet debts and obligations—is a **9–01** state of affairs which confronts many people. For some, the situation becomes so acute that the law intervenes. Someone legally declared unable to pay his debts is referred to as a bankrupt. The law of bankruptcy is to be found principally in the Bankruptcy (Scotland) Act 1985. The 1985 Act was amended by the Bankruptcy (Scotland) Act 1993. The process whereby a person is legally declared bankrupt and his assets removed from him is known as sequestration. Where a person is unable to pay debts there are alternatives to sequestration—namely, private agreement or formal voluntary arrangement.

INSOLVENCY AND ITS EFFECTS

Absolute insolvency is a state that exists where, on a particular date, the person's total **9–02** assets if realised would not meet his total liabilities. The inability to meet a particular debt when demanded to do so may be defined as "apparent insolvency".[2] In a general sense, insolvency of either form has only a limited impact on the debtor's contractual capacity. It will not affect his capacity to pursue and defend legal actions. More importantly, on the face of things, it does not stop the debtor continuing to trade or deal with a view to turning his financial situation around[3] (although there are some restrictions on the behaviour and actions of the insolvent). Some contractual situations which provide for one of the parties to the contract becoming insolvent. Moreover, an unpaid seller of goods has the right to stop any goods in transit to the buyer who has become insolvent.[4]

---

[1] Corporate insolvency is discussed in Chapter 11; the lack of a statutory definition of the word insolvency is mentioned in McKenzie Skene, *Insolvency Law in Scotland* (1999), p 3; see also McBryde, *Bankruptcy* (2nd edn, 1995), p 1.
[2] Bankruptcy (Scotland) Act 1985, s 7. See para 9–04.
[3] *Ehrenbacher and Co v Kennedy* (1874) 1 R 1131.
[4] Sale of Goods Act 1979, s 44.

SEQUESTRATION—AN OVERVIEW

9–03   The literal meaning of sequestration is closely allied to seclusion. In its legal context the insolvent debtor is secluded from his assets and, more importantly, he is largely secluded from pressure by his creditors to pay debts due to them. Although there is often a stigma attached to personal insolvency which may be undesirable to the debtor, many debtors voluntarily seek sequestration as a means whereby they can, in the medium and long term, escape their insolvency and, after a period of sequestration, start again free from the obligations they have to existing creditors. Sequestration of a person's estate is granted by the court and thereafter will be the subject of supervision of the Accountant in Bankruptcy.[5] Sequestration is applicable to an estate belonging to or held by a trust, a partnership (against the partnership alone and/or also against the individual partners), a body corporate (not a company), or an unincorporated body as well as an individual (living or deceased).[6]

Irrespective of who seeks the sequestration of an insolvent debtor, a petition is presented to the court for sequestration. If it is granted, a person called an interim trustee, will be appointed to safeguard the interest of the creditors at an early stage. Some time thereafter, a meeting of creditors will be called and a permanent trustee will be appointed who will see the sequestration process through to conclusion and arrange for the distribution of the value of the assets of the debtor. The sequestrated debtor remains in sequestration for a period of time (usually three years) and is thereafter discharged from bankruptcy and allowed to recommence normal financial life.

THE SIGNIFICANCE OF "APPARENT INSOLVENCY"

9–04   The phrase "apparent insolvency" was introduced by the 1985 Act. The Act defines it as occurring where

(1) the debtor's estate has been sequestrated or he is declared bankrupt;

(2) the debtor has given written notice to his creditors that he has ceased to pay his debts in the ordinary course of business;

(3) he grants a trust deed for his creditors generally;

(4) he has been served with a charge and the 14 days have expired and he has not paid;

(5) a poinding or seizure of goods for rates or taxes and 14 days have elapsed without payment of his debt;

(6) a decree of adjudication is granted against his heritable estate;

---

[5]   Discussed below at para 9–09; Bankruptcy (Scotland) Act 1985, s 1A, as inserted by the Bankruptcy (Scotland) Act 1993; see McBryde, *Bankruptcy* (2nd edn, 1995), Chap 2.
[6]   Bankruptcy (Scotland) Act 1985, s 6.

(7) his goods are sold under a sequestration for rent;

(8) a receiving order has been made against him in England; or

(9) a creditor has demanded payment of a liquid debt of £750 or more[7] and a period of three weeks has elapsed without payment, or challenge of the demand.

The concept of "apparent insolvency" has considerable importance in bankruptcy law in that it is necessary that there be "apparent insolvency" for a creditor to petition the court for a sequestration.[8]

WHO MAY PETITION FOR SEQUESTRATION?

The Court of Session or, more usually, the sheriff court may hear a petition for seques- **9–05** tration. A creditor may lodge a petition in court for sequestration either on his own or with the concurrence of other creditors so long as the total indebtedness due to the petitioning creditor(s) is not less than £1,500. If a debtor is to raise proceedings alone without the concurrence of the qualified creditor(s) the debt due to him must be £1,500 or more, there must have been no award of sequestration against the debtor in the preceding five years and the debtor must be apparently insolvent or have granted a trust deed to his creditors which has been objected to by one third or more creditors.[9] A trustee under a trust deed can also petition for sequestration under certain conditions.[10] Where the debtor is deceased a petition for sequestration of his estate may be sought by his executor, one or more creditors, or a trustee acting under a trust deed.[11]

THE PERSONNEL INVOLVED IN INSOLVENCY PROCEEDINGS

INTERIM TRUSTEES

The court must appoint an interim trustee in any sequestration.[12] The role of the **9–06** interim trustee is, at an early stage of the sequestration, to safeguard the debtor's estate or what is left of it, pending the appointment of a permanent trustee. The interim trustee will be a qualified insolvency practitioner.[13] His role will include meeting with

---

[7] See, *eg*, *Arthur* v *SMT Sales and Service Co Ltd (No 2)* 1999 SC 109.
[8] Bankruptcy (Scotland) Act, s 5 (2)(b); see also McBryde, *Bankruptcy* (2nd edn, 1995), Chap 3.
[9] ss 5(2A) and 5(2B), as inserted.
[10] ss 5(2) and 5(2C).
[11] s 5(3).
[12] Bankruptcy (Scotland) Act 1985, s 2, as substituted.
[13] An insolvency practitioner is an individual who is a member of a relevant professional body (an accountant or a lawyer) who provides a guarantee (caution) and who is not an undischarged bankrupt. See Bankruptcy (Scotland) Regulations 1985 (SI 1985/1925), reg 3. See also McKenzie Skene, *Insolvency Law in Scotland* (1999), pp 32–37.

the sequestrated individual to ascertain the reasons for the insolvency and its circumstances, the compiling of an inventory of assets and liabilities and notifying the Accountant in Bankruptcy. He will continue to administer the sequestrated person's estate until a permanent trustee is appointed.

PERMANENT TRUSTEE

9–07   A permanent trustee may be elected following the holding of a statutory meeting of creditors.[14] If no permanent trustee is elected then the court appoints one. Following election/appointment of the permanent trustee, the debtor's whole estate vests in that person and he takes over from the interim trustee. It is commonplace for the interim trustee and the permanent trustee to be one and the same person.[15] The role of the permanent trustee is one of recovering, managing and realising the debtor's estate and thereafter to arrange for the distribution of assets realised to the creditors of the sequestrated person.[16] In several respects his role must duplicate that of the interim trustee in that he must ascertain the true extent of liabilities and assets of the sequestrated person. His work may, or may not, be supervised by Commissioners.

COMMISSIONERS

9–08   Creditors at the statutory meeting may, if they so wish, elect up to five Commissioners.[17] Commissioners may be creditors themselves or others mandated by the creditors. Commissioners are not endorsed by the court and assume office on appointment. The role of the commissioner is to supervise the activities of the permanent trustee. In this regard, they may advise the permanent trustee in his activities. Commissioners can be removed by the convening of a further meeting and a vote to remove. There is automatic removal where the commissioner is a mandatory of the creditor and the mandate is revoked. The permanent trustee need not follow directions of the commissioner unless such a direction is endorsed by the court. The permanent trustee must, however, obtain commissioner consent where he wishes to carry on the business of the debtor, defend or continue any legal proceedings, create any security, make payments or create liabilities.[18]

ACCOUNTANT IN BANKRUPTCY

9–09   The Accountant in Bankruptcy supervises the work of the interim trustees, permanent trustees and commissioners. He will deal with any complaints regarding their activities and may petition the court for their removal. He is responsible for collating, registering and publishing information in relation to insolvency in Scotland. The register of insolvencies, which he maintains, will be open to public inspection. He may receive reports from trustees regarding the debtor's financial affairs including any suspicion that the debtor may have committed an offence in relation to the

---

[14] Bankruptcy (Scotland) Act 1985, ss 3 and 24.
[15] For the implications of this see *The Laws of Scotland: Stair Memorial Encyclopaedia* Vol 2 "Bankruptcy", para 1313.
[16] s 31.
[17] See McBride, *Bankruptcy* (2nd edn, 1995), Chap 14.
[18] s 39(2).

sequestration. Notices of petition for sequestration are served upon the Accountant in Bankruptcy. Where no commissioners are appointed to oversee the work of the permanent trustee, the Accountant in Bankruptcy will fulfil the supervisory role. Accounts prepared by the permanent trustee must be submitted to the Accountant in Bankruptcy where there are no Commissioners. Where there are Commissioners, the accounts will be copied to the Accountant in Bankruptcy.

PETITIONING FOR SEQUESTRATION

The commencement of the sequestration process will begin with the presentation of a **9–10** petition for sequestration to the court. If the debtor is petitioning for his own sequestration he is required to lodge with the petition a statement of assets and liabilities. Where the debtor presents a petition the court must award sequestration forthwith unless there is cause for it not to be granted.[19] Where the petition is lodged by a creditor or a trustee acting under a trust deed, the debtor is ordered to appear to show cause why the sequestration should not be granted.[20] If, after proper notice, the debtor does not respond, the court must award sequestration if it is satisfied that all proper formalities have been complied with. The debtor may forestall the award of sequestration by paying the debt or by exhibiting or providing sufficient security for the payment of the debt (and other debts due) to the creditor or by showing the petition is incompetent for some other reason.

An interim trustee will be appointed upon the award of sequestration. In the absence of a nominated interim trustee the Accountant in Bankruptcy will be appointed as interim trustee. The interim trustee must notify the debtor of his appointment as soon as practicable.[21]

As soon as sequestration has been awarded by any court, the clerk of that court is required to send forthwith a certified copy of the relevant court order to the Keeper of Inhibitions and Adjudications so that the court order may be recorded. Registration of the court order has the effect of diligence[22] at the instance of creditors on any heritable property of the debtor. In addition a copy of the court order must be sent to the Accountant in Bankruptcy.[23] The interim trustee will arrange for publication of a notice of the sequestration in the *Edinburgh Gazette*.

THE APPOINTMENT AND DUTIES OF THE INTERIM TRUSTEE

Following his appointment, the interim trustee must publish in the *Edinburgh Gazette* **9–11** a notice of the sequestration and invite creditors of the debtor to submit claims to him. His principal duty is to safeguard the debtor's estate. In this regard he has a broad array of powers. He may give directions to the debtor regarding management of the

---

[19] s 12(1), as substituted by the 1993 Act, s 4(2).
[20] s 12(2).
[21] s 2(7).
[22] See Chapter 8 for a discussion of diligence.
[23] s 14(1).

debtor's estate. He may order the debtor to deliver to him money, valuables or documents for safekeeping. He may arrange for the sale or disposal of perishable goods belonging to the debtor. He may insist on the debtor compiling an inventory of his estate. Moreover, he may insist that the debtor implement transactions he has entered into or effect insurance over part of the debtor's estate. The interim trustee may also carry on or suspend business operations of the debtor and borrow any money to safeguard the debtor's estate.[24] Where the interim trustee makes a request of the debtor in pursuance of his powers and the debtor fails to comply, the debtor commits an offence.[25] The interim trustee may also apply to the court for the power to enter and search the debtor's home, house or business premises or, in fact, any other order for the purpose of securing the creditor's interests.[26]

Where the debtor petitioned for his own sequestration, he must within seven days of the interim trustee's appointment send him a copy of the assets and liabilities lodged in court with the sequestration petition. Where the debtor did not petition for his own sequestration, he must nevertheless within seven days of being notified of the appointment of the interim trustee send to that trustee a statement as to his assets and liabilities, and a note of his income and expenditure all in a prescribed form. The interim trustee also conducts his own inquiries to ascertain the true extent of the debtor's state of affairs. The interim trustee on the basis of his inquiries and the information supplied to him must, for the purposes of informing the creditors, prepare a statement of assets and liabilities and indicate whether the debtor's assets are likely to be sufficient to pay a dividend to creditors (that is, a *pro rata* payment based on the extent of the indebtedness and the assets available for distribution).

CONVENING A STATUTORY MEETING OF CREDITORS

9–12   The interim trustee (if he is not the Accountant in Bankruptcy) must convene a statutory meeting of creditors. Four days prior to the convening of the meeting, the interim trustee must send a report to the Accountant in Bankruptcy containing a statement of assets and liabilities and a commentary on the reason for insolvency. The statutory meeting will ordinarily take place within 28 days of the grant of sequestration although the sheriff does have the power to allow further time. The interim trustee must give at least seven days' notice of the meeting to all creditors known to him and the Accountant in Bankruptcy. At the same time he will invite any further claims. The interim trustee will initially chair the statutory meeting but will invite the creditors to elect one of their number to chair the meeting if they so wish. The interim trustee must accept or reject in whole or in part the claims of creditors submitted to him.

The interim trustee will make known to the creditors his statement of assets and liabilities of the debtor. He will answer questions put to him by the creditors and consider any representations made to him. He will give an indication as to whether a dividend is likely to be paid. Usually, it will be obvious from the statement whether such a dividend is likely.

---

[24] s 18(2) (as amended by 1993 Act, Sched 1, para 6).
[25] s 18(5) and (6).
[26] See, *eg*, *Scottish and Newcastle, Petitioners* 1992 SCLR 540 (Notes) where a power of sale was sought in respect of licensed premises.

Where the interim trustee is the Accountant in Bankruptcy he must decide ordinarily within 60 days whether to convene a statutory meeting or not and to notify the creditors accordingly. Where creditors of one quarter of the total indebtedness request a meeting, the Accountant in Bankruptcy must convene a meeting.[27]

THE ELECTION AND FUNCTION OF THE PERMANENT TRUSTEE

One of the primary functions of the statutory meeting is to elect a permanent trustee.[28] **9–13** This will be done at the end of the statutory meeting. Where there is a dispute an election will take place with the basis of voting the value of the indebtedness to each creditor. The election of the permanent trustee requires to be endorsed by the sheriff.[29] Objection may be made by the debtor, any creditor, the Accountant in Bankruptcy, the interim, or the permanent trustee as to any issue connected with the election within four days of the election. Endorsement by the sheriff in the absence of objection is a formality. If the sheriff upholds an objection then a new meeting must take place for the election of the permanent trustee.[30] If the permanent trustee is not the interim trustee he must publish a notice in the *Edinburgh Gazette* notifying his appointment.[31] The interim trustee (if not confirmed as the permanent trustee) must hand over all matters pertaining to the sequestration to the permanent trustee.

There may be situations where no creditor turns up at the statutory meeting thus preventing the appointment of a permanent trustee. The interim trustee must report this to the Accountant in Bankruptcy and also report this to the sheriff who will appoint the interim trustee as the permanent trustee.[32]

If the Accountant in Bankruptcy is the interim trustee and he does not convene a statutory meeting he will report to the sheriff and be confirmed as the permanent trustee.

THE DEBTOR'S ESTATE VESTS IN THE PERMANENT TRUSTEE

On his appointment, the estate of the debtor vests in the permanent trustee and he **9–14** must administer it for the benefit of the creditors.[33] The basic common law position is that the debtor's estate vests *tantum et tale* which means that the trustee only acquires the property as far as the bankrupt had the property. If the debtor acquired the property through fraud it remains reducible even in vesting.

Certain things do not form part of the debtor's estate. For example, furnishings necessary for the maintenance of family life do not vest in the permanent trustee. Solatium payments in actions for damages raised after sequestration will form part of the debtor's estate.[34] Property held in trust by the debtor does not vest in the permanent trustee.

In respect of heritable property, the permanent trustee will register a notice of title

[27] s 27A.
[28] s 24(1).
[29] s 25.
[30] s 25(4).
[31] s 25(6).
[32] s 24(4).
[33] s 31(1).
[34] *Coutts' Tr v Coutts* 1998 SC 798.

using the act and warrant issued to him upon appointment as a link in title and by registration he will have conferred upon him a real right to the heritage. The debtor may be required to leave the property.[35] In a recent case it was held that the registration of an act and warrant of the permanent trustee could defeat a special destination in a house title deed (where parties indicate that the house is disponed to them or the survivor of them). The court took the view that the share of the house passes to the surviving spouse of the sequestrated deceased but that the share of the deceased continues to attract the liabilities of the debtor.[36] One may speculate that the decision in *Sharp v Thomson*[37] may have some effect upon the issue of heritable property vesting in the permanent trustee. The delivery of a disposition to a third party may be thought to have conferred a beneficial interest which takes the property outside the scope of vesting. *Sharp v Thomson* concerned receivership and it is unclear as yet whether it applies to bankruptcy.

Moveable property which requires delivery, possession or intimation of assignation immediately vests in the permanent trustee. Some property requires further formalities for the property to vest in the permanent trustee.

If the debtor acquires property after sequestration that too vests in the permanent trustee. Income from the estate vested in the permanent trustee also vests in the permanent trustee. Ordinary income (not related to the estate that has vested) of the debtor remains with the debtor although the permanent trustee may apply to the sheriff to secure amounts over a limit sufficient to support the debtor and his family and to make any reasonable alimentary or periodical allowance payments to the person supported by him.[38] This need not correspond to any existing order. The sheriff will make an order as to what is a suitable amount of income to be retained by the debtor.

Any part of the debtor's estate, which another person says is rightfully his, may be the subject of court proceedings to have that part of the estate excluded from vesting.[39]

RECALLING SEQUESTRATION

9–15   The award of sequestration cannot be reviewed but it may be recalled. The procedure for recall entails the debtor, the Accountant in Bankruptcy, the interim trustee, or any creditor or other "interested" party presenting a petition for recall to the Court of Session. The court may recall sequestration where: (1) the debtor has paid his debts in full or given security for payment; (2) creditors reside in another country and it is more appropriate for the debtor's estate to be administered in that other country; or (3) there have been other awards of sequestration or analogous remedies.[40] Beyond this the court has broad discretion to recall sequestration including where there has been procedural impropriety.[41] Moreover, the court may entertain an application from a

---

[35] *White v Stevenson* 1956 SC 84.
[36] *Fleming's Tr v Fleming* 2000 SC 206.
[37] 1994 SLT 1068.
[38] s 32.
[39] s 31(6).
[40] s 17(1).
[41] See *Ritchie v Dickie* 1999 SC 593, *cf Bell v McMillan* 1999 SLT 947; *Sutherland v Inland Revenue* 1999 SC 104.

non-entitled spouse to recall the sequestration where the purpose behind the seques-tration is to defeat occupancy rights.[42] Where one is seeking to rely on the court's general discretion, recall of sequestration should ordinarily be presented within 10 weeks of the initial grant of sequestration. In situations where one is relying on the specified grounds of recall an application for recall can be made at any time. Recall has the effect of restoring the parties to their original position immediately prior to the grant of sequestration.[43]

THE RIGHT TO CHALLENGE PRIOR ACTIONS OF THE DEBTOR WHICH DISADVANTAGE CREDITORS

The permanent trustee has a role in securing the interests of creditors. In that capacity   **9–16**
he has the power to challenge transactions entered into by the debtor which prejudiced the creditors. The debtor, though technically insolvent prior to formal sequestration, may continue to trade and in this way gather income or utilise assets. In the best scenario he will turn around his finances. The granting of sequestration, however, brings the debtor's past actions under scrutiny to ensure that he has not done something while insolvent which prejudices the creditors. In his dealings prior to sequestration, the debtor is expected to act in a fashion consistent with his obligation not to harm the interests of the creditors. He must be open with his finances and cannot conceal assets or income. He cannot give away, dissipate or destroy assets, nor can he create any preferential right or security over assets hitherto owned by him. There are rules which prohibit gratuitous alienations (the giving away of assets for free), the granting of unfair preferences, or the creation of fraudulent preferences on particular creditors which advantages them and disadvantages the other creditors.

The right of challenge may arise under common law or under specific statutory provisions contained within the 1985 Act. In addition to the main types of challengeable transactions there are statutory rights of challenge to orders on provision on divorce,[44] extortionate credit transactions,[45] and excessive pension contri-butions.[46]

GRATUITOUS ALIENATIONS

At common law, the debtor is prohibited from passing on assets or money without   **9–17**
a reasonable consideration being obtained for the assets traded. The debtor can-not surrender rights without obtaining some consideration in exchange. The debtor cannot purchase something at an exorbitant price (which is tantamount to alienation of money). All such alienations while in the state of insolvency are frauds on the creditors and, consequently, any creditor or any permanent trustee subsequently

---

[42] s 41; on occupancy rights, see para 9–20.
[43] s 17(4). See McKenzie Skene, *Insolvency Law in Scotland* (1999), p 50.
[44] s 35.
[45] s 61.
[46] s 36A, s 36B and s 36C (not yet in force), added by the Welfare Reform and Pensions Act 1979.

appointed in a sequestration may challenge any such transaction seeking to have it reduced and the asset or money restored to the debtor's estate.

The 1985 Act also provides for challenge of gratuitous alienations following sequestration.[47] The gratuitous alienation may be challenged by any creditor who is a creditor by virtue of a debt incurred on or before sequestration where the gratuitous alienation took place in a period two years before sequestration. Where the alienation is to an associate (a spouse or close relative, partner or an associate of any partner, employee or employer, or the firm itself) then the period extends to five years prior to sequestration.[48]

Those challenging the alienation must prove the fact of sequestration and the alienation.[49] If the court is satisfied that a gratuitous alienation has taken place it will reduce the alienation and restore the asset to the debtor's estate or it will order such other appropriate remedy if reduction is not possible.[50] Where the goods have been passed in good faith for proper consideration to a third party, the party who has acquired them is protected from relinquishing the asset. The party who received the asset in the gratuitous alienation (gift) is not so protected and may be ordered to pay the proper price. Those funds will go into the debtor's estate. Any defences are for the defender to establish in contrast to the common law challenge where the onus is on the pursuer to prove the situation.

UNFAIR PREFERENCES

9–18   Under statute, transactions which have as their effect the creation of an unfair preference for one creditor over others[51] are challengeable and reducible on the basis that they are "unfair" if they are entered into up to six months before the sequestration.[52] Any creditor on or before sequestration may seek to challenge a transaction on the basis that it is an unfair preference. If convinced that it is an unfair preference, the court will reduce the transaction and order restoration of the asset to the debtor's estate. The right to challenge is also conferred on the permanent trustee, the trustee acting under a trust deed or any appointed judicial factor. As with the gratuitous alienation, third parties who acquire assets from a person to whom it has been passed enjoy protection from restoration. The court may order such other remedy as appropriate to rectify the position of the creditors.[53] Where the challenge is presented under statute, the challenger need only prove that the unfair preference was created in the period set down in the statute. There is no need to prove that the debtor was at that time insolvent.

The following are not unfair preferences: (1) a transaction in the ordinary course of trade or business; (2) a payment in cash for a debt that had become due unless there is

---

[47] s 34(1); see, eg, *Short's Tr v Chung (No 2)* 1999 SC 471; *Reid v Ramlort Ltd* 1998 SC 887.
[48] s 74(5).
[49] See *Lombardi's Tr v Lombardi* 1982 SLT 81; *Hunt's Tr v Hunt* 1984 SLT 169.
[50] See *Short's Tr v Chung* 1991 SLT 472; *Cay's Tr v Cay* 1998 SC 780.
[51] See, eg, *T v L* 1970 SLT 243 (delivering a disposition over property in security for a prior debt); *Newton and Sons Tr v Finlayson and Co* 1928 SC 637 (making arrangements to pay creditor direct).
[52] Or the granting of a trust deed which has become a protected trust deed or within 12 months of death where the deceased estate has been sequestrated or where a judicial factor has been appointed under s 11A of the Judicial Factors (Scotland) Act 1889. See the Bankruptcy (Scotland) Act 1985, s 36.
[53] s 36(5).

an attempt by both parties to prejudice other creditors; (3) transactions where there are reciprocal obligations again unless there is collusion between the parties to subvert the position of other creditors; and (4) the granting of a mandate to pay over arrested funds provided there has been a decree for payment or a summary warrant for diligence preceded by an arrestment on the dependence or followed by an arrestment in execution.[54] In respect of the last of these four there is no prejudice to the other creditors as it implements already preferential rights secured by one creditor.

FRAUDULENT PREFERENCES

Fraudulent preferences are challengeable at common law. A fraudulent prefer- **9–19** ence arises where the insolvent debtor before sequestration confers a right of preference over other creditors on a particular creditor.[55] Where the preference is entered into voluntarily in the course of absolute insolvency and the debtor has full knowledge of what he is doing and of his insolvency, fraud is presumed.[56] The following are not fraudulent preferences: (1) cash or cheque payment of debts which are due unless there is a deliberate attempt to defraud the other creditors[57]; (2) transactions in the ordinary course of trade including goods supplied on credit; and (3) transfers for a consideration at the time of transfer, such as the taking of a security at the time of granting a loan of money.[58] Advance payment of a debt yet to fall due may constitute a fraudulent preference.[59] It would also be contrary to the statutory provisions.

THE EFFECT OF SEQUESTRATION

Because moveable property of the debtor vests in the permanent trustee on his **9–20** appointment, those who have a personal right in any property of the sequestrated debtor are unable to enforce that right against the debtor. The permanent trustee may, in respect of moveable property, take delivery or intimate his appointment and the assumption of rights in the property. Moveable property rights which require registration (such as registration of shares) can be so registered by a purchaser without being caught by the vesting in the permanent trustee.[60]

In respect of heritable property, a buyer from the debtor may be allowed to complete title and record property purchased from the debtor in the Land Register or the Register of Sasines.[61] Unless the lease so states, sequestration does not terminate a lease. Where there is a right of vesting in a lease the lease immediately vests in the

---

[54] s 36(2).
[55] For example, where the debtor confers a right in security over previously unsecured debts: *Thomas* v *Thomson* (1865) 5 M 252.
[56] *McCowan* v *Wright* (1853) 15 D 494.
[57] *Whatmough's Tr* v *British Linen Bank* 1932 SC 525.
[58] See, for example of security taken, *Thomas Montgomery and Sons* v *Gallacher* 1982 SLT 138.
[59] *Blincow's Tr* v *Allan and Co* (1828) 7 S 124.
[60] *Morrison* v *Harrison* (1876) 3 R 406.
[61] *Cormack* v *Anderson* (1829) 7 S 868.

permanent trustee to the exclusion of any assignees who have not yet entered into possession.[62] If the trustee adopts the lease he is thereafter liable for the rent.

Sequestration also has important consequences in respect of diligence.[63] The awarding of sequestration has the effect in relation to any diligence done before or after the award of sequestration of a decree of adjudication of the heritable estate of the debts recorded in the Register of Inhibitions and Adjudication or an arrestment in execution and decree of furthcoming, an arrestment in execution and a warrant of sale, and a completed poinding.[64]

Diligence effected in the period 60 days prior to, and any time after, the award of sequestration do not rank as they ordinarily would in date order but rather all rank equally as if they had been effected on the same day.[65] Where arrestment or poinding is effected in the period 60 days prior to, or at any time after, sequestration, no preferential right is created for the person who effects that diligence. Any proceeds their diligence obtains must be given to the permanent trustee although the arrestor may recoup his expenses.[66] Arrestments executed prior to the 60-day period must be given effect to by the permanent trustee.[67] Inhibition of heritable property of another if carried out in the period 60 days prior to sequestration, or at any time after, is rendered invalid by the award of sequestration.[68]

THE DEBTOR'S DUTIES IN SEQUESTRATION

9–21 The bankrupt must act in good faith with the permanent trustee. He is under a duty to perform matters so as to enable the permanent trustee to fulfil his role of identifying, inventorying and realising the debtor's estate. Where the debtor impedes the functions of the permanent trustee, an application may be made to the sheriff court for a court order to force compliance.[69] It is an offence for a bankrupt to knowingly make a false statement to a creditor or anyone concerned in the administration of his estate in relation to his assets or dealings. Furthermore, anyone (whether the debtor or any other person acting in his interest) who destroys, damages, conceals or removes from Scotland any part of the debtor's estate or any relevant document is also guilty of an offence unless that person can show that what was done was not with the intention of prejudicing creditors of the debtor.[70] The debtor in trade or business is guilty of an offence if he fails to keep records necessary to give a fair view of his assets or business and financial affairs for the two years immediately preceding the award of sequestration.[71] It is an offence for a bankrupt or anyone acting in his interests to falsify documents or for the debtor to fail to report the falsification to the permanent trustee. The debtor cannot transfer property for inadequate consideration. It is also an offence

---

[62] *Clark* v *West Calder Oil Co* (1882) 9 R 1017.
[63] See para 9–20; see also McKenzie Skene, *Insolvency Law in Scotland* (1999), pp 249–254.
[64] s 37(1).
[65] s 37; note also the provisions in Sched 7, para 24 which relate to the effect of apparent insolvency on diligence and which may be equally relevant.
[66] s 37(4) and (5).
[67] *Berry* v *Taylor* 1992 SCLR 910.
[68] s 37(2).
[69] s 64.
[70] s 67(1); see *Ferguson* v *McGlennan* 1999 GWD 2–90 (sentence of three months for failing to declare timeshare and using cheque to pay employees and creditors).
[71] s 67(8) It is a defence to show that the failure to keep records was neither reckless nor dishonest.

for an undischarged bankrupt to obtain credit of more than £100 without disclosing his status to the person providing the credit.[72] Where the permanent trustee becomes aware of conduct which may amount to an offence he must report it to the Accountant in Bankruptcy who may refer the matter to the Lord Advocate for prosecution.

One of the controversial features of bankruptcy arises in the context of the debtor's interest in the family home. Because of the operation of the concept of separation of property, the spouse's property survives intact from the sequestrated estate of the debtor. The permanent trustee may only sell or dispose of any right or interest of the debtor in the matrimonial home with the consent of the spouse or, failing which, by court order. Even in circumstances where the non-insolvent spouse has no title to the matrimonial home the permanent trustee must obtain his consent or that of the court before sale.[73] It is ordinarily the case that the permanent trustee will afford the spouse the opportunity of buying the *pro indiviso* share of the sequestrated debtor. The practicality of this will depend on the independent means of the non-sequestrated spouse.

CLAIMS, PREFERRED DEBTS AND DISTRIBUTION OF THE DEBTOR'S ESTATE

Creditors are expected to submit claims to the permanent trustee (though they may already have done so to the interim trustee[74]). The permanent trustee will adjudicate on claims which will involve assessing the validity of claims and thereafter establishing the amount of the claim.[75] As well as submitting the claim (which in any event must have certain vouchings attached to it) to the permanent trustee, the creditor may wish to submit other evidence of the debt due. Unsurprisingly, the word of the debtor or writings of the debtor which post-date the sequestration are not good authority that the debt is valid.[76] The submission of a claim properly validated (and accepted by the interim trustee as conferring a qualifying right) will give the creditor the right to attend and vote at the statutory meeting. If the creditor is to receive a dividend from the debtor's estate, it will be necessary for him to submit his claim at least eight weeks prior to the accounting period.[77] Where a claim is rejected, the permanent trustee must offer a reason in explanation of his decision. The creditor has the right of appeal against the permanent trustee's decision to the sheriff.[78]

9–22

The permanent trustee is required to account either to commissioners (if there are any) or the Accountant in Bankruptcy at six-month intervals from a date starting with sequestration. There is scope within the legislation to shorten the period of accounting after the first such period where the permanent trustee thinks it expedient to do so and he obtains the consent of the commissioners or the Accountant in Bankruptcy. At the end of each six-month period the permanent trustee will prepare a report of his

---

[72] s 67.

[73] s 40; see also *Salmon's Trs* v *Salmon* 1989 SLT (Sh Ct) 49.

[74] Claims submitted to the interim trustee are automatically resubmitted to the permanent trustee: s 48(2). The creditor can submit another claim for a different amount. The permanent trustee is not bound by any earlier decision of the interim trustee in respect of the claim.

[75] See *Crighton* v *Crighton's Tr* 1999 SLT (Sh Ct) 113 (where refusal was overturned in the sheriff court).

[76] See *Carmichael's Tr* v *Carmichael* 1929 SC 265.

[77] The accounting period is discussed below at para 9–23. It is a date on which the trustee must account to the creditors.

[78] s 49.

accounts in respect of the debtor's estate and also a proposed scheme of division in respect of the remainder of the debtor's estate. This report will be delivered to the commissioners or the Accountant in Bankruptcy within two weeks of the end of the accounting period. There is scope to appeal to the commissioners or the Accountant in Bankruptcy against the fixing of any of the provisional amounts stated in the accounts of the permanent trustee. Such appeals must occur within eight weeks of the end of the accounting period. Once the accounts and the sums therein are fixed, the permanent trustee will arrange to distribute the dividend to creditors as proposed in his accounts.[79] The permanent trustee may decide to put some of the debtor's estate on deposit pending validation of a claim. Dividends distributed but not cashed or uplifted must be placed on deposit receipt at a bank or analogous institution.

In distributing the debtor's estate the 1985 Act sets down the following order of priority:

(1) the outlays and remuneration of the interim trustee;

(2) the outlays and remuneration of the permanent trustee;

(3) where the debtor is deceased, his reasonable funeral expenses and expenses incurred in administering his estate;

(4) where a creditor has petitioned for sequestration the costs of the petition by the creditor;

(5) preferred debts;

(6) ordinary debts;

(7) interest on any preferred debts and ordinary debts between date of sequestration and date of payment;

(8) any postponed debt.[80]

There may, of course, be some creditors who rank above the permanent trustee and whose claims from the debtor's estate will be given priority. For example, someone with a right in security, such as a standard security over heritable property, or someone with a lien over documents held on behalf of the debtor but delivered to the permanent trustee in order that he may complete his functions, will not have their rights in security affected. That person will have the right to be paid first out of the secured property. Secured creditors have the right to utilise their security to compel payment from the debtor's estate. In the case of heritable property it will be necessary to intimate the security to the trustee.[81] The permanent trustee may compel the secured creditor to discharge the security in return for payment to the creditor of the sum stipulated by the creditor.

---

[79] s 53(7).
[80] s 51(1).
[81] s 39.

DISCHARGE OF THE DEBTOR AND THE END OF SEQUESTRATION

The debtor may be discharged in one of two ways. He may effectively recoup his **9–23** position and make an offer to his creditors via the permanent trustee which, if acceptable to them, will result in discharge. Alternatively, the debtor may await the expiry of time (usually three years) and obtain "automatic" discharge.

At any time after the sheriff clerk has issued the Act and warrant to the permanent trustee, the debtor may seek a discharge by making an offer in respect of his debts to the permanent trustee. This is known as an offer of composition. The debtor may make only two such offers during the course of his sequestration. The debtor will be expected to outline the guarantee or security to be provided in satisfaction of the discharge. If such an offer is made to the permanent trustee he must report on it to the commissioners or, if there are no commissioners, the Accountant in Bankruptcy. The commissioners or the Accountant in Bankruptcy as appropriate will decide if the offer should go before the creditors. Where it is believed that the offer will be timeously implemented, that a dividend of at least 25 pence in the pound in respect of ordinary debts would be payable and that there would be adequate further security, the offer must be placed before the creditors.

To have an offer placed before the creditors, the permanent trustee will have an advert placed in the *Edinburgh Gazette* informing that an offer of composition has been made, where it can be inspected, and invite the acceptance or rejection of the offer. If not less than two-thirds of the creditors elect to accept the offer the permanent trustee must report this to the sheriff. The sheriff, following the report by the permanent trustee, may approve the acceptance of the offer. Any decision the sheriff may make in this matter may be appealed. If the offer is approved, once its terms have been implemented, the sheriff will make an order discharging the debtor from sequestration and also discharging the permanent trustee. The order discharging the debtor and the permanent trustee may be recalled following application to the Court of Session where the court is satisfied that there has been, or is likely to be, default on the part of the debtor. The Court of Session will, on recall, appoint a judicial factor to administer the estate if the permanent trustee has been discharged.

Ordinarily, the debtor will be discharged "automatically" from sequestration after three years.[82] However, the permanent trustee or any creditor may apply to the sheriff court for an order of deferment of up to two years of the discharge from the sequestration.[83] The application for deferment of discharge must be made no later than two years and nine months after the date of sequestration. Further applications for deferment may be made as long as they are made not less than three months before the intended discharge date.[84] If discharge is deferred in this way, the debtor may apply at any time to the sheriff for discharge.

Once discharged, the debtor may apply to the Accountant in Bankruptcy for a certificate confirming his discharge from bankruptcy.[85] Discharge from bankruptcy

---

[82] s 54(1); *Pattison* v *Halliday* 1991 SLT 645.
[83] s 54(3); see McKenzie Skene, *Insolvency Law in Scotland* (1999), pp 36–37; *Clydesdale Bank PLC* v *Davidson* 1994 SLT 225.
[84] s 54(9).
[85] s 54(2).

has the effect of discharging the debtor from all debts and obligations existing at the time of sequestration in the UK,[86] with the exception of any liability to pay a fine due to the Crown, any forfeiture of bail, any liability incurred through fraud or breach of trust, aliment or periodical allowance or child support maintenance, any liability in respect of a student loan, or the obligation to co-operate with the permanent trustee.[87] To all intents and purposes the discharged bankrupt may resume his life unencumbered by his prior debts. He may acquire assets and property without it vesting in the permanent trustee.[88] However, assets or interests properly acquired during the sequestration period which come to fruition shortly after discharge may be clawed back by the permanent trustee.[89]

Once the permanent trustee has disbursed the debtor's estate and completed his accounts he may seek his own discharge. If there are unclaimed dividends these must be placed on bank deposit. The permanent trustee will deliver to the Accountant in Bankruptcy his audited accounts. The creditors have the right to make representation about the possible discharge to the Accountant in Bankruptcy within 14 days. Thereafter, the Accountant in Bankruptcy must grant or refuse the request for the application for discharge. Not only does the grant of discharge exonerate the permanent trustee from further action but also exonerates him from all liability except that which arises from the fraudulent actions of the permanent trustee.

WHERE THE ACCOUNTANT IN BANKRUPTCY IS THE INTERIM TRUSTEE

ADAPTED SEQUESTRATION PROCEDURES

9-24   There are two adapted procedures. The first is contained in Schedule 2 to the 1985 Act and is referred to simply as the "Schedule 2 procedure". Schedule 2 procedure is pertinent where the assets involved are relatively small, or the Accountant in Bankruptcy acts as the interim trustee, or where no creditor attends the statutory meeting, or where no permanent trustee is elected. The Accountant in Bankruptcy applies for a certificate of summary administration. The modifications to procedures include that the Accountant in Bankruptcy need not consult with anyone regarding the recovery, management and realisation of the debtor's estate.[90]

The second of the adapted procedures is summary administration. This procedure was specifically introduced in 1993 to deal with small asset cases. The interim trustee may apply to the court for a grant of summary administration and it may be granted where the debtor's unsecured liabilities are less than £20,000 and the debtor's assets (excluding heritage and property which would not vest in any permanent trustee) are less than £2,000. The main effect of summary administration is that the permanent

---

[86] s 55(1).
[87] s 55(2).
[88] s 32.
[89] See *Ross v HJ Banks and Co Ltd* 1998 SCLR 1109.
[90] See Forte, *Scots Commercial Law* (1996), pp 255–256.

trustee need only carry on his function to the extent that it is in the beneficial interests of the creditors to do so. He need not waste time and financial resources if it will not recover anything for the creditors.[91]

ALTERNATIVES TO SEQUESTRATION

As an alternative to sequestration, the insolvent may wind up his affairs by private **9–25** agreement with his creditors. Such private agreements may be so informal as simply to be arrangements to pay by instalments or at some future date. However, there are also formal voluntary arrangements alternate to sequestration itself. Accordingly, a debtor may make a voluntary arrangement with his creditors which is effected by a trust deed[92] or a composition contract.

VOLUNTARY TRUST DEEDS FOR CREDITORS/PROTECTED TRUST DEEDS

To create a private trust deed the debtor will convey his estate (which would have **9–26** vested in the permanent trustee if the debtor had been sequestrated) to a trustee for the benefit of his creditors generally.[93] A private trustee appointed in this way must take title to the estate conveyed to him as there is no automatic vesting of such estate. He may register a notice of inhibition in the Register of Inhibitions and Adjudications after the trust deed has been created. If he fails to do so, creditors who are not party to the trust deed or those who become creditors subsequent to the creation of the trust deed may effect diligence against the estate.

Even where a private trust deed has been effected the debtor may still be sequestrated by other creditors who did not accede to (that is, agree to and become a party to) the trust deed or who are new creditors,[94] or by the debtor himself with the concurrence of non-acceding creditors.[95] Indeed, the private trustee may present a petition for sequestration of the debtor. It should be noted that the granting of a private trust deed by a debtor creates apparent insolvency which allows other creditors to raise sequestration proceedings. Because of this fact, a voluntary arrangement naturally works best where all existing creditors are party to it.

If sequestration is granted after a private trust deed has been effected, the trust deed is not reduced but is brought within the sequestration and those who have acquired rights under it must assert their rights before the permanent trustee.[96]

In private trust arrangements the trustee must provide for all claims made to him. Even if a creditor has not acceded to the making of the private trust deed, he is entitled to make a claim and receive a distribution from the debtor's estate.

---

[91] McBryde, *Bankruptcy* (2nd edn, 1995), pp 152–156.
[92] The advantages of the trust deed are discussed in McBryde, *Bankruptcy* (2nd edn, 1995), pp 424–426.
[93] s 5(4A), inserted by the 1993 Act, s 3(4).
[94] *Kyd* v *Waterson* (1880) 7 R 884.
[95] *McAlister* v *Swinburne & Co* (1874) 1 R 958.
[96] However, the effect of sequestration on an earlier trust deed is problematic: see *Salaman* v *Rosslyn's Trs* (1900) 3 F 298.

Ordinarily, the private trustee cannot challenge prior transactions of the debtor prior to the creation of the trust deed. However, a creditor may do so and may assign his right to the private trustee.[97]

Where the trustee obtains a discharge from a creditor, he must notify the Accountant in Bankruptcy and the non-acceding creditors (those not party to the trust deed) of this. A non-acceding creditor may challenge the discharge where he can establish that it is unfairly prejudicial.

Private trust deeds can last a long time. As private arrangements, deeds are likely to provide for discharge of the debtor, the trustee and the end of the trust deed.[98]

PROTECTED TRUST DEEDS

9–27 A private trust deed may be made a "protected trust deed".[99] The conditions for the creation of a private trust deed are that:

(a) the deed must conform to the statutory definition;

(b) the trustee would not be disqualified from acting as a permanent trustee;

(c) publication by the trustee of a notice in the *Edinburgh Gazette* and to every creditor known to him a copy of the trust deed;

(d) no more than one-third in value of the creditors object or do not wish to accede to the trust deed (failure to respond is equated with accession); and

(e) the forwarding by the trustee of a copy to the Accountant in Bankruptcy of the trust deed for registration and certification of (d) above.

The impact of protection is that the debtor may not petition for his own sequestration while the protected trust deed exists.[100] However, the primary benefit is that creditors are compelled to give a speedy decision on whether they accede to it or not and failure to object equals accession. Creditors who have not received a notice, or who have indicated that they do not accede, have the right to petition for sequestration but only for a period of up to six weeks. Thereafter the right is lost,[101] and such creditors have only the same rights as those who have acceded to the protected trust deed. A further benefit of the protected trust deed status is that the trustee, following its creation, may challenge gratuitous alienations and fraudulent preferences.[102] The protected trust deed comes to an end once the trustee has made the final distribution of the debtor's estate and the trustee reports to the Accountant in Bankruptcy. At the conclusion of the trust deed's duration, the trustee will recall the inhibition in the Register of Inhibitions and Adjudications. Creditors who are not party to the protected trust deed may challenge any distribution under it on the basis that it is unfairly prejudicial but they will be required to prove this.

---

[97] *Fleming's Trs* v *McHardy* (1892) 19 R 542.
[98] See McBryde, *Bankruptcy* (2nd edn, 1995), pp 438–439.
[99] Defined in s 73(1). See also Sched 5, para 8.
[100] Sched 5, para 6 (as amended by the 1993 Act, Sched 1, para 32(3)).
[101] Sched 5, para 10; if they can show that the distribution under the protected trust deed arrangement is likely to be or is unduly harsh to them they may still assert their rights to petition for sequestration.
[102] ss 34(1) and 36(1).

COMPOSITION CONTRACTS

A composition contract entails the debtor entering into an obligation to pay the **9–28** creditor or creditors so much in the pound. There is an inference that accession by a creditor is on the basis that all creditors have so acceded. For one to remain outside the fold of the agreement may weaken the position of those who enter the contract of composition. Under the contract the debtor grants to creditors bills confirming his obligation to pay instalments to meet the dividend payment. Generally, where an instalment is not forthcoming the entire debt is reinstated. This is a purely voluntary arrangement which does not in any way preclude sequestration or diligence on the property of the debtor by any creditor who has not acceded to the composition contract.

SUMMARY

OVERVIEW

- The law of bankruptcy is principally found in the Bankruptcy (Scotland) Act 1985 (as amended). Bankruptcy is overseen by the Accountant in Bankruptcy.

INSOLVENCY AND ITS EFFECTS

- Insolvency will not affect the debtor's capacity to pursue and defend legal actions. More importantly, on the face of things it does not stop the debtor continuing to trade or deal with a view to turning his financial situation around.

THE SIGNIFICANCE OF "APPARENT INSOLVENCY"

- The inability to meet a particular debt when demanded to do so may be defined as "apparent insolvency".
- The concept of "apparent insolvency" has considerable importance in bankruptcy law in that it is necessary that there be "apparent insolvency" for a creditor to petition the court for sequestration.

SEQUESTRATION—AN OVERVIEW

- The process whereby a person is legally declared bankrupt and his assets removed from him is known as sequestration.
- Many debtors voluntarily seek sequestration as a means whereby they can, in the medium and long term, escape their insolvency and, after a period of sequestration, start again free from the obligations they have to existing creditors.
- Sequestration of a person's estate is granted by the court and thereafter is subject to the supervision of the Accountant in Bankruptcy.
- Sequestration is applicable to an estate belonging to or held by a trust, a partnership (against the partnership alone and/or also against the individual partners), a body corporate (not a company), or an unincorporated body as well as an individual (living or deceased).

WHO MAY PETITION FOR SEQUESTRATION?

- A creditor may lodge a petition in court for sequestration with or without the concurrence of other creditors so long as the total indebtedness owed to the petitioning creditor(s) is not less than £1,500.
- If a solitary debtor is to raise proceedings alone without the concurrence of creditor(s) the debt due to him must be £1,500 or more.

PETITION FOR SEQUESTRATION

- The commencement of the sequestration process will begin with the presentation of a petition for sequestration to the court.
- An interim trustee will be appointed upon the award of sequestration. In the absence of a nominated interim trustee the Accountant in Bankruptcy will be appointed as interim trustee.

RECALLING SEQUESTRATION

- The award of sequestration cannot be reviewed but it may be recalled.

THE PERSONNEL INVOLVED IN INSOLVENCY PROCEEDINGS

- interim trustee
- permanent trustee
- Accountant in Bankruptcy

INTERIM TRUSTEE

- The principal duty of the interim trustee is to safeguard the debtor's estate. In this regard he has a broad array of powers.
- The interim trustee (if he is not the Accountant in Bankruptcy) must convene a statutory meeting of creditors.

PERMANENT TRUSTEE

- One of the primary functions of the statutory meeting is to elect a permanent trustee.
- On appointment of the permanent trustee, the estate of the debtor vests in the permanent trustee and he must administer it for the benefit of the creditors.
- The bankrupt must act in good faith with the permanent trustee.

THE RIGHT TO CHALLENGE PRIOR ACTIONS OF THE DEBTOR WHICH DISADVANTAGE CREDITORS

- The permanent trustee has a role in securing the interests of creditors and has the power to challenge transactions entered into by the debtor which prejudiced the creditors.
- The insolvent debtor must act in a fashion consistent with his obligation not to harm the interests of the creditors. He must be open with his finances and cannot conceal assets or income. He cannot give away, dissipate or destroy assets, nor can he create any preferential right or security over assets hitherto owned by him.
- There are rules which prohibit gratuitous alienations (the giving away of assets for free), the granting of unfair preferences or the creation of fraudulent

preferences on particular creditors which advantage them and disadvantage the other creditors.

• Once the accounts and the sums therein are fixed the permanent trustee will arrange to distribute the dividend to creditors as proposed in his accounts.

DISCHARGE OF THE DEBTOR AND THE END OF SEQUESTRATION

• The debtor may be discharged in one of two ways. He may effectively recoup his position and make an offer to his creditors via the permanent trustee which if acceptable to them will result in discharge. Alternatively, the debtor may await the expiry of time, usually three years, and obtain "automatic" discharge.

ALTERNATIVES TO SEQUESTRATION

• As an alternative to sequestration the insolvent may wind up his affairs by private agreement with his creditors. Such private agreements may be so informal as simply to be arrangements to pay by instalments or at some future date.

• However, there are also formal voluntary arrangements alternate to sequestration itself. Accordingly, a debtor may make a voluntary arrangement with creditors which is effected by trust deed or a composition contract.

CASE DIGEST

The property of the bankrupt vests in the permanent trustee [see para 9–14]
  White v *Stevenson* 1956 SC 84
The bankrupt owned a mansion house. Following bankruptcy he refused to move. It was held that the bankrupt had no right to occupy the house as his rights in it had vested in the trustee. Accordingly, he could be ejected.

Gratuitous alienations during insolvency may be subsequently challenged [see para 9–17]
  Lombardi's Tr v *Lombardi* 1982 SLT 81
The bankrupt had granted a disposition in favour of his wife. His solicitor had the deed but did not record it until 18 months later. The husband subsequently became insolvent and four months after the recording of the title deed a permanent trustee was appointed in his sequestration. It was held that the insolvency of the debtor at the time of granting the disposition allowed the gratuitous alienation of the property to be reduced and the property of the debtor restored to the estates of the bankrupt.

The debtor's word after sequestration is not conclusive evidence of the validity of a creditor's claim in sequestration [see para 9–22]
  Carmichael's Tr v *Carmichael* 1929 SC 265
The mother of a bankrupt made a claim to be ranked as a creditor in his seques-

tration in respect of two loans she made to him prior to his insolvency. There was no written documentation of the loan other than a letter from the bankrupt acknowledging the debt after his sequestration. It was held that this letter was not sufficient evidence to establish the loans.

Deferment of discharge from bankruptcy may be sought [see para 9–23]
  Clydesdale Bank PLC v *Davidson* 1994 SLT 225
The bank successfully sought a deferment from discharge from bankruptcy within the prescribed time. The sheriff only granted the deferment more than three years after the date of sequestration. It was held that discharge was not automatic and that the lodging of the application for deferment within the prescribed time was sufficient to forestall the discharge pending the outcome of the application.

Property which comes to fruition after the discharge of sequestration may nevertheless vest in the permanent trustee [see para 9–23]
  Ross v *HJ Banks and Co Ltd* 1998 SCLR 1109
S entered into an arrangement whereby he would be paid a commission for introducing purchasers to a third party. He was discharged from sequestration in 1996. Prior to that he had introduced a purchaser to the third party. The commission to S was payable only on conclusion of the missives which were completed after the discharge from sequestration. The sheriff held that the right to the commission arose during sequestration and that it was an interest which vested in the permanent trustee who accordingly was entitled to have the commission paid to him.

FURTHER READING

Books
Adie, *Bankruptcy* (W Green, 1995)
Cusine and Forte, *Scottish Cases and Materials in Commercial Law* (2nd edn, Butterworths, 2000)
Forte (ed), *Scots Commercial Law* (Butterworths, 1997), Chapter 7
Gloag and Henderson, *Introduction to the Law of Scotland* (10th edn, W Green, 1995)
Hughes, *Scottish Insolvency Casebook* (W Green, 1994)
The Laws of Scotland: Stair Memorial Encyclopaedia (Law Society of Scotland/ Butterworths), Vol 2 "Bankruptcy"
McBryde, *Bankruptcy* (W Green, 2nd edn, 1995)
McKenzie Skene, *Insolvency Law in Scotland* (T&T Clark, 1999)

Articles
Aird, "The Liquidator, the Permanent Trustee and the Adjudication of Complicated Claims" (1997) 42(6) JLSS 229
Crawford, "A Question of Jurisdiction in Respect of Sequestration" 1999 JR 203
Franks, "The Permanent Trustee in Bankruptcy: Duties on Moving Firms" (1995) 63(4) SLG 142
Gordon, "The Effect of Bankruptcy on Personal Pension" (1997) 42(8) JLSS 329

Grahame, "Petitions for Recall of Sequestration" 1995 JR 453

Jones, "Deferral of Debtor's Discharge" (1995) 40(10) JLSS 388

McKenzie Skene, "The Past is a Foreign Country, they do things differently there" (1998) 14(5) *Insolvency Law and Practice* 312

McKenzie Skene, "Forthwith and Avoiding Sequestration: Some Observations" 1995 SLT (News) 151

Walker, "Bankruptcy" (1997) 246 SCOLAG 196

10 PARTNERSHIP

THE DEFINITION AND NATURE OF PARTNERSHIP

The law of partnership is largely regulated by the Partnership Act of 1890.[1] This legis- **10–01** lation served to codify a number of common law rules of partnership which predated the Act. The term "partnership" suggests parties working together towards some common goal. Not all such collaborations, however, are treated as partnerships under the Act. Section 1 of the Act defines a partnership as "the relationship which subsists between persons carrying on business in common with a view to profit".

ESSENTIAL ELEMENTS OF A PARTNERSHIP

More than one person

As the name "partnership" suggests, a partnership must consist of more than one **10–02** person. The maximum number of partners is generally set at 20 although there are certain notable exceptions to this rule. This is examined at para 10–12.

Business

The term "business" denotes that the partnership must be involved in some sort of **10–03** commercial venture. Section 45 of the Act defines "business" in very wide terms to include "every trade, occupation or profession". Even if parties work together in pursuance of a single business transaction, this may be sufficient to amount to a partnership.[2]

By virtue of section 1(2), companies, either registered under the Companies Acts or incorporated by an Act of Parliament, Letters Patent or Royal Charter are specifically excluded from the partnership definition.[3]

Profit motive

Before a partnership exists, the parties must participate with profit in mind. Thus non- **10–04** profit-making organisations such as clubs, charitable associations and church groups are not treated as partnerships under the Act.

---

[1] All further statutory references in this chapter are to this Act unless the contrary is stated.
[2] *Winsor* v *Schroeder* (1979) 129 NLJ 1266.
[3] See Chapter 11. In addition, persons working together for the purposes of forming a company have also been held not to be in partnership: *Keith Spicer Ltd* v *Mansell* [1970] 1 All ER 462.

RULES DETERMINING WHETHER A PARTNERSHIP EXISTS

10–05   In most cases it will be readily apparent whether a partnership exists or not. In other cases the situation may not be so clear cut. As will be examined below, if a firm cannot pay its debts then the partners may themselves incur personal liability for those debts. Determining whether a partnership exists and what persons are to be treated as partners are therefore extremely important issues: section 2 of the Act sets out a number of rules which assist in resolving them.

As a general point it should first be noted that each rule by itself will not provide conclusive evidence of whether a partnership exists or not—every case must be examined having due regard to the full facts and circumstances of the business relationship involved. Moreover, it is worth noting that the courts will not be unduly concerned with how the parties to the business relationship themselves term their arrangement. Rather, courts take an objective view of whether, in all the circumstances, a partnership has been constituted.

JOINT OR COMMON INTEREST IN PROPERTY[4]

10–06   By virtue of section 2(1), if the parties have a joint or common interest in property or any part ownership of property then this *by itself* will not create a partnership in relation to that property.[5]

THE SHARING OF GROSS RETURNS

10–07   Again the sharing of gross returns will not by itself give rise to a presumption that a partnership exists. The sharing of gross returns is a common method by which employees are paid in terms of commission and this will not have the effect as to make these employees partners. For example, in *Cox v Coulson*,[6] C, a theatre manager, entered into an agreement with M, that he (C) would be responsible for the provision of the theatre and associated lighting and advertising costs in exchange for 60 per cent of the gross returns of ticket sales. When a member of the audience was injured during the performance, she sought to recover monies from C on the basis that he was in partnership with M. The court held that the mere sharing of gross returns did not by itself establish a partnership.[7]

SHARING OF NET PROFITS.

10–08   On the other hand, by virtue of section 2(3), if a person receives a share of net profits then this will amount to prima facie evidence (*ie* a presumption) that a partnership exists.[8] This test is not conclusive, however, and the Act sets out a number of circum-

---

[4]   See Chapter 7.
[5]   See *Sharpe* v *Carswell* 1910 SC 391; *Dawson* v *Counsell* [1938] 3 All ER 5.
[6]   [1916] 2 KB 177.
[7]   See also *Clark* v *Jamieson* 1909 SC 132.
[8]   This presumption was first established in *Badeley* v *Consolidated Bank* (1888) 38 Ch D 238 (CA).

stances in which a share in net profits will not *by itself* be regarded as constituting a partnership. These include:

(a) where a person receives payment of a debt out of the profits of a business[9];

(b) where an employee is paid or partly paid by way of a share in the net profits of the business[10];

(c) where the widow or child of a deceased partner receives a share of net profits as an annuity[11];

(d) where a person has loaned money to the partnership under an agreement which provides that the lender will be paid back at an interest rate which varies with the net profits of the firm *and* that agreement is in writing and signed by all the parties[12];

(e) where someone sells the goodwill of the business and receives a portion of the profits as payment.[13]

THE SEPARATE PERSONALITY OF THE FIRM

Partnerships are commonly referred to as "firms".[14] A firm is a separate legal person **10–09**
distinct from the partners of whom it consists.[15] The partnership does not, however, exhibit the full characteristics of a separate legal personality. It is probably better therefore to think of the firm as being a quasi-legal person. Most notably perhaps, unlike the position as regards registered companies which exhibit the full character-istics of a separate legal personality,[16] if the partnership cannot pay its debts then the partners become jointly and severally liable for the firm's debts.[17]

Nonetheless there are a number of repercussions which arise from the separate legal personality of the firm: the firm can enter into contracts with the partners and can be sued by or can sue any other partners; the firm can enter into contracts with third parties in its own name; the firm can own property in its own name (although not heritable property held on feudal tenure)[18]; the firm can itself be declared bankrupt.

---

[9] s 2(3)(a).
[10] s 2(3)(b).
[11] s 2(3)(c).
[12] s 2(3)(d).
[13] s 2(3)(e). See also *Pratt v Stick* (1932) 17 TC 459. Goodwill is an intangible asset that generally speaking represents the monetary value which can be placed upon the customer base and good reputation of the business.
[14] s 4(1). It should be borne in mind that confusion can arise as the term "firm" is often used colloquially to refer to other types of business organisation including companies and sole traders.
[15] s 4(2).
[16] See Chapter 11.
[17] The term "joint and several liability" means that all and any of the partners may be sued personally for the firm's debts. If one partner settles a firm's debt then he has a right of relief against the others.
[18] See Chapter 7.

FORMATION OF A PARTNERSHIP

10-10 Unlike the position relating to registered companies, there are no particular formalities to be followed in forming a partnership.[19] From a practical point of view this brings obvious advantages in terms of flexibility and the time and costs expended in setting up the firm. A written document which sets out the terms and conditions of the partnership is referred to as a contract of "co-partnery". While for commercial convenience and reasons of proof it may be preferable to have a written document setting out the terms of the partnership, there need be no written contract. A partnership can be constituted orally or be inferred from the course of dealing between the parties.

RESTRICTIONS ON PARTNERSHIP FORMATION

Capacity

10-11 The general law relating to contractual capacity applies in relation to partnership formation.[20] For example, a person of unsound mind can have no capacity to form a partnership and hence any such purported partnership would be void.[21] A young person between the ages of 16 and 18 has full contractual capacity to enter into a partnership.[22] This is subject to the right of the young person to challenge the transaction if it is prejudicial to him in the sense that he has suffered (or is likely to suffer) financially and a reasonable adult would not have entered into the agreement. This right to challenge is unlikely to be of any import in the partnership context as it does not apply where the young person acts in the course of his trade or business. It should also be noted that it is illegal to contract with an enemy alien—that is a citizen of a nation that the UK is at war with. When war breaks out and a partner in a firm becomes an enemy alien, the partnership is automatically deemed to have dissolved.[23]

Number of parties

10-12 By virtue of the Companies Act 1985, s 716(1), there are restrictions placed upon the number of partners which a partnership can have. Generally a partnership cannot consists of more than 20 partners. However, certain professional groupings are explicitly excluded from this limitation. These include solicitors, accountants, and members of the stock exchange. Additionally, members of other professional groupings are granted exemptions from the provisions of section 716 from time to time by the Secretary of State through a series of Partnership (Unrestricted Size) Regulations. If a partnership fails to comply with the statutory limits on the number of partners then it will be deemed illegal and each partner will be subject to unlimited liability in respect of the firm's debts.

---

[19] See Chapter 11.
[20] See Chapter 4.
[21] An insane person can never be regarded as having ever been a partner, hence he can never be liable for partnership debts.
[22] Age of Legal Capacity (Scotland) Act 1991, s 1(1).
[23] *Hugh Stevenson & Sons* v *AG fur Cartonnagen-Industrie* [1918] AC 239 (HL); *R* v *Kupfer* (1915) 112 LT 1138.

Illegality

A partnership agreement will be void if it is formed for an illegal purpose. An old case, **10–13**
Everet v *Williams*,[24] held that two highwaymen who entered into an agreement to share
in the expenses and profits of their illegal activities could not be held to be in
partnership. One of the highwaymen was therefore unable to compel the other to
account for certain profits from their ventures which he had failed to declare.[25]

Statutory restrictions on the firm's name

The Business Names Act 1985 sets out restrictions on the use of certain names. This Act **10–14**
applies not only to partnerships but also to sole traders and limited companies. In
relation to partnerships, the Act only comes into effect when the firm's name does not
consist of the names of the partners themselves.[26]

One of the main purposes of the Act is to ensure that third parties dealing with the
firm are able to ascertain who the partners of the firm are. Hence a partnership trading
under a name which does not consist of the partners' names must display the true
names of all partners on all business correspondence of the firm. It should be noted
that these provisions do not apply to partnerships where there are in excess of 20
partners; although in such cases the names of all partners must be displayed at the
partnership's place of business.

Additionally, certain names are expressly disallowed by the Act. In particular,
names which convey the impression that the firm is connected with local or central
government require the approval of the Secretary of State. Other names which imply
a certain status require the approval of the Secretary of State and are specified in
regulations issued by the Minister from time to time (current examples are the words
"trade union", "University" and "Scottish").[27]

Common law restrictions on the firm's name

In addition to the statutory rules, the common law also has an impact in this area. In **10–15**
circumstances where a new business trades under a name which is either identical or
very similar to the name of an established firm, the existing firm may bring an action
of interdict to prevent further use of the name. This ensures that firms do not (intentionally or otherwise) dupe customers who may be labouring under the misconception
that they are dealing with another firm, into dealing with their firm. Such an action for
interdict is known as a "passing off" action.

---

[24] (1787) unreported.
[25] See also *Michael Jeffrey & Co* v *Bamford* [1921] 2 KB 351; *Lindsay* v *Inland Revenue* 1933 SC 33.
[26] The Act does allow a small measure of leeway here, however. In relation to firms, the initials of the
partners may be substituted for their forenames, or if the partners share the same surname, a plural of that
name with or without initials is acceptable.
[27] See the Company and Business Names (Amendment) Regulations 1995 (SI 1995/3022).

RELATIONSHIP BETWEEN THE PARTNERS AND THIRD PARTIES

THE AGENCY RELATIONSHIP[28]

10–16 Under the common law, a partner is an agent of the firm. Obviously, where the partner is authorised to carry out a certain act by the firm, his actions will bind the firm in relation to third parties. This is set out in section 6 of the Act which states that where a partner with authority to carry out an act in relation to the business of the firm does so in the firm's name he will bind the firm and the other partners.

A third party will be unlikely, however, to be aware of the extent of the partner's express powers under the partnership agreement. Given the agency relationship between partners and the firm, a partner binds the firm with third parties by the commission of acts which are carried out in the usual way that business is carried out. This rule is underpinned by section 5 of the 1890 Act. The section states:

> "Every partner is an agent of the firm and his other partners for the purpose of the business of the partnership; and the acts of every partner who does any act for carrying on in the usual way business of the kind carried on by the firm of which he is a member bind the firm and the partners, unless the partner so acting has in fact no authority to act for the firm in the particular matter, and the person with whom he is dealing either knows that he has no authority, or does not know or believe him to be a partner."

Clearly what amounts to the implied authority of a partner (and what type of acts third parties can rely on) is a crucial question. The scope of the implied authority that a partner has depends on interpretation of the phrase "carrying on business in the usual way". What this amounts to will depend on the type of partnership concerned.

In "trading partnerships"—those in which buying and selling goods and materials are core activities of the firm—partners will enjoy a very wide implied authority, which extends to such activities as borrowing money and granting a security over partnership property.[29] In "non-trading partnerships" where buying and selling are not core activities, there will be no such implied authority to borrow money and grant securities. In *Paterson Brothers* v *Gladstone*[30] a partner in a firm of builders borrowed money from a money lender, G, at an exorbitant rate of interest and pledged that the firm would repay the loan at a specified date. It was held that the firm was not bound to repay the loan as G ought to have known that a partner in such a (non-trading) firm would not have authority to raise money on behalf of the firm in this fashion. As such, G should have taken measures to ensure that the partner had express authority to act for the firm in this way.

Even where a partner's implied authority has been expressly restricted in some way by the firm, a third party who does not know of the restriction will be entitled to enforce the transaction against the firm as the partner has "apparent authority" which he has relied upon in entering into the transaction.[31]

---

[28] See Chapter 6.
[29] *Bryan* v *Butters Bros & Co* (1892) 19 R 490.
[30] (1891) 18 R 403.
[31] s 8; see *Mercantile Credit Co Ltd* v *Garrod* [1962] 3 All ER 103.

By contrast, when a partner enters into a contract on behalf of the firm for a purpose not connected to the firm's business, the firm will not be bound to honour the transaction except where the partner has express authority.[32] In such a case the partner will become personally liable in respect of the transaction. For example, in *Fortune* v *Young*[33] a partner signed a letter guaranteeing the financial standing of an individual seeking a tenancy. This was written on partnership stationery. It was held, however, that as this was outside the scope of the normal business of the partnership, the partner and not the firm was liable under the guarantee.

LIABILITY OF THE FIRM FOR THE ACTS OF NON-PARTNERS

Any person having either express or implied authority to carry out acts related to the business of the partnership will bind the firm.[34] Therefore agents or employees may bind the firm in a similar fashion to partners.   **10–17**

LIABILITY OF THE FIRM FOR ADMISSIONS OF PARTNERS

An admission or representation made by a partner concerning the business of the firm in the ordinary course of business can be used as evidence of that admission against the firm.[35] Any notice relating to partnership affairs given to any partner who habitually acts in the partnership business is tantamount to notice of this information to the firm.[36] An exception to this rule operates where the partner in question commits or consents to the commission of fraud against the firm.[37]   **10–18**

LIABILITY OF THE FIRM FOR WRONGS OF THE PARTNERS

Under section 10 of the Act, where, by any wrongful act or omission of any partner acting in the ordinary course of business of the firm, or with the authority of his co-partners, loss or injury is caused to any person not being a partner of the firm, or any penalty is incurred, the firm is liable thereof to the same extent as the partner so acting or omitting to act.   **10–19**

In essence, the firm becomes vicariously liable for the actions of its partners in a similar fashion to which employers may be held liable for the negligent acts that their employees commit in the course of business.[38] A pertinent example, is *Kirkintilloch Equitable Co-operative Society* v *Livingstone*.[39] In this case there was some doubt as to whether a partner in an accounting firm, J, had been acting within the course of the firm's business. J had for some time acted as official auditor of the Kirkintilloch Equitable Co-operative Society. It was alleged that his negligence had resulted in the

---

[32] s 7.
[33] 1918 SC 1.
[34] s 6.
[35] s 15.
[36] s 16.
[37] It has further been held that the general rule does not apply to solely partner/client matters where the partner may be under a duty of confidentiality and hence cannot communicate such information to the firm: *Campbell* v *McCreath* 1975 SLT (Notes) 5 (OH).
[38] See Chapter 12.
[39] 1972 SC 111.

Society suffering a loss and an action was raised against J's firm in this regard under section 10. The firm argued that as it was illegal for the firm to be acting as official auditor to the Society, J's actings could not be in the course of business and hence the action was irrelevant. The court held, however, that what was important was whether or not the auditing of accounts was within the firm's contemplation of what business activities it might undertake. The answer to this question, the court viewed, was undoubtedly in the affirmative. Further, the court also held that in any case the other partners had approved of J's actions. The firm was therefore liable for the losses.

It should be noted that under section 10 the firm is not liable if one partner injures another.[40] In such a case, of course, the partner who commits the act remains responsible.[41]

MISAPPROPRIATION OF PROPERTY OR MONEY OF A THIRD PARTY

10–20 Special provision is made for circumstances in which the money or property of a third party is misappropriated by a partner of the firm.[42] The firm will be rendered liable for any resulting loss where money or property is received by a partner acting within the course of the firm's business and that money or property is misappropriated by him, and where the money or property is received by the firm in the course of its business and one or more partners misapplies that money whilst in the firm's custody. A pertinent example of this is *Rhodes* v *Moules*,[43] in which a client seeking a loan was informed by a partner that additional security in the form of share warrants[44] was required. After the partner had misappropriated the warrants, the court upheld a claim by the client against the firm in respect of the losses suffered on the grounds that, in accordance with section 11, the warrants had been appropriated by the firm in the normal course of business.

JOINT AND SEVERAL LIABILITY OF PARTNERS FOR DEBTS AND OBLIGATIONS OF THE FIRM

10–21 Partners are jointly and severally liable for all debts and obligations incurred by the firm while they are partners.[45] If the firm is unable to pay its debts and cannot make due payment through the sale of its assets then each partner becomes personally liable. The term "joint and several liability" means that each party can be sued by a third party for any and all of the debts and obligations owed. If any partner is made liable for such debts of the firm, he may seek relief from the other partners.[46]

In relation to a deceased partner, the estate of that partner can be made liable for debts which were incurred while he was part of the firm.[47] Similarly, the estate of a

---

[40] See *Mair* v *Wood* (1886) 1 Ch 326. This position contrasts with the situation relating to vicarious liability in employment law—see Chapter 12.
[41] *Parker* v *Walker* 1961 SLT 252 (OH).
[42] s 11.
[43] [1895] 1 Ch 236.
[44] A right to take up shares. See Chapter 11.
[45] s 9.
[46] s 4(2).
[47] *Bagel* v *Miller* [1903] 2 KB 212.

bankrupt partner[48] is only liable for debts of the partnership incurred whilst the bankrupt was a partner in the firm.[49]

JOINT AND SEVERAL LIABILITY OF PARTNERS FOR OBLIGATIONS INCURRED UNDER SECTIONS 10 AND 11

In a similar fashion, section 12 stipulates that all partners are joint and severally liable   **10-22** with the firm for all liabilities incurred under sections 10 and 11.

LIABILITY THROUGH HOLDING OUT

In this situation, liability occurs not because the person concerned is a partner in the   **10-23** firm, but because he has either represented himself to a third party as being a partner or has knowingly allowed himself to be represented (or "held out") in such a manner. Such representation can come into being either orally, in writing or be implied by the conduct of the person concerned. In *Hosie* v *Waddle*,[50] W owed H a debt and had in fact paid that debt to C, whom he had believed to have been H's partner. When C absconded with the money, H claimed that C had never been a partner but was merely an employee. The court held, however, that C had been held out as a partner by H and hence payment of the debt had been duly made.

A partner who has retired may often place himself at the risk of being held out as a partner if he does not ensure that all customers are notified of his departure from the firm.[51] Section 14(2) makes express provision, however, that where a deceased partner's name continues to be used in the firm's name that does not in itself make the deceased's estate liable for partnership debts arising after his death.

LIABILITY OF INCOMING AND OUTGOING PARTNERS

The partners who comprise a firm commonly change over time as existing partners   **10-24** retire or die and new partners are appointed. The issue of what debts of the firm the various incoming and outgoing partners are liable for becomes an important one.

Liability of incoming partners

Under section 17(1), an incoming partner does not become liable for any debts or liabil-   **10-25** ities incurred by the firm before he became a partner in the firm. However, the situation is not as clear cut as section 17 would suggest. First, an incoming partner may assume liabilities for existing debts of the firm where an agreement is reached to that effect between the new partner, the firm and the creditor. Second, where a new partner is assumed into a firm, circumstances may show that the newly constituted firm has taken over liabilities of the former firm. This can result from the express agreement of the partners or by an equitable presumption which arises to this effect. The rule is designed primarily to protect third parties where, for example, a sole trader transfers all assets (and liabilities) to a firm and assumes a new partner who himself has

---

[48] See Chapter 9.
[49] s 36(3).
[50] (1866) 3 SLR 16.
[51] See para 10-27.

invested no new capital. In the event of the firm being unable to pay the debts, the new partner may be found personally liable for the firm's debts incurred before he became a partner.[52] In addition, where a continuous running account is operated with a creditor, then an incoming partner may become liable for debts existing at the time he was assumed into the firm.[53]

Liability of retiring partners for debts incurred prior to retiral

10–26 A partner who retires from the firm remains liable for debts of the firm incurred prior to his retiral.[54] A retiring partner can, however, be freed from this obligation by way of an express agreement to this effect between himself, the members of the partnership and the creditor(s) concerned.[55] This agreement may be either in express terms or implied by the course of dealing between the new firm and the creditor. It should be noted that such an agreement reached merely between the partners is of no effect in freeing the retiring partner from liability for pre-existing debts.[56] This is in keeping with the general law of contract that delegating a debt to another requires the consent of the creditor.[57]

Liability of retiring partners for debts incurred after retiral

10–27 As would be expected, the general rule here is that a partner is not liable for debts incurred by the firm after his retiral. However, a retiring partner might become so liable for debts on the basis of "holding out"[58] if he continued to represent himself or allowed himself to be represented as a partner in the firm at a time when he had in fact retired. Where a person deals with a firm after a change in its constitution he is entitled to continue to treat all members of the old firm as partners until he has received notice of the change.[59]

The Act enlightens little on the nature that this notice must take. In practice, however, a notice is generally sent out to all customers of the firm notifying them of the change in the partnership's constitution. A change would also be made in particulars of the business correspondence of the firm. Anything short of personal notification of customers is likely to be regarded as inadequate notice. In relation to persons who have had no prior dealings with the firm, acceptable notice of the change in the firm's constitution can be made by placing an advert to this effect in the *Edinburgh Gazette*.[60]

Under section 36(3), a retiring partner will not be liable for debts contracted after his retirement if he has never been known to the person dealing with the firm to have been a partner.[61] Section 36(3) also provides that the estate of a deceased partner or a

---

[52] See *Miller* v *Thorburn* (1861) 23 D 359; *Heddie's Exrx* v *Marwick & Hourston's Tr* (1888) 15 R 698; and *Miller* v *Macleod* 1973 SC 172.
[53] *Devaynes* v *Noble* (*Clayton's Case*) (1816) 1 Mer 529.
[54] s 17(2).
[55] s 17(3).
[56] *Campbell* v *Cruickshank* (1845) 7 D 548; *Muir* v *Dickson* (1860) 22 D 1070.
[57] See Chapter 4.
[58] See above.
[59] s 36(1).
[60] s 36(2). For firms whose principal place of business is in England or Wales, the appropriate advertisement should be placed in the *London Gazette*.
[61] *Tower Cabinets Ltd* v *Ingram* [1949] 2 KB 397.

bankrupt partner does not become liable for debts incurred after the partner's death or sequestration.

Single continuing contracts

Retiring partners may find themselves liable in respect of contracts and obligations **10–28** which were entered into at a time when they were partners of the firm and which can be viewed as continuing obligations in the sense that once entered into, the partners must see them to their conclusion. In *Court* v *Berlin*[62] a firm retained C as a solicitor to instigate legal proceedings in pursuance of a debt. During the course of the debt action, two partners in the firm retired. After the proceedings were completed, C sued the two partners for his fees. The court held that notwithstanding that the two partners had retired prior to the end of the legal proceedings, the contract with C was a continuing contract to see the action through to the end. The partners were therefore liable for the full amount.[63]

RELATIONS OF PARTNERS TO ONE ANOTHER

This section examines the legal relationship that exists between the partners *inter se* **10–29** ("between themselves") and the repercussions of this relationship. Detailed provisions governing this relationship are set out in sections 19–31 of the Act. Some general observations regarding the nature of the relationship can be made, however, prior to examining the statutory provisions in detail.

GENERAL PRINCIPLES

There are three general principles which govern the relationship between the partners. **10–30** The first is that central to the partnership relationship—the element of *delectus personae* (or "choice of person"). What this means is that the personal qualities of a partner are important to his co-partners. To give an example of this principle in operation, a new partner cannot be assumed into a partnership without the agreement of all the other partners.

The second principle is that the relationship between partners is of a fiduciary nature—that is one of trust where the utmost good faith must be maintained by partners in their dealings with each other. This results in a number of duties that partners owe one another, such as an obligation to disclose all relevant information regarding the business of the partnership to their fellow partners and a duty not to make a personal gain from their partnership dealings.

The third guiding principle is that the partners are largely free to decide on the form and substance of their partnership agreement. As has previously been noted, the agreement between the partners may arise in the form of a written agreement (known

---

[62] [1897] 2 QB 396.
[63] Another pertinent example here would be a bank loan. As the law presumes that the obligation to repay the loan occurs when the debt arises (even though repayment is not to be sought until a later date), retiring partners will be personally liable in respect of loans secured by the firm prior to their retiral.

as a contract of "co-partnery"), through an oral contract or may be implied by the conduct of the parties. It should be noted here that the provisions of the Act regarding the relationship of partners *inter se* are therefore default provisions—they apply only where provision regarding these issues has not been made in the partnership agreement. This is made explicit by section 19 of the Act:

> "The mutual rights and duties of partners, whether ascertained by agreement or defined in this Act, may be varied by the consent of all the partners, and such consent may be either express or implied from a course of dealing."

With this firmly in mind, the following section examines the default provisions.

PARTNERSHIP PROPERTY

10–31   Partnership property can be defined as "all property and rights and interests in property originally brought into the partnership stock or acquired, whether by purchase or otherwise, on account of the firm, or for the purposes and in the course of the partnership business".[64] Such partnership property belongs to the firm and not to the partners themselves. Given the artificial nature of the partnership's status as a separate legal entity, in practice such partnership property will be managed by and be in the possession of the partners themselves. It does not follow from this, however, that partners may treat such assets as their own personal property.[65] Such property must only be used for the purpose of the partnership and in accordance with the partnership agreement.[66]

It should be noted that legal title to partnership property may be either in the firm's name or in the name of the individual partners. In the case of heritable property which is held on feudal tenure,[67] legal title cannot be held in the firm's name. Generally speaking such property will be held in the partners' names as trustees for the firm.[68]

Property which is paid for out of partnership profits is presumed to be the property of the firm.[69] This presumption can be rebutted, however, if contrary evidence is brought.

It is important to note that it does not always follow that where partners are co-owners of property and split profits which have been derived from ownership of that property, such property is partnership property. In what may seem a somewhat difficult provision to follow, section 20(3) provides that where partners derive profits from heritable property of which they are co-owners and such profits are not partnership profits, and if they make use of these profits to purchase more heritable property, that property so purchased is not deemed to be partnership property unless evidence is brought to the contrary.

---

[64] s 20(1).
[65] *Munro* v *Stein* 1961 SC 362.
[66] s 20(1). The court will take an objective view of all the circumstances relating to property in determining whether such property has been acquired as partnership property or not: see *McNiven* v *Peffers* (1868) 7 M 18; *Davie* v *Buchanan* (1880) 8 R 319.
[67] See Chapter 7.
[68] See Chapter 7. It should be noted that feudal tenure may soon be abolished as at the time of writing a Bill is currently being processed through the Scottish Parliament to this effect. This would have the effect of making this provision obsolete.
[69] s 21.

DUTIES OF PARTNERS

The fiduciary nature of the relationship between the parties is exemplified in a number of duties that partners are bound to adhere to, set out in sections 28–30 of the Act. **10–32**

Duty to account

Under section 28, "partners are bound to render true accounts and full information on any matter concerning the partnership to any partner or his legal representative". Non-disclosure may give rise to a claim for damages[70] or an action may be raised for accounting and the payment of any balance due.[71] Additionally, a contract of sale between partners where one party has failed to provide all relevant information may be set aside. In *Law v Law*,[72] W and J were partners; W was effectively a sleeping partner. J bought W's share in the business for £21,000. W subsequently discovered that the business was worth much more and that the true value of the business had been shielded from him. It was held by the court that J had a duty to disclose all relevant facts relating to the firm's assets and therefore the contract of sale could be set aside. **10–33**

Duty not to make a personal profit

Under section 29(1) "every partner must account to the firm for any benefit derived by him without the consent of the other partners from any transaction concerning the partnership, or from any use by him of the partnership property, name or business connection". In *Pathirana v Pathirana*,[73] R and A were partners in a service station which belonged to a company, of which they were agents. R terminated the partnership and then formed a new arrangement with the company in his own name. It was held that the agency agreement with the firm was a partnership asset and R's use of it for his own purposes was a breach of his fiduciary duty. A was therefore entitled to a share in the profits of the new venture.[74] **10–34**

The duty to account for personal profits also applies to transactions after a partnership has been dissolved by the death of a partner undertaken either by surviving partners or the representatives of the deceased partner.[75]

Duty not to compete with the firm

It is further provided that "if a partner, without the consent of the other parties, carries on any business of the same nature as and competing with that of the firm, he must account for and pay over to the firm all profits made by him in that business".[76] A pertinent example here is the case of *Pillans Bros v Pillans*[77] in which three brothers were partners in a nut, bolt and rivet manufacturing business. One of the brothers subsequently bought a similar business situated only four miles away. **10–35**

---

[70] *Ferguson v Mackay* 1985 SLT 94 (OH).
[71] *Smith v Barclay* 1962 SC 1.
[72] [1905] 1 Ch 140.
[73] [1967] 1 AC 233.
[74] See also *Finlayson v Turnbull* 1996 SLT 613, where a number of solicitors who left a firm, taking client files with them, were bound to pay back profits to their original firm.
[75] s 29(2).
[76] s 30.
[77] (1908) 16 SLT 611 (OH).

The court held that he had a duty not to compete with the firm and accordingly he had to account to the partnership for the profits of the new business.[78]

RIGHTS OF PARTNERS

10–36   Section 24 sets out a number of provisions relating to the contractual rights which partners will enjoy in the absence of any agreement to the contrary.

Profit/loss sharing and rights to remuneration

10–37   Partners are entitled to an equal share in the capital of the firm and the firm's profits. On the other hand, however, partners are bound to contribute equally to losses.[79] In addition, no partner has an automatic right to payment for work undertaken in respect of partnership business.[80] It is, of course, common to deviate from the statutory rules to specify other profit-sharing arrangements, and in particular to make provision for "salaried partners" who are paid a fixed rate, prior to profits being shared amongst the other partners.[81]

Right to be indemnified

10–38   By virtue of section 24(2)(a), each partner has a right to be indemnified in respect of any payments made or any personal liabilities incurred in the ordinary course of the partnership business. The corresponding duty is that every partner must indemnify any other partner if he incurs liability "in or about anything necessarily done for the preservation of the business or property of the firm".[82]

Interest on advances and on capital

10–39   A partner who advances capital to the firm above the agreed initial capital investment is entitled to interest thereon at a rate of 5 per cent.[83] A partner is not, however, entitled to interest on his ordinary capital contribution until the amount of profit has been determined.[84]

Managing the firm

10–40   Every partner has a right to participate in the management of the firm.[85] This is often varied by express agreement where certain partners, known as "sleeping partners", are merely financial investors in the firm and are precluded from taking an active part in the firm's management. Business decisions taken by the firm, in so far as they relate to ordinary business matters of the firm, can be decided by majority.[86] However, no alteration in the nature of the firm's business can be made without the unanimous consent of all partners.[87]

---

[78] See also *McNiven* v *Peffers* (1868) 7 M 181 and *Stewart* v *North* (1893) 20 R 260.
[79] s 24(1).
[80] s 24(6).
[81] See Styles, "The Salaried Partner" (1994) 39 JLSS 254.
[82] s 24(2)(b).
[83] s 24(3).
[84] s 24(4).
[85] s 24(5).
[86] s 24(8).
[87] *ibid.*

It is further specified that no new partner can be assumed within the firm without the unanimous consent of all parties.[88] However, it should be noted that appointing new employees of the partnership has been held to be within the ordinary nature of business and hence can be determined by a majority of partners.[89]

Partnership books

Every partner has a right to inspect and take a copy of the partnership books (of accounts) which must be kept at the principal place of the partnership's business.[90] This right does not, however, extend to assignees of a partner.[91]

10–41

Expulsion of partners

No partner can be expelled by any majority of the other partners unless the power of expulsion is expressly set down in the partnership agreement.[92] Even if such a power is provided for in the contract of co-partnery, there are limitations on the manner in which it may be enforced. First, the expulsion must fall within the ambit of the clause. In *Carmichael* v *Evans*[93] the partnership agreement made provision for the power of expulsion by six days' notice where a partner was found to be "addicted to notorious intemperance or immorality or other scandalous conduct detrimental to the partnership business" or in "flagrant breach of the duties of a partner". Byrne, a partner expelled from the firm on the basis that he was found travelling on a train without a ticket, sought to have this overturned on the basis that his expulsion fell outwith this clause. The court refused to uphold his case, however, on the footing that it was a primary duty of a partner to be an honest man not only in relation to his partners but also to third parties.

10–42

Any expulsion must also be carried out in accordance with procedure laid down in the clause (*eg* this may relate to a prescribed period of notice or a particular disciplinary process) and, further, any such procedure must have due regard to notions of natural justice (*eg* any partner subject to dismissal proceedings should be given an opportunity to put forward his case). As a final constraint, any expulsion must be carried out bona fide in the best interests of the company. In *Bisset* v *Daniels*[94] the majority of partners sought to expel another partner so as to obtain his shares at a discounted value. This manipulation of the expulsion clause was held to be for the benefit of the majority partners and not in the best interests of the company. The purported expulsion was therefore void.

Partnership at will

The term "partnership at will" can be used to refer to one of two situations. First, it may be used to describe a situation where a firm exists without any time limit being placed upon the duration of the partnership. Second, the term may be used to describe

10–43

---

[88] s 24(7). This is a reflection of the doctrine of *delectus personae* which is central to the partnership agreement. The provision is commonly deviated from: a partner may hold a right to appoint a successor or, on the partner's death, a representative may be appointed to replace him.

[89] *Highley* v *Walker* (1910) 26 TLR 685.

[90] s 24(9)—the partner may delegate this right to an agent.

[91] s 31(1).

[92] s 25.

[93] [1904] 1 Ch 486.

[94] (1853) 10 Hare 493.

a partnership where, although provision has been made for it to exist for a fixed period of time, the parties have continued the partnership beyond that period and no new express agreement has been put in place.[95]

Where the parties continue their partnership on such an ad hoc basis, the rights and duties of the partners shall remain the same as set out in the original agreement.[96]

Assignation

10-44   Any partner may assign his share in the partnership to another. In keeping with the doctrine of *delectus personae* which is central to the partnership agreement, this does not have the effect of making the assignee a partner in the business.[97] The assignee therefore enjoys no right to take an active part in the business of the firm, nor has he a right to inspect the partnership books. He is bound to accept the partners' account of what any firm profits are.[98]

DISSOLUTION OF THE PARTNERSHIP

10-45   A partnership can be dissolved on a number of grounds. It is noteworthy that the term dissolution applies both to situations where the firm ceases to exist perpetually and also to situations where the firm to all intents and purposes continues to trade but where in fact assets have been transferred over to a new firm (with the same name). This, for example, would occur where the constitution of the partnership has altered after one partner has left the firm. Dissolution is governed by sections 32–35 of the Act.

NOTICE OR EXPIRATION

10-46   A partnership entered into for a fixed period is dissolved automatically when the term expires.[99] Similarly, where a partnership is constituted for the purpose of engaging in a single transaction, the partnership is dissolved automatically when that transaction comes to an end.[100]

A partnership entered into where no time limit is specified (a "partnership at will") can be dissolved at any time by a partner by giving notice.[101] The date of the dissolution will be the date specified in the notice. If no date is specified then the date of dissolution will be the date that the notice is communicated to the other partners. In *Macleod* v *Dowling*[102] a partner sent notice of dissolution of the partnership to his co-partner who died before he received it. The court held that dissolution did not come

---

[95] This is known as "tacit relocation" (silent renewal).

[96] s 27(1). The rights and duties set out on the agreement will only endure in so far as these provisions are consistent with the new status of the firm as partnership at will: see *Neilson* v *Mossend Iron Co* (1886) 13 R (HL) 50 and compare with *McGown* v *Henderson* 1914 SC 839.

[97] s 31.

[98] s 31(1).

[99] s 32. Although if the partners continue to carry on the business, the firm will continue as a partnership at will.

[100] s 32(b).

[101] s 26(1).

[102] (1927) 43 TLR 655.

into effect until notice was received. Hence the partnership was dissolved by the death of the partner rather than by notice.

Where a partnership at will is constituted in writing, notice in written form, signed by the partner giving notice, will be sufficient.[103] The intention to dissolve has been implied from the actions of the parties in cases where there is no written contract.[104]

DEATH OR BANKRUPTCY

A partnership is dissolved automatically when any partner dies or becomes bankrupt.[105] This provision can be varied, however, by the agreement of the partners.[106]   **10–47**

ILLEGALITY

A partnership is automatically dissolved if any event makes it illegal for the firm to carry on its business or for the partners to work together.[107]   **10–48**

RESCISSION

It should be noted that a partnership may also be rescinded in the same way as other contracts where parties have entered into the agreement on the basis of some form of misrepresentation which may be either innocent, negligent or fraudulent. If the misrepresentation is either negligent or fraudulent this may also give rise to a claim for damages.[108]   **10–49**

SECTION 35: DISSOLUTION BY THE COURT

Section 35 sets out six prescribed grounds under which the court may dissolve the partnership agreement on an application made by any partner. This is a discretionary power and thus, even if any of the following grounds are proven, it does not necessarily follow that the remedy will be granted. As an additional point, it has been held that the court's jurisdiction under section 35 cannot be ousted by a clause in the partnership agreement stipulating that all disputes relating to the partnership be settled by reference to arbitration.[109]   **10–50**

Insanity

If a partner is found to be of permanent unsound mind then any other partner or the insane person's *curator bonis* (a guardian appointed to look after his affairs) can petition the court for the dissolution of the partnership.[110]   **10–51**

---

[103] s 26(2).
[104] see *Jassal's Exrx* v *Jassal's Trs* 1988 SLT 757 (OH).
[105] s 33(1). The term bankruptcy refers to a situation where a person is sequestrated under the Bankruptcy (Scotland) Act 1985—see Chapter 9.
[106] *William S Gordon & Co Ltd* v *Mrs Mary Thomson Partnership* 1985 SLT 122.
[107] See para 10–11.
[108] See Chapter 4.
[109] *Roxburgh* v *Dinardo* 1981 SLT 291 (OH).
[110] s 35(a).

Permanent incapacity

10–52   A partner may petition the court to have the firm wound up if a partner (otherwise than by virtue of insanity) becomes permanently incapable of carrying out his partnership functions.[111] Much will depend here on the nature of the incapacity and how the court determines what functions the partner is required to undertake in respect of partnership business. On the facts of the case in *Eadie* v *MacBean's Curator Bonis*,[112] the court held that it was not an essential component of the partnership agreement that a partner who had been paralysed need take any active part in the firm's business. The petition of the other partners for the winding up of the firm was therefore refused.

Prejudicial conduct

10–53   This arises where any partner (other than the partner bringing the action) has conducted himself in such a manner as to prejudice the carrying on of the firm's business.[113] Due regard must be paid here to the nature of the firm's business and how this might be affected by a partner's actings.

Breach of the partnership agreement

10–54   Where a partner breaches the partnership agreement or acts in such a fashion in relation to partnership business as serves to break down the mutual trust between the partners, any other partner may petition the court for a dissolution.[114] A clear illustration of this provision in action is the case of *Thomson, Petitioner*,[115] where a partner drew a cheque in the firm's name and absconded with the proceeds. This was a blatant breach of the partnership agreement and the court granted an order for dissolution at the behest of one of the other partners.

Where business can only be carried out at a loss

10–55   If, in practical terms, it has become impossible for the firm to make a profit, any partner may petition the court to have the partnership wound up.[116] Care must be taken to distinguish this situation from one in which profit could be made if the firm were to be managed more effectively.[117]

Where it is just and equitable to wind up the firm

10–56   This final provision is in some sense a catch-net clause under which the court may wind up a partnership at the behest of any partner in circumstances where it deems it is "just and equitable" to do so.[118] This power is very similar to the provisions of section 124 of the Insolvency Act 1986 which relate to the just and equitable winding up of registered companies.[119]

---

[111] s 35(b).
[112] (1885) 12 R 660. See also *MacCreadie's Trs* v *Lamond* (1886) 24 SLR 114.
[113] s 35(c).
[114] s 35(d).
[115] (1893) 1 SLT 59.
[116] s 35(e).
[117] See *Handyside* v *Campbell* (1901) 17 TLR 623.
[118] s 35(f).
[119] For examples of this general approach, see *Cleghorn* (1901) 1 SLT 409 (OH); *Re Yenidje Tobacco Ltd* [1916] 2 Ch 426; *Baird* v *Lees* 1924 SC 83; and *Ebrahimi* v *Westbourne Galleries Ltd* [1972] 2 All ER 492.

APPOINTMENT OF JUDICIAL FACTOR

Generally speaking, the onus to wind up the affairs of the firm after the partnership **10–57** has been dissolved lies with the partners themselves. In limited circumstances the court will, however, appoint a judicial factor whose remit will be to wind up the firm's affairs on behalf of the partners. By virtue of section 39, any partner (or his representatives) may apply to the court to appoint a judicial factor to wind up the affairs of the firm.[120] A judicial factor is likely to be granted where there are no surviving partners capable of winding up the firm, it seems either that the partners will be unable to reach agreement on how the firm is to be wound up or that some sort of judicial protection is required for any partner.[121] A useful example is *Carabine* v *Carabine*,[122] where a husband and wife were partners in a hotel business in which both had contributed capital and there was no written contract of co-partnery. The husband sought to carry on business against the wife's wishes at a time when a building society was threatening to force the sale of business premises. The court appointed a judicial factor in order that the wife's interests be protected.[123]

RIGHTS ARISING ON DISSOLUTION

Right to notify dissolution

Every partner has the right to give public notice of the dissolution and can require his **10–58** fellow partners to concur in any action necessary for this.[124] This is especially important from the point of view of protecting the interests of retiring partners who, under section 36, may continue to be held liable for debts of the firm until customers are notified of the change in the constitution of the partnership.[125]

Continuing authority of partners

After the partnership has been dissolved, partners continue to have authority to bind **10–59** the firm in so far as their actions are necessary to wind up the affairs of the firm.[126] This authority may endure for some time after the dissolution of the firm. In *Dickson* v *National Bank of Scotland Ltd*,[127] it was held that the continuing authority of a partner under section 28 continued to have effect when some eight years after the dissolution of the firm, a former partner signed the firm's name on a deposit sheet and uplifted and embezzled certain trust monies payable to the firm.[128]

The partners are also empowered to complete transactions already entered into but not completed at the time of dissolution. Indeed, partners may also be subject to a corresponding duty to complete firm transactions which have been commenced prior

---

[120] The Law Reform (Miscellaneous Provisions) (Scotland) Act 1980, s 14 provides that sheriff courts have the same jurisdiction to appoint a judicial factor as the Court of Session.
[121] If there are surviving partners who were neither at fault for the dissolution nor are incapacitated in some way, the court will not appoint a judicial factor: see *Dickie* v *Mitchell* (1874) 1 R 1030, per Lord President Inglis at 1033.
[122] 1949 SC 521.
[123] See also *Allan* v *Gronmeyer* (1891) 18 R 784.
[124] s 37.
[125] See para 10–27.
[126] s 38.
[127] 1917 SC (HL) 50.
[128] See Chapter 15.

to the dissolution of the partnership. In *Lujo Properties Ltd* v *Green*,[129] a firm of solicitors let property from L. The firm was subsequently dissolved prior to the expiry of the rental period. The court held that section 38 imposed a liability on the partners to pay a sum equivalent to the rent that the firm would have paid to L in respect of the remainder of the lease.[130]

Partners may also find themselves liable for professional negligence where they fail to complete a transaction which they have begun. This arose in *Welsh* v *Knarston*,[131] where a firm of solicitors acting on behalf of a client failed to raise a court action which subsequently became time-barred.[132]

It should be noted that this continuing authority does not extend to partners who are bankrupt and thus the firm will not be bound by the actions of a bankrupt partner.[133]

Partner's rights in respect of application of partnership property

10–60 When the partnership is dissolved every partner is entitled to have the partnership property applied in payment of the firm's debts and surplus assets distributed amongst the partners.[134]

Rights to return of premium

10–61 It is not unknown for firms to charge a premium (that is a sum of money over and above the normal amount invested in the partnership) in return for the privilege of becoming a partner in the firm. Where this premium is paid in respect of the entering into a partnership for a fixed period of time, and the firm is dissolved prior to the expiry of this term, the court may order repayment of a part of the premium.[135] The court will not order repayment in such circumstances where:

(a) dissolution is caused by the death of a partner;

(b) dissolution has been wholly or mainly caused by the partner who is seeking repayment of the premium;

(c) where the partners have agreed to dissolve the firm and that agreement makes no provision for the returning of any part of the premium.

Rights of retired or deceased partner to share in profits made after dissolution

10–62 If a partner dies or retires from the partnership and the remaining partners continue to carry on business without giving the partner (or his estate) his share of the assets and capital of the business then in the absence of any agreement to the contrary the former partner will be entitled to either a share of the profits attributable to his share of the assets or interest at 5 per cent per annum on the value of the firm's assets.[136] In

---

[129] 1997 SLT 225 (OH).
[130] The lease agreement may well provide, however, that the lease is to lapse on the dissolution of the partnership.
[131] 1973 SLT 66.
[132] See Chapter 5.
[133] Although this will not serve to affect the liability of any person who represents himself or knowingly allows himself to be represented as a partner of the bankrupt.
[134] s 39.
[135] s 40.
[136] s 42(1).

the absence of provision in the partnership agreement as to how the partner's share is to be evaluated, it will be for the court to determine how this should be done.[137]

Final settlement of accounts

The rules regarding the settlement of accounts between the partners are set out in **10–63** section 44 but these may be varied by the agreement of the partners. Section 44 stipulates that any losses (including deficiencies of capital) shall be paid first out of profits, second out of capital and third by the partners themselves to the same extent as they are entitled to share profits.

The assets of the firm will first be applied to pay debts owed to the firm's creditors; second, to pay partners for any advances they have made other than capital; third, paying partners their share of capital; the remainder will then be paid to partners in proportion to their entitlement to share profits.

LIMITED PARTNERSHIPS

As a final point some mention should be made here of the concept of the limited **10–64** partnership. This type of partnership is governed by the Limited Partnership Act 1907. In a limited partnership, some of the partners may enjoy a limited liability in respect of the debts of the partnership in the event that the firm is unable to pay these. The amount will be limited to the capital contributed by the partner at the time of his entry to the firm. These partners must be "sleeping partners" in the sense that they have no powers of management and their actions do not bind the firm in the usual way. At least one partner, however, known as the "general partner", cannot limit his liability in such a manner and he suffers unlimited liability for partnership debts in the event that the firm cannot meet them.

Limited partnerships must be registered with the Registrar of Companies in Edinburgh and certain formalities must be observed and documents lodged with the Registrar. Limited partnerships are not common. The principal reason for this is that it may be more advantageous to set up a limited company to ensure that all investors restrict their liability to the amount of their investment.

It should be noted that at the time of writing the Limited Partnership Bill is moving through the UK parliamentary process—it would facilitate a new kind of limited partnership within which all partners would enjoy limited liability tantamount to that which they have invested in the firm on their entry.[138] This new limited partnership would combine the organisational flexibility and tax status of a partnership with limited liability for all partners. Such limited partnerships are likely to prove particularly attractive to those in professions that are precluded from setting up companies either by statute or by the rules of the professional bodies. This new business forum

---

[137] See *Clark* v *Watson* 1982 SLT 450 (OH) and compare with *Thom's Exrx* v *Russel and Aitken* 1983 SLT 335 (OH).
[138] This is based upon proposals set out in *Limited Liability Partnership: A New Form of Business Association for Professions* (DTI, 1997). A summary of the Bill is available at http://www.publications.parliament. uk/pa/cm199900/cmbills/143/2000143.htm.

should also provide increased scope for businessmen to protect their financial investment than is currently the case in small limited companies.[139]

---

[139] The major danger in limited companies is that a director may be removed from office (and hence from taking part in the day-to-day running of the business) by majority vote of shareholders—see Chapter 11. This contrasts starkly with partnerships, where partners may only be removed by their fellow partners if there is an express agreement to this effect.

SUMMARY

THE DEFINITION AND NATURE OF PARTNERSHIP

- Partnerships are governed by the Partnership Act 1890. Section 1 of the Act defines a partnership as "the relationship which subsists between persons carrying on business in common with a view to profit".
- The essential elements of a partnership are that more than one person is involved, parties are involved in some kind of business together and that there is a profit motive.

RULES DETERMINING WHETHER A PARTNERSHIP EXISTS

- There are a number of statutory rules which can be applied if doubt exists over whether a partnership exists or not: neither the joint or common interests nor the sharing of gross returns will by themselves create a partnership; the sharing of net profits will lead to a presumption that a partnership exists. Such a presumption can be rebutted, however, in a number of circumstances set out in the Act.

THE SEPARATE PERSONALITY OF THE FIRM

- The firm has a separate legal personality to that of the partners and accordingly the firm can sue and be sued, enter into contracts and own property in its own name. The firm does not exhibit a full legal personality, however, and hence partners are joint and severally liable for the debts of the firm in the event that the firm cannot meet them.

FORMATION OF A PARTNERSHIP

- A partnership can be constituted in writing, orally or by a course of dealings between the parties.
- There are a number of restrictions under both statute and common law regarding partnership formation: some parties lack legal capacity to enter into the partnership agreement; statutory restrictions exist concerning the number of partners that a firm may have; a partnership will be void if formed for an illegal purpose; certain business names are precluded under both statute and common law.

RELATIONSHIP BETWEEN THE PARTNERS AND THIRD PARTIES

- The partner acts as an agent for the firm and binds the firm with third parties in relation to actions undertaken in the firm's name where the partner has either express, implied or apparent authority.

- If a partner acts on behalf of the firm without any form of authority then the firm will not be bound to honour the contract and the partner becomes personally liable.
- If money which is taken from a third party in the course of a firm's business is misappropriated by any partner, the firm will be liable for any resultant losses.
- Any partner may be rendered liable as a partner if he has held himself out or allowed himself to be so represented as a partner to third parties.
- Incoming partners are generally not liable for partnership debts incurred before they joined the firm. Retiring partners will be liable for debts incurred prior to their retiral. They will generally not be liable for debts incurred after their retiral although customers must be notified of their departure or retiring partners may continue to be rendered liable under the doctrine of holding out.

RELATIONS OF PARTNERS TO ONE ANOTHER

- Partners owe a number of fiduciary duties to one another: to render true accounts and provide full information to their fellow partners; not to make a personal profit from the firm's business; and not to compete with the firm.
- Partners have a general right to be involved in the management of the firm and no partners can be expelled unless there is an agreement to the contrary.

DISSOLUTION OF THE PARTNERSHIP

- Partnerships may be dissolved on a number of grounds: where one partner gives the others notice; where the designated time-scale of a firm has expired; or where a partner dies or is made bankrupt.
- Further, the court may dissolve the partnership generally at the behest of one of the partners if a partner is insane or of permanent incapacity, if there is prejudicial conduct or a breach of the partnership agreement, where business can only be carried out at a loss or where it is "just and equitable" to wind up the firm.
- The Act sets out a number of statutory rights partners have on the winding up of the firm, ranging from continuing authority to carry out necessary transactions to a return of capital investment and rights to partnership property and profits.

CASE DIGEST

Determining whether a partnership exists is an objective question [see para 10–05]
Adam v *Newbigging* (1888) 13 AC 308
At p 315, Lord Halsbury said: "If a partnership in fact exists, a community of interest in the adventure being carried on in fact, no concealment of name, no verbal equivalent for the ordinary phrases of profit and loss, no expedient for enforcing control over the adventure will prevent the substance and reality of the transaction being adjudged to be a partnership ... and no phrasing of it by a dextrous draughtsman will avail to avert the legal consequences of the contract."

Sharing in gross returns does not by itself lead to a presumption of a partnership [see para 10–07]

Cox v *Coulson* [1916] 2 KB 177

A theatre manager was held not to be a partner when he was responsible for the provision of the theatre and associated costs in return for 60 per cent of the gross returns of ticket sales.

A partnership agreement is void if it is formed for an illegal purpose [see para 10–13]

Everet v *Williams* (1787) unreported

A highwayman who had entered into agreement with another setting out how the proceeds from their crimes should be shared could not enforce the terms of the partnership agreement.

Acts carried out by partners in the course of the business bind the firm and the other partners [see para 10–16]

Mercantile Credit Co Ltd v *Garrod* [1962] 3 All ER 103

G and P were partners in a firm which let lock-up garages and repaired cars, but did not buy and sell cars. P, on behalf of the firm, sold a car, to which he had no title, to Mercantile Credit. Mocatta J said: "I consider … that when [P] entered into this … [he] was doing an act of a like to the business carried on by persons trading as a garage, and on that ground … my decision … must be in favour of the plaintiffs. The firm and G were liable for the contract."

Partners in non-trading firms do not have implied authority to borrow money on behalf of the firm [see para 10–16]

Paterson Bros v *Gladstone* (1891) 18 R 403

When G, a partner in a builders, borrowed money on behalf of the firm at an exorbitant rate, the firm was held not liable to repay the loan as the actions of G did not fall within his implied authority.

When a partner enters into a contract on behalf of the firm which is not connected with the firm's business, the firm will not be liable [see para 10–16]

Fortune v *Young* 1916 SC 1

When a partner signed a letter (on partnership stationery) guaranteeing the financial status of a would-be tenant, the firm was held not to be liable as this act fell outwith the scope of the normal business of the firm.

Retiring partners may continue to be held liable after retiral for debts which arise from continuing obligations [see para 10–28]

Court v *Berlin* [1897] 2 QB 396

Two partners who retired after a firm had instructed a solicitor to instigate legal proceedings on the firm's behalf were liable to compensate the solicitor for his actions when the firm was unable to pay.

Partners have a duty to render full accounts and provide full information on any matter concerning the partnership to their co-partners [see para 10–33]

> *Law* v *Law* [1905] 1 Ch 140

When one partner sold his share to another partner and the buyer failed to disclose the full worth of the seller's assets to him, the court set the sale aside.

Partners cannot make a personal profit from transactions of the firm [see para 10–34]

> *Pathirana* v *Pathirana* [1967] 1 AC 233

When one partner dissolved the firm and used an agency relation with a third party that was previously an asset of the firm for his own devices, the court ruled that he must account a share of the profits in his new venture to his former partner.

Partners have a duty not to compete with the firm [see para 10–35]

> *Pillans Bros* v *Pillans* (1908) 16 SLT 611 (OH)

When one partner set up a rival business to that of his firm's, he was bound to account to the partnership for the profits of the new business.

The right to expel partners from the firm must be exercised in the firm's best interests [see para 10–42]

> *Bisset* v *Daniels* (1835) 10 Hare 493

When certain partners sought to expel another with the purpose of obtaining his shares at a discounted value, this was held not to be in the best interests of the company and expulsion was therefore void.

The court may wind up the partnership if a partner breaches the partnership agreement [see para 10–54]

> *Thomson, Petitioner* (1893) 1 SLT 59

When a partner drew a cheque in the firm's name and absconded with the proceeds, this amounted to a blatant breach of the partnership agreement and petition to wind up the firm was accordingly granted.

The court may appoint a judicial factor to wind up the firm if one of the partners requires protection [see para 10–57]

> *Carabine* v *Carabine* 1949 SC 521

The court appointed a judicial factor to wind up the firm where both partners had invested capital and one partner wished to carry on business at a time when a lender was threatening to force the sale of business premises.

FURTHER READING

Forte (ed), *Scots Commercial Law* (Butterworths, 1997), Chap 9

Gloag and Henderson, *The Law of Scotland* (10th edn, W Green, 1995)

The Laws of Scotland: Stair Memorial Encyclopaedia (Law Society of Scotland/ Butterworths), Vol 16 "Partnership"

Marshall, *Scottish Cases on Partnerships and Companies* (W Green, 1980)

Miller, *The Law of Partnership in Scotland* (2nd edn by GH Brough, W Green, 1994)

11   COMPANY LAW

GENERAL PRINCIPLES

The legal regulation of registered companies in the UK is mainly administered **11–01** through compliance with the provisions of the Companies Act 1985.[1] This Act consolidated the various Companies Acts passed between 1948 and 1983 and, although it has been amended (most recently by the Companies Act 1989), it remains the main source of regulation in this respect. Although the Act applies to registered companies in both Scotland and England (and Wales), there are certain differences with respect to the historical development in the two jurisdictions.

THE DEVELOPMENT OF COMPANY LAW IN SCOTLAND

Legal intervention came about as a reaction to the growing diversification of trad- **11–02** ing companies during the eighteenth century in both legal systems. Prior to 1720, trading companies in both England and Scotland were organised in such a way that each member traded with his own stock subject to the rules of the company, with each member being personally liable for any losses sustained. The emergence of the "joint stock company" at the beginning of the eighteenth century saw the earliest form of what has developed into today's registered company. The joint stock company traded as a single entity with stock which was jointly contributed by its members and was recognised, at common law, as a legal entity in its own right. Thus, it followed that the members were not liable for the company's debts.

    The separation of control and legal liability encouraged rogue traders to become involved in the administration of such companies and the Bubble Act of 1720[2] was introduced in order to suppress their development. In England the Act was largely successful and it was not until the middle of the nineteenth century that corporate status could be obtained through the process of registration and personal liability could be limited.[3]

---

[1]   Hereinafter referred to as "the Act" and "CA 1985" in footnote references.
[2]   Repealed in 1825.
[3]   Joint Stock Companies Act 1844; Limited Liability Act 1855—neither of which applied to Scotland. Legislation introducing the registered company in Scotland did not appear until the Joint Stock Companies Act 1856.

Although the Bubble Act had application in Scotland, its effect was less significant than in England due to the fact that this form of business arrangement was sanctioned by Scots common law, by its recognition of the co-partnery company. The courts in Scotland recognised companies with transferable shares which were managed by directors and had a personality separate from that of their members.[4]

Over the last century, a framework of legal regulation common to both jurisdictions has emerged and it is this framework that will be discussed here. There are some important differences, notably the rules relating to floating charges and receivership, and, where such differences exist, the appropriate Scottish provisions will be set out and discussed. Much of the case law has application in both jurisdictions but, wherever possible and appropriate, Scottish cases will be referred to.

THE CLASSIFICATION OF COMPANIES

The company as a corporation

11-03   A company is a corporation. The term "corporation" is used to refer to two distinct sub-categories: corporations sole and corporations aggregate. A "corporation sole" consists of only one member at a time holding a perpetual office. The office is given separate legal status from the person holding it. This type of arrangement is very rare, and would apply, for example, to a civil service post where the post-holder acts as a public trustee. A "corporation aggregate" consists of a number of persons who, in law, form a single person. Corporations aggregate can be further broken down:

Chartered companies

11-04   Chartered companies are formed by the grant of a Royal Charter. This method of formation, which is rarely used nowadays, is the means by which professional bodies and educational institutions are formed.

Statutory companies

11-05   Statutory companies are formed by incorporation by a special Act of Parliament. This was the method of formation originally used in the case of the old public utility companies. The enshrinement of such organisations in statute enabled specific powers to be granted to them. However, the privatisation of such concerns has seen the old statutory companies replaced by public limited companies.

Registered companies

11-06   Such companies are formed under the relevant company legislation, currently the Companies Act 1985. This chapter is concerned with the legal regulation relevant to this form of business entity.

Classification of registered companies

11-07   The Companies Act 1985 provides for three types of registered company.[5]

---

[4] *Stevenson & Co v Macnair and Others* (1757) M 14.
[5] CA 1985, s 1.

Companies limited by shares

11–08 The liability of the members of such companies is limited to the amount (if any) that remains unpaid on their shares and this concept is explored below. The limitation of liability offers obvious benefits and this is by far the most popular type of registered company. However, the following should be noted with respect to the operation of limitation of liability: first, although members' liability is limited, the liability of the company itself is *un*limited as it must discharge its debts as long as it has assets to do so. The separation between the liability of the members and the company is a consequence of the "veil of incorporation", which is considered below. Second, in private limited companies, the concept of limited liability can be illusory as the individual director/member will often have to put his personal property at risk in order to finance the company—for example, by offering his own house as a guarantee in order to secure a loan.

Companies limited by guarantee

11–09 A company which is limited by guarantee has "the liability of its members limited by the memorandum to such amount as the members may ... undertake to contribute to the assets of the company in the event of its being wound up."[6] Only companies that are limited by guarantee without a share capital must be registered.

Unlimited companies

11–10 The members of an unlimited company are guarantors of the company's debts and, thus, are personally liable without limitation. Such companies enjoy a high degree of privacy as they are not required to file accounts and directors' and auditors' reports with the Registrar.

Registered companies may be either private or public. The different statutory requirements pertaining to each type of company will be covered in detail, but the main differences, in summary, are set out below.

Public companies

11–11 Section 1(3) of the Act defines a public company as a company limited by shares or guarantee with a share capital. A minimum of two persons is required to form a public company, which must also have a minimum of two directors. The company's name must end with the words "Public Limited Company" or plc. The authorised capital of a public company must be at least £50,000 under section 25 of the Act.

Private companies

11–12 The minimum membership requirement for a private company is now one. The Single Member Company Regulations 1992 permit the formation of single member private companies. These Regulations were introduced in order to implement the 12th EC Company Law Directive. Private companies are required to have at least one director. The Act does not define a private company; therefore, any company which is not deemed to be a public company will be a private company. There is no minimum authorised capital and private companies are not as strictly regulated as public

---

[6] CA 1985, s 1.

companies. The reason for this is that only public companies can offer their shares for sale direct to the public and, therefore, greater protection is required in respect of the operation of such companies. The methods by which membership in a private company can be acquired are considered below.[7] A further categorisation exists in respect of private companies, some of which are classified as being small and medium-sized companies (SMEs). This classification enables such companies to benefit from the financial advantages that arise due to certain accounting requirement exemptions.[8] The indicators used to establish whether the company is small or medium-sized are annual turnover,[9] balance sheet total[10] and number of employees.[11]

DEFINITION OF THE REGISTERED COMPANY

11–13   A registered company is a corporation and, as such, has an existence, rights and duties which are distinct from those persons who are, from time to time, its members. Although there are several different forms of organisation through which business may be carried out, the process of incorporation under the Act and associated legislation confers special legal status on the registered company. The main effects of incorporation are that the registered company is a *persona at law* (an artificial, not real person) and that it has perpetual succession, by which the company's existence is independent of its members who may be replaced due to death or for some other reason.

The registered company is so called because it is brought into existence by registration of certain documents (the most important being the "memorandum of association") with a Registrar of Companies. The Act provides:

> "Any two or more persons associated for a lawful purpose may, by subscribing their names to a memorandum of association and by otherwise complying with the requirements of this Act in respect of registration, form an incorporated company, with or without limited liability."[12]

Furthermore, the Act makes provision for the formation of "single member" private limited companies,[13] which are formed in the same way but by one person.

THE REGISTERED COMPANY CONTRASTED WITH OTHER FORMS OF BUSINESS ARRANGEMENT

Contrast with a "sole trader"

11–14   A sole tradership is one person in business on their own account, where the business has not been registered as a company. Sole traders retain the right to control and manage their businesses as they see fit. They enjoy all of the profits of the business; however, they will be personally liable for all debts incurred.

---

[7] See para 11–98.
[8] CA 1985, ss 246–249.
[9] £2.8 million or less for a small company and £11.2 million or less for a medium company.
[10] £1.4 million or less for a small company and £5.6 million or less for a medium company.
[11] An average of 50 or less for a small company and 250 or less for a medium company.
[12] CA 1985, s 1(1).
[13] CA 1985, s 1(3A), inserted by SI 1992/1699.

Contrast with a partnership

Persons (natural or artificial) who carry on a business in common with a view of profit without being incorporated are said to be engaged in "partnership".[14] To the outside world, the partnership may look very similar to the registered company, in that both may share common features such as the acquisition of business and the profit motive. However, the effects of incorporation which are enjoyed by the registered company are not generally applicable to partnerships; this important distinction provides an interesting contrast between the two types of business organisation which highlights the particular effects of incorporation. **11–15**

Liability for business debts[15]

Scottish partnerships enjoy a certain degree of separate legal status in that the partnership can, to a certain extent, be distinguished from the partners. However, this is really an artificial distinction. Partnerships have separate legal personality and creditors must look to the firm for payment, but, if assets of the partnership are insufficient to meet its debts, the partners will be jointly and severally liable. **11–16**

Formation

There are no special requirements for the formation of a partnership and it may be agreed or constituted verbally. This is in contrast to the registration procedures relating to companies, which will be covered later. **11–17**

Carrying on the business

Partnerships are not subject to any special requirements regarding the day-to-day running of the business. There is no need for public disclosure of information and except for tax returns (that are submitted to the Inland Revenue) there is no need for information to be disclosed to government departments. Therefore, a high degree of privacy exists. Registered companies are subject to many formalities: for example, their accounts are open to inspection, annual audits must be carried out and annual returns must be filed with the Registrar of Companies. They, therefore, lack privacy and there may be increased administration costs. **11–18**

Number of members

The general rule for partnerships is that they must have a minimum of two partners and a maximum of 20, although there are exceptions in the case of professional partnerships—for example, accountants, solicitors, stockbrokers. Public limited companies must have at least two members and private companies, limited by shares or guarantee, may have one member, but there is no upper limit. **11–19**

Transferability of shares

Section 24(7) of the Partnership Act 1890 provides that, unless otherwise agreed, no person is to be introduced as a partner without the consent of the existing partners. A shareholder in a public company can transfer shares freely without the consent of the **11–20**

---

[14] See Chapter 10.
[15] The Limited Partnership Bill which is, at the time of writing, making its passage through Parliament, will, if successful, introduce the "limited partnership" to UK law. See Chapter 10.

company. Private companies must retain the right of pre-emption—that is the existing members have "first refusal" if a member sells his shares. If the company refuses the option, the member can then sell to a third party outside the company.

Changes in membership

11–21   Section 33 of the Partnership Act 1890 provides that the partnership is automatically dissolved by the death or bankruptcy of any partner. This can be contrasted with the effect of a change in membership on a registered company, which is subject to the principle of perpetual succession.

Management of the business

11–22   Section 24(5) of the Partnership Act 1890 provides that, unless otherwise agreed, all partners must take part in the management of the business. To give effect to this provision, section 5 provides that all partners are agents of the firm. Company members are not agents and there is no right to take part in the management of the company. The managers are, in effect, the directors of the company who have certain agency powers.

Security when borrowing

11–23   Registered companies have more opportunity to secure capital by the creation of "floating charges". This is a form of secured loan which a company may create, but a partnership may not.

THE EFFECTS OF REGISTRATION

11–24   The effect of the company's existence as a *persona at law* means that the company has its own legal personality and, therefore, has the capacity to make contracts in its own name. In practical terms this means that the company can sue and be sued and can own property. This concept is sometimes referred to as the "Salomon principle", in reference to the celebrated English case *Salomon* v *Salomon & Co Ltd*[16] in which the principle was first expounded and which provides an interesting insight into the historical development of company regulation.

Mr Salomon had carried on a business as a sole trader for 30 years. His business was profitable and he formed a registered company in 1892 for the purposes of transferring the business to the company. The sale price of £39,000 was paid by an allotment of 20,000 £1 shares, £9,000 cash and the issue of a £10,000 debenture[17] in Salomon's name. The shares were divided equally between Salomon and the members of his family, although all the shares were held in trust for Salomon. Soon after its formation the company failed and went into liquidation[18] with £6,000 of assets, but owing £7,000 to unsecured trade creditors and the £10,000 secured debenture. The unsecured creditors argued that the security given by the debenture was invalid as, "the company was Mr Salomon in another form". However, the House of Lords held that Salomon was entitled to recover all the remaining assets with respect to the debenture as "[t]he company has a legal existence separate from that of its members".

---

[16] [1897] AC 22.
[17] See para 11–81.
[18] See para 11–147 *et seq.*

Salomon's principle is often referred to as the "veil of incorporation" in reference to the separation between the ownership and management of the company which occurs as a consequence of incorporation.[19] The registered company enjoys certain features as a result of its legal status.

Perpetual succession

It follows that, as a consequence of the company's "persona at law", its existence is **11–25** independent of its members. A change in the company's membership by a transfer of shares or death does not represent a change in the company itself, which will continue to exist as a legal entity regardless of the identity of its members.

Limitation of liability

The company, as a persona at law, is liable, without limit, for its debts. The majority of **11–26** registered companies are formed on the basis of limited liability[20] (by shares or, less commonly, by guarantee). In the event of a winding up, the members of such companies are required to contribute only the amount, if any, which remains unpaid on their shares or the amount of their guarantee.

The members of an unlimited company[21] are guarantors of the company's debts and, as such, are liable in the event of a winding up without any restriction on the amount.

"Lifting the veil"

Although the principle set out in *Salomon's* case continues to be a cornerstone of **11–27** company law, there are certain circumstances where the degree of protection offered by its application may lead to incidences of unlawful or rogue practice. In order to counteract such problems, a number of exceptions to the general principle have developed. Where, for specific reasons, the general principle is set aside, the veil of incorporation is said to be "lifted" or "pierced" in order for consideration to be paid to the human and commercial reality. Such exceptions arise by way of a number of statutory provisions and, in certain circumstances, by judicial lifting of the veil.

Statutory provisions

Section 24 of the Act provides that, if a company carries on business without having at **11–28** least two members for more than six months, the remaining member who, knowing this fact, carries on business thereafter will be jointly and severally liable with the company for any debts incurred during that period. Single member private companies are excluded from this provision.[22]

Section 349(4)[23] of the Act states that an officer of a company who, on the company's behalf, signs or authorises any bill of exchange, promissory note, endorsement, cheque or order for money or goods on which the company's name is not mentioned,[24] will be

---

[19] See also *Lee v Lee's Air Farming Ltd* [1961] AC 12; *Macaura v Northern Assurance Co Ltd* [1925] AC 619 (HL).
[20] See CA 1985, s 1(2)(a) and (b).
[21] See CA 1985, s 1(2)(c).
[22] Such companies have been possible since July 1992—see para 11–12.
[23] Applied by the Companies Act 1989, s 112(8).
[24] As required by s 349(1).

personally liable to the holder of the document unless the company honours the obligation. Such an individual will also be liable to a fine.

A public limited company which commences trading before it has received a trading certificate in contravention of section 117 of the Act will, along with any officer in default, be liable to fine.[25] Furthermore, if such a company enters into a transaction prior to receipt of its trading certificate within 21 days of being called upon to comply with the provisions of section 117, the directors will be jointly and severally liable to indemnify the other party to the transaction in respect of any loss or damage suffered by reason of the company's failure to comply.[26]

Certain provisions intended to protect the interests of third parties against the effects of fraudulent or wrongful trading are offered by the Insolvency Act 1986. Section 213 provides that if, in the course of winding up, it appears that the company's business has been carried on with intent to defraud creditors or for any fraudulent purpose, the court may declare that any persons (eg directors) who were knowingly parties to that fraud shall be liable to make a contribution to the company's assets.[27] The director of a company may also be liable to contribute to the company's assets if found guilty of wrongful trading.[28]

Section 216 of the Insolvency Act 1986 places restrictions on the reuse of company names by making it a criminal offence for a director or shadow director of a company that has gone into insolvent liquidation to be involved directly or indirectly with the promotion, formation or management of a similarly named company for five years. Such an individual may be held personally liable[29] for the debts incurred by a company in the event of a contravention of section 216.

The Company Directors Disqualification Act 1986, s 15 provides that a person who acts in contravention of the Act by taking part in the management of a company following disqualification[30] will be personally liable for the debts of the company.

Finally, certain statutory provisions exist for the purposes of determining the existence of the relationship of holding company and subsidiary. This may be necessary in order to confirm that accounting requirements have been complied with as, generally, a holding company must produce group accounts in which the profits and losses and assets and liabilities of subsidiary companies are consolidated.[31] Section 227 of and Schedule 4A to the Companies Act 1985 set out the duty to prepare group accounts and the form and content of such accounts. This area is further explored below by way of the common law principles applied to cases concerning holding and subsidiary companies.

Judicial lifting of the veil of incorporation

11–29 Although it is difficult to identify a common set of circumstances in which courts will lift the veil, consideration of the case law does identify some relevant factors that have

---

[25] s 117(7).
[26] s 117(8).
[27] Such individuals may also be subject to criminal proceedings under s 458 of the Companies Act 1985 which applies to cases of fraudulent trading whether or not the company has been, or is in the course of being, wound up.
[28] Insolvency Act 1986, s 214. See *Re Produce Marketing Consortium Ltd (No 2)* [1989] 1 WLR 745.
[29] Under s 217 of the Insolvency Act 1986.
[30] Under the provisions of the Company Directors Disqualification Act 1986, s 11.
[31] See the provisions of the Companies Act 1985, s 229.

lead judges to carry out such investigations in order to enforce the law in certain respects. Such practice is generally applied to assist in the identification of fraud and illegality. The possibility of trading with the enemy would constitute such further investigation,[32] as would the need to identify a company's residence in order to determine liability for corporation tax.[33]

The formation of a company for a fraudulent purpose has commonly served as justification for lifting the veil, as in *Gilford Motor Company v Horne*[34] in which it was discovered that a company had been formed for the purposes of breaching a restrictive covenant. In such circumstances, where the veil is used as a device for escaping existing liabilities, the resultant company is referred to as a "sham" company.[35]

Where a private company has been founded on the basis of a personal relationship between its members, and the relationship has soured leading to a breakdown in mutual trust and confidence, the court will require to discover the reality of the association to order its winding up under the "just and equitable rule".[36]

Perhaps the most commonly applied criterion for judicial lifting of the veil is to establish the existence of a holding and subsidiary companies. Such determination is often necessary in order to establish compliance with legislative provisions[37] and the application of common law duties. It is surprising that, despite the existence of a plethora of case law, the judiciary have not developed any consistently applied principles in this respect. Thus, the decision in *DHN Food Distributors Ltd v Tower Hamlets London Borough Council*,[38] in which a holding company and its subsidiary were treated as one entity for the purposes of determining the payment of compensation for disturbance, appears prima facie to be in sharp contrast with the decision in *Woolfson v Strathclyde Regional Council*.[39] In the latter case, the House of Lords held that a holding company and subsidiary were to be treated as separate entities, thus entitling the subsidiary to recover damages for disturbance to the business from its holding company. The distinction between the two cases appears to rest on the specific facts, with the relationship between the two entities in the earlier case being comprised of a straightforward parent and subsidiary and, in the latter case, arising from a more complex arrangement whereby the company running the business which had suffered the disturbance (the subsidiary) had no control over the owners of the premises (the holding company).[40]

PROMOTION AND INCORPORATION

A company cannot form itself. Before a company can be incorporated it is often **11–30** necessary to make certain preparations for the commencement of trading. Such

---

[32] *Daimler Co Ltd v Continental Tyre and Rubber Co (GB) Ltd* [1916] 2 AC 307.
[33] *Unit Construction Co Ltd v Bullock* [1960] AC 351 (HL).
[34] [1933] Ch 935 (CA).
[35] See also *Jones v Lipman* [1962] 1 All ER 442; *Re FG Films* [1953] 1 All ER 615; *Creasey v Breachwood Motors Ltd* [1992] BCC 638.
[36] Insolvency Act 1986, s 122(g); see *Ebrahimi v Westbourne Galleries* [1973] AC 360 (HL), *Re Yenidje Tobacco Co* [1916] 2 Ch 426 (CA).
[37] See para 11–28.
[38] [1976] 1 WLR 852 (CA).
[39] (1979) 38 P & CR 521.
[40] See also *Smith, Stone and Knight Ltd v Birmingham Corporation* [1939] 4 All ER 116; *Lonrho v Shell Petroleum* [1982] AC 173; *Ord v Bellhaven Pubs Ltd* [1998] BCC 607; *Bank of Credit and Commerce International (Overseas) Ltd v Price Waterhouse* [1998] BCC 677.

preparations may include taking the necessary steps to incorporate the company, ensuring that the company has share and loan capital (if appropriate), acquiring property on the company's behalf and acquiring the business which the company is formed to control. In addition, it may be necessary to attend to other tasks prior to incorporation, such as appointment of the company's first directors and, in the case of a public company, arranging for the company's shares to be offered to the public by relevant means. Individuals who undertake such tasks on behalf of companies are referred to as "promoters".

The definition of promoter

11–31   Although there is no general definition of the term "promoter" contained in company legislation, the relevant case law does offer some useful definitions that describe the nature of the tasks undertaken by such persons. In *Twycross v Grant*,[41] Cockburn, CJ defined a promoter as, "One who undertakes to form a company with reference to a given project and to get it going, and who takes the necessary steps to accomplish that purpose." In *Whaley Bridge Callico Printing Co v Green*,[42] Bowen J set down a further definition which emphasises the commercial nature of the promoter's undertakings:

> "The term 'promoter' is a term not of law, but of business, usefully summing up in a single word a number of business operations familiar to the commercial world by which a company is generally brought into existence."

From these judicial definitions it can be seen that it will be necessary to consider the facts of a particular case in order to determine whether or not an individual has acted as a promoter. Those who give advice in a professional capacity such as accountants or solicitors will not generally be deemed to have acted as promoters, unless responsible for the production of an expert report which is included in listing particulars or in a prospectus.[43]

Those who act as promoters of modern companies will generally become the first directors on incorporation so that the issues concerning personal liability which may arise with relation to such individuals are of no consequence. However, where this is not the case, it may be essential to determine the status of the individuals involved in the setting up of a company due to the distinct duties owed by promoters and the personal liability which may arise in the context of contracts entered into prior to incorporation.

Duties of promoters

11–32   The relationship between the promoter and the company is a "fiduciary" one (*ie* based on mutual trust), although the promoter cannot act as an agent for the company before it is incorporated due to the fact that it has no recognised legal status at this stage in its development.[44] Promoters have certain duties in respect of their relationship with

---

[41] (1877) 2 CPD 459.
[42] (1880) 5 QBD 109.
[43] See the Financial Services Act 1986, s 152 (for listed companies) and s 168 (for unlisted companies), which exempt those who act in a professional capacity from liability (in certain respects) for false statements.
[44] See the obiter statements of Lord McLaren in *Edinburgh Northern Tramways Co v Mann* (1896) 23 R 1056, in which the promoter is likened to an agent in respect of the duties owed.

the company that are based on the fiduciary nature of the relationship and can be illustrated by reference to case law.

The first of these is a duty to disclose any profit made through transactions undertaken on the company's behalf either to an independent board of directors or, in the common event that the promoter becomes one of the first directors following incorporation, the company's shareholders. In *Gluckstein* v *Barnes*[45] a syndicate failed to make full disclosure of the profits made in respect of mortgage debentures held following the sale of property to a company for which they had acted as promoters. The company subsequently went into liquidation and, although a certain amount of the profit had been disclosed, it was held that it was a breach of the promoter's duty not to disclose the full amount. The members of the syndicate were found to be jointly and severally liable to repay the secret profit.[46]

Second, where the promoter sells property to the company he owes a duty to disclose his identity and his interest in the property. This duty applies whether the promoter's interest in the property predates his association with the company[47] or not. The appropriate remedies in such cases may be rescission of the contract[48] and/or damages for breach of fiduciary duty.[49]

Promoters' remuneration

Prior to incorporation the company lacks the legal capacity to enter into a contract to pay for promotional services or related expenses.[50] Although it is possible to make express provision in the articles of association for such remuneration,[51] such provision will not constitute a legally binding agreement.[52] In Scots law, the directors of a company may make payment for promotional services by way of a future allotment of shares at the company's discretion, providing such payment is authorised by the articles and is made in good faith.[53]

11–33

PROMOTION AND PRE-INCORPORATION CONTRACTS

The lack of legal capacity of the unincorporated company means that, in certain circumstances, individuals who enter into contracts on the company's behalf may encounter certain difficulties where disputes arise concerning the enforcement of such contracts which are known as "pre-incorporation" contracts.

11–34

First, the company will not be bound by a pre-incorporation contract.[54] The company is entitled to ratify an unauthorised contract made in its name, but this will only be possible where the company was in existence at the time the contract was made. Where the contract was made prior to incorporation, the person or persons concerned who purported to act on the company's behalf will be treated as if acting on

---

[45] [1900] AC 240.
[46] See also *Erlanger* v *New Sombrero Phosphate Co* (1878) 3 App Cas 1218 (HL).
[47] *Re Cape Breton* (1887) 12 App Cas 652.
[48] *Erlanger* v *New Sombrero Phosphate Co* (1878) 3 App Cas 1218.
[49] *Re Leeds and Hanley Theatres of Varieties Ltd* [1902] 2 Ch 809.
[50] *Re National Motor Mail Coach Co Ltd* [1908] 2 Ch 515.
[51] See Companies (Table A–F) Regulations 1985, Table A.
[52] *Re English and Colonial Produce Co Ltd* [1906] 2 Ch 435.
[53] *Park Business Interiors Ltd* v *Park* 1990 SLT 818 (OH).
[54] *Re English and Colonial Produce Co Ltd* [1906] 2 Ch 435.

his or their own behalf and will be personally liable.[55] Section 36C of the Companies Act 1985 provides that the promoter's liability is "subject to any agreement to the contrary", meaning that the promoter could agree with the third party to exclude his personal liability at the time that the contract is made. However, this will generally be unsatisfactory for the third party concerned as, should the company refuse to honour the resulting obligations at a later date, the contract will be unenforceable.

Second, where a contract is made by a promoter on the company's behalf, the third party is not bound.[56] This has the effect that the company, following incorporation,[57] will be unable to sue the third party on the contract.

Although the law may appear to be unsatisfactory in this respect, with little protection offered to promoters or companies prior to incorporation, it should be noted that those acting in a promotional capacity will generally become the first directors of a company, thus ensuring that such contractual obligations transfer to the company following incorporation. In other circumstances, there are certain steps a promoter can take to protect against personal liability for pre-incorporation contracts. The first of these would be to incorporate the company before making contracts. The expenses of incorporation are not prohibitive, so this is a real option. Second, the purchase of an "off the shelf" company may offer a solution as such a company is already incorporated and so any contracts made in its name will be binding from the start. Finally, the promoter may undertake to make a draft agreement with the other party. Such an agreement would be morally binding and the company, on incorporation, would enter into the contract. As the draft is not legally binding, the constitutional documents of the company should be drafted to include a provision binding the directors to adopt the agreement as a contract on incorporation. The promoter thus avoids entering into a contract prior to incorporation.

THE REGISTRATION DOCUMENTS

11–35   As noted above, the registered company becomes incorporated under the provisions of the Companies Act 1985 by applying for registration. This is achieved by filing certain documents with the Registrar of Companies for Scotland based in Edinburgh.[58] Under the provisions of the Companies Act 1985, certain documents must be submitted to the Registrar. Each of these will be outlined here and considered in more detail below.

Constitutional documents

11–36   These comprise the memorandum of association and the articles of association. The memorandum deals with the external constitution of the company. As regards the form and content of this document, public companies must follow the pro-forma set out in Table F of the Companies (Table A–F) Regulations 1985.[59] Such a company must state its status as a public limited company and its name must end with the

---

[55] *Kelner* v *Baxter* (1866) LR 2 CP 174; *Phonogram Ltd* v *Lane* [1981] 3 All ER 182.
[56] *Tinnevelly Sugar Refining Co Ltd and Others* v *Mirrlees, Watson and Yaryan Co Ltd* (1894) 21 R 1009 (IH).
[57] *Natal Land and Colonisation Co* v *Pauline Colliery & Development Syndicate Ltd* [1904] AC 120.
[58] For English and Welsh companies the main Registry is in Cardiff.
[59] SI 1985/805.

words "public limited company" (or the abbreviation "plc"). A public company's authorised share capital, which is provided for in the memorandum, must be at least £50,000.[60]

The articles of association deal with the internal constitution of the company. Companies limited by shares (public or private) may adopt Table A as set out in the 1985 Regulations.

Statutory declaration of compliance[61]

This is a document confirming that the company has complied with the requirements **11–37** of the Companies Act 1985.[62] It will usually be drawn up by the solicitor engaged in the formation of the company.

Statement naming and signed by the subscribers to the memorandum[63]

This document sets out the names, former names, addresses, dates of birth, business **11–38** occupations and nationalities of the company secretary and directors and the existing directorships of the directors. It must also state the address of the company's registered office.

THE REGISTRATION PROCEDURE

This is a simple process that can be summarised as a five-step procedure: **11–39**

(1) The constitutional documents are drawn up on the company's behalf.

(2) The relevant documents are submitted to the Registrar with the appropriate fee.

(3) The Registrar examines the documents to ascertain that all the relevant provisions of the Companies Act have been complied with.[64] For example, that the company is being formed for a lawful purpose, that the correct number of persons have subscribed to the memorandum and that the company's name is acceptable.

(4) The Registrar issues the certificate of incorporation. A notice is published in the *Edinburgh Gazette*.

(5) The company commences business at the appropriate time depending on whether it is a public or private company. Private companies may commence business on the date of issue of the certificate of incorporation. Public companies may commence business on receipt of a section 117 trading certificate.

---

[60] CA 1985, s 11.
[61] Companies Form 12.
[62] s 12(1) states that the Registrar shall not register the company until he is satisfied that all the relevant provisions of CA have been complied with.
[63] Companies Form 10.
[64] CA 1985, s 12(1) and (2).

Re-registration and change of status

11–40   In certain circumstances it may be necessary to re-register a company. This will usually arise where the company is about to undergo a change in its capital arrangements (for example, a decision has been taken to offer shares direct to the public for the first time) and so will generally apply to a private company which wishes to re-register as a public company.[65] In such circumstances, conversion will be permitted as long as a special or written resolution has been passed which alters the company's memorandum and articles in line with the statutory requirements relating to public companies, including the requirement that a public company's share capital must be at least £50,000. The altered documents must be submitted to the Registrar along with a copy of the company's balance sheet prepared not more than seven months before the date of application, and a report from the company's auditor.

A company wishing to undergo a change of status from public to private must pass a special resolution altering its memorandum of association which must be submitted to the Registrar along with a written application signed by a director or secretary.[66] Members retain the right to apply to the court for cancellation of the re-registration as long as certain conditions apply. Such application must be made by the holders of not less than 5 per cent of the nominal value of the company's issued share capital or any class thereof (or, in the case of an unlimited company, 5 per cent of its members), or not less than 50 of the company's members. The application must be made within 28 days after the passing of the resolution.[67]

An unlimited company can re-register as a limited company under section 51 of the Act as long as a special resolution has been passed, a copy of which must be sent to the Registrar within 15 days, along with an application for the company to be so re-registered. Section 49 sets out the procedure necessary for re-registration from limited to unlimited, which will be prohibited if the company has previously been re-registered as limited.

THE COMPANY'S CONSTITUTION

THE MEMORANDUM OF ASSOCIATION

11–41   The memorandum of association contains a company's constitution and sets out certain information relevant to the external relations of the company. As well as determining a company's name, domicile, amount of share capital and liability of its members, it also sets out the objects which the company may pursue. Together with the articles of association (considered below), the memorandum constitutes the company's constitutional documents, and both must be submitted to the Registrar of companies as part of the registration procedure. However, the memorandum is the dominant document and its contents will prevail in the case of conflict between the provisions of the memorandum and those of the articles.[68]

Section 2 of the Act provides that the memorandum of every company must state

---

[65] CA 1985, ss 43–47.
[66] *ibid* s 53.
[67] *ibid* s 54.
[68] *Scottish National Trust Co Ltd, Petitioners* 1928 SC 499.

certain information and this is contained in what are commonly referred to as the "compulsory clauses". These clauses will be considered in turn along with the regulatory provisions pertaining to each.

The name of the company

The memorandum must contain a clause setting down the name of the company. **11–42** Section 25 of the Act provides that the name of a public company must end with the words "public limited company" and that a private company limited by shares or guarantee must have the word "limited" as part of its name. The abbreviations "plc" or "Ltd" will suffice.

Under section 26 of the Act, certain names will be prohibited from registration. This includes any name which already appears on the Registrar's index of company names. Under the common law doctrine of "passing off", it is possible for an action to be brought against a company if its name is the same as, or similar to, that used by an existing business. In such circumstances, the company may be prevented, by court order, from using the name and ordered to give an account of profits.[69]

Any name that would be likely to give the impression that the company is, in any way, connected with the Government or any local authority will also be prohibited under section 26.[70] The main reason for such regulation of company names is to give protection to third parties who may contract with the company in good faith. Also prohibited from use is any name that would, in the opinion of the Secretary of State, constitute a criminal offence or be offensive.[71]

Procedure for change of name

A company may change its name by special resolution under the procedure provided **11–43** for by section 28 of the Companies Act 1985. A copy of the resolution must be sent to the Registrar within 15 days of the passing of the resolution, along with the amended memorandum and articles and a re-registration fee. After carrying out the usual checks applicable to all proposed company names, the Registrar will issue a new certificate of incorporation in the company's new name.

Disclosure of the company name

A company must display its name outside each of its offices or places of business.[72] **11–44** The company name must be disclosed in all business correspondence, bills of exchange, promissory notes, invoices, receipts and letters of credit.[73] Failure to comply with these requirements may result in a fine being imposed upon the company and its officers.[74]

Misuse of name and personal liability

An officer of the company who misnames the company on documents used in an **11–45** official capacity may be held personally liable for business undertaken on the

---

[69] *Ewing v Buttercup Margarine Co Ltd* [1917] 2 Ch 1; *Chill Foods (Scotland) Ltd* v *Cool Foods* [1977] SLT 38 (OH).
[70] See also the provisions of the Business Names Act 1985.
[71] *R* v *Registrar of Companies, ex p Attorney General* [1991] BCLC 476.
[72] CA 1985, s 348.
[73] *ibid* s 349.
[74] Throughout the Act, reference is made to "officers" of the company, and s 744 defines an officer as including "a director, manager or secretary".

company's behalf under the provisions of sections 348–350 of the Companies Act 1985.

Public companies—statement of status

11–46 The memoranda of all public companies must contain a statement of status to that effect. This will, of course, be explicit in the choice of company name, but the inclusion of such a statement remains mandatory.

The location of the registered office

11–47 The memorandum of every company must state the location of the registered office,[75] which, for companies registered in Edinburgh, must be in Scotland.

A statement of the objects of the company

11–48 The memorandum of every company must contain a statement of the areas of business in which the company proposes to become involved, commonly referred to as the "objects clause". This statement delimits the acts that the company is permitted to undertake as transactions entered into by a company beyond the scope of the objects will be *ultra vires* and, thus, void.[76] However, as will be illustrated later, the operation of the *ultra vires* rule, once of paramount importance in company law, is now severely restricted by statute.[77]

The objects clause and the ultra vires *doctrine*

11–49 Originally, a company's objects clause was intended to provide a succinct statement as to the nature and purpose of the company.[78] The rationale for such a statement is twofold. First, it serves as a means of protection to the subscribers to the memorandum who are made aware of the purposes for which their money can be used and, second, it informs those dealing with the company of the company's contractual powers. The scope of the *ultra vires* doctrine at common law traditionally served to restrict the range of activities in which a company could engage. Such restriction was based upon the premise that persons dealing with the company would be deemed to have knowledge of the company's objects even if they had not inspected the memorandum as, under the provisions of section 719 of the Act, the memorandum is open to public inspection.[79]

A strict interpretation of the objects of a company as provided for by the objects clause may result in a reduction of such protection for either side, because agreements found to be outwith its scope and therefore *ultra vires* would be unenforceable by or against the company. The difficulties inherent in such strict interpretation have long been recognised (at least in part) by the judiciary, which has been open to the concept of implied powers, as long as such powers are exercised for the benefit of the company and are pursued in furtherance of the company's objects.[80]

---

[75] CA 1985, s 287.
[76] *Ashbury Railway Carriage & Iron Co* v *Riche* (1875) LR 7 HL 653; *Rolled Steel Products (Holdings) Ltd* v *British Steel Corporation* [1986] Ch 246 (CA).
[77] See CA 1985, s 35A, inserted by the Companies Act 1989.
[78] *Cotman* v *Brougham* [1918] AC 514 (HL).
[79] *Mahony* v *East Holyford Mining Co* (1875) LR 7 (HL) 869.
[80] *Hutton* v *West Cork Railway Co* (1883) 23 ChD 654; *Parke* v *Daily News* [1962] Ch 927; *Re Halt Garage (1964) Ltd* [1984] 3 All ER 1016.

Drafting of the objects clause

It is common practice in the drafting of the modern objects clause to include a large **11–50** number of objects contained in sub-clauses, thus giving the company a wide range of powers to conduct transactions alongside its main area of business. Such drafting recognises the reality of the modern commercial environment in which future diversification may be imperative, as well as circumventing any restrictions that may be unforeseeable at the time of incorporation. It is also standard practice to make provision for each sub-clause to contain a main self-standing object which can be viewed independently of the others.[81]

The substratum rule

The objects pursued by a company are still subject to certain limitations, despite the **11–51** broadening of the common law principles governing interpretation of the objects clause and statutory restrictions on the application of the *ultra vires* doctrine, which will be considered below. The main restriction constitutes what is known as the "substratum rule" which provides that objects set out in sub-clauses of the memorandum of a company cannot be pursued unless the main object (substratum), usually contained in the first sub-clause, is being carried on.[82] If this is not the case, the substratum is said to have been destroyed and application can be made to the court to have the company wound up on the "just and equitable" ground provided for by section 122(1)(g) of the Insolvency Act 1986.

The effect of section 35

Section 35 of the Companies Act 1985 was inserted by the Companies Act 1989 in **11–52** response to the first EC Directive on company law[83] and following consultation on the findings of the Prentice Report,[84] which was commissioned by the government to look at the area of company objects and the *ultra vires* doctrine. Although the provisions contained in the new section 35 may appear far-reaching, the development of the modern objects clause and its acceptance by the common law meant that these changes merely served to make explicit what was already happening in practice in many respects. There are two main effects of the new statutory provisions. First, the issue arising from the company's lack of capacity is dealt with by section 35 (as amended), which provides: "The validity of an act done by a company shall not be called into question on the ground of lack of capacity by reason of anything in the company's memorandum". This restricts the right of the company to refuse to honour transactions entered into in its name on the basis that to do so would entail acting *ultra vires* the company's objects and, thus, enables third parties to enforce such transactions. Certain safeguards exist in respect of the rights of members over *ultra vires* transactions entered into by directors on the company's behalf. In such circumstances, section 35(2) provides that any member of a company can petition the court in order to prevent the directors from entering into such a transaction as long as the members have not ratified it by special resolution.[85]

---

[81] See *Cotman v Brougham* [1918] AC 514.
[82] *Re German Date Coffee Co* (1882) 20 ChD 169.
[83] Art 9.
[84] *Reform of the Ultra Vires Rule: A Consultative Document* (1986) based on the findings of Dr Dan Prentice.
[85] *Simpson v Westminster Palace Hotel Co* (1868) 8 HL Cas 712.

Second, the powers of directors to bind the company are dealt with specifically by section 35A(1) which provides that, in favour of a person dealing with the company in good faith, the power of the board of directors to bind the company shall be without any limitation under the company's constitution. Furthermore, section 35B provides that a third party entering into a transaction with the company is not obliged to examine the constitutional documents of the company in order to ensure that the transaction is within the capacity of the company or within the powers of the directors to bind the company.

Directors' liability

11–53   Directors entering into a transaction which is *ultra vires* the company's objects and which results in loss to the company may be liable to pay damages. However, section 35(3) enables the members to relieve the directors of such liability by passing a special resolution or, in the case of a private company, a written resolution.

Alteration of objects

11–54   The company may, by special (or written) resolution make changes to the objects clause.[86] Application may be made to the court for cancellation of such alteration by the holders of 15 per cent of the company's issued share capital or 15 per cent of the holders of any class of shares within 21 days of the passing of the resolution. The dissenters must not have voted for the resolution.[87]

A statement of the limitation of liability of the company

11–55   The memorandum of every limited company must state that the liability of members is limited, whether by shares or by guarantee.

A capital clause

11–56   Under section 2 of the Act, a company which is limited by shares must contain in its memorandum a statement of the amount of share capital which the company is authorised to issue and the division of such capital into shares of a stated amount.

THE ARTICLES OF ASSOCIATION

11–57   The articles of association contain the internal constitution of the company and regulate the rights of members *inter se* (between themselves). The articles govern issues such as the holding of meetings; the voting rights of members; the appointment of directors; the declaration of dividends (if appropriate); and the appointment of company secretaries.[88] Unlike the memorandum, there are no compulsory clauses as the contents of the articles will depend on the internal arrangements of each individual company. However, model sets of articles of association are provided by the Companies (Tables A–F) Regulations 1985,[89] which companies may choose to adopt, Table A of which applies to companies limited by shares, both public and private.

---

[86] CA 1985, s 4.
[87] *ibid* s 5.
[88] Under the provision of s 283 of the Act, every company must have a secretary; a sole director may not also act as a secretary.
[89] SI 1985/805.

Articles must be printed, divided into paragraphs which are numbered consecutively and must be signed by each subscriber to the memorandum in the presence of at least one witness who must attest the signature.[90]

Alteration of the articles

Under section 9 of the Act a company may alter its articles by special resolution in a general meeting. A copy of the resolution, containing the alteration, must be sent to the Registrar within 15 days of passing the resolution.[91] It is also possible to alter articles without a special resolution if the consent of all the members is obtained. Changes must comply with the requirements of the Act and be bona fide for the benefit of the company as a whole.[92] A company cannot exclude or restrict the right of its members to alter the articles as such action would be contrary to section 9(1) and void.

11–58

Restrictions on alteration

Articles cannot be altered for the following purposes:

11–59

(1) To contravene the provisions of company legislation.

(2) To make provision in contravention of the memorandum, as the memorandum is the dominant document.[93]

(3) To impose a liability on members to take more shares than they already hold.[94]

(4) To deprive members of rights given to them by the court.[95]

(5) To undertake any act which is not for the benefit of the company as a whole.[96]

Breaches of contract arising from alteration of articles

In certain circumstances, an alteration to a company's articles may result in a breach of a pre-existing contract. Such alteration will still be valid as long as the correct procedure (as stipulated in CA 1985, s 9) is adhered to and none of the restrictions outlined above are applicable. In such cases, the company may be liable to the party to the original contract for damages for breach of contract.[97] However, where the terms of such a contract are contained, in full or in part, within the articles themselves, the other party to the contract will be deemed to have accepted that the articles are subject to change.[98]

11–60

---

[90] CA 1985, s 7(3).
[91] *ibid* s 380.
[92] *Sidebottom v Kershaw, Leese and Co* [1920] 1 Ch 154; *Greenhalgh v Arderne Cinemas* [1951] Ch 286 (CA).
[93] *Guinness v Land Corporation of Ireland* (1882) 22 ChD 349.
[94] Such an alteration would be contrary to s 16 of the Act and, thus, void. Section 16 provides for written agreement to be made to such alteration by the member affected.
[95] For example, by s 461 of the Act which provides for remedies arising due to unfair prejudice.
[96] *Allen v Gold Reefs of West Africa Ltd* [1900] 1 Ch 656.
[97] *Southern Foundries (1926) Ltd v Shirlaw* [1940] AC 701.
[98] *Shuttleworth v Cox Bros & Co (Maidenhead) Ltd* [1927] 2 KB 9.

Alteration/abrogation of class rights

11–61　Where an alteration to the articles would result in an alteration or abrogation of the rights of a particular class of shareholder, the provisions of sections 125–127 of the Act relating to variation of class rights must be complied with.[99]

THE LEGAL EFFECT OF THE MEMORANDUM AND ARTICLES

11–62　Section 14 of the Act provides that the memorandum and articles, when registered, bind the company and its members in contract as if they had been signed and sealed by each member and contain covenants on the part of each member to observe their provisions. The effect of this provision is that the memorandum and articles constitute a contract between the company and each member[100] and between the members themselves.[101] However, the memorandum and articles are not a contract with outsiders[102] unless an express agreement exists to the contrary or a provision of the constitutional documents is deemed to constitute an implied term of a contract between the company and a third party.[103]

THE CAPITAL OF A COMPANY

CLASSIFICATION OF CAPITAL

11–63　Before the statutory controls relating to a company's capital can be considered, it is necessary to consider the terminology that is used.

Authorised capital refers to the amount that the company is entitled to issue as provided for by the capital clause of the memorandum.[104]

Allotted capital is the amount of capital that the company has allotted to its shareholders. A public company must allot at least £50,000 of its authorised capital.[105]

Share capital is allotted capital. It may be divided into various classes of shares. It is not necessary for the shares to be uniform or to carry equal rights. The various classes of shares that a company may allot and the rights generally attaching to each will be considered below.[106]

Paid-up capital is the amount of allotted capital that has been called up by the company and paid by the shareholders. Unpaid capital refers to the proportion of the capital that has been called up by the company but, as yet, remains unpaid.

---

[99] See para 11–73.
[100] *Hickman* v *Kent or Romney Marsh Sheepbreeders' Association* [1915] 1 Ch 881.
[101] *Rayfield* v *Hands* [1958] 2 All ER 194.
[102] *Eley* v *Positive Government Security Life Assurance Co* (1876) 1 Ex D 88.
[103] *Muirhead* v *Forth and North Sea Steamboat Mutual Insurance Association* (1893) 21 R (HL) 1; *Re New British Iron Co, ex p Beckwith* [1898] 1 Ch 324.
[104] CA 1985, s 2.
[105] *ibid* s 25.
[106] See para 11–72.

Uncalled capital is the amount of allotted capital which has not been called up by the company.

Reserve capital is the amount of the uncalled capital which may only be called upon in a winding up.[107]

METHODS OF RAISING CAPITAL

Companies may raise capital by various means. A public company obtains finance from public investors but a private company cannot raise capital in this manner.[108] **11–64**

Private companies

Private companies, which are prohibited from offering shares direct to the public, may raise capital in the following ways: a rights issue in which the company offers shares to its existing members in proportion to their current shareholding; a private placing in which contracts for the allotment of shares are made with individuals; an offer of shares for subscription to a class of persons (*eg* the employees of the company). **11–65**

Public companies

The Financial Services Act 1986 imposes strict regulation on companies seeking a stock exchange listing.[109] Generally, capital can be raised by these types of companies in the following ways: by making a direct offer to the public; by selling the issue to an issuing house which then offers the shares for sale to the public; by way of a rights issue whereby shares are offered to the existing members in proportion to their current shareholding; by placing the shares with an issuing house which then invites its clients to purchase the shares; by an offer by tender whereby investors are invited to bid for shares subject to a minimum price. Section 97 of the Act provides that a public company may only pay commission in respect of an allotment of shares if authorised to do so by its articles, the provisions of which are subject to a maximum rate of commission of 10 per cent of the issue price. **11–66**

ALTERATION OF SHARE CAPITAL

If so authorised by its articles, a company may alter the conditions of its memorandum in order to: increase its share capital by creating new shares; consolidate and divide its share capital into shares of a greater denomination; subdivide its shares into shares of a smaller amount; or cancel shares which have not been taken and reduce the amount of its share capital accordingly. In order to undertake such a reorganisation of capital, the appropriate resolution as provided for by the articles must be passed. If no such provision is made, an ordinary resolution will be sufficient.[110] Under section 122 notice must be given to the Registrar within one month of the passing of the resolution. **11–67**

---

[107] CA 1985, s 120.
[108] *ibid* s 81.
[109] Financial Services Act 1986, Pt IV.
[110] CA 1985, s 121.

ALLOTMENT OF SHARES—STATUTORY CONTROLS

11–68 There are a number of statutory provisions which are relevant to the allotment of shares in a company. Section 80 of the Companies Act 1985 provides that the directors of a company shall not exercise any power to allot shares unless given authority to do so by the articles or by the company in general meeting.

The right of pre-emption is set out in section 89 of the Act. This will apply where the company proposes to issue new shares. In such circumstances, existing shareholders must be offered a part of the issue pro rata to their existing shareholding. This provision is intended to ensure that the rights of existing shareholders are not affected by the issue of new shares to outsiders. The offer must be in writing and must be delivered to each shareholder who must respond within 21 days if wishing to accept the offer. Where the right of pre-emption is not exercised by the shareholder, the issue can be made available to outsiders. Failure to comply with the provisions of section 89 will result in the liability of the company and any officer who is knowingly in default to compensate the shareholders affected.[111]

A company may issue shares at a premium by requiring allottees (recipients of the shares) to pay a price above the nominal value of the share. The difference between the nominal value of a share and its issue price is called the "share premium". The issue of shares at a discount is prohibited by section 100 of the Act. If shares are allotted at a discount, the allottee will be liable to pay the company an amount equal to the amount of the discount plus interest at the appropriate rate.[112] This provision applies to both public and private companies.

Public companies

11–69 Certain restrictions on allotments operate in the case of public companies. Section 84 of the Act provides that no allotment of shares in a public company can be made unless the capital is subscribed in full or, if this is not the case, the prospectus states that the allotment is made subject to any specified conditions. If the minimum subscription is not met within 40 days of the issue of the prospectus, all the money received must be repaid to the applicants within the following eight days. If any of the money is not repaid within 48 days after the issue of the prospectus, the directors of the company will be jointly and severally liable to repay it with interest at the rate of 5 per cent per annum unless they can show that the delay was not due to any misconduct or negligence on their part.

Section 101 of the Act sets out what is commonly referred to as the "25 per cent rule". This provides that shares in a public company cannot be allotted until 25 per cent of the nominal value and the whole of the premium have been received by the company. Although such payment may be made in cash or by some other consideration, section 103 of the Act provides that, where an allotment is made in exchange for a non-cash consideration, the non-cash asset must have been valued by an independent accountant who must produce a report[113] stating that the value of the asset is at least equal to the value of the shares being allotted. Furthermore, under section 102 of the Act, a public company is only entitled to allot shares in exchange for

---

[111] CA 1985, s 92.
[112] *Ooregum Gold Mining Co of India Ltd* v *Roper* [1892] AC 125 (HL).
[113] CA 1985, s 108.

a non-cash asset if the transfer of the asset is to take place within five years from the date of the allotment.

Share certificates

Under section 185 of the Act, a company must, within two months after an allotment **11–70** of shares, have share certificates complete and ready for delivery. The provisions of section 185 can be excluded if the conditions of issue provide otherwise. Such a certificate serves as sufficient evidence of the member's title to his shares.[114]

Calls on shares

The articles of most companies provide that the full nominal value of a share need not **11–71** be paid on allotment, but rather by contractual instalments either at a date fixed at the time of issue or by a call at some undetermined time in the future. In the case of public companies, the terms of issue generally provide for sums owing to be paid by fixed instalments within a relatively short period of time, thereby enabling the shares to be converted into stock.

Types of shares

The most common types of shares are ordinary and preference, although other types **11–72** of shares, such as deferred shares, redeemable shares or employers' shares, may be issued depending on the provisions of the articles.

The rights attaching to different classes of shares generally relate to the payment of dividends to shareholders, voting rights and the entitlement of shareholders in a winding up and will be provided for in the articles. For example, the holders of ordinary shares will be entitled to the surplus profits after prior interests have been met, as well as the payment of a fixed rate of dividend before payment is made to the holders of deferred shares. The holders of preference shares will be entitled to payment of a fixed rate of dividend before payment is made to any other class of share-holder. In a winding up, the holders of ordinary shares will generally be entitled to the surplus profits after payment of the company's liabilities and the return of capital to all other classes of share unless, as is often the case, the holders of preference shares are given the right to participate in the distribution of the company's assets. Alternatively, the holders of preference shares will have the right to receive a proportionate part of the company's capital in the event of a winding up. Ordinary shares generally carry one vote per share and preference shares are usually without voting rights.

Variation of class rights

Under the provisions of section 125, a company may seek to amend or vary the rights **11–73** attaching to one or more of its classes of shares. The procedure applying to such variation will depend upon where the rights are provided for. Generally, class rights are to be found in the articles but may also be provided for in the memorandum, the terms of issue relating to the shares or contained in a special resolution. If the rights are contained in the articles, they can be changed by a special or written (in the case of

---

[114] s 186(b). It should be noted that in England and Wales the certificate serves as prima facie evidence (s 186(a)).

private companies) resolution. Rights conferred by the memorandum must be changed in accordance with the type of resolution that the memorandum provides for. If contained in the terms of issue, alteration must be by the method prescribed therein.

The dissentient members of a class of shareholding may object to a variation.[115] In order for a variation of class rights to have taken place, the rights of a particular class of shareholders must be different in substance from their condition before the particular act affecting the rights took place.[116] In such circumstances, the dissenting members may apply to the court to have the variation cancelled. The dissenters must hold not less than 15 per cent of the issued shares of the class affected and must not have voted in favour of the resolution. Application must be made to the court within 21 days of the resolution being passed.

THE MAINTENANCE OF CAPITAL

11–74   The limitation of liability enjoyed by the members of a registered company means that such members cannot be required to contribute further to the capital structure once they have paid for their shares in full. In order to provide protection of the capital contributed by the members and, in turn, to provide protection to creditors dealing with the company, certain statutory provisions exist. These provisions include regulation of the ways in which a company's capital may be reduced and the methods by which a company's shares can be acquired.

Reduction of capital

11–75   A limited company may, by special resolution, reduce its share capital in any way provided that authority is given by the articles[117]and the reduction is confirmed by the court.[118] The procedure for such alteration will be by special (or, in the case of private companies, written) resolution. In addition, if the share capital is divided into shares of different classes, the consent of three-quarters of each class of shareholders is required.[119] Application must be made to the court to protect third parties dealing with the company and to ensure that the reduction is fair and equitable between various classes of shareholders.

Section 135(2) provides for certain specific methods of reduction. First, the liability on partly paid-up shares may be eliminated or reduced. For example, in the case of shares of £1 of which 75p is paid up, the company may eliminate the outstanding liability of 25p on each share by reducing the nominal value of each share to 75p. Second, paid-up capital which has been lost or which is not represented by available assets may be cancelled. For example, where the company has £1 fully paid shares, but assets only represent 50p per share, the company may seek to reduce the nominal value of each share to 50p. Third, any paid-up share capital in excess of the company's needs may be paid off. This method may be applied where "over capitalisation" has occurred—for example, if the company has sold off part of the undertaking and wishes to restrict its future activities to the remaining part of the business.

---

[115] CA 1985, s 127.
[116] *Greenhalgh* v *Arderne Cinemas* [1951] Ch 286 (CA).
[117] Table A, art 34.
[118] CA 1985, s 135.
[119] *Re Northern Engineering Industries plc* [1993] BCLC 1151.

Rules of capital maintenance applying to public companies

A promoter is not bound to be a subscriber to the memorandum of a public company **11–76** on incorporation. However, it is likely that he will be in his capacity as a first director. In such circumstances, the following provisions of the Act relating to capital maintenance will apply. Under the provisions of section 104, the company may not acquire (in exchange for cash or shares) non-cash assets from subscribers to the memorandum who hold one-tenth or more of the nominal value of the issued share capital for two years following the date of the issue of the section 117 certificate. This provision operates as a form of control to prevent such individuals from off-loading property onto the company at an inflated price. If section 104 is breached, the company can recover what it has paid for the asset.

There are certain specific exceptions to this general rule. The first exception applies where the valuation rules set out in section 109 are complied with. Under section 109, the asset must have been valued by an independent accountant who must confirm that the transaction represents "good value"—that is, that the consideration offered by the company is equal to the asset to be purchased. The second exception applies where the acquisition of the asset and the terms of the acquisition have been approved by an ordinary resolution of the company. These provisions also apply to private companies which re-register as public companies.

Restrictions on the acquisition of shares in a company

The Companies Act 1985 imposes certain restrictions with respect to the purchase of **11–77** shares in a company. Generally, such restrictions apply where the company itself, or those acting on its behalf, seek to finance the acquisition of shares—for example, by providing financial assistance for the purposes of acquiring shares and in the purchase of shares by the company itself.

Purchase of own shares

Under section 162 of the Act, a company limited by shares or guarantee is permitted **11–78** to purchase its own shares subject to certain safeguards.[120] Such a purchase must be authorised by the articles.[121] The shares must be fully paid and, in the case of public companies, the purchase must be financed by profits or by the proceeds of a fresh issue made for the purpose of the purchase. For private companies, the purchase may be financed out of capital. Following the purchase, a public company must satisfy the capital requirements of the Act in that its allotted capital must amount to £50,000.[122]

Membership of the holding company

Under the provisions of section 23 of the Act, a company cannot be a member of its **11–79** holding company.

Financial assistance

Under section 151 of the Act, a company and its subsidiaries are prohibited from **11–80** giving financial assistance, directly or indirectly, to a person for the purpose of

---

[120] *General Property etc Co Ltd* v *Mathieson's Trs* (1888) 16 R 282.
[121] Art 35.
[122] CA 1985, s 25.

acquiring shares in the company. This prohibition covers gifts, loans, guarantees and securities, assignments of rights (*ie* a waiver or release from its right to recover a debt) and any other financial assistance.[123] If the company's principal purpose in giving the assistance is incidental to some larger purpose and it is given in good faith and for the benefit of the company, the prohibition will not apply.[124] Breach of section 151 will result in the application of criminal sanctions.

DEBENTURES AND SECURITIES

11–81   A company wishing to raise loan capital will generally issue debentures, which are documents issued by a company setting out the terms of the loan and providing for its repayment at some future specified date. Under the provisions of section 744, the term "debenture" includes debenture stock, bonds and any other securities of a company, whether constituting a charge on the assets of the company or not. Debentures are similar in nature to shares and many of the statutory regulations applying to the allotment of shares also apply to the issuing of debentures. However, the holder of a debenture is a creditor of the company and there are no restrictions with respect to the purchase of its own debentures by a company. The interest on a debenture represents a debt of the company which, unlike dividends, can be paid out of capital.

A debenture may be secured by a fixed charge or a floating charge. This means that, if the company defaults in repayment of the debt, the holder can enforce the debt by calling on the company's assets. In the case of a fixed charge, the debenture is attached to a specific asset at the time of its creation. Floating charges, which are only available to companies, do not attach to specific property until the appointment of a receiver.[125]

Registration of charges

11–82   Most forms of fixed charges and all floating charges must be registered within 21 days of their creation.[126] Registration is achieved by the delivery of relevant particulars to the Registrar. Failure to register a charge constitutes an offence by the company and any officer in default. Although a charge which is not registered will be rendered void, the debt will still be valid. Further to the requirement to register charges with the Registrar, the company must keep its own register of such charges.[127] Failure to comply with this requirement may render those responsible liable to a fine.

Ranking of floating charges

11–83   Section 464 of the Act provides for the ranking of floating charges in Scotland. Generally, a fixed charge will take priority over a subsequent fixed charge and over any floating charge. The ranking of floating charges will be considered further in the section dealing with liquidation below.[128]

---

[123] CA 1985, s 152.
[124] *ibid* s 153(1).
[125] See para 11–123
[126] CA 1985, s 410.
[127] *ibid* s 422.
[128] See para 11–157.

Discharge of charges

Where a charge has ceased to apply to a company property, the company must inform **11–84**
the Registrar[129] by way of a memorandum of discharge signed on the company's
behalf and by the chargee.

THE DIRECTORS OF A COMPANY

Section 741(1) of the Act provides that the term "director" includes "... any person **11–85**
occupying the position of director, by whatever name called". Public companies must
have at least two directors, private companies at least one director.[130] There is no upper
limit on the number of directors imposed by the Act and such provision will generally
be made in the articles.

APPOINTMENT OF DIRECTORS

A company's first directors are usually appointed in writing by the subscribers to the **11–86**
memorandum which must, in accordance with the provision of section 10 of the Act,
contain the names of the first directors and their consent to act. Alternatively, the first
and subsequent directors will be appointed in accordance with the provisions of the
articles. Table A provides for appointment by ordinary resolution in a general
meeting. The board of directors can make appointments in two circumstances: first, to
fill casual vacancies that may occur on resignation, removal or death; and, second,
to appoint additional directors to a given maximum set out in the company's articles.
This applies where the number of directors falls below the minimum number
provided for in the articles—for example, by the death of a director. This is a
temporary measure and directors appointed to the board in these circumstances will
only hold office until the next general meeting, at which the temporary director may
be put in front of the members who then vote as per the procedure in Table A.

Although there is no legal requirement that a company must impose a share qualification for directors, the articles will generally provide that such a qualification may
be fixed in general meeting.

Classes of persons excluded

Certain classes of persons may not be appointed as directors, while others may become **11–87**
disqualified under certain statutory provisions. For example, persons aged 70 or over
are disqualified from appointment as directors of public companies under section 293
of the Act and existing directors must vacate office at the conclusion of the annual
general meeting after reaching the age of 70. This provision may be modified or
excluded by the articles or such appointment may be approved by the passing of an
ordinary resolution in a general meeting of which 28 days' notice has been given to the
company.

---

[129] CA 1985, s 419.
[130] *ibid* s 282.

The Company Directors Disqualification Act 1986 (CDDA) contains provisions which make it a criminal offence for certain individuals to act as directors. Under section 11, an undischarged bankrupt cannot act as a director of any company without the permission of the court. Furthermore, under section 6 of the CDDA, the court may make a disqualification order against a person prohibiting him from acting as a director for a period specified by the order. The grounds on which such an order will be granted include conviction for certain offences in connection with the promotion, formation or management of a company, fraudulent trading or breach of duty. Persons convicted of fraud may be barred for up to 15 years.

The company's articles may specify other grounds for disqualification. Article 81 of Table A provides for the following additional grounds: if a director becomes of unsound mind, if a director resigns his office by writing to the company, or if a director is absent for six months or more from the meetings of the directors held within that period without the permission of the directors.

REMUNERATION OF DIRECTORS

11–88 The director of a company has no automatic right to remuneration for his services[131] and the arrangements pertaining to directors' remuneration are generally expressly provided for in the articles. Table A provides for such remuneration to be determined by the company by ordinary resolution and, unless the resolution provides otherwise, that the remuneration shall be "deemed to accrue from day to day".[132] Companies generally vote on directors' fees annually or stipulate a fixed sum payable every year. These are debts owed by the company which can be paid out of capital if insufficient profits have been made.[133] Directors are, of course, free to negotiate a service contract with the company. In such circumstances, the right to remuneration would exist independently of the articles of association.

LOANS TO DIRECTORS

11–89 Under the provisions of the Act, a company may not make a loan to a director or to a director of its holding company.[134] Public companies are subject to further regulation in this respect and are prevented from making quasi-loans, acting as a guarantor or providing any security in respect of a loan to a director.[135] A quasi-loan is defined as a transaction under which a third party provides goods or services to a director and is then reimbursed by a company which, in turn, recovers the sums owing from the director. An example of the type of transaction prohibited would be an arrangement whereby a company arranges for goods to be taken by a director on credit and pays for those goods, recovering the sum payable from the director at a later date. There are exceptions to these general rules,[136] notably, in the case of quasi-loans, where the aggregate amount owing does not exceed £2,500 and the sum is to be repaid within

---

[131] *Hutton* v *West Cork Railway Co* (1883) 23 ChD 654.
[132] Art 82.
[133] *Re Lundy Granite Co* (1871) 6 Ch App 462.
[134] CA 1985, s 330(2).
[135] *ibid* s 330(3) and (4).
[136] Provided for by CA 1985, ss 334–338.

two months[137] or, in the case of loans, where the aggregate amount owing does not exceed £5,000.[138] Breaches of the provisions relating to loans to directors may give rise to criminal liability under section 342 of the Act which provides for both imprisonment and the imposition of a fine.

POWERS OF DIRECTORS

The powers delegated by the company to its directors will be set out in its articles. **11–90** Table A provides: "Subject to the provisions of the Act, the memorandum and the articles and to any directions given by special resolution, the business of the company shall be managed by the directors who may exercise all the powers of the company."[139] It should be noted that, through this process of delegation, directors are restricted in terms of their powers by any limitations imposed on the company generally. Therefore, the *ultra vires* rule will place certain restrictions upon the acts of directors in the same way that it serves to restrict the acts of the company. Furthermore, delegation of the company's powers to its directors is provided for by the company's articles, which are subject to alteration by a special (or written) resolution[140] passed by its members. This gives rise to a division of power between the members of a company and its directors, the former retaining the right to appoint and remove directors in accordance with the provisions of the articles. However, directors can be said to be responsible for the day-to-day running of the company and, in the execution of their duties, will be subject to particular common law and statutory provisions.

In their role as managers of the company's affairs, a wide discretion is generally conferred upon the directors to act on behalf of the company. Although the directors may delegate part of their managerial function to subordinate employees, it will generally be the directors themselves who are responsible for the formulation and execution of company policy. In this respect, it can be seen that directors are agents of the company[141] and the normal rules of agency will thus apply.[142]

The ability of the directors to bind the company

If the board of directors acting together, or one director or other officer of the company **11–91** acting on his own, has authority to contract on the company's behalf, the acts of the director(s) will be binding on the company. As considered above, section 35A provides added protection in this respect so long as the other party to the transaction acts in good faith and there is no obligation on the third party to enquire as to the powers of the board of directors to bind the company or authorise others to do so.[143] This will apply whether the directors are acting within their powers or not and even where the correct internal procedures have not been observed.[144]

Under the common law, the ability of directors to bind the company will not generally be open to question as the company retains the right to manage its own

---

[137] CA 1985, s 332.
[138] *ibid* s 334.
[139] Art 70.
[140] Under the procedure set out in s 9 of the Act.
[141] *Ferguson* v *Wilson* (1866) 2 Ch App 77.
[142] See Chapter 6.
[143] CA 1985, s 35B.
[144] *TCB* v *Gray* [1987] 3 WLR 1144.

affairs and such management will be executed by the board of directors.[145] This is commonly referred to as the "indoor management rule" and will apply where such transactions are *intra vires* the company but beyond the powers of the directors. In such circumstances, the third party will be deemed to have knowledge of any limitations imposed upon the authority of the directors to bind the company, as provided for by the company's memorandum or articles, but may assume, in the absence of any actual notice to the contrary, that the internal procedures of the company have been complied with.[146]

DUTIES OF DIRECTORS[147]

11–92   Directors have a fiduciary relationship with the company and, therefore, owe a duty to act honestly and in the best interests of the company. They must manage the company's affairs in accordance with the provisions of the common law and statute and are bound by the provisions of the memorandum and the articles of association. Directors must manage the affairs of the company in accordance with the "Proper Purpose Rule". This means that, in all their transactions for and on behalf of the company, directors must act bona fide in the best interests of the company as a whole and not to further their own interests.[148] In exercising the powers granted to them by the company in accordance with the principles outlined above, there are certain specific duties owed by the directors of the company, the nature and scope of which are best illustrated by consideration of the relevant case law and, where appropriate, statutory provisions.

To act bona fide in the best interests of the company

11–93   In order to determine what they honestly consider to be in the company's best interests, directors must exercise their own discretion. In *Re Roith Ltd*[149] a company's memorandum and articles were altered to allow pensions to be paid to the dependants of employees. A director in poor health was appointed general manager for life. One of the terms of his service agreement stated that if he died in office, the company would pay his widow a pension for the rest of her life. He died shortly thereafter. The court held that the agreement was not binding as it was not reasonably incidental to carrying on the company's business and it was not, therefore, for the benefit of the company.

To avoid a conflict of interests

11–94   A director must not allow his personal interest to conflict with his duty to the company. There is statutory support for this under section 317 of the Act, which states that a director is required to disclose any interest in a contract between the company and himself or persons connected with him, namely his spouse or infant child. Such

---

[145] *Royal British Bank* v *Turquand* (1856) 6 E&B 327; *Gillies* v *Craigton* 1935 SC 423 (IH).
[146] *Irvine* v *Union Bank of Australia* (1877) 2 App Cas 366.
[147] At the time of writing the results of a consultation exercise relating to the regulation of directors' duties are awaited. The Law Commissions of England (and Wales) and Scotland published a joint consultation document in 1998 entitled *Company Directors: Regulating Conflicts of Interest and Formulating a Statement of Duties* (Scot Law Com No 105).
[148] *Bamford* v *Bamford* [1970] Ch 212.
[149] [1967] 1 All ER 427 (ChD).

disclosure must be made to the board or to the shareholders. Non-compliance may result in a fine. In *Aberdeen Railway Co v Blaikie Bros*[150] a company entered into a contract with a firm for the supply of manufactured goods. At the time of making the contract the company's chairman was the managing partner of the firm. The House of Lords held that the company was not bound by the contract.

To act for the benefit of the company as a whole

This duty is owed to the company rather than to individual shareholders. In *Percival v Wright*[151] a shareholder sold his shares to three of the directors at a price based on his own valuation. He later discovered that negotiations for the sale of the company's shares were taking place. If the negotiations were successful, the price for each share would have been greater than that paid to him. The negotiations were unsuccessful, but Percival brought an action to set aside his sale to the directors. The court held that the directors were not under a duty to inform him of the negotiations as their fiduciary duty was to the company as a whole and not to individual shareholders.

11–95

A duty of care and skill

In *Re City Equitable Fire Insurance Co*[152] the following guidelines were established with respect to the extent of the director's duty of care and skill. First, a director must show the degree of care and skill which would be reasonably expected from someone with his knowledge and experience; second, a director is not bound to give continuous attention to the affairs of the company and, third, a director may trust a company official to perform duties, which may properly be delegated.

11–96

Breach of directors' duties

As directors owe their duties to the company, enforcement of such duties will generally be by the company.[153] In some circumstances, a minority shareholder may bring an action and this area will be considered later.[154] As noted above, where a director exceeds his powers to contract on the company's behalf, subject to the provisions of section 35, he may be liable to the company in damages. Where a breach of duty is discovered during the process of liquidation, the liquidator will bring an action against the director on the company's behalf. The provisions of sections 212–214 of the Insolvency Act 1986, which provide remedies against those involved in misappropriation of company assets and fraudulent and wrongful trading, may be relevant. In such circumstances, directors or officers of the company may be held personally liable for the company's debts in whole or in part.

11–97

PERSONAL LIABILITY OF DIRECTORS TO OUTSIDERS

In certain circumstances directors may be personally liable to outsiders. Such liability may arise as a consequence of breach of contract, breach of a delictual duty or may be imposed by statute.

11–98

---

[150] (1854) 1 Macq 461 (HL).
[151] [1902] 2 Ch 421.
[152] [1925] 1 Ch 407.
[153] *Foss* v *Harbottle* (1843) 2 Hare 461—see para 11–107 *et seq.*
[154] See para 11–109.

Under the general rules of contract, a director may find himself personally liable to a third party if he purports to have authority to conclude a transaction on behalf of the company where no such authority exists.[155] Delictual liability may arise in cases of fraud[156] or negligent misstatement.[157] The statutory provisions which impose personal liability include section 50 of the Financial Services Act 1986, under which a compensation order may be made in relation to misstatements or omissions in listing particulars, and section 85 of the Companies Act 1985 which applies to the irregular allotment of shares. Liability arising due to the improper use of the company name, as provided for by section 349(4) of the Companies Act 1985, has already been considered.[158]

MEMBERSHIP OF A COMPANY

11–99 The acquisition of membership of a company is dealt with in section 22 of the Act, which provides that a person becomes a member of a company when he agrees to become a member and his name is entered in the register of members. In effect this may occur by way of one of the following:

(1) by subscribing to the memorandum—on company registration, subscribers to the memo automatically become members,

(2) by application under a prospectus or offer of sale for an allotment of shares,

(3) by acceptance of a transfer from an existing member,

(4) by succession to shares on the death or bankruptcy of a member,

(5) by the acquisition of shares through an employee share scheme,

(6) by signing and filing an undertaking as a director to take and pay for a qualification share,

(7) by holding oneself out as a member and allowing one's name to be entered on the register of members.

As the relationship between a company and its members is one of contract, it follows that the general rules of contract will apply to membership issues. Therefore, anyone who has the capacity to make a contract may become a member of a company. In the case of minors, unless the articles provide otherwise, a minor may become a member of a company. In Scotland, the age of full contractual capacity is 16[159] and, therefore, although a young person may hold shares in a company, if permitted by the articles,

---

[155] Breach of warranty of authority—see Chapter 4.
[156] *Derry* v *Peek* (1889) 14 App Cas 337.
[157] *Hedley Byrne and Co Ltd* v *Heller and Partners Ltd* [1964] AC 465.
[158] See para 11–45.
[159] Age of Legal Capacity (Scotland) Act 1991, s 1.

he may not transact to purchase them but must acquire them by one of the other means listed above. Persons under the age of 21 have special rights to apply to the court to have prejudicial transactions set aside in respect of contracts entered into while aged 16 and 17. Such a right may enable a young person to repudiate a contract in respect of partly paid shares.[160]

If authorised by its memorandum, a company may become a member of another company and, in such circumstances, a representative may be appointed to attend meetings and vote on the company's behalf or the company may act by proxy. However, a company cannot become a member of itself. It cannot purchase its own shares because such a purchase would amount to a return of capital to the shareholders from whom the shares were bought—this would act as a reduction of capital which would normally require to be sanctioned by the court.[161]

REGISTER OF MEMBERS

11–100 Under section 352, every company is to keep a register of its members. This must contain the following information: the names and addresses of members; a statement of shares held by each member (if applicable) and classes of shares; the amount paid on each member's shares; the date on which each member was entered in the register and the date on which any person ceased to be a member. Under section 356, any member of a company may inspect the register and may apply to the court for an order for rectification of the register if certain information is withheld or misrepresented.[162]

DISCLOSURE OF SUBSTANTIAL SHAREHOLDINGS—PUBLIC COMPANIES

11–101 Various provisions are contained in sections 198–202 of the Act to secure disclosure of substantial shareholdings in public companies. However, these have proved extremely difficult to enforce. A person must inform a company when, to his knowledge, he acquires a 3 per cent interest in the voting share capital or ceases to be interested in the shares. Every public company must keep a register of interests in shares notified to it in accordance with this rule.

INVESTIGATION OF INTERESTS IN A COMPANY'S SHARES

11–102 Under section 212, a public company may require any person whom the company knows or has reasonable cause to believe has been, during the last three years, interested in the company's shares to confirm or deny that fact. Furthermore, members of a company who hold 10 per cent or more of the company's equity capital may requisition the board of directors, acting on the company's behalf, to investigate the ownership of shares.

---

[160] *Steinberg* v *Scala (Leeds) Ltd* [1932] 2 Ch 452.
[161] CA 1985, ss 136 and 137.
[162] *ibid* s 359.

THE ANNUAL RETURN AND DISCLOSURE OF INFORMATION

11–103   Under Part XI, Chapter III of the Act a company is required to file an annual return with the Registrar and, in doing so, must disclose certain information relevant to membership. The system for annual returns is by pro-forma and is known as the "shuttle concept". The Registrar issues form 363s to the company setting out all the information relevant to the annual return currently held. Such information includes: the company's name and the address of its registered office; its principal business activity; the address where registers of members and debenture holders are kept; details of the company's issued share capital and a list of current members and those who have ceased to be members since the last return. The company is required to confirm or amend the information and return it. Failure to make the return may result in a fine[163] or, in cases of persistent failure, the disqualification of directors.

TERMINATION OF MEMBERSHIP

11–104   A person ceases to be a member of a company when his name is removed from the register of members. This may arise, *inter alia*, in the following circumstances: a transfer of shares to another person; the forfeiture or surrender of shares; the sale of shares by the company under a provision in the articles; expulsion, death, bankruptcy or the dissolution of the company.

THE RIGHTS OF MEMBERS

11–105   The members of a company are entitled to certain rights in respect of their membership. For companies with a share capital, the rights enjoyed by members will be determined by the type of shares that the members hold. The memorandum and articles may provide for the issue of different classes of shares which may carry different rights. Table A provides that "without prejudice to any rights attached to any existing shares, any share may be issued with such rights or restrictions as the company may, by ordinary resolution, determine."[164] The rights attaching to the various classes of shares will generally be with respect to the payment of dividends, the distribution of assets in a winding up and voting rights.[165] Members' entitlements in a winding up will be considered below[166] and the rights of members to participate in the passing of resolutions will also be considered.[167]

The payment of dividends

11–106   A dividend is that part of the profits which is distributed to the members of a company in proportion to their shareholding and in accordance with their rights as shareholders. There is no automatic right to a dividend as such distribution will depend on the company's profits. The declaration and payment of dividends is provided for in the articles. Table A provides for the declaration of dividends in a general meeting, but

---

[163] CA 1985, Sched 24.
[164] Art 2.
[165] See para 11–72.
[166] See para 11–147 *et seq.*
[167] See para 11–117 *et seq.*

no dividend may exceed the amount recommended by the directors.[168] If the articles so provide, interim dividends may be paid if justified by the company's profits.[169] Dividends must be paid in cash unless the articles provide otherwise.[170]

Majority rule and minority protection

The members of a company are contractually bound to the company and to each other **11–107** by virtue of the company's articles.[171] Therefore, if a resolution is passed at a general meeting to which an individual shareholder is opposed, he will nonetheless be bound by the decision of the appropriate majority so long as the correct procedure provided by the articles and subject to the provisions of the Act has been adhered to. This is known as the principle of majority rule.

This principle was established in the English case, *Foss v Harbottle*.[172] The effects of the rule are that (a) the company as a legal person is the proper plaintiff[173] in proceedings where an alleged wrong has been done to a company, and (b) where the alleged wrong is a transaction which might be made binding on the company by a simple majority, no individual member is allowed to maintain an action in respect of that matter. The rule established in *Foss* also serves to avoid a multiplicity of actions from being brought by individual shareholders or groups of shareholders in respect of a wrong done to the company.[174]

Exceptions to the rule in Foss

There are certain exceptions to the rule established in *Foss*. Although the "new" **11–108** section 35[175] enables the company to ratify *ultra vires* acts,[176] the majority cannot confirm: an act which is illegal; an act which is a fraud on the minority and the wrong-doers are in control of the company[177]; or a resolution passed by means of a trick.[178]

Statutory protection of the minority

There are certain statutory provisions designed to protect the interests of minority **11–109** shareholders. These provisions amount to exceptions to the "proper plaintiff" rule set down in *Foss* and to the indoor management rule[179] and they are only applicable in specified circumstances and at the discretion of the court.

Sections 122–124 of the Insolvency Act 1986 provide that a company may be wound up if the court is of the opinion that such action is just and equitable. In such circumstances a minority shareholder or a group of minority shareholders may petition the court. The procedure for winding up will be considered later.[180] It should be noted

---

[168] Art 102.
[169] As provided by art 103.
[170] *Wood v Odessa Waterworks Co* (1889) 42 Ch D 636.
[171] CA 1985, s 14. See para 11–62.
[172] (1843) 2 Hare 461. For an equivalent Scottish case, see *Orr v Glasgow, Airdrie and Monklands Junction Railway Co* (1860) 22 D (HL) 10.
[173] "Pursuer" in Scots law terminology.
[174] *Gray v Lewis* (1873) 8 Ch App 1035.
[175] See para 11–52.
[176] See *Parke v Daily News* [1962] Ch 927 for the position prior to the Companies Act 1989.
[177] *Cook v Deeks* [1916] 1 AC 554.
[178] *Kaye v Croydon Tramways* (1898) 1 Ch 358 (CA).
[179] Discussed at para 11–91.
[180] See para 11–149 *et seq.*

that, due to the drastic nature of this particular course of action, the court will only grant such a remedy if it is satisfied that no other course of action is applicable.[181]

Section 459 of the Companies Act 1985 provides an alternative remedy. If the rights of the minority shareholder are unfairly prejudiced[182] by the manner in which the company's affairs are being or have been conducted, the member may petition the court for an order[183] regulating the affairs of the company or to restrain the company from doing or continuing the prejudicial act. In certain circumstances, the court may authorise the company to bring a claim or may order the company or other members to purchase the shares of the minority at a fair price.[184]

MEETINGS AND RESOLUTIONS

PURPOSE AND PROCEDURE OF MEETINGS

11–110   Although the company's directors are responsible for managing the day-to-day running of the company and attending to its business as appropriate, certain acts of the company require the agreement of a majority of its members. For this reason, the members must attend or, in certain circumstances, be represented at company meetings. There are three different kinds of company meetings: annual general meetings; extraordinary general meetings and meetings of a particular class of shareholders. The nature of proceedings and the types of business dealt with at each kind of meeting will be subject to the statutory requirements and the provisions of the articles.

Annual general meetings

11–111   Under the provisions of section 366 of the Act, every company is required to hold an annual general meeting (AGM) in each calendar year. No more than 15 months must elapse between the date of one AGM and the next, except in the case of a newly formed company which may hold its first AGM within 18 months of incorporation. The articles will specify the nature of business which may be transacted to an AGM. There is generally a distinction between "ordinary" and "special" business.

"Ordinary" business is deemed to be: the declaration of a dividend; consideration of the company's accounts and balance sheets; consideration of the directors' and auditors' reports; the election of directors; the appointment and fixing of the remuneration of the auditors. Any other business transacted at an AGM and all business transacted at an extraordinary general meeting is deemed to be "special business".

Extraordinary meetings

11–112   Any general meeting other than the AGM will be deemed to be an extraordinary meeting. Table A provides for the directors to be given powers to call an

---

[181] *Gammack v Mitchells (Fraserburgh) Ltd* 1983 SC 39 (OH).
[182] *Re A Company (No 004475)* [1983] 2 WLR 381.
[183] CA 1985, s 461(1) sets out the remedies available to the court.
[184] *Re Cumana Ltd* [1986] BCLC 430.

extraordinary meeting whenever they see fit.[185] Under section 368, the directors must convene such a meeting if required to do so by members holding at least one-tenth of paid-up capital. In such circumstances, the directors have 21 days in which to convene the meeting, which must be held within 28 days after the date of the notice convening the meeting. Under section 371, the court has a residual power to order the calling of an extraordinary meeting if an application is made by a director or member(s) of the company. A resigning auditor may request that an extraordinary meeting be called in order for the company to consider the reasons for his resignation.[186] A public company must convene an extraordinary meeting if a serious loss of capital has occurred in order to consider what measures should be taken in relation to the matter.[187]

Meetings of classes of shareholders

Such meetings are usually held to enable the holders of a particular class of shares **11–113** to consider and vote on variations of the rights of that class.[188] The articles generally provide that, in order for a company to effect a variation of class rights, it must attain either the written consent of the holders of three-quarters of the issued shares of that class, or an extraordinary resolution at a separate meeting of holders of shares of that class. Under section 425, the court may order a class meeting to be convened.

Notice of meetings

A meeting cannot be properly convened unless and until the correct period of notice **11–114** has been given to every person entitled to receive notice. The notice must state the time, date and place of the meeting and the nature of the business to be transacted. Failure to give such notice invalidates the meeting. The following notice periods are provided for under the Act: 21 days for an AGM[189] or for an extraordinary meeting at which a special resolution is to be proposed[190]; 14 days' notice for any other meeting of a limited company.[191] An AGM can be called at shorter notice if all the members entitled to attend and vote so agree. Certain periods of notice must be given if the transactions proposed require specific types of resolution and these are set out below.[192]

Quorum

The quorum of a meeting can be defined as the necessary number of members present **11–115** for the meeting to take place. If the correct quorum is not present, any transactions undertaken at the meeting will be invalid.[193] The quorum for a meeting is generally fixed by the articles[194] but, if the articles are silent on this matter, section 370(4) of the Act provides that the quorum for a company meeting shall be two members

---

[185] Art 37.
[186] CA 1985, s 392A.
[187] *ibid* s 142.
[188] See para 11–73.
[189] CA 1985, s 369.
[190] *ibid* s 378.
[191] *ibid* s 369.
[192] See para 11–118 *et seq.*
[193] *Re London Flats Ltd* [1969] 2 All ER 744.
[194] Article 40 fixes a quorum at two members present in person or by proxy.

personally present. In the case of single member companies, one member present in person or by proxy shall constitute a quorum.[195]

The role of the chairman

11–116   The chairman of the board of directors or, in his absence, any other director nominated by the board generally presides over company meetings.[196] The chairman's function is to take the meeting through the agenda and to put matters to the vote as appropriate.

RESOLUTIONS

11–117   There are three types of resolution that may be passed at general meetings: ordinary, special and extraordinary. The type used will depend on the provisions of the articles and the nature of the business being transacted. The provisions of the Act stipulate that certain resolutions be used for certain transactions.

Ordinary resolutions

11–118   An ordinary resolution is passed by a simple majority of those attending and voting. "Special notice" of at least 28 days must be given for the following: the removal of a director before expiry of his period of office[197]; the appointment or reappointment of a director who is over 70; the removal of an auditor before the expiry of his period of office; the appointment of a new auditor.

Special resolutions

11–119   Special resolutions are defined under section 378(2) of the Act as requiring the authority of at least three-quarters of the members voting. Notice of 21 days is to be given if a transaction requiring a special resolution is proposed. Special resolutions are required, *inter alia*, for the following: alteration of the objects clause[198]; alteration of the articles[199]; alteration of the memorandum[200]; the creation of a capital reserve[201]; the reduction of share capital[202]; the re-registration of companies[203]; a change of company name.[204]

Extraordinary resolutions

11–120   An extraordinary resolution is passed by three-quarters of the members voting in person or by proxy. Section 378 of the Act provides that notice of the intention to propose the resolution as an extraordinary resolution must have been given. The periods of notice applicable are 14 days in the case of a limited company and seven days in the case of an unlimited company. Extraordinary resolutions are required for a variation of class rights[205] and in order to initiate a voluntary winding up.[206]

---

[195] CA 1985, s 370A.
[196] Table A, art 42.
[197] CA 1985, s 303.
[198] *ibid* s 4.
[199] *ibid* s 9.
[200] *ibid* s 17.
[201] *ibid* s 120.
[202] *ibid* s 135.
[203] *ibid* ss 43, 51 and 53.
[204] *ibid* s 28.
[205] *ibid* s 125.
[206] Insolvency Act 1986 ("IA 1986"), s 84.

Registration of resolutions

Resolutions relating to certain transactions must be registered. Section 380 of the Act **11–121** provides a list of these, which includes all special resolutions and all extraordinary resolutions. Failure to register such resolutions will result in criminal liability.

RECEIVERSHIP

Where a company defaults in satisfying the terms of a debenture which is secured by **11–122** a floating charge, the holder of the charge will have the right to appoint a receiver for the purposes of recovering the debt. The law relating to receivership in Scotland has developed separately from its English counterpart. The Insolvency Act 1986 (IA 1986) governs receivership in both jurisdictions, with sections 28–40 providing the English regulations and sections 50–71 regulating receivership in Scotland.

THE APPOINTMENT OF A RECEIVER

Under section 51 of the Insolvency Act 1986, a receiver can be appointed by the holder **11–123** of a floating charge or by the court under the circumstances set out in section 52. These arise if the company fails to pay within 21 days of a demand for payment; or the company is two months in arrears in the payment of interest; or an order is made to wind up the company; or a receiver is appointed by another holder of a floating charge. The receiver is appointed to enforce repayment of sums owed to the holder of the floating charge.

TERMINATION OF RECEIVERSHIP

Under IA 1986, s 61, the termination of receivership occurs by the removal or resig- **11–124** nation of the receiver. This generally occurs when he has completed his duties, at which time he must give 14 days' notice to the Registrar that he is ceasing to act.[207]

THE POWERS OF A RECEIVER

Under IA 1986, s 55, the receiver may exercise any powers set out in the document **11–125** creating the floating charge. In addition, Schedule 2 to the Insolvency Act provides for certain specific powers. In exercising his duties, the receiver may take possession of any attached property and sell or dispose of it, he may borrow money or grant securities in the company's name, he may bring or defend legal proceedings on the company's behalf, he may carry on the business of the company, call up unpaid capital and present or defend a petition for the winding up of the company.

---

[207] IA 1986, s 62.

THE DUTIES OF A RECEIVER

11–126   A receiver owes a general duty to the company to exercise powers without negligence and to obtain a reasonable price when selling attached property. The relationships between the receiver and the company and between the receiver and the floating charge holder are fiduciary in nature and, therefore, conflicts of interest must be avoided. Under the provisions of section 57, the receiver acts as an agent in relation to property attached by the floating charge and in this respect the general rules of agency will apply.[208] He also owes specific duties which are provided for by Part III, Chapter II of IA 1986. Under section 65, the receiver must notify the company and all known creditors of his appointment within 28 days and all documents issued in the company's name must disclose that the company is in receivership.[209] Section 66 places a duty on the receiver to request a statement of the company's affairs to be prepared by the directors, other officers or employees of the company. The statement must verify the assets and liabilities of the company. Within three months of his appointment the receiver must prepare a report and send it to the Registrar and all creditors of the company.[210] The report must contain details of the events leading to the receiver's appointment, a summary of the statement of affairs, the disposal and proposed disposal of the company's property, the amounts payable to the holder of the floating charge and to the preferential creditors and the sum available for other creditors. This report must be laid before a meeting of the unsecured creditors,[211] who may form a committee which may request the receiver to attend a meeting with at least seven days' notice.[212]

Distribution of money

11–127   Section 60 of the Insolvency Act 1986 sets out the order in which the receiver must distribute any money realised from the sale of attached property.

> (1) The holder of any fixed security over attached property which ranks prior to or equally with the floating charge.
>
> (2) Creditors who have effectually executed diligence on any part of attached property.
>
> (3) Creditors in respect of all expenses incurred by the receiver.
>
> (4) The receiver's remuneration and expenses.
>
> (5) Preferential creditors provided for by section 59 rank equally:
>   (a) Inland Revenue;
>   (b) Customs and Excise;
>   (c) Social security contributions;

---

[208] See Chapter 6.
[209] IA 1986, s 64.
[210] *ibid* s 67.
[211] *ibid* s 67.
[212] *ibid* s 68.

(d) Occupational pension scheme contributions;

(e) Employees' remuneration.

(6) The holder of the floating charge.

ADMINISTRATION AND VOLUNTARY ARRANGEMENTS

Administration and voluntary arrangements provide different means by which a **11–128**
company experiencing financial difficulties may seek to reorganise its affairs.
Although the difficulties experienced by the company may eventually lead to a
winding up, the temporary relief provided by these types of arrangement may help to
facilitate an improvement in the company's performance and, therefore, they are
often referred to as constituting different methods of "company rescue". The process
of administration is a distinct arrangement which is provided for by sections 8–27
of the Insolvency Act 1986, whereas voluntary arrangements consist of a range of
different options all regulated by a simple procedure set out in sections 1–7 of the
Insolvency Act 1986.

ADMINISTRATION ORDERS

An administration order is made by the court only if the company is, or is likely to **11–129**
become, unable to pay its debts,[213] or the court is satisfied that the making of an order
is likely to achieve one or more of the purposes set out in section 8 of IA 1986. These
purposes are: (a) that the company will survive as a going concern in whole or in part;
(b) that a voluntary arrangement will be approved under Part I of the Act; (c) that a
scheme of arrangement will be sanctioned under section 425 of the Companies Act
1985; or (d) that such an order would result in a more advantageous realisation of the
company's assets than would be effected in a winding up. The likelihood of such a
purpose being achieved must be on the balance of probabilities if the court is to be
persuaded to grant such an order.[214]

Application for an administration order

An application for an administration order is by the presentation of a petition by one **11–130**
or more of the persons listed in section 9 of IA 1986: the company itself, the director(s)
of the company, the creditor(s) of the company.

The effects of application

Section 10 of IA 1986 provides that, once an application has been made, the carrying **11–131**
out of certain acts in the company's name will be prohibited. These are that (a) no
resolution may be passed or order made to wind up the company; (b) no steps can be

---

[213] IA 1986, s 123; see para 11–148.
[214] *Re Consumer and Industrial Press Ltd* [1988] BCLC 177; *Re Harris Simons Construction Ltd* [1989] 5 BCC 11.

made to enforce security of the company's property or to repossess goods under a hire purchase agreement without leave of the court; (c) no legal proceedings may be commenced/continued; (d) no diligence can be carried out or continued against the company without leave of the court.

Process of administration

11–132   The process of administration is set out in section 11 of IA 1986. First, the court makes the order and appoints an administrator (who must be a qualified insolvency practitioner) in accordance with the provisions of IA 1986, s 13. Any petition for winding up the company and any administrative receiver in place must then be dismissed. While the administration is in progress, all company documents must state this and contain the administrator's name.

Powers of the administrator

11–133   Under section 14 of and Schedule 1 to the Insolvency Act 1986, the administrator has the power to do whatever is necessary for the management of the company's affairs, business or property. The specific powers of an administrator include the power to take possession and dispose of the company's property and the power to bring or defend legal proceedings in the company's name and on its behalf.

Duties of the administrator

11–134   The general duties owed to the company are similar to those owed by a receiver in that the administrator has a fiduciary relationship with the company. He is also charged with specific duties provided for by the Insolvency Act, which are as follows. He must send a notice to the company and the Registrar within 14 days following his appointment; he must also inform all known creditors of his appointment within 28 days.[215] Under section 23 of IA 1986, the administrator must request the company to prepare a statement of affairs.[216] The administrator may dispose of any property which is subject to a floating charge without the leave of the court.[217] Within three months of his appointment, the administrator must send a report detailing his proposals for achieving the purpose(s) set out in the order. All the members are entitled to receive notice of the contents of the administrator's report. The administrator must present a copy of his report to a meeting of the company's creditors,[218] at which the creditors may approve or modify the proposals.

Variation or discharge of the order

11–135   The administrator may, at any time, apply to the court for a variation or discharge of the administration order.[219] Such application may be made if it appears that the purpose(s) specified in the order has/have been achieved, if the purpose(s) is/are incapable of achievement or if the creditors have requested that the terms of the order be varied.

---

[215] IA 1986, s 21.
[216] See para 11–126.
[217] IA 1986, s 15.
[218] *ibid* s 24.
[219] *ibid* s 18.

Vacation of office and release

An administrator may be removed from office by the court but, generally, will vacate **11–136** his office once the administration order is discharged, which will be on completion of the purposes for which the order was granted.[220]

VOLUNTARY ARRANGEMENTS

The Insolvency Act 1986, Part I (ss 1–7) provides the opportunity for a proposal to be **11–137** made to a company and its creditors for a mutually agreed arrangement to be put in place which will take the form of either a composition in satisfaction of the company's debts or a scheme of arrangement of affairs.

The proposal

Under section 1 of IA 1986, the proposal may be made by the director, the adminis- **11–138** trator (if an administration order is in place) or by the liquidator if the company is being wound up. The proposal must provide that a qualified insolvency practitioner ("the nominee") supervise the arrangement. If the nominee is not the administrator or liquidator he must receive notice of the terms of the proposal and a statement of affairs of the company.[221]

Actions of the nominee

After considering the proposal and the state of the company's affairs, the nominee **11–139** must compile a report for submission to the court in accordance with the provisions of section 2 of the IA 1986. If the nominee is not the company's administrator or liquidator, the report must state whether, in the nominee's opinion, a meeting of the company and its creditors should be called to enable consideration of the proposal. If the nominee is the company's administrator or liquidator, he should call meetings of the company and its creditors in accordance with the provisions of IA 1986, s 3(2). The meeting will consider whether to accept or modify the arrangement proposed. Certain items are not open to the approval of the meeting and these include a proposal for a course of action which would affect the rights of a secured creditor or the withdrawal of the priority of a preferential debt over other debts unless such actions are approved by the creditor(s) concerned. Under the Insolvency Rules, the proposal must be agreed by majority approval. This will be achieved by gaining the support of three-quarters in value of the creditors present and voting and by a simple majority of the members.

Where a voluntary arrangement is approved in the event of winding up or while an administration order is in force, the court may sist all the proceedings in the winding up or discharge the administration order or give such directions as it thinks appropriate to facilitate the implementation of the voluntary arrangement.[222] Under section 6 of IA 1986, a member may challenge the agreed proposal on the grounds of unfair prejudice, for which there is a 28-day period for application to the court.

---

[220] *ibid* s 19.
[221] *ibid* s 2. See para 11–126.
[222] *ibid* s 5(3).

Procedure for voluntary arrangement

11–140　Under the terms of the arrangement, the nominee becomes the "supervisor" over the composition of the arrangement. The supervisor may apply for a winding up order or an administration order to be made. Section 7 of IA 1986 gives any third party affected by the arrangement the right to apply to the court if he is dissatisfied with any act, omission or decision of a supervisor. The court may confirm, reverse or modify the act or decision, give the supervisor directions or make any other order as it thinks fit.

RECONSTRUCTIONS: TAKEOVERS AND MERGERS

11–141　In the modern commercial environment, companies or groups of companies may be subject to changes in corporate structure. Such changes may occur as the result of a takeover by one company of another or a merger between two or more companies into a new company. Collectively, such reorganisations may be termed "reconstructions". Although the term reconstruction is not defined by the Companies Act, it is generally used to refer to the transfer by a company of its assets to another company or a change in the capital structure of a company or group of companies.

　　The terms "takeover" and "merger" refer to business transactions and are not legal terms. However, the transactions that they describe are highly regulated by certain provisions of company law which have been increasingly used in recent years. Regulation in these areas is provided by the Companies Act 1985, as modified by the Financial Services Act 1986. In addition, the City Code on Takeovers and Mergers regulates negotiations and transactions with respect to takeovers and mergers involving public companies.

SCHEMES OF ARRANGEMENT

11–142　Sections 425–427A of the Companies Act 1985 provide for the making of a compromise or arrangement between the company and its creditors (or any class of creditors), its members (or any class of members) or both its creditors and members. Such an arrangement will be necessary where existing obligations may be affected by a transfer of one company or group of companies to another. To effect such a scheme under section 425 the following procedure must be followed. Any member, creditor or, in the case of a winding up, the liquidator will make an application to the court for an order that a meeting or meetings of relevant creditors and/or members be called. The terms of the proposed scheme are then considered by the court and, if appropriate, the meetings are called. In order for the scheme to be put in place, it is necessary to obtain the support of a three-quarters majority of the class of members and/or creditors affected. If the support is obtained, application must be made to the court to sanction the scheme.

　　Section 427A provides a special regulatory regime applicable to public companies in certain circumstances. This will be relevant where a transfer is proposed between two public companies, or between two existing public companies to a new company (public or private) formed for the purpose of the scheme, or where it is proposed that a public company is to be divided into two or more companies which are either public or formed for the purposes of the scheme. In such circumstances, the court may not sanction such a scheme unless a three-quarters majority of the shareholders of the transferee company agree and reports from experts and the directors containing relevant information and company accounts have been made available to the shareholders.

TAKEOVERS

11–143 The term "takeover" is generally used to refer to the acquisition of shares in a company by another company. The company that is to be taken over is sometimes called the "target" company. The acquiring company makes an offer to the shareholders of the target company, the terms of which can then be accepted or rejected. Such an offer may be made by agreement (*ie* with the consent of the board of directors) or, in the case of a hostile bid, without such consent. Following the successful completion of the necessary transactions, the acquiring company becomes the holding company of the acquired or "target" company, which becomes a subsidiary of the holding company.

Compulsory acquisition of shares

11–144 Takeovers are subject to sections 428–430F of the Companies Act 1985, which provide for the compulsory acquisition of shares under what is commonly referred to as the "10 per cent Rule". The 10 per cent rule arises where an offer is made to acquire all the shares or all the shares of a particular class that the offeror does not already hold. If the offer is accepted by at least 90 per cent in value of shareholders within four months of it being made, the offeror can give notice of his intention to acquire the other 10 per cent within two months of receiving the acceptance. The shares must be acquired on exactly the same terms—usually market value. This may give an advantage to those who delay in making a decision, as they will be able to observe movement in the share price before deciding whether to accept the offer or to refuse and accept another offer that may have been made.

Under section 430C, the dissentient member (reluctant seller) may apply to the court within six weeks of the notice for an order stating that the offeror shall not be entitled to acquire the shares. In exceptional circumstances, the court may exercise its power to prevent acquisition. This is rare, but such power may be exercised where the reason for the takeover is not based on genuine commercial grounds but for some other reason—for example, to get rid of a dissentient member.[223]

MERGERS

11–145 A merger (also referred to as an amalgamation) occurs where two companies are brought together to form one company and is usually a mutually convenient arrangement. A merger can take one of two forms. First, two companies may merge to form a third company, and, second, one company may be subsumed by another company. The latter form demonstrates the overlap which exists with respect to the terms "takeover" and "merger".

---

[223] *Re Bugle Press Ltd* [1960] 3 All ER 791.

THE CITY CODE ON TAKEOVERS AND MERGERS

11–146   Public companies listed on the Stock Exchange that are involved in takeovers and mergers will be subject to specific regulation as provided for by the City Code. Its provisions apply to all listed and unlisted public companies. Compliance with the Code is enforced by the City Panel on Takeovers and Mergers and the Stock Exchange has the power to remove or suspend a listing due to non-compliance. The Code contains general principles and detailed rules governing the conduct of takeovers. Where a takeover involving a public company is proposed, the holder of 30 per cent of the company's shares must make an offer for the remainder of the shares to all the holders of all the shares which carry voting rights. The price offered must be the highest price which has been paid by the offeror for the target company's shares in the previous 12 months. Rules 2 and 4 of the Code seek to ensure that that any bid and the terms of the bid are kept secret before public announcements are made in order to avoid insider dealing.

LIQUIDATION

11–147   A company may be dissolved and its name removed from the Register of Companies if the procedure contained in the Act is followed. This procedure, referred to as liquidation or winding up, is carried out by a liquidator. The liquidator's functions are to realise the company's assets, use them for payment of its debts and distribute any surplus among its members. There are two main methods by which a company may be wound up: compulsory liquidation and voluntary liquidation which may be initiated by the members or creditors of the company.

THE GROUNDS FOR COMPULSORY LIQUIDATION

11–148   In certain circumstances, the court may order the compulsory winding up of a company. The grounds are provided by section 122(1) of the Insolvency Act 1986 and are as follows:

(a) The company has resolved, by special resolution, that the company be wound up.

(b) The company is a public company which has not been issued with a section 117 certificate and more than a year has passed since it was registered.

(c) The company is an old public company within the meaning of the Companies Consolidation (Consequential Provisions) Act 1985.

(d) The company has not commenced business within a year of incorporation.

(e) The number of members of the company has fallen below two, unless it is a single-member private company.[224]

---

[224] See para 11–12.

(f) The company is unable to pay its debts.

(g) The court is of the opinion that it is just and equitable that the company be wound up.[225]

A company's inability to pay its debts is defined by section 123 of the IA 1986. Under the Act, a company will be deemed to be unable to pay its debts if: a creditor is owed a debt exceeding £750 for three weeks after making a written request for payment of the debt; execution or process on a judgment is returned unsatisfied in whole or in part; the court is of the opinion that the company is unable to pay its debts as they fall due; the company's assets are worth less than its liabilities; a charge for payment on an extract decree or registered bond or protest have expired without payment.

PROCEDURE FOR COMPULSORY LIQUIDATION

The petition for a compulsory winding up may be presented by the company itself, a creditor, a contributory, the Secretary of State, an administrator or supervisor of a voluntary arrangement. If the court grants an order for winding up, an interim liquidator[226] is appointed.[227] The interim liquidator remains in office until a liquidator is appointed by meetings of the creditors and members. On completion of the winding up, the court will make an order dissolving the company. **11–149**

THE COMMENCEMENT OF VOLUNTARY LIQUIDATION

Section 84 of IA 1986 provides that voluntary liquidation may commence in the following ways: **11–150**

(a) If a fixed period has been settled for the duration of the company and the fixed period has now passed or if the company is to come to an end, after a certain event, then the company may be wound up by special resolution.

(b) If the company resolves to be wound up voluntarily by special resolution.

(c) If the company resolves by special resolution to be wound up on the basis that it cannot by reason of its liabilities continue its business.

PROCEDURE FOR VOLUNTARY LIQUIDATION

Once the required resolution is obtained, a notice of resolution must be published within 14 days in the *Edinburgh Gazette*.[228] The winding up commences on the day the resolution is passed.[229] Under the Insolvency Act, there are two procedures available in voluntary liquidation, the use of which will depend on whether the winding up is initiated by the members or the creditors of the company. **11–151**

---

[225] *Re German Date Coffee Co* (1882) 20 ChD 169; *Re Yenidje Tobacco Company* [1916] 2 Ch 426 (CA); *Ebrahimi v Westbourne Galleries* [1973] AC 360 (HL).
[226] See para 11–154.
[227] IA 1986, s 135. It should be noted that the Official Receiver, who acts in this capacity in England, has no powers in Scotland.
[228] IA 1986, s 85(1).
[229] *ibid* s 86.

Members' voluntary winding up

11–152   A statutory declaration of solvency[230] is passed by a majority of the directors and delivered to the Registrar. The winding up proceeds as a members' voluntary winding up. A general meeting of the members must then be held to appoint a liquidator and fix his remuneration.[231]

Creditors' voluntary winding up

11–153   If the directors are unable to make a declaration, the winding up proceeds as a creditors' voluntary winding up.[232] The company must summon a meeting of its creditors within 14 days of the meeting at which the resolution for voluntary winding up is to be proposed.[233] The directors must lay before the meeting a full statement of the company's affairs together with a full list of creditors and of the amounts owing. The creditors may appoint a liquidation committee with a maximum of five persons.[234] The creditors may apppoint a liquidator subject to the right of any director member or creditor to apply to the court for an order that a liquidator nominated by the company should be appointed.

In a voluntary winding up, the role and functions of the liquidator and the order of priority of creditors are generally the same as for compulsory winding up.

THE LIQUIDATOR

11–154   The appointment of the liquidator will depend on the nature of the winding up. Under a compulsory winding up by the court, an interim liquidator will be appointed until the creditors and members of the company meet to make such an appointment. Often the interim liquidator will be retained by the members and creditors. If the liquidation is voluntary, the appointment of the liquidator will depend on how the winding up was initiated.[235] In any event, a liquidator must be a qualified insolvency practitioner.

The powers and duties of a liquidator

11–155   The actions of a liquidator are subject to the control of the court and the extent of such supervision will vary depending on the nature of the winding up. In a compulsory winding up, approximately half of the liquidator's powers will be subject to the approval of the court.[236] In a creditors' voluntary winding up, the liquidator can exercise his powers without the sanction of the court, except for the payment of creditors and the making of compromise agreements for which he will also need the approval of the creditors.[237] The liquidator may act in a similar capacity as an agent or an officer of the company and will generally owe the corresponding duties pertaining

---

[230] IA 1986, s 89.
[231] *ibid* s 91.
[232] *ibid* s 90.
[233] *ibid* s 98.
[234] *ibid* s 101.
[235] See paras 11–152 and 11–153.
[236] IA 1986, s 167.
[237] *ibid* s 165.

to each of these roles. In the execution of his tasks, he takes over the powers of directors and so owes a fiduciary duty to the company and must act in the best interests of the company as a whole.

In disposing of the company's assets prior to distribution, there are certain provisions of the Insolvency Act that will be relevant to the conduct of the liquidation. These are commonly referred to as the "fair dealing" provisions.

Fair dealing provisions

Section 242 provides for an application to be made to the court by an administrator or **11–156** liquidator for the purpose of acquiring an order of reduction or restoration of property to the company's assets. Application for such an order may be made with respect to a transaction between the company and a connected person if the transaction was made within five years of the company becoming insolvent or, if the transaction was between the company and an unconnected person, within two years of the company becoming insolvent. A third party may challenge such an order if it can be shown that the company was solvent at the time of the transaction or the company received adequate consideration or that the transaction was reasonable in the circumstances.[238] The Insolvency Act also provides for the setting aside of extortionate credit transactions entered into by the company in the three years leading up to the commencement of the liquidation.[239]

DISTRIBUTION AND THE ORDER OF PRIORITY

11–157

When the liquidator has realised the company's assets, he must pay off the company's debts. The relevant order of priority is as follows:

(1) The liquidator's remuneration and costs of the liquidation.

(2) Debts owing to preferential creditors.[240] These rank equally and are as follows:
   - PAYE contributions due in the 12 months prior to the commencement of liquidation;
   - VAT due for the 6-month period prior to the commencement of liquidation;
   - motor vehicle tax due in the 12 months prior to the commencement of liquidation;
   - general betting duty, bingo duty and pool betting duty payable in the 12-month period prior to the commencement of liquidation;
   - NIC contributions which are due for the 12-month period prior to the commencement of liquidation;
   - any sums owing to occupational and state pension schemes;
   - wages owed to employees for the 4-month period prior to the commencement of liquidation, subject to a maximum of £800 per employee;
   - any accrued holiday pay owed to employees.

(3) Charges secured by way of a floating charge.

---

[238] *McLuckie Bros Ltd* v *Newhouse Contracts Ltd* 1993 SLT 641 (OH).
[239] IA 1986, s 244.
[240] *ibid* Sched 6.

(4) Unsecured trade creditors.

(5) Deferred debts such as dividends which have been declared but not paid.

Any surplus assets will be distributed to the company's members according to their class rights. Any unclaimed assets will vest in the Crown.

DISSOLUTION

11–158 Once distribution is complete, the liquidator must call a meeting of the relevant parties in order to present the accounts of the winding up: in a compulsory winding up the creditors are entitled to attend[241]; in a members' voluntary winding up the members are entitled to attend[242]; in a creditors' voluntary winding up the members and creditors are entitled to attend.[243]

The liquidator will be released at the meeting and his final accounts will be filed with the Registrar, along with a return of the meeting. On receipt, the Registrar lodges the accounts and, within three months of receipt, the company will be dissolved.[244]

---

[241] IA 1986, s 146.
[242] *ibid* s 94.
[243] *ibid* s 106.
[244] *ibid* s 201.

SUMMARY

GENERAL PRINCIPLES

- The legal regulation of registered companies in the UK is mainly administered through compliance with the provisions of the Companies Act 1985.
- The Companies Act 1985 provides for three types of registered company: companies limited by shares, companies limited by guarantee and unlimited companies.
- Registered companies may be either public or private and both are subject to some different statutory provisions with regard to certain registration and capital issues.
- Once registered, the company has its own legal personality and the veil of incorporation is drawn between the company and its members, subject to certain statutory exceptions.
- Courts will, on occasion, lift or pierce the veil of incorporation in order to investigate allegations of unlawful or rogue practice.
- Promoters act on behalf of the company prior to registration and the fiduciary nature of the relationship means that they owe specific duties to the company.
- The company will not be bound by a pre-incorporation contract.
- Company registration in Scotland is achieved by filing certain documents with the Registrar of Companies in Edinburgh.

THE COMPANY'S CONSTITUTION

- The constitutional documents are comprised of the articles of association and the memorandum of association and the provisions of the latter will prevail in any conflict between the two.
- The memorandum of the association sets out information relevant to the external relations of the company. The most important clause is the objects clause which provides for the areas of business in which the company will operate.
- The articles of association set out information relevant to the internal relations of the company. A company retains the right to alter its articles of association, which is usually accomplished by special resolution.

THE CAPITAL OF A COMPANY

- A public company can raise finance from public investors but a private company cannot.
- The allotment of shares in a company is subject to a number of statutory provisions and public companies are subject to a higher degree of regulation in this respect than private companies.
- Different types of shares will carry different rights, the terms of which will generally be contained in the articles of association.

THE MAINTENANCE OF CAPITAL

- The limitation of members' liability for the debts of registered companies means that members cannot be required to contribute further to the capital structure once shares are paid in full. Certain statutory provisions relating to capital maintenance exist in order to provide protection to creditors dealing with the company.

THE DIRECTORS OF A COMPANY

- Company directors have specific powers which are provided for by the articles but the acts of the directors will generally be binding on the company.
- Directors owe certain duties in respect of their fiduciary relationship with the company and their powers must be exercised in the best interests of the company as a whole.

MEMBERSHIP OF A COMPANY

- The relationship between a company and its members is essentially one of contract.
- Members are entitled to certain rights in respect of their membership which are generally dependent on the type of shares held.
- The decisions of the majority will be binding on minority shareholders so long as the correct procedure as provided for by the articles and subject to the provisions of company legislation has been followed.
- There are exceptions to the principle of majority rule, which are only applicable in specified circumstances and are subject to the sanction of the court.

MEETINGS AND RESOLUTIONS

- In order to obtain the consent of the majority of members for decision-making purposes, members are required to attend or be represented at company meetings.
- The nature of proceedings and the types of business dealt with at such meetings will be subject to the relevant statutory requirements and the provisions of the articles.
- Company business is done at meetings by the passing of resolutions. There are different types of resolution requiring varying majorities and the type of resolution used will depend on the nature of the business being transacted and the corresponding provisions of the articles.

RECEIVERSHIP

- Where a company defaults in satisfying the terms of a debenture, which is secured by a floating charge, the holder of the charge will have the right to appoint a receiver for the purposes of recovering the debt.
- The appointment of the receiver and the duties and functions of receivers are regulated by the provisions of the Insolvency Act 1986.

ADMINISTRATION AND VOLUNTARY ARRANGEMENTS

- Administration and voluntary arrangements provide different means by which a company experiencing financial difficulties may seek to reorganise its affairs.
- The process of administration is a distinct arrangement which is provided for by sections 8–27 of the Insolvency Act 1986, whereas voluntary arrangements consist of a range of different options all regulated by a simple procedure set out in sections 1–7 of the Insolvency Act 1986.

RECONSTRUCTIONS: TAKEOVERS AND MERGERS

- In the modern commercial environment, companies or groups of companies may be subject to changes in corporate structure. Such changes may occur as the result of a takeover by one company of another or a merger between two or more companies into a new company. Collectively, such reorganisations may be termed "reconstructions". Regulation in these areas is provided for by the Companies Act 1985 as modified by the Financial Services Act 1986.

LIQUIDATION

- A company may be dissolved and its name removed from the Register of Companies if the procedure contained in the Act is followed. A liquidator carries out this procedure, referred to as liquidation or winding up.
- The liquidator's functions are to realise the company's assets, use them for payment of its debts and distribute any surplus among its members.
- There are two main methods by which a company may be wound up: compulsory liquidation and voluntary liquidation which may be initiated by the members or creditors of the company.

CASE DIGEST

The registered company as a "persona at law" [see para 11–24]
  Salomon v *Salomon* [1897] AC 22 (HL)
The veil of incorporation is drawn between the company and its members subject to certain statutory and judicial exceptions.

Judicial lifting of the veil of incorporation [see para 11–29]
  Gilford Motor Company v *Horne* [1933] Ch 935 (CA)
The formation of a company for a fraudulent purpose has commonly served as justification for judicial lifting of the veil.

  Ebrahimi v *Westbourne Galleries* [1973] AC 360 (HL)
Where a private company is formed on the basis of a personal relationship between two or more parties and the relationship has soured, the court may lift the veil in order to investigate the relationship for the purposes of determining whether to grant a winding up order on just and equitable grounds.

Duties of promoters—remedies for breach of duty [see para 11–32]
  Erlanger v *New Sombrero Phosphate Co* (1878) 3 App Cas 1218 (HL)
Breach of a duty owed by a promoter may result in rescission of the contract if the parties can be restored to their former position.

Pre-incorporation contracts [see para 11–34]
  Re English and Colonial Produce Co Ltd [1906] 2 Ch 435
The company will not be bound by a pre-incorporation contract. This will apply in respect of remuneration claimed by those who carry out promotional activities on behalf of the company prior to incorporation.

The company's constitution [see para 11–41]
  Scottish National Trust Co Ltd 1928 SC 499
The provisions of the memorandum of association will prevail in the context of any conflict between the provisions of the memorandum and those of the articles.

Drafting of the objects clause [see para 11–50]
  Re German Date Coffee Co (1882) 20 ChD 169
The objects set out in sub-clauses of the memorandum cannot be pursued unless the main object (substratum) is being carried on. This is despite the statutory restrictions on the operation of the *ultra vires* doctrine which were introduced into the Companies Act 1985, s 35 by the Companies Act 1989, s 108(1).

Alteration of the articles of association [see para 11–58]
  Sidebottom v *Kershaw, Leese & Co* [1920] 1 Ch 154
Alterations to the articles of association must be bona fide for the benefit of the company as a whole.

The legal effect of the memorandum and articles [see para 11–62]

Hickman v *Kent or Romney Marshes Sheepbreeders' Association* [1915] 1 Ch 881

The memorandum and articles, once registered, constitute a legally binding contract between the company and each member.

Rayfield v *Hands* [1958] 2 All ER 194

The memorandum and articles, once registered, constitute a legally binding contract between the members themselves.

Variation of class rights [see para 11–73]

Greenhalgh v *Arderne Cinemas* [1951] Ch 286 (CA)

In order for a variation of class rights to have been effected, the rights of the class of shareholders must be substantially different from those in existence before the particular act affecting the rights took place.

The ability of directors to bind the company [see para 11–91]

Royal British Bank v *Turquand* (1856) 6 E&B 327

The "indoor management" rule means that the company retains the right to manage its own affairs. The fact that such management will be exercised by the directors of the company means that acts of the directors will be binding on the company.

Duties of directors [see para 11–92]

Bamford v *Bamford* [1970] Ch 212

Directors must exercise their duties for the "proper purpose". This means they must act bona fide in the best interests of the company as a whole and not to further their own interests.

The principle of majority rule [see para 10–107]

Foss v *Harbottle* (1843) 2 Hare 461

The minority members of a company will generally be bound by the decisions of the majority. The company, as a legal person, is the proper plaintiff in proceedings where an alleged wrong has been done to a company. Where the alleged wrong is a transaction which might be made binding on the company by a simple majority, no individual member is allowed to maintain an action in respect of that matter.

FURTHER READING

Farrar and Hannigan, *Farrar's Company Law* (4th edn, Butterworths, 1998)

Goldenberg, *Guide to Company Law* (4th edn, CCH Publications, 1997)

Keenan and Bisacre, *Company Law for Students with Scottish Supplement* (11th edn, Pitman Publishing, 1999)

Mayson, French and Ryan, *Company Law* (14th edn, Blackstone Press Ltd, 1998)

Pillans and Bourne, *Scottish Company Law* (2nd edn, Cavendish Publishing Ltd, 1999)

12 EMPLOYMENT LAW

OVERVIEW

Anyone who agrees to provide labour in return for payment enters into a contractual **12–01** relationship with the party providing the payment. Both parties will be subject to the imposition of general rights and obligations. Thus, all working relationships are governed by the law of contract. Where the contract is based on the premise of employment, however, there are certain other applicable statutory and common law provisions. The existence of a contract of employment is not always immediately apparent and issues of identification may arise. Where such a contract does exist, however, it will be made between an employer and an employee and will be regulated by specific legislation and, at common law, by certain express and implied terms. Together these provisions constitute a system of employment law.

HISTORICAL DEVELOPMENT

The employment relationship has long been the subject of legal intervention. As the **12–02** socio-political and economic environment relevant to the relationship has changed, so too has the nature and extent of such intervention. Traditionally, the State's approach to industrial relations in the UK has been one of legal abstentionism based on the notion of voluntary arrangement between the parties, with claims of breach of contract pursued by virtue of the common law provisions through the civil courts. In the contemporary context, the relationship between employer and employee is characterised by considerable statutory regulation which attempts to achieve a balance between the interests of the two parties. The programme of legislation pursued by the Labour Government of the 1970s heralded a move towards a system of employment protection[1] aimed at redressing the imbalance of bargaining power between the

---

[1] *eg* the rights brought together and strengthened by the Employment Protection (Consolidation) Act 1978 (now contained in the Employment Rights Act 1996); the Sex Discrimination Act 1975; the Race Relations Act 1976; the Equal Pay Act 1970; and the Health and Safety at Work etc Act 1974.

individual and the employing organisation. In recent years, this approach has been further strengthened by implementation of the social provisions of European Community law. However, the operation of such regulation depends to a great extent on the existence of a contract of employment and, thus, the relationship is still primarily one of contract.

In contrast to the increased regulation of individual employment rights, legislative intervention in the area of collective rights has been aimed at deregulation in recent years. The legislation introduced by the Conservative Governments during the 1980s and 1990s attempted to reduce the role of the law in the context of collective bargaining while imposing legal restrictions on the operations of trade unions. The pursuance of free market principles lead to the imposition of strict legal requirements on trade unions contemplating industrial action and a reduction in legal protection for those involved in such action.[2] These developments have lead to a greater emphasis on the rights of the individual and it is with this aspect of employment law that this chapter is primarily concerned. Legislation is be introduced later this year which is aimed at providing statutory recognition of trade unions for collective bargaining purposes in certain specified circumstances.[3] It may well be that this development signals a change of direction for industrial relations in the UK. Collective rights and those pertaining to individuals with regard to trade union membership will be dealt with in the context of employment protection.

One further caveat relates to the treatment given to the legal regulation of occupational health and safety. Although an important and dynamic aspect of the employment relationship which undoubtedly influences and shapes the environment in which the contract of employment operates, it is outside the scope of this chapter to provide a comprehensive guide to this aspect of the law. Reference will be made to health and safety requirements which are supported by the application of employment protection measures, but students wishing to develop a more detailed understanding of such issues are directed to the specialist texts available.[4]

EMPLOYMENT LAW IN THE TWENTY-FIRST CENTURY

12–03 Employment law has been the subject of considerable legislative action in recent years. Since 1995, the area has been the subject of several Acts of Parliament and countless sets of regulations. Some of this new law has been concerned with the consolidation of existing provisions,[5] some with amendments to legislation relating to substantive law[6] and procedural aspects[7] and some with the introduction of legislation in previously

---

[2] See the Employment Acts 1980–1990; the Trade Union Act 1984; the Wages Act 1986; the Trade Union Reform and Employment Rights Act 1993 (repealed by the Employment Rights Act 1996).
[3] Under the provisions of the Employment Relations Act 1999.
[4] *eg* Craig and Miller, *The Law of Health and Safety at Work in Scotland* (2000).
[5] Employment Rights Act 1996.
[6] *eg* the provisions relating to maternity rights contained in the Employment Relations Act 1999.
[7] Employment Rights (Dispute Resolution) Act 1998 which, *inter alia*, changed the name of Industrial Tribunals to Employment Tribunals and laid down the necessary statutory provisions for the ACAS arbitration scheme.

unregulated areas.[8] As always, the tribunal system and civil courts have continued to interpret existing provisions as well as adding clarification to certain aspects of the new legislation. Some, although not all, of this new law has arisen due to the UK's obligation to implement European Community law. The impact of the UK's membership of the European Economic Community (EEC, now the European Union) on its national system of employment law cannot be overestimated. EC law is part of our domestic law and, accordingly, European legislation and case law emanating from the European Court of Justice (ECJ) are incorporated into the relevant passages of this chapter rather than being given separate consideration.

The introduction of so much new law arises in part from the current Labour Government's electoral victory in May 1997 which brought with it certain manifesto pledges, including the introduction of a national minimum wage. Labour had also promised to reverse the opt-out from the European Community Charter of Fundamental Social Rights for Workers which had been negotiated by the previous Conservative administration and this was duly done, with the effect that certain aspects of European legislation have recently been implemented in the UK.[9]

The result of all this "new law" has been the creation of an increasingly dynamic environment within which the employment contract operates. Given this fact, it may seem timely to undertake an analysis of current employment law provisions. However, legal reform gives rise to certain factors connected with the operation of the law and it is worth considering the following words of caution. At the time of writing, certain areas of employment legislation have been amended so recently that no related case law yet exists—the new maternity and parental leave provisions were introduced in December 1999.[10] Other areas already dealt with extensively by the Tribunal system are likely to be the subjects of appeals, particularly in hitherto unencountered areas of regulation such as the Disability Discrimination Act 1995 and the Working Time Regulations 1998. The overall effect of this is a current climate of legal uncertainty with respect to certain issues.

Some comfort can be offered to students new to the area in that the proposals contained in the Government White Paper *Fairness at Work*,[11] many of which have now come to fruition in the shape of the Employment Relations Act 1999 and associated Regulations, signal the end of the current Government's programme of employment law reform. However, this does not mean that the next administration will not embark on an equally intensive programme or that the European Commission will cease to propose Directives in related areas. Indeed, new initiatives already on the way from Europe include the introduction of specific legislation providing equal treatment for part-time workers[12] and a proposal for a new equality directive which would introduce protection in respect of discrimination on the grounds of, *inter alia*, sexual orientation.[13] For these reasons, the reader is strongly advised to keep an eye on future developments.

---

[8] Disability Discrimination Act 1995; Working Time Regulations 1998 (SI 1998/1833); National Minimum Wage Act 1998; Public Interest Disclosure Act 1998 and the right to parental leave introduced by the Employment Relations Act 1999.

[9] Parental Leave Directive (96/34/EC); European Works Council Directive (94/45/EC).

[10] By the Maternity and Parental Leave, etc. Regulations 1999 (SI 1999/3312).

[11] Cd 3968, May 1998.

[12] 97/81/EC.

[13] Using, as its legal base, the new Art 13.

THE CONTRACT OF EMPLOYMENT

IDENTIFYING THE EXISTENCE OF A CONTRACT

12–04   All working relationships are governed by the general law of contract. For example, a plumber called out to a private household to fix a leaky tap will enter into a contractual relationship with the householder. In such circumstances, the expectations and obligations of both parties are clearly defined at the outset—the plumber will attend to the tap in exchange for payment. Once the work has been carried out satisfactorily and payment has been received, the relationship is at an end and the contract is discharged. There is no ongoing commitment for the householder to continue to provide work for the plumber and the plumber is not obliged to perform further duties for the householder and both would resist any claims to the contrary. However, where a contract of employment has been made, the relationship is subject to certain statutory and common law provisions. These provisions regulate the contract from its commencement and throughout its currency up to, and including, the point of its conclusion. The expectations and obligations of the parties involved will be very different from those of the plumber and householder. For example, the statutory provision of employment protection rights will generally be available only to those who work under contracts of employment. Such contracts are also subject to certain implied terms at common law. Liability for tax and National Insurance contributions will generally fall to the employer and only employees will be entitled to receive certain social security benefits. In determining when employment law provisions will apply, it is necessary to examine the nature of the relationship between the two contracting parties. This is because it is not always clear whether the contract is in fact one of employment or one formed between a self-employed worker and another party.

The main distinction that arises in this context is between those who work under contracts for service (generally self-employed contractors) and those who work under contracts of service (employees). In the UK there is no general definition of an "employee" provided by statute. The statutory provisions pertaining to the employment relationship vary in scope. For example, the protection offered under the Sex Discrimination Act 1975 is available to workers in general, whereas the maternity and unfair dismissal rights provided by the Employment Rights Act 1996 (ERA) (as amended), apply to employees only. The definition contained in the ERA refers to those who work under contracts of employment, which are in turn defined as being contracts of service or apprenticeship. This is not helpful in identifying whether a contract of employment actually exists, so the common law must be considered.

THE COMMON LAW TESTS OF EMPLOYMENT

12–05   In most instances, the existence of a contract of employment is not difficult to determine. This is particularly true where there is a written contract. However, as detailed below[14] it is not necessary for the contract to be in writing and, even where it is, the written contract will not always reveal its true nature. Problems will occur where the parties to the contract have different views regarding its basis, particularly

---

[14] See paras 12–11 *et seq.*

where one party seeks to escape liability relevant to the employment relationship. This may arise out of an intention knowingly to deceive or as a result of a genuine misunderstanding. In either circumstance, it will generally fall to the courts to determine the true nature of the relationship as a matter of fact before any relevant claim can be discharged or further considered. To assist in this task, the courts have developed a series of common law tests which have been applied to varying effect. Although the tests have developed over the last century or so in line with the changing socio-political and economic environment in which the employment relationship operates, certain constituents of all the tests are still applied today in order to determine employment status. The tests will be considered in chronological order and, together, they provide an interesting journey through the historical development of the employment relationship.

The control test

In the nineteenth century the relationship was viewed as existing between the **12–06** "master" (the provider of payment) and the "servant" (the provider of labour). Much of the work provided was unskilled and the relevant test related to the degree of control exerted over the servant in the fulfilment of his duties by the master. The greater the degree of control, the more likely that the relationship was one of employment. The control test was expounded by Bramwell, LJ, in *Yewens v Noakes*[15] thus: "A servant is a person subject to the command of his master as to the manner in which he shall do his work".[16]

This test is useful in that it tells us something about the dependent nature of the employment contract in contrast to the autonomy inherent in the fulfilment of a contract for services. However, as the nature of work has become more sophisticated in terms of the levels of skill and expertise required in order to perform certain tasks, the limits of control as a single-factor test are apparent. Furthermore, as organisations have expanded in terms of size and degrees of diversification, the worker is unlikely to be in regular contact with the employer, the latter often being a company or public authority. Consider the example of a surgeon employed by a hospital trust to carry out operations of a highly specialised nature. The degree of control exerted over the way in which the surgeon actually operates is likely to be non-existent. The individual may be the only person present within the whole of the organisation who possesses the skills and knowledge pertaining to his specialism. There is little or no control, but this does not mean that the surgeon is not operating under a contract of employment. In the contemporary context, it is not necessary to look to examples of such specialisation as that pertaining to a surgeon in order to identify the high degree of separation and corresponding decrease in control between employer and employee. Although the level of control is still a relevant factor in distinguishing between contracts for service and contracts of service, it cannot be used in isolation reliably to determine the status of a worker.[17]

---

[15] (1880) 6 QBD 530, at 532.
[16] See also *Performing Rights Society v Mitchell & Booker (Palais de Danse) Ltd* [1924] 1 KB 762; *Hitchcock v Post Office* [1980] ICR 100.
[17] Note the unsatisfactory decision in *Hillyer v Governors of St Bartholomew's Hospital* [1909] 2 KB 820, in which, due to a strict application of the control test, it was held that nurses who worked in an operating theatre were not employees of the hospital.

The integration test

12–07   In attempting to develop an alternative approach to that of the control test, Lord Denning set down a new test in *Stevenson, Jordon and Harrison Ltd* v *MacDonald and Evans*.[18] In the post-war climate of full employment and "jobs for life", the test of employment status was deemed to be dependent on the worker's integration into the organisation. Under a contract of service, "a man is employed as part of the business and his work is done as an integral part of that business".[19]

This test had certain clear advantages over the test of control—skilled workers who enjoyed high levels of autonomy (such as the surgeon considered above) would be found to be employees using the test of integration. However, the application of a single-factor test has limitations, in particular those arising from the lack of a clear definition of the terms "integration" and "organisation". Furthermore, as the economic climate in which the employment contract operates has changed, so too has the nature of the relationship between employer and employee. For example, the huge increase in the level of part-time employment has created a new and diverse group of workers whose contributions may be central to the operation of the organisation but who may be deemed to be less well "integrated" in certain respects than those who work full time. The move towards new forms of work such as tele-working and homeworking in some employment sectors, which may be difficult to categorise in terms of the worker's degree of "integration", also illustrates the shortcomings in the application of the integration test.

The multiple test

12–08   The problems arising from the application of a single factor in determining employment status are illustrated by the tests outlined above, which relied on the elements of control and integration respectively. However, although such factors are not particularly useful if applied in isolation, when combined with other factors they become good indicators of the real nature of the relationship under scrutiny. This multi-factor approach has become known as the "multiple test" and it has been used extensively by the judiciary since the late 1960s.[20] The range of factors which may be considered is endless but will normally include the degree of control exerted by the employer which may be measured by the levels of supervision and training provided and the provision and maintenance of equipment and materials. The parties' performance of both express and implied contractual terms will also be considered. For example, the arrangements for payment of income tax, National Insurance contributions and corresponding benefits such as Statutory Sick Pay and Statutory Maternity Pay may be particularly indicative of the true nature of the relationship. The extent of the obligations on the parties to provide and perform work can also be very revealing and the courts will question the extent to which the worker has the opportunity to work for other employers and to delegate work to a third party.

This approach is particularly useful when the court is faced with conflicting evidence in that it enables consideration to be given to all relevant factors, some of

---

[18] 1952 1 TLR 101.
[19] See also Denning's judgment in *Bank voor Handel en Scheepvaart NV* v *Slatford* [1953] 1 QB 248 and the later case of *Whittaker* v *Minister of Pensions* [1967] 1 QB 156, [1966] 3 All ER 531.
[20] See *Ready Mixed Concrete (South East) Ltd* v *Minister of Pensions* [1968] 2 QB 497, [1968] 1 All ER 433; *Market Investigations Ltd* v *Minister of Social Security* [1969] 2 QB 173, [1968] 3 All ER 732.

which may, on further examination, prove to be more persuasive than others. In cases involving "mixed evidence" it may be necessary for the court to select a deciding or determining factor from the range of evidence before it. For reasons of consistency and clarity, it is important that this selection is made cautiously. For example, the non-payment of income tax and National Insurance in respect of a worker may, on face value, indicate that the individual concerned is a self-employed contractor operating under a contract for services and, thus, liable for his own tax and insurance contributions. However, if this aspect were always to be treated as the most important factor for determining status, it would be very easy for an employer to escape his liability under employment protection legislation by also avoiding his PAYE obligations. Conversely, a worker who agrees to be engaged as a self-employed contractor and enjoys the associated tax benefits, must be prevented from claiming to be an employee merely for the purposes of gaining protection from unfair dismissal.[21] A balanced approach is therefore needed, in which all relevant factors are considered and, if necessary, a determining factor selected on the basis of the individual circumstances of each individual case.[22]

Economic reality

In recent years the courts have often selected the level of independence enjoyed by the **12–09** worker concerned in fulfilment of his contractual obligations as a particularly persuasive indicator of employment status. This makes good sense in most cases as, if the individual is deemed to be "[i]n business on his own account",[23] he will rightly be held to be an independent contractor and not, therefore, engaged under a contract of employment. In determining whether the individual is indeed genuinely self-employed, courts are likely to consider the level of financial risk and managerial prerogative exercised by the worker as well as the control factor and delegation of duties referred to above. This has become known as the test of economic reality or the "entrepreneurial test", although it is not really a self-standing test, but rather a factor employed in the application of the multiple approach. It is unlikely that this factor will be easy to determine in every case and an over-reliance on any one indicator will surely suffer from the difficulties inherent in the application of the control and integration tests. Furthermore, in the contemporary employment context, where practices such as outsourcing and homeworking are increasingly utilised along with the engagement of external consultants in many sectors, the determination of employment status has become increasingly complex. Recent changes to company formation in the UK[24] have further added to such complexity, in that an individual worker may now form a private limited company for the purposes of carrying out his or her work.

---

[21] *Massey v Crown Life Insurance Co* [1978] IRLR 31.

[22] See the *Ready Mixed Concrete* case (n 20), in which the "determining factor" was held by the Court of Appeal to be the potential for the workers concerned to hire substitute drivers to perform duties on their behalf thus deeming the claimants to be self-employed contractors rather than employees.

[23] From the judgment of Cooke, J in the *Market Investigations* case: n 20.

[24] Regulations permitting the formation of single-member private companies have been in operation in the UK since 1992: see Chapter 11.

THE SCOPE OF THE "NEW LEGISLATION"

12–10   The growing complexity in working arrangements which operate within an increasingly flexible labour market may create conditions in which some workers will be particularly vulnerable to the denial of their employment rights, without adequate enforcement measures. In turn, it is important that employing organisations are fully aware of the extent of their potential obligations towards workers and are able to pay due consideration to such factors during the human resource planning process. In recent years, the UK Government appears to have given recognition to these issues when proposing and drafting associated legislation. The three main additions to UK employment legislation introduced by the current Labour Government[25] have adopted a consistent approach in their scope so that there are now three types of workers recognised for the purposes of regulation, two of which have generally been included within the scope of the new legislation, with the "genuinely self-employed" being excluded. Employees and those engaged on contracts for personal services (except where provided for a customer or client of a profession or business carried on by the individual) will fall within the scope of the new legislation.[26] If this approach continues to be applied, it would appear that this area of difficulty has at last become the subject of some consistency.

THE CONSTRUCTION OF THE CONTRACT

12–11   The standard definition of a contract as an agreement which is legally enforceable has obvious application in the context of the employment contract. However, the constituent features which together comprise a legally enforceable agreement are often of a particular nature when the contract is one of employment. For example, the notion of "exchange" will have a particular meaning in this context as it will generally relate to the provision of labour in return for payment. The element of "promise" which characterises the contractual relationship serves to illustrate the moralistic nature of the relations between the parties which, in turn, give rise to the specific rights and duties endemic in the employment sphere.

In terms of its construction, the employment contract is subject to the same rules which apply generally to the law of contract in that the agreement will arise out of an offer and acceptance between two parties. In order for the contract to be legally enforceable, there must be agreement in material matters (*consensus in idem*), an intention to create legal relations and the contract must be formed for a lawful purpose. As noted above, when considering the concept of employment, performance of the contract may be crucial in the determination of the nature of the relations between the contracting parties. The importance of this element can be clearly seen at the commencement of the contract and throughout its currency and is of particular significance due to the fact that, despite the highly regulated nature of the employment contract, there is no legal requirement for the contract to be in writing.

---

[25] Working Time Regulations 1998 (SI 1998/1833); National Minimum Wage Act 1998; Employment Relations Act 1999.
[26] This is in fact the definition of a "worker" contained in s 230(3) of the Employment Rights Act 1996.

FREEDOM TO CONTRACT?

The contractual nature of the employment relationship implies that the obligations **12–12** and duties arise from it as a matter of agreement between the parties. However, the operation of the employment contract within a specific market order makes it difficult in practice to ascribe the usual rules of contract law to that relationship. The most obvious difference between the employment contract and other types of contract arises out of the respective roles of the parties to it, illustrated by consideration of the negotiation phase. The relationship between employer and prospective employee is not an equal one within which true negotiation can take place—the employer is usually in a stronger bargaining position than the job candidate in that he may have, at his disposal, a ready pool of suitable labour from which to select. The bargaining power of the prospective employee may be seriously impeded due to the economic conditions under which the relationship operates. This is not only true of the recruitment period, but may also affect the day-to-day operation of the contract and the method by which it is terminated. The law recognises this and legal intervention in the context of employment protection is aimed at redressing such inequality by providing a basic floor of rights which serves to support the employee's position in certain respects. From the employer's perspective, the imposition of certain terms of employment by the common law and statute means that the employment contract is not purely the result of negotiation as it brings with it certain obligations. For example, the Equal Pay Act 1970[27] implies an equality clause into every contract of employment—there is no scope for negotiation and the parties cannot contract out of this provision. Before considering the different elements of employment protection and the impact of each on the employment contract, it is important to explore the various ways in which a contract of employment may be formed and the nature of the terms and conditions which constitute it.

FORMATION OF THE EMPLOYMENT CONTRACT

A contract of employment may be entered into formally or informally, orally or in **12–13** writing. It may occur following formal interviews, as a result of negotiations or by written offer and acceptance, but it can also result from a casual conversation. Its terms and conditions may be defined entirely by performance in that the contract may commence by the worker carrying out certain tasks in return for payment with little or no prior discussion having taken place. The existence of a written contract will not always be helpful in settling disputes as the written agreement may not always truly reflect what happens in practice or may have become outdated as the relationship has developed and matured. Furthermore, there are many important terms which regulate the employment contract but which, due to their nature, are implied rather than express and which will not, therefore, appear even in the best-drafted employment contract. However, a written contract will serve as a useful source of certain information and, for this reason, it is recognised as good practice to provide one.

---

[27] s 1(1).

TERMS AND CONDITIONS OF EMPLOYMENT

12–14   The terms and conditions, which together constitute the contract of employment, originate in different ways. Those which are provided for by a written contract, or which have been discussed and agreed, comprise the express terms of the contract. Other terms are "read into" the contract, either because they are provided for by statute and apply to all contracts of employment or because the contract is interpreted as containing such a term under the common law—these are the implied terms of the contract.

Express terms

12–15   The express terms of an employment contract will depend on what has been agreed between the parties, which will in turn be influenced by custom and practice and the prevailing general economic conditions. Express terms will generally cover such basic matters as the hours of work, rate of pay and a general job description. Procedures relating to the specific workplace, such as those relevant to grievance and discipline, may also comprise express terms, as will other general work rules. Even where the employer does not provide a written contract of employment, certain information must be given in written form to employees: this is known as the written statement of terms and conditions.

Written statement of terms and conditions

12–16   The EC Directive on proof of an employment relationship[28] requires that a written statement of the essential aspects of the contract or employment relationship should be given to all employees within two months of the start of the employment. This requirement is now implemented in the UK by the Employment Rights Act 1996 ("ERA" 1996).[29] The statement must contain the following information:

- The names of the employer and employee

- The date on which the employment commenced

- The date on which the employee's period of continuous employment commenced including any previous period of employment which counts for the purposes of continuity

- The scale or rate of remuneration, or the method of calculating remuneration

- The intervals at which remuneration is paid

- The terms and conditions relating to hours of work

- The terms and conditions relating to holiday entitlement and holiday pay; arrangements for sickness absence and sick pay; pensions and pension schemes

- The relevant periods of notice

- The job title

---

[28]   91/533/EEC.
[29]   s 1(1) and (2).

- If the employment is for a fixed term, the date on which the employment is to end

- The place of work or, if the employee is expected to work at various locations, an indication of that

- The address of the employer

- Details of any collective agreement which directly affects the terms and conditions of employment

- Where the employee is required to work outside the UK for more than one month:

  (a) the period of employment outside the UK

  (b) the currency in which remuneration will be paid

  (c) details of additional payments or benefits due by virtue of working abroad

  (d) terms and conditions relating to the employee's return to the UK.

Status of the written statement

The written statement does not, in itself, constitute a written contract of employment, **12–17** although it will provide strong evidence of the existence of a contract if a dispute arises. In *System Floors (UK) Ltd* v *Daniel*,[30] Browne-Wilkinson, J described the significance of the statement in the following terms:

> "[i]t provides very strong prima facie evidence of what were the terms of the contract between the parties, but does not constitute a written contract between the parties. Nor are the statements of the terms finally conclusive: at most they place a heavy burden on the employer to show that the actual terms of contract are different from those which he had set out in the statutory statement."

Failure on the part of the employer to supply the statutory statement within two months, or the issue of a statement which does not comply with the requirements of the Act, may result in an application to an Employment Tribunal. The tribunal will determine the particulars that ought to have been included in the statement,[31] which will apply as if they had been supplied to the employee by the employer.[32]

Restrictive covenants

It is possible, by express agreement, to restrict the present or future freedom of **12–18** employees to form contracts of employment in certain circumstances. This is achieved by the inclusion of a clause in the contract of employment, which must state the terms of the restrictive covenant by specifying aspects such as the nature and duration of the restriction and the geographical area relevant to it. The use of restrictive covenants arises due to the employer's desire to protect himself from future acts of the employee which may prove damaging to the employer's business as a result of either the sharing of confidential information with third parties[33] or the poaching of clients or

---

[30] [1982] ICR 54.
[31] ERA 1996, s 11(1).
[32] *ibid* s 12(1).
[33] *Forster & Sons Ltd* v *Suggett* [1918] TLR 87.

customers.[34] As the basis of the covenant is the need to protect the business from unfair competition, its terms must be restricted to what is reasonable for the protection of the employer's business interests.[35] If the covenant is found to be too restrictive, it will be void.[36] If the covenant is found to be reasonable[37] and in the public interest,[38] and therefore binding, the court may restrain the ex-employee from fulfilling existing obligations under any contracts made which breach the covenant, as well as preventing him from entering into new contracts.[39] Further protection for employers in this respect is offered by way of the implied term of mutual trust and confidence. This term has been the subject of substantial development in recent years and is considered below.

Implied terms

12–19   There are two main methods by which terms may be implied into a contract of employment. The first of these arises by virtue of certain statutory provisions which will have application in the context of all contracts of employment and are, therefore, said to be "implied by statute": for example, the equality clause relating to equal pay which is implied into all contracts by the Equal Pay Act 1970[40] and the right not to be unfairly dismissed which is implied by the Employment Rights Act 1996.[41] Such provisions provide certain fundamental employment rights which cannot generally be excluded by the process of "contracting out".[42] Until recently, those employed under fixed-term contracts could be asked to contract out of the right to claim unfair dismissal at the expiry of the fixed term. However, the Employment Relations Act 1999 has amended this provision,[43] although it is still possible to exclude the employee's right to a redundancy payment by agreement.

The second method by which terms may be implied into employment contracts arises where the existence of the term in order to ensure the effective performance of the contract is so obvious that the common law allows for it to be read into the contract as if it had been discussed and agreed by the parties.[44] Although certain terms will be implied into all contracts of employment, the implication of other terms will depend on the nature of the individual contract. For example, the employer's common law duty[45] to take reasonable care for the health and safety of his employees will be implied into all contracts,[46] whereas the existence and extent of the duty of confidentiality owed by the employee will depend on the nature of the employment and of the information involved.[47] The establishment of

---

[34] *John Michael Designs plc* v *Cooke* ([987] ICR 445 (CA).
[35] *Stenhouse Australia Ltd* v *Phillips* [1974] 1 All ER 117; *Cantor Fitzgerald (UK) Ltd* v *Wallace* [1992] IRLR 215.
[36] *Fellows and Son* v *Fisher* [1976] QB 122.
[37] *Spafax Ltd* v *Harrison* [1980] IRLR 442.
[38] *Nordenfelt* v *Maxim Nordenfelt Guns & Ammunition Co Ltd* [1894] AC 535.
[39] *Littlewoods Organisation* v *Harris* [1976] ICR 516; *Office Angels Ltd* v *Rainer-Thomas and O'Connor* [1991] IRLR 214.
[40] s 1.
[41] s 94.
[42] For the statutory restrictions relevant to contracting out, see ERA 1996, s 203.
[43] Employment Relations Act 1999 (Commencement No 2 and Transitional and Savings Provisions) Order (SI 1999/2830).
[44] *Shirlaw* v *Southern Foundries* [1926] Ltd (1939) 2 KB 206.
[45] As distinct from the statutory duty imposed by s 2(1) of the Health and Safety at Work etc Act 1974.
[46] *British Aircraft Corporation* v *Austin* [1978] IRLR 322, (EAT); *Johnstone* v *Bloomsbury Health Authority* [1991] IRLR 118.
[47] *Faccenda Chicken Ltd* v *Fowler* [1986] IRLR 69.

certain modes of behaviour through custom and practice may also be indicative of the existence of certain terms. Some of the duties arising from implied terms are owed by one party to the other, whereas others impose "two-way" duties on employer and employee concurrently. The most well-developed "two-way" term is the mutual duty placed on both employer and employee to treat the other party with trust and confidence. The case law resulting from breaches of this particular term relates largely to breaches committed by the employer and, accordingly, it has been included as an employer's duty in the following categorisation.

Duties of employers

(a) To pay wages

The rate and regularity of payment will generally be included as express terms of the contract.[48] However, where this is not the case, this duty will apply to work carried out by the employee or to periods when the employee is available for work. Where there is no work available[49] or where the employee is not available for work,[50] the employer will not be expected to pay the employee unless an express provision provides otherwise. The payment of contractual sick pay should not be presumed if custom and practice suggests otherwise.[51]   **12–20**

(b) To provide work

Although there is no general duty to provide work,[52] such a duty will be implied in certain circumstances—for example, where the employment is based on a piecemeal or commission basis and the withdrawal of work would prevent the employee from earning any money. Furthermore, if a failure to provide work would result in a loss of the employee's reputation, the courts may be willing to imply such a duty on the part of the employer. This would appear to have particular application in cases involving those in the public eye, such as actors or performers[53] and the office holders of senior managerial positions.[54]   **12–21**

(c) To treat the employee with mutual trust and confidence

This term was described by Lord Denning as implying that the "employer must be good and considerate to his servants."[55] In recent years it has been applied to a variety of situations and has been shown to imply duties on both employer and employee. The term implies a duty to treat each other with respect,[56] trust and fairness.[57] Notably, it   **12–22**

---

[48] Either in the written contract of employment, if one exists, or in the written statement of terms and conditions which must be provided under s 1 of the ERA 1996.

[49] *Browning* v *Crumlin Valley Collieries* [1926] 1 KB 522.

[50] *Sim* v *Rotherham Metropolitan Borough Council* [1986] IRLR 391; *Miles* v *Wakefield Metropolitan District Council* [1987] AC 539.

[51] *Mears* v *Safecar Security Ltd* [1982] IRLR 183 (CA).

[52] *Collier* v *Sunday Referee Publishing Co* [1940] 2 KB 647.

[53] *Clayton and Waller* v *Oliver* [1930] AC 209.

[54] *Bosworth* v *Angus Jowett & Co Ltd* [1977] IRLR 374.

[55] *Woods* v *WM Car Services (Peterborough) Ltd* [1982] ICR 693.

[56] *Bliss* v *SE Thames Regional Health Authority* [1985] IRLR 308; *Lewis* v *Motorworld Garages Ltd* (1985) IRLR 465.

[57] *Robinson* v *Crompton Parkinson Ltd* [1978] IRLR 61.

has recently been applied to identify an employer's liability for damage caused to an ex-employee's future employment prospects.[58]

Although the duty goes both ways, in practice it is the employer who is more frequently found to be in breach of it. A breach may arise in various ways, such as demoting the employee or through unfounded accusations of theft. Any behaviour by the employer which can be shown to have made the employee's time at work unbearable could result in a finding of breach of this implied term which forms the basis for many claims of constructive dismissal.[59]

(d) To deal properly and promptly with grievances

12–23   The employer's duty to deal effectively with grievances is clearly supported by the statutory provisions which apply to unfair dismissal.[60] However, it is an implied term in a contract of employment that the employer will reasonably and promptly afford an opportunity to employees to obtain redress for any grievance they may have.[61] Details of the organisation's scheme and procedure for dealing with grievances must be included in the statement of terms and conditions which all employees are entitled to receive under statute.[62]

(e) To exercise care in writing references

12–24   This is a specific duty to exercise care and skill in the writing of references for existing or ex-employees.[63] Failure to comply by the giving of false or misleading information may result in liability for any losses sustained by the employee as a result of the reference.[64]

Duties of Employees

(a) To provide labour

12–25   The employee is expected to be ready and willing to provide labour by performing work duties in return for remuneration. Industrial action in the form of a strike will result in breach of contract through non-compliance with this implied term.[65]

(b) To obey reasonable and lawful orders

12–26   Refusal to obey a reasonable order may result in dismissal without notice.[66] The central issue in cases arising from alleged breaches of this term has generally been the

---

[58] *Malik v Bank of Credit and Commerce International SA* [1997] IRLR 462 (HL). See Brodie, "Beyond Exchange: The New Contract of Employment" (1998) 27 *Industrial Law Journal* 79.

[59] See para 12–107. See *Isle of Wight Tourist Board v Coombes* [1976] IRLR 413; *Bracebridge Engineering Ltd v Darby* [1990] IRLR 3; *White v Reflecting Roadstuds Ltd* [1991] IRLR 331.

[60] See paras 12–105 *et seq.*

[61] *WA Goold (Pearmak) Ltd v McConnell* [1995] IRLR 516.

[62] Employment Rights Act 1996, s 1.

[63] *Spring v Guardian Assurance plc and Others* [1994] IRLR 460.

[64] See *Coote v Granada Hospitality Ltd (No 2)* [1999] ICR 942 where failure to supply a reference was found to amount to victimisation.

[65] *Simmons v Hoover Ltd* [1977] QB 284 (EAT).

[66] *Laws v London Chronicle* [1959] 1 WLR 698; *Pepper v Webb* [1969] 1 WLR 514.

definition of "reasonable" in this context. It is clear from the case law that refusal on the part of the employee to honour an express term of the contract of employment will result in a breach,[67] although the court will examine the term to ensure that it complies with the requirement of "reasonableness" as interpreted in light of the relevant circumstances of the case.[68]

(c) To adapt to new working methods

The duty to adapt in line with the introduction of new technology or new working **12–27** procedures can be viewed as subsidiary to the duty to obey reasonable and lawful orders. However, in the fast-changing world of employment, it is worth bearing in mind that the employee will be expected to adapt to new working methods, as long as the necessary training or retraining has been provided by the employer.[69]

(d) To use reasonable care and skill

The employee is under a duty to exercise reasonable care and skill in the performance **12–28** of his duties.[70] If the employee is found to be negligent or incompetent, he may be in breach of contract and liable for damages.[71]

(e) To exercise good faith and fidelity

This duty has been interpreted widely and is similar in practice to the duty of **12–29** mutual trust and confidence.[72] Compliance with the duty requires loyalty from the employee who should not do anything to harm the employer's business. This would include disrupting the employer's business interests,[73] dishonesty,[74] working for a competitor[75] or disclosing confidential information.[76] It should be noted that the courts do recognise a distinction between confidential information and employee know-how, with only disclosure of the first amounting to breach of contract.[77]

VARIATION OF CONTRACTUAL TERMS

As with all other types of contracts, changes to the terms and conditions of the **12–30** employment contract must be agreed between the parties. Attempts by the employer to unilaterally vary a main term of the contract may result in a successful breach of contract claim by the employee or a finding of constructive dismissal.[78] Failure to

---

[67] *F G Walmsley v UDEC Refrigeration Ltd* [1972] IRLR 80; *United Kingdom Atomic Energy Authority v Claydon* [1974] ICR 128.
[68] *Ottoman Bank v Chakairan* [1930] AC 277.
[69] *Cresswell and Others v Board of Inland Revenue* [1984] IRLR 190.
[70] *Lister v Romford Ice & Cold Storage Co Ltd* [1957] 1 All ER 125.
[71] *Janata Bank v Ahmed* [1981] ICR 791.
[72] See para 12–22.
[73] *Secretary of State for Employment v ASLEF* [1972] ICR 19.
[74] *Sinclair v Neighbour* (1967) 2 QB 279; *Denco v Joinson* [1991] IRLR 63.
[75] *Hivac v Park Royal Scientific Instruments Ltd* [1946] Ch 169.
[76] *Bent's Brewery v Hogan* [1945] 2 All ER 570.
[77] *Faccenda Chicken Ltd v Fowler* [1986] IRLR 69.
[78] *Marriott v Oxford and District Co-operative Society (No 2)* [1970] 1 QB 186.

lodge a complaint about the alleged variation through the employer's grievance procedure may result in a claim by the employer that the employee has impliedly accepted the change by his behaviour.

Despite the general rule prohibiting the employer from unilaterally varying the terms of the contract, the law does recognise the need for change in certain circumstances. Therefore, although variations should be by mutual agreement, refusal by the employee to accept a proposed alteration may result in lawful termination by the employer in certain circumstances.[79] The relevant circumstances would include the requirement that full consultation had been carried out with the employee which had proved to be fruitless and that the employer was able to show that the reason for the dismissal amounted to "some other substantial reason" in that it constituted a "fair" reason for dismissal.[80]

CLAIMS FOR BREACH OF CONTRACT

12–31   The jurisdiction of Employment Tribunals has only recently been extended to allow breach of contract claims to be heard by them,[81] subject to a maximum award of £25,000 in damages. Prior to this, all claims were dealt with through the civil court structure, which resulted in a somewhat uneven application of the law due to the nature of such cases. For example, breach of contract claims are usually concerned with the termination of employment (particularly the area of constructive dismissal)[82] which, where it was linked to other areas, such as discrimination, fell within the jurisdiction of the tribunals.

THE REGULATION OF WAGES

12–32   The rate of pay and method of payment constitute terms of the contract and will generally be agreed between the employer and employee with arrangements dependent on, *inter alia*, the levels of skill and experience necessary to do the job and the general market conditions in operation. In some sectors of employment, collective agreements will determine the terms and conditions of employment relevant to remuneration. However, all contracts of employment are subject to certain statutory controls in the context of the payment of wages. Until recently, such controls were restricted to protective measures aimed at ensuring that employees were paid the correct amount in respect of work carried out without unlawful deductions being made by or on behalf of employers.

The actual rate of pay has not, traditionally, been an area of statutory intervention, subject to the right to equal pay as provided by the Equal Pay Act 1970.[83] However, in 1998 the National Minimum Wage Act came into force. This Act

---

[79] *Grix* v *Munford* [1997] IRLR.
[80] *Wilson* v *Underhill House School Ltd* [1977] IRLR 475. See para 12–121.
[81] Industrial Tribunals Extension of Jurisdiction (Scotland) Order 1994 (SI 1994/1624).
[82] See para 12–107.
[83] See paras 12–07 *et seq.*

introduced a right to be paid at or above a certain rate and has application across all sectors of employment, subject to some exceptions. The main provisions of the Act will be explored below, but first the regulation of the protection of wages will be considered.

UNAUTHORISED DEDUCTIONS

Section 13 of the Employment Rights Act 1996 ("ERA 1996") provides that an **12-33** employer shall not make any deductions from a worker's wages unless the deduction is authorised by a relevant statutory[84] or contractual provision or the worker has previously given written consen[85] to such a deduction being made. In the case of a relevant contractual provision, the employer must have given the worker written notification of the existence of the term and his intention to make a deduction under it prior to the deduction being made.[86]

A worker can bring a complaint about an alleged unauthorised deduction to an employment tribunal within three months of the deduction being made.[87] Section 14 of the ERA 1996 provides for certain exceptions to section 13 and complaints arising from deductions made in respect of the following will be dealt with by the civil courts as breach of contract claims: an overpayment of wages or in respect of expenses incurred[88] in the course of employment[89]; a deduction made in consequence of any disciplinary proceedings by virtue of a statutory provision[90]; a deduction made in respect of the worker's participation in a strike or other industrial action.[91]

THE NATIONAL MINIMUM WAGE ACT 1998

The National Minimum Wage Act 1998 came into effect in April 1999. Under the **12-34** Act, workers are entitled to be paid at or above a national minimum wage ("NMW").[92] The scope of the Act is wide and covers those who work under a contract of employment and those who undertake to do or perform a personal service except in a professional capacity or if in business on their own account. The genuinely self-employed are excluded from its scope, as are workers under 18 years of age, workers aged 18 who are employed as apprentices, workers aged between 19 and 26 employed as apprentices who have not yet completed one year of service, students employed on placements and workers employed in family households who "live in".[93]

---

[84] For example, under a PAYE scheme for income tax and National Insurance purposes.
[85] *Pename Ltd* v *Paterson* [1989] IRLR 195 (EAT).
[86] *Kerr* v *Sweater Shop (Scotland) Ltd* [1996] IRLR 424 (EAT).
[87] ERA 1996, s 23.
[88] *SIP Industrial Products Ltd* v *Swinn* [1994] IRLR 323 (EAT).
[89] ERA 1996, s 14(1).
[90] *ibid* s 14(2).
[91] *ibid* s 14(5).
[92] National Minimum Wage Act 1998 ("NMWA 1998"), s 1.
[93] *ibid* s 1.

NMW rates[94]

12–35 The NMW rate was introduced at £3.60 per hour for all adult workers (over the age of 21)[95] and, for those aged between 18 and 20, at £3.00 per hour. There is a third rate of £3.20 per hour which is applicable for workers aged 22 and over who are receiving accredited training for six months.

In order to calculate a worker's hourly rate of pay, it is necessary to establish the total pay received in the "pay reference period" (which generally depends on the applicable "wage period") and the total number of hours worked during that period. When calculating "total pay" it is the gross pay which is relevant. The following must be included: incentive payments[96]; any bonuses received; any tips and/or gratuities which are paid through the pay-roll. Payments in respect of the following should not be included: advances of wages or loans; pension contributions; redundancy payments; any benefits in kind.[97]

Accommodation provided by the employer should be included in calculations of the hourly rate of pay subject to a special calculation and a maximum amount of £19.95 per week. Any sums in excess of the lowest rate payable to employees—for example, overtime and shift premium payments—do not count towards the NMW.

The method for calculating the total number of hours worked will depend on the type of work undertaken. For example, if the worker is engaged on "time" work, the hours worked and the hours available for work should be included unless the waiting time is spent at home. For "salaried hours" work, the number of hours should be calculated by dividing the basic hours contracted for over the year by the relevant number of pay periods (usually 12). For "output" work, the employer is required to reach a "fair estimate" agreement or to pay the NMW for every hour worked.

Record keeping and enforcement

12–36 Employers are obliged to keep for a minimum of three years records which are sufficient to establish that each worker is being paid at a rate at least equivalent to the NMW.[98] An employee has the right to inspect those records if he or she suspects that the employer is committing a breach of the Act by paying less than the appropriate rate. Failure to produce the records or to allow the employee to inspect them may result in the worker making a complaint to an Employment Tribunal, which has the power to make a declaration or to award the worker a sum equal to 80 times the hourly amount of the NMW.[99]

Enforcement of the Act is carried out in two ways: by complaints to Employment Tribunals and by inspectors appointed on behalf of the State to carry out inspections of wage records. A complaint to an employment tribunal may be made on the basis of an unlawful deduction from wages under the Employment Rights Act 1996 or as a breach of contract claim. Inspectors have the power to serve enforcement notices on an

---

[94] Under NMWA 1998, s 2 the rate is set by the Secretary of State following a recommendation made by the Low Pay Commission.

[95] In May 2000, the Government announced that, on 1st June 2000, the NMW rate for those aged 18–21 would be increased to £3.20 per hour and, on 1st October 2000, the standard NMW rate would rise to £3.70 per hour.

[96] *eg* for piecework and commission.

[97] *eg* company car.

[98] NMWA 1998, s 9.

[99] *ibid* s 11.

employer requiring him to make payment at a rate at least equivalent to the NMW. Employers who wilfully neglect or refuse to remunerate a worker at the correct rate or who fail to keep or who falsify records may be guilty of an offence under the Act and may be liable to a fine.[100]

The regulation of working time

The Working Time Regulations 1998[101] came into force in October 1998 to implement the European Working Time Directive,[102] which was introduced as a health and safety measure. The Regulations apply to those employed under contracts of employment and those working under a contract to do or perform services, but exclude those working for or on behalf of clients or customers in a professional capacity or in a business undertaking (that is, the genuinely self-employed).[103] **12–37**

There are a number of excluded sectors of employment and activities to which specific regulations do not apply. The latter list of activities arises from the scope given by the Directive to depart from its provisions by way of "derogations" in certain circumstances.

Complete exclusions

The employment sectors which are completely excluded[104] from the Regulations are: air, rail, road, sea; inland waterway and lake transport; sea fishing; other work at sea and the activities of doctors in training, the armed forces, the police and the civil protection services.[105] According to recent case law on the extent of this exclusion, those employed in non-mobile activities within these sectors are also excluded, as it is the nature of the business, not the work performed, that is relevant to the transport exclusion provided by the Regulations.[106] **12–38**

Permitted derogations[107]

Although all employees are subject to some of the requirements concerning annual leave,[108] protection for night and shift work[109] and the provisions concerning patterns of work,[110] the list of derogations in the Regulations severely weakens their impact in certain respects. Specific groups of workers can be excluded from the provisions relating to: daily rest periods; weekly rest periods; the provision of breaks; and the protection for night workers. Such groups may work in: activities where the worker's place of work and his place of residence are distant from one another; security and surveillance activities requiring a permanent presence; activities involving the need **12–39**

---

[100] *ibid* ss 31–33.
[101] SI 1998/1833. (The following references are to these Regulations unless stated otherwise.)
[102] Directive 93/104/EC.
[103] reg 2.
[104] reg 18.
[105] The European Commission have put forward a proposal for a Directive amending Directive 93/104/EC for the purposes of protecting workers not covered by the provisions on working time: see COM (1999) 699 Final.
[106] *Bowden* v *Tuffnells Parcel Express Ltd* Ashford Employment Tribunal 21st January 1999, Case No 1102254/98, unreported.
[107] reg 21.
[108] reg 13—see below.
[109] regs 6, 7 and 22—see below.
[110] reg 8—see below.

for continuity of service or production, such as hospitals, docks, airports, communications or in the production of gas, water or electricity; areas where there is a foreseeable surge of activity, such as agriculture, tourism or the postal service. Furthermore, certain shift workers or those engaged in activities split up over the day may be excluded from daily and weekly rest periods. Where derogations are agreed, equivalent compensating rest periods must be granted.

The provisions of the regulations

Maximum working weekly hours

12–40 The average total working time for each seven-day period should not exceed 48 hours.[111] This can be averaged out over a longer reference period of 17 weeks. Individual workers can agree to contract out of this Regulation by entering into an opting-out agreement. An employee who is dismissed for insisting on the right not to exceed the 48-hour week may bring a claim for unfair dismissal.[112]

Night work/shift work

12–41 The normal hours for night workers should not exceed an average of eight in any 24-hour period.[113] A night worker will be entitled to a free health assessment before taking up night work and at regular periods thereafter. Employers using night workers must keep accurate records of hours worked and existing hazards. If a registered medical practitioner advises an employer that a worker is suffering from health problems connected with the night work undertaken, the employer should transfer the night worker to day work to which they are suited, if possible.

Patterns of work

12–42 Where the health and safety of the worker is put at risk due to the organisation of work, particularly if the work is monotonous or the work-rate predetermined, the employer shall ensure that the worker is given adequate rest breaks.[114]

Daily rest

12–43 An adult worker is entitled to a daily rest period of not less than 11 consecutive hours in every 24-hour period. A young worker is entitled to a rest period of 12 consecutive hours in relation to the same period.[115]

Weekly rest

12–44 In addition to the 11 or 12-hour rest period, adult workers are entitled to an uninterrupted rest period of 24 hours and young workers to an uninterrupted rest period

---

[111] reg 4.
[112] *Brown* v *Controlled Packaging Services Ltd* Bristol Employment Tribunal, 21st January 1999, Case No 1402252/98, unreported.
[113] reg 6.
[114] reg 8.
[115] reg 10.

of 48 hours in each seven-day period.[116] This provision can be altered in certain circumstances.

Rest breaks

Where the working day is longer than six hours, adult workers should be granted a **12–45** rest break of 20 minutes to be spent away from the workstation. Young workers who work for longer than four and a half hours, are entitled to a rest break of at least 30 minutes.[117]

Annual leave

Every worker is entitled to four weeks"[118] paid annual leave during each "leave **12–46** year".[119] The leave year will generally start on commencement of employment if there is no provision to the contrary stipulated in the employment contract or relevant agreement. On termination of employment, the worker will be entitled to payment in lieu for any unused leave that has accrued.[120]

Future developments

Forthcoming European legislation will regulate the working time of those **12–47** employed in sectors which are currently excluded from the Working Time Regulations.

DISCRIMINATION IN EMPLOYMENT

UK law provides for the prohibition of discrimination on three different grounds: **12–48** sex, race and disability. Specific legislation exists which attempts to provide equality of treatment regardless of a person's sex,[121] race or disability. The Sex Discrimination Act 1975 ("SDA")[122] and the Race Relations Act 1976 ("RRA") were introduced at around the same time and, although they deal with different aspects of discrimination, have adopted the same approach to such an extent that some of the case law has been used interchangeably over the years. Although these Acts have been in existence for a quarter of a century, they remain almost in their original form. This is not to say that the law in these areas is no longer open to challenge, as the boundaries of the legislation have been increasingly stretched and renegotiated in recent years. This is particularly true of the SDA,[123] which has been applied in line with the provisions of its European counterpart, the Equal Treatment

---

[116] reg 11.
[117] reg 12.
[118] The original entitlement was to three weeks' leave—this was increased on 23rd November 1999.
[119] reg 13.
[120] reg 14.
[121] The Sex Discrimination Act 1975 also prohibits discrimination on the grounds of marital status.
[122] As amended by the Sex Discrimination Act 1986.
[123] For example, transsexuals have recently been found to be covered by the scope of the SDA: see *Chessington World of Adventures Ltd* v *Reed* [1988] IRLR 56 (EAT).

Directive.[124] Furthermore, the SDA has proved to be one of the most utilised sources of litigation in the employment field, giving rise to an ever-increasing number of cases.

The Disability Discrimination Act 1995 ("DDA") is drafted differently from the other two statutes and, as it is substantially more recent, much of its interpretation is unsettled. For this reason, although the provisions of the legislation dealing with sex and race discrimination can be stated with some degree of certainty, the section dealing with disability discrimination provides an overview of the development of the law in this area in which some of the cases considered are likely to be appealed.

SEX AND RACE DISCRIMINATION

12–49   The SDA and RRA cover job applicants as well as those who are already employed by providing "day-one" rights not to be discriminated against on the grounds of sex or race. Furthermore, independent contractors and agency workers employed on a temporary basis are also protected. The scope of both Acts is far wider than employment and extends to the prohibition of discrimination in the provision of services, education and in advertising. Each Act established a statutory Commission[125] with the power, *inter alia*, to provide financial support for those wishing to pursue a claim.

In attempting to provide equality of treatment to all workers, the Acts make it unlawful to treat an individual favourably[126] on the grounds of sex or race. The law is thus applied comparatively as, for every act of favouritism enjoyed by an individual or group of individuals, there must be an individual or group of individuals who are treated *less* favourably. Such treatment, if on the grounds of sex or race, represents a breach of the provisions. Therefore, the approach taken by the legislation can be described as the provision of negative rights, that is the right to not be treated in a certain way. There are three forms of discrimination prohibited by the Acts.

Different forms of discrimination

Direct discrimination

Under the SDA

12–50   Section 1 (1) (a) of the SDA provides that an employer discriminates against a woman[127] in any circumstances if, on the ground of her sex, he treats her less favourably than he treats or would treat a man. Direct discrimination occurs where the less favourable treatment is blatant and can be directly attributed to the person's sex or marital status. For example, a refusal to employ a woman on the grounds

---

[124] 76/207/EEC.
[125] The Equal Opportunities Commission (EOC) was established by SDA 1975 s 53; the Commission for Racial Equality (CRE) was established by s 43 of RRA 1976.
[126] Thus, positive discrimination is prohibited by the legislation.
[127] It should be noted that, although the SDA refers to "a woman" as the potential victim of discrimination, its provisions offer equal protection to men: SDA 1975, s 2.

that women are less reliable workers than men due to family responsibilities,[128] or a refusal to interview a female candidate where male candidates with identical qualifications and experience are interviewed, would amount to direct discrimination.

Where the treatment arises out of the application of a gender-based criterion and results in less favourable treatment, it will be found to amount to direct discrimination. For example, a dismissal which is based on the grounds of pregnancy or childbirth can only be suffered by a woman and, therefore, amounts to unlawful direct discrimination.[129] The employer or prospective employer may not have intended to discriminate,[130] since it is the effect of the employer's action not the reason for it that is relevant. The application of this provision has been characterised as the "but for" test, under which the treatment complained of would not have been experienced "but for" the sex of the applicant.[131]

Under the RRA
Section 1 (1) (a) of the RRA provides that direct racial discrimination occurs where a **12–51** person treats another less favourably than he treats or would treat others on racial grounds. The Act defines racial discrimination as occurring where the less favourable treatment is based on the person's "colour, race, nationality or ethnic or national origins".[132] As with sex discrimination, the employer need not have intended to discriminate to be in breach of the Act.[133]

Although apparently straightforward, it has proved difficult in practice to define the term "racial grounds", particularly with respect to a person's ethnic origins.[134] The important, and in some respects contentious, distinction appears to be between a person's religion and his or her race, with some examples of the former categorisation being deemed to denote a racial as well as religious grouping. Thus, Sikhs,[135] Jews[136] and Gypsies[137] have been held to comprise distinct ethnic groups but Rastafarians have not.[138] As with direct sex discrimination, the approach taken in applying the provision is comparative so that the treatment complained of by an applicant will be compared with that received by someone not of the applicant's race in order to determine whether it is, in fact, less favourable.

Indirect discrimination
The definition of indirect discrimination under the SDA[139] provides three potential **12–52**

---

[128] *Hurley v Mustoe* [1981] ICR 490.
[129] *Webb v EMO Air Cargo (UK) Ltd* [1993] IRLR 27 (HL); this point is discussed further under the auspices of maternity rights—see para 12–87.
[130] *Greig v Community Industry* [1979] IRLR 158.
[131] *James v Eastleigh Borough Council* [1990] IRLR 288 (HL).
[132] RRA, s 3(1).
[133] *Hafeez v Richmond School* [1981] COIT 1112/38, unreported; *Ministry of Defence v Jeremiah* [1979] IRLR 436 (HL).
[134] *Mandla v Dowell Lee* [198]) IRLR 209 (HL).
[135] *ibid.*
[136] *Seide v Gillette Industries Ltd* [1980] IRLR 427 (EAT).
[137] *Commission for Racial Equality v Dutton* [1989] IRLR 8 (CA).
[138] *Dawkins v Crown Suppliers* [1993] IRLR 284 (CA).
[139] s 1(1)(b).

hurdles that must be cleared by claimants wishing to invoke this provision. Indirect discrimination occurs where, an employer applies to a woman employee

> "a requirement or condition which applies or would apply equally to a man, but—
>
> (i) which is such that the proportion of women who can comply with it is considerably smaller than the proportion of men who can comply with it, and
>
> (ii) which he cannot show to be justifiable irrespective of the sex of the person to whom it is applied, and
>
> (iii) which is to her detriment because she cannot comply with it."[140]

Section 1(1)(b) of the RRA gives an almost identical definition of indirect discrimination except that the requirement or condition must be applied to persons "not of the same racial group" and the employer's defence will depend on the act being justifiable "irrespective of the colour, race, nationality or ethnic or national origins of the person to whom it is applied".

Indirect discrimination arises from covert discrimination in that its effects may not necessarily be immediately apparent. The requirement or condition complained of will require further investigation in order to assess its impact on groups of men and women[141] or racial groups.[142] Examples of factors which have been deemed to constitute requirements or conditions within the meaning of the legislation include: age specifications[143]; the imposition of a shift system[144]; a mobility clause[145]; and a requirement to work full time.[146]

At the second "hurdle" which offers the possibility of justification, the employer is able to defend his actions on the basis that the requirement or condition is gender or racially neutral and has been applied objectively. Circumstances such as the needs of the employer will be considered in deciding whether the discriminatory act can be justified.[147] The discriminatory effect of the requirement or condition will be assessed against the justification advanced by the employer and a balance will be struck.[148]

One of the main issues for the courts in the context of claims relating to indirect discrimination on both sexual and racial grounds, has been whether the imposition of the requirement or condition must serve as an absolute bar. For example, would a job applicant, in order to be successful, have to have been denied employment (or promotion) due to her inability to meet the requirement or condition which had been considered as essential during the selection procedure?

There appears to be some divergence of opinion between different courts in this

---

[140] s 3(1)(b) provides a definition of indirect discrimination on the grounds of marital status.
[141] *Price* v *Civil Service Commission* [1978] 1 All ER 1228; *University of Manchester* v *Jones* [1993] IRLR 218.
[142] *Meer* v *London Borough of Tower Hamlets* [1988] IRLR 399 (CA).
[143] *Perera* v *Civil Service Commission* [1983] IRLR 166 (CA).
[144] *London Underground Ltd* v *Edwards* [1995] IRLR 355 (EAT).
[145] *Meade-Hill and NUCPS* v *British Council* ([995] IRLR 478 (EAT).
[146] *Home Office* v *Holmes* [1984] IRLR 299 (EAT).
[147] Case 170/84, *Bilka-Kaufhaus GmbH* v *Weber von Hartz* (1986) ECR 1607.
[148] *Hampson* v *Department of Education and Science* [1989] IRLR 68 (HL); *R* v *Secretary of State for Employment, ex parte Equal Opportunities Commission* [1994] IRLR 76 (HL).

respect with the leading race case[149] having been decided on the basis that it was necessary for the applicant's inability to meet the requirement to serve as an absolute bar, and the cases concerning sex discrimination following the line of reasoning adopted by the European Court[150] that the requirement or condition need not be absolute.[151] Perhaps such separate development of the provisions relating to indirect discrimination is illustrative of the level of influence that the European legislation[152] and its application by the European Court of Justice has undeniably had over the area of sex discrimination.

Victimisation

Under both the Acts,[153] it is unlawful to victimise a person because he has brought **12–53** legal proceedings, given evidence or information in connection with legal proceedings, or made allegations of a contravention of the legislation, unless the allegation was false and the person making it knew this.

Genuine Occupational Qualifications

Both the SDA and the RRA recognise certain circumstances in which an employer will **12–54** be able to discriminate lawfully by favouring someone of a particular sex or racial grouping. In such situations the person's sex or racial grouping will be deemed to be a "genuine occupational qualification" for the job.

Under the SDA[154] genuine occupational qualifications would apply in specific circumstances where the job needs to be done by a person of a specific sex for the following reasons:

(a) physiology or authenticity—*eg* an actor or model is required for a particular role;

(b) decency or privacy—*eg* a shop assistant who measures customers for clothing;

(c) the job requires someone to live in and the accommodation provided is only suitable for one sex and it is not reasonable to expect the employer to make adjustments;

(d) the job involves working in a single-sex hospital or prison;

(e) the job entails the provision of personal services promoting welfare or education to clients—*eg* youth leader for a single-sex organisation such as the Girl Guides;

(f) the job involves working outside the UK in a country where the laws or customs would prevent a woman from performing the job effectively;

(g) the job is one of two to be held by a married couple.

---

[149] *Perera* v *Civil Service Commission* [1983] IRLR 166 (CA).
[150] In *Bilka-Kaufhaus GmbH* v *Weber von Hartz* [1986] ECR 1607.
[151] *Falkirk Council* v *Whyte* [1997] IRLR 560 (EAT), but see also *Connolly* v *Strathclyde Regional Council* (EAT/103/94, unreported, in which the EAT appears to have followed the decision in *Perera*.
[152] Equal Treatment Directive 76/207/EEC.
[153] SDA 1975, s 4; RRA 1976, s 2.
[154] s 7.

Where such circumstances are found to exist, the job can effectively be excluded from the provisions of the SDA, providing that the reason for exclusion is genuine.[155]

Similar exclusions operate in the context of the RRA,[156] under which an employer is able to discriminate by favouring someone of a particular race. Genuine occupational qualifications would apply in respect of the following reasons:

(a) authenticity related to a dramatic performance, entertainment or participation as an artist's or photographic model—*eg* an actor is required for a specific role;

(b) the job involves working in a place where food or drink is provided and consumed in a particular setting and a person of a specific race is required for reasons of authenticity;

(c) the job entails the provision of personal services promoting welfare or education to clients of a particular racial group and such services can be more effectively provided by a person from that racial group.[137]

Sexual and racial harassment

12–55 If a person suffers harassment at work on the grounds of his sex[158] or race, this may amount to direct discrimination under the Acts. To succeed in such a claim, the claimant would have to show that he had been or would be treated less favourably than someone of a different sex or racial grouping and that the treatment had caused him to suffer a detriment.[159] The harassment must be sexually[160] or racially[161] motivated and may be of a verbal or physical nature. An employer may be found to be vicariously liable for the actions of his employees[162] and, in certain circumstances, one single act of harassment may constitute "suffering a detriment".[163]

Codes of Practice

12–56 Both the Equal Opportunities Commission (EOC) and the Commission for Racial Equality (CRE) have issued Codes of Practice[164] which seek to eliminate discrimination and promote equal opportunities. Although they are not legally binding, the Codes may be used as evidence in tribunal hearings.

DISABILITY DISCRIMINATION

12–57 The employment provisions of the Disability Discrimination Act 1995 ("DDA") came into force in December 1996. The Act applies to a wider range of activities than just

---

[155] *Sisley* v *Britannia Security Systems* [1983] IRLR 404; *Etam plc* v *Rowan* [1989] IRLR 150.
[156] s 5.
[157] *Tottenham Green Under Fives Centre* v *Marshall* [1989] IRLR 147.
[158] The European Commission's Recommendation on the Protection of the Dignity of Women and Men at Work No 93/121 and the attached Code of Practice contain useful guidance relating to this recently developed area of the law.
[159] As for any direct discrimination claim under s 1(1)(a) of the SDA 1975 or s 1(1)(a) of the RRA 1976.
[160] *Porcelli* v *Strathclyde Regional Council* [1986] ICR 564.
[161] *Burton and Rhule* v *De Vere Hotels* [1996] IRLR 596.
[162] *Jones* v *Tower Boot Co Ltd* [1997] IRLR 168.
[163] *Bracebridge Engineering* v *Darby* [1990] IRLR 3.
[164] EOC 1985, *Code of Practice for the elimination of discrimination on the grounds of sex and marriage and the promotion of equal opportunities in employment*; CRE 1983, *Code of Practice for the elimination of racial discrimination and the promotion of equality of opportunity in employment*.

employment and has application in the provision of education and public transport and in relation to access to goods, facilities, premises and services. The employment provisions make employers of 15 or more employees liable for discrimination against job applicants and employees in relation to recruitment and selection, terms and conditions of employment, promotional opportunities, the provision of training, employment benefits, dismissal or any other detrimental treatment.[165]

Different forms of discrimination

The Act recognises three forms of discrimination. **12–58**

Direct Discrimination

Section 5 of the DDA defines direct discrimination as occurring if "for a reason relating **12–59** to the disabled person's disability, the employer treats the disabled person less favourably than others who are not disabled, and the employer cannot show that this treatment is justified."

The Act is similar in its approach to the legislation prohibiting direct sex and race discrimination, in that it is applied comparatively. However, the nature of the comparison is somewhat different than under the other Acts. To discover if a disabled person has been treated less favourably it is necessary to compare the treatment received to that which would have been received had the person not been disabled and to question whether the employer would have acted in the same way.

Failure to make reasonable adjustments

Section 6 of the DDA imposes a duty on employers to make reasonable adjustments to **12–60** any arrangements made by or on behalf of the employer or to any physical feature of the premises occupied by the employer. Such adjustments will be required where the disabled person concerned is placed at a substantial disadvantage in comparison with persons who are not disabled due to the existing arrangements or premises. The employer will only be required to make adjustments if considered reasonable in all the circumstances, and issues such as inconvenience or cost to the employer will be considered.[166] Failure to make such adjustments may result in an action for direct discrimination.

"Reasonable adjustments" might include modifications made to premises, such as widening doorways for improved access, providing wheelchair ramps, altering working hours or accommodating the disabled employee's absence during working hours to attend for medical treatment.[167]

Victimisation

Under section 55 of the DDA it is unlawful to discriminate against a person because he **12–61** has brought proceedings under the provisions of the Act or has given evidence in any such proceedings. An employer may be able to defend an allegation of victimisation if he can show that the original allegations were false or were not made in good faith.

---

[165] DDA 1995, s 4.
[166] *Kenny v Hampshire Constabulary* [1999] IRLR 76.
[167] The EAT has provided guidance on the approach to be taken by tribunals in *Morse v Wiltshire County Council* [1998] IRLR 352.

Definition of "disability"

12–62 One of the main areas of difficulty for employers and employees that has been identified through the fast-developing case law is the definition of "disability" that applies under the Act. The DDA defines a disability as "a physical or mental impairment which has a substantial and long-term adverse effect on a person's ability to carry out normal day-to-day activities".[168] A physical or mental impairment may include any clinically recognised mental illness, but will exclude conditions such as alcoholism, drug addiction, hay fever, pyromania, kleptomania or voyeurism.[169] The meaning given to the phrase "substantial and long-term" by the Act[170] is that the disability must be likely to last for at least 12 months. "Day-to-day activities" will include mobility, manual dexterity, physical co-ordination, continence, the ability to lift, carry or otherwise move everyday objects, speech, hearing and eyesight, as well as the use of memory, concentration, the ability to learn or understand or the individual's perception of physical danger.[171]

Accompanying guidance and Code of Practice

12–63 Section 3 of the Act enables the Secretary of State to issue guidance concerning the factors which should be taken into account in determining the meaning of the definition of disability. Such guidance has subsequently been issued[172] and includes, *inter alia*, specific examples of the degree of incapacity required in respect of each of the relevant day-to-day activities in order to comply with the definition. There is a Code of Practice[173] which came into force on 2nd December 1996. As with the codes relating to sex and race discrimination it is not legally binding but can be used in evidence before a tribunal hearing.

The Disability Rights Commission

12–64 The Disability Rights Commission was formally launched in April 2000. The organistion's role will include education, conciliation and enforcement of the law.

Enforcement of the Discrimination Acts

12–65 Any job applicant or employee who feels he has been discriminated against on the grounds of sex, race or disability, may make a complaint to an Employment Tribunal within three months of the alleged act of discrimination. There is a questionnaire procedure in operation in respect of each type of discrimination, which is intended to enable the complainant to find out more about the employer's reasoning. Under this procedure, a standard questionnaire will be sent to the employer, who may choose whether or not to complete the questionnaire. Refusal to answer all or any of the questions or evasive or inaccurate responses will be taken into account in any tribunal proceedings.

---

[168] DDA 1995, s 1.
[169] Disability Discrimination (Meaning of Disability) Regulations 1996.
[170] DDA, Sched 1, para 2.
[171] DDA, Sched 1, para 4.
[172] *Guidance on matters to be taken into account in determining questions relating to the definition of disability*, 25th July 1996.
[173] *Code of Practice for the elimination of discrimination in the field of employment against disabled persons or persons who have had a disability.*

The burden of proving that discrimination has occurred is on the party making the complaint. Once this has, prima facie, been achieved, the burden shifts to the employer, who must defend the claim by proving that discrimination did not occur or that it was justified in the circumstances. If the employer is unable to defend or justify his actions, the tribunal will find in favour of the applicant.

Remedies for discrimination

There are three types of remedy available to employment tribunals in respect of discrimination claims: declarations; recommendations; and compensation.   **12–66**

Declarations

A declaration may be made alongside an award for compensation. The tribunal states the rights of the employer and employee, which may be useful in preventing further acts of discrimination from occurring.   **12–67**

Recommendations

Under a recommendation, the tribunal orders the employer to take specific action in order to eliminate the discriminatory behaviour or make recompense to the employee. Examples of recommendations include an order that the employer should provide a written apology to the employee or an order that the employer should modify certain practices or procedures. Refusal by the employer to comply with a tribunal recommendation may result in an increase in the amount of compensation made to the employee.   **12–68**

Compensation

This is the most common type of remedy awarded. Calculation of the amount of compensation applicable may include consideration of such items as loss of future wages or injury to feelings, as well as the more direct forms of financial loss sustained. Expenses incurred as a result of the discrimination, such as counselling or medical bills, may be reimbursed. There is no maximum ceiling on the amount of compensation that may be awarded in cases of discrimination.[174]   **12–69**

EQUAL PAY

The provision of equal pay for men and women has been enshrined in domestic legislation since the 1970s. The Equal Pay Act 1970 ("EqPA") came into force in 1975. The five-year period between the Act receiving Royal Assent and its commencement was intended to give employers an opportunity to comply with its provisions on a voluntary basis and enabled its introduction to coincide with the parallel rights necessary for its enforcement contained in the Sex Discrimination Act 1975. The provision of equal pay between the sexes has its origin in the Treaty of Rome,[175] and   **12–70**

---

[174] Sex Discrimination and Equal Pay (Remedies) Regulations 1993 (SI 1993/2798); Race Relations (Remedies) Act 1994.
[175] Art 119, now Art 141.

the developments in European Community law, which stem largely from the European Court of Justice's interpretation of the provisions of the Equal Pay Directive,[176] continue to shape domestic law in this area.

DEFINITION OF "PAY"

12–71 When defining what actually constitutes "pay", the House of Lords[177] has held that each of the terms of the contract should be considered separately and individually, not as a total package. The applicant is entitled to equality in respect of each term.

The European Court of Justice[178] has held that benefits paid under a contracted-out occupational pension scheme amount to "pay" under Article 119. Employees are entitled to equal benefits under such occupational schemes—for example, if a woman has the option to take her pension at 60, a male employee has a right to insist on the same terms. This decision overrides UK law which previously allowed discrimination in respect of pension entitlements and benefits and its impact is confined to periods of employment subsequent to the date of the decision—17th May 1990—except where legal proceedings had already been initiated before that date.[179]

Occupational social security benefits do fall within the meaning of "pay" under Article 119, statutory social security benefits do not.[180] Payments which do fall within the definition of "pay" include redundancy payments and *ex gratia* payments[181]; sick pay[182]; paid leave or overtime pay for participation in training courses given by the employer in accordance with statutory provisions.[183]

THE EQUAL PAY ACT 1970

12–72 The EqPA 1970[184] aims to ensure that men and women receive the same rate of pay for performing the same or similar work. The Act applies to all employees, independent contractors and trainees. Benefits other than in cash are also covered by the Act: for example, bonuses, holidays and hours of work may all be relevant factors in the determination of the provision of equal pay. There is no right to contract out of the provisions of the Act, which means that employers cannot ask employees to waive their rights to make a claim for equal pay. Although the provisions of the Act apply equally to men and women, as with the provisions of the Sex Discrimination Act, it has generally been women who have sought legal protection.

The equality clause

12–73 Under section 1 (1) of the Act an equality clause will be read into every contract of employment. This clause will serve as an implied term of the contract and provides the

---

[176] Directive 75/117/EEC.
[177] In *Hayward* v *Cammell Laird Shipbuilders Ltd* [1988] AC 894.
[178] In *Barber* v *Royal Guardian Exchange Assurance Group* [1991] 1 QB 344.
[179] On related issues, see the following ECJ decisions: *Ten Oever* v *Stichting Bedrijfpensioenfonds voor het Glazenwassersen Schoonmaakbedrijf* [1993] IRLR 601; *Neath* v *Hugh Steeper Ltd* [1994] IRLR 91; *Moroni* v *Firma Collo GmbH* [1994] IRLR 130; *Roberts* v *Birds Eye Walls Ltd* [1994] ICR 338.
[180] *Griffin* v *London Pension Fund Authority* [1993] IRLR 248.
[181] *McKechnie* v *UBM Building Supplies (Southern) Ltd* [1991] ICR 710.
[182] *Rinner-Kühn* v *FWW Spezial-Gebaudereinigung GmbH* [1989] IRLR 493.
[183] *Arbeiterwohlfahrt der Stadt Berlin EV* v *Botel* [1992]IRLR 423.
[184] As amended by the Equal Pay (Amendment) Regulations 1983 (SI 1983/1794).

right to receive equal pay in specified circumstances. The application of the term will be by comparison with a named comparator of the opposite sex who receives a higher rate of pay than the claimant. An actual, not hypothetical, comparator must be offered for the comparison, although it is acceptable to base a claim for equal pay on a predecessor[185] or a replacement employee.[186] The comparator must be employed by the same employer as the claimant or by an associated employer.[187]

There are three different types of claims that can be made under the provisions of the Act.[188] The choice of claim will depend on the circumstances in which the claimant finds herself. For example, the woman may be employed in "like work" with a man in the same establishment, she may be employed in "work rated as equivalent" to that undertaken by her comparator, or she may be employed in "work of equal value" to that performed by him. Each of these terms has a distinct meaning under the Act and will be considered in turn.

"Like work"

This is defined in section 1(2)(a) of the EqPA as being work which is "the same or **12–74** broadly similar" as that performed by the comparator. This is the most straightforward type of claim although success will depend on the woman having access to the necessary information on which to base her claim. It is important to note that the jobs to be compared need not be identical but similar. The tribunal will look at the jobs performed by the two workers in order to assess what they actually entail. This is undertaken by applying the "broad brush" approach.[189] The skills and knowledge required for the job should be considered, but a minute examination of the work involved is not necessary. Any differences between the two jobs should not be of any practical importance. Claims by the employer that higher pay rates for men are based on factors such as the performance of different duties will be examined by the tribunal in order to determine the frequency with which the different duties are actually performed.[190]

Nature of the job

If the work performed by men and women can be shown to be substantially different **12–75** in nature, it will not be deemed to be "like work". Factors such as different levels of responsibility[191] and different duties may be relevant in distinguishing one job from another, even if the difference only applies to part of the time spent working.[192]

The time at which a person works is to be disregarded in that the payment of a higher rate of basic pay to males on night shift and a lower rate to women on day shift cannot be justified. Premium payments could be made to night workers for anti-social

---

[185] *Macarthys v Smith* [1979] ICR 500.
[186] *Diocese of Hallam Trustee v Connaughton* [1996] ICR 860.
[187] EqPA, s 1(6).
[188] s 1(2).
[189] *Capper Pass v Lawton* [1977] ICR 83 (EAT).
[190] *Electrolux Ltd v Hutchinson* [1977] ICR 252; *Shields v E Coomes (Holdings) Ltd* [1978]) ICR 1159.
[191] *Eaton v Nuttall* [1977] ICR 272.
[192] *Maidment v Cooper & Co (Birmingham) Ltd* [1978] ICR 1094.

hours, but basic rates must not be distinguished[193]—although the time of work will be important if it results in additional responsibility.[194]

"Work rated as equivalent"

12–76 Section 1 (2) (b) of the Act provides that where a woman is employed in work rated as equivalent to that of a man in the same employment, she is entitled to equal pay. The rating must have been made following the use of a job evaluation scheme[195] by which all jobs in the workplace are given numerical values according to their components and graded. In order to be valid, such a scheme ought to consider all matters connected with the nature of the work, such as effort, skill and responsibilities.[196] Employers should avoid the use of subjective judgments regarding the value of an employee's work by ensuring that the scheme is analytical and objective.[197] Once undertaken, the results of the job evaluation scheme will generally form the basis of the organisation's pay scale and can thus be used in order to claim equal pay. The courts have had different views on whether the implementation of the results of such a scheme is a compulsory requirement.[198]

Not all employers have undertaken job evaluation and there is no way in which they can be forced to do so. When the EqPA originally came into force, the only methods by which a woman could claim equal pay were by proving that she was engaged in "like work" or by relying on the results of a job evaluation scheme. This left a legal loophole through which employers who had not undertaken job evaluation could escape by continuing to pay men and women different rates as long as the work undertaken could not be classified as "like work". It was, therefore, not in the interests of an unscrupulous employer to employ such a scheme which may, after all, have merely served to reveal such inequality. In 1983, the Act was amended[199] following a decision by the European Court of Justice[200] in which the Court found that the Act did not fully comply with the provisions of European law. The amendment corrected this anomaly by making it possible to bring an equal value claim.

"Equal value"

12–77 Under section 1(2)(c) of the Act, a woman is entitled to equal pay for work which is of equal value to that performed by her male comparator. Such a claim will be made where the woman is unable to bring her claim under either of the previous two types. In deciding what will constitute "equal value", the tribunal will look at the demands made upon the employee with regard to effort, skill and decision-making. The tribunal may make such assessment purely on the evidence before it or it may appoint an independent expert in order to investigate the case and prepare a report based on his or her findings. Independent experts are appointed from an ACAS panel.

The comparator in such a claim may be engaged in work which, on the face of it,

---

[193] *Dugdale v Kraft Foods Ltd* [1977] ICR 48; *National Coal Board v Sherwin* [1978] ICR 700.
[194] *Thomas v National Coal Board* [1987] ICR 757.
[195] EqPA, s 1 (5).
[196] *Eaton v Nuttall* [1977] ICR 272.
[197] *Bromley v H & J Quick Ltd* [1988] ICR 623.
[198] See the conflicting decisions in *O'Brien v Sim-Chem Ltd* [1980] ICR 573 (HL) and *Arnold v Beecham Group* [1982] ICR 744 (EAT).
[199] By the Equal Pay (Amendment) Regulations 1983 (SI 1983/1794).
[200] *Commission of the European Communities v UK* [1982] ICR 578.

appears to be completely different from the job undertaken by the claimant as it is the values ascribed to the jobs that must be determined and compared, not the similarities in the nature of the work itself. Thus, in the leading case, a female catering assistant was found to be entitled to equal pay with male apprenticed painters, engineers and joiners.[201]

A woman who has brought a claim for equal pay on the basis of "like work" will be prevented from claiming equal value. However, where no such claim has actually been made, equal pay for work of equal value may be claimed even though the woman works with men doing the same work who are paid the same rate. This is because the House of Lords[202] has held that, in order to interpret the EqPA in line with the provisions of European law, an extra condition should be read into section 1(2)(c), so that the section should be interpreted as reading, "An equality clause is a provision which relates to terms (whether concerned with pay or not) of a contract under which a woman is employed and has the effect that ... *as between the woman and the man with whom she claims equality*, is in terms of the demands made on her (for instance under such headings as effort, skill and decision), of equal value to that of a man in the same employment".

The employer's defence—genuine material difference

Under section 1(3) of the EqPA an employer may be able to defend an equal pay claim **12–78** on the basis that the differences in pay rates are due to the existence of a "genuine material difference"[203] between the case of the claimant and that of her comparator. This difference must be due to a factor other than sex. The European Court of Justice has held[204] that the defence provided under Article 119, whereby an employer is permitted to show that a pay policy is "objectively justified", must be based on legitimate economic grounds. The EqPA has been interpreted by the House of Lords accordingly as applying to administrative needs, so long as the employer's needs are shown to be "significant and relevant".[205]

As well as the more obvious forms of genuine material difference on which an employer's defence could be based, such as levels of qualification, skill, experience and responsibility, employers have succeeded in justifying different rates of pay for men and women on some more surprising grounds. For example, statutory promotion structures and financial constraints have been accepted as comprising genuine material differences,[206] as have market forces.[207] In the case of market forces, the employer must be able to show that the difference in pay was necessary in order to attract employees to a particular occupation.[208]

The European Court has held that, where pay grading structures are not transparent (that is when it is unclear to employees why they have been placed on a particular point of the scale), the onus is on the employer to show that such a practice is not

---

[201] *Hayward v Cammell Laird Shipbuilders Ltd* [1988] AC 894.
[202] *Pickstone v Freemans plc* [1989] AC 66.
[203] *Jenkins v Kingsgate (Clothing Productions) Ltd* [1981] ICR 592.
[204] Case 170/84, *Bilka-Kaufhaus GmbH v Weber von Hartz* [1986] ECR 1607.
[205] *Rainey v Greater Glasgow Health Board* [1988] IRLR 361.
[206] *Strathclyde Regional Council v Wallace* [1998] 1 WLR 259.
[207] *Rainey v Greater Glasgow Health Board*, [1988] IRLR 361.
[208] *Enderby v Frenchay Health Authority* [1994] IRLR 591; *Ratcliffe v North Yorkshire County Council* [1995] IRLR 439.

discriminatory. Employers should assess the criteria used for paying increments or grading to ascertain whether they have an adverse impact on women and, if so, whether this is justifiable. It is acceptable to pay more for quality but not for flexibility or adaptability.[209]

CODE OF PRACTICE ON EQUAL PAY

12–79   The Equal Opportunities Commission has issued a Code of Practice[210] on equal pay which is admissible before Employment Tribunals. The code offers useful definitions of the terminology adopted by the legislation and sets out a suggested equal pay policy.

MATERNITY RIGHTS AND PARENTAL LEAVE

12–80   In December 1999, the Employment Relations Act 1999 made some important amendments to the system of maternity rights in the UK and introduced a right to unpaid parental leave.[211] The changes made to maternity rights represent the latest in a long line of amendments to this area of law and, although these recent changes simplify the operation of the law to some extent, finding and understanding the relevant provisions remains a complex task. This is largely because, as well as the various pieces of legislation dealing directly with the rights to maternity leave[212] and pay,[213] the anti-discrimination legislation[214] will also have application in certain respects. Furthermore, the UK system differentiates between different groups of workers with respect to length of service, so that all women are entitled to some rights relating to pregnancy and maternity, but those with one year's continuous employment enjoy enhanced statutory benefits.

PROTECTIVE MEASURES

12–81   Certain provisions are intended to protect the health and safety of pregnant workers and, therefore, apply to all women regardless of length of service or hours of work. For example, all women will be entitled to paid time off to attend for ante-natal care and the employer may not reasonably refuse such a request.[215] Where the work undertaken by a female worker poses specific risks to her health and safety during or following pregnancy, there are certain rights that will apply. The employer is obliged to assess

---

[209] *Handels-og Kontorfunktionaerernes Forbund i Danmark v Dansk Arbejdsgiverforening (acting for "Danfoss")* [1989] IRLR 532.
[210] Effective from 26th March 1997.
[211] Which were implemented by the Maternity and Parental Leave etc. Regulations 1999 (SI 1999/3312), the maternity leave provisions of which have effect from 30th April 2000.
[212] Pregnant Workers Directive 92/85/EEC; Employment Rights Act 1996; Employment Relations Act 1999 and associated Regulations.
[213] Statutory Maternity Pay (General) Regulations 1986 (SI 1986/1960).
[214] Sex Discrimination Act 1975; Equal Treatment Directive 76/207/EC.
[215] Employment Rights Act 1996, ss 55–57.

the work, taking into account the woman's pregnancy, in order to identify any potential risks or hazards to her health or that of her unborn child.[216] If the woman has recently given birth and is breastfeeding her child, this should also be considered. Following such an assessment, any risks should be removed or, where this is not possible, the woman offered suitable alternative employment.[217] Where there is no suitable alternative available, the woman should be suspended from work on full pay for the duration of the specified risk.[218] Furthermore, all women are prohibited from working for the two weeks following childbirth on health and safety grounds, regardless of any individual arrangements concerning maternity leave.[219]

THE PROVISION OF STATUTORY MATERNITY LEAVE

In the provision of maternity leave, the law operates to impose certain minimum periods of leave with which all employers must comply. Of course, employers are free to "trade up" by providing extra contractual entitlement or enhanced pay during the maternity leave period, as long as the minimum standards imposed by the statutory scheme are recognised in respect of all employees. The UK had a maternity leave scheme in operation before the intervention of European Community law[220] in this area and the existing scheme provided a more generous period of leave than the Directive, although the right to leave was restricted to those with two years' continuous employment and the Directive provided a universal right to maternity leave. When the provisions of the Directive were implemented in the UK, the existing entitlement was retained due to the fact that it is not possible to level down in order to comply with European law. This means that the UK now has a "two-tiered" system of maternity leave in operation, under which certain workers are entitled to an enhanced period of leave. The general scheme is referred to as "ordinary maternity leave" and the enhanced scheme as "additional maternity leave". **12–82**

Ordinary maternity leave

All female workers, regardless of length of service, are entitled to 18 weeks' maternity leave.[221] During this time, the contract will continue to exist so that all its terms will apply[222] and all relevant benefits will continue to accrue. Following the period of maternity leave, the woman will be entitled to return to the same job. **12–83**

Additional maternity leave

Female workers who have completed at least one year's continuous service at the beginning of the eleventh week prior to the expected week of confinement (EWC) will be entitled to a period of additional maternity leave.[223] Such workers have the right to **12–84**

---

[216] Management of Health and Safety at Work Regulations 1999, (SI 1999/3242).
[217] Employment Rights Act 1996, s 67.
[218] *ibid* s 66.
[219] Maternity (Compulsory Leave) Regulations 1994 (SI 1994/2479).
[220] By the Pregnant Workers Directive 92/85/EC.
[221] Employment Rights Act 1996, ss 71–85, as amended by reg 7 of the Maternity and Parental Leave etc Regulations 1999 (SI 1999/3312).
[222] The usual rate of remuneration may be suspended in favour of statutory maternity pay: see *Gillespie* v *Northern Health and Social Services Board* [1996] IRLR 214 and the Maternity and Parental Leave etc Regulations 1999 (SI 1999/3312), reg 9.
[223] Employment Rights Act 1996, s 79(1), as amended by reg 5 of the Maternity and Parental Leave etc Regulations 1999 (SI 1999/3312).

return at any time up to the twenty-ninth week after the week of childbirth. During the period of additional maternity leave, the contract of employment continues, although only certain obligations will remain in place.[224]

PROCEDURE FOR TAKING MATERNITY LEAVE

12–85 The employee wishing to take maternity leave should notify her employer of her pregnancy, the expected week of confinement (EWC) and the date on which she wishes to start her leave. There is no legal requirement for this information to be given in writing and although employers would be well advised to request written notification as a matter of good practice, they cannot insist on this or take any punitive measures if the notice is not given in writing. At least 21 days before maternity leave is to commence, the employee must notify her employer of the date on which maternity leave is to commence, which must be no earlier than the eleventh week prior to the EWC.[225] The maternity leave period will commence on the date notified, or, if the woman is absent on pregnancy-related grounds, the first day after the beginning of the sixth week prior to the EWC,[226] or, if the leave period has not commenced, the date on which childbirth occurs.[227]

EXERCISING THE RIGHT TO RETURN

12–86 Following ordinary maternity leave, once the 18-week period has passed, the woman simply returns to work on the date on which she is due back. She does not need to inform the employer that she intends to return to work as she has an automatic right to resume work at end of the 18-week period. If the woman wishes to return to work early, she should give her employer seven days' notice of this fact.[228] The right to return to work early will be subject to the prohibition from working within two weeks of childbirth.

Following a period of additional maternity leave, the employee should give written confirmation of the date that she intends to return at least 21 days before the end of the maternity leave period.[229]

PREGNANCY-RELATED DISMISSAL

12–87 Dismissal for any reason related to pregnancy or childbirth will amount to an automatically unfair dismissal.[230] The duration of this "special protection" has become known as the protected period, which has been deemed to last from the start of the pregnancy until the end of the maternity leave period.[231] Furthermore, any detriment suffered during this period as a result of childbirth or pregnancy will comprise direct discrimination[232] without the need for a male comparator.[233]

---

[224] Maternity and Parental Leave etc Regulations 1999 (SI 1999/3312), reg 17.
[225] Employment Rights Act 1996, s 74(2).
[226] *ibid* s 72(1)(b).
[227] *ibid* s 72(2).
[228] *ibid* s 76(1).
[229] *ibid* s 82(1).
[230] *ibid* s 99. See para 12–111.
[231] *Brown v Rentokil Ltd* [1998] IRLR 445 (ECJ).
[232] As defined by s 1(1)(a) of the Sex Discrimination Act 1975.
[233] *Webb v EMO Air Cargo UK Ltd* [1994] IRLR 482 (ECJ); [1995] IRLR 645 (HL).

STATUTORY MATERNITY PAY

The right to take maternity leave is separate from the right to receive statutory **12–88** maternity pay (SMP) which is provided for by the Social Security Contributions and Benefits Act 1992 and the Statutory Maternity Pay (General) Regulations 1986.

To qualify for SMP, the woman must be an "employed earner" who has been employed continuously for a minimum of 26 weeks up to the "qualifying week" (that is the fifteenth week before the EWC) and must be paid at or above the lower earnings limit at which National Insurance contributions are payable. She must also be able to produce a medical certificate stating the EWC and should inform her employer, at least 21 days before her maternity leave period is due to begin that she intends to stop work. The maternity pay period lasts for 18 weeks and may commence at any time between the eleventh week prior to the EWC up to the week following the actual week of childbirth. There are two rates of pay that are applicable: for the first six weeks, the woman receives 90 per cent of her average gross weekly earnings (referred to as the "higher rate"); for the remaining period of maternity leave, she receives maternity pay at the standard rate. Women who are not eligible for SMP may qualify for maternity allowance, which is paid direct by the Benefits Agency.

PARENTAL LEAVE

In order to implement European law,[234] and as part of its general package of **12–89** reforms intended to promote "family friendly" policies,[235] the UK Government introduced a right to take unpaid parental leave in December 1999. The Employment Relations Act 1999 provided the framework for this additional employment right, but the right itself was introduced by the Maternity and Parental Leave etc Regulations 1999.[236]

Qualifying conditions[237]

In order to qualify for the right to unpaid parental leave, the following conditions must **12–90** be satisfied: the employee must have one year's continuous service and must be the parent of a child born after 15th December 1999 (who is under five years old) or have adopted a child under the age of 18 after 15th December 1999.

Length of the leave period[238]

The total length of the parental leave entitlement will be 13 weeks for each child. For **12–91** part-time employees, the leave entitlement will be in proportion to time worked—for example, if an employee works for two days per week, he will be entitled to 26 days' leave per child.

---

[234] In the form of the Parental Leave Directive 96/34/EC.
[235] Comprising the amendments to the maternity leave system, discussed above, and the right to time off for dependents, discussed below. For details of the Government's original proposals, see the White Paper *Fairness at Work* (Cd 3968, May 1998).
[236] SI 1999/3312. (The following references are to these regulations.)
[237] reg 13.
[238] reg 14.

Terms and conditions of employment[239]

12–92   The only terms and conditions that will apply during the period of leave will be in relation to mutual trust and confidence. On return to work, the employee will be entitled to the same job or a job with the same terms, conditions and status. Any rights which accrued prior to the leave period, such as pensions rights, will stand.

Timing of the leave[240]

12–93   Leave will have to be taken in blocks of one week at a time, subject to a maximum amount of four weeks' leave per year. Where part of a week is taken as leave, this will count as a full week.

Employees must give at least four weeks' notice of the intention to take leave in respect of each week requested. The employer will have the right to postpone the leave for up to six months on the grounds of "business needs". Fathers requiring paternity leave immediately after the birth of a child must give three months' notice before the expected week of childbirth.

TIME OFF FOR URGENT FAMILY REASONS

12–94   This right, which was introduced by the Employment Relations Act 1999,[241] entitles an employee to take a reasonable amount of unpaid leave in order to deal with a domestic incident. A "domestic incident" is an incident which occurs in the employee's home or affects a member of the employee's family or a person who relies on the employee for assistance. Examples include sudden illness or accident, a family crisis, or an unavoidable domestic crisis such as severe damage or disruption to property through flooding, fire or burglary.

TRANSFER OF UNDERTAKINGS

12–95   The contract of employment is a contract formed between two parties: the employer and the employee. Prior to 1981, if the employer's business was sold or transferred to another employer, the contract was terminated. The new employer (purchaser of the business) could choose whom to employ and offer employment to those individuals, and the employees who were offered work could choose whether to accept or not. If they did, the offer and acceptance constituted an agreement which, along with other relevant factors, constituted a new contract between the two parties. In the absence of any legislation to the contrary, this position had developed at common law and existed until 1981, although the changes that were introduced into UK law in that year had their origins in European Community legislation dating back to 1977.[242] Under the

---

[239] regs 17 and 18.
[240] reg 15.
[241] s 8 and Sched 4, Pt II.
[242] Acquired Rights Directive 77/187/EEC.

UK's obligation to implement European law, the Transfer of Undertakings (Protection of Employment) Regulations 1981 ("TUPE") were introduced.

TRANSFER OF UNDERTAKINGS (PROTECTION OF EMPLOYMENT) REGULATIONS 1981 ("TUPE")[243]

A transfer of an undertaking occurs when a business or part of a business is sold (or **12–96** otherwise given) to another. Once the business is sold, the employees of the original owner (transferor) become the employees of the new owner (transferee). The Regulations apply to an employee described as "any individual who works for another person, whether under a contract of service or apprenticeship or otherwise".[244] This definition includes agency-supplied workers and casual workers. The purpose of legal intervention in this area is to protect the rights[245] of the existing employees during the transfer period. Regulation 5(2) states: "... on the completion of a relevant transfer—(a) all the transferor's rights, powers, duties and liabilities under or in connection with any such contract should be transferred by virtue of this regulation to the transferee." The question frequently posed by the resulting case law has been, "What constitutes a relevant transfer?"

Relevant transfers

The TUPE Regulations provide that "... these Regulations apply to a transfer from one **12–97** person to another of an undertaking situated immediately before the transfer in the UK or a part of one which is so situated."[246] Non-commercial ventures are included in this definition.[247] In order for the Regulations to apply, the business which is transferring must be an existing economic entity.[248] It is not necessary to establish a direct contractual link between the transferor and the transferee, so that a change in ownership of a franchise or in the holder of a lease may still constitute a relevant transfer.[249] A "contracting out" situation will not necessarily constitute a relevant transfer,[250] nor will transfers of shares or of assets only.[251] The main test to determine whether the Regulations will apply is to ask if the transfer is of an existing economic entity. If it is, and so will retain its identity on transfer, the Regulations will apply.[252]

Definition of "an undertaking"

Under the Regulations, an undertaking is defined as including any trade or **12–98** business.[253] TUPE will apply if only part of the undertaking is transferred, as long as the part that is transferred is a separate and self-contained part of the original business and the employee(s) concerned are employed in that part of the business. Problems

---

[243] SI 1981/1794
[244] reg 2(1).
[245] It should be noted that, under reg 7, occupational pension schemes are excluded from the protection of rights provided by TUPE.
[246] TUPE, reg 3 (1).
[247] *Dr Sophie Redmond Stichting* v *Bartol* [1992] IRLR 366.
[248] *Rask* v *Christensen ISS Kantinenservice* [1993] IRLR 133.
[249] *Foreningen af Arbejdsledere i Danmark* v *Daddy's Dance Hall A/S* [1988] IRLR 315.
[250] *Suzen* v *Zehnacker Gebaudereinigung* [1997] IRLR 255; *Betts* v *Brintel Helicopters* [1997] IRLR 361.
[251] *Premier Motors (Medway) Ltd* v *Total Oil GB Ltd* [1983] IRLR 471.
[252] *Spijkers* v *Gebroeders Benedik Abattoir CV* [1986] 3 ECR 1119.
[253] reg 3.

may arise if the employee works partly for a holding company and partly for a subsidiary company.[254]

Dismissal due to a relevant transfer

12–99   TUPE provides: "Where either before or after a relevant transfer, any employee of the transferor or transferee is dismissed, that employee shall be treated ... as unfairly dismissed if the transfer or any reason connected with it is the reason or principal reason for his dismissal."[255] In bringing an action for unfair dismissal, the dismissed employee's rights lie against the transferee not the transferor. This is the case even where the dismissal took place before the transfer, as the liability transfers with the business.[256]

The employer's defence to a claim of unfair dismissal on such grounds offered by the Regulations is that it arose due to an "economical, technical or organisational reason".[257] The onus will be on the employer to show that such a reason existed and formed the basis for the dismissal. It has been established that, in order to justify a dismissal, such a reason must be related to the conduct of the business.[258]

The reason for dismissal may be redundancy, in which case the employee would be entitled to a redundancy payment. The employer must still show that he acted reasonably, and must adhere to the relevant consultation and other procedural provisions relating to redundancy.[259]

Duty to inform and consult with appropriate representatives

12–100   This provision[260] originates from the corresponding duty to inform and consult prior to a collective redundancy situation.[261] Before any transfer takes place, the employer has a duty to consult with appropriate representatives during which time he should provide them with information about the proposed transfer and the relevant time-scale. The consultation must take place with a view to reaching an agreement. Failure to consult, which can not be justified as being due to special circumstances, may result in an award of compensation from an employment tribunal.

PROPOSED CHANGES TO THE LAW

12–101   The Acquired Rights Directive has recently been amended.[262] Member States have until July 2001 to implement the changes which include the following: contracting-out situations are to constitute relevant transfers; non-commercial organisations must be explicitly provided for under transfer legislation; Member States are to have the option of making specific provision for occupational pension rights to transfer alongside contracts of employment.

---

[254] Case 186/83, *Botzen* v *Rotterdamsche Droogdok Maatschappij BV* [1985] ECR 519; *Duncan Webb Offset (Maidstone) Ltd* v *Cooper* [1995] IRLR 633; *Sunley Turriff Holdings Ltd* v *Thomson* [1995] IRLR 184, (EAT).
[255] reg 7.
[256] *Allen* v *Stirling District Council* [1995] ICR 1082.
[257] reg 8(2).
[258] *Meikle* v *McPhail* [1983] IRLR 351.
[259] See paras 12–134 *et seq.*
[260] reg 10.
[261] Collective Redundancies and Transfer of Undertakings (Protection of Employment) (Amendment) Regulations 1995 (SI 1995/2587) See para 12–135.
[262] By Directive 98/50/EC.

TERMINATION OF THE CONTRACT

An employment contract will usually come to an end by employee resignation or   **12–102**
dismissal by the employer. Employee resignation generally occurs because the
individual wishes to take up employment with another employer, but there are
circumstances in which the resignation may be based on a claim that the employer's
behaviour has made it impossible for the contract to continue. In such circumstances,
the employee will claim that he has been constructively dismissed due to a breach of
the contract on the part of the employer. This type of claim amounts to a form of unfair
dismissal and will be considered below. Conversely, there are circumstances in which
the employer may claim that the employee has breached the contract and may,
therefore, be dismissed quite fairly. The type of behaviour and the possibility of
contributory behaviour by the other party will both be relevant factors in determining
whether or not the act complained of does, in fact, amount to a breach which is serious
enough to constitute termination of the employment contract. These issues are
important as those employed under contracts of employment enjoy certain rights in
relation to termination of the contract. There are three main types of claim that may
result from termination of an employment contract: wrongful dismissal, for which
there is a common law remedy, and unfair dismissal and redundancy, which offer
statutory remedies.

WRONGFUL DISMISSAL

Under the provisions of the common law, an employer can lawfully dismiss an   **12–103**
employee by giving him the correct amount of notice or payment in lieu of that notice.
Wrongful dismissal arises where the employment contract is terminated without any
notice or with an insufficient period of notice. In such circumstances, the employee can
make a claim of wrongful dismissal which, if found to be genuine, will result in the
employer being ordered to pay the sum owing in respect of the notice to which the
employee was entitled, as well as any other losses sustained by the employee as a
result of the dismissal.[263] This type of claim may be distinguished from a claim for
unfair dismissal (see below) which arises out of the relevant statutory provisions.[264]

In order to defend a claim of wrongful dismissal, the employer will have to show
that the termination was for a reason other than dismissal, such as employee resignation, or that it amounted to a summary dismissal and was, therefore, justified in the
circumstances.

SUMMARY DISMISSAL

In certain circumstances, the employer will be justified in dismissing the employee   **12–104**
without any notice under the provisions of the common law.[265] This will arise where
the employee has committed an act that amounts to gross misconduct and is,
therefore, in breach of contract. The behaviour which may amount to gross

---

[263] See *Malik v BCCI* [1997] 3 All ER 1.
[264] Contained in Part X of the Employment Rights Act 1996.
[265] *Pepper v Webb* [1969] 1 WLR 514; *Sinclair v Neighbour* [1967] 2 QB 279; *Denco v Joinson* [1991] IRLR 63.

misconduct will vary depending on the type of employment and each case must, therefore, be decided in the context of its own circumstances. Generally the employer's disciplinary procedure will set out the types of relevant behaviour. If an employee is dismissed and his actions do not amount to gross misconduct, he may make a claim for wrongful dismissal.[266]

UNFAIR DISMISSAL

12–105   As outlined above, at common law an employer can lawfully terminate a contract of employment by giving the required period of notice or payment in lieu. The only remedy available to the dismissed employee in such circumstances will be a claim for wrongful dismissal. The law on unfair dismissal attempts to improve the position of the employee in respect of termination by providing a statutory right only to be lawfully dismissed if that dismissal can be shown to be fair. The right to claim unfair dismissal has been in existence since 1972[267] and the relevant statutory provisions can now be found in the Employment Rights Act 1996 ("ERA"),[268] section 94 of which provides an employee with the right not to be unfairly dismissed.

Scope of the rights on unfair dismissal

12–106   Those employed under contracts of employment will be protected, subject to a period of one year's continuous service.[269] Certain groups of employees are excluded from the scope of the legislation, including those who ordinarily work outside Great Britain, those who have reached retirement age and those employed in the police service.[270] Specific provisions apply to those in Crown employment[271] and in the armed forces.[272]

Definition of dismissal

12–107   Before a claim for unfair dismissal can be made, it is necessary to establish that a dismissal has actually taken place. Misunderstandings relating to the course of events often arise in cases where the employment contract has been terminated. For this reason it is important to distinguish an actual dismissal from an employee resignation[273] or a breakdown in communications.[274]

Under the provisions of the ERA, dismissal can arise in four different ways. Section 95 (1) of the ERA defines three of these. First, the employer may terminate the contract with or without notice. Second, a contract which is for a fixed term expires without being renewed. In such circumstances, it may be necessary for the employer to show that the contract has genuinely come to an end and that failure to renew it was not merely an attempt to avoid statutory obligations.[275] For this reason, it has become increasingly common for employers to insert waiver clauses in fixed term contracts, by

---

[266] *Laws* v *London Chronicle* [1959] 1 WLR 698.
[267] Originally introduced by the Industrial Relations Act 1971, now repealed.
[268] ss 94–107.
[269] Unfair Dismissal and Reasons for Dismissal (Variation of Qualifying Period) Order 1999 (SI 1999/1436).
[270] ERA 1996, s 196 provides a list of excluded classes of employees.
[271] *ibid* s 191.
[272] *ibid* s 192.
[273] *Elliot* v *Waldair (Construction) Ltd* [1975] IRLR 104.
[274] *Futty* v *D and D Brekkes Ltd* [1974] IRLR 130.
[275] *Terry* v *East Sussex County Council* [1977] 1 All ER 567.

which employees agree to contract out of their right to claim unfair dismissal on termination. However, this practice has recently been outlawed.[276] Third, the employee may terminate the contract (with or without notice) due to the employer's conduct. This is known as constructive dismissal and will only apply in the case of a significant breach which goes to the root of the contract.[277] Alleged breaches of implied terms have been advanced as the bases for claims of constructive dismissal with varying degrees of success.[278] The fourth method of dismissal is provided by section 96, which states that a failure to permit a woman to return to work following childbirth will be treated as a dismissal under the provisions of the Act. This is referred to as "deemed dismissal" and the qualifying period of one year's continuous service will not apply to this type of dismissal.

Fair or unfair dismissal?

Once it has been established that a dismissal has taken place, it is necessary to determine whether the dismissal was fair or unfair.   **12–108**

Automatically unfair reasons

There are certain situations in which it will be automatically unfair to dismiss an employee.   **12–109**

Discrimination

Dismissal on the grounds of a person's race, sex or disability will amount to unfair dismissal.   **12–110**

Pregnancy or childbirth

Section 99 of the ERA 1996 provides that a woman dismissed due to her pregnancy or any reason connected with it will be found to be unfairly dismissed.   **12–111**

Trade union membership/non-membership

Participation in or refusal to participate in trade union activities at an appropriate time will amount to unfair dismissal under section 152 of the Trade Union and Labour Relations (Consolidation) Act 1992.   **12–112**

For the assertion of a statutory right

Where an employee is dismissed for bringing proceedings to assert a statutory right or alleging in good faith that the employer has infringed such a right, this will amount to unfair dismissal.   **12–113**

---

[276] As of October 1999, by virtue of the Employment Relations Act 1999 (Commencement No 2 and Transitional and Savings Provisions) Order 1999, (SI 1999/2930).
[277] *Western Excavating (ECC) Ltd* v *Sharp* [1978] IRLR 27 (CA).
[278] *British Aircraft Corporation* v *Austin* [1978] IRLR 332; *Dryden* v *Greater Glasgow Health Board* [1992] IRLR 469.

Health and safety reasons

12–114   Section 100 of the ERA 1996 states that it is automatically unfair to dismiss an employee for any reason relating to health and safety.

Disclosure under the Public Interest Disclosure Act 1998

12–115   Under this Act, those making disclosure of certain types of information related to their employment are protected against dismissal as long as such disclosure is made in the way(s) specified by the Act.

Potentially fair reasons for dismissal

12–116   Of course there are certain circumstances in which the employer will be entitled to legally dismiss an employee. Section 98 of the ERA 1996 sets out five reasons for dismissal which amount to potentially fair reasons (below): this list is not intended to be exhaustive and, in practice, there have been many other reasons for dismissal which have been held to be fair.

Capability or qualifications of the employee

12–117   If an employee is dismissed due to his inability to perform his job properly, such a dismissal will be deemed to be fair so long as the correct procedure has been followed. The employer must have behaved reasonably in all the circumstances and this will include ensuring that the employee has received adequate instructions[279] and offering the employee the opportunity to improve his performance.

Conduct of the employee

12–118   The conduct of the employee may amount to a fair reason on which to base a dismissal if it amounts to gross misconduct.[280] The employee's conduct may give rise to dismissal due to one event or a series of events.

Redundancy

12–119   A dismissal which is genuinely for reason of redundancy will be held to be fair if the correct procedure has been followed.[281]

Contravention of a statutory duty

12–120   If the employee's continuing employment would be in contravention of the law, then a dismissal on such grounds will be potentially fair. For example, disqualification

---

[279] *Davison v Kent Meters Ltd* [1975] IRLR 175.
[280] See para 12–104.
[281] *Williams v Compair Maxam Ltd* [1982] IRLR 83. See para 12–134.

from driving may justify dismissal if driving constituted a substantial element of the job.

Some other substantial reason

This is a catch-all provision and there is no exhaustive list of reasons that will **12–121** constitute "some other substantial reason". Employers seeking to justify dismissals arising from a business reorganisation, which do not constitute redundancy, will often attempt to claim a fair reason under this provision.

It is important to note that the reasons set out above are merely *potentially* fair reasons. Even where the employer can show that the reason for dismissal is genuinely based on one of the above, the fairness of the dismissal will still remain to be determined based on the procedure followed and the other circumstances relevant to the particular case. The question that the tribunal will ask is, "Did the employer act reasonably in treating the reason as sufficient grounds for dismissing the employee?"

As regards procedure, the employer will have to show that he has conducted a thorough investigation and held a disciplinary hearing (with the opportunity for appeal) before dismissing the employee. Particular attention should be paid to such factors as the use of warnings, consideration of alternative courses of action, custom and practice, and the employee's previous work record.

ACAS Code of Practice

ACAS have published a Code of Practice on Disciplinary Practice and Procedures in **12–122** Employment which recommends, *inter alia*, that three warnings should be given before a dismissal in all cases except where an act of gross misconduct has occurred. Although not legally binding, as with all approved Codes of Practice, the ACAS Code may be considered by the tribunal and failure to follow the advice therein taken into account in reaching its decision.

Procedure in cases of unfair dismissal

The procedure in such cases follows a specific order and the burden of proof shifts **12–123** from one party to the other.

(a) The employee shows that he was dismissed.

(b) If the reason for dismissal was one of the automatically unfair reasons, a case of unfair dismissal has been made out. If not—

(c) The employer must prove that the reason for dismissal was one of the "five potentially fair reasons" (see above).

(d) The Tribunal will then decide, on the basis of evidence presented, whether or not the employer acted reasonably[282] in treating that reason as sufficient grounds for dismissal.

---

[282] See ERA 1996, s 98(4) for "range of reasonable responses" and *Iceland Frozen Foods* v *Jones* [1982] IRLR 439.

(e) Failure to prove that the reason was one of the "five potentially fair reasons" will amount to unfair dismissal.[283]

Remedies for unfair dismissal

12–124 There are three remedies available to tribunals in unfair dismissal cases: reinstatement, re-engagement and compensation. Orders for reinstatement or re-engagement are often accompanied by an award of compensation.

Order for reinstatement[284]

12–125 Such an order must be made by agreement with the employee. The employee will be reinstated in his job and must be treated, in all respects, as if no dismissal has taken place. This means that all the usual terms and conditions, including accrued benefits, will apply. If an employer unreasonably refuses to reinstate an employee, the tribunal may make an additional award of compensation.

Order for re-engagement[285]

12–126 Under this order, the employee will be re-engaged in employment comparable to that from which he was dismissed. When considering whether to make such an order, the tribunal must take account of the wishes of the applicant, whether re-engagement is practicable in the circumstances, and whether the applicant caused or contributed to his dismissal. If the employer unreasonably refuses to carry out an order for re-engagement, the tribunal may make an additional award of compensation.

Compensation[286]

12–127 Compensation may be made if the terms of the above orders are not complied with or if either order is made but not carried out, or as an alternative. There are three types of compensation that may be awarded, consisting of: the basic award; the additional award; and the compensatory award.

The basic award

12–128 The award is calculated on the basis of age and length of service subject to a maximum of £6,900.

The additional award

12–129 The amount awarded will be between 26 and 52 weeks' pay, subject to a maximum of £11,960.

---

[283] *Raynor* v *Remploy Ltd* [1973] IRLR 3; *Whitaker* v *Milk Marketing Board* [1973] IRLR 300.
[284] ERA 1996, s 113.
[285] ERA 1996, s 115.
[286] ERA 1996, ss 117–125.

The compensatory award

This award is intended to compensate the employee for his loss, subject to a maximum of £50,000. **12–130**

REDUNDANCY

A statutory redundancy scheme was introduced in 1965[287] and the current provisions are now to be found in the Employment Rights Act 1996.[288] Under section 135, a redundancy payment will be due when an employee is dismissed by reason of redundancy. The purpose of the redundancy is to compensate the employee for the loss of employment. It is, effectively, a reward for past service.[289] **12–131**

Eligibility for redundancy payment

The qualifying period for a redundancy payment is two years.[290] Excluded classes of employees include those who have reached normal retirement age and those who ordinarily work outside the UK.[291] **12–132**

Dismissal for reason of redundancy

Section 139 of the Employment Rights Act 1996 provides that redundancy occurs in the following circumstances: (a) the employer ceases or intends to cease carrying on the business for the purposes of which the employee was employed[292]; (b) the employer ceases or intends to cease carrying on that business at the place where the employee was so employed[293]; or (c) the requirements of the business relevant to the employment have ceased or diminished.[294] It can be seen, therefore, that a redundancy will arise where the job, for some reason or another, has ceased to exist. The employee will only be eligible to receive a redundancy payment if he can show that his dismissal was for one of these reasons. **12–133**

Fair procedure

Even where the dismissal does fall within one of the reasons outlined above, it may be found to amount to an unfair dismissal rather than a redundancy if the procedure followed by the employer is found to be unfair. It is a requirement that the employer can show that there was no alternative course of action available and that redundancy has been implemented as a last resort. The Employment Rights Act 1996 lays down certain requirements relating to procedure in cases of redundancy and the Trade Union and Labour Relations (Consolidation) Act 1992[295]governs the procedure applicable in case of collective redundancy. **12–134**

---

[287] By the Redundancy Payments Act 1965, now repealed.
[288] Part II.
[289] *Mairs (Inspector of Taxes)* v *Haughey* [1993] IRLR 551.
[290] ERA 1996, s 155.
[291] *ibid* s 196(6).
[292] *Gemmell* v *Darngavil Brickworks Ltd* [1967] 2 ITR 20.
[293] *Bass Leisure Ltd* v *Thomas* [1994] IRLR 104.
[294] *Carry All Motors Ltd* v *Pennington* [1980] IRLR 455; *Johnson* v *Nottinghamshire Combined Police Authority* [1974] 1 WLR 358.
[295] ss 188–192.

Consultation

12–135 The Trade Union and Labour Relations (Consolidation) Act 1992[296] provides for consultation in cases of collective redundancy which arise where the employer is proposing to dismiss as redundant 20 or more employees within a period of 90 days or less. In such circumstances, the employer shall consult with an appropriate representative in good time in order to discuss ways of avoiding the redundancy or avoiding its effect.

Fair selection criteria

12–136 Although it is the job that has become redundant, not the individual filling it, in practice it is often necessary to select employees for redundancy as some of the particular workforce will be retained. In observing the correct procedure in such cases, it is important that the employer selects the employees to be made redundant in an objective and fair manner. Selection on the grounds of any of the "automatically unfair reasons"[297] for dismissal will amount to unfair dismissal[298] not redundancy.

Redundancy payments

12–137 The calculation of a redundancy payment is based on age and length of service at the time of dismissal. For every year of employment over the age of 41, the employee will be entitled to one and a half weeks' pay; for every year in which he was aged over 22, he will be entitled to one weeks' pay; for every year of employment he was aged over 18 but under 22, he will be entitled to half a weeks' pay. Employment under the age of 18 does not count.

---

[296] As amended by the Collective Redundancies and Transfer of Undertakings (Protection of Employment) Regulations 1999 (SI 1999/1925).
[297] See paras 12–109 *et seq.*
[298] ERA 1996, s 105.

SUMMARY

OVERVIEW

- Although the employment relationship is essentially one of contract, there are specific statutory and common law provisions that regulate contracts of employment.

THE CONTRACT OF EMPLOYMENT

- There are several common law tests that have been developed by the courts for the purposes of identifying the existence of a contract of employment, the most recent of which is the multiple test.
- The terms of an employment contract may be express or implied.
- Express terms will be included in the written statement of terms and conditions required by section 1 of the Employment Rights Act 1996.
- Implied terms may be implied by statute or "read into" contracts by the courts.
- The terms and conditions of an employment contract cannot generally be varied unilaterally but will require the agreement of both parties.

THE REGULATION OF WAGES

- It is generally unlawful for an employer to make deductions from a worker's wages unless authorised by a statutory or contractual provision or by the worker's written consent.
- The National Minimum Wage Act 1998 introduced a right to be paid at or above a specified rate.
- The Working Time Regulations 1998 contain provisions governing working hours, night work, patterns of work, rest periods and breaks, and annual leave.

DISCRIMINATION IN EMPLOYMENT

- There are three forms of discrimination that are prohibited by statute: sex discrimination, race discrimination and disability discrimination.
- The provisions of the Sex Discrimination Act 1975 and the Race Relations Act 1976 are similarly drafted, although there are differences in their interpretation due to the influence of European Community law over sex discrimination.
- Direct discrimination on the grounds of sex, race or disability arises due to "less favourable" treatment and so requires a comparative approach to be taken.
- Indirect discrimination on the grounds of sex or race arises due to the application of a requirement or condition which has a disproportionate detrimental impact on the members of one sex or racial grouping and which cannot be justified by the employer.
- There are certain specified circumstances in which an employer may discriminate lawfully by favouring someone of a particular sex or racial grouping. This will arise where sex or race is deemed to be a genuine occupational qualification.

- Harassment on the grounds of sex or race may amount to unlawful direct discrimination under the legislation.
- There are Codes of Practice in operation with respect to both sex and race discrimination which may be used as evidence in tribunal hearings.
- The Disability Discrimination Act 1995 ("DDA") prohibits direct discrimination on the grounds of disability and imposes a duty on employers to make reasonable adjustments to premises and working arrangements in certain circumstances.
- The DDA uses a specific definition of "disability" which continues to be interpreted by associated guidance and case law.
- Enforcement of the discrimination legislation is by application to employment tribunals and three potential remedies are available: declarations, recommendations and compensation.

EQUAL PAY

- The provision of equal pay between the sexes is regulated by the Equal Pay Act 1970 which continues to be interpreted by reference to European law.
- The Equal Pay Act 1970 inserts an equality clause into every contract of employment which provides the right to receive equal pay with a comparator of the opposite sex in specified circumstances.
- There are three types of claim that can be made under the provisions of the Equal Pay Act 1970 which must be based on "like work", "work rated as equivalent" or work of equal value.
- In order successfully to defend a claim of equal pay, an employer must show that the difference in pay rates is due to a "genuine material difference" between the case of the claimant and the comparator.
- There is a Code of Practice on equal pay which is admissible before employment tribunals.

MATERNITY RIGHTS AND PARENTAL LEAVE

- The system of maternity rights in the UK provides specific rights for pregnant workers, some of which apply universally, whereas others are dependent on qualifying periods of continuous employment.
- There are two types of maternity leave: ordinary and additional.
- Ordinary maternity leave of 18 weeks is available to all female workers regardless of length of service.
- Additional maternity leave is available to those who have completed one year's continuous service and lasts up to the twenty-ninth week following childbirth.
- Dismissal for any reason related to pregnancy or childbirth will automatically be unfair.
- Statutory maternity pay is available for 18 weeks to employees who satisfy certain requirements linked to duration of employment and earnings.
- The right to take unpaid parental leave for up to 13 weeks in respect of each child under the age of five has recently been introduced in the UK.

TRANSFER OF UNDERTAKINGS

- The Transfer of Undertakings (Protection of Employment) Regulations 1981 (TUPE) protect the rights of employees during the transfer of a business.
- Providing the transfer is covered by the TUPE Regulations, the contracts of employment and all related benefits, except occupational pension rights, will transfer to the new owner of the undertaking.
- A dismissal based on the transfer of an undertaking will amount to an unfair dismissal unless the employer can show that it was necessary due to an "economical, technical or organisational" reason.

TERMINATION OF CONTRACT

- Termination of the employment contract may arise due to employee resignation or employer dismissal.
- Summary dismissal (which is dismissal without notice) may be justified where the behaviour of an employee amounts to gross misconduct.
- There are three main types of claim that may result from termination of an employment contract: wrongful dismissal, unfair dismissal and redundancy.
- Wrongful dismissal is a common law claim which arises where the contract is terminated with insufficient notice causing a breach of the terms of the contract.
- The remedy for wrongful dismissal will be the payment of compensation.
- Those who work under contracts of employment have a statutory right not to be unfairly dismissed.
- The Employment Rights Act 1996 provides specific definition as to what constitutes a dismissal.
- There are certain situations in which it will be automatically unfair to dismiss an employee. These are for a reason related to discrimination, pregnancy or child-birth, trade union membership, the assertion of a statutory right, a health and safety reason or due to a disclosure made under the provisions of the Public Interest Disclosure Act 1998.
- Section 98 of the Employment Rights Act 1996 provides five potentially fair reasons for dismissal.
- There is an ACAS Code of Practice on disciplinary practice and procedure, the provisions of which may be considered by an employment tribunal.
- There are three remedies available to tribunals in cases of unfair dismissal: an order for reinstatement or re-engagement or compensation.
- The statutory scheme governing redundancy payments is contained in the Employment Rights Act 1996.
- Section 139 of the ERA 1996 provides that redundancy occurs where a job or work of a particular type ceases to exist.
- In order to avoid claims for unfair dismissal, it is important that employers observe fair procedures when dealing with potential cases of redundancy.
- The redundancy payment is based on the employee's age and length of service at the date of dismissal.

CASE DIGEST

The test of control [see para 12–05]
  Yewens v Noakes (1880) 6 QBD
The greater the degree of control exerted by the "master" over the way in which the "servant" performs the job, the more likely that the relationship is one of employment.

The test of integration [see para 12–07]
  Stevenson, Jordon and Harrison Ltd v MacDonald and Evans (1952) 1 TLR 101
An individual whose work is done as an integral part of a business is deemed to be an employee of that business.

The multiple test [see para 12–08]
  Ready Mixed Concrete (South East Ltd) v Minister of Pensions (1968) 2 QB 497
The correct approach for identifying the status of a working relationship is to consider a range of factors relevant to the relationship. If the evidence reveals the existence of an employment contract or if such consideration indicates the presence of a determining factor, the worker concerned will be deemed to be an employee.

The written statement of terms and conditions of employment [see para 12–17]
  System Floors (UK) Ltd v Daniel (1982) ICR 54
A written statement does not constitute a written contract of employment but does provide strong evidence of the terms of such a contract where it exists.

Restrictive covenants [see para 12–18]
  Spafax Ltd v Harrison (1980) IRLR 442
The court will uphold the terms of a restrictive covenant if they are found to be reasonable and in the public interest.

Implied terms—existence and scope will vary depending on the duty implied and the nature of employment [see paras 12–19]
  Johnstone v Bloomsbury Health Authority (1991) IRLR 118
The employer's duty to take reasonable care for the health and safety of his employees is implied into all contracts of employment

  Faccenda Chicken Ltd v Fowler (1986) IRLR 69
The existence and extent of the employee's duty of confidentiality will depend on the nature of employment and the information involved.

Direct sex and race discrimination [see paras 12–50 and 12–51]
  Hurley v Mustoe (1981) ICR 490
An employer discriminates against a woman if, on the grounds of her sex or marital status, he treats her less favourably than he treats or would treat a man. This is the definition of direct discrimination, which also applies in race cases where the less favourable treatment will be on the grounds of a person's colour, race, nationality or ethnic or national origins.

Webb v *EMO Air Cargo (UK) Ltd* (1993) IRLR 27 (HL
Less favourable treatment on the grounds of pregnancy or childbirth can only be
experienced by a woman and, therefore, constitutes direct discrimination.

Mandla v *Dowell Lee* (1983) IRLR 209 (HL)
For the purposes of applying the Race Relations Act 1976, it is necessary to interpret
the term "ethnic" widely. In order to constitute an ethnic group under the
provisions of the Act, such a group must regard itself as a distinct community with
a long shared history and a specific cultural tradition.

Indirect discrimination [see para 12–52]
Meer v *London Borough of Tower Hamlets* (1988) IRLR 399 (CA)
Indirect discrimination arises from covert discrimination in that its effects may not
necessarily be immediately apparent. The requirement or condition complained of
will require further investigation in order to assess its impact on groups of men or
women or diferent racial groups.

Bilka-Kaufhaus GmbH v *Weber Von Hartz* (1986) ECR 1607
The emnployer is able to defend an act of indirect discrimination on the grounds
that the requirement or condition is gener or racially neutral and has been applied
objectively. Circumstances such as the needs of the employer will be considered in
deciding whether the discriminatory act can be justified.

Genuine occupational qualifications [see para 12–54]
Etam plc v *Rowan* (1989) IRLR 150
Where sex or race is deemed to be an essential requirement for the job, the
provisions of the Sex Discrimination Act 1975 or the Race Relations Act 1976 can be
disapplied providing that the reason for the exclusion is genuine.

Equal pay [see paras 12–70, 12–74, 12–75, 12–77, 12–78]
Hayward v *Cammell Laird Shipbuilders Ltd* (1988) AC 894 (HL)
For the purposes of determining what constitutes "pay" under the provisions of the
Equal Pay Act 1970, it is necessary to consider each of the terms of a contract separ-
ately not as a package.

Capper Pass v *Lawton* (1977) ICR 83
An equality clause providing the right to equal pay will be applied where the
claimant is employed on "like work" with her comparator under s 1(2)(a) of the
Equal Pay Act 1970. This work need not be identical but may be "broadly similar"
to that performed by the comparator.

Eaton v *Nuttall* (1977) ICR 272
In order for a job evaluation scheme to be suitable for the purposes of s 1(2)(b) of
the Equal Pay Act 1970, it must must consider all matters connected with the nature
of the work such as effort, skill and responsibilities.

Hayward v *Cammell Laird Shipbuilders Ltd* (1988) AC 894 (HL)

In deciding on the relative values ascribed to different jobs for the purpose of assessing an equal value claim under s 1(2) (c) of the Equal Pay Act 1970, the demands made upon the employee with regard to effort, skill and decision making must be considered.

Jenkins v *Kingsgate (Clothing Productions) Ltd* (1981) ICR 592

Under s 1 (3) of the Equal Pay Act 1970, an employer is able to defend a claim for equal pay on the basis that a genuine material difference exists. In order to be successful, such justification must be based on some non-discriminatory objective.

Maternity rights [see para 12–80]

Brown v *Rentokil Ltd* (1998) IRLR 445

The protected period during which dismissal for any reason related to pregnancy or child-birth will amount to unfair dismissal lasts from the start of the pregnancy until the end of the maternity leave period.

Transfer of undertakings [see para 12–95]

Rask v *Christensen ISS Kantinenservice* (1993) IRLR 133

In order for the TUPE Regulations to apply, the business which is transferring must be an existing economic entity.

Summary dismissal [see para 12–104]

Pepper v *Webb* (1969) 1 WLR 514

Where the employee has committed an act which amounts to gross misconduct, an employer will be justified in dismissing the individual without any notice under the provisions of the common law.

Unfair dismissal [see paras 12–105, 12–107, 12–119]

Elliott v *Waldair (Construction) Ltd* (1975) IRLR 104

In order to claim protection under the statutory provisions relating to unfair dismissal, it is necessary to ascertain that a dismissal (as distinct from an employee resignation) has taken place.

Western Excavating (ECC) Ltd v *Sharp* (1978) IRLR 27 (CA)

In order for an employee termination to amount to a constructive dismissal, the breach of contract committed by the employer must be significant and go right to the root of the contract.

Williams v *Compair Maxam Ltd* (1982) IRLR 83

A dismissal which is for reason of redundancy will be held to be fair only if the correct procedure has been followed.

Redundancy [see paras 12–131, 12–133]
Gemmell v *Darngavil Brickworks Ltd* (1967) 2 ITR 20
A temporary cessation of business will constitute suitable grounds for redundancy within the meaning of s 139 of the Employment Rights Act 1996.

Bass Leisure Ltd v *Thomas* (1994) IRLR 104
When identifying an employee's place of work for the purposes of applying s 139 of the Employment Rights Act 1996, the actual place of work, not the contractual place of work that should be considered.

Carry All Motors Ltd v *Pennington* (1980) IRLR 455
A situation where the employer requires fewer employees to carry out existing work will constitute a cessation or dimunition of the relevant requirements of the business for the purposes of defining a redundnacy situation within the meaning of s 139 of the Employment Rights Act 1996.

FURTHER READING

Bercusson, *European Labour Law* (2nd edn, Butterworths, 2000)
Mackay and Simon, *Employment Law* (W Green, 1998)
Painter, Holmes, and Migdal, *Cases and Materials on Employment Law* (3rd edn, Blackstones, 2000)
Pitt, *Employment Law* (4th edn, Sweet & Maxwell, 2000)
Selwyn, *Selwyn's Law of Employment* (12th edn, Butterworths, 2000)
Smith, & Wood, *Industrial Law* (7th edn, Butterworths, 1999)

13 CHILD AND FAMILY LAW

THE CHILD, LEGAL PERSONALITY AND CAPACITY

As a basic proposition of law, legal personality begins at birth.[1] However, like many **13–01** statements in law, the basic proposition does not convey the full extent of the law relating to legal status and personality. There are some explicit legal exceptions to the rule. Specifically, the unborn child is regarded as having legal capacity in relation to rights in succession and rights in delict. However, the enforcement and application of these matters can only take place subsequently, after the child has been born alive. Accordingly, it is the basic rule of law that the unborn child who is not referred to in the will of a deceased parent will be deemed to have similar rights to any other child where that person decrees in their will that the legacy is for his "children". It also the case that a child *in utero* (in the womb) can sue for damages under the law of delict for the negligence or intentional conduct of a third party that results in the death of his parent. Again this right would be activated if the child was subsequently born alive albeit that the delict took place while the child was in the womb. Parents may sue in circumstances where a third party injures a child while *in utero* again as long as the child is subsequently born alive. The child naturally has similar rights of action against a third party in respect of injury sustained by the child while in the womb. This extends to the ability of the child once born to sue his parent for negligence or wrongful conduct. The "wrongful" conception and delivery of a child (even a healthy one) may itself give rise to a delictual action where birth arises following failed sterilisation and negligent advice as to the safety of sexual relations. However, there will be no right to recover the cost of the upbringing of a child in respect of wrongful life; although compensation may be obtained for the pain and suffering arising from the resultant pregnancy.[2]

---

[1] One may suppose that the illegality of procuring an abortion (unless in conformity with the Abortion Act 1967) presupposed an implication that the foetus had a right to life and that as a consequence one could assume that, in this respect at least, the concept of personality and status commences at conception. However, it has been stated in a modern case that in respect of the foetus there is no presumed right to life. See *Kelly* v *Kelly* 1997 SC 285.

[2] *McFarlane* v *Tayside Health Board* 2000 SLT 154; Thomson, "Delictual Liability of State Agencies—Further Confusion?' 1999 SLT (News) 245; Thomson, "Abandoning the Law of Delict?" 2000 SLT (News) 43.

Although the law is reasonably clear as to when legal personality commences, the issue of the child's capacity is somewhat more complicated. Capacity is a broad concept, embracing not only rights but also responsibilities. Capacity may be thought to be an evolutionary matter; at certain stages in the child's life his capacity expands.

THE AGE OF LEGAL CAPACITY (SCOTLAND) ACT 1991

13–02   The Age of Legal Capacity (Scotland) 1991 Act states that a person under the age of 16 years shall have no legal capacity to enter into any transaction. The Act goes on to state that a person 16 years or over shall have full legal capacity to enter into any legal transaction.[3] There is an exception to the rule that under-16 year olds have no contractual capacity in that such a person does have capacity to enter into a transaction of a kind commonly entered into by a person of his age and circumstances and on terms which are not unreasonable. As noted elsewhere, children aged 12 and over have the capacity to make a will[4] and to consent to adoption or freeing for adoption.[5] Moreover, a person under the age of 16 years has the legal capacity to consent on his own behalf to any surgical, medical or dental procedure or treatment where, in the opinion of a qualified medical practitioner attending him, he is capable of understanding the nature and possible consequences of the procedure or treatment.[6]

A person under the age of 21 years may make an application to the court to set aside any transaction which he entered into while he was of, or over, the age of 16, but under the age of 18, and which is a prejudicial transaction.[7] There is scope for a court to approve of any transaction involving a person between 16 and 18 years old, which will preclude subsequent challenge in the court. Transactions entered into in respect of a young person's trade, business, or profession cannot be challenged.

THE CHILD AND THE LEGAL PROCESS

13–03   A person under the age of 16 has legal capacity to instruct a solicitor in connection with any civil matter where that person has an understanding of what it means to do so.[8] A person of 12 years of age or more is presumed to be of sufficient age and maturity to have such understanding. As well as having the right to consult a solicitor, a child also has the right as a legal person to initiate, pursue and defend proceedings. A child may apply and qualify for legal aid.

A child may not only be involved in litigation or court proceedings as a principal participant, but may also be the subject of the dispute or appear as a witness. In respect of family actions which involve a child-related matter, a child who is thought competent has the basic right to express a view and to have that view taken into account.[9] Children are competent witnesses in legal proceedings and there is one recorded instance where a child as young as three gave evidence in

---

[3]   Age of Legal Capacity (Scotland) Act 1991, s 1(1).
[4]   See para 13–03.
[5]   See para 13–16.
[6]   Age of Legal Capacity (Scotland) Act 1991, s 2(4); cf *Gillick v West Norfolk and Wisbech Area Health Authority* [1985] 3 All ER 402.
[7]   Age of Legal Capacity (Scotland) Act 1991, s 3.
[8]   *ibid* s 2(4A).
[9]   Children (Scotland) Act 1995, s 11(7).

court.[10] Children over the age of 14 usually take the oath like any other adult witness. Children under that age are likely to undergo a competency exam at the behest of the presiding judge, who will seek to ensure that they understand the difference between right and wrong, truth and lies, and are in other respects competent to give evidence. Special arrangements are often made for taking the child's evidence, including video recording, screening and video linking to the courtroom.[11] Such steps are pertinent in respect of children who are victims of sexual or physical abuse or of very young children who may be intimidated by the court environment.

CHILDREN'S RIGHTS, RESPONSIBILITIES, RESTRICTIONS AND PROTECTIONS

Historically, the law has treated children as less than full legal citizens. Throughout **13–04** much of that time, it has exhibited "paternalism" towards children, offering various protections and restrictions of their activities. In the period from the late 1980s, largely at the prompting of the United Nations Convention on the Rights of the Child but also because of a number of major and important developments, the child has emerged as an altogether more significant legal actor.[12] As well as having important rights, it is perhaps inevitable that, as a consequence, children also have a number of responsibilities. Responsibilities seem likely to grow as the move towards full legal citizenship gathers momentum.

CHILDREN'S RIGHTS

The child's rights can be grouped under three broad headings: **13–05**

- the right to financial support
- succession rights
- delictual rights.

Right to financial support

Until 1991 and the advent of child support, the main method by which absent parents **13–06** financially supported a child was through aliment. Notwithstanding the new system of child support, aliment may be sought in a number of circumstances. It remains pertinent particularly for those children who reside with both parents or those who are undergoing further education or training and are over 18 years of age and not covered by child support.[13] The payment of aliment is regulated by the Family Law (Scotland) Act 1985. As part of their obligation to nurture and care for the child through to

---

[10] *HMA v Miller* (1870) 1 Coup 430.
[11] See Field and Raitt, *Evidence* (2nd edn, 1996), pp 233–236.
[12] See Tisdall, *The Children (Scotland) Act: Developing Policy and Law for Scotland's Children* (1997), pp 1–47.
[13] For a recent example of aliment see *Kuzub v Kuzub* 1999 SCLR 902.

adulthood, parents may have a duty to aliment a child by providing such financial support as is reasonable for his upkeep. Aliment may also be payable by a person who has accepted a child as a member of his or her family.[14] In determining the amount of aliment payable, the courts shall have regard to the needs and resources of the party, the earning capacity of the party and all other circumstances of the case.[15] Other provisions relating to aliment are similar to those pertaining in respect of aliment between husband and wife.[16]

The system of child support, introduced under the Child Support Act 1991, has proved rather controversial. It was a system designed largely to ensure that absent parents maintained financial responsibility for their children and that the burden of their upbringing did not fall unduly upon the state. The system operates under the auspices of the Child Support Agency, who may carry out an assessment of an absent parent's liability for child support based on a complicated formula. Although there may be private ordering (agreements between parents) of financial arrangements in respect of a child, the Child Support Act 1991 overrides this. Even where a voluntary agreement has been made, it may subsequently be displaced by a child support assessment. This may occur where there is a mandatory assessment activated by the fact that the parent with whom the child resides is claiming state benefits, or indeed a voluntary assessment requested by the absent parent, the parent with residence, or the child himself. The 1991 Act applies to a child under the age of 16 or a child who is in full-time education (but not tertiary education) under the age of 19 or under 18 and available for work or youth training. An absent parent will have his level of child support contribution assessed using the formula. Decisions are made by child support officers of the Child Support Agency. There is concern that their calculations have not always been accurate. A review may be undertaken either through the agency or by an appeal to a Child Support Appeal Tribunal and from there to a Child Support Commissioner. Further appeal may be had to the Inner House of the Court of Session on a point of law.

When a calculation has been made as to appropriate payments, the Child Support Agency enforces the order. The Agency has at its disposal two types of order to secure payment: a deduction from earnings order whereby payments due by the absent parent may be deducted at source from that person's wages and paid directly to the Child Support Agency; alternatively, if the absent parent is not in regular employment, a "liability order" may be sought which may be enforced in addition to other normal types of diligence.[17] Ultimately, the wilful failure to pay any sum due may result in civil imprisonment. The child support will be paid to the parent with whom the child resides.

Succession rights of the child

13-07   Children have important rights in succession in Scots law. Principal amongst those rights is the common law right to *legitim* (or legal rights). Under this, any child or children have the right where there is a surviving spouse of up to one-third of the deceased parent's moveable estate to be placed in a legal fund from which they may inherit. Where there is more than one child, they will share equally in that legal fund.

---

[14]   Family Law (Scotland) Act 1985, s 1(1)(d); *Inglis* v *Inglis* 1987 SCLR 608.
[15]   Family Law (Scotland) Act 1985, s 4(1).
[16]   Discussed at para 13–48.
[17]   On the meaning and types of diligence see Chapter 8.

Where there is no surviving spouse one-half of the deceased parents' moveable estate will be set aside in a legal fund.

In circumstances where the parent has left a will and that will contains a legacy for the child, the child will require to elect whether to claim the legacy or a share of the legal fund. It is possible for deductions to be made from a child's share where he has had an advance in his lifetime. Legal rights may therefore be rejected on the basis that the child has accepted the terms of the will or indeed has renounced the right to claim legal rights during the lifetime of the now deceased parent. There is no age restriction on the definition of child in the context of legal rights. Where there is no will a child will also have legal rights in succession but these must be considered in the context of any surviving spouse's prior rights.[18]

Rights in delict

As noted earlier, a child has the juristic capacity to pursue a delictual action either in **13–08** respect of any injury or wrong occasioned to himself (including injury or wrong by his own parent) and in respect of any delict by a third party which results in death or injury of his parent. As a simple proposition of law, where a third party wrongfully injures or kills the parent of the child, that child will have a right to seek compensation. Any other surviving parent may pursue that right on behalf of the child. The child can sue the third party for damage or injury to his or her father even though that person is not married to the mother of the child. The child will be able to claim for "loss of support" and "loss of other non-patrimonial benefits".

It is commonplace for actions entailing intentional or negligent injury occasioned to the child by his or her parent to arise in respect of road traffic incidents. However, a compensation claim may also be possible where a child sustains damage arising from culpable behaviour on the part of the parents such as the ingestion of drugs or alcohol or smoking during pregnancy.

Miscellaneous rights of the child

A child has the right to make a will at the age of 12,[19] and the right to consent to or veto **13–09** adoption or freeing from adoption at the age of 12.[20] A child at that age also has a right to seek a child maintenance assessment order under the Child Support Act 1991.[21] In addition, a child of any age has a right to have his or her views considered in any action in which a decision pertaining to him is being taken.[22]

CHILDREN'S RESPONSIBILITIES

A child has responsibilities under the law of delict, the law of contract[23] and, from the **13–10** age of eight, criminal responsibility.[24] Children remain liable for their own delicts

---

[18] Discussed at para 13–47.
[19] Age of Legal Capacity (Scotland) Act 1991, s 2(2).
[20] *ibid* s 2(3).
[21] Child Support Act 1991, s 7(1).
[22] Children (Scotland) Act 1995, s 6; see, *eg*, *Oyeneyin v Oyeneyin* 1999 GWD 38-1836; *McGrath v McGrath* 1999 SLT (Sh Ct) 90.
[23] See para 13–02 on contractual capacity of children.
[24] Although most child offenders are referred to the Children's Hearing System. See para 13–23 on children's hearing system. The subject of criminal responsibility is currently under review by the Scottish Parliament.

although actions against them are largely ineffectual. Parents will only be vicariously liable[25] for the delicts of a child where they have instructed the child to perpetrate the delict and the child is thought to be an agent of the parent.

RESTRICTIONS AND PROTECTIONS

13–11 The law also contains restrictions on the activities of children and also several provisions designed to protect children. The protections applicable to children may be grouped under the headings of sexual exploitation and protection from abuse or neglect. For example, it is an offence for a man to have sex with a girl under the age of 16 even with that girl's consent. It is rape for a man to have sex with a girl under the age of 12. The following are also offences designed to protect young persons from sexual exploitation: for a man to have sexual intercourse with a child in breach of trust; procuring a girl for unlawful sexual intercourse; intercourse with a step-child; incest; indecent behaviour with a girl aged between 12 and 16; and a number of offences designed to deter the procurement or involvement of children in prostitution, or to have a child in or around a brothel. A woman over the age of consent who has sexual relations with a boy under the age of 16 commits the offence of shameless indecency. Non-consensual sexual relations by a male with a child of the same sex will be prosecuted as indecent assault. A recent lowering of the age of consent to homosexual sexual behaviour ensures that there will be no prosecution of consensual homosexual acts where both parties are over the age of 16, and the sexual behaviour involves no more than two persons at any one time and takes place in a private place.[26]

The criminal law also operates to protect children from neglect.[27] Anyone aged 16 or over having custody or charge or care of a child, or young person under 16 years of age, who wilfully assaults, ill-treats, neglects, abandons or exposes a child in a manner likely to cause unnecessary suffering or injury to health, resulting in loss of sight, hearing, limb, organ or body or any other mental derangement shall be guilty of an offence.[28] The existence of such a statutory offence does not prevent such criminal activity against children being prosecuted under specific named crimes such as assault, indecent assault and lewd and libidinous practices.

PARENTHOOD AND PARENTAL RESPONSIBILITIES AND RIGHTS

13–12 In the law of parent and child there can be fewer fundamental questions than the identity of the parent. The answer to the question is no longer solely determined by genetics. The advancement of medical science and the expanded capacity for assisted parenthood has ensured that the law now has to deal with a number of complex social

---

[25] For concept of vicarious liability see Chapter 5.
[26] These protective offences are discussed in para 13–34 and Chapter 14.
[27] See generally Sutherland, *Child and Family Law* (1999), pp 290–310.
[28] Children and Young Persons (Scotland) Act 1937, s 12.

issues. A child's mother automatically has parental responsibilities and rights in relation to her child irrespective of her age or her marital status.[29] In contrast, a child's genetic father only acquires parental rights automatically if he is married to the mother of the child at conception, or subsequently.[30] This raises one of the most controversial aspects of family law: the apparent discrimination against unmarried fathers.[31] A genetic father who is unmarried to the mother at the time of the child's birth may acquire parental rights by subsequently marrying the mother of the child, or by reaching a formal agreement with the mother that he will have responsibilities and rights,[32] or alternatively by applying to the courts for a parental responsibilities and rights order.[33]

Ordinarily, in respect of children conceived normally, parenthood is largely an issue of genetics although the law often proceeds with a number of legal presumptions. These presumptions are contained in section 5 of the Law Reform (Parent and Child) (Scotland) Act 1986. The first of these presumptions is that a man is presumed to be the father of the child if he is married to the mother of the child at any time during the period beginning with the conception and ending with the birth of the child. Second, there is a presumption that a man is the father of the child where both he and the mother have acknowledged that he is the father and he has been registered as such in an appropriate register of births, deaths and marriages. Both presumptions can be disproved on the balance of probability,[34] although in respect of the first presumption the courts have been prepared to recognise unusually long gestation periods in upholding that presumption.[35] Disputed genetic parentage is now a relatively simple matter to resolve using blood testing and DNA profiling. A court may request a party to any proceedings to provide a blood sample or other bodily fluids or tissue for the purpose of blood or DNA test.[36] Refusal to comply with such a request may result in the court drawing an adverse inference from such refusal. Consent to obtain a blood sample from a child for such a purpose may be given either by a parent or by the child himself.

In modern times, the law has been forced to respond to the problem of assisted parenthood in situations where there has either been artificial insemination, *in vitro* fertilisation, egg donation, or surrogacy. Provisions in the Human Fertilisation and Embryology Act 1990 have resolved some confusing issues of maternity and paternity. A woman giving birth to a child will be considered for all purposes as the mother of that child.[37] Where a child is conceived and delivered following artificial insemination by sperm donation, paternity will be granted to the husband or partner of any woman undergoing artificial insemination donation or similar treatment where both the woman and the man consent to that treatment and are undergoing it in a joint venture.[38] A husband may not be considered to be the father of the child if he is able

---

[29] Children (Scotland) Act 1995, s 3(1)(a).
[30] *ibid* s 3(1)(b).
[31] *Sanderson* v *McManus* 1997 SC (HL) 55; note that the position of unmarried fathers is under review by the Scottish Parliament.
[32] Children (Scotland) Act 1995, s 4.
[33] *ibid* s 11.
[34] See *eg*, *J* v *Aberdeen City Council* 1999 SC 404.
[35] *eg Currie* v *Currie* 1950 SC 10; *Jamieson* v *Dobie* 1935 SC 415.
[36] Law Reform (Miscellaneous Provisions) (Scotland) Act 1990, s 70.
[37] Human Fertilisation and Embryology Act 1990, s 27(1).
[38] *ibid* s 28(2).

to establish that he did not consent to his wife undergoing such treatment. The onus of proof will be firmly on the husband. A sperm donor is not to be considered as the father of any child conceived by artificial insemination.[39]

In respect of surrogacy, the gestational mother—the mother who carries the child—is deemed to be the mother of the child in law and, if she is married, her husband (if he has consented to the surrogacy) is deemed to be the father.[40] There are three options open to the commissioning parent or parents of a surrogate baby. First, they may seek a parental responsibilities and rights order under section 11 of the Children (Scotland) Act 1995.[41] Second, they may seek an adoption order.[42] The other alternative is to apply within six months of the child's birth for a parental order under section 30 of the Human Fertilisation and Embryology Act 1990. Following the granting of a parental order, a child is treated for all purposes as the child of the applicant party. The surrogate mother (and her husband or partner if she has one) must consent to the making of the order. However, the court must be satisfied that there has been no exchange of money to procure the child. The section 30 parental order is only open to applicants who are married and both over the age of 18. There is no scope for overruling the withholding of the agreement of the surrogate parent or parents and in such situations the commissioning parents will require to seek an alternative order.

PARENTAL RESPONSIBILITIES AND RIGHTS

13–13   Parenthood carries with it a number of responsibilities and rights. There is for the first time a statutory statement of key responsibilities and rights, contained in the Children (Scotland) Act 1995. A "relevant person" (including parents, guardians or someone who has parental responsibilities and rights in respect of a child) has the responsibility: (a) to safeguard and promote the child's health, development and welfare; (b) to provide direction and guidance to the child in a manner appropriate to the stage of the child's development; (c) if the child is not living with the parent, to maintain personal relations and direct contact with the child on a regular basis; and (d) to act as the child's legal representative.[43] In fulfilment of these responsibilities, parents also have a number of rights: (a) the right to have the child living with him or her or otherwise to regulate the child's residence; (b) to control, direct and guide the child's upbringing in a manner appropriate to the child's stage of development; (c) if the child does not live with the parent, to maintain personal relations and direct contact with the child on a regular basis; and (d) to act as the child's legal representative.[44]

These statutory provisions are still relatively novel and illumination of several key concepts is awaited in the emerging case law. The statutory statement of responsibilities and rights displaces any analogous common law rights but does not displace specific statements of parental rights and responsibilities in particular statutes. Other than parental guidance, which subsists until the child is aged 18, all other statutory parental responsibilities end when the child attains the age of 16. A parent is expected to have regard to the views of the child in reaching any major decision affecting the

---

[39] Human Fertilisation and Embryology Act 1990, s 28(6).
[40] *ibid* s 28(2).
[41] See para 13–13.
[42] C v S 1996 SLT 1387. See paras 13–14 to 13–16.
[43] Children (Scotland) Act 1995, s 1(1).
[44] *ibid* s 2(1).

child if the child wishes to express them. For the avoidance of doubt, a child 12 years of age or over is presumed to be of sufficient age and maturity to express a view, although that age is not prescriptive.[45]

The first of the statutory responsibilities to safeguard and promote the child's health development and welfare is a broad responsibility. It presupposes a proactive strategy on the part of parents. It is incumbent upon parents to ensure the safety of the child and ensure that adequate care arrangements are in place during parental absences. It is also incumbent on parents to ensure that their child is exposed to experiences which promote their development, such as playing with friends and exposure to the wider community.

The issue of health is somewhat more controversial. The basic premise that a parent has the right to consent to, or refuse, medical treatment of a child is now overshadowed by a number of exceptions and caveats. Ordinarily, the parent will be the party giving consent. However, it should be noted that a person under 16 years of age may herself agree to medical treatment or undergo medical procedures, without first obtaining parental consent. Where, in the opinion of a medical practitioner, the child knows the nature and consequences of the medical treatment, the child may transact for medical services.[46] In cases of dispute or controversy, where parents refuse consent or medical practitioners refuse to comply with the parents' wishes, or indeed the child refuses urgent medical treatment, the matter will be determined by the court. It will determine the issue simply on the basis of the "welfare principle". The court will ask whether it is in the interest of the child and, having asked this question, may override the wishes of the parent or indeed those of the child.[47]

As part of the requirement to promote the child's development, it will be incumbent upon the parent to ensure that the child is educated, though this responsibility is covered specifically in the Education (Scotland) Act 1980.[48]

The parental responsibility to provide guidance and direction again may be thought to cover education but it also may address the issue of chastisement and discipline. Although not specifically mentioned in the statute, the provision must be interpreted in line with the parents' right reasonably to chastise their child.[49]

An interesting aspect of the new statutory responsibilities is the requirement to maintain personal relations and direct contact with the child on a regular basis. Failure to do so may impact on other dimensions of child-care law. However, it has recently been pointed out that the statutory provisions do not create a presumption in favour of contact: it must still be established that contact is in the best interests of the child.[50] A parent has the right to have the child living with him or her or otherwise to regulate the child's residence, or, if the child is not living with the parent, to maintain personal relations and direct contact with the child on a regular basis. The new terminology of "contact" and "residence" has displaced the traditional terms of "access" and "custody". Any rights of residence or contact must operate under the "welfare

---

[45] Children (Scotland) Act 1995, s 6.
[46] Age of Legal Capacity (Scotland) Act 1991, s 2(4).
[47] Wilkinson and Norrie, *The Law Relating to Parent and Child in Scotland* (2nd edn, 1999).
[48] See Wilkinson and Norrie, *The Law Relating to Parent and Child* (2nd edn, 1999), Chapter 12 (on educational responsibilities of parents).
[49] See *A v UK* [1998] 2 FLR 959 (ECHR); *B v Harris* 1990 SLT 208; *Peebles v Macphail* 1990 SLT 245.
[50] *White v White* 1999 SLT (Sh Ct) 106; see though *Sanderson v McManus* 1997 SC (HL) 55.

principle."[51] Such rights cannot be viewed as absolute rights. Courts will always determine such issues on the basis of what is in the best interests of the child. In situations where there is a dispute relating to residence or contact with the child, application may be made to the court under section 11 of the Children (Scotland) Act 1995. An application may be made by a person who already has parental responsibilities and rights or a person who claims such responsibilities and rights,[52] or by the child himself. An application cannot be made where the child is the subject of a supervision order from the children's hearing.[53] Where an application is lodged under section 11, the courts will convene a special hearing called a Child Welfare Hearing designed to resolve any child-related issues.[54] Section 11 applications might be stand-alone proceedings or may be an integral part of divorce actions. A pursuer may seek a residence order, a contact order, a specific issue order,[55] an interdict, an order depriving a parent of parental responsibilities or rights, an order imposing upon a person parental rights or responsibilities, or an order appointing or removing a person as guardian of that child. In determining any child-related issues, section 11 insists on three key criteria to be applied by the court. First, the welfare of the child is to be the paramount consideration.[56] Second, the court should only make an order where it considers it is better to do so than to make no order at all. And third, the court, as far as practical, shall have regard to the views of the child, taking account of the child's age and maturity.

The determination of what is in the welfare of the child has attracted considerable controversy in recent years, particularly in relation to the issue of maternal preference. Should mothers (as a matter of course) be viewed as the parent with whom a child should live?[57] Notwithstanding the view of some that there should be maternal preference, the dominant issue in the context of residence of a child is perhaps continuation of the status quo rather than the sex or age of the child or the sex, age or financial wherewithal of the respective parents. The fact remains that in roughly 80 per cent of all cases, residence remains with the female party to any dispute. The courts have, however, repeatedly made it clear that their sole criterion is the child's welfare.

Other parental rights and responsibilities relate to the naming of the child, educating the child, and the religious upbringing of the child. In all matters of parental rights and responsibilities, the parent's power must be exercised with the welfare of the child in mind. Moreover, because the child continues to mature in the parent/child relationship, his or her rights will undoubtedly impact upon those of the parent. There is a fine balance between parental rights and responsibilities and the rights, views and wishes of the child.

---

[51] *Porchetta* v *Porchetta* 1986 SLT 105.
[52] Such as an unmarried father or grandparents: see *Wright* v *Wright* 1999 GWD 3–119, or foster-parents: *Osborne* v *Matthan (No 3)* 1998 SC 682.
[53] *P* v *P* 1999 SCLR 679.
[54] See Christie and Mays, "The Role of the Child Welfare Hearing in the Resolution of Child Related Disputes in Scotland" 2000 (forthcoming – *Child & Family Law Quarterly*).
[55] See *G* v *H* 1999 GWD 24–1125.
[56] For a recent example, see *Dosoo* v *Dosoo* 1999 SLT (Sh Ct) 86.
[57] *Brixey* v *Lynas* 1994 SLT 847; *Senna-Cheribbo* v *Wood* 1999 SC 328; *cf Early* v *Early* 1989 SLT 114.

ADOPTION

Adoption is a legal process whereby the relationship between a child and his or her **13–14** (natural or adopted) parents is terminated, and a new legal relationship of parent and child created between the child and his or her adoptive parents. While adoption may arise from many different circumstances, there are principally two common sets of circumstances. First, there may be state-sponsored adoption of a child probably already in the care of the local authority, where that child's natural family does not exist or is dysfunctional. Second, a large proportion of adoptions arise through individual sponsorship: for example, relatives adopting children of a family member, adoptions arising out of surrogacy, step-parent adoptions where a natural parent and/or the child wish to regulate the relationship with the step-parent, or inter-country adoption.

The requirement of a court order and the operation of state or state-sponsored agencies in respect of adoption ensure that there is considerable judicial and state supervision of the whole process of adoption. Local authorities are required to provide an adoption service for their area. They may, as part of that service, have an adoption agency although the law also recognises the right of other adoption societies to constitute approved adoption agencies.[58] The mechanisms that exist are designed to ensure that the best interests of the child are paramount in considering that there is no abuse of the process and that there is no trading in children.[59]

Only children under 18 years of age who are not married or have not been married can be adopted. It is possible for a child to be adopted and thereafter readopted. Where a child is placed by an adoption agency, or the adoption is by a step-parent, parent or relative, the child must be at least 19 weeks old by the time the order is made by the court. In addition, the child must have lived with the prospective adopters for the preceding 13 weeks.

In respect of adoption sponsored by local authorities and adoption societies, it is likely that the local authority will be looking after the child.[60] An adoption agency is required to put in place appropriate mechanisms for assessing the suitability of the child and the prospective adopters and to facilitate the bringing together of both. Adoption agencies are required to have adoption panels who will assess whether it is in the best interest of a particular child to be adopted, whether there are alternatives to adoption, the suitability of prospective adopters and whether the prospective adopters would be suitable adoptive parents for a specific child. Parties who wish to become adoptive parents must complete an application form and thereafter be assessed as prospective adopters. Part of the assessment process will include medical and police checks. It may thereafter be the case that the child is temporarily placed with prospective adoptive parents and, if that placement is successful, a decision is likely to be made that the prospective adopters lodge an adoption petition in court for approval by the court.

The local authority may seek to "free" the child for adoption.[61] Such an order has the

---

[58] Organisations such as Barnardos may be an approved adoption society.
[59] Adoption is governed by the Adoption (Scotland) Act 1978, as amended by the Children (Scotland) Act 1995; see McNeil, *Adoption Law in Scotland* (3rd edn, 1998).
[60] See para 13–17.
[61] For a recent example, see *J v Aberdeen City Council* 1999 SC 405.

purpose of severing the connection between the natural parents and the child with a view to the smooth facilitation of adoption at some subsequent stage. By obtaining an order freeing for adoption it will be unnecessary to obtain parental consent to the actual adoption at some future stage. It will be necessary for the child to have been placed for adoption, or that the child is likely to be so placed, before the court will grant a freeing for adoption order.

In respect of family initiated adoptions by step-parents or some other closely connected member of the family, the child is not placed by the adoption agency but is likely to be already in place with the prospective adopters. Notwithstanding this, there is a role for the adoption agency in that they must be notified of the intention of the adopters to lodge an adoption petition in court. Thereafter, the adoption agency will have the opportunity to visit the parents and the child to carry out some assessments with a view to reporting to the court on the situation pertaining to the child.

WHO CAN ADOPT?

13–15   An unmarried person aged 21 or over may apply to adopt a child alone. Applications can be made to adopt a child jointly only if the applicants are a married couple both of whom are 21 or over, or one of the spouses is the child's parent and is 18 or over and the other spouse is 21 or over. A married person can adopt the child alone if the court is satisfied that the other spouse cannot be found, or the spouses have separated and are living apart and the separation is likely to be permanent, or the other spouse is incapable of making a joint application because of physical or mental ill health.[62] There is no restriction on the sexual orientation of prospective adopters and in one celebrated case a single gay person in a stable relationship was entitled to adopt the child.[63] Where there is only one applicant seeking to adopt, the court will need to be satisfied that he or she is single, or that his or her spouse cannot be found, or that the party's spouse is incapable of making an application through mental or physical ill-health, or that the parties have separated and are living apart and that separation is likely to be permanent. Cohabitees cannot make a joint application to adopt. It is possible for a step-parent on his or her own to make an application for adoption.[64]

THE ADOPTION PROCESS

13–16   An application to adopt may be made to the Court of Session or, more usually, to the sheriff court. Adoption hearings are held in private. A *curator ad litem*[65] will be appointed, to safeguard the interests of the child. The *curator ad litem* will also provide the court with a report in respect of the child's interest. A court is required to regard the need to promote the welfare of the child concerned as its paramount consideration. It must also have regard to the views of the child if he wishes to express them, taking into account his age or maturity, and must have regard to his religious persuasion, racial origin, cultural and ethnic background.[66] A child aged 12 or more is presumed

[62]   See Thomson, *Family Law in Scotland* (3rd edn, 1996), p 240.
[63]   *T, Petitioner* 1997 SLT 724.
[64]   Adoption (Scotland) Act 1978, s 15(1)(aa), as amended by the Children (Scotland) Act 1995.
[65]   Wilkinson and Norrie, *The Law Relating to Parent and Child* (2nd edn, 1999), pp 506–508.
[66]   Adoption (Scotland) Act 1978, s 6, as amended.

to be of sufficient age or maturity to form a view. More importantly, in respect of all adoption applications, it is necessary that a child 12 years or over gives his consent to the adoption. The child's refusal to consent cannot, unlike that of the natural parents, be overridden by the court.

It is an important requirement that the parent or guardian of any child must freely, and with full understanding of what is involved, agree unconditionally to the making of an adoption order (or an order freeing a child for adoption). A parent in this context is defined as the mother of the child or the father of the child where both or either have parental responsibilities and rights. Unmarried fathers do not automatically have parental rights and responsibilities although they may acquire them under section 4 or section 11 of the Children Scotland Act 1995.[67] A guardian is someone appointed by a deed or a court order. A mother cannot give her consent to the adoption of her child until six weeks after the birth. While parental agreement is an integral and important part of the adoption process, it is possible for the court to dispense with the parental agreement in the following circumstances:

(a) the parent or guardian is not known, cannot be found[68] or is incapable of giving agreement;

(b) the parent or guardian is withholding agreement unreasonably[69];

(c) the parent or guardian has persistently failed without reasonable cause to fulfil one or other of his parental responsibilities in relation to the child[70];

(d) the parent or guardian has seriously ill-treated the child whose reintegration into the same household as the parent or guardian is, because of serious ill-treatment, or for other reasons, unlikely.[71]

Having reflected upon the report and the evidence before it, the court may grant the adoption order or may refuse it. The court may postpone it for up to two years or refer the matter to a Children's Hearing when the court considers that a ground of referral has been established.[72] Where the child in question is the subject of a supervision requirement, the Children's Hearing must be asked to review the child's case and to offer the court advice on whether the adoption should proceed or not.

Following the granting of an adoption petition, the child will be registered in the adopted children register. When the child reaches the age of 16 years, he or she will be entitled to obtain information in respect of his natural birth and subsequent adoption.[73] The adopted person may be allowed access to the court records relating to the adoption and also to see his original birth certificate. Such a child will be offered advice and counselling at this stage. Children under 16 years of age have no right of access to this information.

---

[67] See para 13–13; see also *J v Aberdeen City Council J* 1999 SC 405.
[68] *S v M* 1999 SC 388.
[69] For a recent example, see *Edinburgh City Council v B* 1999 SCLR 694.
[70] See *G v M* 1999 SC 439.
[71] Adoption (Scotland) Act 1978, s 16.
[72] See para 13–27.
[73] Adoption (Scotland) Act 1978, s 45(4) and (5) and Sched 1, para 1(1); see Wilkinson and Norrie, *The Law Relating to Parent and Child* (2nd edn, 1999), pp 184–186.

THE CHILD IN NEED OF CARE

13–17   For the most part, children are nurtured in their own relatively autonomous family environment. From time to time such family life, however constituted, either becomes dysfunctional or is not possible. In such circumstances children may be in need of care and it is necessary that the state, principally in the form of the local authority, intervenes to secure that care and protection.

The Children (Scotland) Act 1995 places important duties on local authorities in respect of children. A local authority is required to provide services to children in need. It is specifically under a duty to: (a) safeguard and promote the welfare of children in its area who are in need, and (b) so far as consistent with that duty, promote the upbringing of such children by their families.[74]

Fundamental to the provision of services to children is the local authority's duty to assess children's needs. A child is deemed to be in need of care if he falls within one of the following categories: (a) he is unlikely to achieve or maintain or to have the opportunity of achieving or maintaining a reasonable standard of health and development unless the local authority provides services for him; (b) his health or development is likely to be impaired unless such services are provided; (c) he is disabled; or (d) he is affected adversely by the disability of any other person in his family.[75]

The structure of child care law presupposes that local authorities will assess referrals and, where appropriate, offer advice and assistance, undertake assessment of the child's needs and make enquiries in respect of the child's welfare or safety. In an attempt to address the varying situations that one encounters in respect of the child, the 1995 Act confers a number of important powers upon the local authority. Given the basic premise that the child is best nurtured in the confines of his own family, it is incumbent upon the local authority to attempt to secure that where appropriate. To this end, assistance may be given to a particular child or his family or any other member of the child's family with a view to safeguarding or promoting the child's welfare. Such assistance may be in kind or exceptionally in cash.[76]

Where it is necessary, a local authority shall provide accommodation for any child who, residing[77] or having been found in their area, appears to require such provision because: (a) no one has parental responsibility for him; (b) he is lost or abandoned; or (c) the person who has been caring for him is prevented, whether or not permanently, and for whatever reason, from providing him with suitable accommodation or care.[78] The duty is mandatory in respect of qualifying children who are under 18 years of age, although it is open to a local authority, on a voluntary basis, to provide similar assistance to young persons between the age of 18 and 21. Before providing a child with accommodation the local authority must have regard to his views if he wishes to express them.

The local authority cannot provide accommodation where there is a person with

---

[74] Children (Scotland) Act 1995, s 22.
[75] *ibid* ss 22 and 93(4).
[76] *ibid* s 22.
[77] See *S v Stirling* 1999 Hous LR 73.
[78] Children (Scotland) Act 1995, s 25(1).

parental responsibilities and rights in respect of the child and that person wishes either to have care or arrange care for the child. Where a child is received into care, any person with parental responsibilities and rights has the right to remove the child from the accommodation provided by the local authority. Generally speaking, parental rights and responsibilities are unaffected by the authority providing accommodation for the child. In cases where the child has been in the care of the local authority for a period exceeding six months, the person wishing to remove the child must give the local authority 14 days' written notice of his intention to remove the child. The practical fulfilment of the duty to provide accommodation may be carried out either by placing the child in a residential establishment run by the local authority, or by placing the child with another of his own relatives, or by placement with a foster parent or with any other person deemed suitable by the local authority. Children received into care are deemed to be "looked after" by the local authority. Where a child is being "looked after" by a local authority it is required: (a) to safeguard and promote the child's welfare, taking the child's welfare as the paramount consideration; (b) to make use of services that would be available for children were they cared for by their parents; (c) to take steps to promote regular and direct contact between the child and any person with parental responsibilities as far as practical or appropriate and consistent with the duties to safeguard the child's welfare; (d) to provide advice and assistance with a view to the time when the child is no longer looked after by them; (e) to find out and have regard to the views of the child, parents and any other relevant person, when making decisions about the child; and (f) to take account, as far as practicable, of the child's religious persuasion, racial origin and cultural and linguistic background.[79]

In addition to the broad duty to provide assistance and in appropriate circumstances accommodation for children in need of care, there are a number of orders at the disposal of local authorities, designed to give them further powers to tackle the growing problem of child abuse and neglect. The orders are:

- child assessment orders
- exclusion orders
- parental responsibility orders
- child protection orders
- other emergency measures.

CHILD ASSESSMENT ORDERS

The Child Assessment Order (CAO) may be sought by a local authority to undertake preliminary investigation and assessment where there are suspicions of neglect or abuse. The findings of the assessment may in turn lead a local authority to seek a further court order in respect of the child. The purpose of the child assessment order is to assess the state of the child's health or development. A sheriff may grant an application for the child assessment order if he is satisfied: (a) the local authority have

13–18

---

[79] Children (Scotland) Act 1995, s 17.

reasonable cause to suspect that the child in respect of whom the order is sought is being so treated (or neglected) that he is suffering, or is likely to suffer, significant harm; (b) such an assessment is required in order to establish whether or not there is reasonable cause to believe that the child is being so treated (or neglected); and (c) such assessment is unlikely to be carried out, or carried out satisfactorily, unless the order is granted.[80]

The child assessment order must specify the date on which the assessment is to begin and the dates for commencement and duration of the assessment, which must not be for more than seven days. An order will require that person to produce the child to an authorised person and to permit that person (or another authorised person) to carry out the assessment. Compliance with the order should not normally entail the forced separation of the child from his family, although it may do so. In the course of hearing an application for a child assessment order, if the sheriff is convinced that the grounds for any of the other orders contained in the Children (Scotland) Act 1995 are satisfied, he should accordingly pronounce that order rather than grant a child assessment order.

EXCLUSION ORDERS[81]

13–19   A local authority may seek to exclude an abuser (or alleged abuser) from the child's family home in circumstances where there is thought to be an ongoing risk to the child. The orders are modelled closely on the exclusion orders contained in the Matrimonial Homes (Family Protection) (Scotland) Act 1981.[82] Child abuse exclusion orders are designed to be reasonably temporary measures to facilitate a period of time where other alternatives may be canvassed and put in place. Rather than remove the child from the family home to an environment alien to him, the order operates to exclude the abuser and to allow the child to remain with other family members in the family home, thus minimising the distress. Such an approach to child abuse may not always be relevant and there may be some circumstances where it is preferable that the child is indeed removed properly to secure their safety. It is only open to local authorities to seek an exclusion order. The granting of the order has the effect of excluding a named person from the child's family home: the named person need not necessarily be a parent—it may simply be someone who is living in the child's home. Before granting the order, the sheriff must be satisfied:

(a) that the child has suffered, is suffering, or is likely to suffer, significant harm as a result of any conduct, or any threatened or reasonably apprehended conduct, of that named person;

(b) that the making of an exclusion order against a named person—

(i) is necessary for the protection of the child, irrespective of whether the child is for the time being residing in the family home; and

(ii) would better safeguard the child's welfare than the removal of the child from the family home; and

---

[80] *ibid* s 55.
[81] See, generally, Children (Scotland) Act 1995, ss 76–80.
[82] See para 13–49.

(c) that, if an order is made, there will be a person specified in the application who is capable of taking responsibility for the provision of appropriate care for the child and any other member of the family who requires such care and who is or will be residing in the family home.

Given the terms of the test set down for the sheriff, it is apparent that it is an order that is not appropriate in respect of single parent families.

In determining an application for an exclusion order, the sheriff must have the welfare of the child as his paramount consideration. It is thought that this must qualify any interpretation of the word "necessary" in the test for granting an exclusion order. The sheriff shall not make an exclusion order if it appears to him that to do so would be unjustifiable or unreasonable in all the circumstances of the case. There will be few circumstances where an exclusion order is thought to be unjustifiable or unreasonable where it has already been assessed to be in the welfare of the child that the exclusion order is granted. An interim exclusion order can be obtained under the Act and this has the same effect as the exclusion order proper, albeit on a temporary basis. Interim orders may be sought where the matter is deemed to require some urgency. Once granted, an interim order is likely to become a matter for review at a further hearing held to afford the opportunity to a party who has not yet been heard in the proceedings. If the sheriff is satisfied that the conditions exist for a child protection order (discussed below), he will make such an order rather than grant the exclusion order.

As with the matrimonial homes exclusion orders, the granting of an exclusion order has the effect of suspending the excluded person's occupancy rights in the home. That person is prohibited from entering the home without the express permission of the local authority. In conjunction with the exclusion order, the sheriff may grant a number of incidental orders designed to put in effect the exclusion and to prevent the named person from returning or entering the home or being within its vicinity. The sheriff may also make an incidental order as to contact between the child and the person who has been excluded. Exclusion orders are likely to have attached to them the power of arrest which will allow the police immediately to apprehend anyone suspected of being in breach of the order or any incidental interdict attached to it.

PARENTAL RESPONSIBILITIES ORDERS

When it becomes apparent to a local authority that it is not possible or that it would be **13–20** detrimental to the child's welfare to reintegrate the child within his own family, the local authority may seek a parental responsibilities order (PRO). The seeking and granting of a parental responsibilities order is a fairly major step and only likely to be undertaken where the child is thought to be in need of long-term care outwith his family. The local authority may already "look after" the child but this is not a prerequisite for the making and granting of such an order. The PRO has the effect, during the subsistence of the order, of transferring appropriate parental responsibilities and rights to the local authority.

Parental responsibilities orders cannot be granted by the sheriff unless he is satisfied that each relevant person has either (a) freely and with full understanding of what is involved agreed unconditionally that the order be made; (b) withheld such agreement unreasonably[83]; (c) persistently failed, without reasonable cause, to fulfil one or other of the following parental responsibilities in relation to the child: the responsibility to safeguard and promote the child's health, development and welfare or the responsibility of maintaining personal relations and direct contact with the child on a regular basis[84]; or (d) seriously ill-treated the child, whose reintegration into the same household as that of that person is, because of the serious ill-treatment or for other reasons, unlikely.[85]

Following the granting of a parental responsibilities order, the local authority must undertake full parental responsibilities in respect of the child. Almost bizarrely, one of the things the local authority may do is allow the child to remain and reside with the parent, guardian, relative or friend. Even if this is not the case, the sheriff may in granting a PRO make an order as to contact between the child and any other person. The impact of the PRO means that the local authority will exercise judgement about the various issues of parental responsibilities. Anyone who has hitherto had parental rights and responsibilities retains the right to consent or object to a freeing for adoption order or adoption in respect of the child. Parental responsibilities orders automatically end when the child attains the age of 18 years, or is adopted or becomes subject to a freeing for adoption order. The child, the relevant person or persons and the local authority, or indeed anyone with an interest, may make an application to the sheriff to vary or discharge the order or any order incidental to it.

THE CHILD PROTECTION ORDER

13–21 The Child Protection Order (CPO) is the principal order available to protect the child in situations of neglect or abuse. It is an order which is open to the local authority to seek, but, unlike other orders, any other person may also seek it.

There are two possible routes to obtaining a CPO. First, the sheriff will grant a child protection order where he is satisfied that there are reasonable grounds for believing that the child is being so treated or neglected that he is suffering significant harm, or that he will suffer such harm if he is not removed to a place of safety and it is necessary to make the order to protect the child.[86] Second, the sheriff will grant an order if he is satisfied that: the local authority has reasonable grounds for believing that the child is suffering or will suffer significant harm as a result of the way the child is being treated or neglected; the local authority is making inquiries to allow it to decide if it should take action to safeguard the welfare of the child; and those inquiries are being frustrated by access to the child being unreasonably denied and the authority has reasonable cause to believe that the access required is a matter of some urgency.[87]

The CPO as an emergency protection order will be sought and dealt with on the same day. In determining an order, the sheriff must consider the welfare of the child

---

[83] See *eg, Glasgow City Council* v M 1999 SLT 989.

[84] See, *eg, Edinburgh City Council* v A 1999 GWD 37–1785.

[85] Children (Scotland) Act 1995, s 86. ("Relevant person" in relation to a child means—"(a) any parent enjoying parental responsibilities or parental rights under Part I of this Act; (b) any person in whom parental responsibilities or rights are vested by, under or by virtue of this Act; and (c) any person who appears to be a person who ordinarily (and other than by reason only of his employment) has charge of, or control over, the child": 1995 Act, 93(2).)

[86] *ibid* s 57(1).

[87] *ibid* s 57(2).

as the paramount consideration but there is no mandatory obligation to obtain the child's views. The child protection order acts in a way that requires a person in a position to do so to produce the child, and thereafter authorises the child's removal to a place of safety. As an alternative it may actually prevent the child being removed from a place where he is currently accommodated. It may order that a child's whereabouts not be disclosed. In making a child protection order, the sheriff may make a direction as to contact between the child and any other person. The child protection order may authorise the examination of the child's physical or mental state or some other assessment or interview and related treatment. The child protection order will also be served on the Reporter to the Children's Hearing[88] for the area. The child, or indeed anyone with whom the notification is served, may seek a variation or discharge of the child protection order. The notification to the reporter to the Children's Hearing activates the second stage of the child protection order proceedings.

The Reporter may, on the basis of the information he has or on making further enquiries, decide to discharge the CPO or any condition or direction attached to it. If the Reporter does not discharge the hearing he must arrange for the case to go before a Children's Hearing.[89] This "initial hearing" will determine whether or not the CPO should be continued. An initial hearing must take place on the second working day after the CPO has been implemented. The Children's Hearing may continue that order with or without variation until a second Children's Hearing which will deliberate upon what measures of care are required for the child.

Notwithstanding the convening of an initial hearing, it is open to any party to seek a variation or discharge of the granting of a child protection order by having the case go back before a sheriff. Given the speed with which the initial hearing is convened, it is highly unlikely that parties will be sufficiently organised to lodge an appeal before the sheriff—nevertheless such an approach is possible. Any applicant seeking variation or discharge must notify the Reporter forthwith. Even where variation or review is sought before the sheriff, it is open to the Reporter to convene a Children's Hearing with a view to giving the sheriff some advice in respect of the child. In cases where the discharge or variation is sought after the initial hearing the sheriff has the power to recall any order, vary, cancel or continue that order.

When, either immediately before the initial hearing or after the initial hearing, no variation or discharge of a child protection order is sought before the sheriff, a second Children's Hearing is convened. It will take place on the eighth working day after the order was implemented. The second hearing has the power to deal with the child as if it was a referral under section 52.[90]

OTHER EMERGENCY MEASURES

13–22 Whilst the principal emergency protection is a child protection order, there are two other emergency measures designed to protect a child. First, a Justice of the Peace, where he is satisfied that the conditions exist for the making of a child protection order, may authorise the removal of a child to a place of safety. This authorisation lasts for 24 hours and will allow time for the local authority to seek a child protection order. Second, there is power

[88] For a discussion of the role of the Reporter, see para 13–25.
[89] For procedure of the Children's Hearing, see paras 13–25 to 13–26.
[90] See para 13–27.

conferred upon a police constable, who believes that the conditions exist for a child protection order, to intervene and remove a child to a place of safety. Intervention can only result in the child being detained for up to 24 hours in a place of safety and again is designed to offer an opportunity to seek a child protection order in the normal fashion.[91]

THE CHILDREN'S HEARING SYSTEM

13–23 The scheme of Children's Hearings, first mooted by the Kilbrandon Committee in 1964, is to be found in its modern incarnation in Part 2 of the Children (Scotland) Act 1995.[92] Kilbrandon's original concern was, of course, juvenile justice but the system introduced, and that now in operation, has a much broader remit rooted in a welfare philosophy towards children. As a basic premise, children who offend and children who are victims of abuse and neglect are for the most part equally both in need of care and supervision. The Children's Hearings System provides a means whereby measures of compulsory supervision may be instituted in respect of a child.

REFERRING THE CHILD TO THE CHILDREN'S HEARING SYSTEM

13–24 Any person who believes that a child requires compulsory measures of supervision may make a referral to the Reporter to the Children's Hearing. It is commonplace that such referrals are at the instance of social workers, school authorities, police or some other person known to the child. Given that one of the major reasons why a child comes before a hearing is that he or she has committed an offence, there is a strong working relationship between the police, the Procurator Fiscal and the Reporter to the Children's Hearing. Where a child is suspected of committing an offence, the police will notify the Reporter at the same time as the report goes to the Procurator Fiscal. Local authorities are under a statutory duty where a matter is brought to their attention to "cause enquiries to be made".[93] After having made such enquiries, the local authority may if so minded pass a report to the Reporter in connection with the child. It is also the case that a child may come before a Children's Hearing arriving out of a referral by a court. Such referrals arise out of "relevant proceedings" (*ie* where, for example, in an action of divorce the court forms the view that a ground of referral has been established). Referrals may also be made to the hearing system arising out of the making of child protection orders or from criminal court cases involving children where the court makes a referral for guidance and disposal.

THE PROCEDURE FOLLOWING REFERRAL TO THE REPORTER

13–25 Following a referral to the Reporter, which suggests that a child may be in need of compulsory measures of care, the reporter will undertake an initial investigation. He will gather information, and obtain reports from social workers or the child's school. The Reporter is expected to undertake a preliminary investigation to ascertain whether

---

[91] Children (Scotland) Act 1995, s 61.
[92] For a complete view of the system, see Norrie, *Children's Hearings in Scotland* (1997).
[93] Children (Scotland) Act 1995, s 53(1).

a hearing should be convened. It is commonplace for the Reporter to make a fairly speedy decision and in a number of instances to decide that a hearing is unnecessary, perhaps because the issue is being tackled at source, is not sufficiently serious to warrant convening of a hearing, or the family voluntarily agrees to social work help.

Having obtained information, the Reporter must decide whether to convene a hearing or not. If he decides not to convene a hearing, he must notify the relevant parties and perhaps the local authority so that it can provide advice and guidance or assistance to the child and his family. Alternatively, the Reporter may decide to arrange for the convening of a hearing to consider the child's case: before so doing he must be convinced that one of the grounds of referral contained in section 52 of the Children (Scotland) Act 1995 exists.

COMPOSITION AND PROCEDURE OF A CHILDREN'S HEARING

Children's Hearings operate under the supervision and guidance of a locally consti- **13–26** tuted Children's Panel Advisory Committee. One of the primary functions of the Children's Panel Advisory Committee is to compile a panel of members for the Children's Hearings from amongst members of the local community. From this list will be drawn the names of the three members of the panel who will conduct the Children's Hearing. It is a requirement that of the three members comprising a hearing there is one member of either sex. One of the three members will act as chairman of the hearing but will carry no more authority than any of the others involved. It is a requirement that the hearing be conducted as informally as possible. The hearing is conducted in private. The chairman should take all reasonable steps to ensure that numbers are kept to a minimum. Generally speaking, at the hearing the following will be present: three panel members, the Reporter, the parents or relevant persons, the child or the children, and perhaps other professional staff such as a social worker or a child psychologist. Although legal aid is not available for the conduct of the hearing, families will frequently be represented or accompanied by a lawyer who is admitted to the hearing as a "friend". Whilst it is possible for a bona fide member of the press to be in attendance, they are prohibited from publishing information which identifies or is likely to identify any child concerned in the proceedings, the child's address, or school.[94]

The issue of whom should be in attendance at Children's Hearings attracted considerable controversy in the 1990s. The matter has now been resolved following modifications to the law contained in the Children (Scotland) Act 1995. Generally speaking, a child has the right to attend all stages of the hearing and is obliged to do so. In certain circumstances a child may be excused attendance where it is not necessary for him to attend a hearing of that type or where it is detrimental for him to be in attendance as he has been the victim of bodily injury or sexual abuse. The Reporter will notify the child of the hearing and is responsible for ensuring the child's attendance. If it is necessary, the Reporter may apply to the Children's Hearing for a warrant for the child to be removed and detained in a place of safety and thereafter be brought before a Children's Hearing.

Relevant persons[95] also have a right and obligation to attend but may be similarly

---

[94] Children (Scotland) Act 1995, s 44.
[95] See definition at note 85 above.

excused where their attendance is thought to be unreasonable or unnecessary. Rather more controversially, however, a relevant person may be excluded if the hearing is satisfied that it is in the interest of the child and that the presence of that person is causing or is likely to cause the child significant distress or that it is necessary in order to attain the child's view. This may be particularly pertinent in respect of cases where there is an allegation of child abuse by the relevant person. The procedure is that the excluded person will return to the room later and be informed by the chairman of the proceedings that have taken place.

In advance of the hearing, relevant persons may be served with the papers that the Reporter intends to place before the hearing although they have been sent to the chairman and members of the hearing. The child himself will not be entitled to receive such documents but may be made familiar with the substance of the report prior to the hearing unless the chairman decrees that such disclosure would be detrimental to the interest of the child. As an alternative, a safeguarder[96] may be appointed by the hearing to represent and protect the interests of the child. Such a person would be entitled to the papers of the case and be entitled to make appropriate enquiries. The safeguarder has the right to become a party to the action.

THE GROUNDS OF REFERRAL

13–27   At the beginning of the hearing, there will be enquiry as to the child's age. This is important as the Children's Hearing only has jurisdiction over a child.[97] It is necessary to establish that the young person is indeed a person over whom the hearing has jurisdiction. The chairman of the hearing will thereafter explain the ground of referral asserted by the Reporter. The possible grounds of referral can be summarised as:

(a) the child is beyond the control of any relevant person;

(b) the child is falling into bad associations or is exposed to moral danger;

(c) the child is likely (i) to suffer unnecessarily; or (ii) to be impaired seriously in his health or development, due to lack of parental care[98];

(d) the child is one in respect of whom any of the offences mentioned in Schedule 1 to the Criminal Procedure (Scotland) Act 1995 has been committed;

(e) the child is, or is likely to become, a member of the same household as a child in respect of whom any of the offences referred to in paragraph (d) above has been committed[99];

(f) the child is, or is likely to become, a member of the same household as the person who has committed any of the offences referred to in paragraph (d) above;

(g) the child is, or is likely to become, a member of the same household as a person in respect of whom an offence under sections 1–3 of the Criminal Law

[96] See McGhie, "The Role of the Safeguarder" (1994) 39 JLSS 26.
[97] For the definition of "child" see the Children (Scotland) Act 1995, s 93(2).
[98] *H v Harkness* 1998 SC 287.
[99] *G v Scanlon* 1999 SC 226; *cf M v Constanda* 1999 SC 348.

(Consolidation) (Scotland) Act 1995 (incest and intercourse with a child by a step-parent or person in a position of trust) has been committed by a member of that household;

(h) the child has failed to attend school regularly without reasonable excuse;

(i) the child has committed an offence;

(j) the child has misused alcohol or any drug, whether or not a controlled drug within the meaning of the Misuse of Drugs Act 1971;

(k) the child has misused a volatile substance by deliberately inhaling a vapour other than for medicinal purposes;

(l) the child has been provided with accommodation by a local authority under section 25 of the Children (Scotland) Act 1995 or is the subject of a parental responsibilities order obtained under section 86 of the Act, and, in either case, his behaviour is such that special measures are necessary for adequate supervision in his interests or in the interests of others.

Establishment of the ground of referral is vital. It founds the jurisdiction of the hearing and its acceptance or establishment allows the hearing to go on to deliberate a solution for the child's circumstances. At the outset of the hearing the grounds of referral will be put to the child and any relevant person. The hearing can only proceed if the grounds of referral are accepted in full or in part. In circumstances where either the child or the relevant person rejects the grounds of referral or the child is too young to understand the ground of referral, the hearing cannot proceed and the matter will be referred to the sheriff court for a hearing to establish whether a ground of referral is established. An application by a Reporter for the sheriff to deliberate on the establishment of the ground of referral must be made within 28 days of the original hearing. The child has a right and duty to attend such a hearing at this stage in the proceedings. The child or relevant persons have the right to be represented and legal aid is available. The onus is on the Reporter to convince the sheriff that the grounds of referral are established. In the course of the reference to the sheriff, the child or the relevant persons may accept the ground of referral and the matter may at that point be referred back to the Children's Hearing. In circumstances where the sheriff considers that a ground of referral is established the matter will be referred back to the hearing for disposal. Where the sheriff does not find the ground or grounds of referral established he will discharge the referral to the Children's Hearing. In the hearing before the sheriff, the ground of referral will be established on the balance of probabilities, except the ground that the child has committed an offence which will require to be established beyond a reasonable doubt.

Where the ground or grounds of referral are accepted or have been established following reference to the sheriff, the Children's Hearing will discuss the most appropriate disposal of the case. The hearing may continue the case to seek further information, it may require the child to attend or reside in a clinic, hospital or other establishment for the purpose of investigation, and it has the power to issue warrants for the removal and detention of the child in a place of safety. The Children's Hearing may discharge the referral, offering advice and assistance, where it is convinced that there is no need for any formal compulsory measure of supervision and that the issue is being tackled at source. Second, it may make a supervision requirement which requires the child to be under the supervision of the local authority whilst remaining within his or her own home. Before making a supervision requirement it is necessary for the hearing to consult the child and to be convinced that it is better that such an order is made in respect of the child than that no order be made at all. The hearing has the power to control conditions additional to the supervision required. A supervision requirement will require a child to reside in a particular place or places. In some circumstances this may require the child to reside in accommodation provided by the local authority. The making of a supervision requirement in respect of a child does not affect parental rights and responsibilities. The Children's Hearing may also make a recommendation that a child be freed for adoption.[100]

APPEAL AND REVIEW

13–28 Supervision requirements imposed by a Children's Hearing are intended to endure for as long as is necessary in the interest of promoting or safeguarding the welfare of a child. They may be reviewed or varied and indeed, unless reviewed, they will only last up to one year. Any supervision requirement in place will terminate when the child attains 18 years of age. Review of the supervision requirement may be at the instance of the child or the relevant person or the local authority. Review may be sought through the office of the Reporter. The local authority has the power to call for review at any time. The child or any relevant person may seek a review not less than three months after the supervision requirement has been imposed or at least three months after the most recent continuation or variation of the supervision requirement. Following a request for a review, the Reporter will arrange a Children's Hearing. A review hearing has the power to terminate a supervision requirement, vary a requirement or impose further conditions, or simply continue without variation. The Reporter has no power to seek variation.

As well as the mechanisms for review within the hearing system itself, there is also scope for judicial redress before the sheriff. Within three weeks of a Children's Hearing making a decision in respect of a child, the child or a relevant person may appeal to the sheriff against that decision. An appeal may be made against the actual decision of the hearing or any condition imposed as incidental to that decision. The sheriff may hear evidence, question the Reporter, consider the report or seek further report. The sheriff has the power to confirm the decision of the Children's Hearing, vary or remove any condition attached to that decision, or substitute a decision for that of the Children's Hearing. There is scope in the legislation for further appeal on a point of law to the sheriff principal and to the Court of Session.

THE CHILDREN'S HEARING AND THE CRIMINAL COURTS

13–29 On those occasions where a child is prosecuted in the criminal courts (for example, where the offence is serious, such as murder or rape) and pleads guilty or has been found guilty of an offence where the punishment is not fixed by law, instead of disposing of the case the court may remit the case to the Reporter for the purpose

---

[100] *H* v *Taylor* 1999 GWD 34–1608.

of arranging a hearing which may dispose of the case or for the obtaining of advice as to how the court can best dispose of the child's case. Where the court has sought a hearing with a view to obtaining advice, the court may on the basis of that advice dispose of the case or remit the case back to the Children's Hearing for disposal. In cases where the child is already the subject of a supervision requirement and has pled guilty to an offence, the High Court may remit the case back to the Children's Hearing and the sheriff court must ask for the Reporter to arrange a hearing for the purposes of obtaining advice. Any court which has referred a matter to the Children's Hearing system for advice may, on the receipt of that advice, dispose of the case or remit the case back to the Children's Hearing for disposal, thus ending the court's jurisdiction over the case.[101]

MARRIAGE

The law relating to marriage in Scotland is largely contained in the Marriage (Scotland) Act 1977. Although there is always debate about its continuing social and legal importance, marriage remains the most common form of adult relationship. Whilst there has been focus on the numbers of people who divorce, it is still the case that each year large numbers of adults enter into marriage. The relationship is quasi-contractual, whereby two persons—a man and a woman—agree to be married and to enter into the legal consequences that follow from that relationship. Marriage may be constituted by "regular" means by civil ceremony or by religious ceremony, and also by one irregular method whereby the courts declare that two parties are married by cohabitation with habit and repute. Many regular marriages are, of course, preceded by the parties' formal announcement of engagement. Engagement is now nothing more than a social arrangement and no longer has legal significance.[102]

13–30

MARRIAGE (SCOTLAND) ACT 1977

The Marriage (Scotland) Act 1977 sets down the process of regular marriage and at the same time details the legal requirements and restrictions as to who can be married. Where two persons wish to be married they must submit a notice of intention to marry to the District Registrar in the area where they intend the marriage ceremony to be solemnised.[103] Parties to the marriage need not be resident in the area where they intend to marry though it is usual that they are. In practical terms the parties will usually attend the registrar's office and the notice of intention to marry will be completed on a computer pro-forma, printed off and signed by the parties. In other situations a form may be obtained, completed and returned to the registrar. Along with the notice of intention to marry, parties must submit their birth certificates, and other prescribed

13–31

---

[101] Criminal Procedure (Scotland) Act 1995, s 49; see Norrie, *Children's Hearings in Scotland* (1997), pp 125–130.
[102] The action of breach of promise was abolished by the Law Reform (Husband and Wife) (Scotland) Act 1984, s 1.
[103] Marriage (Scotland) Act 1977, s 3(1).

certificates such as the decree of divorce of a prior marriage, the decree of nullity or a death certificate of one's former spouse.[104] Where such a certificate is unavailable the parties may be permitted to make a declaration in its place. Where one of the parties is a foreign national he or she must submit a certificate from the authorities in his or her country certifying that the person has capacity to be married. In an effort to ensure up-to-date information on the parties' capacity, notices of intention to marry should not be submitted more than three months prior to the proposed ceremony. On receipt of the notice of intention to marry, the appropriate accompanying documentation and the relevant fee, the registrar will enter the details in the marriage notice book. Thereafter, the registrar will display the names of the parties and their proposed date of marriage in a conspicuous place (usually a notice board outside the registry office).[105] The purpose of the display is fairly obvious in that it allows anyone to have notice of the marriage in order that they may raise an objection as to the probity of the proposed marriage. Any person wishing to raise an objection to the marriage may inspect the marriage book free of charge. Objections must be submitted in writing to the registrar.[106] Where the objection relates to the mental capacity of one of the intending spouses it will be necessary to submit a medical certificate in support of this contention.[107] Where the registrar decides that the objection is trivial and does not affect the validity of the proposed marriage, he may simply correct the details of the marriage and proceed. Where, however, the objection strikes at the validity of the marriage, the registrar must notify the Registrar General and carry out an investigation. If the objection is substantiated it is incumbent on the district registrar to make sure that the marriage does not proceed. The minimum notice period is ordinarily 14 days but the registrar has a power to dispense with this minimum period.

In the ordinary course of events no objection is taken to the marriage and the registrar will proceed to make up the marriage schedule.[108] Depending on whether the proposed marriage is to be solemnised in a civil ceremony or by religious ceremony, the marriage schedule will respectively be retained by the registrar or be issued to the parties seven days prior to the date of marriage. Civil ceremonies are usually conducted in the Registry Office, although in cases of illness or where the parties are unable to attend for some other reason, the parties may apply to have the marriage solemnised at any other venue.[109] The marriage will take place in normal working hours. Both parties must be present and there must be two witnesses who profess to be 16 years of age or more.[110] In the course of the ceremony, the parties declare that there are no legal impediments to their marriage and that they consent to take each other as man and wife. Once pronounced husband and wife, the parties will sign the marriage schedule, as does the celebrant of the marriage and the two witnesses. The registrar then takes the schedule and enters the details in the register of marriages.

The religious ceremony, like the civil ceremony, can take place anywhere. The marriage schedule will state the date and venue of the marriage.[111] An "authorised

---

[104] Marriage (Scotland) Act 1977, s 3(1)(b).
[105] *ibid* s 4(2).
[106] *ibid* s 5.
[107] *Mears* 1969 SLT (Sh Ct) 21.
[108] Marriage (Scotland) Act 1977, s 6(1).
[109] *ibid* s 18.
[110] *ibid* s 19(2).
[111] *ibid* s 6(5).

celebrant" must carry out all religious marriages.[112] The 1977 Act states that an authorised celebrant is a Minister of the Church of Scotland or a minister, clergyman, pastor, priest or other religious celebrant of churches and religious orders. Authorised celebrants must be over 21 years of age. Authorised celebrants will be placed on a list held by the Registrar General. He may reject nominees if they are from a non-religious body or he considers them not to be fit and proper persons. As with the civil ceremony, the parties must be present and there must be two witnesses purporting to be 16 years of age or over. The parties will express their consent and confirm that they know of no impediment. After the ceremony they will sign the marriage schedule in the presence of the witnesses. The authorised celebrant and the witnesses will also sign the schedule. The authorised celebrant or the parties must return the schedule within three days to the registrar. The district registrar will thereafter register the marriage.

The formal procedure of regular marriage is designed to ensure that the parties have capacity to enter into marriage. Where there is some procedural defect, which does not raise issues of capacity, the marriage may nevertheless be valid. Where the particulars of any marriage at which both parties are present are entered in the marriage book, the validity of the marriage shall not be questioned on the ground of any failure to comply with provisions of the Act.[113] This cures most procedural defects but it is equally clear that certain procedural defects cannot be cured.[114] It cannot be used to remedy a marriage where the parties are of the same sex, where there is a prior subsisting marriage or an incapacity based on age or one of the forbidden degrees of matrimony.[115]

RESTRICTIONS ON MARRIAGE

Age

A person must be 16 years of age or over before he or she can lawfully marry in Scotland.[116] No parental permission is required for those aged between 16 and 18 years. Where a marriage is entered into in Scotland and one or both of the parties is under 16 years of age, the marriage is void. No person below the age of 16 and domiciled in Scotland can marry; a person domiciled in Scotland who is 16 years of age or over can marry someone below the age of 16 who is domiciled abroad.   **13-32**

Forbidden degrees of relationship

Principally for public policy reasons, though arguably for genetic and medical reasons, certain persons who stand in particular relationships to each other are forbidden to marry one another. Those forbidden degrees arise through blood connection (consanguinity), through marriage (affinity) and through adoption. Although there is a clear correlation, it is not the case that the forbidden degrees of marriage are the same as the relationships governed by the law of incest. A list of the forbidden relationships is contained in section 2 of the Marriage (Scotland) Act 1977. Following an amendment by the Marriage (Prohibited Degrees of Relationship) Act 1986, it is possible for two   **13-33**

---

[112] Marriage (Scotland) Act 1977, s 8(1).
[113] *ibid* s 23A.
[114] *Saleh v Saleh* 1987 SLT 633.
[115] Clive, *Husband and Wife* (4th edn, 1997), p 80.
[116] Marriage (Scotland) Act 1977, s 1.

persons who might otherwise stand in a forbidden degree of relationship due to affinity to each other to marry.

Parties of the same sex

13–34   In the modern era there has been acceptance of same sex relationships. That acceptance has not, however, expanded towards legal recognition of same sex marriage. The issue of sex is determined by genetic composition at birth.[117] As a consequence, rather ironically, where a man and a woman have undergone sexual realignment surgery and now consider themselves to be members of the opposite sex, there is no impediment to the marriage. Other legal systems recognise a form of contract analogous to marriage but in Scotland there is no sign that the law is about to be modified to reflect the growing acceptance of same sex relationships. Challenges to the law before the European Court of Human Rights have also been unsuccessful.

Prior subsisting marriage of one or both parties

13–35   One of the core values enshrined in Scots family law is that of monogamy. A prior subsisting marriage is therefore an impediment to marriage in Scotland. Anyone who marries another in Scotland while already married commits the criminal offence of bigamy. A bigamous marriage is void although, where at least one of the parties thought the marriage valid, children born of the relationship are considered legitimate. Children may continue to exercise any rights they may have against their parents. An innocent spouse who enters into a bigamous marriage may sue for damages.[118]

Marriages void through lack of true consent

13–36   Marriage requires the true consent of the parties for it to be valid. Where consent is improperly obtained or has not been truly given, the marriage is void. Consent may be invalidated in a number of ways.

(a) Mental incapacity

13–37   It is not a complete impediment to marriage that one spouse suffers from a mental disorder or defect. Many such persons enter into marriage. The law only operates to exclude those who do not properly understand the relationship which they wish to enter. The lack of mental capacity impedes their ability to give true consent to the marriage. It is likely that only medical evidence may be adduced to prove or disprove a person's mental capacity to marry.

(b) Error and fraud

13–38   The concepts of error and fraud in the context of contract are of major importance. Although they are of limited value in relation to marriage, nevertheless there have been attempts to utilise the concepts to have a marriage declared void. Notably, in *McLeod* v *Adams*[119] the court held that it was not error as to identity for a woman to marry a man who fraudulently used the wrong name and who lied about his status. Error as to identity could only be applicable as a ground of vitiating true consent to be married in the almost unconscionable circumstances of a party mistakenly marrying a

---

[117] *Corbett* v *Corbett* [1970] 2 All ER 33.
[118] *Burke* v *Burke* 1983 SLT 331.
[119] 1920 1 SLT 229.

person under the erroneous belief that it was in fact someone else. An error as to quality, whilst possible in ordinary contract law, is not a ground of invalidating consent.[120]

(c) Intoxication

Although there is an ancient authority which gives expression to the proposition that intoxication (through drink or drugs) may be advanced as a basis of establishing the lack of true consent to be married,[121] the procedures pertinent to modern regular marriage effectively operate to preclude such a claim. The preparatory plans and notices will all point to a willingness to be married. The prospect of being intoxicated for such a period of time as to include the preliminaries and the ceremony are highly unlikely.   **13–39**

(d) Force and fear

The contractual concept of force and fear operates in the context of marriage to invalidate consent and leads, where it is proved, to the marriage being declared void. Consent to marry must be freely given and not improperly coerced. Many people may feel some moral compulsion to enter into marriage—for example, if there is a child of the liaison—or some other emotional pressure. This is not sufficient compulsion to amount to force and fear. For force and fear to pertain there must be sufficiently induced fear as to have overcome the person's true consent. In Scotland the issue has come to be considered in the context of arranged marriages of persons of ethnic origin who have been pressurised into marrying someone not of their own choice but that of their parents. The question has accordingly come to be asked whether such pressure can amount to force and fear. Initially it was thought that it could not, but latterly there has been recognition that parental pressure and the threat of familial ostracisation can be so great that it truly does amount to force and fear, and as such the marriage should be declared void.[122]   **13–40**

(e) Sham marriages

In the context of consent, the courts have further come to consider whether persons who enter into what are known as "sham marriages" have truly consented to the marriage or whether their pretence of consent should allow them at some later date to seek to have the marriage annulled on the basis that consent was absent. Sham marriages are those where the parties go through a ceremony of marriage (thus being married in law) for some ulterior purpose (perhaps rights of residency that are accorded to those who marry British citizens) but who do not consider themselves to be married in fact. Although there is some dissatisfaction,[123] the law appears well settled. If the court is satisfied that the marriage is a sham and that the parties did not give their consent, then it will declare the marriage void.[124]   **13–41**

---

[120] *Lang v Lang* 1921 SC 44, where husband sought to invalidate the marriage under the alleged erroneous belief that his wife was a virgin, when in fact she was pregnant by another man.
[121] *Johnston v Brown* (1823) 2 S 495.
[122] *Mahmud v Mahmud* 1994 SLT 599—in this case the man was the victim.
[123] See *Akram v Akram* 1979 SLT (Notes) 87 where the sheriff thought that parties who enter into a sham marriage should be personally barred from seeking to have it annulled subsequently.
[124] *Orlandi v Castelli* 1961 SC 113; *Mahmud v Mahmud* 1977 SLT (Notes) 17; *McLeod v Adams* 1920 1 SLT 229.

Voidable marriage through incurable impotency

13–42   A marriage may be voidable on the basis of incurable impotency where one or both of the parties have an incurable incapacity to engage in sexual relations. Where a successful challenge is made to the marriage the courts will declare the marriage void from the date of the marriage. Incurability is not the absolute incapacity to engage in any sexual relations. The absence of full and complete sexual intercourse constitutes incapacity[125] and incurability is established even if it could be cured by extensive or protracted medical treatment.[126] A pursuer can rely on his/her own incurable incapacity. A person may personally barred from seeking annulment on the ground of incurable impotency: where he or she had prior knowledge of the incurable impotency but proceeded with the marriage; where a party has derived benefits from the marriage; or where the parties have adopted children.

MARRIAGE BY COHABITATION WITH HABIT AND REPUTE

13–43   Despite criticism by the Scottish Law Commission and a desire on their part to see it abolished, Scots law continues to recognise one form of irregular marriage—marriage by cohabitation with habit and repute.[127] Anyone can raise an action of declarator of marriage in the Court of Session, whereby they seek to convince the court that there was tacit consent of the parties to be married, which can be inferred from their cohabitation with habit and repute. Over the years several rules have emerged which will require satisfaction before the court will grant a declarator. First, the parties must live together; simply engaging in sexual relations is not enough. The cohabitation must be as husband and wife; the parties must not be cohabiting in some other capacity.[128] The cohabitation must be in Scotland[129] and must be of sufficiently long duration to warrant the inference of tacit consent.[130]

THE LEGAL CONSEQUENCES OF MARRIAGE

13–44   Notwithstanding that the legal consequences of marriage continue to diminish, there remains a number of implied and explicit legal consequences relating to the relationship of marriage. Some of these consequences are rooted in common law and some are rooted in statute.

Name, nationality, domicile and citizenship

13–45   There is no legal requirement that a spouse assume the surname of the spouse he or she marries. It is purely by conventional arrangement that a wife may assume the surname of the husband. Although there is no legal requirement to do so, it is common practice to utilise both the wife's maiden name and her husband's surname when referring to her in formal legal documents.

Marriage now only has an indirect impact upon British citizenship. Citizenship

---

[125] *J* v *J* 1978 SLT 128.
[126] *M* v *M* 1966 SLT 152.
[127] See Ashton-Cross, "Cohabitation with habit and repute" 1961 JR 21.
[128] *Nicol* v *Bell* 1954 SLT 314; *Low* v *Gorman* 1970 SLT 356.
[129] *Walker* v *Roberts* 1998 SLT 1133.
[130] *Campbell* v *Campbell* (1866) 4 M 867; *Wallace* v *Fife Coal Co* 1909 SC 682; *Shaw* v *Henderson* 1982 SLT 211.

may be acquired through a process of naturalisation based on residence within the UK. The indirect impact comes from the fact that one may have a right of residence arising from marriage but, moreover, the rules relating to naturalisation for a married person facilitate a speedier process of naturalisation than that for the unmarried applicant. The period of naturalisation required before a spouse of a British citizen may obtain citizenship is three years with permitted absences. Marriage does not carry with it an automatic right of entry into the United Kingdom or indeed the right to remain. Restrictions do continue to apply but it seems likely that a spouse will be treated more favourably than others might be. Where an overseas person marries a British citizen or a person already settled in the United Kingdom, he must obtain a current entry clearance certificate to enter the country. The rules relating to the issue of such a certificate is purely designed to preclude sham marriages and also to ensure that those entering this country to join a spouse have sufficient financial support without the need for recourse to public funds. When a person has entered the UK with permission and marries a person settled here, he may apply to be allowed to remain here. It is common practice for an extension of 12 months to be granted and further extensions thereafter if the authorities are satisfied that the marriage is genuine and the parties have independent means of supporting themselves and their dependants. A national of a European Community country seeking to enter or remain in Britain following marriage to someone settled here is subject to very limited restrictions.

A wife's domicile of dependence on that of her husband has been abolished. On marriage, she will retain the same domicile, be it her domicile of origin or domicile of choice. A husband no longer has the right to determine where the parties to the marriage will reside.

Contractual and delictual consequences of marriage

There are now no complications engendered by marriage in the contractual capacity **13–46** of the spouses. Previously, married women had no power to enter into contract. Following statutory amendment in 1920 both parties to the marriage are on an equal footing. It is possible for one spouse to appoint the other as his or her agent either expressly or by implication or by acquiescence. However, the mere existence of the relationship of marriage does not in itself impute the existence of a relationship of agent and principal. It is possible for one spouse to be sued or sue the other in a legal action arising from a contractual dispute between them. Marriage does not, however, operate so that both parties to the marriage are automatically jointly and severally liable for any debts or other contractual obligations or delictual acts of only one spouse.

Intentional wrongs or negligent actions are substantially unaffected by the advent of marriage, although certain basic rules can be enunciated. First, a spouse can sue his or her own spouse for any injury arising out of a delictual act. Where one spouse is killed or injured by a third party, the other spouse may sue that third party for loss of support, personal services, funeral expenses and loss of society. A surviving divorced spouse can sue but only for loss of support and funeral expenses (where another has not claimed these). Where a spouse is injured, only that spouse can pursue the claim, although that person can include in their claim a quantification of their immediate family's loss, including that of the spouse. He can seek compensation for failure to provide services to his immediate family.

Succession rights[131]

13–47   One of the most significant legal consequences which arise from marriage are the succession rights that a spouse has in his or her deceased spouse's estate. Where a spouse dies, leaving no will, the other will be entitled to claim prior rights and legal rights. Prior rights comprise rights in respect of three types of property left by the deceased. First, the surviving spouse will be entitled to the dwelling house in which he or she was ordinarily resident prior to death, up to a value of £130,000. Where there is more than one house, the surviving spouse may elect which house to obtain from the deceased's estate. Where the value of the house is greater than £130,000, the surviving spouse will be entitled to claim the equivalent value in money terms. A second facet of prior rights is that the surviving spouse will be entitled to claim furnishings and plenishings up to a sum of £22,000. The third aspect of prior rights relates to remaining estate left by the deceased. Where there are surviving children of the deceased, the surviving spouse's entitlement is to a sum of £35,000, and where there are no children surviving the deceased, the surviving spouse is entitled to £58,000.[132] Prior rights will be settled first out of the intestate estate (estate where there is no will) of the deceased, and thereafter, the surviving spouse may claim legal rights, as may any surviving children. Any estate left following satisfaction of prior rights and then legal rights will be settled in accordance with the ranking of succession as laid down in the Succession (Scotland) Act 1964.

Irrespective of whether there is a will or not, a spouse will be entitled to claim legal rights. Where the deceased is survived by children, the legal rights fund set aside will be such that the surviving spouse is entitled to claim one-third of the moveable estate of the deceased. The child (or children collectively) can likewise claim a further one-third of that moveable estate. Where there are no children surviving the deceased, the surviving spouse is entitled to claim one-half of the deceased's moveable estate. Legal rights do not apply to heritage. They may be discharged by acceptance of the will's provisions or by renunciation of the right to claim legal rights during the lifetime of the spouse now deceased. The end of the marriage does not automatically revoke a testamentary disposition and it may be that a former spouse may acquire some rights from a deceased's will by merely having been described as "my wife". The rules relating to succession between married persons stand in marked contrast to the absence of similar provisions relating to persons in cohabiting relations, irrespective of how longstanding those relationships are.[133]

The right to aliment

13–48   A spouse has a legal obligation financially to support the other during the subsistence of the marriage, whether or not they are residing together.[134] It is a requirement that a spouse pay such support as is reasonable in the circumstances having due regard to the needs and resources of the parties, the earning capacity of the parties and all the circumstances of the case. Account may be taken of anyone the alimenting spouse (that is, the person making the payment of aliment) is supporting, whether that support is

---

[131] See also Chapter 16.
[132] Prior Rights of Surviving Spouse (Scotland) Order 1999 (SI 1999/445).
[133] See para 13–72.
[134] Family Law (Scotland) Act 1985, s 1.

under a legal obligation or not. Support from another party to the alimenting spouse may be taken into account only to such extent as the impact upon his needs. Thus, where a spouse has separated and is residing with another, the cost of accommodation may be thought to be considerably less than it would be were that spouse living on his own. No account may be made of the party's conduct unless it is manifestly inequitable to disregard it. It is a defence to a claim that the defender to the action is willing to allow the pursuing spouse to stay within the matrimonial home and support him, or her, there; such an offer must be deemed to be reasonable. An award of aliment may take the form of a periodical payment that may initially involve occasional payments for particular expenses. It cannot be awarded as a lump sum. There is provision for the backdating and variation of any amount awarded, particularly where there is a material change in circumstances. The parties may reach a voluntary deal as to aliment. Such voluntary agreements are enforceable through the courts. Aliment terminates when the marriage ends, or when either party dies, or the parties voluntarily terminate any agreement they may have.[135]

The matrimonial home and protection from domestic violence

The matrimonial home retains crucial significance in the relationship. It may, if **13–49** privately owned, represent the single biggest asset of matrimonial property. Notwithstanding its monetary value, it is the seat of nearly all that transpires in the domestic relationship.

The Matrimonial Homes (Family Protection) (Scotland) Act 1981 introduced protection against domestic violence. These protections can be listed as:

- occupancy rights

- exclusion orders

- matrimonial interdicts

- protection from dealings in the matrimonial home.

Occupancy rights

The 1981 Act identifies two types of spouse: an entitled spouse and a non-entitled **13–50** spouse. An entitled spouse is a spouse who has legal title to occupy the matrimonial home either as an owner or as a tenant. His or her name is likely to appear on the title to the house or in the tenancy agreement. Conversely, a non-entitled spouse has no legal title to the property. The 1981 Act confers upon the non-entitled spouses the right to occupy (and to continue to occupy) the matrimonial home. These rights are exercisable with any child of the family. In addition to these occupancy rights, non-entitled spouses may seek an order of court giving them ancillary rights to use furniture and furnishings, to make payment of rent or mortgage, to carry out essential repairs and under certain circumstances non-essential repairs, and, generally, to take any steps that the entitled spouse would be able to take in an effort to secure the occupancy of the house. Conferment of occupancy rights protects the non-entitled spouse from ejection from the family home when the relationship breaks up. The

---

[135] Family Law (Scotland) Act 1985, ss 1–7.

simple act of marriage creates the circumstances where one may be determined as an entitled or a non-entitled spouse, thus conferring rights to occupy the matrimonial home. Such conferment is automatic but it may be that a court order is sought to regulate the various occupancy rights of the spouses.

Exclusion orders

13–51 More importantly, there is power under section 4 to seek an exclusion order. Even the spouse who is non-entitled may seek to have their occupancy rights declared and the entitled spouse excluded. The courts will make an exclusion order if it appears to the court that the making of the order is necessary for the protection of the applicant spouse, or any child of the family, from any conduct, or threatened or reasonably apprehended conduct, of the non-applicant spouse, which is or would be injurious to the physical or mental health[136] of the applicant or child.[137] The court shall not make an exclusion order if it would be unjustified or unreasonable having regard to all the circumstances including the conduct of the spouses in relation to one other along with the respective needs and financial resources of the spouses, the need to involve any child of the family and the extent to which the matrimonial home is used in connection with the trade or professional situation of either spouse and whether the entitled spouse is offered or offers to make available to the non-entitled spouse any suitable accommodation.[138] In seeking and being granted an exclusion order, a spouse is likely also to be granted a number of ancillary orders designed to ensure the ejection of the other spouse from the home: an interdict stopping the excluded spouse from entering the home without the express permission of the spouse remaining in the house, and an interdict preventing the removal of furniture and furnishings unless consent is given. In addition there may be interdicts preventing the excluded spouse from entering or remaining in the vicinity of the matrimonial home.

Matrimonial interdicts

13–52 As a prelude, alternative, or adjunct to the pursuit of an exclusion order, the spouse who is the victim or is fearful of domestic violence from the other spouse may seek a matrimonial interdict.[139] Such interdicts are designed to restrain or prohibit any conduct on the part of one spouse towards the other, or a child of the family, or to prevent a spouse from entering or remaining in the matrimonial home or in a specified area in the vicinity of the matrimonial home. Such interdicts cannot be used on their own as a means of excluding an entitled spouse from the home. It is necessary that an exclusion order proper be sought. Matrimonial interdicts, a special form of interdict, can have attached to them a power of arrest which permits a police officer to arrest any spouse suspected of being in breach of the interdict. The power of arrest is of crucial importance in that it allows police officers immediately to apprehend a spouse, thus removing any fear and alarm from the occupying spouse or the spouse in fear of violence. The obtaining of a matrimonial interdict is not an essential prerequisite of an exclusion order. It is made quite clear in cases of domestic violence that one may seek an exclusion order without first assessing the impact of a matrimonial interdict. One

---

[136] On mental health, see *Roberton* v *Roberton* 1999 SLT 38.
[137] Matrimonial Homes (Family Protection) (Scotland) Act 1981, s 4(2).
[138] *ibid* s 4(3).
[139] *ibid* s 14.

of the great criticisms of matrimonial interdicts is that they automatically come to an end when the marriage ends and yet the need for protection may persist beyond the duration of the relationship. Reform of the law on this matter is under consideration within the Scottish Parliament.

Dealings in the matrimonial home

The third arm of the protection of a spouse is the restriction of the entitled spouse from **13–53** defeating occupancy rights by "dealing" (selling, sub-letting, disposing, granting a loan or creating a trust) in the matrimonial home. The law is such that an entitled spouse is still entitled to sell the property but the non-entitled spouse's occupancy rights remain, and as a consequence any purchaser will be unable to exercise his proprietor's right of occupancy. A third party is not by reason only of such a deal entitled to occupy the matrimonial home or any part of it, nor can the third party purchaser demand rental from the occupying spouse.[140] More importantly the third party purchaser cannot evict the occupying spouse.

Where a non-entitled spouse consents in writing to the entitled spouse dealing in the property the entitled spouse will not be inhibited from dealing. The court may dispense with the consent of the non-entitled spouse where consent is being unreasonably withheld, when the spouse's consent cannot be obtained because of a physical or mental disability, or the spouse cannot be found. A non-entitled spouse may renounce by affidavit the right to occupy the matrimonial home. A third party will not be prejudiced where he has acted in good faith and has received an affidavit declaring that the subjects of sale were not at the time of dealing a matrimonial home in relation to which the spouse of the seller has or had occupancy rights, or renouncing occupancy rights, or a consent to the dealing which purports to have been properly made or given by the non-applicant spouse.[141] The solicitor acting for the purchaser will naturally require to be satisfied that such an affidavit or renunciation is in place. The non-entitled spouse who has occupancy rights and who is the subject of a fraudulent dealing by the entitled spouse has the remedy of seeking compensation from the entitled spouse. The unwitting purchaser has the right to occupy and the occupancy rights of the non-entitled spouse are defeated. Where the matrimonial home is held under a lease, it is open to either spouse to seek an order regulating occupancy of the matrimonial home or an exclusion order of one spouse against the other, or indeed to obtain any of the matrimonial interdicts.

Fiscal matters

Until recently, marriage had some consequences in respect of taxation, though it had **13–54** no special significance in respect of social security benefit entitlement. As a consequence of taxation changes introduced in April 2000, the married person's allowance has been abolished along with any tax relief for the payment of aliment to a spouse or dependent children. As a consequence there will no longer be any tax benefits in being married other than the ability to pass property on death to a spouse without incurring inheritance tax.

As regards social security matters, it matters not that the parties are married but

---

[140] Matrimonial Homes (Family Protection) (Scotland) Act 1981, s 6(1)(b).
[141] *ibid* s 6(3)(e).

rather that they are cohabiting together. Any assessment or means-tested benefit operates on the basis that the aggregate income of persons in the same household is taken into account.

Privilege in court proceedings

13–55　In all cases civil or criminal involving one spouse, the other spouse is a competent witness—that is, he or she is allowed to give evidence. In civil cases it appears that a spouse is also a compellable witness (they can be forced to give testimony and must answer any questions put to them). The one notable exception in this matter is that "marital communications" attract a privilege whereby a spouse can refuse to answer any questions relating to a communication between that person and his or her spouse. In a criminal case, where a spouse elects to give evidence on behalf of the accused spouse, she must answer any questions put to her and cannot select those questions which she will answer. However, in criminal matters a spouse is not compellable at the instance of either a co-accused or a prosecutor unless the accused consents to his or her spouse being called. A spouse of the accused is a competent and compellable witness for the accused in criminal cases.

Property

13–56　As a general proposition of law, marriage does not affect ownership of property. Entering into marriage does not give either spouse the right to deal in or to acquire the property of the other spouse. However, that simple statement does not convey the full extent of its impact upon property. It may more properly reflect the situation at the point the parties enter into the marriage. As the marriage continues, individually held and commonly held property may be assimilated into what is known as matrimonial property and may be the subject of dispute or division on termination of the marriage.[142]

The single largest item of property likely to be owned by either spouse or both in common is the matrimonial home. The home is acquired by a written document called a disposition and this document will indicate the owner or owners of the property. Where a property is bought prior to marriage and is not intended as the matrimonial home, ownership remains with the purchasing spouse. This inevitably raises questions where improvements have been carried out at the non-owning spouse's expense. There appears to be little remedy in Scots law for such occurrences.[143] Where two spouses own property in common, as is the more usual modern practice, they do so as *pro indiviso* owners (they each own one-half of the whole property). This means that they have the right to occupy the whole of the house. The spouse seeking to recover his share of such property prior to divorce will require to raise an action for division and sale forcing the property to be sold and the proceeds divided between the parties. A spouse may ask the court under section 19 of the Matrimonial Homes (Family Protection) (Scotland) Act 1981 to refuse to grant the petition for division and sale on the basis that it will defeat his/her occupancy rights.

Section 25 of the Family Law (Scotland) Act 1985 states: "If any question arises (whether during or after a marriage) as to the respective rights of ownership of the

---

[142] See para 13–67.
[143] See Edwards and Griffiths, *Family Law* (1997), pp 326–333.

parties to a marriage in any household goods obtained in prospect of or during the marriage other than by gift or succession from a third party, it shall be presumed, unless the contrary is proved, that each has a right to an equal share in the goods in question." Household goods are defined as any goods including gifts (including decorative or ornamental goods) kept or used at any time during the marriage in any matrimonial home for the joint domestic purposes of the parties to the marriage but not money or securities (shares etc), a motor car, caravan or other vehicle or any domestic animal.[144] Gifts and inheritances are specifically excluded. The ownership of wedding or engagement presents will fall to be determined by the intention of the donor of the gifts. Any cash held or bank account held, whether in joint names or single name, will require proof of ownership: one will require to show who contributed what amount to such accounts. Money saved from any housekeeping allowance is presumed to be property owned and indeed co-shared unless the contrary can be proved.[145]

Children

The mere fact of marriage may lead to legal consequences relating to the children. **13–57** There are presumptions as to paternity and there is the conferment of automatic parental responsibilities and rights on a father married to the child's mother at any time from conception until birth.[146]

DIVORCE

GROUND OF DIVORCE

The sole ground of divorce is that the marriage has irretrievably broken down.[147] **13–58** Irretrievable breakdown may be proved in five ways.

Adultery

Adultery occurs where, since the date of the marriage, a married person voluntarily **13–59** has sexual intercourse with a person of the opposite sex. One solitary post-marital act of sexual intercourse is sufficient. Other forms of sexual act with a person of either sex do not constitute adultery but may constitute unreasonable behaviour (discussed below). Artificial insemination is not adultery.[148] A man who rapes a woman engages in adulterous sexual relations whereas the vicitm does not.[149] It is a defence to an allegation of adultery that the "innocent" spouse actively encouraged the adulterous liaison (known as lenocinium).[150] One may also defend an accusation of adultery on the basis that the other spouse has "condoned" the act of adultery. Condonation is

---

[144] Family Law (Scotland) Act 1985, s 25(3).
[145] *ibid* s 26.
[146] See para 13–12.
[147] Divorce (Scotland) Act 1976, s 1(1).
[148] *MacLennan* v *MacLennan* 1958 SC 105.
[149] *Andrews* v *Andrews* 1971 SLT (Notes) 44.
[150] *Gallacher* v *Gallacher* 1928 SC 586; *cf Thomson* v *Thomson* 1908 SC 179.

more than verbal forgiveness and entails the resumption of marital relations in the full knowledge of the adulterous act.[151]

Behaviour

13–60   Irretrievable breakdown of marriage may be proved by the fact that one of the spouses has at any time since marriage behaved either actively or passively (whether or not as a result of mental abnormality) in such a way that the other spouse cannot reasonably be expected to live with that spouse.[152] Behaviour before marriage is irrelevant.[153] Depending on the gravity of it, one single act may be sufficient. Behaviour has been described as an act rather than an event.[154] It is an action or way of conducting oneself, which affects the other spouse.[155] A physical condition is not "behaviour". Unreasonable behaviour can be drawn very widely and as a consequence it is the most common method of proving irretrievable breakdown of marriage.[156] Examples of unreasonable behaviour include assault, accusations of an incestuous association,[157] obsessive working,[158] sexual behaviour, bestiality, homosexuality, neglect, obsessive behaviour, drunkenness, exposure to disease, and behaviour towards a third party, such as a relative or a child. As the statute states, the behaviour may be passive, such as ignoring the other spouse. There need be no injury to health. Proof of unreasonable behaviour is on the balance of probabilities. It is not a bar to proving unreasonable behaviour that the parties are continuing to cohabit.

Desertion

13–61   Although it has existed for a considerable period of time as a means of founding a divorce action, in the modern era irretrievable breakdown of marriage based on desertion is relatively rare. The statute provides that irretrievable breakdown may be proved where one spouse has wilfully and without reasonable cause deserted the other and throughout a two-year period after the desertion there has been no cohabitation, and the deserted spouse has not refused a genuine and reasonable offer to adhere.[159] Due to the requirement of wilfulness, imprisonment or being separated against one's will is not desertion. Moreover, an agreement to separate does not amount to desertion.

Two years' non-cohabitation with consent

13–62   The second most common method of establishing irretrievable breakdown of marriage is where the spouses have not cohabited for a continuous period of two years after the marriage and immediately prior to divorce and both consent to decree of divorce passing.[160] Unlike desertion, the reason for separation is irrelevant; the parties may have been separated against their will.[161] The prime consideration is that the parties

---

[151] Divorce (Scotland) Act 1976, s 1(3).
[152] *ibid* s 1(2)(b).
[153] *Hastings* v *Hastings* 1941 SLT 323.
[154] Clive, *Husband and Wife* (4th edn, 1997), p 379.
[155] *Katz* v *Katz* [1972] 1 WLR 955 at 960.
[156] See, *Untying the Knot: Characteristics of Divorce in Scotland* (Scottish Office, 1993).
[157] *Hastie* v *Hastie* 1985 SLT 146.
[158] *Ross* v *Ross* 1997 SLT (Sh Ct) 51.
[159] Divorce (Scotland) Act 1976, s 1(2)(c).
[160] *ibid* s 1(2)(d); *Untying the Knot* (1993).
[161] Note the English case of *Santos* [1972] 2 All ER 246, where it is suggested that there must be a mental intent not to live together; Meston, "Divorce Reform in Scotland", 1977 SLT (News) 13.

are not cohabiting as man and wife. The absence of sexual relations will not be conclusive proof of that, although it may be an indicator. The parties may be living in the same house but not cohabiting together as man and wife. For example, in the case of *Fuller* v *Fuller*[162] a woman took her husband back into the matrimonial home to nurse him through a serious illness. The law also recognises that parties may be experiencing difficulties within their marriage and that there may be attempts to save the marriage. With this in mind, where parties separate and resume cohabitation for a period of less than six months the continuity of the period of non-cohabitation is not broken. The court will not enquire into why there is a refusal to grant consent and has no power to overrule a refusal to consent, no matter how unreasonable such a refusal may appear.[163] Consent may be withdrawn at anytime during the divorce proceedings.

Five years' non-cohabitation without consent

In the absence of consent, a party may seek a divorce on the basis that the marriage has **13–63** irretrievably broken down as evidenced by no cohabitation between the parties for a continuous period of five years after the marriage and immediately preceding the divorce. The statute does provide that the court may decline to grant decree of divorce where there is likely to be grave financial hardship on the defender.[164] The current law and practice relating to financial provision on divorce make such an eventuality highly unlikely. The Scottish Law Commission has recommended abolition of the court's discretion in the matter.[165]

FINANCIAL PROVISION ON DIVORCE

Given the large number of divorce actions each year, it is hardly surprising that this **13–64** area of law gives rise to a substantial body of case law. From what was once an issue largely determined by judicial discretion,[166] a system of flexible court powers and five key principles has emerged to introduce a measure of consistency into this hotly disputed area of law. The significance of the law lies not only in the settlement of disputes that actually go before the courts but also in the large number of negotiated settlements between parties prior to divorce in anticipation of a complete ending of the parties' relationship.[167]

THE LEGAL FRAMEWORK OF FINANCIAL PROVISION ON DIVORCE

In the early 1980s the Scottish Law Commission pressed for reform of the law relative **13–65** to financial provision on divorce. The desire for a flexible system of principles and court orders was given effect to in the Family Law (Scotland) Act 1985. It was an

---

[162] [1973] 2 All ER 650.
[163] *Boyle* v *Boyle* 1977 SLT (Notes) 69, per Lord Maxwell.
[164] *Boyd* v *Boyd* 1978 SLT (Notes) 55.
[165] SLC, *Report on Family Law* (1992), para 13.12.
[166] For a discussion of the pre-1985 position, see Thomson, *Family Law in Scotland* (2nd edn, 1991), pp 99–119.
[167] For a discussion about private ordering in family law matters, see Edwards and Griffiths, *Family Law* (1997), pp 393–414.

underpinning philosophy of the new law that where possible a clean break settlement was to be preferred. The courts now have the power to order:

- the payment of a capital sum

- a property transfer order

- periodical allowance

- an order relating to pension benefits

- various incidental orders

- an anti-avoidance order.

A capital sum (or lump sum) or a property transfer order can be effective immediately on divorce or at some future time specified by the court (for example, on receipt of a pension, a lump sum or sale of a house)[168] or, alternatively, within a period of time specified by the court.[169] The presumption is that orders will be effective immediately and that postponement will only occur in special circumstances. A capital sum can be paid in instalments.[170] A capital sum may be related to the value of the asset rather than a fixed amount, although any percentage must be fixed. The property transfer ordered may be postponed.[171] The court also has the power to make a pension benefit order,[172] which compels the trustees and managers of a pension fund to pay a lump sum to a former spouse when the lump sum falls as due to be paid.[173] Before making a pension benefit order, the court must first have made an order for a capital payment, the liable party must have rights and interests in a pension fund which are matrimonial property, and the benefits must include the payment of a lump sum to a liable party or on his or her death.[174]

Before making an order for periodical allowance the court must satisfy itself that a transfer of property order or a capital sum is inappropriate or insufficient in the circumstances to settle the issue of financial provision.[175] Moreover, periodical allowance can only be made if it is justified by one of the principles listed in section 9(1) (c), (d), or (e). The instinctive preference of the courts should always be to promote a clean break and thus the case law is illustrative of a reluctance to order periodical allowance and, where it is ordered, for the duration of it to be limited.[176] An award of periodical allowance can be for a definite period, an indefinite period or until the happening of a specific event.[177] A periodical allowance order may be recalled, varied or converted to a capital sum or a property transfer order by the court. Although it may continue to be paid from the payer's estate if the payer dies, periodical allowance

---

[168] See, *eg*, *Little* v *Little* 1990 SLT 785.
[169] *Neill* v *Neill* 1987 SLT (Sh Ct) 143.
[170] See, *eg*, *Bell* v *Bell* 1988 SCLR 457 where £10,000 was ordered to be paid at £200 per month; see also *Gracie* v *Gracie* 1997 SLT (Sh Ct) 15.
[171] Family Law (Scotland) Act 1985, s 12(1).
[172] *ibid* s 12A.
[173] *ibid* s 8(1)(ba).
[174] *ibid* s 12A(1).
[175] See *Cunniff* v *Cunniff* 1999 SC 537, where it was said that it would be unusual to leave one party insolvent.
[176] *Dever* v *Dever* 1988 SCLR 352.
[177] Family Law (Scotland) Act 1985, s 13(3).

automatically ends with the death or remarriage of the recipient. In addition to the foregoing powers, the court has the power to order disclosure of assets and resources in matrimonial proceedings.[178] The court can also vary or block transactions, which have as their purpose the avoidance of financial provision.[179]

The incidental powers of the courts referred to above include the power to order the sale of matrimonial property, to order the valuation of property,[180] to issue a declarator of ownership or to make an order in respect of occupancy of the matrimonial home or in respect of the furnishings contained therein.

The section 9 principles of division

Section 9 of the Family Law (Scotland) Act 1985 affords the court discretion to make **13–66** an order relating to financial provision on divorce which is reasonable having regard to the resources of the parties. Before it can make any order, financial provision has to be justified by one or more of five key principles.

Section 9(1)(a): the net value of the matrimonial property should be shared fairly between the parties to the marriage

This principle is the dominant one in that it is used in most divorce settlements. **13–67** Although brief, it contains many matters which require interpretation. First, the inclusion of the words "net value" dictates that all permitted matrimonial debts are deducted from the assets before a division of matrimonial property takes place. Thus, for example, mortgages must be deducted from the value of the matrimonial home. Fair sharing is ordinarily interpreted as equal sharing although circumstances set down in section 10(1) of the 1985 Act may dictate that settlements are skewed in favour of one spouse or another. In making a calculation it is important to determine exactly what is matrimonial property. Matrimonial property is all property belonging to spouses or either of them at the relevant date, that being the date when the parties separate. This includes property acquired before marriage for use as or in the matrimonial home and all property acquired by the parties during the marriage before the relevant date. From any calculation of matrimonial property there can be excluded: property acquired by individual spouses prior to the marriage which was not used during the marriage and was kept distinct from matrimonial property; any property acquired by a spouse after the relevant date unless it is something which pertains to an occurrence which happened prior to separation; and any gifts or successions during marriage. Accordingly, matrimonial property includes rights and interests under a life policy or an occupational pension scheme.[181] It also includes compensation for personal injury sustained during the marriage before separation[182] and redundancy payments relating to the relevant period.[183] Property purchased in the name of one spouse intended for use as the matrimonial home becomes matrimonial property and may be divided upon the termination of the marriage.

The principle is a general one and a number of reasons for departure from the

---

[178] Family Law (Scotland) Act 1985, s 20.
[179] *ibid* s 18.
[180] *Demarco v Demarco* 1990 SCLR 635.
[181] *Little v Little* 1990 SLT 230; it does not include a right to share in a pension benefit which only arises through marriage, such as a widow's benefit: see *Dibie v Dibie* 1997 SC 134.
[182] *Skarpaas v Skarpaas* 1991 SLT (Sh Ct) 15.
[183] See, *eg, Tyrrell v Tyrrell* 1990 SLT 406.

principle are recognised within the statute.[184] First, where any agreement exists between the parties on ownership and division of matrimonial property the courts may give effect to this.[185] There is scope within the legislation for the courts to vary agreements where they contain provisions to that effect, although courts are reluctant to intervene.[186] Second, the courts will deviate from the basic tenet of the principle to recognise that the source of the funds or assets used to acquire the matrimonial property has come from the efforts or income of one of the parties during the marriage. The case law on this matter betrays an inconsistency of approach in the courts. There are instances where the utilisation of one party's assets to acquire what is admittedly matrimonial property simply results in the property being submerged into matrimonial property with all the inherent unfairness that that brings.[187] The third reason whereby the courts will not simply divide the net matrimonial property is when there has been destruction, dissipation, or alienation of property by either spouse.[188] A fourth factor, which may result in a deviation from the norm, relates to the nature of the matrimonial property[189]—for example, where the matrimonial property is used as a business asset, or is compensation for a specific injury which requires the party to engage medical help or support care. Finally, the courts will take into account any expenses incurred in transferring property.

In determining financial provision on divorce, the conduct of either party is largely irrelevant unless it adversely affects the relevant financial resources.[190] There may be exceptions to this rule where the conduct of either party impacts upon the matrimonial property. Under this principle, the courts cannot make an order for periodical allowance but can make a capital transfer order, an order relating to a pension or a property transfer order.

One of the thornier issues addressed under this principle relates to the situation where the matrimonial home, or indeed any matrimonial property, has increased in value after the relevant date but before the date of divorce. Is the increase in value a matrimonial asset to be shared between the parties? It would appear, following the controversial decision by the House of Lords in *Wallis v Wallis*,[191] that the valuation of the property is tied to the date of separation.[192]

Section 9(1)(b): fair account should be taken of any economic advantage derived by either party from contributions by the other, and of any economic disadvantage suffered by either party in the interests of the other party or of the family

13–68 The second of the section 9 principles permits the court to take account of any economic advantage or disadvantage which may arise in the circumstances of the parties. It has been used in a variety of ways to introduce fairness into the distribution of matrimonial assets.[193] It has been used to recompense mortgage payments by one

---

[184] Family Law (Scotland) Act 1985, s 10(6).
[185] *Anderson* v *Anderson* 1991 SLT (Sh Ct) 11.
[186] Family Law (Scotland) Act 1985, s 16.
[187] See *Fulton* v *Fulton* 1998 SLT 1262 (shares purchased by gift).
[188] Family Law (Scotland) Act 1985, s 18.
[189] *ibid* s 10(6)(d).
[190] *ibid* s 11(7)(a).
[191] 1993 SLT 1348.
[192] A solution is suggested by Elaine Sutherland in *Family Law Basics* (1999), p 91; *Jacques* v *Jacques* 1997 SC(HL) 20.
[193] See *Wilson* v *Wilson* 1999 SLT 249 (assistance in developing company); *Cahill* v *Cahill* 1998 SLT (Sh Ct) 96 (repairs to a cottage).

spouse after the parties have separated.[194] Advantage or disadvantage in the context of this principle can relate to periods during or before[195] the marriage, including gains and losses in capital, income or earning capacity.[196] In responding to this principle the courts have the power to order a capital transfer or a property transfer but not a periodical allowance.[197]

Section 9(1)(c): any economic burden of caring, after divorce, for a child of the marriage under the age of 16 years should be shared fairly between the parties

This principle relates to any child of the marriage including children of both spouses **13–69** and any child accepted by them as part of their family.[198] Although it is not to be confused with child support or financial provision for children (discussed above), nevertheless in calculating financial provision on divorce, child support or aliment may be taken into account, as can the child's needs and whether or not the payer is supporting another in his or her household irrespective of any legal obligation to do so.[199] The court may make a capital transfer order, a property transfer order and/or an order for periodical allowance.[200]

Section 9(1)(d): a party who has been dependent to a substantial degree on the financial support of the other party should be awarded such financial provision as is reasonable to enable him to adjust, over a period of not more than three years from the date of the divorce, to the loss of that support on divorce

Although the statute has a basic premise that where possible a clean break settlement **13–70** should be promoted, the fourth of the section 9 principles permits the courts to make an order designed to allow a former spouse to adjust to the changed circumstances where that person has previously been dependent to a substantial degree on the other. In the first instance the court should attempt to utilise the first three principles and the power of a capital sum and/or a property transfer order to provide for the adjustment.[201] However, where that is not possible the court may look to making an order for periodical allowance. In assessing the circumstances, the court may decide not to award a large sum or if an award for periodical allowance is made it may only be for a short duration.[202] The court is empowered to look at a number of factors including the age of the claiming spouse, his or her earning capacity, his or her plans for retraining and the duration of dependence prior to divorce.[203] The court may consider the conduct of the parties as adversely affecting financial resources where it would be manifestly inequitable to disregard it.[204]

---

[194] *Kerrigan v Kerrigan* 1988 SCLR 603.
[195] See *Dougan v Dougan* 1998 SLT (Sh Ct) 27.
[196] Family Law (Scotland) Act 1985, s 9(2); see *Loudon v Loudon* 1994 SLT 381.
[197] *ibid* ss 8(1), 12(3) and 13(2).
[198] *ibid* s 27(1).
[199] *ibid* s 11(6).
[200] *ibid* ss 8(1) and 13(2).
[201] *Wilson v Wilson* 1999 SLT 249.
[202] See *Dever v Dever* 1988 SCLR 352 (award for six months); *Sherett v Sherett* 1990 SCLR 799 (award for 13 weeks).
[203] Family Law (Scotland) Act 1985, s 11(4).
[204] *ibid* s 11(7)(b).

Section 9(1)(e): a party who at the time of divorce seems likely to suffer serious financial hardship as a result of the divorce should be awarded such financial provision as is reasonable to relieve him of hardship over a reasonable period

13–71 The fifth principle is often used in respect of long-standing spouses of mature years. It provides a flexible principle, which permits deviation from the notion of clean break.[205] The court will consider the age and health of the spouses, the duration of the marriage, and their needs and resources. In addition, the court will consider whether either of the spouses is supporting another in their household whether under a legal obligation or not. Again, the courts will only consider conduct if it is inequitable not to do so. In addition the courts will look at the conduct of the parties which affects resources (such as destruction or alienation of property). The court may make a capital sum order and/or a property transfer order and/or a periodical allowance order. Orders can subsist until remarriage or death.

COHABITATION

13–72 Previously, family law concentrated on marriage as the dominant adult relationship. The changing nature of societal relationships calls for the reappraisal of such an approach. Families are no longer nuclear families in the traditional sense. Large numbers of families are now single-parent families or those where the adult partners are cohabitees. The law remains discriminatory in many respects, although the diminution in the legal consequences of marriage has brought some convergence of the status, treatment and rights of cohabitees and those of married persons. There is pressure from the "gay" community for reform of the law relating to those in same-sex cohabiting relationships. That pressure includes demands for recognition of same-sex "marriage" and all the attendant legal consequences that flow from formal recognition of the relationship.

It is certainly the case that any discussion of adult family law no longer pertains solely to the discussion of marriage. The legal effect of cohabitation is rarely given separate treatment in law books but this seems likely to change in the future. For the moment, discussion of cohabitation centres on comparison with the legal consequences pertaining to marriage and the extrapolation from general principles of law those applicable to cohabiting couples, irrespective of the formal relationship between the parties.

The status of cohabitation has not attracted as many legal rights as the relationship of marriage. It is true that cohabiting parties receive similar treatment to those in the more formalised relationship of marriage in a few key respects. First, in relation to the fiscal matters of taxation and social security, marriage attracts no special status and there can be said to be parity in these respects between the two forms of relationship. It is also the case that it is a basic premise of property law that there is a presumption

---

[205] See Thomson, "Financial Provision on Divorce—The current state of play", 1989 SLT (News) 33; *Johnstone v Johnstone* 1990 SLT (Sh Ct) 79.

in favour of the separation of property between the marital spouses and the same can be said of those who are in cohabiting relationships.

However, as has been seen elsewhere in this chapter, there are a number of situations where marriage has important legal consequences and, irrespective of the duration and quality of the cohabitation, those same rights are not afforded to cohabiting couples. Thus, for example, the provisions of the Family Law (Scotland) Act 1985 in respect of household goods, savings and life policies only pertain to married couples and not to cohabiting couples. The rights that a spouse has in succession are not conferred on the cohabitee. Furthermore, the obligation of aliment implicit in the marital relationship does not exist in the cohabiting relationship. Likewise, there are no provisions for the making of financial provision following the termination of a relationship in the same way that there are for financial provision on divorce. These are fundamental situations, which give rise to a great deal of unfairness in many cohabiting relationships.

Ownership of the home where two persons are cohabiting is determined solely by title. The taking of title in the sole name of one of the cohabitees can often result in unfairness when the relationship comes to an end. Though there may be solutions to such unfairness (see below), the pursuit of fairness is fraught with great complexity.[206]

Cohabitees are given some rights in respect of protection from domestic violence but these are not the same as those afforded to persons in a marital relationship. A non-entitled cohabitee may seek a declarator of occupancy rights. There is no automatic conferment of occupancy rights and, indeed, before engaging the statutory protections a cohabitee will require to prove that he or she is in a cohabiting relationship. This can be contrasted with marriage, which automatically confers occupancy rights. A further difference is that the cohabitee cannot seek a grant of interim occupancy rights under the statute but must raise an action for full occupancy rights with all the delay that entails. Occupancy rights can be granted to cohabitees initially only for a period not exceeding six months, although this may be extended by further periods of six months. Exclusion orders granted to cohabitees under section 4 are similarly limited to a six-month duration, albeit that again one can seek renewal. The cohabitee is not protected to the same extent as the spouse in relation to third party dealings. Only cohabitees who have been granted occupancy rights can seek a court order transferring a tenancy. An entitled cohabitee cannot seek to utilise an exclusion order against a violent non-entitled cohabitee. It is believed that he simply has the right to eject the non-entitled cohabitee and to enforce this through interdict. The discrimination between spouses and cohabitees in respect of domestic violence has been strongly criticised. It is thought likely that this will be an area for reform in the not too distant future by the Scottish Parliament. One positive aspect of the treatment of cohabitees under the 1981 Act has been the relatively recent decision of *Armour* v *Anderson*,[207] where it was held that the cohabitee who has fled the family home may seek an exclusion order notwithstanding that she is no longer within the former home.

A further controversial area relates to the care and upbringing of children. The issue is not, by and large, dominated by consideration of whether the parents are married. However, it has been noted elsewhere that the existence of marriage has the effect of

---

[206] See Sutherland, *Child and Family Law* (1999), Chap 11; Edwards and Griffiths, *Family Law* (1997), Chap 12.
[207] 1994 SCLR 642.

conferring automatic parental responsibilities and rights on fathers who are married to the mother. A cohabiting father does not receive such automatic conferrance and instead must seek recognition by the mother or through agreement with the mother or through the pursuit of a court order conferring such rights and responsibilities.

Indirectly, the absence of the relationship of marriage does have an impact upon an unmarried father in respect of a whole range of matters and decisions affecting the care and upbringing of a child. It does not, however, affect certain key obligations, principally that of aliment, which the cohabiting father may have in respect of the child. As already noted, cohabitees may assume the right to aliment a child that is not naturally their own where they have accepted that child as a member of the family. Natural fathers cohabiting with the child's mother naturally do retain the obligation to aliment the child.

The differential treatment of cohabiting couples has led to many academic commentators calling for reform. The three ideas most often canvassed to attempt to resolve some of the problems are the creation of cohabitation contracts, remedies under the law of unjustified enrichment, and finally solutions in the law of constructive trusts.[208] It would be fair to say that cohabiting contracts have not been fully tested before the Scottish courts and that there is doubt in respect of the other two concepts as to their true scope for remedying unfair treatment. Pursuit of legal reform to equalise the positions of marriage and other forms of cohabiting relationships appears to be a far better solution; one that may nevertheless take some time to bring about.

SAME-SEX COHABITATION

13–73   A further area that requires some comment is that of same-sex relationships. In many respects all that has been said in respect of cohabiting couples can similarly be addressed to those in same-sex cohabiting relationships. Some campaign for the legal recognition of such relationships but all legal attempts have, so far, failed. Same-sex couples are treated even less fairly than heterosexual cohabiting couples in that the protections afforded in the Matrimonial Homes (Family Protection) (Scotland) Act 1981 to cohabitees only apply to those cohabiting as "man and wife".

There are those who campaign for those in same-sex relationships to be allowed to marry but this would appear to be (certainly in the medium term) a forlorn hope. There is evidence of increasing recognition of the status of such relationships and, in a recent case, of some enlightenment on the part of the judiciary. In *Fitzpatrick v Sterling Housing Association*,[209] the House of Lords ruled that a gay man in a cohabiting relationship could have the tenancy of his former partner transferred to him following the death of that man. It had been argued that the male partner of the deceased could not count as part of his family but the House of Lords took the view that this was not the case.

Those seeking further support of the incremental advancement of recognition of same-sex relationships may be drawn to consider the case of *T, Petitioner*,[210] where a homosexual was allowed to adopt a young child. In addition, there is a recent case in England involving Scottish men who had commissioned a surrogate baby in America

---

[208] See Edwards and Griffiths, *Family Law* (1997), pp 328, 330, 339, 404–413.
[209] [1999] 3 WLR 1113.
[210] 1997 SLT 724.

and have now been given leave to have the child enter and remain in the United Kingdom. For cohabitees and same sex cohabitees there is doubtless a long way to go before there will be an equalisation or parity with the rights conferred upon those in a marital relationship.

SUMMARY

THE CHILD, LEGAL PERSONALITY AND CAPACITY

- As a basic proposition of law, legal personality begins at birth, although the unborn child (subsequently born alive) is regarded as having legal capacity in relation to rights in succession and rights in delict.
- Capacity is a broad concept, embracing not only rights but also responsibilities. In many circumstances capacity begins with the commencement of personality. However, capacity may be thought to be an evolutionary matter. At certain stages in the child's development, capacity may be expanded.
- Ordinarily a person under the age of 16 years shall have no legal capacity to enter into any transaction.
- Children 12 years and over have the capacity to make a will and to consent or otherwise to adoption or freeing for adoption.
- A person under the age of 16 years has legal capacity to consent on his behalf to any surgical, medical or dental procedure or treatment where in the opinion of a qualified medical practitioner attending him he is capable of understanding the nature and possible consequences of the procedure or treatment.
- A person under the age of 16 years of age has legal capacity to instruct a solicitor in connection with any civil matter where that person has an understanding of what it means to do so. As well as having the right to consult and instruct a solicitor, a child also has the right as a legal person to initiate, pursue and defend legal proceedings.

CHILDREN'S RIGHTS, RESPONSIBILITIES, RESTRICTIONS AND PROTECTIONS

- There is a broad array of rights, responsibilities, restrictions and legal protections applicable to the child. The child's rights can be grouped under three broad headings: the right to financial support, succession rights, and delictual rights.
- The main method by which absent parents financially support the upbringing of their children is child support. Liability for child support is assessed and it is collected by the Child Support Agency. Parents cannot exclude the operation of the Child Support Agency. There will be automatic assessment where the custodial parent is in receipt of state benefits. Parents, guardian, other relevant persons or the child may seek an assessment. The calculation of the extent of liability is based on a formula.
- Although substantially replaced by child support, aliment remains as a basis of financial support of children in certain circumstances. Parents and other relevant persons (custodial and non-custodial) are obliged to give such support as is reasonable in the circumstances having regard to various factors. Aliment may be privately agreed or sought through the courts.
- Any child has legal rights in succession in his parents' moveable estate.
- A child has the juristic capacity to pursue a delictual action either in respect of any injury or wrong occasioned to himself (including injury or wrong

perpetrated by his own parent(s)) and in respect of any delict by a third party which results in the death or injury of his parent(s).

- From the age of eight a child is criminally responsible.
- Children are protected by law from sexual exploitation, abuse and neglect.
- A child may have certain responsibilities under the law of delict, and also under the law of contract.

PARENTHOOD AND PARENTAL RESPONSIBILITIES AND RIGHTS

- A child's mother automatically has parental rights and responsibilities in relation to her child, irrespective of her age or her marital status.
- In contrast, a child's genetic father only acquires parental rights automatically if he is married to the mother of the child at conception or subsequently.
- A genetic father who is not married to the mother at the time of the child's birth may acquire parental rights by subsequently marrying the mother of the child, or by reaching a formal agreement with the mother that he will have responsibilities and rights, or alternatively by applying to the court for a parental responsibilities and rights order.
- A man is presumed to be the father of the child if he is married to the mother of the child at any time in the period beginning with the conception and ending with the birth of the child.
- A man is presumed to be the father of the child where both he and the mother have acknowledged that he is the father and he has been registered as such in an appropriate register of births, deaths and marriages.
- In assisted parenthood a woman giving birth to a child will be considered for all purposes as the mother of that child.
- Where a child is conceived and delivered following artificial insemination by sperm donation, paternity will be granted to the husband or partner of any woman undergoing artificial insemination donation or similar treatment where both the woman and the man consent to that treatment and are undergoing it in a joint venture.
- In surrogacy cases the gestational mother—the mother who carries the child—is deemed to be the mother of the child in law and, indeed, if she is married, her husband (if he has consented to the surrogacy) is deemed to be the father.
- A "relevant person" (including parents, guardians or someone who has parental responsibilities and rights in respect of a child) has the responsibility:

  (a) to safeguard and promote the child's health, development and welfare;
  (b) to provide direction and guidance to the child in a manner appropriate to the stage of the child's development;
  (c) if the child is not living with the parent, to maintain personal relations and direct contact with the child on a regular basis; and
  (d) to act as the child's legal representative.

- Relevant persons also have a number of rights:

(a) to have the child living with him or her or otherwise to regulate the child's residence;

(b) to control, direct and guide the child's upbringing in a manner appropriate to the child's stage of development;

(c) if the child does not live with the parent, to maintain personal relations and direct contact with the child on a regular basis; and

(d) to act as the child's legal representative.

ADOPTION

- Adoption is a legal process whereby the relationship between a child and his or her parents is terminated, and a new legal relationship of parent and child is created between the child and his or her adoptive parents.
- The requirement of a court order and the operation of state or state-sponsored agencies in respect of adoption ensure that there is considerable judicial and state supervision of the whole process of adoption.
- A court is required to regard the need to promote the welfare of the child concerned as its paramount consideration.
- There is no restriction on the marital status or sexual orientation of those who can adopt.
- Only children under 18 years of age who are not married or have not been married can be adopted. It is possible for a child to be adopted and thereafter readopted.
- It is an important requirement that the parent or guardian of any child must freely and with full understanding of what is involved agree unconditionally to the making of an adoption order (although this may be dispensed with in certain circumstances).
- It is necessary that a child 12 years or over gives his consent to the adoption. The child's refusal to consent cannot be overridden by the court.
- The adopted child will be registered in the adopted children register. When the child reaches the age of 16, he or she will be entitled to obtain information in respect of his natural birth and subsequent adoption.

THE CHILD IN NEED OF CARE

- In some circumstances children may be in need of care and it is necessary that the state, in the form of the local authority, intervenes to secure the care and protection of the child.
- A local authority is under a duty to: (a) safeguard and promote the welfare of children in its area who are in need, and (b) so far as consistent with that duty, promote the upbringing of such children by their families.
- Where it is necessary, a local authority shall provide accommodation for any child who, residing or having been found in their area, appears to require such provision because: (a) no one has parental responsibility for him; (b) he is lost or abandoned; or (c) the person who has been caring for him is prevented, whether or not permanently, and for whatever reason, from providing him with suitable accommodation or care.

- There are a number of orders at the disposal of local authorities, designed to give them further powers to tackle the growing problem of child abuse and neglect. The orders are:

  (a) child assessment orders;
  (b) exclusion orders;
  (c) parental responsibilities orders;
  (d) child protection orders.

THE CHILDREN'S HEARING SYSTEM

- The Children's Hearings system provides a means whereby measures of compulsory supervision may be instituted in respect of a child.
- Any person who believes that a child requires compulsory measures of supervision may make a referral to the Reporter to the Children's Hearing. It is also the case that a child may come before a Children's Hearing as the result of a referral by a court.
- There are 12 different grounds of referral of a child to a Children's Hearing.
- Establishment of the ground of referral is vital. It founds the jurisdiction of the hearing and its acceptance or establishment allows the hearing to go on to deliberate a solution for the child's circumstances.
- In circumstances where the grounds of referral are rejected either by the child or by the relevant person, the hearing cannot proceed and the matter will be referred to the sheriff court for a hearing to decide whether a ground of referral is established.
- A children's hearing may be continued to seek further information; it may require a child to attend or reside in a clinic, hospital or other establishment for the purpose of investigation; and it has the power to issue warrants for the removal of the child and detention in a place of safety.
- The main powers open to a Children's Hearing are: it may discharge the referral, offering advice and assistance, if convinced that there is no need for any formal compulsory measure of care and that the issue is being tackled at source; alternatively, it may make a supervision requirement which requires the child to be under the supervision of the local authority either while remaining at home or in the care of the local authority.
- The decisions of a Children's Hearing may be reviewed or varied.
- As well as the mechanisms for review within the hearing system itself, there is also scope for judicial redress in the courts.

MARRIAGE

- Marriage may be constituted by "regular" means by civil ceremony or by religious ceremony and also an "irregular" method whereby the court declares that two parties are married by cohabitation with habit and repute.
- There is a formal process involved in regular marriage designed to ensure that the parties have capacity to enter into marriage.

- A person must be 16 years of age or over before he or she can lawfully marry in Scotland.
- Certain persons who stand in particular relationships to one another are forbidden to marry each other.
- Same-sex marriage is not recognised in Scotland.
- A prior subsisting marriage is an impediment to marriage.
- Where consent is improperly obtained or has not truly been given the marriage is void.
- A marriage may be voidable on the basis of incurable impotency where one (or both) of the parties has an incurable incapacity to engage in sexual relations.
- Anyone may raise an action of declarator of marriage in the Court of Session, whereby they seek to convince the court that there was tacit consent of the parties to be married, which can be inferred from their cohabitation with habit and repute.
- There remains a number of implied and explicit legal consequences relating to the relationship of marriage.

DIVORCE

- The sole ground of divorce is that the marriage has irretrievably broken down.
- Irretrievable breakdown may be proved in five ways: adultery; behaviour of one of the parties; desertion by one of the parties; the failure of the parties to cohabit for two years and both parties consent to the divorce; and both parties live apart for five years.
- Financial provision on divorce is determined by a system of flexible court powers and five key principles.
- The courts now have the power to: order the payment of a capital sum; make a property transfer order; order a periodical allowance; make an order relating to pension benefits; make various incidental orders and an anti-avoidance order.

COHABITATION

- The status of cohabitation has not attracted as many legal rights as the relationship of marriage.
- The law remains discriminatory in many respects, although the diminution in the legal consequences of marriage have brought some convergence of the status, treatment and rights of cohabitees and those of married persons.
- The cohabitee does not have legal or prior rights in succession.
- The obligation of aliment implicit in the marital relationship does not exist in the cohabiting relationship, irrespective of the quality, duration and circumstances of the cohabitation.
- There are no provisions concerning the making of financial provision following the termination of a relationship in the same way that there are following divorce.
- Same-sex cohabitees are treated even less favourably than heterosexual cohabitees.

CASE DIGEST

The rights of the foetus and the rights of the father in abortion [see para 13–01]

Kelly v *Kelly* 1997 SLT 896

A husband and wife separated while the wife was in the early stages of pregnancy. The husband sought interim interdict and interdict to prevent the wife from terminating the pregnancy. The court held that a foetus had no right to exist in the mother's womb and that injury to the foetus was not actionable before birth. As a consequence the father had no right to prevent any damage to the child while in the womb.

Damages for the upbringing of a child are not recoverable in cases of wrongful life arising from medical negligence [see para 13–01]

McFarlane v *Tayside Health Authority* 2000 SLT 154

A husband and wife sought damages from a health board alleging that after the husband's vasectomy they were advised that it was safe to resume sexual relations. The wife became pregnant and after a normal pregnancy gave birth to a baby boy. The couple sued for the costs of upbringing concerning the child and for the pain and suffering arising from the pregnancy. The couple were awarded damages for pain and suffering but not the costs of upbringing concerning the child.

The rights of the unmarried father [see para 13–12]

Sanderson v *McManus* 1997 SLT 629 (HL)

An unmarried father raised an action for paternity and access (contact). He was initially granted interim access but this was withdrawn after an allegation that he hit the child during one access visit. The father appealed, alleging that the intrinsic value of the parent and child relationship should be an important factor in deciding the issue of contact. It was held by the House of Lords that this was only one factor of which proper account should be taken but that it was always a case of what was in the best interests of the child's welfare that should prevail. The father's appeal was dismissed.

Chastisement of children [see para 13–13]

A v *UK* 100/1997/884/1096, ECHR, September 1998

A child had been beaten with a stick by his step-father. The step-father was prosecuted but found not guilty. The child applied to the European Court of Human Rights for a ruling on whether his human rights had been violated. The court held that there had been a violation of Article 3 of the Convention, which states: "No one shall be subjected to torture or to inhuman or degrading treatment or punishment."

Fathers can be suitable custodial parents [see para 13–13]

Early v *Early* 1989 SLT 114

A divorced father who already had custody of two children sought custody of a third. He argued that custody of the child should not be divided and that the mother's lesbian relationship would put pressure on the child within the child's peer group. The judge held that the father would be a suitable custodial parent and that it was in the best interests of the child that he be awarded custody.

The best interests of the child [see para 13–13]
Porchetta v *Porchetta* 1986 SLT 105

The parties had divorced when their child was very young. The mother was awarded custody (residence) of the child. A father sought access (contact) but there was evidence that the mother was hostile to the father and that his presence was causing her, and consequently the child, some distress. It was held that a parent has no absolute right of contact with his or her child and that the true test was "what is in the best interests of the child?"

There is no presumption of maternal preference in residence cases involving very young children [see para 13–13]
Brixey v *Lynas* 1996 SLT 908

The parents of a child separated when the child was only four months old. The mother obtained interim custody but after proof the father secured custody of the child on the basis of an unfavourable impression of the mother's lifestyle. The Inner House overturned the sheriff's ruling (and the sheriff principal's confirmation of it) on the basis that the sheriff had failed to consider the long-term interests of the child with the advantage of maternal care to a very young child. The House of Lords held that there was no presumption or principle as to maternal preference but the advantage to a very young child of being with the mother was a consideration which had to be taken into account in deciding the best interests of the child.

Rectification of informalities in the ceremony of marriage [see para 13–31]
Saleh v *Saleh* 1987 SLT 633

A couple lodged a notice of intention to marry at Grangemouth. No marriage schedule was issued. The parties subsequently went through a marriage ceremony in a different registration district. The woman raised an action for declarator of nullity. The validity of the marriage was not saved, as it had not been registered. Lord Clyde in judgment said: "This is a case where there has been no compliance with any of the relevant statutory preliminaries to a regular marriage ... The validity of the marriage is not saved by s 23A because there was no registration."

Parties of the same sex cannot marry [see para 13–34]
Corbett v *Corbett* [1970] 2 All ER 33

Parties went through a ceremony of marriage. Both of the parties had been registered at birth as male. One of them had undergone a sex-change operation with reconstructive surgery. One of the parties sought a declarator of nullity. It was held that marriage was a relationship between a man and a woman; any other "marriage" was void.

The effect of force and fear on marriage [see para 13–40]
Mahmud v *Mahmud* 1994 SLT 599

A man sought declarator of nullity alleging that he had entered into an arranged marriage with his cousin under pressure from his family. It was held that the pressure was sufficient force and fear to invalidate his true consent to marriage.

Artificial insemination by donor does not amount to adultery [see para 13–59]
MacLennan v *MacLennan* 1958 SC 105
A divorce action was raised alleging adultery. Over one year after the parties had separated the wife gave birth to a child. The wife denied adultery, alleging that she had been artificially inseminated. It was held that artificial insemination was not adultery.

Financial provision on divorce [see para 13–67]
Wallis v *Wallis* 1993 SLT 1348
It was held that the section 9 principles only applied to fair sharing of matrimonial property at the "relevant" date and that any subsequent changes in value had to be left out of any calculation. The result could not be viewed as an economic disadvantage under section 9(1)(b). The House of Lords commented on the need for amending legislation.

Rights of same-sex couples to be treated as families [see para 13–73]
Fitzpatrick v *Sterling Housing Association Ltd* [1999] 3 WLR 113
A homosexual man had been in a long-standing cohabiting relationship with another man who was a tenant of the Housing Association under a protected tenancy. The provisions of the relevant legislation (Housing Act 1988) provided that when the tenant died the tenancy may be transferred to the spouse of the deceased or a member of his family living with him. The tenant died in 1994 and Mr Fitzpatrick sought a declaration that he was entitled to succeed to the tenancy on the basis that he was the tenant's spouse or a member of his family. The House of Lords held that Mr Fitzpatrick for the purposes of this legislation (and only this legislation) was indeed a member of the former tenant's family.

FURTHER READING

Clive, *The Law of Husband & Wife in Scotland* (4th edn, W Green, 1997)
Edwards & Griffiths, *Family Law* (W Green, 1996)
Hogget, Pearl, Cooke & Bates, *The Family, Law & Society: Cases & Materials* (4th edn, Butterworths, 1996)
Jamieson, *Parental Responsibilities & Rights* (W Green, 1995)
McNeill, *Adoption of Children in Scotland* (3rd edn, W Green, 1998)
Norrie, *Children (Scotland) Act 1995* (Revised edn, W Green, 1998)
Norrie, *Children's Hearings in Scotland* (W Green, 1997)
Scottish Law Commission, *Family Law: Pre-Consolidation Reforms* (Discussion Paper No 85, 1990)
Scottish Law Commission, *Family Law* (No 135, 1992)
Sutherland, *Child & Family Law* (T&T Clark, 1999)

Sutherland, *Family Law Basics* (W Green, 1999)
Sutherland & Cleland (eds), *Children's Rights in Scotland* (W Green, 1996)
Thomson, *Family Law in Scotland* (3rd edn, Butterworths, 1996)
Travers, *Money Matters on Separation & Divorce* (W Green, 1996)
Wilkinson & Norrie, *The Law Relating to Parent & Child in Scotland* (2nd edn, W Green, 1999)

14 CRIMINAL LAW

THE NATURE AND SCOPE OF CRIMINAL LAW

Criminal law may be described as a body of rules designed to ensure the peaceful co-existence of citizens within the community. The purpose behind enforcement of the criminal law may be said to have the (often irreconcilable) goals of deterrence, rehabilitation, retribution, and reparation. In Scotland, the criminal law remains uncodified (that is, not brought together in one single Act of Parliament): it is a combination of offences at common law and statutory offences. Writers have commented upon the peculiarity of the Scottish criminal justice system.[1] It is a system which straddles, without falling neatly into one or the other, the Anglo-American common law tradition and the civil law systems of Western Europe.

14–01

Several of the common law crimes—for example, murder, culpable homicide and rape—represent the apex of criminal conduct. These are often seen as "true" crimes, rooted deeply in long-held notions of morality. However, a major feature of modern development of the criminal law has been the considerable expansion of statutory criminal law, in some instances overlapping or overtaking the common law, but in most cases, simply expanding the criminal law generally. The common law dimension of much of Scots criminal law has provided considerable flexibility, allowing for development of the law when it is confronted with changes in social acceptability. While it is commonplace to link the criminal law and morality, it is not always the case that crimes are representative of an infraction of human morality. Many of the modern statutory crimes are more concerned with regulation than with sanctioning morally reprehensible conduct. These "regulatory" crimes remain equally significant for social cohesion and protection from harm.

For the most part, the Scots common criminal law has retained much of its own integrity. The highest appeal court in criminal matters is the High Court of Justiciary, there being no appeal in criminal matters to the House of Lords. The development of statutory criminal law has introduced many laws of generic application throughout the UK.[2] More

---

1 See McCall Smith and Sheldon, *Scots Criminal Law* (2nd edn, 1997), p 2; See also L Farmer, *Crime Law and Tradition* (1997), pp 21–56.
2 See Misuse of Drugs Act 1971; Road Traffic Act 1988 discussed below at para 14–39.

than this, however, it is debatable the extent to which any legal system can lay claim to indigenous integrity. The historic and contemporary influences brought to bear on Scots law undoubtedly have a global flavour.

As a basic premise, the Scottish criminal courts respect limits to their territorial scope or jurisdiction. Principally, they are concerned with crimes committed within Scotland or within the territorial waters pertaining to Scotland. However, recognition that crime increasingly has an international element has stretched this supposition and, accordingly, there are instances where the Scottish criminal courts are concerned with crimes committed outwith Scotland which may have an impact within Scotland, or crimes committed within Scotland that may have an impact outwith Scotland.[3]

The temporal scope of Scots law is much more certain. The prosecution of common law crimes suffers from no restriction and as such it is commonplace for crimes of some antiquity to come before the courts for prosecution. Notwithstanding this, a judge has discretion to halt proceedings where the lapse of time between the date of the offence and prosecution is thought to be oppressive (that is, highly prejudicial) to the accused.[4] It seems likely that this will apply more frequently to minor charges. There may be time limits for the bringing of prosecutions prescribed for statutory offences. Otherwise, the issue of whether to prosecute is one of discretion as to whether it would be in the public interest.[5]

A controversial feature of Scots criminal law is the capacity of the High Court of Justiciary to declare conduct hitherto not recognised as a crime, as criminal. Thus, someone can be punished for engaging in conduct thought to be lawful, but subsequently declared to be unlawful by the High Court of Justiciary.[6] Such power offends the notions that the criminal law should be certain and, more significantly, that a person, legal or natural, can infringe only *known* criminal law

COMPONENTS OF A CRIME—THE CRIMINAL ACT OR OMISSION (*ACTUS REUS*) AND THE CRIMINAL MIND (*MENS REA*)

14–02   As a general proposition, for criminal liability there must be a criminal act or omission *and* a criminal mind. The need for concurrency of both criminal act and criminal mind is true of all the common law crimes and in many of the statutory

---

[3]   Accordingly, one can observe in the bombing of the PAN-Am flight over Lockerbie an instance of a crime committed in Scotland which had consequences for nationals of another country. Another example is the manufacture and exportation of drugs to another country, or, indeed, offences committed in another country which have as their object the importation of drugs into Scotland. See Misuse of Drugs Act 1971. A further example of a crime committed elsewhere but triable in Scotland is that of war crime under the War Crimes Act 1991. On the issue of territorial scope of Scots law see McCall Smith and Sheldon, *Scots Criminal Law* (2nd edn, 1997), pp 13–16; Sexual Offences (Conspiracy and Incitement) Act 1996; Brown 1997 SLG 18–20.
[4]   *Connachan* v *Douglas* 1990 JC 244.
[5]   For comment on the sensibility of prosecuting some historic crime see McCall Smith and Sheldon, *Scots Criminal Law* (2nd edn, 1997), pp 16–17.
[6]   Willock, "The Declaratory Power—Still Indefensible", 1996 JR 97; Crichton-Styles, "The Declaratory Power: Inevitable and Desirable" 1996 JR 99; *Greenhuff* (1838) 2 Swin 236; *Grant* v *Allan* 1987 SCCR 402.

crimes. Some statutory offences do not require a criminal mind for conviction, liability being strict.

THE CRIMINAL ACT OR OMISSION (*THE ACTUS REUS*)

For each crime there is an *actus reus*, that is, a criminal act or omission. No matter how **14–03** evil or ill-disposed an individual in society is, he will face criminal prosecution only if his wickedness finds expression in the form of some criminal act or omission. The *actus reus* of a particular crime may be a solitary act or omission or a series of acts or omissions. For criminal liability, all such acts or omissions must be *voluntarily* engaged in by the actor. There is no criminal liability for involuntary acts or omissions. Thus, there may be no liability in respect of external events, which are beyond the control of the actor or where the act is a consequence of a reflex action. Similarly, Scots law recognises that there may be a range of situations which arise where the perpetrator of an otherwise criminal act is in a state of unconsciousness. There have been frequent attempts by accused persons to escape liability in the Scottish courts on the basis that their acts or omissions were not criminal as they were undertaken in the course of a comatose state, somnambulism, concussion, epilepsy, other medically recognised states of unconsciousness or extreme psychological stress.[7]

In certain circumstances, the criminal law imposes liability where the *actus reus* is an omission on the part of someone or some persons. Criminal liability for omissions is a controversial area, principally because it is often difficult to establish that the failure to do something actually led to the result in question (what is known as causation). Nevertheless, it is accepted that criminal liability for an omission may arise in one of four situations: first, where the accused has a duty to act (such as a doctor attending a patient) and fails to do so; second, where the accused has an obligation under the law of contract and he fails to fulfil those duties; third, where the accused has engaged in prior dangerous actings and has created a situation which compels him to act; and fourth, where there is a close relationship and the "victim" is dependent on the actings of the accused and the accused fails to act.[8]

THE CRIMINAL MIND (*MENS REA*)

As noted earlier, all common law crimes and many statutory crimes require not only **14–04** a criminal act or omission, but also a guilty or criminal mind (as *mens rea*). Scots law, in common with most jurisdictions, recognises several species of guilty mind. Where a crime requires *mens rea*, the requisite standard (or level of culpability) will require to be met before a conviction can be secured. For all the common law crimes, the standard of guilty mind required is to be found in the established case law. In respect of statutory crimes, the situation is more confusing. Some statutes will stipulate the necessary standard of criminal mind, others may be silent on the issue, and yet others may impose strict liability.

The standards of criminal mind commonly recognised and applied in Scots law may

---

[7]   See paras 14–16 and 14–22.
[8]   See Jones and Christie, *Criminal Law* (2nd edn, 1996), pp 46–48; McCall Smith and Sheldon, *Scots Criminal Law* (2nd edn, 1997), pp 32–35; prior dangerous actings—*McManimy and Higgins* (1847) Arkley 321; duty to act—*Bonar v McLeod* 1983 SCCR 161.

be listed as intention (and wicked recklessness), recklessness (and gross negligence), and negligence.[9] Differing standards of criminal mind are variously identified in particular crimes as necessary for criminal liability. Because the thought processes of an accused person are known only to that person, it is commonplace in the Scottish criminal courts for the mental state of the accused to be inferred from the nature and quality of the accused's actions prior to, during, and after the crime.

It has been said that to act intentionally is to act with a view to bringing something about. It is an action which the actor wants to happen, either for itself or as a means to a further end.[10] Intention is something more than mere contemplation: it is a resolve or purposive desire to act in a particular way.[11]

Recklessness occurs where one acts without regard to the consequences of one's action and one is aware of risk to the public at large. It is not the simple failure to address any risk, but rather indifference to that risk.[12] In Scots law, recklessness is usually assessed objectively. The standard of behaviour is assessed against the standard one might reasonably expect from other ordinary members of the public.[13] Where the recklessness is severe enough to be viewed as "wicked recklessness" it is equated with intention. Indeed, some commentators have even described "wicked recklessness" as an objective assessment of intention.[14]

Although it is not a sufficiently culpable mind for most common law offences, there are, nevertheless, some statutory crimes which recognise negligence as the appropriate standard of criminal mind. For example, there is an offence in the Road Traffic Act 1988 of careless (equivalent of negligent) driving.[15] It is said that negligence is similar to recklessness and that it involves the individual in risk-creating conduct, which deviates from the standards of the reasonably careful citizen.[16] Although some offences (common law and statutory) often refer to "gross negligence", it seems clear in modern law that the concept of gross negligence is to be equated to that of recklessness. It is quite different from simple negligence.

STRICT AND VICARIOUS LIABILITY

14–05 In almost direct contradiction to the notion that criminal liability should attach where moral fault exists, there are a number of statutory offences where strict liability is imposed.[17] The consequence of strict liability is that no *mens rea* is required. The accused individual or corporation[18] is guilty of the criminal act described in the statute. Strict liability is justified by many on the basis that it is necessary to regulate many forms of socially harmful conduct. If foresight and knowledge (implicit in the criminal mind) were required in every case, successful prosecution would be problematic. It has been suggested that although strict liability implies inflexibility,

---

[9] On criminal minds generally see Jones and Christie, *Criminal Law* (2nd edn, 1996), pp 51–57.
[10] McCall Smith and Sheldon, *Scots Criminal Law* (2nd edn, 1997), p 35.
[11] *Sayers and Others* v *HMA* 1981 SCCR 312 at 318.
[12] *Cameron* v *Maguire* 1999 JC 63.
[13] See *Gizzi and Another* v *Tudhope* 1983 SLT 800; *Thomson* v *HMA* 1995 SLT 827.
[14] Jones and Christie, *Criminal Law* (2nd edn, 1996), pp 51–52.
[15] Road Traffic Act 1988, s 3.
[16] Jones and Christie, *Criminal Law* (2nd edn, 1996) p 57.
[17] *ibid* pp 342–350.
[18] Corporate criminal liability is discussed at para 14–08.

there is, nevertheless, flexibility in prosecutorial discretion so as to avoid the potentially harsh impact of such liability.[19] Ironically, some strict liability offences concede some defences, such as insanity, automatism[20] and nonage. Rather more pertinently, many statutory offences contain what is referred to as a "due diligence" defence. The accused will escape liability where he has taken all "due diligence" (every care) to avoid the commission of the act.[21]

Many statutes are silent on the question of *mens rea* and where that is the case there is a presumption in favour of the need for *mens rea*.[22] The presumption in favour of *mens rea* can be overcome where the court forms the view that the offence in question is simply a regulatory offence. Some statutes, in describing the offence, use words which may imply *mens rea*. Thus, words such as "knowingly", "wilfully", "fraudulently" or "maliciously" are all words which suggest that *mens rea* is required.

The concept of vicarious liability, readily accepted in civil law, is contentious in the criminal law context. The controversy arises from the belief that as criminal liability is personal, it is wrong that one may be criminally liable for the acts of another. However, for the same reasons as it is accepted in civil law, there are some limited instances where it is accepted as a concept in criminal law. It is not accepted in respect of "true" crimes, which invariably involve moral fault. It is, however, accepted in some statutory crimes, which impose liability on an employer. Under the operation of vicarious liability, criminal liability for these statutory crimes attaches to the employer through the conduct of the employee.[23]

THE NEED TO HAVE CAUSED THE CRIME (CAUSATION)

It is a principle of criminal law that a person must cause the prohibited result before **14–06** he will be criminally responsible.[24] Where some intervening act breaks the chain of causation one cannot be criminally liable for the end result. Accordingly, where someone is stabbed by an accused and is admitted to hospital for medical treatment for non-life-threatening injuries and, as a result of medical negligence, dies, the accused will not be liable for the murder of the victim. In many situations, it is possible that the original act may have caused the result regardless of the intervening factor and criminal liability for the caused event will then ensue. In respect of medical treatment, the law will not recognise that there has been an intervening act breaking the chain of criminal causation unless the medical treatment substantially departs from the accepted medical practice. In summary, it may be said that for causation, the accused's act must be a significant act which materially brings about the event; it need not be an exclusive event—there may be other contributory factors.

---

[19] See McCall Smith and Sheldon, *Scots Criminal Law* (2nd edn, 1997), p 48.
[20] Laurie, "Automatism and Insanity in the Laws of England and Scotland", 1995 JR 253–265.
[21] *Ahmed* v *MacDonald* 1995 SLT 1094; see Jones and Christie, *Criminal Law* (2nd edn, 1996), p 350.
[22] *Sweet* v *Parsley* [1970] AC 132, per Lord Reid at 148.
[23] Jones and Christie, *Criminal Law* (2nd edn, 1996), pp 350–351.
[24] *Hendry* v *HMA* 1987 JC 63, *cf Lourie* v *HMA* 1988 SCCR 634.

Implicit to any understanding of causation is the notion that the accused must take his victim as he finds him. Accordingly, the accused may be liable where the victim has a thin skull or a medical predisposition and, as a consequence, the impact or result of the criminal act or omission is greater than it would be otherwise.[25]

The law recognises that an act of the victim himself may impact upon the question of causation.[26] The victim's own act may operate to interrupt causation but to do so it must be an unreasonable act, or an act which is an unforeseeable result of the accused's conduct. For example, the voluntary consumption of illegally supplied and obtained controlled drugs may break the chain of causation in homicide cases between the accused's criminal activity in supplying the drugs and the eventual fatality. Similarly, there will be no liability for homicide where a victim takes his own life as a consequence of some prior criminal act perpetrated against him, or, where the victim sustains minor injuries but acts so irrationally as to elevate those injuries to the point where what may otherwise have been non-life-threatening injuries result in fatality of the victim. In cases where the victim attempts to escape from the scene of the crime the accused will be liable for any consequences of the escape unless it can be shown that the escape mode is utterly unreasonable.

WHO CAN BE A PARTY TO A CRIME?

14-07 For many commentators, only the individual human actor can be a moral actor and, as a consequence, only the individual acting together with another or others can be criminally liable. In historic times, such an approach had validity and little challenged this conception of criminal law. However, the advent of the corporation as a legal person has, ultimately, led to reappraisal. Notwithstanding this, it remains the case that the individual human actor (the natural person) is the principal focus of the criminal law.

THE CORPORATION

14-08 The criminal liability of the corporation in Scots law is less than clear.[27] The Criminal Procedure (Scotland) Act 1995 offers mechanisms for the prosecution of the "body corporate" either in summary[28] or solemn proceedings.[29] Notwithstanding this, there is limited illumination in the case law of the true extent of corporate criminal liability. While it is clear that a number of statutory crimes apply, there has never been a definitive statement as to the applicable common law crimes. The problem revolves around the exhibition of the criminal mind. Where an offence (common law or

---

[25] *Bird* v *HMA* 1952 JC 23 at 25; *McDonald* v *Smellie* (1903) 5 F 935.
[26] Jones and Christie, *Criminal Law* (2nd edn, 1996), pp 99–107.
[27] See Mays, "The criminal liability of corporations and Scots Law—The Lessons of Anglo-American Jurisprudence" (2000) 1 (1) ELR 46–73; Ross, "Corporate Criminal Liability—one form or many forms?" 1999 JR 49; Stuart, "The case of a shameless company" (1986) 31 JLSS 176; Ross,"Corporate Liability for Crime", 1990 SLT (News) 265; Whyte, "Corporate Criminal Liability", 1987 SLT (News) 348.
[28] Criminal Procedure (Scotland) Act 1995, s 143(2).
[29] *ibid* s 70.

statutory) requires *mens rea* the courts face the problem of how to identify in a legal person what are usually notions of will or mind in a natural person. There are two principal cases in Scots law which deal with the issue of corporate criminal liability. In the first case, *Dean v John Menzies Ltd*,[30] a limited company was charged with the common law offence of shameless indecency for stocking indecent and obscene publications. A divided court decided that the corporation could not commit the crime of shameless indecency. All three judges offered different insights into corporate criminal liability. Two of the judges made comments which suggested limitations on the extent of the offences for which a corporation could be criminally liable. They suggested that such limitations might be based upon the inability of the corporation to exhibit intention, and that the corporation could only be liable for those crimes for which it could be sanctioned.

In the second case, *Purcell Meats (Scotland) Ltd v McLeod*[31] it was held that a corporation could be convicted of a crime of intention (in this case, attempted fraud). The case is also thought to have accepted into Scots law, the English method of identifying the criminal mind of the corporation in the minds of those who control the company (sometimes referred to as the controlling mind theory or the alter ego or identification doctrine).[32] Thus, it appears that a corporation can commit those common law crimes for which it can be sanctioned (obviously not murder which requires life imprisonment[33]) and which do not require specifically human characteristics (for example, rape, perjury, and shameless indecency). It can also commit statutory crimes where liability is strict or vicarious, or those which require *mens rea*. In respect of statutory crimes requiring *mens rea* the method of ascribing the appropriate criminal mind is the "identification" approach.

ACTING WITH ANOTHER OR OTHERS IN THE CRIMINAL ACT (ART AND PART GUILT)

When more than one person is involved in the commission of a crime, the doctrine of **14–09** "art and part" guilt operates to hold each of the parties involved equally liable for the commission of the crime. It may be that, among the co-accused, only one of those involved actually commits the *actus reus* while others play a lesser, but nevertheless vital, role in the commission of the crime. The perpetrator of the *actus reus* of the crime may be termed the "principal actor" while those who are accessories to the crime may be referred to as "actors art and part". Art and part guilt is a common feature of crimes where there is collective involvement such as gang assault, robberies involving more than one person, and indeed in any crime where more than one party acts in concert.[34] Sheriff Gordon has said:

> "it is a basic principle of Scots law that all persons who are concerned in the commission of a crime are equally guilty and that each is responsible for the whole of

---

[30] 1981 JC 23.
[31] 1987 SLT 528.
[32] *Tesco Supermarkets Ltd v Nattrass* [1972] AC 153; see Mays, "Towards Corporate Fault as a basis of ascribing criminal liability to corporations" (1998) 2 *Mountbatten Journal of Legal Studies* 31–64.
[33] See Mays, "A new offence of corporate killing—solution or further problems in corporate homicide cases" 2000 JR (forthcoming).
[34] See Ferguson, "Joint responsibility for Criminal Homicide", 1998 SLT(News) 177–180.

the ultimate *actus reus*, whatever his own part in the criminal conduct; the subordinate nature of the participation of any one of the persons involved is irrelevant to the question of guilt, although, it may of course, influence his sentence."[35]

Ironically, it is possible that someone may be convicted of a crime as an art and part actor while the principal actor is acquitted either through insufficiency of evidence or because of some procedural defect in the case laid against him.[36] Alternatively, one may find art and part guilt where the principal actor is acquitted on the basis that the principal actor is an innocent agent of the other or others. It may also be the case that the principal actor does not have the requisite *mens rea* for the commission of the crime (*eg* insanity) and is, on that basis, not convicted whilst those who acted in concert are liable, as art and part actors.[37]

The role of the co-accused may be simply to instigate the crime or provide counsel and advice as to its perpetration; or, it may be to provide the principal actor with material assistance in the perpetration of the offence; or, it may involve various modes or levels of assistance or participation in the actual commission of the crime. In respect of the counselling or instigation of the crime it is clear that a party must do more than simply express enmity towards another or a desire that something happens.[38] It is important to distinguish between expressions of desire, mere thoughts or simple suggestions, and actual persuasion of a party to engage in a crime.

In relation to the provision of material assistance, naturally, it is important that the person who is accused had prior knowledge of the intention to commit a crime, that the assistance has a connection with the crime, and that there is some proximity between the assistance and the commission of the crime. Thus, for example, an innocent hardware merchant who sells a knife, which is thereafter used in a murder, will not be charged as an art and part actor in that murder. Assistance or involvement in the perpetration of the crime may arise from some long-standing (or at least prior) agreement to engage in the perpetration of the crime, or through spontaneous assistance or involvement at the time of commission of the criminal offence.[39] Mere presence at the scene of a crime, unless it is for the purposes of encouragement of that crime or to act as a lookout, will not amount to art and part guilt.[40]

Where the concerted crime involves a number of people engaging in the *actus reus* itself as joint principal actors, there are complex issues of proof. A group is responsible for the actions of the group and therefore each member of the group is responsible for the acts of all other members. However, it seems clear that this will only be the case if it can be shown that there is a common plan between members of the group and it can be established that the consequences of their common plan were therefore foreseeable.

Questions often arise as to the criminal responsibility for the unintended consequences of a concerted action. Here again it is important to determine the parameters of the common plan, the extent of the knowledge of the participants, and the foreseeability of the consequences of their action.[41] Where one of the actors engages in an act

---

[35] Gordon, *Criminal Law* (2nd edn, 1978), p 129.
[36] Jones and Christie, *Criminal Law* (2nd edn, 1996), pp 135–136; *Vaughan v HMA* 1979 SLT 49.
[37] *R v Cogan and Leak* [1976] 1 QB 217 (an English case, but contains a significant discussion of this issue).
[38] *Little v HMA* 1983 JC 16; *Spiers v HMA* 1980 JC 36.
[39] Jones and Christie, *Criminal Law* (2nd edn, 1996), pp 130–131.
[40] *Quinn v HMA* 1990 SCCR 254.
[41] *HMA v Lappen* 1956 SLT 109; *Mathieson and Murray v HMA* 1996 SCCR 388, *cf Codona v HMA* 1996 SCCR 300.

outwith the common purpose, which is unforeseeable by the others, then that act may not be attributed to those with whom he acts in concert. In a situation where a bank robber, in the course of a robbery, produces a gun of which the other participants are unaware, and where there is prior agreement that no one would be hurt, there can be no art and part guilt on the part of the others if that person were, in the course of the robbery, to shoot someone. This situation must be distinguished from a situation where the other parties know of the presence of the gun irrespective of whether they have previously agreed that the gun is not to be used. The presence of the gun makes its use a much more foreseeable consequence and, as a result, the parties may be liable for any art and part guilt that arises from any shooting that may occur.

A final issue is whether someone, having prior participation in preparing for a crime may, at a later stage, withdraw and thus negate any art and part guilt for the eventual commission of that crime? This will always be a matter of facts and circumstances. The courts have taken a fairly harsh view of this matter and have, on occasion, decreed that the participant must recant to the extent that he intervenes to prevent the crime either directly, by stopping the commission of the *actus reus*, or by reporting the matter to the police.[42]

CRIMINALISING THE INCOMPLETION OF CRIME (INCHOATE CRIMES)

Scots criminal law punishes not only completed crimes where the conception of the crime has been carried through to fruition, but also instances where criminality is exhibited in the development stage. It is sometimes appropriate that the law punishes the wrongfulness of the conduct, as it would had the crime been completed. These are known as inchoate crimes. Inchoate crimes are often divided into three categories—criminal attempts, conspiracy and incitement. **14–10**

CRIMINAL ATTEMPTS

There is, of course, no criminal liability for merely thinking about committing a crime.[43] There is, however, considerable controversy regarding the question of what amounts to an attempt. Several theories have been expounded in Scots law to determine whether actions have gone beyond contemplation. The test, which appears to have been accepted, is the preparation/perpetration test where, as a matter of fact and degree, the jury or court will decide whether the accused has moved beyond simple preparation down the path of perpetration.[44] **14–11**

The law is less than clear on the issue of whether an attempt can be renounced. It seems likely, however, that this would require ensuring that the crime attempted is not completed. For the most part, it is highly unlikely that an attempt, once engaged upon,

---

[42] *McNeil* v *HMA* 1986 SCCR 288, per Lord President Emslie at 318.
[43] *Andrew* v *HMA* 1999 GWD 32–1517.
[44] *HMA* v *Camerons* 1911 SC (J) 110.

can be revoked. The final issue in respect of the law of attempt relates to whether one can be guilty of an impossible attempt—that is, where the crime attempted is legally or factually impossible.[45] It seems clear in Scots law that an accused will be convicted unless he can prove that he knows of the impossibility of what he is attempting, or that the crime he believes he is attempting does not, in fact, exist in law.

CONSPIRACY

14-12 Conspiracy is the agreement of two or more persons to effect any criminal purpose, whether as their ultimate aim, or as a means to it, and the crime is complete if there is such agreement, even though nothing further is done.[46] Conspiracy (as opposed to incitement) is something more than contemplation or suggestion. There is no requirement that the conspirators have met. Because conspiracy operates to penalise the agreement to perpetrate a crime, the fact that the actions proposed are impossible does not preclude the relevancy of the charge.[47] There can be no withdrawing from conspiracy, as the crime is committed following the reaching of agreement to perpetrate the criminal purpose.[48]

INCITEMENT

14-13 Incitement is the attempt to form a conspiracy.[49] The crime is committed where the accused approaches another seeking either his participation jointly in a crime or, with a view to the incitee perpetrating the crime on his own.[50] The criminal mind of incitement is that the accused intends that the person approached will be incited to commit the crime.

There is a close link between conspiracy and incitement, and the doctrine of art and part guilt.[51] A person may be art and part guilty of a crime or attempted crime depending on the crime's stage of development. Incitement and conspiracy appear appropriate only where little or no progress has been made towards the eventual crime. Where progress has been made such as to raise the possibility that a person may be art and part guilty of a crime or attempted crime then that will overtake conspiracy or incitement.

GENERAL DEFENCES TO CRIMINAL CHARGES

14-14 The criminal law of Scotland recognises various general defences that an accused may deploy to negate criminal liability. Some of those defences are known as "special defences" and require to be intimated before trial to the prosecution. The special

---

[45] Oliver,"Impossible Attempts, Settled at Last" (1997) 42 JLSS 157.
[46] *Crofter Hand Woven Harris Tweed Co Ltd* v *Veitch* 1942 SC (HL) 1, per Viscount Simon LC at 5.
[47] *Maxwell* v *HMA* 1980 JC 40.
[48] See Jones and Christie, *Criminal Law* (2nd edn 1996), p 144.
[49] Ferguson, "Criminal Incitement" (1997) 42 JLSS 407; *HMA* v *Baxter* 1997 SCCR 437.
[50] *Baxter* v *HMA* 1998 JC 219.
[51] See para 14-09.

defences are self-defence, alibi (the accused was in another location at the time of the crime), incrimination (claiming another committed the crime), and insanity. Some defences are general defences, applicable in a number of situations, while particular defences apply to particular crimes. For example, some statutory crimes lay down specific defences applicable only to that offence or statute.

SELF-DEFENCE

Ordinarily, one is justified in engaging in what would otherwise be a criminal act in **14–15** defence of oneself, or another, or one's own property. Self-defence arises most commonly in relation to crimes of personal injury, homicide or sexual assaults. It may also arise in the context of property offences where one is defending property. Defending one's property will permit a person only to "assault" another and not to kill him.[52]

The successful pleading of self-defence results in acquittal. However, before it can be successfully pled, certain conditions must be met.[53] In the context of justifying homicide on the basis of self-defence, it is necessary that the accused must be in imminent danger to life, either to the accused himself or another, or, in the case of a woman, under threat of rape.[54] Simple physical threat of a non-life threatening nature will not justify killing. It may be that one responds to a physical threat which is non-life-threatening and, as a consequence, death ensues. For example, when facing an assault, where an accused person pushes someone back who then stumbles and hits his head, he may properly lead a defence of self-defence in a culpable homicide case.

The threat of some future action will not allow retaliatory action—it is not immediate enough. The court must base its assessment on whether one acted in self-defence on the basis of whether one's belief of imminent threat was genuine.[55] It is possible that one may have the erroneous but reasonable belief that one's life is in danger when it is not.[56]

A further requirement of self-defence is that one is expected to flee from the threat where that is possible and reasonable.[57] In addition, there must be reasonable proportionality between the force used and the threat. One is expected only to use sufficient force to repel the attack. Gross over-reaction or wildly excessive force may preclude a plea of self-defence.[58] Excessive force does not reduce the homicide from murder to culpable homicide.[59] Self-defence is not open to an accused where the threat or physical violence arises from lawful force. Even in circumstances where the incident is initiated by the accused and his conduct elicits a serious life-threatening response, he may be entitled to react and shelter behind the defence of self-defence.[60] Even in cases not involving homicide (*eg* assault or property defence) the issues of immediacy of threat and proportionality of response are still relevant.

---

[52] *McCluskey* v *HMA* 1959 JC 39. (This issue has been highly debated in recent times in England).
[53] *HMA* v *Docherty* 1954 JC 1.
[54] But not sodomy—see *McCluskey* v *HMA* 1959 JC 39; *Elliott* v *HMA* 1987 SCCR 278.
[55] *Owens* v *HMA* 1946 JC 119; see Connelly, "Women who kill violent men" 1996 JR 215.
[56] *Crawford* v *HMA* 1950 JC 67; *Jones* v *HMA* 1990 JC 160.
[57] *HMA* v *Doherty* 1954 JC 1.
[58] *Pollock* v *HMA* 1998 SLT 880.
[59] *cf Kizileviczius* v *HMA* 1938 JC 60.
[60] *Boyle* v *HMA* 1993 SLT 577 at 587; *Burns* v *HMA* 1995 SLT 1090.

INSANITY

14–16   Due to the common requirement of *mens rea*, for the most part, mental capacity is important in the context of crime. Mental health deficiency such as diminished responsibility may act as a mitigatory factor. However, where the accused is insane the impact is altogether more significant and has a bearing on liability itself. Insanity amounts to complete alienation of reason.[61] It is a severe and high test. Insanity may act in bar of trial or it may result in acquittal where the accused is found to have been insane at the time of commission of the offence. In the latter circumstance, the accused must lodge a special defence of insanity. The prosecutor will investigate the offence and where the court is satisfied that the accused was insane at the time of commission of the offence, he will be acquitted and it will be recorded that he is being acquitted on the grounds of insanity. This will not be the end of the matter—the person found insane at the time of the act may be committed to hospital for treatment under a variety of court orders.[62] A person found to be insane at the time of commission of a murder must be detained under a restriction order which requires the Scottish Executive to assent to that person's release.

Insanity might also be raised as a plea in bar of trial because the accused is not fit to plead or to instruct a defence. Medical evidence will be the determinant of the accused's mental state. A person found to be insane in bar of trial is likely to be committed to hospital for treatment. If he subsequently recovers mental capacity then he may stand trial.[63]

ERROR

14–17   Error may act as an exculpatory factor in a number of crimes. The person who acts in error may be thought not to have the requisite *mens rea* for commission of the crime in question. However, not all errors exculpate. For the most part, error as to the applicable law is no excuse.[64] There has been criticism of the concept of constructive notice of the criminal law. On the face of things, it hardly seems fair to hold that all criminally responsible citizens are deemed to know the entire criminal law in existence at any one time (and, indeed, those crimes not yet declared by the High Court of Justiciary). The notion is rooted in public policy. To concede that a person may escape liability on the basis that he is unaware of the law would be to open the doors to challenge of each and every prosecution. The one exception is that a person who erroneously, but reasonably, believes he is acting under an entitlement of civil law may escape liability on the basis that he does not have the necessary intent to commit the crime.[65]

Although errors as to the identity of the victim, the object of the crime, or the method will have no impact on criminal liability, some errors may mitigate any sanction. More importantly, certain factual errors may actually exculpate an accused from criminal

---

[61] *HMA v Brennan* 1977 JC 38; *HMA v Kidd* 1960 JC 61 at 70; *Cardle v Mulrainey* 1992 SLT 1152.
[62] See Mays, Smith and Strachan, *Social Work Law in Scotland* (1999), pp 194–202; Connelly, "Insanity and Unfitness to Plead", 1996 JR 206; Brown, "Insanity in Bar of Trial" 1996 64(1) SLG 23.
[63] *HMA v Bickerstaff* 1926 JC 65.
[64] *Ignorantia juris neminem excusat*, "ignorance of the law is no excuse"—see Jones and Christie, *Criminal Law* (2nd edn, 1996), pp 162 *et seq.*
[65] For example, the removal of property in the belief that one is the owner—see McCall Smith and Sheldon *Scots Criminal Law* (2nd edn, 1997), pp 119–120.

liability. Thus, for example, it is a defence to a charge of rape to mistakenly believe that a woman is consenting to sexual intercourse. There is no requirement in rape cases that such an error be reasonable.[66] Reasonableness is an important part of error in respect of other crimes.[67] The variation between rape cases and other cases may be justified on the basis that in the rape cases the error affects intention: one cannot intend to overcome the will of the woman if one believes that she is consenting. In other cases such as self-defence, coercion or necessity, the accused is asserting that he did engage in a particular course of conduct and it is perhaps right that he should justify that conduct on the basis of reasonableness.[68]

INTOXICATION

Intoxication arising from the ingestion of alcohol, drugs or some other intoxicant, or any combination thereof, may impact upon criminal liability. On the one hand, medical science notes the psychological impact of intoxication but to concede that it should act as an exculpatory factor on each and every occasion would be to open the floodgates to defendants who had voluntarily consumed intoxicants preceding the criminal act. It would appear that Scots law now distinguishes voluntary intoxication from involuntary intoxication, although the law on the matter is not crystal clear. There are two principal decisions. In *HMA v Brennan*[69] it was argued that in the intoxicated state one could not exhibit intent. However, it was held that voluntary intoxication could not reduce a charge of murder to that of culpable homicide. The person who knowingly and voluntarily ingests intoxicants may well exhibit intention or wicked recklessness. The decision in *HMA v Ross*[70] appears to accept that involuntary intoxication is materially different and that, if successfully pled, may result in acquittal.

    In respect of those offences where liability is strict, intoxication will be of no consequence.[71]

14–18

PERSON IS BELOW AGE OF CRIMINAL RESPONSIBILITY

Criminal responsibility begins at the age of eight.[72] No child under the age of 16 should be prosecuted in the criminal courts without the approval of the Lord Advocate. The vast majority of Children who commit offences in Scotland are referred to the Children's Hearing system.[73] No child may be prosecuted in the district court on the basis that it deals with minor matters and, in such cases, children should be referred to the Children's Hearing System.

14–19

---

[66] *HMA v Jamieson* 1994 SCCR 181; *HMA v Meek* 1982 SCCR 613.
[67] *HMA v Crawford* 1950 JC 67; *Owens v HMA* 1946 JC 119.
[68] McCall Smith and Sheldon, *Scots Criminal Law* (2nd edn, 1997), p 123.
[69] 1977 SLT 151; see also *Donaldson v Normand* 1997 JC 200.
[70] 1991 JC 210.
[71] For a full discussion on intoxication see McCall Smith and Sheldon, *Scots Criminal Law* (2nd edn, 1997) pp 123–130.
[72] Criminal Procedure (Scotland) Act 1995, s 41.
[73] See para 13–23.

COERCION (AND NECESSITY)

14–20 In the ordinary course of events only voluntary acts are punishable under the criminal law. Where the accused undertakes some action because it is necessary for him to do so (events coerce a response), or under coercion by another (another party compels the criminal act), he may be able to enter this as a defence.[74] Both situations are viewed as variants of coercion. Because of the capacity to abuse such a defence, a claim that it was necessary to engage in some conduct will only rarely be accepted as a defence. In a recent controversial case an accused successfully pled necessity to a charge of drink-driving claiming that she had previously been raped by a person and, on seeing him again, had driven away in order to avoid him.[75] The test of coercion is that the accused had no real alternative but to do what he did. As a consequence, it seems clear that there must be an immediate danger to life or the imminent threat of bodily harm.[76]

MITIGATION OF CRIMINAL LIABILITY

14–21 Criminal liability can be mitigated. Mitigation has the effect of reducing the charge that might otherwise be brought, or lessening the punishment that might be meted out for the infraction of the criminal law. Scots law recognises two principal mitigatory pleas—diminished responsibility and provocation.

DIMINISHED RESPONSIBILITY

14–22 Diminished responsibility acts as a mitigatory factor reducing a homicide from what would otherwise be murder to culpable homicide.[77] The leading modern authority is that of *HMA* v *Savage*[78] where it was said that:

> "there must be aberration or weakness of mind: there must be some form of mental unsoundness: ... there must be a state of mind bordering on, though not amounting to, insanity; ... there must be a mind so affected that responsibility is diminished from full responsibility to partial responsibility—in other words the prisoner is only partially accountable for his actions ... there must be some form of mental disease".[79]

Evidence of some mental disorder or disease is important for, without it, there can be no finding of diminished responsibility.[80]

PROVOCATION

14–23 One of the more commonly advanced pleas in mitigation, particularly in respect of assault or homicide crimes, is that of provocation. This occurs where the accused

---

[74] See Jones and Christie, *Criminal Law* (2nd edn, 1996), pp 173–178.
[75] See note 196; see also *Ruxton* v *Lang* 1998 SCCR 1.
[76] *Moss* v *Howdle* 1997 SCCR 215; *Thomson* v *HMA* 1983 JC 69; see also Ferguson, "Necessity and Duress in Scots Law" [1986] Crim LR 103; Christie, "The Mother of Invention? Moss *v* Howdle" 1997 1(4) ELR 479.
[77] *Dingwall* (1867) 5 Irv 466.
[78] 1923 JC 49.
[79] *ibid* at 51; see also *HMA* v *Blake* 1986 SLT 661.
[80] *HMA* v *Connelly* 1990 SCCR 504.

concedes that he has engaged in the criminal act but has done so in response to the actions of the victim.

Where, as is common, provocation is pled in conjunction with self-defence it is the duty of the court first to assess whether the accused acted in self-defence, which has exculpatory effect.[81] If self-defence is rejected, the jury should then assess whether the accused's actings can be mitigated by provocation.

In respect of intentional homicide, provocation may act to reduce the charge from murder to culpable homicide. For provocation to be admitted as mitigation in homicide cases, it is necessary that the victim's provocation took the form of an assault on the accused.[82] Verbal provocation (other than admission of sexual infidelity[83]) is not sufficient.[84] Further requirements of provocation in homicide cases are that the criminal act should follow immediately upon the provocation and that the provoked response[85] must be proportionate to the provocative act.[86] Similar general rules apply to assault cases in that the provoked act must follow immediately upon the provocation and be proportionate to the victim's provocation.

THE SUBSTANTIVE CRIMES OF SCOTLAND

Most writers attempt to categorise offences by grouping them together under broad headings. The generally accepted categories of criminal offences in Scotland are— offences against the person; sexual offences; public order offences; offences aimed at social protection; offences related to property; offences against the state; and offences against the administration of justice.[87]   **14–24**

OFFENCES AGAINST THE PERSON

Murder

Murder ranks most heinous of all the common law crimes recognised by Scots law. It may be defined as the unlawful killing of another where the accused exhibits intention to kill or such wicked recklessness as to his conduct as to imply a disposition depraved enough to be regardless of whether death ensues from his actions.[88]   **14–25**

Murder can be divided into voluntary murder and involuntary murder. Voluntary

---

[81] See *Pollock* v *HMA* 1998 SLT 880.
[82] Assault is defined at para 14–27.
[83] *HMA* v *Callender* 1958 SLT 24; *HMA* v *McKean* 1996 SCCR 402, although note where parties have long separated it is not thought that verbal admission of infidelity can amount to provocation: see *McKay* v *HMA* 1991 SCCR 364.
[84] *Cosgrove* v *HMA* 1990 SCCR 358.
[85] *Parr* v *HMA* 1991 SCCR 180.
[86] *Lennon* v *HMA* 1991 SCCR 611.
[87] This chapter does not attempt to cover all the crimes recognised in Scots law but attempts rather to summarise the position in respect of the most commonly referred to crimes.
[88] McDonald, *Criminal Law* (1949), p 89; conduct after the incident could be indicative of wicked recklessness: see *Reid* v *HMA* 1999 GWD 19–871; *Halliday* v *HMA* 1999 SLT 485.

murder is where the accused intentionally kills the victim. Such intention may be inferred from the accused"s actings. Involuntary murder is committed unintentionally through the exhibition of wicked recklessness. It would appear that for this type of murder it is necessary that, as a minimum, the accused exhibited an intention to cause personal injury,[89] although in *Cawthorne* v *HMA*[90] the accused was held to have exhibited wicked recklessness by simply intending to fire a gun into a room where persons had taken refuge. Some commentators suggest that the distinction between the two types of murder is rather blurred and that wicked recklessness is merely an objective assessment of intent.[91] The crime of murder carries a mandatory penalty of life imprisonment.[92]

Culpable homicide

14–26   Culpable homicide represents the lesser of the two homicide crimes. Culpable homicide is committed where death is caused by improper conduct and where the guilt is less than murder.[93] It does not carry a mandatory penalty and can be subdivided into involuntary culpable homicide and voluntary culpable homicide.

Voluntary culpable homicide occurs where the accused intends his actions but the mental element is less than *mens rea* for murder because of the mitigatory effect of diminished responsibility or provocation.[94]

Involuntary culpable homicide arises where the accused has no intention to kill but, nevertheless, death ensues from his actions, which are either lawful or unlawful. It often involves the commission of an assault.[95] Such an assault would, in the normal chain of events, not in itself be life-threatening but because of some extraneous circumstance, death results. Thus, for example, fatality may arise in what would ordinarily be a relatively minor or moderate assault but because of some weakness or infirmity on the part of the victim that victim dies. An accused is expected to take a victim as he "finds him".

Where an accused person perpetrates an unlawful act, not directed at the physical integrity of the victim (such as damaging property) but as a consequence of that act someone dies, a charge of culpable homicide may be brought.[96] An example of this is setting fire to buildings which the deceased inhabits or occupies, with an intention to do damage but without the intention to do bodily harm. A further example would be illegally providing substances to another knowing that they may cause death. It has been held that to provide drugs to another, even in circumstances where the victim administers drugs to himself, may constitute culpable homicide.[97]

There is no requirement for culpable homicide that the unlawful act should be a dangerous act.[98] Where the unlawfulness arises because of a failure to perform a lawful duty then culpable homicide, rather than murder, is the appropriate charge.

---

[89] Although see Jones and Christie, *Criminal Law* (2nd edn, 1996), pp 210–211.
[90] 1968 JC 32.
[91] Jones and Christie, *Criminal Law* (2nd edn, 1996), pp 51–52.
[92] Criminal Procedure (Scotland) Act 1995, s 205.
[93] McDonald, *Criminal Law* (1949), p 96.
[94] Discussed above at paras 14–22 to 14–23; see also *Strathearn* v *HMA* 1996 SCCR 100; *Carracher* v *HMA* 1946 JC 108; *Williamson* v *HMA* 1994 JC 149.
[95] Jones and Christie, *Criminal Law* (2nd edn, 1996), pp 215–216.
[96] *Sutherland* v *HMA* 1994 SCCR 80.
[97] *Lord Advocate's Reference (No 1 of 1994)* 1994 SLT 248.
[98] See McCall Smith and Sheldon, *Scots Criminal Law* (2nd edn, 1997), pp 182–183.

Involuntary lawful act homicide involves engaging in reckless conduct (sometimes equated with gross negligence) where fatality ensues. It often arises in the context of road traffic matters and also in respect of medical negligence which results in death.

Assault

An assault is an attack upon a person of another. It will (but need not) often take the form of physical attack. Assault may be perpetrated by means of threatening gestures if they place the victim in fear. Thus, brandishing a fist or a weapon of some type at the victim is sufficient to constitute an attack on that person. Assault may involve various degrees of violence, ranging from the absence of any physical contact through to very serious personal injury. It has been held to be assault to spit at someone,[99] or to pour petrol on someone thus placing that person in fear of injury,[100] or to throw acid at someone.[101] It is also possible to indirectly perpetrate an assault either by setting a dog on someone,[102] or undertaking some action which propels the victim to injury.[103] Although threatening gestures are accepted as sufficient to constitute an attack on the person of another, there is some debate in Scots law as to whether threatening words in the absence of gestures are enough. Most authorities adopt the position that threatening words are not enough.[104]

14–27

Assault may be aggravated in several ways, making the crime much more serious and therefore requiring harsher punishment. Assault may be aggravated by the method deployed by the accused. Thus, if the accused uses a weapon or punches or kicks his victim, the courts may take a more serious view of this than of other forms of assault. Another aggravation of assault may arise from the consequences for the victim. If the victim is disfigured, or impaired, or the assault endangers his life, the courts are likely to take a severe view. The nature and circumstances of the victim himself may also have a bearing on whether the assault is considered to be aggravated. Where the assault is on an elderly person, or a child, or perhaps an officer of the law, the courts are likely to consider it an aggravated form of assault. Similarly, where the assault involves some form of breach of trust it may also be considered aggravated. Accordingly, schoolteachers assaulting school children, or a care worker in a social work establishment, or a nurse assaulting a patient, are all examples of situations where the courts may consider the offence aggravated. It may also be an aggravation to the crime of assault where the accused intended to commit a further crime. For example, assault is aggravated where the accused commits an assault with an attempt to rape or with intent to rob. A further aggravating factor is the locus of the assault.[105]

The criminal mind necessary for the commission of the crime is the intention to do bodily harm. Assault cannot be committed by a person acting recklessly or negligently.[106]

---

[99] *James Cairns* (1837) 1 Swin 597.
[100] *Williamson v HMA* 1984 SLT 200.
[101] Sheils,"Assault by Throwing Acid" 1999 JR 33.
[102] *Kay v Allan* 1978 SCCR (Supp) 188.
[103] *David Keay* (1837) 1 Swin 543.
[104] However, see Jones and Christie, *Criminal Law* (2nd edn, 1996), p 182.
[105] On aggravation see McCall Smith and Sheldon, *Scots Criminal Law* (2nd edn, 1997), pp 162–163.
[106] *Lord Advocate's Reference (No 2 of 1992)* 1993 JC 43; *HMA v Harris* 1993 JC 150; though see *RHW v HMA* 1982 SLT 420.

There are various recognised defences to the crime of assault. The first relates to the lawful chastisement of children by parents.[107] This remains a controversial area and one where there is diminishing legal tolerance to the affliction of violence upon the child. The whole question of lawful chastisement relates not to the motive of the parent but to the degree of physical chastisement inflicted.[108] In addition, certain categories of people—such as prison officers, nurses or police officers—are lawfully authorised to act in restraint of others. It may be a defence to a crime of assault to convince the court that one was acting in defence of one's own property. It is important not to engage in excessive violence. It will be a defence to establish that the assault was perpetrated in the exercise of crime prevention. Thus, an individual may execute a "citizen's arrest" of someone who has committed, or is in the process of committing, a crime.[109] Where the good citizen exceeds the exercise of reasonable force, he himself will be guilty of the crime of assault and will be prosecuted accordingly.

Finally, the defence may allege that the "victim" consented to the action. Although consent (or at any event a genuine belief that the person consents) may represent a good defence, particularly in assaults involving touching or kissing, there are limitations on the use of consent as a defence. The basic position of the Scottish courts is that the issue will be resolved on whether there is evil intent to inflict bodily harm.[110] Accordingly, where two or more parties decide to resolve their differences by engaging in a fight neither can subsequently expect to rely upon the defence of consent. Similarly, someone who engages in sado-masochist activities cannot subsequently argue that his partner consented to the assault. Consent also arises in the context of sporting activities which involve physical contact. It is clear that in sport there has been narrowing of the courts' and prosecutors' views as to what participants can voluntarily consent to.[111]

Provocation is not a defence to assault but simply a mitigating factor.[112]

SEXUAL OFFENCES

Rape

14–28   Rape is a very serious and distinct form of sexual assault. It is principally a common law crime although there is also a statutory offence of rape by impersonating a woman's husband.[113] There is also a statutory offence of having sexual relations with a girl under 13 years of age which, although the statute makes no mention of the word rape, is often referred to as "statutory rape".[114] The common law crime of rape is defined as: where a man has intercourse with a woman by overcoming her will.[115] The crime may be attended with varying degrees of (physical) violence. However, the important feature of the crime is that the woman is unwilling to engage in sexual

---

[107] See Chapter 13; Spink and Spink, "What is reasonable chastisement?" (1999) 44(6) JLSS 26.
[108] *B v Harris* 1990 SLT 208.
[109] *Wightman v Lees* 1999 SCCR 664.
[110] *Smart v HMA* 1975 JC 30.
[111] See James and Gardiner, 1997 Crim LR 41.
[112] Jones and Christie, *Criminal Law* (2nd edn, 1996), pp 193–194; for provocation see para 14–23.
[113] Criminal Law (Consolidation) (Scotland) Act 1995, s 7(3).
[114] *ibid* s 5.
[115] *Stobbs v HMA* 1983 SCCR 190; *S v HMA* 1989 SLT 469; see Tadross, "No Consent: A Historical Critique of the *Actus Reus* of Rape" (1999) 3(3) ELR 317.

intercourse and not the physical violence which accompanies this. Violence and the victim's resistance will be factors, having a bearing on the case as they are indicative of the fact that the woman was unwilling. However, in keeping with the accepted definition of rape there need be no violence accompanying the sexual assault. It may, for example, be sufficient simply to threaten the victim with violence as a means of overcoming her will to engage in sexual relations.[116] Where threats are the means of overcoming the will, they must be of a serious nature, although not necessarily of physical violence. These threats need not necessarily be directed at the victim but may be directed at another—for example, a child.

In Scots law, the definition of rape makes no specific reference to the absence of consent. Consent does have a major role to play in the prosecution of the crime but it is not the case that the simple absence of consent to sexual relations results in the perpetration of the crime of rape.[117] There are several circumstances where consent may be absent but the will of the woman has not been overcome and, as such, the crime of rape has not been committed (see the discussion of clandestine injury to women below).

The *actus reus* of the crime requires sexual intercourse by a man with a woman. It requires penetration of the female sexual organ by the male sexual organ. It is in that sense a gender-specific crime. There is no recognition of the crime of male rape in Scotland.[118] Penetrative sexual assault by a male against another male will be prosecuted as indecent assault. Anal intercourse and other forms of sexual assault (penetration by something other than the penis) are not rape in Scots law, but again may be prosecuted as indecent assault. A woman cannot be prosecuted for the crime of rape as the principal actor but may, nevertheless, be guilty art and part in the commission of the crime where she assists a male in his perpetration of the offence.

The *mens rea* of the crime of rape has two alternate forms. It can be committed either where the perpetrator intends to overcome the will of the woman or does so through recklessness (simply not caring whether she consented or not). The crime of rape cannot be committed by negligence. It is clear from a now well-established line of authority that where a man believes the woman is consenting to sexual relations he should be acquitted. There have been several attempts at introducing a concept of reasonableness into the man's belief. The Scottish courts have, however, rejected this, pointing out that the question of reasonableness will doubtless be part of the jury's determination as to whether they believe the man had an honest belief that the woman was consenting.[119]

To administer drugs or drink or any other intoxicant to a woman with a view to overcoming her will and thereafter having sexual intercourse with her is rape. This must be distinguished from situations where the woman voluntarily takes intoxicants and is subsequently incapable of resisting. The distinction being drawn is that where a man deliberately uses intoxicants to overcome the will of a woman with the intention of raping her he commits a crime: but where the woman voluntarily consumes the alcohol and is then incapable of resisting, she is deemed in law not to have a will to be overcome (although such a situation may give rise to prosecution of the crime of

---

[116] *Barbour* v *HMA* 1982 SCCR 195.
[117] See Jones and Christie, *Criminal Law* (2nd edn, 1996), pp 29 *et seq.*
[118] *cf* English offence of male rape in Criminal Justice and Public Order Act 1994, s 142.
[119] *Jamieson* v *HMA* 1994 JC 88; *Meek* v *HMA* 1983 SLT 280.

clandestine injury to women). The absence of will may also be encountered if a man has sexual intercourse with an unconscious woman, or has sexual relations with the woman whilst she is asleep. It is not rape to induce sexual relations on the basis of a fraudulent misrepresentation although there is now a statutory offence of having sexual relations with the woman whilst impersonating her husband.[120]

Where a man has sexual relations with a girl aged under 12 years, even in a situation where the girl gives her consent, the law decrees that this is "constructive" rape. The girl is presumed not to be of sufficient maturity to have formed a will, which can then be overcome. An accused will be charged with the common law offence of rape rather than the statutory crime. The consent of the victim will be no defence. One possible defence is the honest belief on the part of the male that the girl was over the age of 12.

A husband can no longer claim immunity from prosecution for raping his wife on the basis that the contract of marriage contains explicit consent to engage in sexual relations throughout the duration of the marriage.[121]

Clandestine injury to women

14–29   Clandestine injury to women, although often regarded as a historic crime, continues to be prosecuted in Scottish courts.[122] It arises in circumstances where a man has sexual relations with a woman without her consent but not by overcoming her will.[123] Accordingly, it arises in situations where the woman is unconscious, asleep, or where the woman is generally capable of giving consent but at the time of intercourse is incapable. The physical aspects of the crime are similar to those of rape. The male perpetrator must engage in vaginal intercourse with the woman. To establish the crime it must be shown that the accused intended to have intercourse with the woman without her consent. It will be a defence for the accused to establish that he had an honest belief that the woman was consenting.

Indecent assault

14–30   Indecent assault is an aggravated form of assault.[124] It ranges from conduct attended with very limited physical violence, such as touching another's private parts, to very serious attacks. As indicated earlier, it covers instances of "male rape", anal inter-course with a woman against her will, and other serious sexual assaults not involving sexual intercourse.[125] Unlike rape and clandestine injury to women, indecent assault is not a gender-specific crime. Likewise, the victim of the assault may be of either sex. As in assault generally there must be an attack upon the victim.[126] Merely exposing oneself is not an attack, whereas menaces, gestures or threats may be. Thus, someone presenting a knife at a victim, threatening them and telling them to strip would indeed be guilty of an offence of indecent assault. There may be no physical contact between the attacker and the victim. Whereas the concept of assault is fairly well defined in Scots law, indecency is somewhat more vague. Indecency is an affront to the sexual modesty of the victim.

---

[120] Criminal Law (Consolidation) (Scotland) Act 1995, s 7(3).
[121] *S v HMA* 1989 SLT 469; see English case of *R v R* [1992] 1 AC 599.
[122] Criminal Procedure (Scotland) Act 1995, s 274 (2)(c).
[123] See, for example, *Charles Sweenie* (1847) Ark 280.
[124] See para 14–27.
[125] It was said in *S v HMA* 1989 SLT 469 that rape itself was a form of sexual assault.
[126] See para 14–27.

The *mens rea* of indecent assault is the evil intent to occasion harm upon the victim.[127] Harm may be interpreted as physical injury or mental injury. It is not possible to commit the crime of indecent assault by recklessness or negligence.[128] In addition to denying that there was an attack, possible defences include lawful authority, such as child chastisement[129] or police or medical restraint.[130] A further possible defence is that of consent. However, there are some victims who are considered too young to give their consent to an indecent assault.[131] Moreover, consent must be narrowly construed. Thus, where a patient gives consent to an examination by a doctor this should not be viewed as consent to examine any part unconnected with the medical ailment.[132] Consent and indecent assault raise the issue of sado-masochistic practices between consenting adults. Even in situations where such activity is engaged in consensually, a charge of indecent assault may be brought. The issue is whether there was an intention to injure or cause harm.[133]

Other statutory sexual offences

Part 1 of the Criminal Law (Consolidation) (Scotland) Act 1995 sets down a number of statutory sexual offences relating to such matters as incest; sexual activity with girls under the age of consent; prostitution and homosexual activity. **14–31**

Incest

Where a person has sexual intercourse with a person related to him within one of the forbidden degrees of relationship, he commits the offence of incest.[134] The list of forbidden degrees of relationship is similar to, but not congruent with, the forbidden degrees of relationship with respect to marriage. It does not matter whether the relationship is established by full-blood or half-blood even where traced through, or to, any person whose parents are not, or have not been, married to one another.[135] There are three defences listed in the statute. First, that he did not know and had no reason to suspect that the person with whom he had sexual relations was so related. Second, that he did not consent to the sexual relations. Third, that he was married to that person at the time the sexual relations took place by marriage entered into outside Scotland but recognised as valid in Scots law. **14–32**

Sexual activity with girls under the age of consent

The 1995 Act also contains important offences relating to sexual intercourse with female children. It is an offence, punishable with up to life imprisonment, for a man to have unlawful sexual intercourse with any girl under 13 years of age.[136] This offence is sometimes referred to as "statutory rape". It is of no consequence that the girl consented to the sexual relations. It is also an offence to attempt to have sex with a girl under 13 **14–33**

---

[127] *Sweeney* v *X* 1982 SCCR 509.
[128] *Young* v *McGlennan* 1991 SCCR 738.
[129] See para 14–27. *Stewart* v *Thain* 1981 SLT (Notes) 2.
[130] *Skinner* v *Robertson* 1980 SLT (Sh Ct) 43 (psychiatric nurse); *Marchbank* v *Annan* 1987 SCCR 718 (police officer).
[131] *C* v *HMA* 1987 SCCR 104.
[132] *Hussain* v *Houston* 1995 SLT 1060.
[133] See *Smart* v *HMA* 1975 JC 30.
[134] Criminal Law (Consolidation) (Scotland) Act 1995, s 1(1).
[135] s 1(2).
[136] s 5(1).

years of age.[137] Where a person has sexual intercourse with a girl under 12 years of age with or without her consent it is usual for that person to be charged with common law rape rather than the statutory offence. It is also an offence for a person to have or attempt to have sexual intercourse with a girl aged between 13 years and 16 years of age.[138] It is a defence to such a charge for a man to prove that he had reasonable cause to believe the girl was his wife, or that he was under 24 and he had not been charged with a like offence and had reasonable cause to believe she was 16 years of age or over.[139] In addition, any person who uses lewd, indecent or libidinous behaviour towards a girl of 12 years of age or over and less than 16, even where she consents, commits an offence.[140] Such behaviour towards a girl under 12 constitutes a common law offence.[141]

It is an offence for any step-parent, or former step-parent, to have sex with his or her step-child or former step-child, if the step-child is either under the age of 21 or has, at any time before attaining the age of 18, lived in the same household and been treated as a child of his or her family. It is a defence to any such charge for a person to prove that he did not know, or had no reason to suspect that the person he had sexual relations with was a step-child or former step-child, or that he did not consent to sexual relations or that he believed on reasonable grounds that the person was of, or over, the age of 21 years or finally, he was married to that person by a recognised marriage entered outside Scotland. [142]

A person over 16 years of age who is a member of the same household as a child (such as a foster carer or partner of a parent) or is in a position of trust in relation to that child commits an offence where he has sexual intercourse with that child.[143] Again, an accused can escape liability if he proves reasonable belief that the person was over 16, there was consent to have sex, or he was married to that person by recognised marriage solemnised outside Scotland.[144]

Prostitution

14–34   There are a number of statutory offences relating to the procuring of women, whether for prostitution or for unlawful sexual intercourse.[145] Accordingly, procuring,[146] allowing premises to be used for prostitution,[147] the seduction of underage girls for prostitution,[148] trading in prostitution,[149] keeping a brothel,[150] or allowing a child to be in a brothel are all offences.[151]

---

[137] s 5(2).
[138] s 5(3); *cf HMA* v *Roose* 1999 SCCR 259.
[139] s 5(5); *Clark* v *Gallacher* 1999 GWD 25–1185.
[140] s 6.
[141] See *Batty* v *HMA* 1995 SCCR 525 where it was suggested the common law charge may be appropriate to older children in certain circumstances notwithstanding the statutory provision.
[142] Criminal Law (Consolidation) (Scotland) Act 1995 ("1995 Act"), s 2.
[143] 1995 Act, s 3; *cf HMA* v *K* 1994 SCCR 499.
[144] 1995 Act, s 3(2).
[145] *ibid* s 7.
[146] *ibid* s 7.
[147] *ibid* s 9 .
[148] *ibid* s 10.
[149] *ibid* s 11.
[150] *ibid* s 11.
[151] *ibid* s 12.

Homosexual activity

At common law, homosexual acts may constitute an offence of sodomy, lewd and **14–35** libidinous practice, indecent assault or shameless indecency. Consensual homosexual acts are given certain protection from prosecution. Acts committed in private involving only two persons over 18 years of age do not constitute criminal offences.[152] A male person who is mentally deficient to the extent that he is incapable of independent living or guarding himself against exploitation cannot give consent. If a person can show that he had no reason to suspect that the other person was mentally deficient to that extent he may still be protected from prosecution.[153] The statute also makes it an offence to commit, or be a party to, or procure a homosexual act not protected by the legislative provisions. Living off the earnings of homosexual prostitution or allowing one's premises to be used as a brothel for homosexual acts are also offences.[154]

Obscenity offences

It is an offence to display, publish or sell or distribute obscene material. Such an **14–36** offence may be prosecuted under statute or as the common law crime of shameless indecency. Simple possession of obscene material, unless it is child pornography, does not amount to an offence. There are also other statutory offences related to the importation of obscene material or the posting of obscene material. It is also an offence to take, or permit to be taken, pictures of children under 16 years of age where such a picture is deemed to be obscene. It is an offence to be in possession of such a picture although one may lead a defence that there is a legitimate reason why one is in possession of such a picture or that one is unaware of the nature of the picture, or that the picture has been sent to that person without prior request and he has not had reasonable time to destroy it. What amounts to indecency in this context is always a matter for the court.

Shameless indecency

The common law sense of shameless indecency operates to regulate a wide array of illegal **14–37** sexual behaviour. It is in every respect a fairly imprecise offence covering, on the one hand, sexual intercourse by a woman with an underage male, and on the other hand, less physically injurious conduct such as sexual exhibitionism,[155] selling, publishing or circulating obscene publications or items,[156] incestuous behaviour,[157] indecent exposure,[158] homosexual acts in public places, a sexual spectacle involving the performance of an indecent act,[159] and indecent conduct stopping short of indecent assault.[160] In *Dean* v *John Menzies (Holdings) Ltd*[161] it was said that it is of the essence of shameless indecency that:

---

[152] 1995 Act, s 13. Note, this is soon to be reduced to 16 years of age.
[153] *ibid* s 13(3).
[154] *ibid* s 13(9) and (10); *Reid* v *HMA* 1999 JC 54.
[155] *Lockhart* v *Stephen* 1987 SCCR 642 (Sh Ct).
[156] *Dean* v *John Menzies (Holdings) Ltd* 1981 JC 23.
[157] Incest is a statutory crime but conduct stopping short of sexual intercourse may be shameless indecency: see *R* v *HMA* 1988 SLT 623.
[158] *McKenzie* v *White* (1864) 4 Irv. 570; *Niven* v *Tudhope* 1982 SCCR 365.
[159] *cf Lockhart* v *Stephen* 1987 SCCR 642.
[160] *McLaughlin* v *Boyd* 1934 JC 19.
[161] 1981 SLT 50.

"the conduct be directed towards some person or some persons with an intention or in the knowledge to corrupt or be calculated to be liable to corrupt or deprave in the manner liable, those to whom the conduct is directed".

Consequently, it is clear that there must be some damaging impact on another for the crime to be committed. If the affect is directed towards a less mature child or someone with less than a normal adult standard of morality it is nevertheless competent to lay the charge of shameless indecency. It has recently been held that passively allowing children to watch a pornographic video was not shameless indecency.[162]

Standards of sexual decency change, as do notions of sexual propriety.[163] Generally, contemporary society is altogether more permissive than previously and there is, therefore, continual redefinition of what amounts to shameless indecency. Where the erotic performance (of another) simply stimulates adult sexual desires it seems clear that Scots courts are not inclined to uphold an accusation of shameless indecency. It will always be a matter of circumstance and degree. Although the locus of the crime is significant and public exhibitionism is more likely to come under the heading of shameless indecent conduct, it is not a requirement of the offence that it is conducted in public.[164] If the act is in a private place to which the public has resort or is able to view, then a charge of shameless indecency may, nevertheless, be competent.[165]

PUBLIC ORDER OFFENCES

Breach of the peace

14–38   Breach of the peace is one of the better-known common law offences in Scotland. Generally, breach of the peace is a relatively minor offence although it can be applicable to fairly serious matters.[166] It covers a broad range of activity often, but not exclusively, linked to public order. In *Montgomery* v *Macleod*[167] it was said that there is no limit to the kind of conduct which may be charged as breach of the peace.

Breach of the peace has often been criticised as an imprecise offence and also one which contains implications for civil liberties. A person may commit breach of the peace engaging in otherwise lawful conduct (even aggressive begging)[168] where it is likely to provoke annoyance or disturbance. Although many of the cases refer to the word "lieges" it is clear that the courts take a very broad view of what is meant by that word. Normally, it will be equated with ordinary people. However, in several breach of the peace cases the only persons present are likely to be police officers.[169] The court's approach has always been to assess whether a reasonable member[170] of the public

---

[162] *Patterson* v *Lees* 1999 JC 159.
[163] McCall Smith and Sheldon, *Scots Criminal Law* (2nd edn, 1997), p 173.
[164] *Usai* v *Russell* 1999 GWD 32–1519.
[165] *Watt* v *Annan* 1978 JC 84.
[166] *eg* serious "stalking" and prison riots. On its application to stalking see Mays, Middlemiss, and Watson, "Scots Law, Stalking and the Protection from Harassment Act 1997" 1997 JR 331; on prison riots see *Ralston* v *HMA* 1989 SLT 474.
[167] 1977 SCCR 14 (Supp); see also Oliver, "Recent Trends in Breach of the Peace", 1997 SLT(News) 293.
[168] *Donaldson* v *Vannet* 1998 SLT 957.
[169] See, for example, *Grogan* v *Heywood* 1999 SCCR 705.
[170] *Farrell* v *Normand* 1993 SLT 793.

might have been alarmed had they been present.[171] It is also clear that breach of the peace need not necessarily be a public offence and may well be committed within the confines of a private house or building or within the back of a police van.[172] It need not involve the creation of noise but may simply relate to an act which causes alarm, such as peering in a window,[173] or repeatedly inviting a young girl up to one's flat.[174] It need not involve an overt act but may simply be passive conduct, such as loitering.[175] Breach of the peace is often simply assessed from the whole circumstances of the matter and rarely is the question of the appropriate criminal mind ever addressed. Breach of the peace may be committed intentionally or recklessly.[176]

OFFENCES AIMED AT SOCIAL PROTECTION

Misuse of Drugs

The prosecution and sanctioning of various offences relating to the misuse of drugs **14–39** has become an everyday occurrence in the Scottish criminal courts.[177] The applicable law is to be found principally in three statutory enactments—the Misuse of Drugs Act 1971, the Customs and Excise Management Act 1979, and the Drug Trafficking Offences Act 1986. There are also several related pieces of delegated legislation.

Control of drug abuse revolves round the control of importation and exportation, the production, supply, and possession of controlled drugs. The appendix to the 1971 Act categorises controlled drugs as either class A, B or C. Such drugs include the opiates, cocaine and derivatives, hallucinogens, amphetamines, and other controlled stimulant drugs. Not all drugs are included in the categories of controlled drugs and in respect of those drugs not listed, drug abuse remains largely unregulated.

The 1971 Act and the 1979 Act both seek to regulate the importation and exportation of controlled drugs. It is an offence to import controlled drugs into the UK or to be knowingly concerned in the fraudulent evasion of the prohibition against the importation of controlled drugs. Even to fulfil fairly limited roles in the importation process may result in the commission of serious offences. Moreover, it is possible to be guilty of an offence in the UK even if one's entire role is performed abroad. It is an offence under section 20 of the Misuse of Drugs Act 1971 for any person to attempt to break the law of a foreign country pertaining to the control of the importation and the exportation of controlled drugs.

It is an offence to supply or produce controlled drugs. Production may involve cultivation or laboratory production. The Scottish courts have interpreted the concept of cultivation fairly liberally and, thus, to place a plant on the window has been held to be sufficient to cultivate the plant. Supply may involve offering to supply, intending to supply, or being concerned in the supply of controlled drugs. The quantity of controlled drugs found in the possession of a person may infer the intention to supply. It is also the case that intention to supply can be inferred from the actings of the

---

[171] *Wilson v Brown* 1982 SLT 361; *Raffaelli v Heatley* 1949 JC 101; *Mackay v Heywood* 1998 SCCR 210.
[172] *Keegan v Friel* 1999 JC 185.
[173] *Raffaelli v Heatley* 1949 JC 101.
[174] *Biggins v Stott* 1999 SLT 1037.
[175] *Montgomery v McLeod* 1977 SLT (Notes) 77.
[176] *Pallazzo v Copeland* 1976 JC 52; *Butcher v Jessop* 1989 SLT 593; *Stewart v Lockhart* 1991 SLT 835.
[177] Bovey, "Misuse of Drugs: Developments and Trends" (1999) 4(1) SLPQ 41.

accused. It is possible to be guilty of a supply offence even if one is not in possession of the drug. It is also an offence to attempt to supply controlled drugs.[178]

It is an offence to be in possession of a controlled drug.[179] Possession is viewed as the least serious of the drug offences. There is pressure in modern society to decriminalise the possession of cannabis and marijuana.[180] Possession of large quantities of drugs may give rise to an inference that one is not merely possessing for personal use but, rather, one is concerned in the supply and this will be a much more serious matter. In respect of possession, it is clear that Scots law requires a physical and a mental element. Not only must there be control of the drugs in terms of possession on the person of the accused or in some place under the control of the accused, but the accused must also be aware that he is in possession (and control) of the drug.[181] One is allowed to be in possession of controlled drugs to facilitate the handing over to police authorities. If a person were the innocent possessor of a quantity of controlled drugs, it would appear that the burden is on him to show his innocence.

Road traffic offences

14–40   The law relating to road traffic offences is found principally in two statutes of generic application throughout the UK—the Road Traffic Act 1988 (as amended by the Road Traffic Act 1991) and the Road Traffic Offenders Act 1988.

It is an offence to cause the death of a person by dangerous driving.[182] "Dangerous" driving can be equated with recklessness. For the accused's driving to be dangerous it is a requirement that an accused has knowledge and foresight of the circumstances of his driving. There must be a link between the death and the dangerous driving and it must be shown that the accused's driving was the material or operative cause of death. The accused must have driven a mechanically propelled vehicle on a road or other public place. The courts will make an objective assessment of the driving and the proved circumstances.[183] It does not just involve deliberate and wilful driving but also driving where there are potential dangers and the accused's approach in attitude and behaviour in such circumstances is dangerous. This is a serious offence, which results in imprisonment for anyone convicted.

It is an offence to engage in dangerous driving.[184] This offence has substantially the same components as the offence of causing death by dangerous driving except in this instance there is no consequential fatality. It relates to standards of driving which are seriously below that expected of an ordinary driver.[185] There may be no collision and the dangerousness may simply relate to excessive speed. In defining the quality of the driving, reference may be made to the Highway Code but this will not be the pure determinant of dangerousness. Dangerousness is not likely to be evidenced by momentary lapse or error but is more akin to a course of conduct. Anyone accused of dangerous driving may be acquitted but, as an alternative, be convicted of careless

---

[178] Misuse of Drugs Act 1971, s 4.
[179] *ibid* s 5.
[180] Greig, "Smoke Screen over Cannabis" (1999) JLSS 44(8) 22.
[181] *Salmon* v *HMA* 1999 JC 67.
[182] Road Traffic Act 1988, s 1.
[183] See *Patterson* v *HMA* 1999 GWD 17–817.
[184] Road Traffic Act 1988, s 2.
[185] *eg Hannigan* v *Hutchison* 1999 GWD 23–1119; *Howdle* v *O'Connor* 1998 SLT 94.

driving which has a lower standard of culpability. Knowledge of the dangerous state of one's vehicle may be enough to constitute dangerous driving.[186]

The most basic of the statutory offences relating to quality of driving is careless driving.[187] It is an offence which may be perpetrated in one of two ways—driving without due care and attention or driving without reasonable consideration. Driving without due care and attention involves an assessment of the accused's driving measured against the standard of the careful and competent driver. The law does not permit any concessions to new or learner drivers nor is there any immunity for emergency services though one may plead necessity (emergency) as a defence. It is possible that the offence may be inferred from the circumstances.[188] Examples of driving without reasonable consideration involve driving too close to the vehicle in front, driving with lights on a full beam, unnecessarily driving on the outside lane or overtaking on the inside. It is not only cars or car drivers who may face criminal sanction for carelessness. There is also an offence of careless cycling.[189] It is an offence to cause death by careless driving while under the influence of drink or drugs.[190] Further, there is an offence under section 4(1) of the 1988 Act to drive or attempt to drive[191] while unfit through drink or drugs. In this context, drink is equated to alcoholic drink and a drug can be any intoxicating drug but not necessarily a controlled drug. The interesting feature of this offence is that there is no prescribed level of alcohol or drugs—a simple test is whether the accused's ability was impaired. That test may be satisfied by medical evidence. Section 4(2) of the Act also contains an offence of being "in charge of" a vehicle while being unfit. In circumstances where the accused has been apprehended when not driving the vehicle, if he appears to be responsible for the control of it, then such a charge may be appropriate. There is a defence that the accused had no likelihood of driving while unfit.[192]

The most renowned of the driving offences is contained in section 5 of the 1988 Act. Under this section it is an offence to drive or be in charge of a vehicle while over the prescribed limit of alcohol – those limits currently stand at 35 milligrams per 100 millilitres in breath tests, 180/100 millilitres in blood tests, or 107 millilitres/100 in urine tests. There are three recognised defences to the offence: that there is no likelihood of driving[193]; (2) that the accused has participated in post incident drinking[194]; and (3) that the accused has driven in such circumstances under necessity.[195]

OFFENCES RELATED TO PROPERTY

Theft

It is theft to appropriate moveable, corporeal things belonging to another person,   **14–41**
without the consent of that person, where the accused knows that those things belong

---

[186] *Niven* v *Heywood* 1999 GWD 15–722.
[187] Road Traffic Act 1988, s 3.
[188] However, see *Crawford* v *O'Donnell* 1999 SCCR 39.
[189] Road Traffic Act 1988, s 28A.
[190] *ibid* s 3A.
[191] *eg Hamilton* v *Vannet* 1999 GWD 8–406.
[192] *Cartmill* v *Heywood* 1999 GWD 22–1075.
[193] *Kelso* v *Brown* 1998 SLT 921.
[194] Mason, "Conversion on the road to Auchtermuchty", 1996 SLT(News) 33.
[195] *Dawson* v *McKay* 1999 SLT 1326 (only where driver faces conscious dilemma between saving life or avoiding serious bodily harm and breaking the law).

to another and he intends to deprive him of them or their use permanently, indefinitely, or (in certain circumstances) temporarily.[196] Although the crime of theft is often attended with dishonesty, dishonest obtaining of the thing stolen is not a central component of the crime. A person may have in his possession goods which he has lawfully obtained and which he subsequently decides to appropriate. It has been said that:

> "it is of no consequence of what character original possession of the property is. The moment the intention of appropriating the property of another is formed then the theft is committed."[197]

In *Herron v Diack and Newlands*[198] the accused were funeral directors who were engaged to conduct a burial at sea. They removed the corpse from a steel coffin and placed it in a substitute wooden container with the intention of keeping the steel coffin for future use. Following problems in conducting the burial, they returned the body to the steel casket and effected the burial. Notwithstanding the circumstances, the accused were charged with theft and convicted. At the time that they had decided to retain the steel casket they had formed the intention to appropriate, thus committing the offence of theft.

Corporeal moveable property can be defined as tangible objects or things, which are moveable, or are capable of being severed from that which is naturally or artificially attached to them. Professor Bell defines it as "all things which being themselves capable of motion or of being moved".[199] Beyond the more obvious objects such as cars, household property and money, corporeal moveables include crops, which may be severed from the land, soil, and animals.

It is a requirement of theft that the goods belong to another. It is not possible for a person to steal his own goods. However, some goods do not have an owner. Accordingly, wild animals, while they remain free and at large in their own environment, cannot be stolen. Once captured and taken into possession (dead or alive) by someone they can, subsequently, be stolen from that person. In modern times, there has been some controversy over the question of ownership of remedial or improvement work to the home. Items such as doors, windows and other fixtures once attached to the property of another thereafter belong to that person and cannot be removed by the person who has fixed them to the property. In circumstances where a contractor's bill remains unpaid his remedy is to seek recompense of breach of contract. If he attempts to remove the goods and take them back into his own possession he may, in the process, commit the crime of theft.

The *actus reus* of theft may be committed in one of three ways—theft by taking, theft by appropriation or theft by finding.

Theft by taking

14–42   Theft by taking conveys the classical imagery of the robber running off with the stolen goods. It represents a particular species of theft. It should be noted, however, that

---

[196] Jones and Christie, *Criminal Law* (2nd edn, 1996), p 239.
[197] per Lord Meadowbank in *John Smith* (1838) 2 S 28.
[198] 1973 SLT (Sh Ct) 27; see also *Dewar v HMA* 1945 JC 5.
[199] Bell's *Principles*, s 1285.

taking involves simply the physical movement of goods. The extent and circumstances of the movement will be crucial in each and every case. Generally speaking, simply touching goods or moving them will be insufficient to constitute the crime of theft. In contemporary society, the advent of the supermarket has given rise to certain types of shopping. Shoppers will collect goods from the shelves and thereafter present them at a check-out for payment. It is not uncommon for such supermarkets to engage store detectives and security agents who will often await the shopper's departure from the shop before apprehending him on suspicion that he may have stolen goods from the shop. This practice has given rise to the notion that the crime of theft is committed only once the person has moved beyond the check-out till. However, this is not the case: the crime of theft is committed when the accused has engaged in actions which indicate that he has formed the intention to appropriate the goods. This may be at the point where he has concealed the goods in an unorthodox location. It is only customary for such shops to await the shopper's departure from the shop so that there can be no doubt that that person intends to appropriate the property of the shop.

Theft by appropriation

This occurs where goods are lawfully in the possession of the accused and he subsequently forms the intention to keep them. It does not involve the taking away of goods as the goods have already been taken from their lawful owner.

14–43

Theft by finding

For purely practical reasons, the law does not recognise that theft occurs the moment something is found but the longer one retains found property the more likely it is that one may be thought to have formed the intention to appropriate the goods. Again, the perpetrator has not taken the goods away from their rightful owner; he has simply found them and thereafter formed the intention to appropriate. There is another related requirement under statute that where one finds goods, one is expected to hand them into a police station. It is an offence to fail to do so.[200]

14–44

   In all cases, the criminal mind requirement to complete the crime of theft is the intention to deprive the rightful owner of their possession and that deprivation may be permanent or on a temporary basis for a nefarious purpose.[201] "Nefarious", in this context, may be defined as wicked or evil. Accordingly, the crime of theft is not committed where one borrows an item without the intention to deprive the owner permanently or temporarily for a nefarious purpose. It will always be a difficult matter of proof to convince the court that one simply intended to borrow something rather than to steal it. There is no requirement in the crime of theft that one retains the goods or intends to retain the goods for one's self. As such, one may find goods in the street and subsequently decide to give them to another. Although this may be viewed by some as an act of generosity, the minute a person decides to retain the goods and pass them on, he forms the intention to deprive the owner and, accordingly, the crime of theft is committed.

   The crime of theft, like the crime of assault, may be aggravated—that is, made more serious and therefore punished more severely. There are three aggravations to the

---

[200] Civic Government (Scotland) Act 1982, s 67.
[201] See *Scott* v *Freil* 1999 SLT 930.

crime of theft—theft by house-breaking; theft by opening lockfast places; and theft by drugging.

Theft by house breaking

14–45   This need not necessarily involve unlawful entry into a house. Any building may be broken into in this way. The house-breaking must precede the theft. House-breaking may be perpetrated by forcing open doors or windows or any other entrance, or by using stolen, found, or lawfully obtained keys to gain unauthorised entry. Entry secured by pretending to be another might also constitute house-breaking and indeed, in very unusual circumstances, it may be possible to house-break without actually entering the house—for example, where one inserts an implement of some kind in order to steal the property of another. All that is required is violation to the integrity of the building, preceding the theft.

Theft by opening lockfast places

14–46   This entails breaking into locked rooms, drawers, cupboards, cars or some other secured or sealed item. A lockfast place is defined as any place that may be locked which is not an entire building.

Theft by drugging

14–47   As the phrase implies, theft by drugging involves the perpetrator drugging the victim with a view to thereafter stealing property from him.

Reset

14–48   The crime of reset is the retention of goods that have been obtained by means of theft, robbery, fraud or embezzlement with the intention of keeping those goods from their rightful owner. Although the crime requires the goods to be retained, the resetter may not be in actual physical possession of the retained goods. All that is required is that the retainer exhibits some control over the goods and is complicit in the deprivation of their rightful owner. The *mens rea* of the crime requires the accused to have knowledge that the goods belong to another and have been obtained by means of theft, robbery, fraud or embezzlement.[202] Furthermore, an accused must exhibit the intention to keep the goods from the true owner. The court will be able to draw an inference of intention from the nature and quality of retention.[203] The longer someone has in his possession goods belonging to another, the more likely the inference that he intended to deprive the true owner of his goods. Notwithstanding this, possession for a very short period of time may be sufficient to constitute the crime of reset. It is a general proposition of law that a spouse will not be guilty of reset in circumstances where he or she receives stolen goods from the other spouse. Although largely to be determined by the circum-stances, there may be situations where husband and wife may be complicit in one of the property offences, and indeed there may be circumstances where the deprivation is joint, rendering both spouses liable for the crime of reset itself.[204] It is believed that reset as a crime pertains only to the retention of improperly acquired goods and not the proceeds from the sale of those improperly required goods. Naturally, receipt of

---

[202] *Shannon* v *HMA* 1985 SCCR 14; *Nisbet* v *HMA* 1983 SCCR 13.
[203] *Hamilton* v *Friel* 1994 SCCR 748.
[204] See *Smith* v *Watson* 1982 JC 34.

the proceeds of improperly required goods may constitute complicity so as to draw an inference of art and part guilt to the commission of the original crime.

Robbery

Robbery is a species of theft effected by means of violence or intimidation (assault).[205] **14–49** The assault must be the means by which the theft is affected. Where the violence arises between the accused and the victim subsequent to the theft it will not be robbery. For example, in situations where a victim pursues someone who has stolen something from him and violence occurs, it is likely to be charged as two separate offences of theft and assault. Where the violence occurs immediately preceding the theft, such as a violent blow inflicted with a view to removing goods belonging to the victim, then robbery is clearly an appropriate charge. Intimidatory threatening gestures may be sufficient violence to constitute the crime of robbery. Words alone are not enough to constitute an attack. Intimidation which takes the form of the threat of immediate violence to the victim is sufficient.

The close proximity in terms of time between the violence and the theft is fundamental to the crime of robbery. For example, it would not be robbery to assault a victim one day and at that time take the means of securing entry to that person's home at a subsequent date, thereby subsequently stealing goods from him. It would be robbery to assault someone with a view to stealing his keys, but the subsequent theft from the home would be theft by house-breaking.

Complications arise where there is simultaneous violence and theft. The act of taking could be so violent in itself that it constitutes an attack and, thus, the crime of robbery. This will always be a matter of fact and circumstance: simply snatching or pick-pocketing from a victim is unlikely to be sufficient violence to constitute the crime of robbery, whereas deliberately knocking a person down whilst snatching something could be robbery. It has been said by Lord Justice-Clerk Aitchison that "it is not necessary to robbery that there should be actual physical assault. It is enough if the degree of force used can even be described as violence."[206] In a situation where, after perpetrating an assault, the accused notices and appropriates some valuables of the victim, he is likely to be prosecuted for assault and theft, not robbery.

Fraud

Fraud is a common law offence although there are, additionally, a number of statutory **14–50** offences that are designed to tackle fraud. The causing of prejudice to another by means of a false pretence constitutes common law fraud. It is necessary for there to be a false pretence; a prejudicial result; and a connection between the two.

A false pretence may be exhibited in a number of ways and may relate to a number of issues, *eg* identity, quality, extent or fact. It is not necessary that the false pretence be made in words, written or verbal. It may be constituted by any false impression created in the mind of the victim of the fraud. Only in situations where there is a clear duty on the part of a person to correct any misapprehension can liability ensue from a situation where a party says and does nothing. Although there is a fine distinction to be drawn, expressions of opinion do not constitute false pretences and thus cannot

---

[205] See para 14–27 for assault; see *Cromar* v *HMA* 1987 SCCR 635; *cf Flynn* v *HMA* 1995 SLT 1267.
[206] *O'Neil* v *HMA* 1934 JC 98.

found a case of fraud. The false pretence must relate to something past or present. One cannot establish liability for fraud in respect of a pretence as to some future act, or a contingent matter.[207]

The second component of fraud is the requirement that a false pretence is accompanied by some result, which is prejudicial to the victim. In many cases, this will be very clear in that the situation will involve some monetary loss. However, it is not an essential prerequisite that the victim has suffered financial loss. The prejudicial loss may take some other form. Nor is there any requirement that the party making the false pretence benefits from it.

Finally, there must be a connection between the false pretence and the prejudicial result. The pretence must have induced the victim to act in a prejudicial way. Fraud is a crime of intention, which requires the perpetrator to have knowledge of the falseness of the pretence. The accused must intend that the victim act on the basis of the statement and thus incur a prejudicial result.

Uttering of forged documents

14–51   It is a common misconception that to forge something is a crime. The crime lies in the "uttering" of a forged document. This is where the accused presents a forged copy, which he falsely purports to be authenticated by another.[208] Forgery can take the form of imitation of another's signature, fictitious signature of a document, or copying and modification of documents. The uttering of a forgery might not relate simply to a document, but also relate to an item such as a painting. The requirement of the crime of uttering is that it is prejudicial to another. Uttering is a crime of intention where, in similar fashion to the crime of fraud, the utteror knows that the document or item is not genuine and thereby intends to defraud another.

Embezzlement

14–52   Earlier authorities point to embezzlement as a crime of breach of an obligation to account. It is suggested that embezzlement has several key features. The first of these is that the goods or money must be in the possession of the accused. The accused is authorised to receive the money or goods and he has an obligation to account to another person. Second, it is necessary for the accused to have embarked upon a course of dealing with the goods or money of another, and third, it is necessary for the appropriation to take place in the course of that dealing. Finally, the accused must hold the goods or fund on behalf of another. The *mens rea* of embezzlement can be stated as an intention to appropriate money or goods due to another without his consent. The subtle distinction between embezzlement and theft in this respect is that, unlike theft, embezzlement is a pure crime of dishonesty. It will have been noted that, in respect of theft, one may obtain the goods of another quite honestly and with his consent and thereafter form the intention to appropriate.

Extortion

14–53   Extortion arises in circumstances where a person gains an advantage at the expense of another and extraction of that gain or advantage is brought about by threat. It can be

---

[207] Although see *Richard* v *HMA* 1971 JC 1.
[208] *MacDonald* v *Tudhope* 1984 SLT 23.

distinguished from robbery on the basis that robbery involves a threat or use of immediate violence. Extortion may arise in circumstances where there is some future contingent threat of violence. The legality or variety of the threat, however, is of no consequence, and the threat may be, for example, to expose the victim's past or some truth about the victim. If the act is done with a view to extracting a gain from the victim, that amounts to extortion. To threaten court proceedings does not amount to extortion. In *Silverstein* v *HMA*[209] Lord Justice-Clerk Thomson said that where the pressure consists in creating in the victim fear that, "unless he yields, his position will be altered for the worse, it is criminal unless the pressure is thought to be exerted as recognised by law as legitimate."

Malicious mischief

Malicious mischief is an offence, which relates to the damage and destruction of property, and involves monetary loss on the part of the owner of the property.[210] It need not involve physical damage. In the case of *Wilson* v *HMA*,[211] an employee pushed an emergency stop button at a power station resulting in considerable loss, albeit that no property was damaged. This was held to be an example of malicious mischief. It seems clear, following *Wilson*, that deliberate interference with the property of another may be sufficient to constitute malicious mischief. For a person to be guilty of malicious mischief the criminal mind required is deliberate disregard or indifference coupled with intent to injure another in respect of his property. The courts have been unprepared to admit a defence that the accused believed he was entitled to perpetrate the damage to the property. In the case of *Clark* v *Syme*,[212] a landowner shot some sheep who were eating turnips on land belonging to him in the belief that he had the right to do so. The court held that this was no defence to the crime of malicious mischief. There is also a statutory offence of vandalism in the Criminal Justice (Scotland) Act 1995, which makes it an offence for someone without reasonable excuse[213] to wilfully or recklessly destroy or damage property belonging to another.

14–54

Fire raising

Fire raising is treated very seriously in Scots law. It involves the deliberate and reckless burning of another's property. Ordinarily, burning one's own property will not constitute an offence but may, nevertheless, amount to a whole range of other offences (for example, breach of the peace).

14–55

There are now two species of fire raising—wilful fire raising, and culpable and reckless fire raising. Wilful fire raising is viewed as a fairly serious crime and is thought to be a crime of intention.[214] Culpable and reckless fire raising requires something more than simple carelessness. Culpability and recklessness will always be assessed by the courts taking into account all the facts as to the exhibited standard of

---

[209] 1949 JC 160.
[210] *Bett* v *Hamilton* 1998 JC 1.
[211] 1984 SLT 117.
[212] 1957 JC 1.
[213] *John* v *Donnelly* 2000 SLT 11.
[214] *Byrne* v *HMA* 2000 SLT 233; see also Chalmers, "Fire Raising: From the Ashes?", 2000 SLT (News) 57; Morrow, "The Development of the Law of Fire Raising", 1995 SLT (News) 51.

criminal mind. It is often the case that culpable and reckless fire raising is laid as an alternative charge to wilful fire raising.

OFFENCES AGAINST THE STATE

Offences relating to official secrets

14–56   It is an offence to disclose information about the security and intelligence services. Where the discloser has been a member of the security services the nature and content of the information is irrelevant. Where the discloser is a government servant or contractor it is necessary to show that the information is likely to be damaging to the security and intelligence services.[215] Where a person receives information and that person knows or has reasonable cause to believe that the information is protected and that disclosure would be damaging, and nonetheless discloses information, he will commit an offence.[216]

OFFENCES AGAINST THE ADMINISTRATION OF JUSTICE

Perjury

14–57   Perjury arises where a person who is on oath affirms something, which he knows to be false. It is a prerequisite that the person intentionally affirms falsehoods in the knowledge of their falsity. It need not be something material to a particular case. It should, nevertheless, not be something trivial or insignificant. It is a requirement of the crime that the uttering of the falsehood must be during competent and relevant evidence. One cannot seek to found a charge of perjury in respect of falsehoods within precognition statements[217] although this may constitute the offence of attempting to pervert the course of justice. It is also an offence to attempt to induce another to perpetrate a falsehood while being questioned by a judge. This offence is known as subornation of perjury. The inducement need not involve bribery or intimidation. For subornation of perjury to occur, the person must utter the falsehood on oath. If that does not happen, but it appears that there has been an attempt at subornation of perjury, then two other offences may be appropriate—contempt of court or attempting to pervert the course of justice.

Contempt of court

14–58   Where something is done which offends the majesty of the court, the judge may deal with that matter immediately (even in the course of a case) or shortly thereafter. Examples of contempt of court include the refusal to answer questions,[218] the refusal to implement a court order, or anything which challenges or affronts the authority of the court, such as being absent from the court on occasions when one should be there or even simply being late where the absence and lateness is a result of wilful conduct. Further examples of contempt of court include being drunk and disorderly in court, being abusive towards the judge, or refusing to do what the judge asks. Solicitors'

---

[215] Official Secrets Act 1989, s 1.
[216] *ibid* s 5.
[217] Statements taken and noted in preparation of a case.
[218] *McNeilage* v *HMA* 1999 SCCR 471.

behaviour may also result in a finding of contempt of court.[219] A number of the contempt of court cases relate to media activity in the judicial process. The Contempt of Court Act 1981 seeks to regulate anything which may prejudice a fair trial or the administration of justice.[220] It is necessary that the act exhibit wilful or reckless disregard of the authority of the court. One can only perpetrate such contempt through speech, broadcast or publication. Restrictions imposed in respect of criminal cases by the Contempt of Court Act 1981 are activated from the point a suspect is arrested. Section 3 of the Act offers a defence to anyone charged with contempt of court that he took all reasonable steps to avoid liability. It is also a defence under section 4 to fairly, and accurately, report contemporaneously proceedings before the court. Section 5 provides yet another defence that the publication has been published in good faith and relates to public affairs or matters of public interest.

THE IMPACT OF THE HUMAN RIGHTS ACT 1998 ON SCOTS CRIMINAL LAW

Although the Human Rights Act 1998 has only recently been implemented into Scots **14–59** law its impact has already been felt in the realms of criminal law and the prosecution of crime. Changes have already been made to the Scottish criminal justice system and more seem likely to follow. Although it is beyond the scope of a book such as this to discuss the impact of the 1998 Act in depth, it is nevertheless important that the student be aware that this legislation is likely to have considerable influence over Scots criminal law in the months and years ahead. Obvious areas of challenge and reform include the imprecision of the offences of shameless indecency and breach of the peace and the declaratory power of the High Court of Justiciary.

---

[219] *Peter Cox, Petitioner* 1998 SLT 1172.
[220] For example, where it was held that an article claiming Colonel Gadaffi ordered the Lockerbie bombing was a contempt of court prejudicing trial of two accused in Netherlands under Scots law: *Al Mehgrahi* v *Times Newspapers Ltd* (High Court of Justiciary, 1999, unreported); see also *HMA* v *Scottish Media Newspapers Ltd* 1999 SCCR 599.

SUMMARY

THE NATURE AND SCOPE OF CRIMINAL LAW

- Criminal law may be described as a body of rules designed to ensure the peaceful co-existence of citizens within the community.
- In Scots law the criminal law remains uncodified and comprises common law offences and a large number of statutory crimes.
- Principally (though not exclusively), the Scottish Criminal courts are concerned with crimes committed within Scotland or within territorial waters pertaining to Scotland.
- There is no time limit for the prosecution of common law crimes; statute may stipulate in respect of particular statutory crimes.
- The High Court of Justiciary has the power to declare new crimes.

COMPONENTS OF A CRIME—THE CRIMINAL ACT OR OMISSION AND THE CRIMINAL MIND

- As a general proposition of law, for criminal liability to attach there must be concurrent a criminal act or omission (*actus reus*) and a criminal mind (*mens rea*). This is true of the common law crimes and of many statutory crimes. It is not, however, an absolute principle—many statutory offences do not require a criminal mind, liability being strict.
- The standards of criminal mind commonly recognised and applied in Scots law may be listed as intention (and wicked recklessness), recklessness (and gross negligence), and negligence.
- Each crime which requires *mens rea* will define the nature of the mind for criminal liability to ensue.
- There are a number of statutory offences where strict liability is imposed.
- Many statutes are silent on the question of *mens rea* and where that is the case there is a presumption in favour of the need for *mens rea*.

THE NEED TO HAVE CAUSED THE CRIME (CAUSATION)

- It is a principle of criminal law that a person must cause the result before he will be criminally responsible for any event.
- Where some intervening act breaks the chain of causation the accused will not be criminally liable for the end result.
- The victim's own act may operate to interrupt causation but to do so it must be an unreasonable act, or an act which is an unforeseeable result of the accused's conduct.

WHO CAN BE A PARTY TO A CRIME?

- The individual acting alone or together with another or others can be criminally liable.

- The Criminal Procedure (Scotland) Act 1995 sets out mechanisms for the prosecution of the "body corporate" either in summary or solemn proceedings.
- When more than one person is involved in the commission of a crime, the doctrine of art and part guilt operates to hold each of the parties equally liable for the commission of the crime.

CRIMINALISING THE INCOMPLETION OF CRIME (INCHOATE CRIMES)

- Scots criminal law punishes not only completed crimes but instances where criminality is exhibited in the development stage and it is appropriate that the law punishes the wrongfulness of the conduct just in the way it would had the crime been completed. These are known as inchoate crimes.
- Inchoate crimes are often divided into three categories: criminal attempts, conspiracy and incitement.

GENERAL DEFENCES TO CRIMINAL CHARGES

- The criminal law of Scotland recognises various general defences to criminal charges. Some of those defences are known as "special defences" and require to be intimated before trial to the prosecution. The special defences are: self-defence, alibi, incrimination, and insanity. Some defences are general defences, applicable in a number of situations. Other defences are particular defences and apply to particular crimes: for example, some statutory crimes lay down specific defences applicable only to that offence or statute.
- Ordinarily, it is justifiable to engage in what would otherwise be a criminal act in defence of oneself, or another, or in defence of one's own property.
- Insanity may act in bar of trial or it may result in acquittal where the accused is found to have been insane at the time of commission of the offence.
- Error may act as an exculpatory factor in a number of crimes.
- Involuntary intoxication may result in acquittal.
- Criminal responsibility begins at the age of eight.
- In the ordinary course of events, only voluntary acts are punishable under the criminal law. Where the accused undertakes some action because it is necessary for him to do so or under coercion of another, he may be able to enter this as a defence.

MITIGATION OF CRIMINAL LIABILITY

- Diminished responsibility acts as a mitigatory factor reducing homicide from what would otherwise be the crime of murder to that of culpable homicide.
- Provocation may act as a mitigating factor.

THE SUBSTANTIVE CRIMES OF SCOTLAND

Murder; culpable homicide; assault; rape; clandestine injury to women; indecent assault; other statutory sexual offences; obscenity offences; shameless indecency;

breach of the peace; misuse of drugs; road traffic offences; theft; reset; robbery; fraud; uttering of forged documents; embezzlement; extortion; malicious mischief; fire raising; offences relating to official secrets; perjury; contempt of court.

THE IMPACT OF THE HUMAN RIGHTS ACT 1998 ON SCOTS CRIMINAL LAW

Although only recently implemented, the 1998 Act has had an impact on criminal law and further challenges and reform will undoubtedly follow.

CASE DIGEST

Corporate criminal liability [see para 14–08]
  Dean v *John Menzies (Holdings) Ltd* 1981 JC 23
The company was charged with shameless indecency, having exhibited for sale pornographic magazines in one of its shops. It was held that while a body corporate could be prosecuted for a common law crime it could not be charged with an offence, which required the exhibition of human characteristics. Lord Cameron said: "The criminal law has long recognised that a corporate body may be guilty of breaches of statute ... If Parliament had intended that a company in its individual capacity should not be liable to prosecution in respect of common law offences it could have said so." (at 28)

Criminal attempt is something more than mere contemplation and occurs where the accused's act has entered the stage of preparation [see para 14–11]
  HMA v *Camerons* 1911 SC (J) 110
Two persons were charged with attempted fraud by insuring a necklace and thereafter claiming the insurance on the pretence that it had been stolen. The prosecution failed to prove that the insurance claim had been made. Nevertheless, the court held that attempted fraud could be established. The Lord Justice-General said "mere conception of a fraudulent scheme is not enough; the fraudulent scheme, in order to be criminal must be carried into effect by some overt act; but if it has begun to be carried into some effect by an overt act it need not come to final fruition." (at 114)

Dealing with self-defence and provocation separately [see para 14–15]
  Crawford v *HMA* 1950 JC 67
The accused was charged with the murder of his father and claimed he was acting in self-defence. The trial judge decided that there was no evidence of self-defence and withdrew the defence from the jury. There was evidence of provocation and the accused was convicted of the alternative charge of culpable homicide. Lord Justice-General Cooper said "exculpation is always the sole function of the special defence of self-defence. Provocation and self-defence are often coupled in a special defence. Provocation is not a special defence" (at 69).

Reasonable belief enough for self-defence [see para 14–15]

Owens v *HMA* 1946 JC 119

Accused claimed he saw what looked like a knife in the deceased's hands and had as a consequence used his own knife. It was held that it was sufficient for an accused to convince the jury that he had reasonable belief of the imminence of danger to himself even in cases where the accused was mistaken. Lord Justice-General Normand said: "self defence is made out when it is established to the satisfaction of the jury that the panel believed that he was in imminent danger and that he held that belief on reasonable grounds. Grounds for such belief may exist though they are founded on a genuine mistake of fact." (at 125)

Voluntary intoxication cannot be used to found the defence of insanity or the mitigatory effect of diminished responsibility [see para 14–16]

Brennan v *HMA* 1977 JC 38

The accused was charged with the murder of his father by stabbing him. He lodged a special defence of insanity induced by the voluntary consumption of alcohol and LSD tablets. He argued that, if it was not insanity, then the mental state following the ingestion of the alcohol and the hallucinogenic drug should reduce the charge from murder to culpable homicide on the basis of diminished responsibility. It was held that voluntary ingestion of intoxicants could not found either insanity or diminished responsibility.

Involuntary intoxication may found a defence [see para 14–18]

HMA v *Ross* 1991 JC 210

The accused was charged with seven charges of attempted murder. He had been drinking lager from a can. It was alleged that, unknown to him, temazepan and LSD had been placed in the can. Following consumption he had gone berserk, lunging at various people with a knife. It was held that involuntary intoxication could affect the issue of *mens rea* and that unforeseen involuntary intoxication could result in insanity or some other mental deficiency.

Wicked recklessness can be the *mens rea* for murder [see para 14–25]

Cawthorne v *HMA* 1968 JC 32

A man fired gun shots at random into a room in which some people had taken refuge. He was charged with attempted murder. The accused argued that he could only be guilty of this offence if he had intended to kill those inside the room. It was held that the *mens rea* for murder could be the reckless disregard of consequences. Lord Justice-General Clyde said: "the reason for this alternative being allowed in our law is that in many cases it may not be possible to prove what was in the accused's mind at the time, but the degree of recklessness in his actings, as proved by what he did, may be sufficient to establish proof of the wilful act on his part." (at 35–36)

Unlawful act culpable homicide [see para 14–26]

Sutherland v *HMA* 1994 SLT 634

The accused was convicted of culpable homicide. He acted with another to set fire to a building and claim insurance. In the course of setting fire to the building there was an explosion, which killed the other alleged participant. It was held no defence to say that the deceased was a willing participant in the common criminal purpose which led to his death.

Consent is limited as a defence in assault cases [see para 14–27]
Smart v HMA 1975 JC 30

Accused sought to defend a charge of assault on the basis that he and the "victim" had engaged in a fight whereby they both consented to being hit by each other. It was held that consent in this instance was not a defence. The *mens rea* of assault is determined by looking at whether there is, on the part of the accused, an intention to injure and do bodily harm. Evil intention is the essence of assault.

A belief that a woman is consenting to sexual relations can lead to acquittal of a rape charge. There is no need for the belief to be reasonable [see para 14–28]
Jamieson v HMA 1994 SLT 537

The accused alleged that the woman consented, or at least that he believed she was consenting. On appeal, it was held that there was no need to establish that there were reasonable grounds for such a belief. However, the jury could be directed to the issue of reasonableness in assessing whether the man genuinely and honestly believed the woman was consenting.

A man can be guilty of raping his wife [see para 14–28]
S v HMA 1989 SLT 469

The accused sought to found on a long-held notion that a man cannot be guilty of raping his wife as a principal actor where the parties were cohabiting as man and wife. The court held that there was no such immunity for a husband in respect of a charge of raping his wife.

Shameless indecency may be committed in a private place [see para 14–37]
Watt v Annan 1978 JC 84

Accused was convicted of shameless indecency having shown a film of an obscene or indecent nature. The film was shown in a private club. It was held that it was not necessary to show that the act took place in public or was a matter of public exhibition. The club had no special qualifications as to membership and the shamelessly indecent acts were directed to anyone who could easily obtain access to the viewing.

Appropriation is central to the crime of theft [see para 14–41]
HMA v Dewar 1945 JC 5

A manager of a crematorium was convicted of the theft of two coffins and a number of coffin lids, which he had removed from coffins received at the crematorium. He had removed the lids for a variety of ulterior purposes. There was no evidence of financial gain or dishonesty in the obtaining of the goods on the part of the accused.

FURTHER READING

Books
Bovey, *Misuse of Drugs* (2nd edn, Butterworths, 2000)
Bradley, *Firearms* (W Green, 1995)
Christie, *Breach of the Peace* (Butterworths, 1990)

Duff and Button (eds), *Criminal Justice in Scotland* (Dartmouth, 1999)

Ferguson, *Crimes Against the Person* (2nd edn, Butterworths, 1998)

Gane, *Sexual Offences* (Butterworths, 1992)

Gane and Stoddart, *Casebook on Scottish Criminal Law* (3rd edn, W Green, 1999)

Gordon, *The Criminal Law of Scotland* (2nd edn, W Green, 1978)

Hunter (ed), *Justice and Crime: Essays in Honour of the Right Honourable the Lord Emslie* (T&T Clark, 1993)

Jones and Christie, *Criminal Law* (2nd edn, Butterworths, 1996)

McCall Smith and Sheldon, *Scots Criminal Law* (2nd edn, Butterworths, 1997)

Shiels, *Offensive Weapons* (2nd edn, W Green, 1996)

Shiels, *Controlled Drugs* (W Green, 1997)

Wheatley, *Road Traffic Law in Scotland* (3rd edn, Butterworths, 1999)

The Scottish Law Commission, *The Mental Element in Crime* (Scot Law Com No 80, 1983)

The Scottish Law Commission, *Attempted Homicide* (Consultative Memo No 61, 1984)

Articles

Crichton-Styles, "The Declaratory Power: Inevitable and Desirable", 1996 JR 99

Ewing, "Obscene Publications", 1982 SLT (News) 55

Ferguson, "Rape and Reasonable Belief", 1983 SLT (News) 89

Ferguson, "Recklessness and the Reasonable Man in Scots Criminal Law", 1985 JR 29

Ferguson, "Murder, Provocation and Self Defence", 1986 SLT (News) 38

Ferguson, "The Doctrine of Self-Defence", 1986 SLT (News) 171

Ferguson, "Art and Part Guilt and the Defence of Disassociation", 1987 JR 131

Ferguson, "The Defence of Automatism", 1991 SLT (News) 415

Ferguson, "The Limits of the Automatism Defence" (1991) 36 JLSS 446

Ferguson, "Automatism, Responsibility and Recklessness", 1992 SLT (News) 375

FORENSIS, "The Logic of Art and Part Guilt" (1985) 30 JLSS 230

FORENSIS, "Vandalism and Malicious Mischief" (1986) 31 JLSS 232

Gill, "Impossibility in Criminal Attempts", 1965 JR 137

Gordon, "Crimes without Laws", 1966 JR 214

Gordon, "Cawthorne and the *Mens Rea* of Murder", 1967 SLT (News) 89

Gordon, "Shameless Indecency and Obscenity" (1980) 25 JLSS 262

Jones, "The Defence of Necessity in Scots Law", 1989 SLT (News) 253

Jones, "Temporary Appropriation as Theft" (1989) 34 JLSS 343

Norrie, "The Defence of Coercion in Scots Law", 1984 SLT (News) 13

Ross, "Housebreaking with Intent", 1994 SLT (News) 323

Ross, "Unlawful Act Culpable Homicide", 1996 SLT (News) 75

Ullmann, "The Reasons for Punishing Attempted Crimes", 1939 JR 353

Willock, "The Declaratory Power—Still Indefensible", 1996 JR 97

15

TRUSTS

THE NATURE OF A TRUST

The law of trusts is complex but the nature of a trust is easier to understand if a simple   **15–01** example is borne in mind. A trust may be created where a person donates money to a friend or an institution, such as a university, in trust for the purposes of providing grants for needy students. In any trust the title to property is vested in a party known as a "trustee" (the friend or the university in the example) to be administered on behalf of other parties known as "beneficiaries" (the students) for certain purposes (to alleviate student need). The party who sets up the trust and who specifies the purposes of the trust is known as the "truster" or "settlor". The essentials of the arrangement are threefold:

(a) the existence of the parties—truster, trustee, beneficiary;

(b) the transfer of property to the trustees;

(c) the laying down of purposes for the trust.

SOURCES OF TRUST LAW

The law of trusts comprises a considerable amount of common law (declared by the   **15–02** courts or set down in the writings of the institutional writers) which has been extensively supplemented by statutory provisions having general application. In addition, there are particular rules which apply only to special types of trusts. These special rules will not be examined here except as occasional illustrations of the variety of trusts. Private trusts are frequently encountered in connection with taxation matters and are the subject of much attention in the taxation statutes. Although the detailed rules of taxation relative to trusts will not be looked at here, a trust should never be set up without first considering the tax implications. The taxation statutes apply generally throughout the UK but it is not to be assumed that there is a unitary law of trusts applicable throughout the UK. The law of trusts in Scotland is different from the law of trusts in England or Northern Ireland, and in any overview of Scottish trusts the law of those two jurisdictions should be ignored for the most part.

INTERNATIONAL PRIVATE LAW

15–03 The rules of law outlined in this chapter are applicable to trusts governed by Scots law. In many cases, however, trusts have foreign and international aspects. A trust of foreign land is invalid if the legal system where the land is situated does not give effect to trusts.[1] There is statutory provision to regulate the situations in which a trust will be governed by the law of Scotland and to determine in what circumstances a trust governed by a foreign legal system will be recognised and thereafter given effect to in Scotland.[2] These provisions were enacted to allow the UK to ratify the Hague Convention on the Law Applicable to Trusts and Their Recognition. The UK ratified this convention in November 1989. The provisions of this Convention are complex but, broadly speaking, under the Hague Convention a trust can become a Scottish trust by the express or implied choice of the truster. Failing such a choice, the law will determine Scots law to be the legal system to which the trust has closest connection.

THE PARTIES

15–04 A trust is a tripartite relationship. That relationship deals with the truster, the trustee and the beneficiary. This is not to suggest that only three persons can be involved in a trust at any one time. In general there may be more than one truster, more than one trustee and more than one beneficiary. In many cases, the three parties—the truster, the trustee and the beneficiary—will exist at the same time. A simple example is an *inter vivos* trust (established during the lifetime of the trustee) where someone sets up a trust for the benefit of his friends with his solicitor acting as the trustee. There must be identifiable beneficiaries and in relation to private trusts these are usually specified individuals personally known to the truster. In relation to public trusts, the beneficiaries will constitute a specified section of the general public and it will not be necessary to name each of the benefited individuals within that section of the public. It is usual that the truster in a public trust will not know all of the beneficiaries personally. Beneficiaries are usually natural persons or juristic parties afforded personality by the law, such as limited companies. Exceptional cases exist in relation to trusts which are set up to benefit animals or to erect gravestones for a deceased truster. Both of these are recognised as valid in Scotland provided, in the case of gravestones, that they are on a suitably modest scale. In such cases it is possible to argue that the true beneficiaries may be the general public who gain the indirect benefit of having the animals looked after and the dead afforded a decent level of respect.

---

[1] *Brown's Trs* v *Gregson* 1920 SC (HL) 87.
[2] Recognition of Trusts Act 1987.

TRANSFER OF PROPERTY

The existence of some trust property and the passing of title to that property to the **15–05** trustees are essential for any trust. In a trust, the trustees have the real right in the property (the right of ownership) which is enforceable against the whole world including, in appropriate cases, the truster and beneficiaries. The beneficiaries are not the owners of trust property.

PURPOSES

A trust cannot exist without certain purposes. Where the trust has been created by the **15–06** voluntary act of the truster—usually by the granting of a trust deed—these purposes will be specified by him—usually in the trust deed where they will be set out at length. Where the trust has been implied by law the purposes will also be implied by law and, in some cases, are set out at length in a statute. The essence of the rights of the beneficiaries is to insist that the trustees implement the trust purposes.

MODERN USES OF TRUSTS

Trusts are commonly encountered in modern practice. Five of the most common **15–07** situations where trusts occur and where there are many additional specialised rules are:

(a) executors;

(b) judicial factors;

(c) improper liferents;

(d) trustees in bankruptcy;

(e) conveyancing matters.

The additional rules will not be detailed in this chapter, but anyone dealing with these forms of trusts should be aware that such rules exist and seek specialist advice. Many solicitors may not specialise in all of these areas of law.

(a) EXECUTORS

Executors feature largely in the law of succession. Although they have some special **15–08** characteristics, executors may generally be regarded as trustees in respect of the estate of the deceased. The principal function or duty of the executor is to gather in (the usual term is "ingather") and distribute the estate according to the appropriate rules of division.[3] Broadly speaking, the duties of an executor are to pay the funeral and testamentary expenses, the deceased's debts and the legacies, the residuary legatee or the persons entitled to the estate on intestacy as circumstances dictate.

(b) JUDICIAL FACTORS

15–09   A judicial factor is a special type of trustee whose function is to protect the interests of certain vulnerable parties in difficult situations. Very broadly speaking, judicial factors are appointed by a court to administer property in cases where the property is the subject of litigation or because it lacks some other competent administration at the date of the factor's appointment. Judicial factors are found in various guises but they commonly include parties such as *curators bonis* to insane persons, judicial factors on insolvent estates and judicial factors appointed on the estates of defaulting solicitors.

(c) IMPROPER LIFERENTS

15–10   The distinction between proper and improper liferents is examined in Chapter 7. Improper liferents (otherwise known as "trust" or "beneficiary" liferents) involve trustees who hold the property for the benefit of two distinct types of beneficiary: the liferenter and the fiar. The liferenter is entitled to enjoy the subjects for the term of the liferent without destroying their substance and is entitled to the income of the property. The fiar is entitled to the capital of the trust property but obviously has little access to this during the existence of the liferent. The interest of the fiar is (a) not to have the subjects diminished and (b) on the termination of the liferent, to have the subjects conveyed to him. Improper liferents may be alimentary or non-alimentary. An 'alimentary' liferent is a special form of liferent in which property is given to trustees for the purpose of providing the liferenter with funds from which his maintenance and support is drawn or his education paid. A non-alimentary liferent may provide funds for the liferenter for much more than mere subsistence or maintenance. In so far as it is not excessive for the liferenter's maintenance at the level to which he is accustomed, an alimentary liferent is protected from creditors of the liferenter. Any excess, however, will be available to his creditors.[4] The common law rule that when an alimentary liferenter accepts the liferent he cannot thereafter renounce or assign it has caused considerable practical difficulty. As a result, it has been modified by statutory provision which allows the court to authorise the variation or revocation of an alimentary liferent.[5]

(d) TRUSTEES IN BANKRUPTCY

15–11   Insolvency is a specialised area of law with many detailed rules laid down in statute.[6] Where a person becomes insolvent, the court may be requested to award sequestration of his estate. When this is done the property of the bankrupt party is no longer his own but is held for the benefit of creditors. The party appointed to oversee the property is

---

[3]   See Chapter 16.
[4]   *Livingstone* v *Livingstone* (1886) 14 R 43.
[5]   Trusts (Scotland) Act 1961, s 1(4).
[6]   Bankruptcy (Scotland) Act 1985.

the trustee in bankruptcy who administers a bankrupt's estate for the benefit of the creditors. The aim of the process is to avoid an unseemly scramble amongst creditors and to pay all the creditors a fair proportion of what is due to them.

(e) CONVEYANCING MATTERS

Trusts arise in the context of the conveyancing of heritable property in a number of situations. One of the most common situations is where, at the settlement of a conveyancing transaction, a minor matter cannot be settled timeously. Frequently, this may be a relatively minor matter such as a lack of a completion certificate on a building warrant relating to an extension to a house. The purchaser may be willing to hand over the bulk of the purchase price in exchange for all other settlement items and to place the balance in a bank account in trust for the seller and purchaser until the outstanding matter is dealt with appropriately. **15–12**

CLASSIFICATION OF TRUSTS

Trusts may be classified into various types.   **15–13**

ENGLISH CATEGORIES

Two types of trust are of English origin and have no general relevance to Scotland.   **15–14**

Discretionary trusts

In contrast to English law there is no special category of trusts known in Scotland as "discretionary trusts" to which different legal rules apply.   **15–15**

Charitable trusts

In English law there is an important class of trusts known as "charitable" trusts which are distinct from "private" trusts. Although many trusts are set up in Scotland to further charitable purposes, this classification as "charitable trusts" does not generally exist in Scots law except in relation to taxation law. However, certain trusts may become what are known as "recognised bodies" in terms of statute,[7] and a "recognised body" is entitled to describe itself as a "Scottish Charity". There are special statutory rules for the administration of Scottish public trusts which have been awarded charitable status for tax purposes.[8] These rules impose duties on all those "concerned in the management or control" of such trusts, particularly in relation to accounting matters, supervision by the court and the Lord Advocate. There is the possibility of disqualification from office in cases of breach of the statutory duties. **15–16**

---

[7] Law Reform (Miscellaneous Provisions) (Scotland) Act 1990, Pt I.
[8] *ibid.*

SIMPLE TRUSTS AND SPECIAL TRUSTS

15–17   In a simple trust there is no special trust purpose but merely an obligation to hold the property and to hand it over to the truster or his nominee when called upon to do so.

INTER VIVOS TRUSTS AND TESTAMENTARY TRUSTS

15–18   *Inter vivos* trusts are set up by trusters whilst they are alive. Testamentary or *mortis causa* trusts are set up to take effect after the death of the truster.

PUBLIC TRUSTS AND PRIVATE TRUSTS

15–19   Private trusts are for the benefit of individuals and cannot continue perpetually or indefinitely. Public trusts are for the benefit of the public or a section of the public and can exist indefinitely although perpetual existence is not required. It may sometimes be difficult to determine whether a trust is a public trust or a private trust because of the difficulty in distinguishing between a large group of individuals and a small section of the general public.[9] As regards private trusts, all the beneficiaries and, in addition, the truster have a separate title to sue the trustees for breach of trust. In relation to public trusts any member of that section of the public who would qualify as a potential beneficiary and, in addition, the Lord Advocate representing the public interest, can bring an action to enforce the provisions of the trust.[10] The courts can exercise a wider jurisdiction over the administration of public trusts than they can over private trusts. A significant instance of this in relation to public trusts is the exercise of the *nobile officium* of the court to sanction a *cy près* scheme.[11]

CREATION OF TRUSTS

TRUSTS CREATED VOLUNTARILY

15–20   Where a truster grants a trust deed that is an instance of a trust created voluntarily. Where a trust is created by legal implication the trust arises independently of the wishes of the parties involved. In a voluntarily created trust the document of trust may be in three different forms:

(a) a disposition to the trustee bearing to be in trust only;

(b) a disposition to the trustee which is *ex facie* absolute (absolute on the face of the deed) but qualified by a separate declaration or acknowledgment of the trust purposes;

(c) a declaration of trust by a person who is already vested in the property.

---

[9]   *Salvesen's Trs v Wye* 1954 SC 440; *Glentanar v Scottish Industrial Musical Association* 1925 SC 226.
[10]   *Ross v George Heriot's Hospital* (1843) 5 D 589.
[11]   See para 15–40.

What all three methods of creation have in common is the passing of property from the truster to the trustee for certain purposes.[12] Trust deeds should be clearly expressed or there may be serious problems ascertaining the intent of the truster. This is why it is best to have a trust deed drawn up by a solicitor. "Precatory" trusts may arise where a person conveys estate to a named party but uses unclear phraseology and there is some uncertainty as to whether he intended to create a trust. In such a case, the courts will attempt to determine the wishes of the party and will decide whether a trust is the method of giving effect to them. This situation crops up most frequently in relation to informally drawn-up wills.

Formal validity

The general rule is that writing is not required for the constitution of a trust.[13] This is subject to three exceptions:

15–21

    (a) where a person declares himself to be sole trustee of his own property or any property which he may acquire[14];

    (b) any trusts which relate to an interest in land will require to be in writing[15] (*inter vivos* trusts which relate only to moveables do not need to be in writing);

    (c) writing is always required for any trust created by a will or testamentary disposition.[16]

Writing is not required for *inter vivos* trusts unless they fall within exceptions (b) or (c) above. Despite the provisions of the statute it is sensible to ensure that, where a client wishes to set up a trust, all the provisions relative to that trust are put into writing.

TRUSTS CREATED BY LEGAL IMPLICATION

The law will imply that a trust is created in certain specific circumstances. There are various types of trusts created by legal implication which include:

15–22

    (a) constructive trusts[17];

    (b) fiduciary fees[18];

    (c) trusts created by statute[19];

    (d) resulting trusts.

---

[12] *Reid's Trs v Dawson* 1915 SC (HL) 47; *Reddie's Trs v Lindsay* (1890) 17 R 558; *Wilson v Lindsay* (1879) 5 R 538; *Barclay's Exr v Mcleod* (1880) 7 R 477.
[13] Requirements of Writing (Scotland) Act 1995 ("1995 Act"), s 1(1).
[14] 1995 Act, s 1(2)(a)(iii).
[15] *ibid* s 1(2)(b).
[16] *ibid* s 1(2)(c).
[17] *Black v Brown* 1982 SLT (Sh Ct) 50; *Cherry's Trs v Patrick* 1911 2 SLT 313; *Soar v Ashwell* [1893] 2 QB 390.
[18] *Snell v White* (1872) 10 M 745; Trusts (Scotland) Act 1921, s 8(2).
[19] See, *eg*, Married Women's Policies of Assurance (Scotland) Act 1880, s 2; Married Women's Policies of Assurance (Scotland) (Amendment) Act 1980, s 1; Conveyancing and Feudal Reform (Scotland) Act 1970, s 27(1).

These areas of law are very complex and will not be examined in detail here. Resulting trusts have been held to arise where the trust purposes are contrary to public policy or impossible to carry out.[20] Similarly, a resulting trust arises where the truster has failed to appoint trustees[21] or where trust purposes fail from uncertainty.[22]

CAPACITY TO BE TRUSTER, TRUSTEE AND BENEFICIARY

15–23 Anyone who can competently alienate (convey away) his property can create a trust. This usually means persons of full age[23] and capacity. It also extends to juristic bodies such as limited companies and local authorities. Persons of unsound mind cannot create a trust. No one may create a trust whilst their powers of understanding are impaired by the effects of drink or drugs. Generally speaking any person who has the legal capacity to hold and deal with property is qualified to act as a trustee but there may be special and more limited provision in the trust deed. For example, a trust set up by a Glasgow Rangers fan may exclude Celtic fans as trustees. Subject to any express provision in the trust deed, the matter is dealt with by the common law which is subject to special statutory provision in special cases. An insane person cannot accept office as a trustee nor can a person under 16 be a trustee.[24] An insolvent party is not generally disqualified from being a trustee. There are, however, a number of special rules which disqualify a bankrupt party from being a particular type of trustee. For example, in charitable trusts there are special rules to disqualify insolvent parties.[25] In certain other cases, the holder of an office from time to time is appointed as a trustee. A good example of this latter case occurs in relation to clubs. In such cases the office-bearers from time to time (such as the president, vice president, treasurer and secretary) are nominated as trustees. Other common examples of this nature include churches where the trustees may be the deacons of the church or a group of other office-bearers such as bishops. Generally speaking, it is the truster who will identify who are the beneficiaries under the trust which he sets up. He may limit the class of persons who may be beneficiaries and such limitations will be applied. Subject to such express limitations, any person, legal or natural, may be a beneficiary. So a hospital trust, a limited company, a firm (partnership), or a corporation such as the BBC may be a beneficiary. A beneficiary may be a foreigner, be insane, not yet born or belong to a prescribed class of unascertained persons.

---

[20] *McCaig's Trs v Kirk Session of the United Free Church of Lismore* 1915 SC 426.
[21] *Angus's Exx v Batchan's Trs* 1949 SC 335.
[22] *Anderson v Smoke* (1898) 25 R 493.
[23] Age of Legal Capacity (Scotland) Act 1991, ss 1(1)(a), 2(1) and (2) and s 3.
[24] *ibid*, ss 1(1) and 9(5).
[25] Law Reform (Miscellaneous Provisions) (Scotland) Act 1990, s 8.

PROPERTY SUBJECT TO A TRUST

As a general rule, any property which can be conveyed may be the subject of a trust. **15–24**
This includes all descriptions of property—heritage, moveables, corporeal property
and incorporeal property. Exceptional items which cannot be subject to a trust include
a right to a peerage[26] and foreign land where the legal system in which the land is
situated does not give effect to trusts.[27] The trustees and not the beneficiaries are the
owners of trust property but the trustees' right to the property is constrained by
the right of the beneficiaries and they cannot use the trust property for their own
purposes as if it were their own property. Where there is more than one trustee
the type of ownership is joint ownership (as contrasted to common ownership). On the
death or resignation of one trustee the share of the deceased or resigning trustee
accresces to the remaining trustees without the necessity of any conveyance. Each
trustee cannot separately dispose of his own share or burden it with a security for his
own purposes.[28] The beneficiaries and the truster have independent personal rights to
require the trustees to carry out trust purposes but they are not the owners and they
do not have real rights in the trust property.

LIABILITY TO THIRD PARTIES

Where third parties contract with a trust (for example, a purchase of trust property) it **15–25**
is the trustees and not the beneficiaries who enter into the contract. Where the trustees
enter into contracts with third parties the general rule is that they are presumed to
undertake joint and several personal liability in respect of those contracts. This means
that each trustee is liable for all debts and obligations incurred in a contract. The
personal liability of trustees may be excluded, varied or limited by means of express
provision in any contract. Where such an exclusion is desired it should be set out in
clear, express and unambiguous terms. Where a contract is not in writing there will
obviously be no written exclusion of personal liability on the part of the trustee. In
such a case, evidence may be led from surrounding circumstances of the common
intention on the part of the trustee and the third party not to hold the trustee
personally liable but it may be difficult to overcome the burden of proof. If a
trustee has had to pay out of his own pocket to discharge a liability properly undertaken on behalf of the trust he is entitled to an indemnity from the trust estate. Where
a trustee properly incurs such personal liability he may proceed to pay the liability out
of trust funds first without the necessity of paying the sum out of his own pocket.
Where he enters into a contract with third parties the personal liability of a trustee to
those third parties extends to liability to pay for any breach thereof. One category of
acquirer in breach of trust can defeat the right of the beneficiaries. This is the bona fide
onerous transferee without notice of the trust. This generally means if a person in good

---

[26] *The Buckhurst Peerage* (1876) 2 App Cas 1.
[27] *Brown's Trs* v *Gregson* 1920 SC (HL) 87.
[28] See Chapter 7.

faith acquires a property from trustees for full value without notice of the trust this will defeat the rights of the beneficiaries to recover the property from the acquirer. The rights of third parties who deal with trustees have been supplemented by a number of statutory provisions. The more commonly encountered of these are:

(a) Trusts (Scotland) Act 1961, s 2. A person carrying out certain dealings with trustees does not need to inquire whether the transaction comes within the implied powers given to trustees by the first six paragraphs of the Trusts (Scotland) Act 1921, s 4(1).[29] These transactions are the sale, feu[30] or lease of trust property, the borrowing of money on the security of trust estate, the excambion (swap) of any part of the trust estate, and the purchase of a suitable home for any of the beneficiaries. Other transactions are not covered by the statutory protection.

(b) Trusts (Scotland) Act 1921, s 7. Where a deed purports to be granted by a body of trustees but is in fact granted only by a quorum the deed is not void and its validity cannot be challenged on the ground that there has been some procedural irregularity.

(c) Succession (Scotland) Act 1964, s 17. This protects a person who, in good faith and for value, has acquired title to any interest in or security over property directly or indirectly from an executor or a person deriving title from the executor. The protection is limited to challenges made on the ground that the executor's confirmation was reducible or has already been reduced or that the executor should not have transferred title to the person from whom the third party, acting in good faith and for value, has obtained title.

The statutory rules concerning the bona fide acquirer do not remove the rights of the beneficiary to seek a remedy against the trustees.

APPOINTMENT OF TRUSTEES

15–26 Normally a truster setting up a trust identifies those parties he wishes to be trustees in the deed of trust. These are known as the "original trustees". These parties must have capacity to be trustees and their appointment is not valid until there is an acceptance by the parties nominated. As a general rule, acceptance is a wholly voluntary act and no one is obliged to accept trusteeship. Executors may be appointed either by the deceased or, failing such appointment, by the court. An executor appointed by the deceased is known as an executor "nominate". An executor appointed by the court is an executor "dative". New trustees may be assumed by the existing trustees unless this power is expressly excluded by the trust deed, which is most unlikely.[31] In rare cases an express clause in the trust deed may give the truster or third parties the power

---

[29] See para 15–35.
[30] Incompetent after the abolition of the feudal system. See Chapter 7.
[31] Trusts (Scotland) Act 1921, s 3(b).

to appoint new trustees. This may be a general power or one restricted in its exercise to such circumstances as the trust deed specifies. New and additional trustees may be appointed by the court in terms of common law and under statute. For almost all practical purposes the statutory power has replaced the common law power. Under statute[32] new trustees may be appointed by the court when trustees cannot be assumed under any trust deed, or when the sole acting trustee has become *incapax* (incapable, for example, due to supervening insanity) or has been continuously absent from the UK or has otherwise disappeared for a period of six months.

CEASING TO BE A TRUSTEE

When a trustee dies he ceases to be a trustee. If a company is a trustee it ceases to be a **15–27** trustee upon its liquidation and striking off. Supervening insanity of an individual who is a trustee does not terminate the office of trusteeship although it may be a ground for removal of the person from the office of trustee. A gratuitous trustee (one who acts without remuneration) has a right to resign unless he is a sole trustee.[33] The trustee's power to resign may only be excluded completely by express provision in the trust deed. A sole trustee cannot resign his office unless he has assumed "new trustees" who have accepted office, or the court has appointed new trustees or a judicial factor.[34] A trustee appointed "on the footing" of receiving remuneration for his services cannot resign in the absence of an express power to do so.[35] Trust deeds are usually drafted to include such a power. The form of a resignation is usually in express and clear language but, in rare circumstances, resignation may be implied from acts and deeds. The fact that a trustee does nothing for a period of time does not amount to resignation. In terms of statute[36] a trustee may be removed from office by the court for (a) insanity; (b) incapacity through mental or physical disability; (c) continuous absence from the UK for at least six months; and (d) disappearance for at least six months. If the first or second ground is established the court must grant the application for removal. If the third and fourth grounds are established the court may grant the removal but it has a discretion in deciding what to do.

TRUST PURPOSES

All trusts must have a purpose whether that purpose be express or implied. Where a **15–28** trust is set up by a trust deed it is usual for there to be an express clause stating the purposes of the trust. The purposes are as chosen by the truster. If the deed is badly

---

[32] Trusts (Scotland) Act 1921, s 22.
[33] *ibid* s 3(a) and proviso (1).
[34] *ibid*; *Kennedy, Petitioner* 1983 SLT (Sh Ct) 10.
[35] Trusts (Scotland) Act 1921, s 3(a) and proviso (2).
[36] *ibid* 1921, s 23.

drafted and it cannot be determined what a truster wishes to be done with trust property the trust may be void for uncertainty either (a) because the wording used by the truster is too vague or (b) because the trust purposes established by the truster are too wide. An example of the former is seen where a trust was set up for the purposes of acquiring premises for the establishment of a bookshop for the sale of books dealing with the subjects of "free thought". The trust was held void for uncertainty because of the uncertain nature of the term "free thought".[37] There are conflicting decisions about the latter aspect of uncertainty. In one case it was held that directions for distribution were void from uncertainty where they directed the trustees to distribute the trust assets "in such manner as they may think proper"[38] but in another case a direction to pay to "those whom you know respect me" was upheld. The judges in that case made the observation that the wording "those who respected me" (without any reference to the knowledge of the trustees) would have been bad because it gave no workable definition of the class of persons entitled.[39] Purposes which are too wide can be a much greater problem with public trusts.[40] A trust purpose will also be void if it is held by the court to be immoral. Thus, a trust to further prostitution would probably still be immoral,[41] and a trust to torture animals would probably be contrary to public policy. A trust will be void if all of its purposes are contrary to public policy. In the main, the courts have restricted application of this doctrine to invalidate trust purposes that are so extravagant and wasteful that they are wholly lacking in benefit to the community.[42] A trust purpose must not be illegal nor be one which has been rendered incompetent by law. An example of the former is where the trust purports to benefit an illegal organisation such as a cartel of drug dealers. Examples of the latter include entails[43] and successive liferents. These are complex devices which purport to restrict dealings with property over a number of generations. Trusts for the accumulation of income are also restricted by statute. Provision is made in statute[44] against accumulation of the income of any property (including land) in whole or in part beyond any one of six specified periods. These are: (a) the life of the granter; (b) 21 years from the death of the granter; (c) the minority of any person living or *in utero* (in the womb) at the date of the death of the granter; (d) the minority of any person who would, under the terms of the trust deed directing accumulation, be entitled to the income accumulated if of full age; (e) 21 years from the making of the settlement or the other disposition; or (f) the duration of the minority of any person living or *in utero* (in the womb) at the date of the making of the settlement or other disposition. If accumulation is directed contrary to the statutory provisions, the direction is void and the income goes to the person who would have been entitled if there had been no direction to accumulate.[45]

---

[37] *Hardie* v *Morison* (1899) 7 SLT 42.
[38] *Sutherland's Trs* v *Sutherland's Trs* (1893) 20 R 925.
[39] *Warrender* v *Anderson* (1893) 1 SLT 308.
[40] *Angus's Exx* v *Batchan's Trustees* 1949 SC 335; *Blair* v *Duncan* (1901) 4 F (HL) 1; *Rintoul's Trs* v *Rintoul* 1949 SC 297; *McConochie's Trs* v *McConochie* 1909 SC 1046; *Wink's Exx* v *Tallent* 1947 SC 470.
[41] *Johnstone* v *Mackenzie's Exrs* (1835) 14 S 106.
[42] *Sutherland's Trs* v *Verschoyle & Ors* 1968 SLT 43; *McCaig* v *Glasgow University* 1907 SC 231; *McCaig's Trs* v *Kirk Session of the United Free Church of Lismore* 1915 SC 426; *Aitken's Trs* v *Aitken* 1927 SC 374.
[43] Abolition of Feudal Tenure etc (Scotland) Act 2000, Pt V; Law Reform (Miscellaneous Provisions) (Scotland) Act 1968, s 18; *Stewart's Trs* v *Whitelaw* 1926 SC 701, per Lord Sands at 718.
[44] Trusts (Scotland) Act 1961, s 5; Law Reform (Miscellaneous Provisions) (Scotland) Act 1966, s 6.
[45] Trusts (Scotland) Act 1961, s 5(3).

ADMINISTRATION OF A TRUST

After a trust is set up and the trustees have accepted office it is the duty of the trustees **15–29**
to begin the administration of the trust. The three sources of the duties and powers of
trustees in relation to this administration are the trust deed, common law and statute.
The duties in the trust deed will vary from case to case and each trust deed must be
examined for its contents. Once he has accepted office, a trustee must act personally
and cannot generally delegate his duties either to another trustee or a third party. This
is a presumption rather than a general rule and it may be rebutted in appropriate
circumstances as would be the case if there is specific provision in the trust deed
permitting trustees to delegate their duties. Unless there is an express exclusion of the
power in the trust deed, a trustee always has power to appoint agents when a person
of reasonable prudence would do so. Under statute[46] a trustee is specifically given the
power to appoint factors and law agents and to pay them suitable remuneration.

SECURING TRUST PROPERTY

A trustee has a duty to identify and gather in all trust property as soon as possible after **15–30**
taking up office. This duty is particularly important in respect of the position of an
executor who has a duty to identify and gather in the whole of the deceased's estate.

DEBTS, PAYMENT AND OBLIGATIONS

It is unusual for there to be outstanding debts and obligations at the start of the trust **15–31**
except in the case of (a) *mortis causa* trusts where the purpose is to distribute the estate
of the deceased to beneficiaries and (b) where the trust involves an existing business.
In the case of testamentary trusts, the trustees usually wait six months after the date of
death before paying any debts (except privileged debts, such as funeral expenses
which can be paid immediately) to allow creditors to lodge claims.[47] An executor
cannot be compelled to pay an ordinary debt until the expiry of six months from the
date of death. Executors may pay out only when the estate is solvent. If they pay out
of an insolvent estate they will be liable to the creditors. The trust may incur new debts
in the course of the administration of the trust and in respect of these debts the trustees
assume personal liability unless they expressly contract to the contrary. A trustee is
entitled to be indemnified out of the trust estate in respect of debts properly incurred
by him in the course of trust administration. Except in exceptional cases, trustees have
a common law duty to keep accounts to show their dealings with the trust estate. A
trustee is under a duty to pay to the correct beneficiaries and may be liable to the true
beneficiary if an incorrect payment is made.

POWERS OF TRUSTEES

The powers of trustees are derived from three sources: (a) the trust deed; (b) statute; **15–32**
and (c) the common law.

---

[46] Trusts (Scotland) Act 1921, s 4(1)(f).
[47] See Chapter 16.

Powers in the trust deed

15–33   Each trust deed is different and a truster should confer on his trustees all powers which are suitable to the purposes for which the trust is set up. In each case, the trust deed must be examined to determine what are the powers of the trustees.

Powers under statutory provisions

15–34   The terms of each statutory power must be examined to determine its extent but they may be classified in the following ways: (a) provisions limited to certain special types of trustees[48]; (b) provisions limited to certain powers conferred without court application; and (c) provisions limited to certain powers conferred only upon court application.

Statutory powers without court application

15–35   Under statute[49] all trustees have 17 general powers where such acts are not at variance with the terms or purposes of the trust. For the full list, reference should be made to the statutory provisions. The first six of these powers are, broadly speaking: (a) the power to sell trust estate; (b) the power to feu trust estate[50]; (c) the power to grant leases; (d) the power to borrow money on the security of the trust estate; (e) the power to excamb (exchange) any part of the trust estate; and (f) the power to acquire with trust funds a residence for any of the beneficiaries. The 17 general powers of trustees will not be implied where such acts are "at variance with the terms or purposes of the trust". This is a twofold test. The word "terms" of the trust denotes the actual words used by the truster himself in the trust deed. This means that if a power is expressly excluded in the trust deed it cannot be implied by this statutory provision. The term "purposes" of the trust relates to the specified aims or the ultimate aim of the trust. Where the trustees enter into a transaction with a third party involving acts under any of the six heads listed above, the validity of the transaction cannot be challenged by the third party on the ground that the act in question is at variance with the terms of the trust or purposes of the trust.[51]

Statutory powers with court application

15–36   Various statutory provisions enable trustees to petition for additional powers. The most important of these are:

(a) Trusts (Scotland) 1921, s 16. This enables the court to authorise trustees to make advances from the capital of a fund destined absolutely or contingently (limited by a condition) to beneficiaries who at the date of the application to the court are not yet of full age. But the scope of the section is limited by the requirements that the advance must be necessary for the maintenance or education of the beneficiaries, that it is not expressly prohibited by the trust

---

[48] For powers of permanent trustee in bankruptcy see Bankruptcy (Scotland) Act 1985. For judicial factors see Judicial Factors Act 1849, s 7; *Bell's CB, Noter* 1999 SLT 33. See also Married Women's Policies of Assurance (Scotland) Act 1880, s 2(2).
[49] Trusts (Scotland) Act 1921, s 4.
[50] This power will disappear with the abolition of the feudal system. See Chapter 7.
[51] Trusts (Scotland) Act 1921, s 2(1).

deed and that the rights of the beneficiaries, if contingent, are contingent only
on their survivance (survival).

(b) Trusts (Scotland) Act 1921, s 5. This permits the court on the petition of the
trustees to grant authority to them to do any of the acts mentioned in the 1921
Act, s 4 (which sets out the general powers of trustees), even though such an
act is at variance with the terms or purposes of the trust. The court must be
satisfied that such act is in all the circumstances expedient for the execution of
the trust.[52]

(c) Trusts (Scotland) Act 1961, s 1. This permits the court to approve an
arrangement for the variation of trust purposes. In certain circumstances, the
variation of trust purposes sought in terms of this provision may involve
the conferring upon the trustees of powers to which they would not otherwise
be entitled (whether under the trust deed or any other statutory provision).[53]

TRUSTEES—DECISION-MAKING

In all decisions relating to the trust administration all trustees have a right to be   **15–37**
consulted. A majority of trustees—no matter how large—cannot exclude the participation of a minority—no matter how small—in the administration of the trust. The
administration of the trust may continue only for so long as a quorum of trustees
participates. The terms of the trust deed may dictate what constitutes a quorum. If the
trust deed is silent on the matter, a majority of the trustees accepting and surviving
shall be a quorum.[54] Acts of trust administration may be undertaken by a majority of
trustees except in the rare case where the appointment of trustees is stated in the trust
deed to be "joint". As a result, in the normal case, a minority of trustees have no veto
on acts of trust administration.

Courts' approach to discretion of trustees

As a general rule, the courts are not proactive in relation to the administration of trusts   **15–38**
and will not readily interfere with the discretion of trustees. The basis for the courts'
view is that the courts take the view that the trustees are in the best position to make
proper judgments in relation to trust circumstances. Only where the improper exercise
of a discretion or the failure to exercise a discretion amounts to a breach of trust or is
clearly unreasonable will the courts interfere.

VARIATION OF TRUST PURPOSES

After a trust is set up it may be desirable to vary the original purposes of that trust for   **15–39**
various reasons. The variation of trust purposes is dealt with at common law and by
statute. At common law, variation of the trust purposes cannot be done unilaterally by

---

[52] *Conage's JF* 1948 SLT (Notes) 12; *Tod's Trs, Petitioners* 1999 SLT 308.
[53] *Henderson, Petitioner* 1981 SLT (Notes) 40.
[54] Trusts (Scotland) Act 1921, s 3(c).

the truster, the trustees or the beneficiaries. It can, however, be done if all the possible beneficiaries consent.[55] For public trusts the common law provided for variation of purposes under the *cy près* doctrine to avoid the lapse of the trust when the initial purposes become impossible by diverting the trust to a similar purpose.[56] Certain statutes provide for the variation of trust purposes generally. The main statutory provision is section 1 of the Trusts (Scotland) Act 1961.

Section 1 of the Trusts (Scotland) Act 1961 allows the trustees or any of the beneficiaries to petition the court to sanction a variation of the terms or purposes of the trust. The court may approve an arrangement varying or revoking all or any of the trust purposes or altering the powers of the trustees in relation to managing or administering the trust estate. The court may also authorise any arrangement varying or revoking any trust purpose that entitles any of the beneficiaries to an alimentary liferent of, or an alimentary income from, the trust estate or any part thereof. The court cannot approve an arrangement on behalf of persons who can consent to it on their own behalf but simply have not done so or refuse to do so. If any of the beneficiaries are capable of giving their consent it must be obtained from them before the variation can take effect. Before the court will grant authority to a variation under the 1961 Act, s 1(4) the court must consider that the proposed arrangement is "reasonable" and the liferenter's consent to the variation must be obtained.

CY PRÈS DOCTRINE

15–40 The *cy près* doctrine is a common law doctrine which applies only to public trusts. It does not apply to private trusts. Using this doctrine the courts may avoid the lapse of a public trust, when the initial purposes become impossible, by diverting the trust to a similar purpose. The situations in which a *cy près* scheme may be appropriate are very varied but include the situation where a trust has been set up to benefit a particular public institution (such as a hospital or a school) which has closed down either before or after the trust was set up. In this case, the court may permit the trust funds to be paid to another similar institution. A *cy près* scheme will be inappropriate if the truster has provided in the trust deed what is to occur to the trust funds if they require to be diverted because the trust cannot be continued. A series of cases has indicated that trust purposes do not become impossible simply because of difficulty in carrying them out, shortage of trust funds or a shortage of qualified beneficiaries.[57] In applying the conditions to be satisfied before the *cy près* doctrine is applied a distinction must be made between supervening impossibility and initial impossibility. In the case of supervening impossibility it is clear that the *cy près* doctrine should be applied. In the case of initial impossibility the interest of the truster will not have been effectively terminated and he retains a residual right in the property if the trust cannot take effect. In such a situation the trust property will revert to the truster as part of a resulting trust[58] and the *cy près* doctrine cannot be applied unless it can be demonstrated that there is an underlying general intention on the part of the truster to benefit public purposes. Where there is initial, but not supervening, impossibility the court

[55] *Earl of Lindsay* v *Shaw* 1959 SLT (Notes) 13.
[56] See para 15–40.
[57] *Scotstown Moor Children's Camp* 1948 SC 630.
[58] This is a type of trust arising by implication of law—see para 15–22.

will grant a *cy près* scheme only if the terms of the trust deed show that the truster had a general intent to benefit public purposes. This may be distinguished from a situation where the truster confers to benefit a particular institution or body which happens to have public purposes.[59] Whether the failure of the original trust purposes is initial or supervening a *cy près* scheme will require that the proposed replacement purposes are approximate to the original purposes.[60]

STATUTORY VARIATION OF PUBLIC TRUSTS

15-41 A statutory power to enable the court to approve a scheme to vary public trusts was introduced in 1990.[61] This power applies to all public trusts whether created before or after the legislation came into operation. The aims of the statute were to make the variation of public trusts simpler, quicker and cheaper. There is also a simplified approach to vary trusts with a very small annual income. The grounds for variation are set out in the statute.

INVESTMENT DUTIES

15-42 Where trustees hold the trust estate for any longer than a minimal period they will be under an obligation to use it in a manner which protects its value in real terms. The investments must comply with three requirements: (a) the interest of no beneficiary is to be exposed to greater risk than any other; (b) any investment must be "authorised"; and (c) any investment must be "proper". The first requirement means that all the beneficiaries are entitled to have their interests secured by the whole trust fund and the trustees will have no power to appropriate particular investments to particular beneficiaries except where the truster directs otherwise in the trust deed either expressly or impliedly or all the beneficiaries consent to the appropriation. The second requirement limits the trustee in the type of investments he can choose. The narrow common law requirements have been superseded by statute[62] but, in turn, the statutory limitations are usually varied by the provisions of the trust deed.[63]

STRUCTURE OF THE STATUTORY LIMITATIONS

15-43 The statutory limitations may be split into three types: (a) those relating to types of authorised investments; (b) those requiring a balanced mix of investments; and (c) those relating to duties falling upon trustees in deciding whether a particular investment is proper. In the statute itself investments are classified into three categories: (a) "Narrower Range Investments not requiring advice". These are the least risky investment such as National Savings Certificates. (b) Part II of the Schedule lists

---

[59] *Hay's JF* v *Hay's Tr* 1950 SC 576; *McRobert's Trs* v *Cameron & Ors* 1961 SLT (Notes) 66.
[60] *Glasgow Royal Infirmary* v *Mags of Glasgow* (1888) 15 R 264; *Glasgow SPCA* v *National Anti-Vivisection Society* 1915 SC 757.
[61] Law Reform (Miscellaneous Provisions) (Scotland) Act 1990, ss 9 and 10.
[62] Trustee Investments Act 1961.
[63] *ibid* s 3(1). See also *Henderson* v *Henderson's Trs* (1990) 2 F 1295; *Clarke* v *Clarke's Trs* 1925 SC 693.

"Narrower Range Investments requiring advice". These are slightly more risky but generally secure investments such as heritable securities, UK company debentures and government securities. (c) Part III of the Schedule lists "Wider Range Investments". These are the most risky of the three types of authorised investment and were not permitted before the passing of the 1961 Act. Part III includes shares in building societies, units in Unit Trust schemes and shares in certain companies. If the provisions of the statute apply to a trust, a trustee cannot invest in any investment of a type which is not listed in the statutory provisions. In addition to choosing authorised investments a trustee must show that overall he has achieved the correct mix of investments.[64] Where a trustee wished to invest in Wider Range Investments he had to divide the whole trust fund into two parts which (until 1996) were required to be equal in value at the time of division and only invest one half in the "wider-range part" and one half in the "narrower-range part". This proportion of each fund to the other has now been amended by a statutory instrument which came into force on 11th May 1996.[65] The statutory instrument permits the wider range fund to be up to three times as large as the narrow range fund. If the trustees do not wish to invest in Wider Range Investments, they do not need to split the fund. There are detailed provisions in the statute for compensating transfers if a transfer between the funds takes place. It is open to the truster to provide for powers of investment in the trust deed which differ from those allowed under that Act. He may waive the requirements of the Act in whole or in part or provide an entirely new scheme of investment. It is common for modern trust deeds to provide that the trustees will have wider powers of investment than those provided for in statute.

PROPER INVESTMENTS

15–44   A trustee has a general duty only to make "proper" investments. A proper investment is one which is authorised but which provides a suitable return for the trust without exposing the trust to excessive risk. This common law standard of care is the same standard of the ordinary prudent trustee that is applied in respect of all other aspects of trust management. The common law duty of care is re-stated in statute.[66] This statute requires a trustee to have regard to the need for diversification of the investments of the trust in so far as is appropriate to the circumstances of the trust and to have regard to the suitability of the investments. The trustee is also obliged from time to time to reconsider whether that investment is still appropriate. To determine whether there is sufficient diversification or if the investments proposed are suitable or when the investments are periodically re-appraised the trustee is obliged to take and consider "proper advice". Proper advice is the advice of a person who is reasonably believed by the trustee to be qualified by his ability in, and practical experience of, financial matters. The advice must be given or confirmed in writing before the trustee is taken as having discharged his duty to take and consider proper advice. There is one exception to the rule that advice must be taken in writing as to suitability of investments, diversification of investments and continued suitability of investments and this is where there are two or more trustees and the person giving the

[64]   Trustee Investments Act 1961, s 2.
[65]   Trustee Investments (Division of Trust Fund) Order 1996, SI 1996/845.
[66]   Trustee Investments Act 1961, s 6.

advice is also a trustee. In such a case, the trustees are still required to consider these matters but the obtaining and considering of advice in writing is not required.

CONFLICT OF INTEREST AND PROPER MOTIVATION

A trustee must keep his personal interest separate from the interests of the trust. This **15–45** has two related consequences: (a) no trustee may place himself in a position where there is a possible conflict between his personal interest and his duty to the trust. This is known as the rule precluding *auctor in rem suam* (which in translation means actor in his own cause); and (b) a trustee should be motivated only by those consequences which are relevant to the trust and not by those which are personal to him.

AUCTOR IN REM SUAM

A trustee should not place himself in a position where his personal interest and his **15–46** duty to the trust may possibly conflict. Where a trustee does breach the rule of *auctor in rem suam* the trustee will be in breach of trust. In addition, where the trustee makes any profit or derives any property from the breach of trust a constructive trust will be created over that profit or property and the beneficiaries in the original trust are the beneficiaries in that constructive trust.[67] Any transaction in which a trustee is *auctor in rem suam* is capable of reduction and is voidable at the instance of a number of parties. Any beneficiary or co-trustee may challenge a transaction on the basis that it is in breach of the rule *auctor in rem suam*. The rules relating to the avoidance of a conflict of interest apply in various circumstances to the following effects. First, the trustee may not carry out transactions with the trust.[68] Second, the trustee cannot take a personal advantage or profit from his position as trustee.[69] Third, the trustee is not entitled to remuneration. The rule may, in some cases, extend to parties or legal entities which are closely associated with the trustee. For example, it has been held that the purchase of shares from a trust by a limited company was invalid because the trustee was a director and shareholder of the company.[70] The charging of fees by a trustee is prima facie a breach of the duty not to act with a conflict of interest. In the absence of contrary provision, trustees are therefore under a duty to act without pay. They are, however, entitled to out of pocket expenses properly incurred in connection with trust administration. The charging of fees by a trustee may be authorised by an express clause in the trust deed. The acts of a trustee which would otherwise be invalid because of a conflict of interest may be sanctioned where the truster foresees the possibility of a conflict of interest and expressly authorises this in the trust deed. It will not avoid application of the principle of conflict of interest to show that a trustee acted with the concurrence of the other trustees. In the absence of authority from the truster, the trustees may obtain the sanction of the consent of all the beneficiaries and potential

---

[67] This is a type of trust arising by virtue of law—see para 15–22.
[68] *eg* sale of goods in *Cherry's Trs v Patrick* 1911 2 SLT 313. See also *Sarris v Clark* 1993 SLT 44.
[69] *University of Aberdeen v Town Council of Aberdeen* (1877) 4 R (HL) 48.
[70] *Adair's Factor v Connell's Trs* (1894) 22 R 116; *Burrell v Burrell's Trs* (1915) 1 SLT 101.

beneficiaries to the transaction. Provided this consent is freely given and the beneficiaries are fully informed in relation to the nature of the transaction and the surrounding circumstances it will prevent the transaction from being avoided on the basis that the trustee acts as *auctor in rem suam*. The Court of Session probably has no power to authorise a transaction which would otherwise render the trustee *auctor in rem suam*.

PROPER MOTIVATION

15–47　In all his dealings with the trust a trustee must do his best to exercise a fair and rational judgment taking into account matters which are relevant to the trust only.[71] Thus, he may not avoid investment in Germany just because he has a personal dislike of Germans. Nevertheless, the transaction may still be upheld if the truster has sanctioned the application of the trustee's personal values to transactions of the nature contemplated. For example, a truster who dislikes smoking may set up a trust and make provision in the trust deed expressly excluding investment in companies manufacturing cigarettes. Alternatively, all the beneficiaries may expressly consent to the transaction in the knowledge that the trustee has applied his personal beliefs and values.

LIABILITY OF TRUSTEES TO BENEFICIARIES

15–48　A trustee is expected to exercise due care in respect of all his actions in relation to trust property. Breach of trust arises where the trustee fails in his duty of care to the beneficiaries. To carry out this general duty of care it is not enough that a trustee acts to the best of his ability or in good faith. The general duty imposes an objective standard of care on trustees. Liability for breach of the duties of trustee may be enforced by any of the beneficiaries or by the truster although most litigation arises in relation to the former. It cannot be enforced by a third party who is neither beneficiary nor truster.

REMEDIES FOR BREACH OF TRUST

15–49　The remedies available to a beneficiary for breach of trust include the following:

(a) Interdict—Any beneficiary, co-trustee or truster may apply to the court for interdict against a threatened breach of trust or the continuation of a breach of trust. Where the breach has been completed and there is no indication of a repetition, interdict will not be granted.

(b) Damages—A trustee will be liable to pay for any loss suffered by a trust as a result of his breach of trust. It is always open to a trustee to avoid having to pay by showing that the loss would have arisen even if he had carried out his duties in full.[72] The measure of damages is the loss suffered by the trust no

---

[71] *Martin v City of Edinburgh DC* 1988 SLT 329.
[72] *Carruthers v Carruthers* (1896) 23 R (HL) 55.

matter whether this is remote or not foreseeable. An action for damages prescribes after five years.[73]

(c) Accounting—Where a trustee refuses to hand over to a beneficiary the full entitlement of that beneficiary in accordance with the provisions of the trust the beneficiary may force the trustee to do so by means of an action of count, reckoning and payment. Such an action may also be used to recover the profit which a trustee has obtained as a result of a breach of trust and is held by him in a constructive trust.[74] The trustee's liability for fraudulent breach of trust is imprescriptible. This means that it may be claimed even after the period of long negative prescription (20 years) has elapsed.[75]

(d) Removal of trustees—the truster, any beneficiary or a co-trustee may petition the court for the removal from office of a trustee in respect of a breach of trust. The court has a common law power to remove a trustee from office and it will do this in cases (i) where the breach is particularly flagrant such as embezzlement[76] or (ii) if the trustee refuses to discontinue the breach of trust.

IMMUNITY AND DEFENCES

The trust deed may have expressly permitted the action which would otherwise be **15–50** regarded as a breach of trust or contain an immunity or indemnity clause absolving the trustee from the usual consequences of breach. Such clauses are construed strictly and will not absolve a trustee from conduct which is in bad faith. There are various statutory defences each of which relates to different matters as follows:

Trusts (Scotland) Act 1921, s 3(d)

Unless the contrary is expressed all trusts are held to include a provision that each **15–51** trustee is to be liable only for his own acts and intromissions (dealings) and is not to be liable for the acts and intromissions of co-trustees or for omissions. The subsection does not prevent a trustee being liable for the breaches of trust of his fellow trustees if he himself commits a breach of his own duty to the trust. Where more than one trustee is in breach of duty to the trust, all the trustees in breach are jointly and severally liable for the whole loss caused to the trust.

Trusts (Scotland) Act 1921, s 30

A trustee is not to be chargeable with breach of trust for lending money on the security **15–52** of any property by reason only of the proportion of the amount of the loan to the value of the property if he has complied with certain requirements. These requirements are that the trustee has relied upon a valuation report prepared by someone the trustee reasonably believed to be a practical valuator and the amount of the loan when taken together with prior ranking loans or *pari passu* (equal) ranking loans secured on the property does not exceed two-thirds of the valuation stated in the report. This means

---

[73] Prescription and Limitation (Scotland) Act 1973, s 6.
[74] See para 15–22.
[75] Prescription and Limitation (Scotland) Act 1973, s 7 and Sched 3, para (e).
[76] *Wishart & Ors, Petitioners* (1910) 2 SLT 229.

that where a trustee is to lend money on the security of heritable property he should always obtain a valuation survey from a professional firm of surveyors.

Trusts (Scotland) Act 1921, s 31

15–53   Where a trustee commits a breach at the instigation or request or consent in writing of a beneficiary the court may make such order as is just to make available the interest of the beneficiary in the trust as an indemnity to the trustee or the person claiming through him. This statute does not confer on the trustee a right of personal action against the beneficiary but allows the court to authorise the trustees not to pay that beneficiary his full entitlement. If the trustee is liable for more than the instigating beneficiary's interest, he must suffer the excess loss himself. For relief to be granted to the trustee it must be shown that the beneficiary not only understood the nature of the act he was requesting but also that the performance of the act would amount to breach of trust. The provision does not give the court an absolute right to indemnity. This is given only if the court thinks fit to grant it.

Trusts (Scotland) Act 1921, s 32

15–54   The court may relieve a trustee from liability if he acted honestly and reasonably and it appears to the court that he ought fairly to be excused for the breach of trust. The trustee must establish both honesty and reasonableness to be granted relief. If the trustee acts honestly, but not reasonably, relief will not be granted.

TERMINATION OF TRUSTS

15–55   Some public trusts may exist in perpetuity. These, however, are exceptional cases and the vast majority of trusts will come to an end when the trust purposes have been implemented and all trust property distributed to the appropriate beneficiaries. This usually happens far short of perpetuity. A trust may be brought to an end by various parties as follows: (a) the truster (revocation); (b) the creditors of the truster (reduction); (c) the trustees; (d) the beneficiaries.

REVOCATION BY THE TRUSTER

15–56   A distinction must be made between testamentary and *inter vivos* trusts. As a general rule, a testamentary trust may be revoked by the testator at any time prior to his death.[77] After his death the truster is obviously in no position to revoke such a trust. A declaration that a testamentary deed is irrevocable is of no effect to prevent revocation prior to the testator's death because it also can be revoked by the testator.[78] The truster retains the right to revoke an *inter vivos* trust for so long as the following apply: (a) the property in the trust estate has not yet passed from the truster to the trustees; (b) there are no beneficiaries in existence, or, if there are beneficiaries in existence, none have a

---

[77] See Chapter 16 in relation to revocation of wills.
[78] See Chapter 16 for further details.

vested interest; and (c) the truster intends the trust to be revocable. In relation to *inter vivos* trusts an express declaration that the trust is revocable by the truster will receive effect except where the trust deed creates an alimentary liferent in favour of a beneficiary other than the truster and the beneficiary has entered into possession.[79] If the deed states that it is irrevocable the trust can be revoked by the truster only if he obtains the consent of all the beneficiaries who have obtained a beneficial interest.

REDUCTION BY THE CREDITORS OF THE TRUSTER

Insolvency of the truster does not entitle the truster to revoke the trust nor is a trust **15–57** revoked without any legal process upon the sequestration of the truster. In certain cases, however, a creditor and a permanent trustee in bankruptcy may reduce a trust deed. In such a case, the trust will come to an end and the property will vest in the permanent trustee for the purposes of the sequestration. Where a sequestrated party has made a gratuitous alienation within a period of two years prior to the sequestration, a creditor and a permanent trustee in bankruptcy may challenge the alienation.[80] If the challenge is successful the court will reduce the alienation. The term gratuitous alienation generally denotes a gift or transfer for insufficient consideration made at a time when the granter's liabilities exceeded his assets. The meaning of the term "alienation" is wide enough to include the granting of a deed of trust.

TERMINATION BY THE TRUSTEES

At common law the general rule is that the trustees may terminate a trust only by **15–58** effectively and completely fulfilling the purposes of the trust. This usually occurs where the trustees distribute all trust property in accordance with the provisions of the trust deed.

TERMINATION BY THE BENEFICIARIES

As a general rule the beneficiaries may compel the trustees to bring the trust to an end **15–59** if they all agree to this course of action. The agreement of every one of the beneficiaries is, however, essential to the operation of this principle. This general rule is subject to two major exceptions: (a) there is no such right if it would prejudice the trustees in the proper administration of the trust; and (b) such a power on the part of beneficiaries cannot be used to renounce any alimentary provision which a beneficiary has started to enjoy.[81] The court may authorise variation of alimentary provisions under statute.[82] The case of all the beneficiaries bringing the trust to an end should be distinguished from the case of one or more beneficiaries renouncing their rights as beneficiaries. In the latter case, the trust does not come to an end but continues in force in respect of the remaining beneficiaries.

---

[79] See paras 15–30 and 15–59.
[80] Bankruptcy (Scotland) Act 1985, s 34.
[81] See paras 15–10 and 15–56.
[82] Trusts (Scotland) Act 1961, s 1(4).

SUMMARY

THE NATURE OF A TRUST

- A trust is a relationship of three parties—the truster, the beneficiaries and the trustees.
- The truster sets up the trust, the beneficiaries are those who are benefited by it and the trustees hold the title to the trust property for the purposes of the trust.
- Property must be transferred to the trustees to set up a trust. Trusts are common in relation to executry estates, judicial factories, liferents, bankruptcy and conveyancing matters.

CLASSIFICATION AND CREATION OF TRUSTS

- Trusts may be categorised as *mortis causa* (created upon the truster's death), or *inter vivos* (created during the settlor's life).
- Public trusts benefit a section of the public whilst private trusts benefit a class of individuals.
- Trusts may be created by a deed or by legal implication. Where created by a deed they require to comply with the rules of formal validity.

CAPACITY TO BE TRUSTER, TRUSTEE AND BENEFICIARY

- Generally, all competent persons may be trusters or trustees.
- The trust deed generally specifies who may be a beneficiary. They may include disabled persons and children.

PROPERTY SUBJECT TO A TRUST

- Most property may be subject to a trust—exceptions include a peerage.
- Where trustees deal with trust property it is they who enter into the missives and sign the disposition as they are the holders of the real right.

LIABILITIES TO THIRD PARTIES

There are certain statutory protections for third parties dealing with trustees.

APPOINTMENT OF TRUSTEES

- The truster normally identifies the original trustees in the trust deed.
- Certain trustees may be appointed by court process as is the case with executors dative.
- New trustees may be assumed by existing trustees and by court process if required.

CEASING TO BE A TRUSTEE

- When a person dies he ceases to be a trustee.
- Trustees generally have a power to resign and may be removed for misconduct.

TRUST PURPOSES

- All trusts must have purposes which must be specific and not illegal.
- Vague purposes cannot be enforced.

ADMINISTRATION OF A TRUST

- Trustees must administer a trust after it has been set up. They must secure trust property, pay debts and carry out obligations.
- The powers of trustees are contained in the trust deed, the common law and statute.
- Courts do not readily interfere with exercise of the discretion of trustees.

VARIATION OF TRUST PURPOSES

- Trust purposes may be varied under statute if required.
- Public trusts may have their trust purposes varied under the *cy près* doctrine and under statute.

CONFLICT OF INTEREST AND INVESTMENT DUTIES

- Trustees have a duty to invest in proper and authorised investments. They must avoid undue risk. If the trust deed does not regulate the matter it is dealt with under statute.
- Trustees must avoid conflict of interest and have a proper motivation, failing which they will be liable to beneficiaries for breach of trust.
- Certain defences are available to trustees under statute and provisions of a trust deed.

TERMINATION OF TRUSTS

- Trusts cease when their purpose is fulfilled.
- In certain circumstances they may be revoked by the truster, his creditors, the beneficiaries or the trustees.

CASE DIGEST

Distinction between private and public trust is sometimes difficult to make [para 15–19]

Glentanar v Scottish Industrial Musical Association 1925 SC 226

In this case the truster donated a silver shield to a musical association for the purpose of having the shield awarded as a trophy to the winner of an annual musical feis organised by the trustees. It was held that this was a private trust and not a public trust but the decision is not free from criticism because there are strong indications of public benefit in the gift.

A trust will be void if its purposes are too vague [see para 15–22]

Angus's Exx v Batchan's Trs 1949 SC 335

A will provided that certain sums were to be paid to "charities". No trustee or executor was appointed. It was held that the gift was void from uncertainty and the court had no power to appoint a judicial factor who could exercise the discretion.

Trust purposes must not be extravagant or wasteful [see para 15–28]

Sutherland's Trs v Verschoyle & Ors 1968 SLT 43

A truster purported to set up a trust to display what she believed was a valuable art collection. In fact it had little artistic value and the court held the purpose to be void on the basis that it was completely wasteful and contrary to public policy.

General intent to benefit public required for *cy près* doctrine [see para 15–40]

Hay's JF v Hay's Tr 1950 SC 576

A testatrix left a will which expressly stated that a particular mansion house was to be maintained by her trustees "either as a home for aged and infirm Shetland seamen, a surgical hospital or a convalescent hospital, whichever the said trustees may consider the most beneficial for the islands of Shetland". After the death of the testator it became clear that it was impossible to open the rest home or hospital but the words used by the testatrix were wide enough to demonstrate a general intent to benefit the public. Therefore the *cy près* doctrine could apply.

Replacement purposes must be similar to original purposes for *cy près* scheme [see para 15–40]

Glasgow Royal Infirmary v Mags of Glasgow (1888) 15 R 264

An existing public trust had as its purpose the building of a convalescent fever home. The town council established a fever hospital. The trustees petitioned the court to sanction a *cy près* scheme to divide the trust funds to support two purposes: (a) the erection of nurses homes at the Glasgow Royal Infirmary, (b) the support of a society for fever and smallpox hospitals. The court approved the scheme but only on the basis that all the funds went to the society as this was closest to the original wishes of the parties who donated funds to the original trust.

Trustees have a duty to check the prudence of investments [see para 15–42]

Henderson v Henderson's Trs (1900) 2 F 1295

A request by a beneficiary that the trust should invest in Canada did not amount to a request to invest in an imprudent way in Canada. Hence, when trustees invested in a Canadian lumber company which failed they were not entitled to indemnity out of the share of the beneficiary. The beneficiary was entitled to assume that the trustees would check it was within their power to make the specific investment.

Trustees cannot avoid risk by investing in unusually low risk investments [para 15–42]

Clarke v *Clarke's Trs* 1925 SC 693

A trustee honestly left a sum of money on deposit receipt for two years instead of investing part of it in an annuity as the trust deed required. It was held that this was not a reasonable course of action since the result was that the annuity would be charged on the whole trust fund and not only on the part that ought to have been invested. Relief under the 1921 Act, s 32 was refused.

Conflict of interest rules do not apply where associate of interested party can show she acted independently [see para 15–46]

Burrell v *Burrell's Trs* 1915 1 SLT 101

It was held that the purchase of shipping shares belonging to a trust estate by the wife of one of the trustees, on her own initiative, out of her separate estate and for an adequate consideration, was valid.

Profit from breach of trust can be recovered by beneficiaries [see para 15–46]

University of Aberdeen v *Aberdeen Town Council* (1877) 4 R (HL) 48

The Town Council of Aberdeen acted as trustees in a trust for the benefit of the professors of the University of Aberdeen. The trust property consisted of the lands of Torry. The Town Council wanted the lands for themselves and sold them secretly at an auction to themselves. They then obtained a lease from the Crown Estate of the salmon fishings *ex adverso* the lands of Torry. The salmon fishings were sublet by the Council and a rent was received by the Council. When the University found out about the sale 80 years later they brought an action against the Town Council for breach of trust. It was held that a breach of trust had occurred and the Council were obliged to return not only the lands of Torry but also the income from the fishings. The latter is significant because at no time were the University ever owners or tenants of the fishings—but the Town Council would never have been in a position to obtain a lease of these fishings if they had not abused their position as trustee.

Conflict of interest may be implicitly sanctioned by truster [see para 15–46]

Sarris v *Clark* 1993 SLT 44

A testator was a farmer who appointed his wife as executrix in his will. Shortly before his death he entered into contracts of co-partnery with his wife and granted a lease of the farms to the partnerships. After his death the executors entered into negotiations with the partnerships to renounce the leases and to compensate the partnerships for the renunciation. The wife was obviously on both sides of the negotiations in different capacities but it was held that this was not a breach of trust as it was the truster who had placed the wife in this position.

Trustees must have proper motivation for investments [see para 15–47]

Martin v *City of Edinburgh DC* 1988 SLT 329

The Edinburgh District Council were trustees in respect of several trusts and took a policy decision to sell all trust funds invested in South Africa. They did so because of their own political antipathy to the then government in South Africa. The decision was challenged and it was held that the decision was in breach of trust as the Council had been motivated by their own values and not by the interests of the beneficiaries.

FURTHER READING

Gordon, *Scottish Land Law* (2nd edn, W Green, 1999), Chapter 16
Norrie and Scobbie, *Trusts* (W Green, 1991)
Paisley, *Trusts* (W Green, 1999)
Wilson and Duncan, *Trusts, Trustees and Executors* (2nd edn, W Green, 1995)

16 SUCCESSION

PURPOSES OF THE LAW

The purposes of the Scottish law of succession are fivefold:

(1) to identify the parties who are entitled to the property of a person who has died. Within certain limitations, Scots law permits the deceased party to identify these persons in a will. This is the law of testate succession.[1] Failing the existence of such a deed or a legally effective substitute the parties entitled to succeed are identified by application of the rules of intestate succession[2];

(2) within limitations, to secure against the disinheritance of certain close family members of the deceased. The chief methods of achieving this in Scotland are the law of aliment[3] and legal rights[4];

(3) to administer the property of the deceased property until its transfer to beneficiaries. This is achieved by the appointment of an executor who falls under certain duties to give effect to the law of succession[5];

(4) to provide for the transfer of that property to the entitled party. This is more an aspect of the law of conveyancing known generally as *mortis causa* or "executry" conveyancing[6];

(5) Scots law does not presume to deal with these matters in respect of the whole world. It limits its attention to certain matters having a connection to Scotland.

---

[1] See para 16–32 to 16–67.
[2] See paras 16–20 to 16–31.
[3] Aliment from the estate of a deceased person is known as aliment *jure representationis*. See the Family Law (Scotland) Act 1985, s 1(4). A detailed treatment of this matter is more appropriate to an examination of family law. For an overview see Gloag and Henderson, *The Law of Scotland* (10th edn, 1995), p 892, para 49.7.
[4] See paras 16–25 *et seq.*
[5] This is a form of trust administration and has been examined in Chapter 15.
[6] This chapter shall not deal with this issue. For details see Gretton and Reid, *Conveyancing* (2nd edn, 1999), Chap 25.

This is an aspect of Scottish international private law which will be examined only briefly here.[7]

The passing of property at the death of an owner is frequently an occasion for the imposition of taxes. The major tax presently exacted is inheritance tax.[8] Although no executry estate should be would up without regard to taxation issues, these will not be dealt with further here.

INTERNATIONAL PRIVATE LAW

16–02   The Scots law of succession applies to the moveable property wherever situated of a person domiciled in Scotland and the immoveable property situated in Scotland whatever the domicile or nationality of the owner of that property. The categorisation of an item of property into moveable or immoveable is made by the law of the place where the property is situated (*lex situs*).[9] The classification which Scots law makes for domestic purposes between heritable and moveable property is not exactly the same as the distinction between immoveable and moveable.

HISTORY, SOURCES AND REFORM

16–03   There has been no comprehensive statutory codification of the law of succession. Although much of the law of intestate succession exists in statutory form,[10] common law principles still apply. Most of the law relating to wills remains governed by the common law. There are, however, a number of important exceptions to this such as in relation to the requirements for proper execution of wills.[11] Wide ranging reforms of the law of succession were proposed by the Scottish Law Commission in its *Report on Succession*,[12] published on 25th January 1990 but these have never been implemented.

ASSETS AND DEBTS

16–04   The law of succession, both testate and intestate,[13] applies to distribution of the net estate of the deceased. This comprises his assets less his liabilities. Where a deceased

---

[7] See also the Wills Act 1963 examined at para 16–42.
[8] Inheritance Tax Act 1984.
[9] *Macdonald* v *Macdonald* 1932 SC (HL) 79.
[10] See particularly the Succession (Scotland) Act 1964.
[11] Requirements of Writing (Scotland) Act 1995, s 1.
[12] Scot Law Com No 124.
[13] Note the references to "heritable debt" in the Succession (Scotland) Act 1964, s 8(6)(d) and "net estate" in the 1964 Act, ss 1(2) and 9(6)(a), and "net moveable estate" in the 1964 Act, s 10(2).

holds property as a trustee and not as part of his personal property it will not form part of his estate on death and he cannot dispose of it by a will.

The assets to which the rules of succession apply comprise certain personal obligations and all real rights in property.

The deceased's delictual claims for patrimonial loss (financial loss resulting from damage to property or earning capacity) pass on his death to his estate and remain enforceable by the executors in so far as they relate to loss incurred in the period between injury and death.[14] Such claims may be transferred by will or intestacy as appropriate. Claims for *solatium* (pain and suffering) are also transmissible on death provided also that they relate to loss incurred in the period between injury and death. Where a *solatium* claim arises in respect of a defamation action it will lapse unless the deceased had raised a court action before his death.[15] Contractual rights and obligations may transmit to the estate of the deceased provided such transmission is not excluded by virtue of express provision in the contract or implication arising from the doctrine of *delectus personae*. Under this doctrine the contract is of such a nature that it is regarded as particularly personal to the deceased with the result that it terminates on his death. A classic example of such a personal contract is a contract of employment.[16]

The real rights in property to which the law of succession applies extend to property of all natures including heritable, moveable, corporeal and incorporeal. In certain exceptional cases some property which belonged to the deceased prior to his death will not pass into the deceased's estate for various reasons as follows:

(a) Some real rights such as a liferent in the sole name of the deceased will come to end when the deceased dies.

(b) Some rights are not transmissible on death. These include some statutory rights such as occupancy rights in terms of the matrimonial homes legislation[17] and peat cutting rights under the crofting legislation.[18] Certain leases also contain an express clause excluding transfer on death.

(c) Where a deceased commits suicide an issue may arise as to whether his estate can benefit from an insurance policy. It will not if the policy expressly or impliedly excludes a payment in cases of suicide. In certain cases the policy may restrict the class of persons who may claim in cases of suicide to assignees for value.[19] Under English law a rule of public policy used to preclude payment[20] but this rule has probably ceased to have effect given that suicide has ceased to be a crime in England.[21] Although suicide was never a crime in Scotland the matter was relevant as many insurance policies

---

[14] See, *eg, Williams' Trs* v *Macandrew and Jenkins* 1960 SLT 246.
[15] Damages (Scotland) Act 1976, s 2, as amended by the Damages (Scotland) Act 1993, s 3.
[16] McBryde, *The Law of Contract in Scotland* (1987), Chap 24.
[17] Matrimonial Homes (Family Protection) (Scotland) Act 1981, s 1, as amended.
[18] Crofters (Scotland) Act 1993, s 17(6).
[19] *Ballentyne's Trs* v *The Scottish Amicable Life Assurance Society* 1921 2 SLT 75.
[20] See, *eg, Beresford* v *Royal Insurance Society Limited* [1938] A C 586.
[21] *Re Giles, Deceased* [1972] Ch 544, per Pennycuick V-C at 552.

contained a clause expressly stating that the proper law of the contract was English law.

(d) A special case arises in relation to unevacuated special destinations. Where before the death of the deceased heritable property was held *pro indiviso* in the names of the deceased and a second party with a survivorship destination, the half share belonging to the deceased will pass automatically to the second party without forming part of the executry estate of the deceased.[22] No title is required from the deceased's executor and the deceased's one-half share in the property does not vest in the executor. There is an exception for certain special destinations where the property vests in the executor purely for him to have it conveyed to the person entitled under the destination.[23]

DEBTS

16–05 Rights of succession arise only if the deceased's estate is solvent after payment of debts, funeral expenses and the expenses of administering the deceased's estate. An executor's first duty is to draw up a list of assets and debts. If the executor deals with the estate but fails to obtain confirmation he may be held liable for all the debts of the deceased without limitation as a "vitious intromittor". After confirmation the executor is liable for the debts of the deceased up to the value of the estate. As a result the executor must be certain that he retains sufficient funds to pay the debts and that the estate is solvent before he proceeds to distribute the net estate. If the estate is insolvent the executor must proceed within a reasonable time to have a judicial factor or trustee in bankruptcy appointed.[24]

Debts intimated to an executor within six months after death rank equally (*pari passu* ranking). The executor has a special power to pay a limited class of debts known as "privileged" debts immediately, even if other debts cannot be paid in full. This class extends to servant's wages, mourning for the widow and funeral expenses. Otherwise he should not (and cannot be obliged to) pay out any part of the estate before the expiry of six months after the death. The reason for this is that if he pays out any other debts and legacies before the expiry of the six-month period and a creditor turns up within that period and cannot be paid, the executor is personally liable to the creditor to the extent of the sums disbursed. If a creditor turns up after the six-month period and finds that the executor has paid out in good faith to creditors who had intimated their claims timeously then that creditor cannot recover from the executor.

Order for payment

16–06 The order for payment of debts is as follows. Within each class debts rank *pari passu*:

(1) expenses of sequestration;

(2) deathbed and funeral expenses;

---

[22] 1964 Act, s 36(2)(a).
[23] *ibid* s 18(2).
[24] Bankruptcy (Scotland) Act 1985, s 8(4); McBryde, *Bankruptcy* (2nd edn, 1995), para 18–16.

(3) secured debts—debts secured over a particular asset such as a mortgage secured by a standard security over a house;

(4) preferred debts—these comprise taxes and social security contributions for a certain period, typically the 12-month period before death, and employees' wages for four months prior to the employer's death up to a maximum of £800;

(5) ordinary debts including aliment of the deceased's wife and children.

Incidence of debts

Subject to any contrary instructions in the will, the type of debt determines which part **16–07** of the estate must ultimately bear liability for it. Moveable debts are paid out of moveable property and heritable debts out of heritage. Ordinary debts arising out of delict or contract are moveable. A debt is heritable if it is secured over heritage. The classic example is a mortgage secured over a house by a standard security.

Where a debt is secured over a particular asset, heritable or moveable, whoever inherits the asset takes it subject to the debt and must pay the debt if he wishes to have the asset unless, of course the will provides otherwise.[25] This may have some unexpected results in respect of a loan secured over a house. Even if an insurance policy provides funds to pay off the mortgage the legatee must reimburse the estate to the extent of the sums paid off. The difficulty can be avoided with a will which confirms that the legatee is to receive the asset free of debts.

Inheritance tax is a debt on the estate chargeable on the value of the deceased's estate immediately before his death. The executor is primarily liable for the inheritance tax payable. Unless there is contrary intention shown in the deceased's will inheritance is a testamentary expense and will fall on the residue of the estate. This means that the legatee in a bequest will obtain the full value of his bequest and the residue will be reduced by the tax bill. This may be confirmed by an instruction in the will that the legatee is to receive a gift "free of tax". Where the will dictates otherwise by requiring the gift to be "net of tax" the tax will be repaid to the executor who takes the assets to which the tax is attributable.

DEATH

Before the law of succession can apply to any property it must be established that **16–08** the owner of that property has died. Thus the law of succession can apply only to the property of natural persons as juristic bodies such as corporations cannot die.[26] There is no Scottish statute which defines what is death and the law is generally willing to recognise that death is what is accepted by members of the medical profession from time to time. In relation to establishing the fact of the death of the deceased the onus of proof lies on the claimant, usually a potential beneficiary. If death cannot be proved

---

[25] See, *eg, Stewart* v *Stewart* (1891) 19 R 310.
[26] The equivalent of death for companies incorporated in terms of the Companies Acts is dissolution: see the Insolvency Act 1986, ss 201–205.

by acceptable evidence the claim will fail. If proof is called for, an extract from the register of deaths (the "death certificate") is regarded as sufficient evidence[27] when taken with some suitable evidence to link the deceased with the person named in the certificate. Practical problems can arise as to the proof of the terms of foreign public records and registers[28] or where such foreign registration systems are inadequate due to inherent inefficiency or external causes such as war.[29]

Problems of proof arise where a person has disappeared and it is not known whether he is still alive or not. Action to resolve the difficulty may be taken at common law or under statute for a declarator of the death of the missing person. At common law there is a rebuttable presumption that life continued up to the extreme limits of human age[30] but the authorities do not agree as to what this age limit is.[31] Given the wide statutory powers the common law has been superseded for all effective purposes, although an action at common law is still competent.

PRESUMPTION OF DEATH (SCOTLAND) ACT 1977

16–09   The relevant statutory provisions are contained in the Presumption of Death (Scotland) Act 1977 which came into effect on 1st March 1978.[32] The 1977 Act provides that where a person who is missing is thought to have died or has not been known to be alive for a period of at least seven years, any person having an interest may raise an action of declarator of the death of the missing person. This covers two types of cases. First, a person may be missing and be thought to have died when he has not been found after a major incident such as a bomb blast or a fire. In such a case the action can be raised immediately after the incident and there is no need to wait seven years.[33] Second, if the person has simply disappeared and no one has heard of him for seven years, the pursuer must wait for the seven-year period to elapse before he can bring the action.

The decree is granted if the court is satisfied on a balance of probabilities. It will specify a date and time of death.[34] If the missing person has not been known to have been alive for at least seven years the court will find that the missing person died at the end of the day occurring seven years after the date on which he was last known to be alive.[35] The court also has power to decide any question concerning any interest in property which arises as a result of the death.

As the effect of a decree is conclusive for all purposes, including any question of rights to property,[36] succession rights will arise immediately in the estate of the missing person. A decree also dissolves the missing person's marriage but the estate

---

[27] Registration of Births, Deaths and Marriages (Scotland) Act 1965, s 41(3).

[28] Anton, *Private International Law* (2nd edn, 1990), pp 758–761.

[29] For example, there are difficulties with the registers in Northern Ireland and the Irish Republic which were largely destroyed by terrorist action in Dublin in 1922. See also Patrick MacKenzie, *Lawful Occasions* (1991), pp 50–52.

[30] *Greig v Merchant Company of Edinburgh* 1921 SC 76; *X v SSC Society* 1937 SLT 87; *Secretary of State for Scotland v Sutherland* 1944 SC 79.

[31] Stair, *Inst*, IV, xlv, 17 (19thly) mentions 80 or 100 years; Bankton, *Institute*, II, vi, 31 mentions 80 years.

[32] Presumption of Death (Scotland) Act 1977 (Commencement) Order 1978, SI 1978/159.

[33] Presumption of Death (Scotland) Act 1977 ("1977 Act"), s 1(1), (2).

[34] 1977 Act, s 2(1).

[35] *ibid* ss 2(1)(b), 3(2).

[36] *ibid* s 3(1).

of the missing person, if married, will be distributed as if he or she were married immediately before his declared death. Thus, the "widow" or "widower" of the deceased will be entitled to legal rights and prior rights, if appropriate.

A situation may arise in which the court is mistaken in presuming that the missing person is dead or where it is discovered that his death occurred at a time other than that stated in the decree (with the result that the succession to his estate would have been different). If this is the case the decree in an action of declarator may be varied by the court issuing a variation order.[37] This variation order is exactly what it bears to be—a variation—it is not an annulment of the original decree. Anyone with an interest may at any time seek to have the presumption of death varied or recalled by a variation order.[38]

The variation order does not automatically affect any property rights which have been acquired as a result of the original presumption of death under the original decree.[39] The exceptional case is where a court makes such a variation order within five years of the original presumption of death. In such an exceptional case the court is required to make such further order concerning property rights as it considers to be fair and reasonable in all the circumstances of the case. It may order restitution of property in kind or in cash. Limitations are placed on the effect of such a variation within the five-year period. First, a variation order of this kind cannot affect any income which has arisen between the date of the original decree and the variation order.[40] Second, where any property right has been acquired by a third party in good faith and for value from a person who has acquired a right under the original presumption of death, the third party's title cannot be challenged. The general aim of the provisions is, on the one hand, to give adequate protection to the interests of the missing person while, on the other hand, enabling other parties, such as his relatives, to be reasonably free from insecurity in transacting with his estate. To cover the situation of a property order made as part of a variation within the five-year period insurance is taken out. The executor appointed to administer the missing person's estate will, in terms of the original presumption of death order, be required to insure against the cost of giving effect to any property order to be made on a variation.[41] Such insurance is still important in relation to land registered titles because there is no entitlement to indemnity from the Keeper in respect of loss arising in consequence of a further order concerning property.[42]

SURVIVORSHIP

To be a beneficiary in a succession, a party wishing to inherit must prove he has survived the deceased.[43] This is usually easy to establish because a beneficiary   **16–10**

---

[37] 1977 Act, s 4.
[38] *ibid* s 4(1).
[39] *ibid* s 5(1).
[40] *ibid* s 5(2).
[41] *ibid* s 6(1).
[42] Land Registration (Scotland) Act 1979, s 12(3)(c).
[43] McLaren, *Law of Wills and Succession As Administered in Scotland* (3rd edn, 1894, with Supplement 1934), I, para 117; *The Laws of Scotland: Stair Memorial Encyclopaedia*, Vol 25, para 655.

simply turns up in the offices of the executor and identifies himself. As regards beneficiaries that are not natural persons, such as limited companies, the equivalent requirement is to show that the company still exists. Thus, where the Crown acts in its public capacity as *ultimus haeres* it may do so without proving the survivance of a particular incumbent of the throne because the institution of the Crown does not die.[44]

There is no minimum period of survivorship at common law and a mere instant will suffice in theory. Many bequests in modern wills, however, require as a condition of vesting that the beneficiary survives the deceased for a period of time such as 30 days.[45] If the beneficiary dies within this period the bequest fails. Particular rules are required for two very different distinct factual situations. These are: (1) common calamities; and (2) unborn children.

COMMON CALAMITIES

16–11 Difficult cases may arise where two or more parties die in a common calamity such as a road accident or their bodies are found after an incident such as a fire. A claimant may wish to inherit an item of property forming part of the estate of one of those deceased parties not directly from that party but indirectly through a second deceased party. To succeed at common law the claimant must show on the balance of probabilities[46] that the second deceased party survived the first deceased party and the second party acquired a vested right to the property if only instantaneously. This often proved impossible as mere speculation as to the order of the deaths was not sufficient evidence.[47] There were no presumptions of survivorship at common law and this led to a number of hard decisions.[48] Reform of the law came with the enactment of the Succession (Scotland) Act 1964 ("1964 Act"), s 31.

The 1964 Act, s 31 is limited in its scope to "all purposes affecting title or succession to property or claims to legal rights or the prior rights of a surviving spouse".[49] As no part of the 1964 Act applies to "any title, coat of arms, honour or dignity transmissible on the death of the holder thereof"[50] the common law of survivorship still applies to inheritance of peerages. For inheritance taxation purposes, parties to a common calamity are deemed to die simultaneously.[51] This avoids an unfortunate double charge to tax which would otherwise arise.

Section 31 of the 1964 Act is entitled "Presumption of survivorship in respect of claims to property" but its provisions consist not of presumptions which can be rebutted but of a general rule with two exceptions. This rule and exceptions apply only

---

[44] See, *eg*, *Drummond's JF* v *HM Advocate* 1944 SC 298.
[45] See, *eg*, Barr, Biggar, Dalgleish and Stevens, *Drafting Wills in Scotland* (1994), paras 5.15–5.17, 5.19, 5.76, 5.104, 5.106, 6.03 and 6.26.
[46] *Lamb* v *Lord Advocate* 1976 SLT 151, reversing 1976 SLT (Notes) 78.
[47] *Wing* v *Angrave* (1860) 8 HL Cas 183; *Re Beare*, *The Times*, 4th October 1957.
[48] *Drummond's JF* v *HM Advocate* 1944 SC 298; *Mitchell's Exrx* v *Gordon's Factor* 1953 SC 176; *Ross's JF* v *Martin* 1955 SC (HL) 56.
[49] 1964 Act, s 31(1).
[50] *ibid* s 37(1)(a).
[51] Inheritance Tax Act 1984, s 4(2). This Act was originally named the Capital Transfer Act 1984 but was renamed in terms of the Finance Act 1986, s 100.

if there is no proof of survivorship and, by definition, cannot be rebutted.[52] The general rule provides that where two persons have died in one or other of two sets of factual circumstances there shall be a presumption of survivorship. The first set of circumstances is where the evidence suggests that they died simultaneously.[53] The second is where it is uncertain which survived the other. In each of these cases the younger person is presumed to have survived the elder.[54] To this general rule there are two exceptions:

(1) First, if the two persons were husband and wife it is presumed that neither survived the other.[55] For married couples this does little more than preserve the common law situation. The effect is that the estates of both the husband and the wife would each be distributed as if the deceased were a widow or widower. In practice this will usually result in the wife's estate passing to members of her own family and the husband's estate to members of his. If the deceased spouse does not have a family and dies intestate the estate will pass to the Crown rather than to his or her in-laws as they have no claim to the deceased's estate under the rules of intestate succession.[56] The exception does not apply to cohabiting couples who are not married.

(2) Second, if the elder person has left a testamentary disposition (a term which includes a will[57]) in favour of the younger containing a provision that, in the event of the younger failing to survive, a third party is to inherit and the younger person dies intestate, then for the purposes of that provision only, the elder person is presumed to have survived the younger.[58] The general aim of this rule is to give effect to the testamentary wishes of the elder party by preventing the property passing to the relatives of the younger person contrary to the wishes of the elder person. Unfortunately the provision is flawed with an overly wide definition of "intestate".[59] As a result, the exception will come into play even if the younger person has left a will if he has omitted to deal in that will with the smallest item of his estate. Another defect is that the second exception does not apply to married couples.

UNBORN CHILDREN

This is the case of the posthumous child. Where a deceased leaves a child who is conceived but not yet born it may be treated as having been born at the date of the death and having survived the deceased. This is expressed in the maxim *qui in utero est, pro iam nato habetur*.[60] The rule applies provided two conditions are satisfied. These are:

16–12

---

[52] *The Laws of Scotland: Stair Memorial Encyclopaedia*, Vol 25, para 658.
[53] Scots law learned from the English experience of *Hickman* v *Peacey* [1945] AC 304; [1945] 2 All ER 215 (HL).
[54] 1964 Act, s 31(1)(b).
[55] *ibid* s 31(1)(a).
[56] Exactly the situation that arose at common law in *Drummond's JF* v *HM Advocate* 1944 SC 298.
[57] See the definition of "testamentary disposition" in the 1964 Act, s 36(1).
[58] 1964 Act, s 31(2).
[59] *ibid* s 36(1).
[60] Erskine, *Inst*, III, viii, 76.

(1) The child must be born alive. A stillborn child or a child which perishes at an earlier stage is regarded as never having existed for these purposes.[61]

(2) The rule cannot be invoked in the interests of a third party but only if the child benefits from its application. It was refused in *Elliot* v *Joicey*,[62] where A left his property to be held in trust for B absolutely in the event of B leaving any "surviving" issue. The House of Lords held that the word "surviving" would not normally mean "posthumous" but, even if it did, it would in this case result in a benefit to B and not to B's unborn child.

The rule applies to both testate and intestate succession but, in the former case, the testator may insert a clause in his will expressly including or excluding a child as yet unborn. In *Cox's Trustees* v *Cox*[63] the testator left a will leaving property to "the descendants alive at the time of my death". It was held that this class included posthumous descendants. This case also confirms that the rule applies whether the unborn child is the child of the deceased or someone else because the relevant children were issue of siblings of the deceased.

Technology may have overtaken the maxim to some extent. It is an unanswered question whether the maxim would apply to children born after the death of their parents where at the date of death the children were frozen embryos or even unconceived in the form of frozen sperm or ova. The birth of a posthumous child may in certain circumstances lead to the revocation of a will made by the deceased conform to the rule *conditio si testator sine liberis decesserit*.[64]

DISQUALIFICATION OF THE BENEFICIARY

16–13

In some cases a person is disqualified as a beneficiary even though he has survived the deceased. In Scotland there are (or have been) a number of examples of this and the matter may be considered in respect of the following types of persons:

(a) illegitimate and adopted children;

(b) separated spouses;

(c) persons involved in the preparation and execution of the will; and

(d) a beneficiary who has unlawfully killed the deceased.

---

[61] Bankton, *Institute*, I, xxxvii, 8; Walker, *Intestate Succession* (1927), p 10.
[62] 1935 SC (HL) 57.
[63] 1950 SC 117.
[64] See para 16–53.

ILLEGITIMATE CHILDREN

At common law an illegitimate child was *filius nullius*, regarded as nobody's child. He **16–14** had no right to inherit from his parents or anyone else.[65] Another more traditional way of viewing this situation is to regard illegitimate children as individuals who were not related to the deceased rather than as relatives who were disqualified. Over the course of this century the discrimination against illegitimate children has been removed increasingly by a succession of statutes[66] and it has now been virtually eliminated.

The modern legislation is contained in the Law Reform (Parent and Child) (Scotland) Act 1986 ("1986 Act"). This provides that the fact that a person's parents are not or have not been married to one another shall be left out of account in establishing the legal relationship between the person and any other person.[67] A child may inherit from anyone on an equal footing with legitimate children. There still remain a number of complications:

(1) The 1986 Act does not apply to deaths occurring or wills executed prior to 8th December 1986. In respect of these deaths and wills the rules under the older law still applies.[68]

(2) The 1986 Act does not apply to succession to titles and honours.[69]

(3) A deceased's executors are protected from liability if they distribute his estate without checking that he left no illegitimate children or, if the deceased is illegitimate, if they fail to discover any of his paternal relatives.[70]

(4) The concept of illegitimacy is not abolished and a testator may still leave a will excluding persons who are illegitimate.

ADOPTED CHILDREN

For all purposes of succession (not just between an adopted person and parents) an **16–15** adopted person is treated as the child of the adopter and no one else. By virtue of the adoption he loses his or her right of succession in the estate of his natural parents.[71] There remain a number of practical qualifications:

(1) This rule does not apply to the succession of those dying before 10th September 1964.

(2) The rule does not apply to the succession to titles or coats of arms.[72]

---

[65] Erskine, *Inst*, III, x, 8; *Clarke* v *Carfin Coal Co* (1891) 18 R (HL) 63, per Lord Watson at 70; Meston, "Bastards in the Law of Succession", 1966 SLT (News) 197.
[66] Including the Legitimacy Act 1926; Law Reform (Miscellaneous Provisions) (Scotland) Act 1966, s 5.
[67] s 1(1).
[68] See *The Laws of Scotland: Stair Memorial Encyclopaedia*, Vol 25, para 663.
[69] s 9(1)(c).
[70] 1986 Act, Sched 1, para 10, inserting a provision into the Law Reform (Miscellaneous Provisions) Act 1968, s 7(b).
[71] Succession (Scotland) Act 1964 ("1964 Act"), s 23(1).
[72] *ibid* ss 23(4) and 37(1).

(3) It remains open to a natural parent to leave a will expressly naming his natural child to be a beneficiary notwithstanding the adoption.

(4) Special rules govern the relationship of the adopted child with collaterals— brothers, sisters and their descendants.[73]

SEPARATED SPOUSES

16–16   All property acquired by a wife after she obtains a decree of judicial separation will pass, if she dies intestate, to her heirs and representatives as if her husband were dead.[74] If the spouses resume cohabitation the disqualification ceases to apply. There is no corresponding disqualification for a wife where a husband obtains a decree of judicial separation. The obtaining of a decree of judicial separation does not revoke a bequest in an existing will and a wife who obtains a decree of judicial separation may competently leave a bequest to her husband, however unlikely such a prospect may be. The statute does not apply to cohabiting couples.

PERSONS INVOLVED IN THE PREPARATION AND EXECUTION OF THE WILL

16–17   Since 1st August 1995 a party who subscribes a will on behalf of a blind granter or a person unable to write may not take benefits under it.[75] The will is invalid to the extent that it confers a benefit in money or money's worth (whether directly or indirectly) on the person subscribing in such circumstances. The exclusion is extended also to the person's spouse and his son or daughter. This does not preclude such a beneficiary inheriting under the rule of intestate succession if this invalidity of the provision in the will results in the whole or a part of estate falling into intestacy.

Under English law a party who witnesses a will (or his spouse) may not take benefits under it.[76] There is no such absolute rule in Scots law but it is inadvisable for a beneficiary to witness the execution of a will as this may lead to a challenge on the basis of a claim of facility and circumvention or duress.[77] If a solicitor drafts a will in which he is granted a legacy he may be required to show that he has not acted in an improper manner.[78]

UNLAWFUL KILLING OF THE DECEASED

16–18   Where the beneficiary has unlawfully killed the deceased he may be disqualified from inheriting even though he is otherwise entitled under the rules of testate or intestate succession. This is generally known as the situation of the "unworthy heir". The rule in Scots law has origins in statute and the common law. The rule applies to both testacy and intestacy and to claims in respect of legal rights.

---

[73] 1964 Act, ss 24(1) and 24(1A).

[74] Conjugal Rights (Scotland) Amendment Act 1861, s 6, as amended by the Family Law (Scotland) Act 1985, s 28(2) and Sched 2.

[75] Requirements of Writing (Scotland) Act 1995, s 9(4). For the date of commencement, see the 1995 Act, s 15(2).

[76] Wills Act 1837, s 15; Williams on *Wills* (7th edn, 1985), Vol 1, pp 84–88.

[77] See para 16–35.

[78] *Grieve* v *Cunningham* (1869) 8 M 317.

The statutory rule arises from the Parricide Act 1594 which applies to the killing of parents and grandparents but not spouses. The Act is obscurely worded and has never successfully been applied in any reported case. The Act requires a conviction for murder before its application.[79] The disqualification may apply only to succession to heritage.[80] As originally framed the statute appears to have involved what is known as corruption of blood. This resulted in the disqualification of the killer and all his descendants. That part of the statute has probably been impliedly repealed with the result that the killer only is disqualified.[81]

The basis of the common law rule is unclear in Scots law. It may be a rule of public policy, as in common law legal systems, a matter of the personal unworthiness of the beneficiary or possibly a mixture of both.[82] The rule applies to murder and culpable homicide.[83] A criminal conviction of the killer is not essential. The rule prevents the killer from acquiring a benefit in the deceased's estate as a result of the killing but it is not clear if it extends to the estate of the victim's heir.[84] The killer is not regarded as "predeceasing" the deceased for the purposes of a destination over clause in a bequest.[85]

The Forfeiture Act 1982 gives the court power to make an order in any particular case modifying the effect of the "forfeiture rule" which it defines as a rule of "public policy".[86] The court is given no express power to modify the effects of the 1594 Act. The Act does not extend to a person convicted of murder.[87] In appropriate cases the court may "modify" the effect of the forfeiture rule only if it is satisfied that the justice of the case requires it in the light of the conduct of the offender and of the deceased and other material circumstances.[88] The Scottish courts have taken the narrow view that only modification and not total exclusion of the forfeiture rule is authorised by the Act. Depending on the circumstances they have allowed the killer to inherit up to 99 per cent of the victim's estate.[89]

INCAPACITATED BENEFICIARIES

A party is not disqualified as a beneficiary because he is *incapax* due to non-age or mental infirmity. In such circumstances a parent or *curator* will administer the gift during the period of incapacity.   **16–19**

---

[79] *Oliphant* v *Oliphant* (1674) M 3429.
[80] MacKenzie, *Laws and Customs*, I, xiv, 5; Bankton, *Institute*, II, cccxxxi, 30.
[81] Criminal Justice (Scotland) Act 1949, s 15(1).
[82] *Hunter's Exrs, Petitioners* 1992 SLT 1141, per Lord Justice-Clerk Ross at 1143.
[83] *Smith, Petitioner* 1979 SLT (Sh Ct) 35; *Burns* v *Secretary of State for Social Services* 1985 SLT 351.
[84] *cf* South African law: *Steenkamp* v *Steenkamp* 1952 (1) SA 744 (T).
[85] *Hunter's Exrs, Petitioners* 1992 SLT 1141; *cf.* English law *Re Callaway* [1956] 2 All E R 451.
[86] 1982 Act, s 1(1).
[87] *ibid* s 5.
[88] *ibid* s 2(2).
[89] *Cross, Petitioner* 1987 SLT 384 (100% of heritable estate and 99% of moveable estate); *Jackson, Petitioner* 1989 GWD 22–947; *Gilchrist, Petitioner* 1990 SLT 494; *cf* English law *Re K, Deceased* [1985] 2 WLR 262.

INTESTATE SUCCESSION

16–20   The rules of intestate succession are largely contained in the Succession (Scotland) Act 1964 ("the 1964 Act"). The rules of intestacy are important because the majority of people in Scotland still do not leave a will. The aim of the rules of intestate succession is to embody broad principles as to how society considers property should be disposed of on death. They represent society's model of what the reasonable testator would have done if he had left a will.

The term "estate" is defined in the 1964 Act, s 36(2) as meaning "the whole estate, whether heritable or moveable, or partly heritable and partly moveable, belonging to the deceased at the time of his death or over which the deceased had a power of appointment and, where the deceased immediately before his death held the interest of a tenant under a tenancy of lease which was not expressed to expire on his death, ... that interest."

Total intestacy occurs when a deceased leaves undisposed of by a will all of his estate. Where this occurs the rules of intestate succession apply to the whole of the estate. Partial intestacy occurs when a deceased leaves part of his estate undisposed of in a will. In such a case the rules of intestate succession apply only to the part undisposed of. Intestacy or partial intestacy may occur when the testator has left a will but that will has failed for some reason. This situation is known as "artificial intestacy".

The rules of intestate succession are largely contained in the Succession (Scotland) Act 1964 but this Act has limitations as follows:

(a) It is not a complete code and one important aspect of the rules of intestate succession, the legal rights of a spouse and a child, derives originally from the common law.

(b) The Act is not retrospective and applies only to deaths on or after 10th September 1964.

(c) The Act does not apply to titles, coats of arms and honours.

The scheme of succession set out in the 1964 Act requires six stages to be implemented in the distribution of an intestate person's estate. These are:

(a) payment of debts[90];

(b) prior rights: right to dwelling house—s 8(1);

(c) prior rights: furniture and plenishings—s 8(3);

(d) prior rights: right to cash—s 9;

(e) legal rights;

(f) free estate—s 2.

---

[90] See para 16–05.

PRIOR RIGHTS—GENERAL

Prior rights arise only in cases of total or partial intestacy. They differ from legal rights **16–21** in that they can be defeated by provisions in the deceased's will. Where prior rights are claimable they rank in priority to legal rights. Only a surviving spouse (widow or widower) is entitled to prior rights. They are not available to cohabitees or children. If the intestacy is merely partial the surviving spouse is entitled to prior rights only out of the intestate part of the estate. Under the 1964 Act a surviving spouse has three prior rights: (i) a right in the dwelling house; (ii) a right to furniture and plenishings; and (iii) a right to a financial provision. The Secretary of State (now the Scottish Minister) has power to fix by order larger amounts for these various rights from time to time.[91] As the amounts of the rights have been changed on several occasions, the date of death will determine the amount to which the surviving spouse is entitled.

Dwelling house—s 8

The surviving spouse has a right to the deceased's interest in the deceased's dwelling **16–22** house or, depending on its value, a monetary sum in lieu. "Dwellinghouse" is defined as including a part of a building occupied as a separate dwelling house and includes garden and amenity ground attached to the house.[92] Several points must be established to determine the quantification of the right:

(a) The prior right applies only to a house in which the deceased was an owner or a tenant.[93] Rent Act tenancies are excluded as are tenancies which terminate on the death of the deceased.[94]

(b) It must be established that the surviving spouse was ordinarily resident in the house at the date of death.[95] Where the deceased was ordinarily resident is immaterial. If the surviving spouse was ordinarily resident in two houses she must chose one within six months after the death.[96]

(c) If the value of the deceased's interest exceeds £130,000 the spouse will receive that amount in cash instead.[97] If there is disagreement about the value of the interest it is to be determined by arbitration.[98] The interest is valued under deduction of heritable debts (mortgages) secured on it.

(d) If the interest is worth under £130,000 the surviving spouse's claim is not to the actual interest of the deceased but merely to a sum of money representing

---

[91] Succession (Scotland) Act 1973; 1964 Act, s 9A.
[92] 1964 Act, s 8(6)(a).
[93] *ibid* s 8(6)(d).
[94] *ibid* s 36(2).
[95] *ibid* s 8(4).
[96] *ibid* s 8(1) proviso.
[97] *ibid* s 8(1)(b). The Prior Rights of Surviving Spouse (Scotland) Order 1999 (SI 1999/445, in force 1st April 1999).
[98] 1964 Act, s 8(5).

the value of the interest if it is one of the two exceptional cases.[99] These are, first, where the house forms part only of the subjects comprised in one tenancy[100] and, second, where the house forms the whole or part of subjects used by the deceased for carrying on a trade, profession or occupation and the value of the estate as a whole would be likely to be substantially diminished if the house were to be disposed of separately from the assets of the trade, profession or occupation.[101]

(e) Earlier values of the maximum value of the right are as follows: 10th September 1964 to 22nd May 1973—£15,000; 22nd May 1973 to 31st July 1981—£30,000; 1st August 1981 to 30th April 1988—£50,000; 1st May 1988 to 25th November 1993—£60,000; 26th November 1993 to 31st March 1999—£110,000.

Furniture and plenishings—s 8

16–23   The surviving spouse is entitled to the furniture and plenishings of a dwelling house in which he or she was ordinarily resident at the date of death.[102] This right exists even although no dwelling house forms part of the intestate estate provided the contents are themselves part of that estate. The term "furniture and plenishings" includes garden effects, domestic animals, plate, plated articles, linen, china, glass, books, pictures, prints, articles of household use and consumable stores. This list is not exhaustive. Excluded from the definition are articles or animals used at the date of death for business purposes (*eg* a sheep dog), money or securities for money (*eg* share certificates) and heirlooms.[103] "Heirlooms" is defined as "any article which has associations with the intestate's family of such a nature and extent that it ought not to pass to some member of that family other than the surviving spouse of the intestate".[104] The definition is vague but it may include items such as a paternal grandfather's war medals. Several points must be established to determine the quantification of the right:

(a) The maximum value of furnishings is £22,000. Where all the furnishings in the house are valued at less than that the spouse may have them all.[105] There is provision for arbitration where there is dispute as to the value of the furniture.[106]

(b) If there are two or more relevant houses, the surviving spouse must chose from which house she shall take the contents which must be exercised within six months of the death. She cannot take some contents from one house and

---

[99] 1964 Act, s 8(1)(a)(ii). The Prior Rights of Surviving Spouse (Scotland) Order 1999 (SI 1999/445, in force 1st April 1999).
[100] 1964 Act, s 8(2)(a).
[101] *ibid* s 8(2)(b).
[102] *ibid* s 8(3).
[103] *ibid* s 8(6)(b).
[104] *ibid* s 8(6)(c).
[105] *ibid* s 8(3)(a). The Prior Rights of Surviving Spouse (Scotland) Order 1999 (SI 1999/445, in force 1st April 1999).
[106] 1964 Act, s 8(5).

other articles from another.[107] She is not, however, obliged to chose the contents of the house chosen by her in fulfilment of her prior right to a dwelling house.

(c) Previous values for the maximum figure are as follows: 10th September 1964 to 22nd May 1973—£5,000; 22nd May 1973 to 31st July 1981—£8,000; 1st August 1981 to 30th April 1988—£10,000; 1st May 1988 to 25th November 1993—£12,000; 26th November 1993 to 31st March 1999—£20,000.

Financial provision—s 9

The surviving spouse has a right to receive a sum of cash from the intestate estate. This **16–24** right arises only after rights to the dwelling house and furnishings have been satisfied.[108] The sum is paid out of both heritable and moveable parts of the remaining intestate estate rateably in proportion to the respective amounts of those parts.[109]

The sum at present is £35,000 if the deceased is survived by issue (children, grandchildren, and any more remote direct descendants); otherwise it is £58,000.[110] Both these sums have been varied from time to time by statutory instrument and the sum to which the surviving spouse is entitled will depend on the date of death.[111] Where the intestate estate is less than the sum to which the surviving spouse is entitled she may receive the entire intestate estate.[112] In both cases interest is due on the sum from the date of death until payment.[113] The rate of interest is presently seven per cent and it can be varied by statutory instrument.[114] Where the intestacy is partial only and the surviving spouse is entitled to a legacy under the deceased's will (other than a legacy of dwelling house or of furniture and plenishings to which the section 8 right would apply), then the surviving spouse is entitled only to the sum necessary to bring the legacy up to £58,000 or £35,000 as the case may be.[115] This is calculated at the date of death.[116]

LEGAL RIGHTS

Legal rights are available to the surviving spouse and children of the deceased. They **16–25** are known as (a) *jus relictae* ("right of the widow"), (b) *jus relicti* ("right of the widower") and legitim (the right of the children, otherwise known as "the bairn's part"). An unmarried cohabitee has no legal rights. Step-children have no claim to

---

[107] 1964 Act, s 8(3) proviso.
[108] See the definition of "intestate estate" in the 1964 Act, s 9(6)(a).
[109] 1964 Act, s 9(3).
[110] *ibid* s 9(1). See the definition of "issue" in s 36(1). The Prior Rights of Surviving Spouse (Scotland) Order 1999 (SI 1999/445, in force 1st April 1999).
[111] The previous figures are as follows: 10th September 1964 to 22nd May 1973—£2,500 and £5,000; 23rd May 1973 to 30th December 1977—£4,000 and £8,000; 31st December 1977 to 31st July 1981—£8,000 and £16,000; 1st August 1981 to 30th April 1988—£15,000 and £25,000; 1st May 1988 to 25th November 1993—£21,000 and £35,000; 26th November 1993 to 31st March 1999—£30,000 and £50,000.
[112] 1964 Act, s 9(2).
[113] *ibid* s 9(1).
[114] *ibid* s 9(1); Law Reform (Miscellaneous Provisions) (Scotland) Act 1980; SI 1981/805. Previous rates have been 4% from 1964 to 1st August 1991.
[115] 1964 Act, s 9(1) proviso.
[116] *ibid* s 9(6)(b).

legitim but illegitimate children have the same rights as legitimate children[117] and adopted children have been treated for the purposes of legitim as children of the adopter.[118] Where a child has predeceased the deceased that child's children (*ie* grand-children of the deceased) and remoter descendants may have an entitlement by reason of the doctrine of representation.[119]

Legal rights apply to both intestate[120] and testate succession and cannot be defeated by any provision in the deceased's will. Legal rights are rights to cash and not rights to specific assets. They are, however, calculated by reference to the value of the moveable estate of the deceased. For the purpose of calculating legal rights it is still necessary to divide the estate into heritage and moveables. As legal rights apply only to moveables a party may defeat or restrict claims on his estate by converting his assets during his lifetime into heritage.

The extent of legal rights depends on who survives the deceased.

(a) If the deceased is survived both by a spouse and by issue the spouse is en-
    titled to a third of the moveables as *jus relictae* or *jus relicti* and the issue are
    entitled to a third of the moveables as legitim. The remaining third is known
    as the "dead's part" and is distributed according to the rules of testate or
    intestate succession.

(b) If the deceased is survived only by a spouse the spouse is entitled to one-half
    of the moveables as *jus relictae* or *jus relicti* and the other half is the dead's part.

(c) If the deceased is survived only by issue, the issue are entitled to one-half of
    the moveables as legitim and the other half is the dead's part.

Representation in legal rights

16–26 The application of the principle of representation in connection with legitim is governed by the 1964 Act, s 11. The general effect is as follows:

(a) If the deceased has had a child who has predeceased him but left issue (grand-
    children or remoter issue of the deceased), the issue have the same right to
    legitim as the child himself would have had if he had survived the deceased.

(b) If all those claiming legitim are related in the same degree to the deceased
    (*eg* if they are all children or all grandchildren), the division amongst them
    is equal. For example, if there are three grandchildren all receive a third
    of the legitim. This is referred to as "division *per capita*" (according to
    individuals).

(c) If, however, the claimants on the legitim fund are not all related in the same
    degree to the deceased (*eg* if there are both children and grandchildren, the
    latter representing children who have already died), the division amongst
    them is based on the class of claimants which is nearest to the deceased. For

---

[117] See para 16–14.
[118] See para 16–15.
[119] 1964 Act, s 11.
[120] Confirmed by the 1964 Act, s 10(2).

example, if there are three children living and one dead but the dead child in turn has left two children, the three children each receive one-quarter of the legitim fund and the grandchildren receive one-eighth each. This is known as "division *per stirpes*" (according to branches of the family tree).

Advances and collation *inter liberos*

Collation *inter liberos* is the legal doctrine which applies where a child has received **16–27** advances of his share of the legitim fund during the deceased's lifetime. The purpose of the doctrine is to maintain equality among the children sharing in the legitim fund. There must be more than one child claiming legitim before the doctrine can apply.[121] It has no application whatsoever in relation to payments made to a spouse during the lifetime of the deceased. Where representation applies and grandchildren or remoter issue of the deceased are entitled to a share of the legitim fund, they must collate not only advances made to them directly by the deceased but also the appropriate proportion of advances made to the person whom they represent.

The effect of the doctrine is that a child who has received an advance of his share of the legitim fund during the deceased's lifetime must collate these advances. This means that when the legitim fund is calculated the advance is brought into the calculation to increase the total legitim fund. In the distribution of that fund the advance will then be set against the child's share, with the result that he will receive on the parent's death that much less than the other children who have had no advances made to them.

A typical advance to be taken into account for collation is an advance made to set up a child in a business[122] or a marriage.[123] Not all payments made by the deceased during his lifetime to a child are advances which require to be collated. The following are not subject to collation:

(a) cash paid by the deceased to a child where it is clear that the deceased wished the sums to be a gift additional to his share of legitim;

(b) loans made to a child (these are not advances but debts due to the estate as a whole);

(c) remuneration for services rendered by the child to his parent;

(d) sums paid by the deceased for the purposes of maintaining and educating a child[124];

(e) gifts of heritage; and

(f) a legacy left by the deceased to a child.

---

[121] *Coats' Trs v Coats* 1914 SC 744.
[122] *Douglas v Douglas* (1876) 4 R 105.
[123] *Elliot's Exrx v Elliot* 1953 SC 43.
[124] Erskine, *Inst*, III, ix, 24.

Extinction of legal rights

16–28   Legal rights may be extinguished by negative prescription if not claimed within 20 years of the death, or when the intestacy arose, or the date when the legitim claimant became 16 years of age. It is relatively rare for legal rights to be extinguished in this manner.

    A more common method of extinction of legal rights is express discharge. This may be done either during the lifetime of the deceased or after the death.

    Jus relictae and *jus relicti* may be discharged before the death by unilateral renunciation or a bilateral agreement. The latter method was common last century where the agreement was usually in the form of a provision in an ante-nuptial marriage contract (a contract made before the marriage). Such agreements are now rare. A claim for legitim cannot now be discharged without the consent of the child or other descendant concerned.[125] Before 1964 intending spouses might, by an ante-nuptial marriage contract, discharge in advance the right of any child of the marriage to claim legitim[126] and pre-1964 discharges remain in force.[127] A discharge by a child will bind any of that child's children who attempt to claim legal rights by representation.[128]

    Discharge of legal rights after the death usually occurs in the context of a will making an express provision for the person entitled to the legal rights. That person cannot chose both the legal rights and the legacy. This is known as the situation of "approbate and reprobate" or "election". The party entitled to the legal rights and the legacy must make a choice between the provisions; usually he will chose the more valuable one. In many cases the terms of the will emphasise the need for an election by containing an express forfeiture clause declaring that a party who claims legal rights will forfeit all provision under the will. Difficulties arise in practice where the party requiring to choose is incapacitated due to mental infirmity or non-age.

    Where there has been a discharge of legal rights during the deceased's lifetime the effect is that the granter of the discharge is treated as dead. This has the effect of increasing the shares of the other claimants to legal rights. Where legal rights are discharged after the death the effect is that the share of the person effecting the discharge falls into free estate and the shares of the other claimants to legal rights are not increased.

INTERPLAY OF LEGAL AND PRIOR RIGHTS

16–29   Legal rights apply in cases of testacy and intestacy but prior rights apply only in cases of intestacy. Prior rights may be excluded by a will but legal rights cannot. On intestacy prior rights are an entitlement calculated prior to legal rights. This means that sometimes where a deceased is survived by a spouse and children the surviving spouse is better off under intestacy than being left everything under the deceased's will. In *Kerr, Petitioner*[129] a widow was left all of her husband's estate in his will. The children of the marriage wished to claim their legal rights. The wife renounced her

---

[125] 1964 Act, s 12.

[126] See, *eg, Callander* v *Callander's Exr* 1972 SC (HL) 70.

[127] 1964 Act, s 12.

[128] *Hog* v *Hog* (1791) M 8193.

[129] 1968 SLT (Sh Ct) 61.

bequest under the will creating artificial intestacy. Upon intestacy her prior rights exhausted the entire estate and the children received nothing.

FREE ESTATE

The free estate is what is left after payment of debts, prior and legal rights. If a **16–30** deceased is not survived by a spouse or issue the free estate comprises the whole net estate. The rules for division of the free estate are contained in Part I of the Succession (Scotland) Act 1964. These rules apply to both heritage and moveables.

The general principles in the 1964 Act applicable to the division of the free estate are as follows:

(a) The succession opens to certain classes of relations in the order set out in the under-noted list. As soon as the succession opens to a class in which there is a possible claimant it stops there and goes no further.

(b) At every stage in the order of succession representation is applied except in the case of parents and spouses. A person who would have succeeded if he had survived the deceased is represented by his issue. They "step into his shoes" and are entitled to take what would otherwise have been his share of the deceased's estate. Issue means issue however remote and there is now no distinction made in the law betweeen legitimate and illegitimate relationships.[130]

(c) Where there are two or more persons with rights of succession, the division between or among them is *per capita* (according to individuals) if the persons are all related in the same degree and *per stirpes* (according to branches of the family tree) in other cases.

(d) Collaterals of the whole blood (*ie* two parents in common with the intestate or an ancestor) exclude collaterals of the half-blood (sharing only one parent). The latter are entitled to succeed only if there are no collaterals of the whole blood. No distinction is now made between collaterals of the half-blood "consanguinean" (half-brothers and half-sisters who have the same father) and collaterals of the half-blood "uterine" (half brothers and sisters who have the same mother).

(e) There is no provision at present for cohabitees, step-children or in-laws to inherit.

Order of succession—s 2

The order of succession is as follows:

(a) children, including adopted children;   **16–31**

---

[130] See para 16–14.

(b) parents and siblings (brothers and sisters)—provided there is at least one from each class, each class is entitled to one-half of the free estate;

(c) siblings (where there is no surviving parent);

(d) parents (where there is no surviving sibling);

(e) surviving spouse;

(f) uncles and aunts (maternal or paternal);

(g) grandparent or grandparents (paternal or maternal);

(h) collaterals of grandparents;

(i) remoter ancestors of the intestate;

(j) the Crown as ultimus *haeres* ("ultimate heir").[131]

TESTATE SUCCESSION

16–32   The law of testate succession deals with wills. This permits a party, within certain limitations, to "contract out" of the law of intestate succession and require his estate to be divided up in a manner different to that provided for under those rules. An individual may choose to make a will in respect of all or part only of his estate. Under Scots law a party is under no obligation to make a will unless he has contracted to do so. In some cases an individual may enter into a contract with another party to leave a will in certain terms in favour of that person. If the individual fails to meet his contractual obligations his estate may be liable in damages and any later will to different effect may be reduced.[132] A gratuitous unilateral obligation to make a will in certain terms must be constituted in writing.[133] Prior to 1995 such an obligation could be proved by the writ or oath of the promiser.[134]

There is no statutorily prescribed form of a will although wills which are drawn up by solicitors usually follow a form which has arisen from years of practice. It is not necessary to use such a will and it is possible to draw up a will in a homemade fashion. These "DIY" wills cause problems in practice, usually because of failings in formal validity or their manner of expression. A will need not be one single document and may consist of several documents of different dates and in different forms. For example, there may be a will followed by later deeds effecting alterations.

TERMINOLOGY

16–33   A person who makes a will is said to "test" and is known as the "testator". A will is also known as a "testament" or a "testamentary document". A more complex will

---

[131] 1964 Act, s 7.
[132] *Paterson* v *Paterson* (1893) 20 R 484.
[133] Requirements of Writing (Scotland) Act 1995, ss 1(2) and 11(2).
[134] *Smith* v *Oliver* 1911 SC 103.

setting up a trust is known as a "trust disposition and settlement". A later deed which alters an existing will is called a "codicil". A person to whom a bequest is left is known as a "legatee".

ESSENTIAL VALIDITY

Essential validity relates to wide-ranging matters such as: (1) capacity to test; (2) intention to test; and (3) restraints on testamentary freedom.   **16–34**

Capacity to test

For a will to be valid the testator must have capacity to test. There are various **16–35** limitations on this affecting different classes of person. The rules are generally aimed at protecting that person from exploitation by others or from his own mistake.

(a) A person has no capacity to test until he or she reaches the age of 12 years.[135] A parent cannot make a will for his child whether under 12 or not.

(b) Where a person is suffering from a mental illness or psychiatric disorder which removes from him the capacity to understand the nature of the act of making a will he cannot make a will. He may, however, make a will during a lucid interval when his understanding briefly returns.[136] Not all mental illnesses will result in a lack of capacity and many persons who are mildly affected may have capacity. Each case should be considered on its own special facts. If a person is not generally insane but suffers from delusions, his will can be set aside if it was affected by his delusions.[137] Mere eccentricity is insufficient. Insanity is the most common ground upon which disappointed relatives challenge a will.[138]

(c) The doctrine of facility and circumvention may protect persons who have a weakness of mind short of insanity. This occurs where the testator has testamentary capacity but is weak in mind ("facile") so that he is easily misled by a person who seeks to obtain some benefit under the will. The machinations of the party seeking to benefit are known as "circumvention". Both facility and circumvention must exist before the ground of reduction is established. This may occur where a testator is old or in ill-health and is being cared for in a nursing home or in the home of a relative. It may also arise in cases involving religious groups.[139]

(d) A will made at a time when the testator was so affected by drink or drugs or otherwise as to be without the necessary understanding of his action is invalid and open to reduction.

(e) A will may be reduced on the basis that the testator made it whilst affected by undue influence. This may occur where the person who benefits under

---

[135] Age of Legal Capacity (Scotland) Act 1991, s 2(2).
[136] *Nisbet's Trs. v Nisbet* (1871) 9 M 937.
[137] *Siveright's Trs. v Siveright* 1920 SC (HL) 63; *Ballantyne v Evans* (1886) 13 R 652.
[138] For a recent example, see *Muirden v Garden's Exrs* 1981 SLT (Notes) 9.
[139] *Anderson v Beacon Fellowship* 1992 SLT 111.

the will stood in a position of trust towards the testator. An example is the relationship of parent and child or solicitor and client. There is nothing wrong in the relationship itself but the problem arises where there has been an abuse of that position. In contrast with facility and circumvention there is no need to establish a weakness of mind on the part of the testator.[140] A solicitor who benefits under a will which he himself has drawn up has the onus (burden) of proving, if the will is challenged, that he did not exercise undue influence.[141]

(f) Where a testator signs a will under a material misrepresentation of what it contains[142] or his consent is obtained by threats, the will is void.

Intention to test

16–36   If a document is to be treated as a will it must be clear that the deceased intended it to be a will. No particular form of words is required in law but it is always best to have a will prepared by a solicitor (rather than to use a homemade document which might contain ambiguous expressions). A common difficulty with homemade wills is that it is sometimes difficult to establish if they were intended to be wills or simply a note to remind the testator of what he was going to put in a will which he never got around to making.[143] This may be illustrated in *Rhodes* v *Peterson*,[144] in which the court considered the terms of a holograph letter from a mother to a daughter. The terms of the letter were held in the circumstances to amount to a complete statement of testamentary intention even though the letter contained a phrase which suggested that a formal will might be made in the future. A mere list of names and sums of money is not sufficient to be regarded as a will.[145]

A different problem of intention arises if a testator leaves a will with a clause which is something like the following: "If I die whilst I am on holiday…". What does this mean? It could mean that the will is to have effect only if the testator dies whilst on holiday. That interpretation, however, is probably too strict and the courts will probably regard such a statement as a reason which induced the testator to make a will rather than a condition precedent to the operation of the will.

Restraints on testamentary freedom

16–37   A testator is not entitled to use a will to dispose of his estate in an unfettered manner. Several different limitations arise. Some of these, such as limitations arising from the law on accumulations, successive liferents, entails, certainty of purposes and beneficiaries, and public policy, have been dealt with in Chapter 15. In this chapter we will consider: (1) legal rights; (2) the nature of the property; and (3) defamation.

Legal rights

16–38   These have been outlined above in the context of intestate succession. They apply

---

[140] *Ross* v *Gosslin's Exrs* 1926 SC 325, per Lord President Clyde at 334.
[141] *Stewart* v *McLaren* 1920 SC (HL) 148.
[142] *Munro* v *Strain* (1874) 1 R 522.
[143] *Colvin* v *Hutchison* (1885) 12 R 947.
[144] 1971 SC 56.
[145] *Waddell's Trs* v *Waddell* (1896) 24 R 189; *Cameron's Trs* v *Mackenzie* 1915 SC 313.

where the testator dies leaving a spouse and/or issue. There are some limitations on
the effectiveness of these rights as constraints on testamentary freedom:

(a) They apply only to moveables and not to heritage and then only to one-, two-
thirds or half, as the case may be, of the moveables. In many cases the most
valuable asset of the deceased is his house and that will be heritable.

(b) Legal rights can be evaded by *inter vivos* transactions. If a testator gives away
all his moveables before his death there will be no estate out of which to claim
legal rights.[146]

Approbate and reprobate (election)

Where a will provides for a bequest of moveables to a beneficiary who is also entitled
to legal rights the doctrine of approbate and reprobate (otherwise known as
"election") applies.[147] That party cannot claim both the legal rights and the moveables
bequest unless the will provides otherwise—which would be unusual. Many wills
expressly contain a forfeiture clause declaring that if the beneficiary claims legal rights
he will forfeit his entitlement under the will. If a testator wishes to encourage a beneficiary not to claim legal rights he usually makes a provision in the will which is greater
than that to which the beneficiary is entitled under legal rights.

A difficulty with the doctrine of election and express forfeiture clauses arises in
connection with the assessment of value of the respective entitlements. Obviously a
beneficiary will wish to claim whichever right will give him a more valuable
provision. The courts have been reasonably sympathetic to widows or children who
wished to undo an election at a later date where they received inadequate advice at the
time of the election.[148]

A particular problem arises where a beneficiary is not of sound mind and is not in a
position to make the election between legal rights and a provision under a will. In such
a case the beneficiary's representative will usually petition the court for authority to
elect one way or the other.[149] A child under 16 cannot elect but if aged 16 or 17 can elect
but potentially challenge the election until aged 21 as a "prejudicial transaction".[150]

In relation to wills executed prior to 1964 the doctrine of equitable compensation
applied to modify the effect of approbate and reprobate in relation to a choice between
legal rights and a testamentary provision.[151] For wills executed after the coming into
force of the 1964 Act this doctrine was excluded.[152]

The nature of the property

Testamentary limitations may arise from the nature of the property within the estate   **16–39**
of the deceased. For example, because a servitude is inseparably linked to a dominant tenement a testator may not leave a bequest of a servitude separate from the

---

[146] *Agnew* v *Agnew* (1775) M 8210; *Lashley* v *Hogg* (1808) 4 Pat App 581.
[147] *Crum Ewing's Trs* v *Bayly's Trs* 1911 SC (HL) 18.
[148] See, *eg*, *Dawson's Tr* v *Dawson* (1896) 23 R 1006; *Walker* v *Orr's Trs* 1958 SLT 220; *Donaldson* v *Tainsh's Trs*
(1886) 13 R 967.
[149] *Burn's CB* v *Burn's Trs* 1961 SLT 166; *Allan's Exrs* v *Allan's Trs* 1975 SLT 227.
[150] Age of Capacity (Scotland) Act 1991, ss 1 and 3.
[151] See, *eg*, *Macfarlane's Trs* v *Oliver* (1882) 9 R 1138.
[152] 1964 Act, s 13.

dominant tenement. As regards a croft, a testator may not leave a bequest of his croft to more than one beneficiary.[153] Where the single beneficiary is not a member of the testator's family the bequest is null and void unless the Crofters Commission otherwise determine.[154]

Defamation

16–40   In certain very unusual circumstances a will may contain passages which are defamatory of another person still living.[155] In such a case the parties defamed may bring an action for defamation against the executry estate for damages. Obviously a testator will wish to avoid having his estate dissipated in this way and this will serve as a practical restraint upon what the testator states in his will.

FORMAL VALIDITY

16–41   Formal validity relates to compliance with the requirements for the execution of wills. There may be a number of reasons for the rules of formal validity. The most commonly suggested reasons are: (1) to avoid fraud; and (2) to impress upon the testator the importance of making a will.

If a will did not comply with the requirements of formal validity it was invalid at common law.[156] There was no general dispensing power on the court to award validity to documents which failed to comply with the rules.[157] The harshness of this rule has been relaxed by certain provisions of the Requirements of Writing (Scotland) Act 1995 ("the 1995 Act").[158]

Foreign wills

16–42   Where a will purports to leave a bequest of heritage in Scotland or where it purports to deal with moveables and the testator is domiciled in Scotland the rules to be applied in relation to formal validity will be the rules of Scots law. There are some complications with a foreign element which are given a privileged position in terms of the Wills Act 1963 ("1963 Act"). The rules as to formal validity may be summarised as follows:

(a) 1963 Act, s 1 provides that a will is formally valid if it is executed according to any of the following:
   (i) the internal law of the testator's domicile, habitual residence or nationality either at the date of the execution of the will or the death; or
   (ii) the law of the place of execution.

---

[153] Crofters (Scotland) Act 1993, s 10(1). Time limits for the acceptance of the bequest, and rights on the part of the landlord to object, are set out in the 1993 Act, s 10(2)–(6). The tenancy cannot be bequeathed to one person in liferent and another in fee: see *Anderson v Barclay-Harvey* (1917) 5 SLCR 65.

[154] Crofters (Scotland) Act 1993, s 10(1). See further MacCuish and Flyn, *Crofting Law* (1990), Chap 7, especially paras 7.02–7.03. The term "family" is defined in the 1993 Act, s 61(2).

[155] See, *eg*, *B's Exr v The Keeper of the Registers* 1935 SC 745.

[156] *Syme's Trs v Cherrie* 1986 SLT 161.

[157] The Scottish Law Commission has recommended the introduction of such a power in *Report on Succession* (Scot Law Com No 124, 1990), Pt IV, pp 39–46, paras 4.1–4.20. A more limited power contained in the Conveyancing (Scotland) Act 1874, s 39 was repealed by the 1995 Act, s 14(2) and Sched 5. See *Williamson v Williamson* 1997 SLT 1044.

[158] These are examined at paras 16–43 *et seq*.

(b) 1963 Act, s 2(1)(b) provides that if the will relates to immoveable property it will be valid if it conforms with the *lex situs* (the law of the place where the property is sited).

(c) 1963 Act, s 2(1)(a) contains special provisions for the execution of wills on aeroplanes and ships. The formal validity of such wills can be referred to the law of the territory to which the vessel or plane is most closely connected.

The Administration of Justice Act 1982, ss 27 and 28 make provision for international wills which will be recognised in a number of countries. These provisions have not been brought into effect.

Domestic law and formal validity

The Requirements of Writing (Scotland) Act 1995 ("the 1995 Act") came into operation on 1st August 1995 and applies to wills executed after that date. For wills executed prior to that date the older law still applies.   **16–43**

Law after 1995

The 1995 Act seeks to set out two things: **16–44**

(a) the minimum requirements of formalities of execution to make a document such as a will valid—this may be referred to as "validity"; and

(b) additional requirements as regards signing by a witness and further subscription on all pages by the granter of the will to give the granter's subscription "self-proving" status. This is known as "probativity". When the testator's subscription is "self proving" it is presumed to be valid and the onus of proof will lie on any party wishing to challenge its validity.

To apply the broad principles of the 1995 Act it is best to ask four questions:

(a) *When is a will valid?* In terms of the 1995 Act, s 1(2)(c) a written document is required to constitute a will. The term "writing" is not defined in the 1995 Act but it is defined in the Interpretation Act 1978 as including typing and printing. A will may be typed, printed, written in the hand of the testator or someone else and any mixture of these. At common law there were special provisions for documents written in the hand of the granter known as "holograph" documents but these were abolished by the 1995 Act.[159] A will requires to be subscribed by the testator only on the last page to be valid.[160]

(b) *What are the additional requirements for self-proving status?* The additional requirements in relation to a will are either of the following alternatives: (i) the will is signed by one witness to the testator's subscription on the last page and, if it consists of more than one page, the will is signed on every

---

[159] 1995 Act, s 11(3)(b).
[160] *ibid* s 2(1).

page by the testator[161]; or (ii) application is made to the court for a decree or certificate to the effect that the subscription of the testator is self proving.[162] Evidence will require to be led to satisfy the court. The second alternative is obviously much more costly and slower than the first alternative.

(c) *Is it necessary for the testator's subscription to be self-proving?* The answer to this question is yes. To enable any estate to be wound up by an executor that executor must receive confirmation from the court. No confirmation will be issued in respect of a will executed after the commencement of the 1995 Act unless the testator's subscription of that will has self-proving status by one of the two alternative means outlined above.[163]

(d) *What is best practice?* The method of obtaining self-proving status of the testator's subscription by means of court procedure should be used to repair omissions only where the testator has executed a will himself without recourse to legal advice. A solicitor when preparing a will should ensure self-proving status by obtaining the signature of a witness on the last page of the will and the signature of the testator on every page. The testing clause of the will should also state the date and place of subscription because this gives rise to a presumption that the statement of the place and date are correct if there is nothing to the contrary in the will.[164] This is useful where the law changes to give a particular interpretation to a particular word used in the will such as the changes in the law relative to illegitimate children.[165]

Law pre-1995

16–45 Before 1st August 1995 the law recognised that a will could be in two forms: (1) holograph wills; and (2) formally attested wills (wills with witnesses).

Holograph wills

A will was a valid holograph will if it conformed to either of the following: (a) it was wholly in the testator's own writing and signed by him at the end of the last page; or (b) if it was written by someone else or typed, if the testator in his own handwriting appended a doquet "adopted as holograph" above his own signature. In neither case were any witnesses required to render the will valid. In both cases the will did require to be signed. Although a holograph will was valid it was not self proving in relation to the testator's signature. To obtain confirmation on a holograph will it had to be proved by affidavit evidence that the writing and signature on the will were those of the testator.[166] Difficult cases arose where the testator was disabled and found difficulty in writing.[167]

---

[161] 1955 Act, s 3(1) and (2).
[162] *ibid* s 4.
[163] Succession (Scotland) Act 1964, s 21A.
[164] 1995 Act, s 3(10).
[165] See para 16–14.
[166] Succession (Scotland) Act 1964, s 21.
[167] *McBeath's Trs* v *McBeath* 1935 SC 471; *Chisholm* v *Chisholm* 1949 SC 434.

Formally attested wills

The requirements for executing formal wills were set out in a number of statutes of the old Scottish Parliament. These statutes were repeatedly and most recently amended in the Conveyancing and Feudal Reform (Scotland) Act 1970, s 44. After the enactment of the 1970 Act the will required to be executed by the testator on every page and annex and also signed by two witnesses on the last page of the will. The law prior to 1995 did not make a clear distinction between the formalities required to render the will valid and the formalities required to render the will "probative" (self proving) as regards the testator's execution. It was generally regarded that the same formalities were required for both.

Subscription and signing

The law pre-1995 and the law post-1995 have two important matters in common: they **16–46** both include in their formalities some element of (a) the subscription by the testator, and (b) the signing by a witness.

Pre-1995

No statute prescribed what subscription or signing amounted to and the matter was dealt with at common law. The term subscription meant signing at the bottom of the page in respect of both formal and holograph wills.[168] The term signing by a testator or a witness meant the applying of a signature. A signature comprised the full surname prefaced by any of the following: (a) the Christian names in full; (b) any recognised contraction of any of the Christian names; (c) the initials of the Christian names; or (d) any combination of (a), (b) and (c). A partially completed signature was invalid.[169] Abbreviations and nicknames might suffice if there was evidence that the testator or the witness usually signed his name in that way. For example, in *Rhodes* v *Peterson*[170] the court upheld a letter as a will in which the testator signed her name "mum". There was a doubt whether signing by a mark was acceptable. The signature had to be the act of the testator or the witness. It was not a signature if the hand was guided by someone else although it was permissible to have the hand supported above the wrist.[171]

Post-1995

The meaning of the terms "subscription and "signing" are generally dealt with by the 1995 Act although some recourse must be made to the common law. In terms of the 1995 Act subscription occurs when a testator signs at the end of the last page of the will.[172] There are two types of signatures of a testator: the formal and the informal.[173] Broadly speaking the formal signature is the same as was required by the common law; an informal signature is a nickname by which the testator commonly signs wills. A mark is also a signature if that is how a testator commonly signs documents. A will with an informal signature of the testator does not give the will self-proving status as regards the signature and further court process is required. What

---

[168] *Taylor's Exx* v *Thom* 1914 SC 79.
[169] *Donald* v *McGregor* 1926 SLT 103.
[170] 1972 SLT 98.
[171] *Noble* v *Noble* (1875) 3 R 74.
[172] 1995 Act, s 7(1).
[173] *ibid* s 7(2).

amounts to the signature of a witness is the same for the signature of a testator except that the informal method is excluded so that a witness may not sign by initials or a mark.[174]

Who can be a witness

16–47 The law pre-1995 and the law post-1995 have the following matters in common. Parties interested in the will are not disqualified but they are best avoided as a matter of practice to remove any suspicion of undue influence. A person under the age of 16 is excluded as a witness. A witness must know the testator but the requirements are slight and a reliable introduction will suffice. The act of witnessing should follow immediately upon the act of signing by the testator so that they form one continuous process.[175]

Notarial execution

16–48 In practice a will is invariably signed by the testator personally or it is executed on his behalf in accordance with the statutory provisions relative to notarial execution. A *curator bonis* cannot execute a will for a testator lacking capacity due to mental illness. There is no reported decision or statute which precludes a will being executed by an agent acting under a power of attorney of the testator[176] but this is never attempted in practice. Provision is made in statute for a party to execute a will on behalf of testators who are blind or who are unable to write.[177] Again, a distinction must be made between the law prior to the 1995 Act and the provisions thereof.

Prior to 1st August 1995 the parties who could execute a will notarily were a solicitor, a notary public, a justice of the peace or a parish minister acting within his own parish.[178] The solicitor did not need to have taken out a practising certificate. If the person who executed a will notarily had any interest therein the will would be completely invalid.

On or after 1st August 1995 the parties who can execute a will notarily are an advocate, a solicitor possessing a valid practising certificate, a justice of the peace or a sheriff clerk or, where wills are executed outside Scotland, a notary public.[179] If the person who executes a will notarily has any interest therein the will is invalid only to the extent of the interest that it confers on the interested party.

Informal writings

16–49 A will which is validly executed according to the statutory formalities frequently contains a provision that future alterations to the will can be made by less formal deeds. Such a provision may be valid but the subsequent informal writings will require to conform strictly with any specially permitted derogations from the general law of execution of deeds.[180] The effect of the 1995 Act on these writings is uncertain and they are best avoided in practice.

---

[174] 1955 Act, s 7(5).
[175] *Walker* v *Whitwell* 1916 SC (HL) 75.
[176] *cf* the view expressed in Blackie and Patrick, *Mental Health: a Guide to the Law in Scotland* (1990), para 3.4.5.
[177] 1995 Act, s 9.
[178] Conveyancing (Scotland) Act 1924, s 18.
[179] 1995 Act, s 9(6).
[180] *Waterson's Trs* v *St Giles Boys' Club* 1943 SC 369.

REVOCATION OF WILLS

Once a will is made it will take effect upon the testator's death unless it is previously **16–50** revoked. There is no legally implied time limitation on the effectiveness of a will. A will is "ambulatory" in nature, meaning that it may be revoked at any time by the testator prior to his death except in so far as he has made a contract not to do so.[181] Delivery of the will to a beneficiary or a statement in a will that it is "irrevocable" will not constitute such a contract. A contract not to revoke a will may arise in relation to mutual wills executed by married couples.[182] Even if there is a contract to make a will in certain terms and not to revoke it the property remains owned by the testator during his lifetime and he is free to alienate it even to the extent of dissipating it altogether in a way which would defeat the purpose of the will and the contract not to revoke it. To prevent this a beneficiary may wish to persuade the testator to convey the property to him during the testator's lifetime.[183]

Revocation may be in whole or in part, express or implied and effected by a subsequent document or the actions of the testator.

Revocation by subsequent deed

A subsequent deed may revoke an earlier will expressly or by implication. The deed **16–51** which purports to revoke a will must be executed with the same formalities as are required for a will but it need not contain alternative provisions for the disposal of the estate. Problems which arise in relation to deeds which revoke wills tend to be ones of interpretation. Care needs to be taken to correctly identify the will being revoked.[184] Where the deed does not expressly revoke an earlier will but makes contradictory provisions the earlier will may be revoked by implication to the extent of the contradiction. If the subsequent will purports to deal with the whole estate of the deceased then the earlier will is impliedly revoked in full.[185] The courts are reluctant to apply the doctrine of implied revocation and will attempt to read the earlier will and the later will as consistent if this is at all possible.[186]

Revocation by the actions of the testator

Actions which may revoke a will take various forms and include matters such as tearing **16–52** it up or putting it in a fire. Lesser acts such as drawing a line through a will may suffice in certain circumstances. The act of destruction may be symbolic such as the cutting off of a seal from the will even when what remained would have been regarded as a validly executed will if looked at in isolation.[187] Revocation may be confined to a part of the will such as where parts of a will were cut out revoking certain legacies only.[188]

To revoke a will the act of destruction must be carried out by the testator himself or someone acting on his authority, such as a solicitor. If destruction is carried out by a third party who does not act on the instructions of the testator then it has no

---

[181] *Paterson v Paterson* (1893) 20 R 484.
[182] See, *eg, Dewar v Dewar's Trs* 1950 SLT 191.
[183] *Curdy v Boyd* (1775) M 15946.
[184] *Gordon's Exr v MacQueen* 1907 SC 373.
[185] *Cadger v Ronald's Trs and Ors* 1946 SLT (Notes) 24.
[186] *Duthie's Exr v Taylor* 1986 SLT 142. For an unusual decision, see *Clark's Exrs v Clark* 1943 SC 216.
[187] *Nasmyth v Hare* (1821) 1 Sh App 65 (HL).
[188] *Thompson's Trs v Bowhill Baptist Church* 1956 SC 217.

effect.[189] If the will was known to be in the possession of the testator himself but cannot be found after his death there is a presumption that it was destroyed by the testator with intent to revoke.[190] A revocation by destruction or cancellation must be effected *animo et facto*. This means that there must be a mental intention to revoke by destruction and some physical act of destruction. The will is not revoked where there is no intention to revoke such as where the will is destroyed by accident[191] or if the testator was insane at the time of the destruction.[192] The onus of proof lies on the party seeking to establish revocation. As it is always difficult to prove what is inside someone's mind this may be the decisive factor in any case.[193] Proof may always be led that an act of cancellation was for a purpose other than to revoke the will. For example, where a testatrix scored out her married name with a view to reverting to her maiden name this did not revoke the will.[194]

Revocation by law

16–53   In Scotland a will is not revoked by the subsequent marriage or divorce of the testator. It may be revoked upon the birth of a child of the testator after the execution of the will. This is known as the operation of the *conditio si testator sine liberis decesserit*. The Latin phrase is misleading. A literal translation gives the impression that it deals with a situation where a testator dies without surviving children. It actually deals with the reverse situation where the testator dies with an unexpected surviving child. The principle applies when a testator has made a will which contains no provision for children who may subsequently be born to the testator. If children are born after the date of execution of the will it is presumed that the testator did not desire his will to remain in effect in the altered circumstances. Unless the presumption is rebutted, the whole will is revoked and the result is usually intestacy. The rule does not operate automatically to revoke the will on the birth of the subsequent child for whom no provision has been made. Instead, it is a presumption for the benefit of the afterborn child and is based on equitable principles. Only the afterborn child himself may seek to found on the *conditio* for the purposes of the revocation of the will and it cannot be used to improve the share of other relatives.[195] The clearest case for applying the rule and regarding the will as revoked would be the case of the posthumous child. However, for the *conditio* to apply the child need not be born after the death of the testator. The child need only be born after the date of the execution of the will. It is possible for the will to be made, a child born and a period of time elapse before the death of the testator.[196] Although the presumption may be overturned by evidence that the testator considered the birth of the child and regarded it as well provided for, it is a strong presumption and the cases in which it has been overturned are rare.[197]

---

[189] *Cullen's Exr v Elphinstone* 1948 SC 662.
[190] *Clyde v Clyde* 1958 SC 343.
[191] *Pattison's Trs v University of Edinburgh* (1888) 16 R 73, per Lord McLaren at 76.
[192] *Laing v Bruce* (1838) 1 D 59.
[193] *Crosbie v Wilson* (1865) 3 M 870.
[194] *Fotheringham's Trs v Reid* 1936 SC 831.
[195] *Stevenson's Trs v Stevenson* 1932 SC 657.
[196] *Milligan's JF v Milligan* 1910 SC 58 (10 years).
[197] For one such instance see *Stuart-Gordon v Stuart-Gordon* (1899) 1 F 1005.

Revival of wills

A problem may arise where an old will is revoked by means of a new will. Does **16–54** the old will revive when the new will is itself revoked? Authority is divided on the point.[198] Until the law is reformed the safest course is for a solicitor to receive his client's instructions to tear up the old will when it is revoked by a new will so that there is no possibility of revival of the old will.

MUTUAL WILLS

A mutual will is a testamentary document in which two or more parties give directions **16–55** for the disposal of their estates after their deaths. Although frequently used up to the middle of the twentieth century these wills have fallen out of favour in practice because of the difficulties in relation to revocation by one of the parties either before or after the death of the other or others.[199] If the mutual will is regarded as "contractual" in nature the unilateral power to revoke will be excluded. If the will is regarded as non-contractual and merely testamentary the power to revoke may be exercised. There is a general presumption that a mutual will is merely two wills within one document and is therefore revocable. If, however, the testators are spouses the court is more easily persuaded that the provisions in the mutual will in favour of the surviving spouse and the children are contractual, and so irrevocable. If the parties to the will make express provision either excluding or permitting unilateral revocation that will be given effect to.

CONSTRUCTION OF WILLS

The expression "construction" of a will denotes the technique of finding out what a **16–56** will means. The task is rendered more difficult as there is no set format for a will. The primary object of construction is to find out what are the testator's intentions. All rules of interpretation will bend to this primary object. Despite this the courts have evolved certain general principles of construction.

The whole will should be read and so far as possible an interpretation should be placed on the clauses so that they are reconciled. A will cannot be valid if it is too vague to be interpreted and in such cases the result is usually intestacy. In so far as is reasonably possible the courts will try to avoid setting aside a will on these grounds. A provision which merely expresses a wish will not be interpreted as a bequest.[200] Nevertheless, where a testator narrates in a will that he has made a provision for a person in the will but he has not, the implication from this false narrative is the equivalent of a legacy.[201] The *ejusdem generis* rule is used to construe lists.[202] The words used should be given their normal grammatical meaning.[203] Where, however, a testator uses

---

[198] *Bruce's JF* v *Lord Advocate* 1969 SC 296 (favourable); *Elder's Trs* v *Elder* (1895) 22 R 505 (unfavourable).
[199] For a rare recent example of such a will see Will of Robert Duncan Wilson and Mrs Catherine Morrison Gowans Wilson dated 27th January 1976 and recorded in the Court Books of the Commissariot of South Strathclyde, Dumfries and Galloway at Stranraer on 21st March 1994.
[200] *Milne* v *Smith* 1982 SLT 129.
[201] *Grant* v *Grant* (1851) 13 D 805.
[202] *Dunbar* v *Dunbar* 1808 Hume 267.
[203] *Stalker's Exrs, Petitioners* 1977 SLT (Notes) 4.

a word with a technical legal meaning there is a presumption, which is stronger where the will is prepared by a lawyer, that he intended it to be given its technical meaning.

Given the vast variety of wills it would be impracticable to list a series of cases which clarify the meanings of all words which are encountered. Furthermore, as words in a will are construed by reference to their context it is debatable how much value can be placed on the meaning given to words in previous cases. Three words, however, are frequently encountered: (a) child; (b) family; and (c) money.

(a) *Child* Normally this means the immediate children of the testator but in particular cases the word may be interpreted to include grandchildren.[204] The meaning of the word has altered because of the change in the law relative to illegitimate children. For wills executed after 8th December 1986 there is a general presumption that any reference to a "child" includes an illegitimate child unless the contrary intention appears from the will.[205] There were similar, but slightly narrower, provisions under earlier legislation.[206] Before 25th November 1968 the word "child" when used in a will was rarely ever construed as including an illegitimate child.[207] There is special provision for children born by modern artificial reproductive techniques.[208]

(b) *Family* In everyday language the word family has a wide and indefinite series of meanings. It can mean everything from a clan to a cult. Despite its variety of meanings, unless one of the wider meanings can be shown to have been intended by the testator, it will be taken as meaning the immediate children of the testator as opposed to remoter descendants or other relatives.

(c) *Money* In everyday language "money" means cash and excludes heritage such as houses and land. Where the term money is used in a will it may include heritage if the context indicates that this is what the testator intended. A factor which would show that the testator did not intend the term to include heritage is the fact that he owned no heritage at the time of the execution of the will.[209]

Extrinsic evidence may be admitted to interpret a will in some exceptional circumstances. It may be used to interpret a will written in a code or a foreign language or to resolve a latent ambiguity.[210] In some cases the named beneficiary may have changed his or its name since the date of the will and extrinsic evidence may be led to link the individual with the party named in the will.

TYPES OF LEGACIES

16–57   Legacies may be classified in various ways as follows:

> (a) *Specific or special legacies.* These are legacies of some definite object, such as a particular house, a particular investment, or the right to receive a debt due to the testator by a particular person. The legacy lapses if the item no longer

---

[204] *Yule's Trs Petitioners* 1981 SLT 250.
[205] Law Reform (Parent and Child) (Scotland) Act 1986, s 5.
[206] Law Reform (Miscellaneous Provisions) (Scotland) 1968, s 5 (wills executed on or after 25th November 1968).
[207] *Purdie's Trs v Doolan* 1929 SLT 273.
[208] Human Fertilisation and Embryology Act 1990, ss 27–30.
[209] *Lawson's Exr v Lawson* 1958 SLT (Notes) 38.
[210] *Wedderspoon v Thomson's Trs* (1824) 3 S 396; *Keiller v Thomson's Trs* (1826) 4 S 724.

belongs to the testator at his death. In these circumstances the legacy is stated to be "adeemed". In *Ogilvie-Forbes Trustees* v *Ogilvie-Forbes*[211] a legacy of a house was adeemed by its transfer to a limited company controlled by the testator.

(b) *Demonstrative legacies*. These are legacies in which the testator indicates the source from which the legacy is to come. Where the fund is insufficient the legatee has a claim against the residue for the excess.

(c) *General legacies*. The subject of the legacy has no individual character distinguishing it from other subjects of the same kind. A typical general legacy is a bequest of a sum of money or a quantity of goods answering to some general description.

(d) *Residue*. This covers the remainder of the testator's estate remaining after payment of debts and all legacies. A well-drafted will should always include a bequest of residue otherwise any bequest which fails will pass to the persons who would have been entitled to the deceased's estate had he died intestate. The person to whom the residue is bequeathed is termed "the residuary legatee".

CUMULATIVE AND SUBSTITUTIONAL LEGACIES

Where a double legacy is given the question arises: are the two legacies cumulative so **16–58** that the legatee takes both of them or substitutional so that he takes only one? The express provision of the testator is paramount and his express statement governs the matter. In the absence of express statement the courts apply a number of presumptions. Where the legacies are created in more than one deed, such as a will and a subsequent codicil, they are presumed to be cumulative. Where the legacies are in the same deed and the exact amount is given twice they are presumed to be substitutional. This, however, is only a presumption and can be rebutted in appropriate cases.[212] Where the legacies are in the same deed but are of different amounts they are presumed to be cumulative.

LEGATUM REI ALIENAE

This is a legacy of a thing which did not belong to the testator when he made the will. **16–59** In such a case the testator is presumed to have made the legacy in the mistaken belief that the thing was his and, because of this error on the testator's part, the legacy fails. If, however, it can be proved that the testator knew that the thing did not belong to him, then the legacy is interpreted as an instruction to the executor to purchase the thing from its owner and hand it over to the legatee. If it cannot be purchased the executor must pay its value to the legatee. It is not enough to show that the testator should have known the true facts: he must actually have done so.[213]

---

[211] 1955 SC 405. See also *Ballantyne's Trs* v *Ballantyne's Trs* 1941 SC 35.
[212] *Gillies* v *Glasgow Royal Infirmary* 1960 SC 438.
[213] *Meeres* v *Dowell's Exr* 1923 SLT 184.

ABATEMENT OF LEGACIES

16–60   Where the testator's estate is insufficient to pay all debts and to satisfy all bequests then the bequests must be cut back according to the doctrine of abatement. If the will does not itself indicate the order in which the bequests are to abate the following rules apply:

(a) residuary legacies abate first;

(b) general legacies abate next, the abatement being *pari passu* ("equally");

(c) demonstrative legacies do not abate until the specified fund is exhausted but then abate like general legacies; and

(d) specific legacies are payable even although the result may be that nothing is left for the general legatees.

The mere numbering of legacies in the will is not considered to indicate the order of priority intended by the testator.

DIVISION *PER CAPITA* AND DIVISION *PER STIRPES*

16–61   Where a legacy is left to a number of named individuals without any indication of how it is to be divided among them, it is presumed that the division is equal. For example, a legacy to A and B and C of £300 is presumed to be a legacy of £100 each. If, however, the legatees are described by reference to some term suggesting a group—for example, "my brother's and sister's children"—a question may arise as to whether the testator intended division among all the beneficiaries as individuals (*per capita*) or division according to groups (*per stirpes*). In the example given this would be important if the number of the children in the two families was not equal. A properly drafted testamentary deed will clarify the point beyond doubt. In the absence of indication to the contrary the testator is presumed to have intended division *per capita*.

ACCRETION

16–62   The simplest introduction to the doctrine of accretion is by means of an example. If a legacy is left to "A and B" and A dies before the testator dies then B will take what A would have inherited in addition to his own share. Otherwise stated, A's share accresces to B.

Accretion is a principle applicable when construing a testamentary provision in favour of more than one person. Accretion does not apply to a testamentary provision in favour of one person. If accretion does apply, then, where one or more legatees have predeceased the testator, the provision in their favour falls to the survivor or survivors. In cases where accretion does not apply the provision passes to the next person identified in the will or, if such a person does not exist, into intestacy. The application of the doctrine of accretion is subject to the rule *conditio si institutus sine liberis decesserit*.

Any doubts as to the application of the principle can be clarified by a well-drawn will. This should make it clear whether accretion does or does not apply. It is unlikely expressly to exclude or include the doctrine but certain phrases used in practice have been interpreted by the courts as excluding or including accretion. Accretion will apply in respect of a legacy in favour of "A and B"[214] or a legacy to A and B which is expressly stated to be "joint" or "joint and several". Accretion is excluded by a provision in a will for the contingency of a beneficiary predeceasing the testator in a provision, known as a destination-over, declaring that the children of that beneficiary will take in the place of that beneficiary. Except in relation to class gifts, accretion is excluded if there are what is known as "words of severance".[215] An example of a legacy employing words of severance is a legacy to A and B "equally among them" or A and B "in equal shares"[216] or A and B "equally and proportionally".[217] Words of severance do not exclude accretion in relation to class gifts.

A class gift is a gift to persons falling within an identifiable class. A good example of a class gift is a gift to "my children" or "my issue".[218] The date for the identification of the members of the class is normally the date of distribution (not necessarily coincident with the date of death).

DESTINATIONS-OVER

A destination-over in a bequest is a provision such as "to A, whom failing, to B". **16–63** A is referred to as "the institute". Depending on the construction placed on the clause B may be either a "conditional institute" or a "substitute". If B is the conditional institute then the following is the effect of the clause. If A survives the testator he will acquire a right to the legacy. The destination-over to B flies off and has no effect. If A does not survive the testator B will acquire the legacy. By contrast, if B is a "substitute" then A will acquire a right to the legacy on the testator's death provided A survives the testator, B will also take on the death of the testator if A does not survive the testator. Even if A survives the testator B will also take on the death of A provided B survives A and the substitution is not defeated by A by *inter vivos* lifetime transfer or *mortis causa* deed. Where the subjects are heritage the presumption is for substitution. Where the subjects are moveables the presumption is against substitution. In any case the terms of the will of the testator will determine the issue.[219]

VESTING OF LEGACIES

There is a difference between vesting in the executors and vesting in beneficiaries.   **16–64**

The deceased's estate, both heritable and moveable, vests, for the purposes of administration, in the executor by virtue of confirmation.[220] It is the confirmation, not

---

[214] *Andrew's Exrs* v *Andrew's Trs* 1925 SC 844. Accretion applied to bequest "to my said sisters Eliza and Alexandrina".
[215] *Fraser's Trs* v *Fraser* 1980 SLT 211.
[216] *Paxton's Trs* v *Cowie* (1886) 13 R 1191.
[217] *Paterson* v *Paterson* (1741) M 8070.
[218] Because of the reform of the law relative to illegitimate children, the term "child" is taken as including illegitimate children: see para 16–14.
[219] *Simpson's Trs* v *Simpson* (1889) 17 R 248.
[220] Succession (Scotland) Act 1964, s 14(1).

the appointment of the executor, which itself constitutes a valid title to heritage and may be used as a link in title.

On intestacy the right of the deceased's heirs to participate in the estate vests by their survivance of the intestate.[221] A legacy is said to "vest" in the legatee when he acquires right to it. At that stage the legatee may dispose of it by *inter vivos* or *mortis causa* deed. On his death intestate it will form part of the legatee's estate. The date of vesting is not necessarily the date upon which the legatee is entitled to payment of the legacy or the date he obtains possession of it. The basic rule is that the date of vesting is determined in accordance with the wishes of the testator as expressed in his will. Further complicated rules of vesting have been developed by the courts to deal with special circumstances but they all yield to the express intentions of the testator. The express statement of the testator as to vesting will be disregarded only where it is irreconcilable as to the terms of the bequest.[222] Where words in the will are obscure there is a general presumption in favour of early vesting. A testator may provide in his will that a particular legacy will vest on the occurrence of an event which may never happen. This is known as a conditional bequest. Conditional bequests may, in turn, be divided into two types: first, bequests which are subject to a condition precedent (otherwise known as a "suspensive condition") which postpones vesting until the fulfilment of the condition; second, bequests which are subject to a resolutive condition (otherwise known as a "subsequent condition") which do not prevent vesting but render it liable to be defeated if the event occurs—this is known as vesting subject to defeasance.[223] As a general rule conditions which are personal to the legatee have the effect of suspending vesting. Typical examples of such conditions are those which relate to a legatee surviving beyond a certain age. Where a bequest is made in favour of a class of beneficiaries, the general rule is that only those members who are in existence when the time appointed for the payment for the gift arrives are entitled to participate in it.

CONDITIO SI INSTITUTUS SINE LIBERIS DECESSERIT

16–65   The effect of the *conditio si institutus sine liberis decesserit* is that in certain circumstances where a testamentary gift has been left to a legatee without reference to the legatee's children, the courts will presume an implied gift to those children if the legatee should die without having acquired a vested right in the legacy.

The *conditio* does not apply to a conveyance of a lifetime gift: it is wholly testamentary in character and applies only to deeds such as wills. The *conditio* applies only in relation to bequests to certain close relatives and not to bequests to persons outside the family circle. The testator's own children and descendants are clearly within the ambit of the *conditio*. It applies to bequests not only to children but also to grandchildren[224] and great-grandchildren.[225] Since 25th November 1968 the *conditio* has applied to illegitimate children.[226] The *conditio* applies to bequests to nieces and

---

[221] Confirmation of Executors Act 1823, s 1; Succession (Scotland) Act 1964, s 1(1) (removing distinction between heritage and moveables).
[222] *Croom's Trs v Adams* (1859) 22 D 45.
[223] See Gloag and Henderson, *The Law of Scotland* (10th edn, 1995), para 44.24.
[224] *Mowbray v Scougall* (1834) 12 S 910.
[225] *Grant v Brooke* (1882) 10 R 92.
[226] See para 16–14.

nephews but not to brothers and sisters.[227] It is sometimes said that the *conditio* applies to bequests to nieces and nephews only if the testator has placed himself *in loco parentis* to them. This carries no implication that the testator must have taken any special interest in them during his lifetime. As a result there is a presumption that legacies to nieces and nephews imply the *conditio* and the onus is on those who challenge it to prove from the terms of the will that the testator had not placed himself *in loco parentis*.[228]

As the *conditio* is a rule of the construction of wills based upon the presumed intention of the testator it may be displaced if it can be shown that the testator had some other intention. An express contrary statement will preclude the operation of the *conditio*. There may be some doubt about the application of the *conditio* if the testator had not overlooked the possibility of issue surviving his descendants or nephews or nieces.[229] Nevertheless, the mere fact that the testator knew of the predecease of the legatee and did nothing to alter his will does not in itself preclude the operation of the *conditio*.[230] Where the legatee dies before the date of the will then the children of that legatee cannot benefit by the *conditio*.[231]

CONDITIONS ATTACHED TO LEGACIES

A legacy may be subject to conditions. The conditions may be classified in various **16–66** ways:

(a) suspensive conditions postpone payment of the legacy until the condition is fulfilled;

(b) resolutive conditions may result in the legacy lapsing if a specified event occurs;

(c) potestative conditions require the legatee to do something before he is entitled to the legacy;

(d) casual conditions render the entitlement to the legacy conditional upon the occurrence of some external event;

(e) mixed conditions involve elements of both potestative and casual conditions.

Conditions attached to legacies may be ineffective for several reasons. If it is ineffective it is regarded as *pro non scripto* and the legacy is given effect to as if it had been unconditional. Conditions may be ineffective if impossible to fulfil, unlawful, contrary to public policy or inconsistent with the bequest. In the last case the condition is stated to fail on the basis of the doctrine of repugnancy.

An example of repugnancy occurs where a testator confers a vested and unconditional right of full ownership on a beneficiary and then subjects it to conditions which are appropriate only to a limited right such as liferent. If a testator leaves a full gift of

---

[227] *Hall v Hall* (1891) 18 R 690.
[228] *Knox's Exr v Knox* 1941 SC 432.
[229] *McNab v Brown's Trs* 1926 SC 387.
[230] *Reid's Trs v Drew* 1960 SC 46.
[231] *Traver's Trs v Macintyre* 1934 SC 520.

property but directs his executors to pay only the income to the beneficiary until he reaches the age of 25, the beneficiary may insist upon immediate payment of the capital unless he is legally *incapax*.[232]

RE-ARRANGEMENTS AFTER DEATH

16–67   Beneficiaries in a deceased person's estate are generally free to make any re-arrangement among themselves after the death of the deceased to vary the provisions made by the testator. The variation is frequently entered into by means of a deed known as a deed of family arrangement. This may apply to variations of rights on intestacy, legal rights or those arising from a will. The beneficiaries who enter into such an arrangement must be of full age and capable of consenting. A deed of family arrangement within two years after death can alter the tax consequences of the dispositions made by the testator or the inheritance tax bill on intestacy. To achieve this tax benefit the beneficiaries require to intimate to the Capital Tax office that they wish to have the variation backdated to the death so that the deceased is treated as having made the variation. The time limit for the intimation is six months after the date of the instrument effecting the alteration.[233] A second variation is competent to make variations to the provisions left by the testator but it does not receive these tax benefits.[234]

SUBSTITUTES FOR WILLS

16–68   Scots law recognises or has recognised that, in addition to wills, there may be several other methods of making provision for beneficiaries and contracting out of, or rendering inapplicable, the rules of intestate succession to a limited extent. These devices may be classified as will substitutes. They include:

(a) gifts *inter vivos*;

(b) *donationes mortis causa*;

(c) verbal legacies;

(d) nominations;

(e) benefits under certain life assurance policies; and

(f) special destinations.

Gifts *inter vivos*

16–69   A genuine gift is an outright transfer of ownership of property to the chosen beneficiary. Neither the donor nor his creditors are entitled to its return except, in the latter case, where the gift is reduced as an unfair preference in terms of the bankruptcy legislation. An outright gift is not an advance for the purpose of *collation inter liberos*.

---

[232] See, *eg, Miller's Trs* v *Miller* (1890) 18 R 301.
[233] Inheritance Tax Act 1984, s 142.
[234] *Russell* v *Inland Revenue Commissioners* [1988] STC 195.

Donationes mortis causa

These are gifts in contemplation of death. They are a sort of halfway-house between **16–70** outright gifts and legacies. The gift is made during the lifetime of the donor but is conditional upon the death of the donor earlier than the donee. Ownership passes to the donee but the gift is revocable at any time by the donor until he dies. The gift must be made in contemplation of death but does not need to be in actual peril of death. Contrary to the position in English law a *donatio mortis causa* in Scotland is not revoked upon the recovery of the donor from a serious illness.

Verbal legacies

Since 1st August 1995 all wills require to be in writing.[235] Prior to that date a will for **16–71** less than £8.33 could be made verbally. Except in so far as permitted by the Wills Act 1963,[236] soldiers' wills which are verbal or informal legacies recognised by the law of England[237] and several Commonwealth jurisdictions have never been part of the law of Scotland.[238]

Nominations

Nominations are a form of testamentary arrangement limited to certain small savings **16–72** in certain institutions of a profit-making nature. Nominations are wholly statutory in character and the limits of the arrangements are set out in the relevant statutes. To effect a nomination all the saver did was to register the identity of the nominated person with the savings institution in question. Nominations are now extremely limited in scope.

Benefits under certain life insurance policies

In certain cases a policy effected under the Married Women's Policies of Assurance **16–73** (Scotland) Act 1880 may serve to transfer property without a will. The policy must be by a spouse on his or her own life and must be expressed to be for the benefit of the surviving spouse or children or both.

Special destinations

A special destination is part of the title to heritable property and it may have testa- **16–74** mentary effects. A typical example is the title to a house of a married couple in the name of H and W and the survivor. Upon death of H or W his or her one-half share will pass automatically to the survivor.

The revocation of special destinations depends on two things: (a) was there a power to revoke the special destination and (b) was that power exercised? The general rule is that special destinations may be revoked. An exception to the general rule occurs where the special destination is regarded as "contractual", in which case it may not be revoked in a will or other *mortis causa* deed. What this means is that there is a contract between the parties to the destination that it may not be evacuated without the other's consent. Even if the special destination is contractual it is always possible to evacuate

---

[235] Requirements of Writing (Scotland) Act 1995, s 1(2).
[236] See para 16–42.
[237] *Re Jones* [1981] 1 All ER 1.
[238] *Stuart* v *Stuart* 1942 SC 510; 1995 Act, s 1(2).

the destination by an *inter vivos* sale or gift to a third party.[239] It is very unlikely that a special destination will expressly declare itself to be contractual. The courts will therefore look to see if there is an implied contract. In determining whether a special destination is contractual it is important to establish if both parties H and W contributed to the price. If both contributed equally to the price this is a strong factor in assessing that the destination is contractual.[240]

In respect of wills executed after 10th September 1964 limitations are placed on the manner of exercise of a revocation in a will. There is no revocation of a special destination unless there is an express reference to the destination in the will and a declared intention on the part of the testator to revoke it.[241]

---

[239] *Steele* v *Caldwell* 1979 SLT 228.
[240] *Gordon-Rogers* v *Thomson's Exrs* 1988 SLT 618.
[241] 1964 Act, s 30; *Stirling's Trs* v *Stirling* 1977 SC 139.

SUMMARY

PURPOSES OF THE LAW

- The law of succession contains the rules whereby the estates of deceased persons are distributed.
- Scots law of succession deals generally with the rules relating to the distribution of the estate of domiciled Scots persons and heritable property in Scotland.

DEATH

- Death is relatively easy to establish except where persons have disappeared or died in common calamities. There are special statutory rules to deal with these extraordinary cases.
- Unborn children in the womb at the time of death are treated as having been born provided this is of benefit to them.

DISQUALIFICATION OF THE BENEFICIARY

- Certain beneficiaries are disqualified—generally because they have been involved in the death of the deceased. Relief is sometimes available in terms of the Forfeiture Act 1982.
- There are special rules for illegitimate children, adopted children, separated spouses and those involved in the preparation of the will.
- Incapacitated persons may be beneficiaries.

ESTATE

- The entire estate of the deceased comprising both personal and real rights is gathered in by the executor for the purposes of distribution.
- Debts are deducted prior to any distribution to beneficiaries.
- Special rules govern the order for payment and incidence of debts.

INTESTATE SUCCESSION

- Where the deceased party has not left a will his property is divided according to the rules of intestate succession. After payment of debts the estate is distributed by payment of prior rights, legal rights and then free estate.

PRIOR RIGHTS

- Prior rights are available only to a spouse and include a right to a dwelling house; a right to furniture and plenishings; and a financial provision. The value of these rights is laid down in statutory rules.

LEGAL RIGHTS

- Legal rights are available to the surviving spouse and surviving children. The spouse's right is known as *jus relictae* or *jus relicti*. The child's right is known as legitim. They are all payable out of moveables only. They vary in amounts according to who survives the deceased.
- Representation and collation *inter liberos* apply to payments of legitim.
- Legal rights can be extinguished by discharge.

FREE ESTATE

- The rules for free estate distribution are set out in the 1964 Act, s 2. They begin with close relatives and end with more distant relatives.
- If someone dies without any relatives the Crown inherits.

TESTATE SUCCESSION

- The rules of testate succession apply where a person leaves a valid will. They are subject to limitations on testamentary freedom. Chief amongst these is the effect of legal rights and public policy.
- A testator may also limit his freedom to make a will by contract.

ESSENTIAL VALIDITY AND FORMAL VALIDITY

- Wills must comply with requirements as to essential and formal validity.
- Essential validity relates to matters such as capacity to test, facility and circumvention, insanity and undue influence. Children under 12 cannot make a will.
- Formal validity relates to the manner of execution and witnessing. Statutory provisions require a will to be in writing and signed by the testator. Certain relaxations are made for foreign wills. Notarial execution is available as an alternative for persons who cannot write or who are blind.

FORM AND CONTENT OF WILLS

- There is no set form of a will so many problems arise as to interpretation.
- Wills may be revoked by another deed, by the actings of the testator or by application of legal implication.
- The order of succession may be rearranged by beneficiaries after death.
- There are limited substitutes for wills including *inter vivos* gifts, nominations and special destinations.

CASE DIGEST

Categorisation of property by *lex situs* [see para 16–02]

Macdonald v *Macdonald* 1932 SC (HL) 79. A domiciled Scotsman died leaving land in various Canadian provinces. It was held that because land was immoveable according to the law of these provinces, it was not subject to Scottish legal rights over moveable estate.

Children unborn at time of death may inherit if the provision is for their benefit [see para 16–12]

Elliot v *Joicey* 1935 SC (HL) 57

A's property was to be held "in trust for [B] absolutely ... in the event of [B] leaving any issue ... surviving". In the House of Lords it was held that "surviving" would not normally mean "posthumous" but even if the maxim *qui in utero est, pro iam nato habetur* was applied it would benefit B's estate and not necessarily his issue. The maxim was therefore inapplicable.

A widow may be better off renouncing bequest under will and claiming prior rights [see para 16–29]

Kerr, Petitioner 1968 SLT (Sh Ct) 61

A widow was left all her husband's small estate. There was no other provision in the will. She would have been better off under intestacy because if she took under the will she could not claim prior rights or legal rights (because of approbate and reprobate) but her children could claim legal rights. She disclaimed her benefit under the will creating intestacy. She took everything under her prior rights leaving the children nothing.

Revoked wills need to be carefully identified [see para 16–51]

Gordon's Executor v *MacQueen* 1907 SC 373

A revocation of "two wills which are recorded in the Books of Council and Session in Edinburgh" was ineffective to revoke the testator's only previous will which did not meet that description.

Uninstructed destruction is ineffective [see para 16–52]

Cullen's Executor v *Elphinstone* 1948 SC 662

A widow instructed her solicitors to prepare a new will which they executed notarily as she was blind. Uninstructed, they destroyed the old will. Their act was legally ineffective.

The presumption of revocation of a will in favour of an after-born child may be overturned in exceptional cases [see para 16–53]

Stuart-Gordon v *Stuart-Gordon* (1899) 1 F 1005

This case concerns the birth of a child before the death of the testator and the effect of the rule *conditio si testator sine liberis decesserit*. The testatrix died shortly after the birth of her child. It was proved she was considering her legacies in view of her bad health and, knowing that the child was well provided for anyway, she had decided to omit her. The will could not therefore be revoked on the basis of the rule.

FURTHER READING

Agnew, *Crofting Law* (T&T Clark, 2000)

Currie, *The Confirmation of Executors in Scotland* (8th edn by Scobbie, W Green, 1996)

Gloag and Henderson, *The Law of Scotland* (10th edn, W Green, 1995), Chaps 42–45

Halliday, *Conveyancing Law and Practice in Scotland* (2nd edn by Talman, W Green 1996), Vol 1, Pt IV, Chaps 18–22

The Laws of Scotland: Stair Memorial Encyclopaedia, (Law Society of Scotland/ Butterworths) Vol 25, "Wills and Succession".

MacCuish and Flyn, *Crofting Law* (Butterworths/Law Society of Scotland, 1990), Chap 7

Macdonald, *Succession* (2nd edn, W Green, 1994)

Meston, *The Succession (Scotland) Act 1964* (4th edn, W Green, 1993)

INDEX

Index entries refer to paragraph numbers.